P9-EAX-904

OKANAGAN COLLEGE LRC

00961201

K

# Women and Mental Health

OKANAGAN COLLEGE LIBRARY
BRITISH COLUMBIA

# WOMEN
# AND
# MENTAL
# HEALTH

EDITED BY

## Elizabeth Howell

AND

## Marjorie Bayes

71929

*Basic Books, Inc., Publishers     New York*

Library of Congress Cataloging in Publication Data

Women and mental health.

Bibliography: p. 639
Includes index.
1. Women—Mental health.  2. Women—Mental health
services.  I. Howell, Elizabeth.  II. Bayes, Marjorie.
[DNLM: 1. Mental health services—United States.
2. Psychotherapy.  3. Women—Psychology.  WM 30 W872]
RC451.4.W6W64      616.89′0088042      81–66982
ISBN 0–465–09202–0 (cloth)                    AACR2
ISBN 0–465–09200–4 (paper)

Copyright © 1981 by Basic Books, Inc.
Printed in the United States of America
Designed by Vincent Torre
10 9 8 7 6 5 4 3 2 1

# CONTENTS

# PART III
## *Diagnosis and Psychopathology*

# Contents

# PART V
## *Therapies*

# Contents

## PART VI
### *Where Do We Go from Here?*

# ACKNOWLEDGMENTS

This book owes its major debt to the authors who have allowed us to reprint their work and to those who have, at our request, written chapters in their areas of specialized knowledge. As we compiled the material for this volume we began to see a network, loosely connected but nevertheless real, of women and men who care about women's lives and who work toward the best possible mental health services for women. To these colleagues, our admiration and respect.

E. H. *and* M. B.

In addition, for my own chapters in this book, I would like to thank Robert Holt, Jody Brown, Emilie Sobel, William Czander, Julia Schulman, Dale Bernstein, and Sandy Swinburne for their careful reviews and many helpful suggestions.

E. H.

# Introductory Comments

ELIZABETH HOWELL AND MARJORIE BAYES

The majority of clients for mental health services are women. Women comprise more than 50 percent of clients in general counseling and psychotherapy services and 100 percent of clients for abortion counseling, rape counseling, and programs for unwed mothers. Despite the preponderance of women as consumers of mental health services, frequently used texts for counseling and psychotherapy focus no specific attention on the particular needs of women clients (Fabrikant 1974). Only a minority of training facilities make any attempt to train students to provide adequate services to women (Kenworthy 1976). The differences in clients' responses to male and female therapists are seldom discussed; most texts are written as if all therapists were male.

However, there is a growing awareness of the need for knowledge and training to counteract the prevalence of gender-role bias that often affects the treatment of female clients. This training should involve not only (1) a raising of consciousness of one's own and others' sexist attitudes and practices, but also (2) specific attention to concepts of feminine development, which have implications for treatment, and (3) attention to some of the special treatment needs of women clients, such as abortion counseling, rape counseling, and treatment for battered women. Despite the growing awareness of the need for such knowledge, and despite the general flood of literature about various aspects of the women's movement, little material is available to help therapists determine the effects of sexism in the etiology of emotional disturbance and to help them deal with the particular treatment needs of women. This book addresses these training aspects.

## Purpose and Organization

*Women and Mental Health* is intended to serve as a resource for those who would like to know more about issues important to the treatment of female clients within mental health services. It consists of six parts, spanning pertinent issues for women in mental health services. Each begins with a general chapter written by the editors. These chapters provide background material and orient the reader to critical issues in the area. Each part ends with a supplementary reading list. The entries cited therein include literature that we would have liked to reprint had space permitted, "landmark" material that is of particular significance, and literature dealing with specific issues in depth.

The book begins with a theoretical background: Part I includes theoretical papers on female development, on the development of gender-role stereotypes, and on female socialization. Part II addresses general issues of sexism in mental health, presenting papers about sexist bias of therapists, discriminatory treatment of female clients, and the over-prescription of psychotropic drugs to women. Part III addresses issues of diagnosis and psychopathology as they are influenced by gender and discusses syndromes that tend to be female-linked, such as anorexia, depression, and hysteria. Part IV provides comprehensive material on specific treatment needs of women, such as those stemming from developmental crises and those brought on by such trauma as rape, abortion, and battering. The importance of these needs within the mental health services delivered to women is evident by a glance at the entries in this section. The papers collected in Part V, "Therapies," address feminist versus traditional therapies and gender issues relevant to the different therapeutic modalities. The sixth and concluding part, "Where Do We Go from Here?," presents papers that discuss recent changes in the field of women's mental health, changes in process, and changes that still need to be made in our practice and in our thinking about women clients.

By now it should be clear that the papers within the collection do not comprise a complete psychology of women and do not present a perfected therapeutic approach. Much work remains to be done. However, we believe that the papers provide some of the most helpful and thoughtful contributions to the field to date.

## Introductory Comments

### Theoretical Orientation

We believe that most psychological theories of personality, of human development, and of psychotherapy contain a substantial amount of gender-role bias. Sexism in the practice of psychotherapy is often a direct result of theoretical bias, but it is also largely unconscious and to varying degrees present in all of us, men and women alike, as a result of having been socialized in this culture. Often it is very difficult for the psychotherapist or psychotherapy theorist to sort out and eliminate the sources of cultural and gender-role bias from his or her work. Many otherwise very good therapists have been limited by their unknowing participation in culturally accepted but detrimental attitudes toward women. The difficulties involved in the identification and elimination of gender-role bias, and the harm incurred by the failure to do so, are enormous.

As a result of cultural and gender-role bias, social inequities are often unknowingly identified as personal inadequacies of the female client. This translation occurs within theory as well as in the work of the individual therapist. We believe it is extremely important to be alert to such tendencies so as to avoid reinforcing or continuing them.

However, we do not intend to suggest the opposite extreme, that the environment should be diagnosed *instead* of the client. There has been a growing tendency among some therapists who have incorporated feminist ideals to discount the importance of theory and technique in support of the belief that all one really needs in order to treat women is the ability to spot sexist bias and, somehow vaguely, "be human." It is not necessary to throw out the whole body of psychodynamic theory because it is riddled with gender-role bias. With full recognition of the sexist bias of the bulk of Freud's psychology of women, we believe it would be a mistake to dismiss his great discoveries, such as those pertaining to unconscious motivation, mechanisms of defense, structure of the personality, and so forth. Indeed, as Lewis (1976) and Dinnerstein (1976) point out, Freud has given us the very tools with which to correct his mistakes.

We cannot overemphasize the importance of theoretical knowledge and technical skill. Dismissal of these, like diminishment of the importance of eradicating sexism from our practice, ultimately can have only a de-skilling effect on the therapist and can only shortchange women clients.

We hope that this collection of readings will help therapists to better address the needs of their women clients; that it will provide useful information, both practical and theoretical; and, of course, that it will help therapists to spot and eliminate sexist bias from their work. In brief, we hope that it will raise not only consciousness, but competence.

REFERENCES

Dinnerstein, D. 1976. *The mermaid and the minotaur*. New York: Harper and Row.
Fabrikant, B. 1974. The psychotherapist and the female patient: Perceptions, misperceptions and change. In *Women in therapy*, ed. V. Franks and V. Burtle, pp. 83–110. New York: Brunner/Mazel.
Kenworthy, J. A., et al. 1976. Women and therapy: A survey of internship programs. *Psychology of Women Quarterly* 1:125–137.
Lewis, H. 1976. *Psychic war in men and women*. New York: New York University Press.

# PART I

# *What Happens to Women?*
# *Some Theoretical Views*

# 1

# Women: From Freud to the Present

## ELIZABETH HOWELL

The theoretical underpinning of any adequate psychotherapeutic treatment of women must be nonsexist. Unfortunately, our psychological theories about women contain far too much sexism. Particularly in recent years there has been widespread criticism of the gender-role bias existing in our theories by practitioners, scholars, and theorists. Accordingly, there have been revisions in theory and additions to it. With a few exceptions, most of this work has been done by women.

Of course, the eradication of sexism is not the only goal of those who study the psychology of women. The overriding goal, which subsumes the eradication of sexism, is veridicality. We are striving for theories and constructs that will most accurately describe the female psyche and its genesis. The object of this chapter is to describe the current state of this endeavor, where it has been, and where it is going.

Currently the field is teeming with investigatory activity about the psychology of women. In the midst of this there are broadly two camps: the "analysts" (predominantly Freudian), whose point of view is intrapsychic, and the "feminists," who tend to have a sociocultural orientation. Those entering the field often have already been indoctrinated into one camp or the other; even when this is not the case, they are likely to feel pressure to "choose up sides" in the hotly charged debates. While the sources of this rift are certainly various (e.g., largely male composition among the analysts and largely female composition among the feminists, as well as the historic antagonism between the intrapsychic and sociocultural outlooks), one particularly important source may be the old conflict between Freud and Karen Horney, buried in its own time but recently unearthed by Fliegel (1973). While most current contributions to the psychology of women take us beyond this conflict, much that is currently being said, particularly in rebuttal to Freud, does not (Sobel 1977). Let us examine what this conflict was about.

## Freud's Psychology of Women

Most of Freud's psychology of women was based on his postulation of anatomical deficiency and its concomitant, penis envy. According to Freud, penis envy is the beginning and the crux of what is the matter with women, but it is also the propelling force behind the development of feminine identity.

Freud stated that children of both sexes believe they were born with penises, but that girls were castrated. When the girl notices that the boy has a penis, she is "overcome by envy" (1953, vol. 7, p. 195) of the boy's penis, which is "strikingly visible and of large proportions," and which she recognizes "as the superior counterpart of [her] own small and inconspicuous organ. . . ." At the moment of seeing the penis, the little girl "makes her judgment and her decision in a flash. She has seen it and knows that she is without it and wants to have it" (1961, vol. 19, p. 252).

According to Freud, it is the little girl's recognition of her penisless state that ushers in the process of her feminine development. Prior to this point her libidinal development was parallel to that of the little boy: there are some differences, but essentially "the little girl is a little man" (1964, vol. 22, p. 118). It is by repression of her masculine, active, clitoral sexuality that she achieves femininity. This repression occurs on a large scale in puberty, when the zone of erotogenic sensitivity is gradually transferred from the clitoris to the vaginal orifice. An important forerunner, however, of the repression that occurs at puberty develops soon after the first occasion of penis envy: a strong current against masturbation occurs as a result of the girl's sense of narcissistic humiliation concerning her inferior organ. This humiliation serves as a reminder:

that after all this is a point on which she cannot compete with boys, and that it would therefore be best for her to give up the idea of doing so. Thus the little girl's recognition of the anatomical distinction between the sexes forces her away from masculinity and masculine masturbation on to new lines which lead to the development of femininity. (1961, vol. 19, p. 256)

Femininity is also achieved by a change in the libidinal object. For the pre-oedipal girl as well as the boy, the first love object is mother. Recognition of the "fact of being castrated," as Freud puts it, causes her to blame her mother for this defect. This, along with other dissatisfactions with her mother, causes the girl to turn away from her mother. Hoping to gain from her father the penis that her mother denied her, she turns to him. Soon, however, the wish for a penis is replaced by the wish for a baby. As a result, she takes her father as a love object and becomes jealous of her mother. Attachment to the mother gives way to identification with her. At this point, "the little girl has turned into a little woman" (1961, vol. 19, p. 256).

As we have seen, penis envy and the castration complex usher in the Oedipus complex for the little girl. For the little boy, the castration complex causes the repression of the Oedipus complex. It is this difference that, according to Freud, causes women to have less stringent moral development. Because they have no built-in developmental incentive, such as castration fears, to give up their oedipal love-object, girls often do remain attached to their objects longer and have less impetus to introject the values and prohibitions of the parent(s) and by this means acquire their morality.

There are other negative outcomes to the alleged fact that girls are so envious of the penis. One is that normal jealous tendencies become excessive as a result of reinforcement by displaced penis envy. Penis envy also makes women more vain, since they attempt to compensate for their genital inferiority by their charms, and it makes them more prone to shame because they wish to conceal their genital deficiency. Women's excessive claim to privileges also results from penis envy, for they feel they have been wronged for having been brought into this world as female rather than male.

Perhaps the most unfortunate negative outcome is that the path of psychic development to womanhood is fraught with difficulties. There are essentially three directions in which a girl may go. First of all, she may refuse to accept "the fact of being castrated" and develop a "masculinity complex" that is a reaction formation or attempt to reverse the aforementioned "fact." In effect, she begins to behave and to think as if she were a man. She "clings to the hope" that someday she will receive a penis, and she may even turn into a manifest homosexual. Another unfortunate path the girl's development may take is that, as a result of her narcissistic disappointment, she may simply give up sexuality in general, becoming sexually inhibited and/or neurotic. Even if the little girl is able to develop along the third, most positive (albeit most circuitous) path, that of acceptance of her condition and development of the feminine Oedipus complex, she is still beset by tremendous limitations. Freud seemed to feel that the developmental tasks confronting the little girl were almost hopelessly difficult. He contrasts a typical woman to a typical man of about thirty coming for analysis:

A woman of the same age . . . often frightens us by her psychical rigidity and unchangeability. Her libido has taken up final positions and seems incapable of exchanging them for others. There are no paths open to further development; it is as though the whole process had already run its course and remains thence forward insusceptible to influence—as though, indeed, the difficult development to femininity has exhausted the possibilities of the person concerned. As therapists we lament this state of things, even if we succeed in putting an end to our patient's ailment by doing away with her neurotic conflict. (1964, vol. 22, pp. 134–135)

Freud emphasized that the analytic task of working through penis envy frequently raised the strongest resistances in women. Indeed:

[the female's wish for a penis] is the source of outbreaks of severe depression in her, owing to an internal conviction that the analysis will be of no use and that nothing can be done to help her. And we can only agree that she is right, when we learn that her strongest motive in coming for treatment was the hope that, after all, she might still obtain a male organ, the lack of which was so painful to her. (1964, vol. 23, p. 252)

He suggested that the reason penis envy was so intractable was that the psychological parameters had been explored as far as possible and the biological "bedrock" had been reached.

Despite the complexities of his theory, Freud felt quite uncertain about female psychology and stated his puzzlement frequently. For instance at the end of his lecture on femininity, after acknowledging that what he has to say is incomplete and fragmentary, he goes on to say:

If you want to know more about femininity, enquire from your own experiences of life, or turn to the poets, or wait until science can give you deeper and more coherent information. (1964, vol. 22, p. 135)

What has often been found so objectionable about Freud's psychology of women is his theory of oedipal and post-oedipal development as motivated by penis envy. Perhaps part of his deficiency in this area stemmed from his greater interest in men and their relationship to their fathers than in women and their relationship to their mothers. Four of his five long case histories were of men. This imbalance seems to stem from his own vigorous attempts to understand his relationship to his father[1] and from his inability to consider the possibility that there were problems in his relationship with his mother (Stolorow and Atwood 1978). As observed by Schafer (1974), "It seems that [Freud] knew the castrate in himself and other men, but not the mother and the woman" (p. 482). Despite these difficulties, Freud's clinical acumen directed him, particularly in his later work, to an interest in the pre-oedipal little girl's relationship to her mother, a relationship that he felt was more important for the little girl than for her male counterpart (Freud 1964, vol. 21). This is indeed the period of development upon which modern investigators have begun to focus. Interestingly, Freud himself suggested that in the future it would be female analysts who would make the most important discoveries in the psychology of women.

As mentioned earlier, Fliegel (1973) has recently unearthed the old controversy between Freud and Horney. According to her, Freud's failing health during the period in which he produced his essays on female psychology (1925–1933) (his cancer was discovered in 1924) and the increasing fragmentation of the psychoanalytic movement caused him to be less responsive to challenges to his theory of feminine development and less inclined to modify it than might otherwise have been the case. When Freud died his followers continued to be doctrinnaire, in part because the cohesiveness of the movement was deemed more important than the resolution of the controversy about feminine development. For almost thirty years after his death little was published that was not in agreement with his formulations. (Fliegel notes that while most current members of the psychoanalytic establishment do not endorse Freud's view of the constitutional inferiority of women, the psychoanalytic literature does not accurately convey the changes in views and therapeutic goals of most practicing analysts. She attributes this to the same constellation of events discussed above.)

In spite of his views on femininity, Freud accepted the contributions of female colleagues in his contemporary society. Among these were Jeanne Lampl-de Groot, Ruth Mack Brunswick, Marie Bonaparte, and Helene Deutsch. (See Part I Supplementary Readings, page 79.) These analysts were in basic agreement with Freud's theories about women, and their work, along with that of others among Freud's contemporaries, may have served to entrench even more solidly the phallocentric viewpoint. In particular, Helene Deutsch was influential in establishing a biologically deterministic and evolutionary-adaptational view according to which the triad, passivity, masochism, and narcis-

---

1. G. Mahl, personal communication, 1976.

sism, became aspects of feminine "nature" (Wimpfheimer and Schafer 1979).

Thus the tenacity of the phallocentric theory is not entirely attributable to Freud. Freud's inestimable contributions to psychology and ultimately to the relief of human suffering were made possible by a quality of mind that worked and reworked theories, but continually integrated new data and had the courage to admit mistakes. The seeds of revisionism are evident in Freud's own work. Ironically, it is due to historical happenstance that his concept of penis envy has been handed down to us in essentially unmodified and, in some cases, rigidified form, resulting in unfortunate destructive applications in clinical practice.

## Karen Horney's Views on Women

Another ramification of this historical omission is that Freud did not give Karen Horney's ideas the notice they deserved. As a consequence, Horney founded her own school. This had the effect of relegating much of her work to relative oblivion (Fliegel 1973). Horney's contributions to the psychology of women are extensive, various, and of current clinical interest. Interestingly, many of them have not received proper credit, having appeared more notably in the later writings of other authors.

Her views on penis envy are of particular interest. Horney recognized penis envy as a problem for women, but she suggested that it had different causes and consequences than those proposed by Freud. She observed two types of penis envy, which she labeled *primary* and *secondary*. Only the secondary type was in itself pathological. In her description of the causes of the primary type of penis envy, which in her view occurs in the pre-oedipal years, she answers a question posed by Freud's concept—"Why should the little girl be envious?" According to Horney, the sources of primary penis envy are threefold. One is urethral eroticism and the desire to urinate like a man. She notes that fantasies of omnipotence are associated with male urination and that children typically display a narcissistic overestimation of the excretory processes. Another motivation is the boy's greater opportunities to have his sexual curiosity satisfied and exhibit himself. The third, and most important, is that as the boy must hold his organ while urinating, he appears to have greater permission to masturbate. This the little girl greatly envies. Horney quotes one of her patients who, upon observing a father reprove his little daughter for touching herself, said, "He forbids her to do that, yet he does it himself five or six times a day."

For Horney what is important about this primary type of penis envy is that it arises from a sense of restriction in the wish to gratify the instinctual impulses that are so important in the pre-genital period. The pre-genital girl, she stresses, *does* have less opportunity for gratification, and, inevitably, this *does* pose developmental complications. However, this does not mean that the kind of consequences described by Freud, such as immediate and profound feelings of inferiority, follow. Nor does it mean that the castration complex is a concomitant of primary penis envy or that denial of womanhood, when it occurs, rests on penis envy.

Indeed, Horney states:

it is true that in these first years, little girls who have not been intimidated very often express themselves in ways which admit of interpretation of early penis envy; they ask questions, they make comparisons to their own disadvantage, they say they want one too, they express admiration of the penis or comfort themselves with the idea that they will have one later on. Supposing for the moment that such manifestations occurred very frequently or even regularly, it would still be an open question as to what weight and place in our theoretical structure we should give them. (1973, pp. 150–151)

She continues, stating that boys of this age give parallel expressions of the wish to have breasts or children. These expressions do not influence the child's total behavior (that is, boys still behave like boys, and girls like girls); furthermore, both boys and girls frequently express bisexual wishes and uncertainty as to their sexual role.

This primary type of penis envy is based simply on anatomical differences. Despite the interaction of various other factors, an anatomical disadvantage does exist for pre-genital little girls, but the disadvantage does not in itself evoke pathological consequences.

This is in contrast to the secondary type of penis envy, which arises as a result of developments relating to the oedipal complex. According to Horney, the oedipal little girl has been disappointed in her expectation of her father's reciprocal love for her. It is wounded womanhood that is the root of this secondary formation.[2] The little girl, in her love for her father, fantasizes that he made love to her. (Indeed, Horney suggests, one source of the castration complex in females is the fantasy that castration occurred in the process of intercourse with the father.)

2. Horney did not consider the route to the feminine Oedipus complex to be as circuitous and difficult as did Freud. Indeed, she thought that the Oedipus complex developed in little girls in a natural way as a result of "the biological principles of heterosexual attraction" (1973, p. 63) and that no psychical mechanism was needed to facilitate the transfer of the object (from the mother to the father).

In addition, the little girl wishes for babies from her father. But her love and her wishes are not reciprocated, and the ensuing disappointment can be so unbearable that a new defensive formation is necessary.

The little girl identifies with her father, Horney continues, and by this means represses her womanly feelings toward him. A concomitant regression to the pre-genital period revives the earlier feelings of penis envy; it is at this point that the penis complex becomes a truly pathological formation. This defensive identification with the father in the little girl, with its homosexual implications, is analogous to the little boy's defensive identification with his mother. Both have the same purpose—coping with the oedipal situation. The little girl's desire for a penis is essentially her wish to *be* father and is exactly the same in function as the psychically wounded oedipal boy's wish to be castrated. The primary difference is that for the boy this development is at variance with conscious narcissism, while for the girl it conveys more of a sense of acquittal, the condition of womanhood in itself being felt to be culpable.[3]

Horney also had some criticisms of Freud's views on penis envy. In her 1933 paper, "Denial of the Vagina," she addressed the bearing of the existence of pre-genital vaginal sensations on penis envy. She argued that an intimate knowledge of their own genitals and, in particular, of vaginal sensations should provide little girls with a sense of their own specific female sexuality and their own sexual role. (And, indeed, she observed that pre-genital girls are coquettish and in many other psychological respects behave like little women: in other words, they behave as if they know they are female.) If little girls are cognizant of their specific female sexuality, she reasoned, then they do not have to repress a masculine sexuality in order to achieve a female sexuality, as Freud suggests. Incidentally, Ernest Jones's position on this issue was quite similar to Horney's, and he was often supportive of her contentions. As he put it, "the ultimate question is whether a woman is born or made" (Fliegel 1973, p. 396). Jones believed that the clitoris was only part of the female genitals, and that very young girls did experience vaginal excitations. On this basis he suggested that a firm theory concerning the masculine primacy of the sexuality of the female infant be held in suspense. As we shall see, the question of vaginal sensations in very young girls has continued to be important in the field.

Horney also had some interpretations of Freud's views on penis

3. Horney made an interesting observation about the possible meaning of the phrase "desire for the penis": "I must mention the analytical discovery that in the association of female patients the narcissistic desire to possess the penis and the object libidinal longing for it are often so interwoven that one hesitates as to the sense in which the words 'desire for it' are meant." (1973, pp. 68–69)

envy. For one thing, she suggested that masculine projection might be clouding his vision and charted a correspondence of the ideas little boys entertain about little girls with the psychoanalytic ideas about feminine development. In addition, she suggested that the male psychoanalytical theorists' (Freud and Ferenzi in particular) insistence on penis envy as a central dynamic in female development might arise in part from the male's intense envy of the capacity for motherhood. This envy may be even greater than that of women's penis envy, giving rise to an unconscious need to depreciate women:

In favor of the greater intensity of the man's envy, we might point out that an actual anatomical disadvantage on the side of the woman exists only from the point of view of the pregenital levels of organization. From that of the genital organization of adult women there is no disadvantage, for obviously the capacity of women for coitus is not less but simply other than that of men. On the other hand, the part of the man in reproduction is ultimately less than that of women. (Horney 1973, pp. 61–62)

Much more than did Freud, Horney emphasized the sociocultural influences on women's psychology, and this emphasis became more pronounced in her later years. Though sympathetic to women's dilemma, she was not one to offer an "out" because of the bad deal given by culture. She was alert, for instance, to the defensive way in which some patients could use "penis envy" to pass on the responsibility for their personal failings in life. One of Horney's most important observations was the harm done to women in this culture by their overvaluation of love. (We will see this theme echoed by more modern writers.) This condition results in excessive dependency on external sources of gratification, such as other people's appreciation, rather than reliance on internal resources. Horney particularly lamented the devaluation of women's mature years that is encouraged by the cultural emphasis on beauty and attractiveness to men. About this she says:

Woman can scarcely take the task of the development of her personality as seriously as she does her love life if she constantly entertains a devaluating attitude toward her mature years, and considers them as her declining years. (1939, p. 116)

## Other Psychodynamic Theorists

Until recently, Horney remained one of the few to challenge the patriarchal view of women as being constitutionally inferior. Such a view of women was by no means confined to Freud, but was characteristic of other prominent psychodynamic theorists, women as well as men. These theorists continued to define women in ways that limited their developmental options and maintained cultural myths about women's "nature" and desires. Not the least pernicious of these myths was that women need to fulfill their "biological destiny" of motherhood (in the context, of course, of being helpmate to their husbands) in order to be mentally healthy. Bettleheim, for instance, stated that women "want, first and foremost, to be womanly companions of men and to be mothers" (cited in Chesler 1972, p. 77). (Let us note that Freud had a teleological viewpoint that assumed the desirability of the fulfillment of women's childbearing potential in order to propagate the species and made this the endpoint of development (Schafer 1974). This viewpoint is no longer an unquestioned assumption of modern society.)

Let us briefly examine the shape that these myths about women take in the writings of two well-known theorists, Carl Jung and Erik Erikson. Jung states:

by taking up a masculine profession, studying, and working like a man, woman is doing something not wholly in accord with, if not directly injurious to, her feminine nature . . . It is a woman's outstanding characteristic that she can do anything for the love of a man . . . Love for a thing is a man's prerogative. (cited in Goldenberg 1976, p. 445)

Jung's anima-animus concept of the personality is often considered to be liberating because it opens the way for androgyny. This may be so, but the initial bipolar assumption as to the respective psychic domains of men and women remains. Further, Jung was "primarily concerned with the integration, or within the tradition of the myth (of androgyny), reintegration, of the feminine into the masculine psyche" (Gelpi, cited in Goldenberg 1976, p. 447). Goldenberg (1976) states that, according to Jung's theory, men were more encouraged to develop their Logos (corresponding to the animus) than were women encouraged to develop their Logos (corresponding to the animus), the latter development being "often only a regrettable accident" (Jung 1971, p. 152). Interestingly, long before Jung used it, the concept of the androgyne was used in historical tradition, as a male construct which enhanced masculine self-sufficiency by incorporating the female (Harris 1979).

Erik Erikson states:

. . . much of a young woman's identity is already defined in her kind of attractiveness and in the selective nature of her search for the man (or men) by whom she wished to be sought. This, of course, is only the psychosexual aspect of her identity. . . . (1974, p. 354)

Further,

the stage of life crucial for the emergence of an integrated female identity is the step from youth to maturity, the stage when the young woman, whatever her work career, relinquishes the care received from the parental family in order to commit herself to the love of a stranger and to the care to be given to his and her offspring. (1974, p. 337)

Though Erikson (1974), like Freud, argues a version of "anatomy is destiny," unlike Freud he believes that the little girl is aware of her vagina and that her "inner space" is more important to her than the penis that she lacks. From his now classic study of the scenes that 150 boys and 150 girls constructed with play objects, Erikson deduced his concept of inner and outer space, characterizing girls and boys respectively. The girls tended to design enclosures that could be entered and intruded upon, whereas the boys' constructions were characterized by protrusions and high towers that were prone to collapse. Erikson dismisses a purely sociological interpretation of the data, suggesting instead that an orientation to "inner space" is an aspect of female nature. Though he admits that he has *proven* nothing, he persists in the exposition of his argument as if he has.

There is no intention here to dismiss the great works of Erikson, Jung, and other theorists because of the sexist bias in them. Critical examination is important in that it isolates what is unsubstantiated and objectionable from what is not. Certainly there is much that is curative of sexism in these works as well. For instance, as early as 1950 Erikson (1963) criticized the scapegoating of "Mom" by the psychoanalytic establishment.

## Dissident Female Voices

Clara Thompson was the first American woman to write a number of papers on the psychology of women (many in the 1940s) (Moulton 1974). Like Karen Horney, Thompson was impressed with the influence of Western culture on women's underprivileged status. Indeed, these two women exchanged ideas before they each formed separate training institutes. Thompson offered no new theories, staying close to clinical observation and focusing on the personal conflicts of women attempting to deal with their changing roles and options in a rapidly changing culture. Yet her clear-voiced interpretation of reality cuts through the theoretical abstraction of others, so that her observations are both profound and commonsensical (Moulton 1974). Thompson observed, for instance, the social and cultural pressures inhibiting women's authentic expression of sexuality and suggested that the problem for women is less that of reconciling themselves to the lack of a penis than that of acknowledging their own female sexuality. Concerning penis envy, she noted that body parts are often symbols in archaic thought, and she suggested that the penis has come to symbolize the greater prestige and power of the male in this culture. Thus envy of it is simply the envy felt by the subordinate in the power relationship. Similarly, Thompson stated that if our culture were a matriarchal one in which women were dominant, the breast might well be the symbol of greater status and power of women. Thus there is "no evidence that the body situation is the cause of the thing it symbolizes" (1964, p. 75).

Thompson interpreted the female personality characteristics (passivity, masochism, narcissism) that the Freudians identified as part of women's nature in the light of social pressures and economic necessity. For example, about "narcissism" she notes:

one cannot help thinking that a woman's greater need to be loved and to have one meaningful sexual relation . . . comes about chiefly in a culture which provides no security for her except a permanent so-called love relationship. It is known that the neurotic need of love is a mechanism for establishing security in a dependency relation. In the same way to the extent that a woman has a greater need of love than a man, it is also to be interpreted as a device for establishing security in a cultural situation producing dependency. Being loved not only is part of woman's natural life in the same way as it is part of man's but it also becomes of necessity her profession. Making her body sexually attractive and her personality seductive is imperative for purposes of security. . . . One sees that woman's alleged narcissism and greater need to be loved may be entirely the result of economic necessity. (Thompson 1964, pp. 133–134)

While Thompson was aware of the problems generated by dependency, she felt that it was also important for women not to copy men in order to fit into a male-dominated world, but to pursue their own interests. So impressed was she with the plasticity of behavior under the influence of sociocultural forces that she stated: "The basic nature of woman is still unknown" (1964, p. 141).

Mabel Blake Cohen was a contemporary of Thompson's, and, like Thompson and Horney, Cohen had a sociocultural outlook. She was among the first to examine gender-role stereotypes, their frequent inaccuracy and deleterious effects. With some humor she describes the devastating demise due gender-role stereotypic behaviors for a couple with a new baby: "This brave, strong, dominant male is expected to get up at night with a colicky infant, and this passive, helpless, and dependent woman is expected to deal courageously and with common sense with all the accidents and upsets of life with a small baby." (Cohen 1973, pp. 161–162)

## The Impact of New Biological and Psychological Research

As mentioned previously, until very recently the question of whether a woman "is born or made" has been a dominant undercurrent in the psychology of women. Whether or not the pre-oedipal little girl experiences vaginal sensations is of particular importance in this question—at least insofar as it rebuts Freud's contention that femininity is a secondary formation arising from renunciation of clitoral (i.e., masculine) sexuality. In this context, pre-oedipal vaginal sensations are supportive of the existence of a primary femininity. Some of Freud's female contemporaries, notably Horney and Melanie Klein, noted the probability of vaginal sensations in very young girls. Later such analysts as Kestenberg, Greenacre, and Barnett also ascribed vaginal sensations to very young girls (Kleeman 1977). Vaginal masturbation in female infants has recently been documented by Galenson and Roiphe (1977).

Mary Jane Sherfey (1966) has noted that Freud's views on penis envy followed quite logically from the biology of his time. This biology did not encompass an understanding of the extent of the interconnectedness of the clitoral and vaginal structures; it did not understand, for example, that the female orgasm is really "an orgasm of the circumvaginal venous chambers" (p. 94). Instead, it was believed that the vagina was a second female erotogenic zone. That left the comparison of the clitoris as a homologue to the penis. This view of the clitoris as a small phallus set the stage for Freud's theory of feminine development concerning penis envy (Sherfey, 1966).[4]

Further challenge to the idea that the girl's sexuality is first masculine and then changes to become feminine, and specifically that erotogenic sensitivity is transferred from the clitoris to the vagina, is pre-

4. Sherfey's careful scrutiny of the literature suggested to her what has now become a widely held view among embryologists: that the situation is the *reverse* of that originally believed by Freud. At conception the embryo of both sexes is believed to be female rather than male in structure, and it is only as a result of the male hormone, androgen, that the male morphological structure is differentiated. Thus it is more correct to say that the penis is an androgenized clitoris than that the clitoris is a small penis. However, the currently held view that the original structure is female is still controversial. (See Heiman 1968)

sented by the recent work of Masters and Johnson (1966). Their discovery that the clitoral and vaginal orgasm are physiologically the same thing has offered new insight into an understanding of feminine development as well as female sexuality.

However, it is the study of gender identity that has offered the most important correction to Freud's theory of feminine development. The research of John Money (1975), Robert Stoller (1974, 1977), James Kleeman (1974), and others is highly supportive of the existence of primary femininity. Their work indicates that the assignment of gender at birth and the parental attitudes and influences that are then conveyed in numerous ways in the first one and a half to four or five years of life are more important than biological sex in the determination of gender identity. For example, Stoller observes that when an otherwise biologically normal female is born with an androgenital syndrome (which causes masculinized external genitals), and sex assignment is male, a male core gender identity develops. If, however, sex assignment is female and the little girl is recognized as such, core gender identity is female. Kohlberg's (1966) cognitive-developmental theory of the acquisition of gender-role concepts has been found useful in explaining this phenomenon. According to this view, it is the self-labeling process as male or female that serves as an organizer for subsequent gender experience. Even vaginal sensations are not necessary for the development of femininity. At last, current theory presents cogent alternatives to Freud's theory that the girl's femininity stems from her disappointment in being confronted with anatomical deficiency. Stoller (1977) comments that probably no one would have bothered to question primary femininity had not Freud offered up his elaborate theory. Let us note, however, that these discoveries do not negate penis envy as a phenomenon of clinical importance. Indeed, the discovery of the anatomical distinction can have a profound effect, but this occurrence is built upon earlier learning experiences and the ways in which the little girl makes sense of the world in which she lives.

Of course, the importance assigned to psychological variables as a result of the recent work on gender identity by no means negates the powerful impact of hormonal differences. These are highly influential in both the behavior and affect of males and females. For instance, normal endocrine changes in the menstrual cycle of human females are found to vary with normal emotional states in predictable ways. High estrogen levels, either alone or in combination with other hormones, are implicated in women's feelings of self-esteem and competitive behavior (Bardwick 1974). Progesterone has been found to have a calming influence on behavior (Scarf 1980). High testosterone levels have been associated with aggressive feelings and behavior (Bardwick

1974). Quite recently, a plethora of biological research has appeared bearing on the question of what it means to be female. The results are just beginning to come in, and the difficulties involved in sorting out the multiple interactions of biological and psychological variables are becoming more and more apparent (Sobel 1980). Thus, the issue is not whether or not biology is influential. Clearly it is. The task before us is to arrive at valid conclusions on the basis of the data available and to sort out these conclusions from the prevailing errors.

## Present-Day Contributions: New Ideas and Theories About Women

Since the 1960s a great many publications presenting new ideas about the condition of women have appeared. The women's liberation movement has made the public more aware of women's political, social, and psychological oppression. Such literature as Simone de Beauvoir's *The Second Sex*, Betty Friedan's *The Feminine Mystique*, Germaine Greer's *The Female Eunuch*, Kate Millett's *Sexual Politics*, and Juliette Mitchell's *Psychoanalysis and Feminism*, for instance, have achieved a wide readership. Coinciding with the flood of the feminist literature, scholars in the field of mental health and in related sciences such as psychology and sociology have been recently proposing numerous new concepts and theories.

Psychology researchers have been taking more note of methodological flaws that generate gender bias and that certainly do not contribute to our pool of accurate information. Examples of such flaws are the frequent lack of attention to the gender of subjects in psychological experiments: The preponderance of subjects has been male—in some experiments, males comprise the entire subject population—and all too often the results have been erroneously generalized to women. When the gender composition of the subject pool is noticed, researchers may be prone to write up their results in a manner that conveys antiwoman distortions (Parlee 1975). Recognition of the frequency of such flaws has spawned a new subfield of psychology, "the psychology of women." As a result of the activity in this new field, more study of experiences particular to women—for example, childbirth—have emerged. Noting that "women have always been studied in relation to men and in the service of the study of man," Mednick (1976) quotes from *The Descent of Woman* by Elaine Morgan:

A very high proportion of thinking [in writings on evolution] . . . is androcentric in the same way as pre-Copernican thinking was geocentric. It's just as hard for man to break the habit of thinking of himself as central to the species as it was to break the habit of thinking of himself as central to the universe. He sees himself . . . as the main line of evolution, with the female satellite revolving around him as the moon revolves around the earth. (p. 769)

While advances in the field of mental health and the related sciences make Freud's notion of woman's inferior organ appear to be a dead issue, the issue has not been given a proper burial. In a landmark essay, "Problems in Freud's Psychology of Women," Roy Schafer (1974) does lay to rest Freud's conclusions (stemming from his theory of penis envy) concerning the inferiority of women's morality and ego development. In his paper Schafer shows how the irrationalities inherent in the legacy of patriarchy pervaded Freud's psychology of women. He notes that without substantiating evidence, Freud simply evaluated certain characteristics generally attributed to women as being inferior to those of men. Schafer points to the logical errors in Freud's linguistic linkage of "male-masculine-active-aggressive-dominant" and "female-feminine-passive-masochistic-submissive," noting their unfortunate and fateful results. He also observes that Freud paid insufficient attention to the period of pre-phallic development in the little girl and describes what he thinks are the reasons for this omission.

Since Freud's time there has been a shift of interest in psychoanalytic theory from the oedipal period to the pre-oedipal period, a time during which the relationship to the mother (as opposed to the father—at least in the most common family arrangements in our current culture) is predominant for both boys and girls. Interestingly, a woman, Margaret Mahler (1975), has furnished the most thoroughly researched account of pre-oedipal development. Until recently the distinguishing features of the mother-daughter relationship have remained largely unstudied. Adrienne Rich's beautifully written *Mothers and Daughters* is evocative and compelling. While Nancy Chodorow (1974) and Jane Flax (1978) have developed new theoretical viewpoints, and Signe Hammer, a psychological journalist, has published the thought-provoking conclusions drawn from her research (1976), much more work remains to be done.

The social learning point of view, which arose out of experimentation, has become increasingly popular among clinicians. One of its advantages is that it does not have to correct, but simply bypasses, some of the difficulties posed by a Freudian perspective. The same is generally true of a humanistic perspective. For both, the major instances of sexist bias occur more as a reflection of the practitioner than as a result of guiding theory.

18

Important new contributions to our understanding of the psychodynamic processes and symptom constellations more usually characteristic of women have been presented notably by Jean Baker Miller (1971, 1973, 1976), Alexandra Symonds (1971, 1974), and Helen Block Lewis (1974, 1976). In various publications Miller elaborates on the theme of the consequences of social inequality between men and women. Compassionately and poignantly, she illustrates for us the deleterious effects of this inequality on everyone: women, men, children, and society. She observes that women frequently feel that they exist to serve others. She attributes this to a coupling of two conditions: women's tendency to have more highly developed affiliative abilities and the fact that often the only forms of affiliation available to women are subordinate ones. In contrast, men are faced with the dilemma of having cut themselves off from the affiliative benefits of the disdained psychic world which they have assigned to women.

Alexandra Symonds has followed in the theoretical tradition of Karen Horney. As was Horney, she is particularly concerned with the excessively dependent personality pattern characteristic of so many women. She notes that overdependency stifles the capability to express aggression and stunts the growth toward autonomy. Symptomatic outlets are phobias, depression, and anxiety. Symonds advocates a more balanced personality development for women, including the cultivation of the qualities of detachment and expansiveness, the latter of which is more characteristic of the masculine style of interaction in our culture. Following Horney's scheme, Symonds states that psychological health involves fulfillment in all of these dimensions.

Helen Block Lewis, in contrast to Miller and Symonds, follows the Freudian tradition within a cognitive framework. While acknowledging Freud's sexism, she points out that we owe the very concept of sexism to his description of psychic defenses. On the basis of her research on gender differences in superego functioning, she has observed a greater propensity on the part of females for the cognitive style of field dependence and the affect of shame and on the part of males to field independence and the affect of guilt. These differences stem from the developmental dilemmas generally encountered by girls and boys. She feels that both sexes are affectionate by nature. In an exploitative society that scorns affectionateness, men are taught to renounce this quality (creating dilemmas for them) while women are taught to develop it. Thus the superego development of the female tends to be bound by affectional ties largely in relation to the "ego-ideal" of the superego. The superego development of the male on the other hand tends to be dominated by internalized castration threats, translatable into the "punishing conscience" aspect of the superego. Lewis's attention to the shame experience of women in daily living and in psychotherapy is new and noteworthy. She links this affect with the symptom expressions so common to women: depression and the hysterias. As does Miller, she notes the dehumanizing consequences for men of their inculcation of patterns of aggressiveness, domination, and exploitation.

Let us note that while Miller, Symonds, and Lewis all emerge from different theoretical traditions and employ different terminology, they all note the greater importance of affiliative and affectional ties for women and connect these with women's greater vulnerability to depression. Aspects of these themes have been noted by other researchers and theorists as well (e.g., Chodorow 1974; Scarf 1980).

There has been a return recently to concern with the issue of the psychical consequences of the anatomical differences between the sexes, this time with more of an emphasis on women's potential to have psychologically healthier resolution of this issue than men. Marjorie Barnett (1968) postulates that an important difference in early experience of boys and girls is that the boys' awareness of his immature penis instills in him a feeling of "I can't (penetrate mother)" while the girl, who knows she "can (be penetrated by father)," has a different dilemma: father "won't." The experience of the boy leads to a hypercathexis of that body part that "can't," leading to the part-object orientation of so many men. In contrast, the girl, who does not feel uncertain about her part, has a better chance to develop whole-object cathexis. Her desire is to "win" a man of her own "who will . . . fill her space."

A most important aspect of the psychical consequences of the anatomical distinction between the sexes was well phrased by Oscar Wilde: "Madam, I cannot conceive." One tradition in our culture stemming from this distinction has been the pattern for women to be the primary caretakers of children. Robert Stoller (1974) and Ethel Person (1974) have addressed the question of impact of primary caretaker's gender on the developing child. Both suggest that because the girl need not switch her object of identification from mother to father, her developmental tasks are in many ways less problematic than the boy's. Observing that men are more vulnerable to gender-identity disturbances (transsexualism, transvestitism), both Stoller and Person suggest that girls and women have a more solid sense of core gender identity. Interestingly, this is the other side of the coin of Freud's hypothesis that the girl's development is more complicated because she must switch her love object.

Stoller further suggests that women have a more solid sense of core gender identity and are therefore the "stronger" (1974, p. 410) sex. He emphasizes that for the little boy, from birth on, his still to be created masculinity is endangered by the primary, profound, primeval oneness with mother, a blissful experience that serves, buried, but active in the core of one's identity. (p. 409)

If the little boy is to achieve an adequate identity as a male, it is crucial that he be able to separate himself from this blissful symbiosis with his mother and her femininity. Stoller's point is well taken, but his suggestion that women's more solid core gender identity makes them stronger may be unfounded. Little girls have to separate from their mothers, too. Different conclusions can be drawn from the information that the girl and her caretaking mother are of the same gender. According to Flax (1978) this can make the task of separation particularly difficult for the little girl. Her perspective is that the mother's own difficulties can impinge on her developing daughter. The mother's identification with her daughter and her attempt to tie her daughter to her in order to secure nurturance for herself can interfere with the daughter's ego development, making the task of separation in particular more difficult. Louise Kaplan (1978) makes a similar observation in her book *Oneness and Separateness: From Infant to Individual.* She notes that while mothers tend to be proud and even in awe of their little boys' masculine prowess, they tend to fear more for the safety of their little girls. An important experience of the practicing period of pre-oedipal development, often called "the love-affair with the world," is the emotion of elation, an elation in feeling body strength and discovering body edges with abandon. Kaplan notes that mothers tend to maintain the erroneous idea that girls are more fragile than boys, despite the fact that they are usually stronger and better coordinated. She says, "Elation cushions disappointments and disenchantment, and many little girls simply haven't had enough elation" (p. 176). This makes the task of separation more difficult.

Almost half a century ago, Karen Horney addressed the psychodynamics behind the cultural devaluation of women. She described how male envy of female procreativity (1926) and dread of women (1932) become transformed into devaluation of women. More recently, Harriet Lerner (1974), Dorothy Dinnerstein (1976) and Joel Kovel (1974) have focused on the psychological processes contributing to the devaluation of women. Lerner and Dinnerstein place particular emphasis on the impact of woman's traditional role as childrearer. Both wish to make us aware of the ways in which the devaluation of women is a defensive response to powerful affects (such as terror, envy, and rage) that the dependent, helpless infant inevitably experiences at the hands of its powerful mother. They suggest that these affects are so strong and so persistent that women as well as men are caught up in the need to depreciate women. Lerner suggests that a process of defensive reversal of early matriarchy contributes to gender-role stereotyping according to which women are typically experienced by men as infantile, physically weak, intellectually helpless—in short, as "babies." Dinnerstein develops an impressively complete, complex, and ultimately sweeping argument. She contends that the crux of our current human dilemma is our gender arrangements according to which women are assigned primary child-rearing responsibilities. This includes the maintenance of a stalemated immaturity of both men and women as well as the massive defilement of "mother" earth and imminent threats of nuclear disaster. She states that while both men and women share some motivation in common for devaluing women, they have different motives according to their respective positions in the social context, leading to a symbiotic interweaving of motivation that tightly holds the status quo. While an identification with the father and other men supports the emotional distancing from mother for the boy, the oedipal triangle offers the girl an "out" for the split of loving and hostile feelings toward her mother. Her father becomes the object of her grateful love (originally felt toward her mother), while her mother remains the object of her derogatory, hostile attitudes. Thus, both men and women turn to patriarchy as a solution to their intolerable feelings toward their mothers. Once symbiotically entrenched, the interplay of benefits, imagined benefits, and fears makes it exceptionally hard for women and men to see their mutually contorted positions and to develop and reclaim independent, whole selfhood. Unless corrected, says Dinnerstein, the cost of our gender arrangements, which typically begin with the delegation of childrearing to women, will probably be global self-destruction.

There has been a resurgence of interest lately in certain older writings that address the theme of the mythically powerful mother. Examples are Erich von Neumann's descriptions of the archetype of the "Great Mother" (*The Great Mother* 1955) and Helen Diner's *Mothers and Amazons* (1973). Diner's book resurrects the earlier work of Bachofen with its hypothesis of the existence of early matriarchal cultures.

Perhaps as theorists' and therapists' interpretations of the devaluation of women filter through to conscious appraisal, images of the powerful women become less threatening, more tolerable, and even uplifting. We are now in a better position than ever before to tap the depths of psychic life with more precision and with less danger of rendering harm to clients. We have corrected Freud's errors with respect to the nature of biological determinism, and revised our theory in accordance. We now have a more sophisticated knowledge of biology, which, in combination with our knowledge of the processes of learning and development, gives us a better framework (than that which, for instance, Freud had) for continued scientific investigation.

Lacking a clear or complete understanding of what it means to be female, we are awaiting the results of further research and thought, and continue to focus on two questions: "What are the (internalizing/cognitive) processes by which social reality, interacting with biology, becomes psychic reality? And, how is intrapsychic reality to be understood in its interaction with the dynamics of the larger social system?" It is only through such understanding that we can continue to improve our approaches to the psychotherapeutic treatment of women.

## REFERENCES

Bardwick, J. 1974. The sex hormones, the central nervous system and affect variability in humans. *Women in therapy*, ed. V. Franks and V. Burtle, 27–49. New York: Brunner/Mazel.

Barnett, M. 1968. "I can't" versus "he won't." Further considerations of the psychical consequences of the anatomical and physiological differences between the sexes. *Journal of the American Psychiatric Association* 16:588–600.

Beauvoir, S. de. 1953. *The second sex.* New York: Alfred A. Knopf.

Chesler, P. 1972. *Women and madness.* New York: Avon Books.

Cohen, M. B. 1973. Personal identity and sexual identity. In *Psychoanalysis and women*, ed. J. B. Miller, pp. 156–182. Baltimore: Penguin Books.

Chodorow, N. 1974. Family structure and feminine personality. In *Women, culture and society*, ed. M. Rosaldo and L. Lamphere, pp. 43–66. Stanford, Calif.: Stanford University Press.

Diner, H. 1973. *Mothers and amazons.* New York: Anchor Press.

Dinnerstein, D. 1976. *The mermaid and the minotaur.* New York: Harper & Row.

Erikson, E. 1963. *Childhood and society.* New York: W. W. Norton.

Erikson, E. 1974. Women and inner space. In *Women and analysis*, ed. J. Strouse, pp. 333–364. New York: Dell.

Flax, J. 1978. The conflict between nurturance and autonomy in mother-daughter relationships and within feminism. *Journal of Feminist Studies* Summer:171–189. [Reprinted herein chapter 4.]

Fliegel, Z. O. 1973. Feminine psychosexual development in Freudian theory: A historical reconstruction. *Psychoanalytic Quarterly* 42 (3):385–407.

Freud, S. 1953. Three essays on the theory of sexuality. In *The standard edition of the psychological works of Sigmund Freud* (hereafter *Standard edition*), ed. J. Strachey, vol. 7, pp. 135–243. London: Hogarth Press. [Originally published 1905.]

————. 1961. Some psychical consequences of the anatomical distinction between the sexes. *Standard edition*, vol. 19, pp. 248–258. London: Hogarth Press. [Originally published 1925.]

————. 1964. Female sexuality. *Standard edition*, vol. 21, pp. 225–243. London: Hogarth Press. [Originally published 1933.]

————. 1964. New introductory lectures on psycho-analysis. *Standard edition*, vol. 22, pp. 7–182. London: Hogarth Press. [Originally published 1931.]

————. 1964. Analysis terminable and interminable. *Standard edition*, vol. 23, pp. 216–253. London: Hogarth Press. [Originally published 1937.]

Friedan, B. 1963. *The feminine mystique.* New York: Dell.

Galenson, E., and Roiphe, H. 1977. Some revisions concerning early female development. In *Female psychology*, ed. H. Blum, pp. 29–58. New York: International Universities Press.

Goldenberg, N. 1976. A feminist critique of Jung. *Signs* 2:443–449.

Greer, G. 1970. *The female eunuch.* New York: McGraw-Hill.

Hammer, S. 1975. *Daughters and mothers: Mothers and daughters.* New York: Quadrangle/New York Times Book Co.

Harris, D. 1979. Book review of *Androgyny: Toward a new theory of sexuality* by June Singer. *Signs* 4:783–784.

Heiman, M. 1968. Mary Jane Sherfy: The evolution and nature of female sexuality in relation to psychoanalytic theory. *Journal of the American Psychoanalytic Association* 16: 406–416.

Horney, K. 1939. New ways in psychoanalysis. New York: Norton.

_____ . 1973. The denial of the vagina. In *Feminine psychology*, ed. H. Kelman, pp. 147–161. New York: Norton.

_____ . 1973. The flight from womanhood. In *Feminine psychology*, ed. H. Kelman, pp. 54–70. New York: Norton.

Jung, C. 1971. *The portable Jung.* New York: Viking Press.

Kaplan, L. 1978. *Oneness and separateness: From infant to individual.* New York: Simon & Schuster.

Kleeman, J. 1977. Freud's views on early female sexuality in the light of direct child observation. In *Female sexuality*, ed. H. Blum. New York: International Universities Press.

Kohlberg, L. 1966. A cognitive-developmental analysis of children's sex role concepts and attitudes. In *The development of sex differences*, ed. E. Maccoby, pp. 82–173. Stanford, Calif.: Stanford University Press.

Kovel, J. 1974. The castration complex reconsidered. In *Women and analysis*, ed. J. Strouse, pp. 162–170. New York: Dell.

Lerner, H. E. 1974. Early origins of envy and devaluation of women: Implications for sex-role stereotypes. *Bulletin of the Menninger Clinic* 38:538–553. [Reprinted herein chapter 2.]

_____ . 1978. Adaptive and pathogenic aspects of sex-role stereotypes: Implications for psychotherapy and parenting. *American Journal of Psychiatry* 135:48–52. [Reprinted herein chapter 44.]

Lewis, H. 1971. *Shame and guilt in neurosis.* New York: International Universities Press.

_____ . 1976. *Psychic war in men and women.* New York: New York University Press.

Mahler, M., Pine, F., and Bergman, A. 1975. *The psychological birth of the human infant.* New York: Basic Books.

Masters, W., and Johnson, V. 1966. *Human sexual response.* Boston: Little, Brown.

Miller, J. 1971. Psychological consequences of sexual inequality. *American Journal of Orthopsychiatry* 41:767–775.

_____ . 1976. *Toward a new psychology of women.* Boston: Beacon Press.

_____ , ed. 1973. *Psychoanalysis and women.* Baltimore: Penguin Books.

Millett, K. 1970. *Sexual politics.* Garden City, N.Y.: Doubleday.

Mitchell, J. 1974. *Psychoanalysis and feminism.* New York: Vintage.

Money, J. 1975. Psychosexual differentiation. In *Women, body and culture*, ed. S. Hammer, pp. 91–105. New York: Harper & Row.

Moulton, R. 1974. The role of Clara Thompson in the psychoanalytic study of women. In *Women and analysis*, ed. J. Strouse. New York: Dell.

Parlee, M. 1975. Psychology. *Signs* 1:119–138.

Person, E. 1974. Some new observations on the origins of femininity. In *Women and analysis*, ed. J. Strouse, pp. 289–302. New York: Dell.

Scarf, M. 1980. *Unfinished business.* Garden City, N.Y.: Doubleday.

Schafer, R. 1974. Problems in Freud's psychology of women. *Journal of the American Psychoanalytic Association* 22(3):459–485.

Sherfey, M. J. 1966. *The nature and evolution of female sexuality.* New York: Vintage.

Sobel, E. 1977. Book review of *Women and analysis* by J. Strouse. *Group Process* 2:271–276.

_____ . 1980. Aggression in women: A perspective for the eighties. Unpublished manuscript. Presented at the New York Academy of the Sciences, 1980.

Stoller, R. 1974. Facts and fancies: An examination of Freud's concept of bisexuality. In *Women and analysis*, ed. J. Strouse, pp. 391–415. New York: Dell.

————. 1977. Primary femininity. In *Female psychology: Contemporary psychoanalytic views*, ed. H. Blum, pp. 59–78. New York: International Universities Press.

Stolorow, R. and Attwood, G. 1978. A defensive-restitutive function of Freud's theory of psychosexual development. *Psychoanalytic Review* 65: 217–238.

Symonds, A. 1971. Phobias after marriage: Women's declaration of dependence. *American Journal of Psychoanalysis* 31:144–52. [Reprinted herein chapter 16.]

Thompson, C. 1964. *On women*, ed. M. Green. New York: Basic Books.

von Neumann, E. 1955. *The great mother*. Princeton, N.J.: Princeton University Press.

Wimpfheimer, J., and Schafer, R. 1979. Psychoanalytic methodology in Helene Deutsch's *The psychology of women*. *Psychoanalytic Quarterly* 16:287–318.

# 2

# Early Origins of Envy and Devaluation of Women: Implications for Sex-Role Stereotypes

## HARRIET E. LERNER

Psychoanalysts have long believed that penis envy is central to the understanding of women and have invoked this concept to explain everything from a woman's desire for a husband and child to her strivings to work and compete in traditionally masculine fields. Those outside psychoanalytic circles have shown less enthusiasm for such explanations—particularly members of the women's liberation movement, who angrily protest that women have cause to be envious of men's position in society for reasons other than their possession of the desired penis. Certain psychoanalysts have, in turn, insisted that the women's liberation movement is itself a manifestation of penis envy and that discontent with the female role is a psychiatric problem.

Narrow and stereotyped notions concerning women's appropriate place in society are not confined to a mere handful of psychoanalysts. The most authoritative of psychoanalysts have concurred that the

The author would like to express her gratitude to Dr. Otto Kernberg, Dr. Paul Pruyser, and Dr. Tobias Brocher for their helpful comments and criticisms.

"true" nature of women is to find fulfillment in the traditional role of wife and mother (Chesler 1972). Without sharing Freud's views of the Oedipus complex and penis envy, Jung (1928) nevertheless stated, ". . . that in taking up a masculine calling, studying, and working in a man's way, woman is doing something not wholly in agreement with, if not directly injurious to, her feminine nature" (p. 169). Bettelheim (1965) commented, ". . . as much as women want to be good scientists or engineers, they want first and foremost to be womanly companions of men and to be mothers" (p. 15). Women who are not happy with this state of affairs, according to Freud (1950), have refused adaptively to come to grips with their sexual inferiority and still have the "hope of some day obtaining a penis in spite of everything . . ." (p. 191).

While I am not in agreement with those who discredit the importance of penis envy, I do believe psychoanalysts who rationalize certain maladaptive aspects of femininity as unavoidable biological necessities court contempt by carrying the concept of penis envy to untenable extremes. As Chesler (1972) has commented, "The 'Freudian' vision beholds women as essentially 'breeders and bearers,' as potentially warmhearted creatures, but more often as cranky children with uteruses, forever mourning the loss of male organs and male identity" (p. 79).

It is unfortunate, however, that feminist anger and misunderstanding have led to a global damnation of all psychoanalytic thinking, as well as a somewhat more benign condemnation of other established modes of treatment. There have been numerous revisions of Freud's viewpoints on women with frequent references to the unfortunate "phallocentric" bias of his theorizing and open acknowledgment that femininity and female sexuality are insufficiently understood (David 1970; Torok 1970). Even Freud expressed reticence and insecurity in the face of that "dark continent" of femininity and never failed to stress the incomplete and tentative nature of his theorizing. Recent psychoanalytic writers have, in fact, shown considerable appreciation of feminist protests and of the intense cultural pressures that combine with intrapsychic factors to encourage "women [to] accept [a] . . . neurotically dependent, self-effacing solution in life" (Symonds 1971–72, p. 224).

Long before the current feminist movement, however, there existed wide recognition that femininity in most cultures is much devalued and that frequent exaltation and idealization of women hardly mask the underlying contempt for them (Horney 1932). Writers from many disciplines, psychoanalysts among them, have written about the quasiracial discrimination that exists against women. David (1970), for example, has noted one primitive tribe that refers to women as "the race which is not entitled to speak" (p. 50); and anthropologists have observed that the devaluation of women in many cultures is no less intense than the oppression of racial or ethnic minority groups.

The oppression of women is unique, however, in one important respect: Women participate as vigorously in their own depreciation as do men. The "masochistic attitude" of many women can be easily recognized, and women's belittling of their own sex is observed daily in our consulting rooms, demonstrated in experimental research (Goldberg 1968), and is inherent in cultural institutions around the world (Lederer 1968).

The devaluation of women is readily documented, but the reasons behind the complicity of both sexes are less than clear. In addition to powerful cultural pressures on women to devalue themselves, there must be strong internal pressures as well, for institutionalized patterns are not so readily established and maintained unless there are advantages for all involved. For men as well, the reasons for complicity with a sexist solution are not obvious. Men have too frequently been described as having all the advantages and power of a "ruling class" when, in fact, the cost for their situation is no less dear. As one psychoanalyst has written:

> . . . on examining the question more closely, it is not obvious a priori that men should naturally want such a relationship of mastery. The falsity, the ambivalence, and the refusal of identifications it conceals should appear to him as so many snags on which his own full and authentic achievement comes to grief. . . . What interest has he in giving in to his need to dominate the being through whom he could understand himself and who could understand him? To discover oneself through the other sex would be a genuine fulfillment of one's humanity, yet this is exactly what escapes most of us. (Torok 1970, pp. 168–169)

For many psychoanalytic theorists, the devaluation of women is an irreducible problem that stems from the genital deficiency (real or imagined) of the female sex. Intense hatred directed toward the mother because of her penisless state and the resulting contempt not only for her but for all women is the inescapable lot of girls (due to their castration complex) and of boys (due to their castration anxiety). As long as men have penises and women vaginas, institutionalized sexism is an inevitable symptom of our anatomical destinies, for which phylogenesis alone must bear the responsibility.

However, by overextending the concept of genital inferiority in explaining the devaluation of women, we have failed to appreciate other important determinants. My opinion is that the devaluation of women as well as the very definitions of appropriate "masculine" and "feminine" behavior stem in large part from a defensive handling of the powerful and persistent affects of the early infant-mother relationship.

The profound affects (i.e., envy, fear, rage, shame) aroused by the child's helpless dependency on an all-powerful maternal figure have indeed received recognition, but their resulting impact on adult life has continually been underplayed and insufficiently elaborated. As Lederer (1968) commented, "of our fear and envy of women, we, the psychoanalytic-papers-writing-men, have managed to maintain a dignified fraternal silence" (p. 153).

## Envy of Women

If the concept of penis envy is familiar even to the layman, psychoanalytic speculations regarding breast envy require a more arduous search through the literature. This fact is surprising, for society's intense idealization, devaluation, and literal obsession with breasts seems to point to the significance of such a phenomenon. Also of relevance is the critical importance of the mother's breast in early infancy: The breast is the earliest source of gratification and frustration, of love and hate, as well as the first vehicle of intimate social contact (Fairbairn 1952). Klein (1957), for example, has highlighted the infant's early relationship to the mother's breast: "in the analysis of our patients . . . the breast in its good aspect is the prototype of maternal goodness, inexhaustible patience and generosity, as well as of creativeness" (pp. 5–6).

Although the idea of breast envy has no formal conceptual status in psychoanalytic theory, it is of central importance in Melanie Klein's theoretical work. Defining envy as "the angry feeling that another person possesses and enjoys something desirable—the envious impulse being to take it away or to spoil it" (1957, p. 6), she writes: "My work has taught me that the first object to be envied is the feeding breast, for the infant feels that it possesses everything he desires and that it has an unlimited flow of milk and love which the breast keeps for its own gratification" (1957, p. 10). To Klein, the desire to internalize and thus possess the breast, so all the power and magic that the infant attributes to it will be his own, is of central importance. She reports that in the analysis of female patients even penis envy can be traced back to envy of the mother's breast (or its symbolic representation, the bottle).

Freud (1955a, b) also recognized that there is a counterpart to penis envy when he described pregnancy fantasies and the wish for a baby

OKANAGAN COLLEGE LIBRARY
BRITISH COLUMBIA

among men. In the analytic literature, one can find case studies describing pregnancy fantasies and enacted pregnancies both in grown men and young boys. Others such as Ruth Mack Brunswick (1940) have elaborated this theme, stating that in girls the wish for a child precedes the wish for a penis and that penis envy itself can be understood as the desire to possess the omnipotent mother and her attributes.

It is not my intention to popularize the notion of breast envy, but rather to suggest that male envy of female sex characteristics and reproductive capacity is a widespread and conspicuously ignored dynamic. Of greater importance is the fact that envy tends to be a larger phenomenon for both sexes, not typically confined to such part objects as penises and breasts. As Torok (1970) points out, it is not the absence of a thing (such as the penis or breast) that produces such profound feelings of envy, despair, and self-hatred, but, rather, such envy is a symptom of unconscious desires, wishes, or fears that may have little to do with objective anatomical realities. Penis envy, for example, frequently has its origin in the dyadic relationship between mother and daughter and may be a symptom reflecting difficulties in identifying with and achieving differentiation from a mother who is perceived as jealous, destructive, and intrusive (Chasseguet-Smirgel 1970; Torok 1970). For men, it is unlikely that envy of women is derived simply from the feeding breast and reproductive capacities, but rather from the varied impressions of infancy and early childhood in which the mother is experienced as an omnipotent object who possesses inexhaustible supplies as well as the power both to inflict and ward off all pain and evil.

## Envy and Devaluation: Reversing an Early Matriarchy

Of central importance to the dynamic understanding of defensive sexism is the close relationship between envy and devaluation. Devaluation of an envied object is a typical defensive maneuver, for as long as an object is devalued it need not be envied. Klein has suggested that spoiling and devaluing are inherent aspects of envy and that the earliest and most important objects of envy and devaluation are the mother and her breast. Kernberg (1972) has also noted in his work with borderline and narcissistic patients that intense envy and hatred of women are conspicuous dynamics that impair the capacity to form love relationships. He finds that envy and hatred are defensively dealt with by depreciating and devaluating women.

The question arises whether envy and devaluation of women is confined to persons with serious psychopathology or whether it is a more pervasive if not universal dynamic. Although Kernberg implies that this constellation is a serious problem only for very disturbed patients, he also notes it is not a circumscribed clinical phenomenon: "One finds intense envy and hatred of women in many male patients. Indeed, from a clinical viewpoint, it seems the intensity of this dynamic constellation in men matches that of penis envy in women . . . " (1972, p. 14).

I agree with Kernberg's statement that devaluation of women is "in the final analysis, devaluation of mother as a primary object of dependency" (1972, p. 14). However, I would further suggest that this dynamic is a pervasive one that is expressed in the institutionalized values and mores regarding gender in cultures around the world. In this culture, for example, I believe that the envy-devaluation constellation is reflected in the selection of what traits, qualities, behaviors, and roles are deemed appropriate for each sex. Our current notions of "masculinity" and "femininity" are such that enormous pressures are put on females to "let the man win"; to avoid direct expressions of aggression, self-assertion, competitiveness, and intellectual prowess; and to suppress wishes to be leader and initiator rather than follower and helpmate (Lerner 1974; Lynn 1972). I suspect these widely accepted gender definitions and sex-role stereotypes are themselves a reflection of a defensive devaluing of women and thus of an early dependency relationship with mother.

Our gender definitions and sex-role stereotypes also reflect an attempt to reinstate and retain in adult relations all the nurturant qualities of the "good mother." Thus, according to most cultural stereotypes, the desirable, "feminine" woman is one who embodies all aspects of the good mother (e.g., cleaning, feeding, providing emotional understanding, comfort, softness, warmth), but who possesses no elements of the power, dominance, and control that are also factors within the imago of the omnipotent, envied mother. To put it somewhat differently, in conventional adult relationships, males stereotypically experience a *defensive reversal* of an early matriarchy, yet retain the nurturant functions of the good mother. A psychic and social situation is created in which the adult male retains the good aspects of mother but is now dominant and in control of a female object on whom, as in the case of his mother, he was initially helpless and dependent; that is, his wife (or female peer) becomes his own child. As long as this defensive reversal of an early dependency situation continues, envy and devaluation of women is subdued or seemingly eliminated; the devaluation of women achieves expression in the reversal itself.

But how are we to understand women's active participation in this system? For although women reverse the helpless dependency of their own infantile situation through the role of mother, they often "choose" in peer relations with men to remain the dependent child. As Kernberg (1972) points out, envy and devaluation of the mother as a primal source of dependency is no less intense in women than in men. Thus women's acceptance and perpetuation of feminine stereotypes (e.g., fragility, dependency, passivity, etc.) as well as idealization of men and the penis may also be an attempt to devalue the omnipotence and power of the maternal figure. This notion is compatible with Chasseguet-Smirgel's (1970) statement that images of women as castrated or deficient are a denial for both sexes of the imagos of the primitive mother (i.e., the good omnipotent mother is symbolized by the generous breast, fruitful womb, wholeness, abundance; the bad omnipotent mother is symbolized by frustration, invasion, intrusion, evil).[1]

Other theorists as well, while not focusing specifically on envy, have linked early maternal power to the depreciation of women. David (1970) speculates that profound narcissistic injuries inflicted on the infant by the omnipotent mother lead to a powerful need for revenge. He suggests that our distorted concept of femininity and female sexuality, the discrimination that women suffer by men and women, and the masochistic attitude that characterizes women are all the result of "revenge" for the radical narcissistic wounds inflicted on both male and female infants at the breast. Horney (1932) relates both the idealization and depreciation of women to the violently aggressive desires for revenge that stem from the mother's dominance and power and the small child's related feelings of weakness, impotence, and humiliation. Brunswick (1940) notes the powerful character of the primitive maternal image and emphasizes the early narcissistic injuries resulting from the child's dependency on the omnipotent mother "who is capable of everything and who possesses every valuable attribute" (p. 304).

Chasseguet-Smirgel (1970) suggests another determinant of the need to reverse the infantile situation, namely the fear and terror of women.

1. Penis envy and castration concerns in women reflect a defensive need to devalue the imagos of the primitive mother. Yet such symptoms may also reflect deep guilt and anxiety in identifying with this imago, especially when mother is experienced as a powerful, malevolent, and castrating figure in her relationship with father. Thus women's self-experience of being "castrated" (and their idealization of men and the penis) is often a reaction formation against their own feared "castrating" and aggressive wishes. (See Chasseguet-Smirgel [1970] for an excellent discussion of this issue.)

I believe that a child, whether male or female, even with the best and kindest of mothers, will maintain a terrifying maternal image in his unconscious, the result of projected hostility deriving from his own impotence.... the child's primary powerlessness ... and the inevitable frustrations of training are such that the imago of the good, omnipotent mother never covers over that of the terrifying, omnipotent, bad mother. (pp. 112–113)

Horney (1932) and Lederer (1968) each present an impressive amount of clinical, mythological, and anthropological evidence regarding man's terror of women. Although both authors comment on the remarkable lack of recognition and attention this topic has received, I suggest that perhaps it is not that the fear of women has gone unrecognized, but that the consequences of that fear for the patriarchal nature of societies have not been sufficiently appreciated. To what extent has our concept of femininity been distorted by a need to discourage women from the recognition and expression of self-seeking, aggressive, competitive, ambitious strivings, in order to assure that the primitive maternal imago can, in adult life, at last be controlled, dominated, and revenged? Similarly, if men were encouraged to experience and express so-called "feminine" qualities (e.g., dependency, passivity, fragility), would they then feel in danger of returning to that dreaded (although wished-for) condition of early maternal omnipotence? In keeping with this theme, Chasseguet-Smirgel (1970) has related religious mythology to the difficulties that maternal dominance and omnipotence present to both sexes.

Man and woman are born of woman: before all else we are our mother's child. Yet all our desires seem designed to deny this fact, so full of conflicts and reminiscent of our primitive dependence. The myth of Genesis seems to express this desire to free ourselves from our mother: man is born of God, an idealized paternal figure.... Woman is born from man's body. If this myth expresses the victory of man over his mother and over woman, who thereby becomes his own child, it also provides a certain solution for woman inasmuch as she also is her mother's daughter: she chooses to belong to man, to be created *for* him, and not for herself, to be a part of him—Adam's rib—rather than to prolong her "attachment" to her mother. (pp. 133–134)

## Sex-Role Stereotypes

At the cost of oversimplifying, I believe it may be worthwhile to examine how the values and mores of traditional male-female relationships in this country can be understood within the stated theoretical framework.[2] The fact that the nurturant functions of the good mother are retained by women in marriage (e.g., feeding, cleaning, providing emotional comfort, support) hardly requires description or elaboration. The following points are offered to support the notion that the cultural stereotypes of adult gender interactions (apart from nurturant functions) involve a reversal for males of their early helplessness and dependency on a powerful female object.

1. Women are encouraged to be dependent and are frequently portrayed as lost and helpless without a male partner. "Little girl" qualities typically make women more attractive, and it is of significance that women are affectionately referred to as "girls," "chicks," "baby," and "doll." Mother tends to foster dependency to a greater degree in female children (Lynn 1972); and research indicates that adult men and women tend to equate assertive, independent strivings in girls and women with a loss of femininity (Baumrind 1972).

Expressions of dependency needs in men are considered unattractive, weak, or effeminate, and are more frequently denied than cultivated. For males, the notion of men's greater independence is a reversal of the infant-mother paradigm, in which it is the child who is helplessly dependent on the powerful maternal figure.

2. In male-female relationships, intellectual ability and competence are frequently seen as the man's domain. A girl's sense of intellectual mastery and skill is progressively discouraged as she is trained to be "feminine"; she is encouraged to be smart enough to catch a man but never to outsmart him (Baumrind 1972; Lerner 1974). In the media, wives are often portrayed as silly, capricious, gossipy, illogical, and intellectually helpless; and mockery of a female's ability to think logically and critically is an extremely popular form of humor. Although women are acknowledged to have a type of wisdom that goes by the name of "feminine intuition," there is a persistent insinuation that for females organized and sustained logical thinking is not critically involved. Research findings indicate that both sexes regard intellectual achievement as "unfeminine" and that college women tend to equate academic success with detrimental social consequences (Baumrind 1972).

Although many men do not value the "dumb blonde" stereotype, few seek love relationships with a female partner who is comfortably

2. It is, of course, naive to assume that the devaluation of women and the establishment and maintenance of traditional sex-role stereotypes can entirely be understood according to the stated theoretical framework that emphasizes the early oral dyadic relationship between mother and child without regard for the complexities inherent in the oedipal triangle. Additional socioeconomic, biological, and psychodynamic factors are relevant to the present discussion, and the narrow focus of this paper is due only to the necessity for brevity. The speculations offered in this paper are to be considered partial rather than exhaustive explanations of complicated phenomena.

acknowledged to be an intellectual equal or superior. Similarly, a woman who assumes an intellectually aggressive, critical, or dominant stance is often labeled "masculine" or "castrating." Again, this social situation appears to be a reversal of the male's position as an infant in which the intellectually helpless child is slowly taught to master his environment by a maternal figure who is experienced as infinitely capable and wise. The role of early teacher (and frustrator) moves systematically from mother to a continuing series of figures (governesses, baby-sitters, elementary schoolteachers) who are predominantly female.

3. Physical strength and prowess, which are glorified and cultivated in men, are considered unattractive in women; the strong athletic female or gymnast is generally not thought to be the most attractive of mates. Although men may be encouraged to go to painful extremes in body building, women are taught to exaggerate and even feign weakness in the interest of "femininity." Men enjoy treating women as weak and delicate creatures who cannot open their own doors or carry their own packages. Similarly, it is typically important for men to be physically taller than their mates. Short or small men are devalued. Again, for men, this paradigm reverses the infant's experiences of the small and weak child who is carried about with ease in the arms of the powerful mother. Horney (1932) emphasized the small boy's feeling of distress and humiliation at being small and weak in comparison with mother.

4. In love relationships, men are typically older than their female partner. While there is nothing unusual about a match between a thirty-five-year-old man and a twenty-three-year-old woman, the reversed situation is evaluated as eccentric if not pathological. Similarly, when a man marries a woman "young enough to be his daughter," the match may be either criticized or condoned by society, but the desires of both parties are considered understandable. Were a woman to marry a man young enough to be her son, society tends to respond with scorn and shock. Again, for males, this situation reverses the infant-mother relationship in which the "older woman" is the sole object of the young child's libidinal desires. One might further speculate that the intense pressures on women to look eternally like adolescent girls (rather than "mothers") stem in part from the matronly woman's capacity to arouse infantile envy of the inexhaustible feeding breast as well as to stimulate anxiety-laden wishes for returning to a helpless state of dependency.

5. The perpetuation of personality characteristics and traits associated with infancy and childhood is encouraged in the female sex only. For example, crying, whining, seductively manipulative and petulant behavior are all acceptable ways for women to make their demands

felt and are portrayed as typical feminine qualities in the media. Such behaviors are unacceptable in men, encouraged as they are to assert themselves in a more "manly" fashion. Similarly, females are most frequently portrayed as emotional and males as intellectual. The stereotype is of the "hysterical," overemotional wife who is kept in check by her husband who allegedly makes decisions by the laws of logic and cool reason. Again, males experience a reversal of the infant's situation in which it is the mother who supplies the intellectual controls to the child who has considerable affective lability and emotionality.

6. In courtship and sexual relations, women stereotypically assume a passive stance and men an overly active one. Men are taught actively to pursue what they want; women are taught to make themselves pretty enough to be sought after. Although females may learn "feminine wiles" to attract the men of their choice, they are discouraged from openly and directly pursuing a male figure. This state of affairs for males is again the reversal of the infant's situation in which the baby is unable actively to determine whether it will get the breast or the mother's affection. The baby may actively attempt to "court" her in a number of ways (e.g., by crying or being cute), but it is the active mother who initiates or fails to initiate contact with the child.

7. Stereotyped notions of feminine sexuality tend to glorify naïveté and "innocence"; whereas for males, "experience" tends to enhance their sexual attractiveness. (One might consider the difference between an "experienced man" and a "loose woman.") Similarly, in regard to the expression of aggressive impulses, Symonds (1971–72) notes that what is called "strength of character" in boys is called "unfeminine" in girls. Stereotypes that have encouraged the stifling of sexual and aggressive expression in women and the frank expression of impulse life in males are also for men a reversal of the infant-mother paradigm: It is the mother who inhibits the expression of "unacceptable" impulses early in the child's life. Many psychoanalytic writers, including Horney, Klein, and Freud, have stressed that mothers are experienced as punitive because they are the first to forbid a child's instinctual activities.

## The Significance of Sex-Role Stereotypes

I anticipate the objection that the generalizations presented in this paper are oversimplified clichés that fail to account for the richness of individual differences in our culture. Clearly, both clinical knowledge and human experience reveal that there are varied bases for successful male-female relationships and that many stable and gratifying marriages involve variations if not thoroughgoing modifications of these general themes. Sydney Smith[3] points out that a common American cliché holds that the woman is the real decision maker in the family despite the man's belief that he is the boss. This understanding of power relationships between the sexes is familiar and is well illustrated by the European saying: "The man is the head of the family but the woman is the neck that carries the head and determines the direction." Underlying the notion that the woman gets her way despite the husband's stated authority as boss is the idea that the woman wields her power in subtle and manipulative ways that allow the husband to retain his fantasies of being in charge. Many families are indeed matriarchal in their power balance, but the cultural ideal is that the man be the "head" of the household rather than a relatively submissive, passive (and thus "effeminate") figure. When we say that the wife "wears the pants" in the family, we imply that she has stepped into the role that rightfully belongs to the man.

That women surreptitiously wield power is further illustrated in movies, novels, and plays where one frequently runs across the theme of the egocentric, unrealistic male who meets his match in an eminently reasonable, practical woman. Smith also mentions A. J. Leibling's psychological and sociological studies of the American soap opera in which men are characteristically portrayed as weak, helpless, and impotent, or who become physically crippled and must be sustained by a good woman who alone maintains contact with the real world.

I do not purport to provide in this paper a factual description of all possible relationships between men and women, which are indeed infinitely variable and complex. Rather, what I present is an outline of widespread cultural values and ideal types—society's definition of the way relationships "should be" if both partners have fulfilled the criteria for appropriate masculine and feminine behavior. Thus a frail, dependent, and intellectually inept man may indeed seek out a strong, assertive, and capable woman to protect and care for him; and the needs and dynamics of the two individuals might "fit" in a manner that results in a stable and rewarding marriage. However, such a man is hardly the prototype of the successful male, and he is likely to be considered a poor if not pathognomonic role model for his son. Similarly, the woman married to such a man is perceived as having made a "bad catch," accompanied by the speculation that some neurotic problem kept her from "doing better." Men may indeed be passive, con-

3. Personal communication.

forming, childlike, and unrealistically dependent but, as Chesler (1972) points out, they are hardly taught to romanticize these qualities as essential aspects of their masculinity.

Furthermore, the sex-role stereotypes I have described are not peripheral to the culture but are powerful and ubiquitous forces affecting even the most "liberated" persons. Some authors (Baumrind 1972; Symonds (1971–72) suggest that lifelong consequences exist for the growing girl whose concept of femininity is based on the model that to be more aggressive, assertive, or intellectually capable than one's male partner is to be unfeminine, unlovable, and even "castrating." Similarly, boys are deeply affected by current notions of masculine attractiveness that glorify such traits as power, dominance, and intellectual skill, and that do not allow for even realistic expressions of fear, dependency, childishness, and weakness. Although in intellectual circles there is a tendency to see such stereotypes as outdated and inapplicable to today's changing patterns of relationships, the psychic and social dynamics persist. Even if recent social changes were indeed substantial, there remains the important task of making sense of the intense subjugation and devaluation of women that has occurred throughout the world. The specifics of male-female sex-role stereotypes may vary across time and place, but the ethos of male dominance and phallocentric prejudice is as old as humanity itself.

## Concluding Remarks

Rather than applying psychoanalytic principles toward understanding how our distorted notions of masculinity and femininity have been established and maintained, we have instead tended to incorporate these stereotypes into our theorizing and language, thus allowing myth and anxiety to prevail over scientific thought. A review of psychoanalytic writings reveals how practitioners and theorists pervasively and glibly label active displays of competitiveness, aggression, and intellectual ambitiousness in women as "phallic" or "masculine," and similarly label manifestations of passivity, submissiveness, malleability, childishness, emotionality, and dependency in men as "effeminate" or "feminine" (Young 1973).

For example, the character of the primitive maternal imago (and women's related fear of their castrating and destructive potential) may be such that the female sex has relatively greater difficulty acknowledging and directly expressing aggressive, competitive, and ambitious strivings. Labeling these qualities as "masculine," however, only serves to increase women's guilt and inhibitions and to reinforce a masochistic position. Similarly, anxiety about reenacting an early matriarchy with its related castration fears may make men more fearful of acknowledging their own passive, dependent, and regressive longings; but it does not follow that these longings are "feminine" ones. There are indeed different developmental tasks that the two sexes must master based on anatomical differences; however, I believe that our present gender definitions are less a reflection of anatomical realities and more an expression of a defensive reaction to the imagos of the primitive mother. It is imperative that we gain greater conceptual clarity regarding the treatment implications and underlying theoretical rationale for labeling specific traits and behaviors as "masculine" or "feminine."[4]

In order to defuse the character of the primitive maternal imago and to prevent excessive envy and fear of women, I suggest that shared parenting may be important. While the psychiatric literature is replete with the hazards of inadequate mothering, there has been only minimal concern with the infant-father relationship. The child's formula for mental health seems to involve spending the early years with a mother who "is always present, alert and responsive to the child's needs . . ." (Mandelbaum 1973, p. 6), the later relationship with father being secondary to and dependent on the quality of this first interaction. While many mental health professionals are protesting that we have held onto this model of mothering at a tremendous cost to women's growth and development, there has been less emphasis on its hazards for the growing infant and child. Is not defensive idealization and devaluation of women one pathological consequence of the child's world being a matriarchal one, where the powerful figures that gratify and frustrate the child's impulses and wishes are predominantly female? We have not as yet applied our sophisticated psychoanalytic principles to understanding the consequences of shared parenting or examining how such a system would affect the developmental tasks that each sex must master. Clearly, shared parenting would affect the maternal and paternal imagos that the child internalizes and may consequently lead to a capacity for adult men and women to relate to each

---

4. Research findings demonstrating sex differences along some dimension (e.g., relatively greater activity and aggressiveness in male infants) are often used to argue that a particular characteristic is a masculine or feminine one. Apart from the fact that there is always considerable overlap between the sexes, such conclusions are arbitrary ones. For example, female children are more verbal and articulate than male children; however, we do not label verbal skills as "feminine" and proceed actively to encourage these skills in girls or call them "feminine" to discourage them in boys. Group sex differences in no way imply that a trait or quality is healthy for one sex and less adaptive or important for the other.

other from a position of greater equality, openness, and mutual respect.

REFERENCES

Baumrind, D. 1972. From each according to her ability. *School Review* 80(2):161–197.

Bettelheim, B. 1965. The commitment required of a woman entering a scientific profession in present-day American society. In *Women and the scientific professions: The M.I.T. symposium on American women in science and engineering,* ed. J. A. Mattfeld and C. G. Van Aken, pp. 3–19. Cambridge, Mass.: M.I.T. Press.

Brunswick, R. M. 1940. The preoedipal phase of the libido development. *Psychoanalytic Quarterly* 9:293–319.

Chasseguet-Smirgel, J. 1970. Feminine guilt and the Oedipus complex. In *Female sexuality: New psychoanalytic views,* ed. J. Chasseguet-Smirgel et al., pp. 94–134. Ann Arbor: University of Michigan Press.

Chesler, P. 1972. *Women and madness.* Garden City, N.Y.: Doubleday.

David, C. 1970. A masculine mythology of femininity. In *Female sexuality: New psychoanalytic views,* ed. J. Chasseguet-Smirgel et al., pp. 47–67. Ann Arbor: University of Michigan Press.

Fairbairn, W. R. D. 1952. *An object-relations theory of the personality.* New York: Basic Books.

Freud, S. 1950. Some psychological consequences of the anatomical distinction between the sexes. In *Collected papers,* ed. J. Strachey, vol. 5, pp. 186–197. London: Hogarth Press. [Originally published 1925.]

————. 1955a. Analysis of a phobia in a five-year-old boy. In *The standard edition of the complete psychological works of Sigmund Freud* (hereafter *Standard edition*), ed. J. Strachey, vol. 10, pp. 3–149. London: Hogarth Press. [Originally published 1909.]

————. 1955b. From the history of an infantile neurosis. *Standard edition,* vol. 17, pp. 3–122. London: Hogarth Press. [Originally published 1918.]

Goldberg, P. 1968. Are women prejudiced against women? *Trans-action.* 5(5):28–30.

Horney, K. 1932. The dread of women. *International Journal of Psychoanalysis* 13:348–360.

Jung, C. G. 1928. *Contributions to analytical psychology,* II. Trans. G. Baynes and C. F. Baynes. London: Routledge & Kegan Paul.

Kernberg, O. 1972. Barriers to being in love. Unpublished manuscript, The Menninger Foundation.

Klein, M. 1957. Envy and gratitude. New York: Basic Books.

Lederer, W. 1968. *The fear of women.* New York: Grune & Stratton.

Lerner, H. 1974. The hysterical personality: A "woman's disease." *Comprehensive Psychiatry* 15(2):157–164.

Lynn, D. B. 1972. Determinants of intellectual growth in women. *School Review* 80(2):241–260.

Mandelbaum, A. 1973. Separation. *Menninger Perspective* 4(5):5–9, 27.

Symonds, A. 1971–72. Discussion of Ruth Moulton's paper, Psychoanalytic reflections on women's liberation. *Contemporary Psychoanalysis* 8:224–228.

Torok, M. 1970. The significance of penis envy in women. In *Female sexuality: New psychoanalytic views,* ed. J. Chasseguet-Smirgel et al., pp. 135–170. Ann Arbor: University of Michigan Press.

Young, E. 1973. A review of feminine psychology. Unpublished manuscript, University of California at Berkeley.

# 3

# Psychological Consequences of Sexual Inequality

## JEAN B. MILLER AND IRA MOTHNER

Our current concern with the role of women should lead to major changes in psychiatric theory. Already the reexamination of women's role has enabled some psychiatrists and psychoanalysts to help a number of women—and even some men—to deal in a new way with feelings of sexual and human inadequacy.

"Reexamination" seems too mild a term for the open conflict likely in the future. For many women, the revolution is at hand. Yet open conflict, if understood, offers far more productive possibilities for both women and men than the covert conflict it can replace. Is this conflict between the sexes the result of various neuroses and psychoses, or does it represent an existential dilemma, unrelated to time and place— the inevitability of the two sexes misunderstanding and thwarting each other?

Before one can settle on either of these explanations, one should examine the implications of another proposition, more obvious yet strangely neglected. In our society there exists a thoroughly realistic basis for conflict: Men and women are irrationally defined as unequal. It is striking that, in a field that attempts to define, differentiate, and promulgate rationality, so few psychiatrists have studied or even recognized the irrationalities with which we all live. Understanding the conflict between men and women requires some exploration of the psychological consequences of irrational inequality.

All relationships that are irrationally unequal (e.g., blacks and whites, women and men) share characteristics that lead to profound psychological results. Many of these seem obvious. Yet we rarely acknowledge them when dealing with situations that are, in fact, caused by characteristics as apparent as these.

1. Both parties are tied to each other in many ways and affect each other profoundly. Indeed, they need each other.

2. Actions of the dominant group tend to be destructive to the less powerful group. (There are also destructive effects on the dominant group.) All historical experience confirms this tendency.

3. The dominant group usually puts down the less powerful group, labeling it defective in varying ways (e.g., "blacks are less intelligent than whites," "women are ruled by emotion"). This derogation can take many subtle forms, even seeming to elevate the subordinate. Artists and intellectuals attempt to find all truth in the soul of the black, or the secret of life in the womb of the woman; any soul or womb will do, and thus they deny the individuality of the black or the woman.

4. The dominant group usually acts to halt any movement toward equality by the subordinate group. It also militates strongly against stirrings of rationality or greater humanity in any of its own members. (It was not too long ago that "nigger lover" was a common appellation, and men who let their women have more than the usual rights are still subject to ridicule in many circles.)

5. The dominant group obscures the true nature of the relationship, that is, the very fact of the existence of inequality itself. It rationalizes the situation by other, always false explanations, such as racial or sexual inferiority. This point has particular application to psychoanalytic theory, which, despite overwhelming evidence to the contrary, is still rooted in the notion that women are meant to be passive, submissive, and docile—in short, secondary. From this premise the outcome of therapy is often determined.

6. By proffering one or more "acceptable" roles, the dominants attempt to deny other areas of development to the less powerful. These acceptable roles usually provide a "service" that the dominant group does not choose to, or cannot, do for itself. The functions that the dominant group prefers to perform are closely guarded and closed off to the subordinates. The ability of subordinates to perform other roles is usually manifest only in emergency situations such as wartime, when inexperienced and untrained blacks and "incompetent" women suddenly "man" the factories with great skill.

7. Since the dominants determine society's ethos, its philosophy, morality, social theory, and its science, they legitimize the unequal relationship and incorporate it into all of society's guiding cultural concepts.

8. The dominant group is the model for "normal human relationships." Thus it may then be "normal" to treat others destructively and derogate them, obscure the truth of what you are doing, create false explanations for it, and oppose actions toward equality.

9. The dominant group, then, is bound to suppress disruption of these relationships and to avoid open conflict that might bring into question the validity of the established situation.

Certainly, the dominant group is setting the stage for conflict with the subordinates; and yet it insists there is no cause for conflict. Its interests are being served by the unequal relationship (clearly oppressive to the less powerful group), but its rationalization of that relationship is so well integrated that the dominants actually come to believe that both groups share the same interests.

The dominants' faith in the *rightness* of the relationship is nowhere more apparent than in their attempts to impose that relationship where it does not exist or does not exist as rigidly as seems proper to them. The great distress of white male social theorists with matriarchal black families would seem evidence of this.

Since the dominants have determined what is "normal" for society, and their ethos prevails, we are not very familiar with how subordinates deal with their part of the relationship. Because the less powerful group is discouraged from free expression and action, we are only now learning about their experience, thoughts, and feelings. The first such expression always comes as a surprise to the dominants, and is usually rejected as strangely atypical. After all, the dominants *knew* that blacks were always happy and cheerful, albeit lazy and shiftless, and that all women really want and need is a man at the center of their lives. What they don't understand is what "they," the first to speak out, are so angry about.

The subordinate group is initially less able to buck the line than the dominants are to hold it. The characteristics that typify their part in the relationship are even more complex.

1. The less powerful group is primarily concerned with its survival. Accordingly, direct, honest reactions to destructive treatment are avoided. Open action in their own self-interest can (and in some places still does) literally result in death. For women in our society this kind of action may mean economic hardship, social ostracism, psychological isolation, and even the diagnosis of personality disorder by some psychiatrists.

2. The underpowered group then resorts to various disguised reactions, to "put on" the oppressor while appearing to please him. Black stories, Jewish stories, and various folk tales are full of such humorous examples. In that sense, the "mother knows best" school of literature (e.g., Herman Wouk) and the television family comedies in which father is absurdly manipulated by mother seem almost the continuation of such folk "wisdom."

3. The less powerful may absorb some of the untruths created by the dominants, so that there are blacks who feel inferior and women who believe they are less important than men. This is more likely to occur if there are few or no alternate concepts at hand. In the short period since the women's movement began, many women in therapy are beginning to raise the issue of their own needs and interests. Previously they would have felt no right to define an issue in this way, rushing on, instead, to question what is wrong with them that makes them unable to fit into their husband's needs and plans.

4. Members of the subordinate group also have experiences and perceptions that more accurately reflect the truth about themselves and the irrationality of their positions. Their own more truthful conceptions are bound to come into opposition with the mythology they have absorbed from the dominant group.

An inner tension between these two sets of concepts and their derivatives is almost inevitable.

5. Despite the obstacles, the subordinate group always tends to move toward free expression and action. There were always some slaves who revolted; there were some women who spoke out. Most records of these actions are not preserved by the dominant culture, thus making it difficult for the subordinate group to find a supporting tradition and history.

6. Within each subordinate group there is a tendency for some members to imitate the dominants and to treat their fellow subordinates just as destructively. Psychologists have described this as "identification with the aggressor." Others may attempt to reverse the roles of oppressor and oppressed. Being a subordinate in one relationship does not necessarily guarantee a benign effect upon one's performance as a dominant in another relationship. (Blacks may put down women; workers may put down blacks and women.)

7. To the extent that the subordinates move toward free expression, exposing the inequality and questioning the basis for its existence, they create open conflict.

What is immediately apparent from the characteristics of these two groups is that mutually enhancing interaction is not probable between unequals. The dominant group is denied any truthful reaction, consensual validation, or feedback to its actions. With no wholly truthful reactions to guide them, the dominants go on dispensing all knowledge and wisdom for the society, building distortions on top of distortions.

The characteristics common to all unequal relationships take on special impact in the case of the man-woman relationship. Each needs to develop individually and also needs growing and intimate affection, satisfaction, and affirmation from the other. In intimate human relationships if growth does not occur, deterioration of the relationship and of each person ensues. Things rarely stand still.

Before today women often pressed for validation of their importance without full awareness of why it was denied them. The facts of denial were plain enough: They were not encouraged, often not allowed, to develop their full capacities; they were told their development was less important and should not interfere with men's development; they were, in short, held less important, less valued, less valuable.

As a result, their search for development and participation in a useful and meaningful life assumed special proportions. Women tended to load their ambitions upon husbands and children. Most women felt valued only if they could win favor in the eyes of men, and useful only if their children repeatedly demonstrated to them that they were so. Clearly, women have desires and capacities that cannot be contained within these narrow boundaries.

It was perfectly apparent to anyone able to observe the psychological problems of men and women that women were struggling against the bonds of inequality, engaging in conflict and using heavy weapons. Their campaign, however, was covert. It had no useful objectives, was aimed at no real enemy, was waged with no plan, no order. Indeed, there was no real recognition by many of the combatants that the battle was underway. They fought secretly, often viciously, and, in most instances, uncomprehendingly. And the battlefield was most often their own families.

Within many homes in which the woman seemed to accept her place as subordinate, one variant or another of the following scenario unfolded. The wife would complain of or even merely mention the family's lacks, the limitations of their budget, the possessions they did not have, the vacations they did not take. She made clear, perhaps without even verbalizing it, her feelings that her husband was less able, less successful, less adequate than other men. She constantly demonstrated his relative unimportance within the home and indicated that his failure to find sufficient time for his family was the result of his own inefficiency. Meanwhile, she flaunted her own qualities as a worker, dramatizing the speed and efficiency with which she cared for the home. She, of course, spent much more time with the family and used the time to demonstrate her greater devotion and "love." She capitalized upon whatever weaknesses her husband possessed. He tended to make impulsive decisions that he himself sometimes regretted. He could never admit this, because his wife magnified these errors, falsely creating the impression that they were the cause of many of the family's problems. By contrasting her own more sober reflections she attempted to establish her superiority. Her husband was unable to defend himself against much of this psychological sabotage. Each charge contained some truth. In family discussions, the wife used his weaknesses to humiliate him and treat him with contempt. In time he came to feel increasingly inadequate, less successful, less "manly," humiliated, and demeaned. His children then regarded him as weak, less masterful and mature than their mother. They turned increasingly to mother for fulfillment of their needs, and simultaneously hated and distrusted her for the destruction of their father.

The wife had waged a devastatingly effective covert campaign, destroying the nominal enemy but gaining no victory. Her husband's effectiveness had been diminished both within the home and outside it. The wife, however, had won nothing. She could not replace the husband she had rendered impotent. She was truly afraid to go out into the world and accomplish anything herself. Indeed, she was ill-prepared and afraid to do so, having earlier surrendered her opportunities for education or work experience in order to advance her husband's. During the course of the campaign, she had also lost much and was made to feel unappreciated as a person and less of a woman.

This woman was not asking for equality. She was not struggling to develop her capacities or interests. If she had been, she undoubtedly would have run into conflict with her husband—but conflict of a very different nature.

There are numerous variations of the theme, some even more subtle. In working-class families similar processes operate, but the husband may appear more dominant and the wife be more restricted in her words and movements. A tyrannical truck driver's recent remark reflected the fact that he harbors an inner feeling that he is not valued, that he and his wife constantly drain rather than augment each other: "No matter what I do, I know she still thinks I'm a jerk."

Such covert conflict tends to have certain constant characteristics. There is no real resolution or satisfaction possible. The winner gains little beyond resentment and the withdrawal of affection. Neither party perceives or learns anything new. Neither is helped toward a new basis for action. The distortions of each are usually reinforced and defended even more strongly. This leads not just to a repetition of the same, but to a progressive deterioration of the personalities of each party and of the relationship between them.

The process of the conflict itself has a fairly regular quality. There is usually an attempt to foreclose the outcome, guarantee the result, insure victory. One tries to avoid a true clash of interest by aiming for the psychological destruction of the opponent without the acknowledgment that a true conflict of interest exists. It is very easy to undercut, diminish, and eliminate the effectiveness of a husband. Any woman who knows a man can convey the notion that he is not very much of one. Meanwhile the real objectives, the factors that create the unequal relationship, are never attacked. The old model of repression remains unchanged, except that the goal of some women has become the reversal of the roles of oppressor and oppressed.

Overt conflict is far more demanding. It takes courage and strength. It involves risk, and women don't have much to fall back on should they lose. The process here is different. Desires are openly stated, and opponents are invited to respond with equal openness and honesty. Although the subordinates in this relationship may have little hope that the male dominants will fight fairly, they keep their own tactics clear. The subordinates engage an opponent who is armed with all of his psychological assets. They do not attempt to deprive him of his psychological resources as an alternative to true conflict over the real issues. The goal is equality and integrity for each, not the destruction of either.

Open conflict offers a chance for resolution. Women, the subordinates, stand to gain their freedom. Men can enjoy the benefits of a more equal relationship, although they may have to admit to old wrongs and reexamine old values. But this is change, not defeat, and growth can occur for both men and women, producing new satisfactions and new ways of valuing each other. The result then includes at least the possibility of new development for each party. Each may perceive some of what the other is trying to express and may be able to utilize this new knowledge to formulate new action. The new action is not forced, but a choice based on new knowledge.

However, when dominants first perceive within the ranks of the less powerful the beginnings of overt conflict, they almost always confuse what they are seeing with the more destructive model, the covert conflict they have never recognized as any kind of conflict at all. These two models of conflict are easily confused. In psychiatric practice one can readily observe this. There is often a shift from one model to the other without any realization of this by the participants. The dominants feel threatened, even though open action for equality is not aimed at their destruction. It is a challenge to change. While this change might free the dominants from the psychological assaults of covert conflict and offer them an opportunity for new satisfaction, it would also destroy their dominant role. It is a threat not to their persons or their psyches, but to their position of privilege.

Unfortunately, the dominants usually fail to count the true cost of their dominance. They do not know the new satisfaction equality can bring. Indeed, they are unaware of what the denial of truthful feedback has already cost them. Losing out on positive reactions, as well as negative ones, has deprived them of pleasure as well as reality.

As we come to better understand the extent to which characteristics of irrational inequality have snarled relationships between races, sexes, and generations, we can only breathe a collective sigh of relief that the conflicts are now coming into the open. With what we now know about the real damage of covert conflict, it seems no accident that the "cause" of one psychological problem after another was "discovered" during the period immediately preceding the current women's movement to be the dominant mother and the weak, ineffectual and emotionally removed father. This was held to be true for schizophrenia, homosexuality, alienation, and a number of other personality disorders.

The dominant mother-ineffectual father theme also pervades fiction and drama (e.g., Philip Roth, Edward Albee, and so on). There is more than a hint here of how important the women's movement may be for psychological theory. When more than half the nation is fighting to establish its sense of self-value, and the other half is defending, with untruths, its irrational dominance, and all of this is going on in disguised and confused ways, there would seem a basis for much of what we now consider "functional psychological disturbance." The serious disturbance of children from families that have been ravaged by this kind of conflict are not simply idiosyncratic occurrences but intensified examples of a situation that exists for all.

Though this formulation of the "dominant mother-ineffectual father" as the cause of practically every serious psychological difficulty was an incomplete description of the situation, it probably did reflect observations that occurred with some degree of regularity. The underlying inequality that leads to such situations was never examined or even recognized. More sophisticated psychiatrists (e.g., Theodore Lidz) have already moved on to more complex delineations of the total family interactions that provide the seedbed of such disorders. They have already gone beyond the image of the mother as the prime "castrating" yet "sick" cause of all problems. But they still do not include a conception of the family as the arena of the conflicts that arise from the inequity sanctioned by the larger society.

Examining the destructive results of inequality can lead to new theoretical understanding of some of the most serious and perplexing psychological problems. Concealed within the hitherto acceptable status of inequality between men and women are destructive forces with far-reaching ramifications. Precisely because women and men affect each other and their children so intimately and so profoundly, this unequal situation is particularly malignant psychologically and especially difficult to confront squarely. Even some of our most humanitarian psychological theorists seem to accept unquestioningly assumptions based upon it.

The existence of irrational unequal relationships has also caused great problems in other vast areas—those relationships in which there do exist real inequalities: parents and children, teachers and students, doctors and patients, and perhaps therapists and clients. What characterizes these relationships is the understanding that one of the parties presumably possesses qualities that it hopes to impart to the other—for example, mental or emotional maturity, experience in the world, a body of knowledge, or a medical treatment. In marked contrast to situations of irrational inequality, society here decrees that the subordinates are to be helped by the dominants to attain their full stature, full equality.

It is striking that all instances of "rational" inequality constitute dilemmas for our society. Possibly our lives are so affected by irrational inequalities, we are so busy denying and falsifying them, that we do not know how to deal with those who are truly not equal in certain ways. Our theories on child rearing swing from strict control, which assumes that youngsters have no rights, to the progressive extreme, which grants them absolute equality. Our confusion about inequality in general may be preventing us from finding sound means to help our children grow from unequals to full equals. Certainly the problem of developing identity, independence, and authentic autonomy in young people is central to psychology today. We admittedly have no good theory of education. It is likely that these dilemmas are related both to each other and to the fact that we have no idea of how to treat unequals constructively and respectfully. We have no full concept of the process of change from unequal to equal, having experience only with enforcing inequality.

We have no guiding notion of how to deal with the challenges of these unequals who are properly unequal in one or another attribute. Instead we tend to apply the values derived from situations of irrational inequality, including the tendency to suppress *all* conflict. We want children to grow. But when their growth challenges us, we shift rapidly to the tactics of closure and intimidation that characterize our irrationally unequal relationships. When children, who often perceive with great accuracy, smite at our weak points, we frequently abandon the struggle so necessary for their growth and either shut it off or surrender unconditionally under the delusion that they somehow "know best." We have never learned how to relate to unequals with the goal of ending their inequality.

In a more direct practical way it is apparent that the current women's movement has already helped many women and some men to work on their personal problems more productively. In a short time some women have changed from feeling no sense of self or of worth except as these were defined and valued by a man to a sense of worth based on their own processes of evaluation. Some women have freed themselves from implicit or explicit condemnation of themselves for desires that did not fit into the definition of a person who is supposed to want first and foremost to submit herself to another. The fuller development of outlooks such as these can ultimately lead to relationships with men and children that are freer and more satisfying for all concerned. It is also clear that this process will not proceed easily and smoothly. For each individual there are many complex issues to work out. It will be difficult for all involved and, as always, most difficult for the subordinates, the women.

If change is to come and to extend beyond a small segment of the middle class, it obviously will involve activity in many areas—economic, social, legal, political. Behavioral scientists, however, can play a particularly important role in clarifying the situation. While they may not have created the problem, they have often provided support and rationalization for the existing situation. Their pronouncements carry great weight in current society and filter into the popular media to provide the current "religion" and morality for a large segment of the public. Discussion about women often revolves around what is "normal" or "natural" or "good for mental health." In general, behavioral scientists and practitioners have played a role in rationalizing and sanctifying the status quo publicly, and in enforcing it with their patients either grossly or subtly in their practices. Instead we can turn to elucidating the destructive effects of inequality, exposing the errors of previous concepts of normality that were based upon it, and presenting evidence of the positive advantages gained by people who have struggled for more equal human relationships.

# 4

---

# The Conflict Between
# Nurturance and Autonomy
# in Mother-Daughter
# Relationships
# and Within Feminism

---

JANE FLAX

---

> For we think back through our mothers if we are women.
> —Virginia Woolf, 1945

> My mother's worst fantasy is that she will end up like her mother. My worst fantasy is that I will end up like my mother, and I know that as soon as I have that fantasy, I am already trapped.
> —Therapy patient, age twenty

After years of psychoanalytic investigation and practice, Freud admitted that he still could not answer the question "What do women want?" Ironically, his own theoretical framework may have prevented

I would like to thank Temma Kaplan for her editorial assistance, encouragement, and sharing of ideas. Kirstin Dahl and Joan Sarnat exchanged clinical experiences and ideas and, most important, have worked to develop friendships that have overcome some of the conflicts described here.

him from answering this question because male development remained the model for general psychological processes and structures. In his later work, Freud realized the particular importance of the pre-oedipal period and the mother-daughter relationship for female development.[1] However, he did not adequately analyze these factors, nor did he integrate his awareness into his metapsychology.

What women want is an experience of both nurturance[2] and autonomy within an intimate relationship. What makes this wish so strong and, for many women, so unattainable, is that psychological development occurs within the patriarchal[3] family—in which the mother is the primary nurturer and the father is the symbol of authority. The psychological difficulties that this arrangement causes are reinforced and compounded in later life by the inability of many men to be nurturers, an inability created as a result of patriarchal family structure, and by homophobia, which makes intimacy between women suspect. Women's need for nurturance is not neurotic, but it can lead to self-defeating behavior under certain conditions that will be discussed.

The sources of information for the theoretical ideas presented in this paper are my own experience working as a therapist for three years in intensive, psychoanalytically oriented practice; my experiences as a feminist; and my research in psychoanalysis and political theory. My therapeutic experience was limited by time (never more than twelve

---

1. Freud's comments on the pre-oedipal period and the psychology of women are, as he himself admits, "incomplete and fragmentary." His most sustained discussion of this period appears in "Female Sexuality" (1949), reprinted in Strouse (1974a). Other relevant comments appear in his "Some Psychical Consequences of the Anatomical Distinction Between the Sexes" (1974b) and "Femininity." However, as Juliet Mitchell (1974) cogently argues, Freud's comments on women are not fully comprehensible without a systematic study of his psychological theory as a whole.

2. By nurturance I mean the expression of love that conveys a deep concern for the well-being of the person receiving it, without requiring that the person prove herself worthy or fulfill the nurturer's own needs, fantasies, and so forth as the condition of receiving such care. Nurturance has a sensual aspect as well because the care extends to the recipient's body as well as to her psyche. The model for nurturance in our society is the love a mother gives her child. Because primary responsibility for child care in our society still rests with women, I have called the caretaker of the child "the mother" throughout. This is not meant to imply that men, or women and men together, could not assume such responsibility.

3. There is much controversy among feminists concerning the use of the term "patriarchy." Some object to its use altogether, arguing that it takes on an ahistorical, universal character and explains nothing. Others wish to restrict its use to the most literal cases, where fathers *qua* fathers rule, such as in ancient Semitic tribes. I think the term is useful because it expresses powerfully a situation in which men as a group oppress women as a group, even though there may be hierarchies among men. Patriarchy has a material base in men's control of women's labor power and reproductive power and a psychodynamic base as a defense against the infantile mother and men's fear of women. It has assumed many different historical forms, but it still remains a dynamic force today. On the material base of patriarchy, see Heidi Hartmann (1979). On reproduction, see Linda Gordon (1976), esp. pp. 3–25 and pp. 403–418. On psychodynamics, see Gregory Zilboorg (1973); Karen Horney (1967); and Dorothy Dinnerstein (1976).

hours in one week, plus an hour of supervision) and by the client population—white college or ex-college students, mostly under twenty-five years of age, and predominately female. The average duration of therapy was one and one-half years, although the range was from two months to three years. The class backgrounds of the patients ranged from very poor to upper middle class; because the therapy was provided within a state university, class backgrounds tended to be more varied than in private practice.

Although my analysis points to the importance of relationships that have persisted historically over long periods—in particular, women's almost exclusive responsibility for child rearing—it is important to note that the *content* of these relationships has varied over time. Thus the specific form of psychological development I will describe is mostly reflective of post-World War I white, middle-class families. However, I believe that certain psychodynamic concepts have more general validity, although there is no way to prove this, and that to the extent that working-class families adopt (or are pressured to adopt) middle-class norms, the analysis will also apply to them.[4] Furthermore, I will argue that investigating the genesis of women's dual needs for autonomy and nurturance will provide insights into feminist and antifeminist politics.

Many therapists[5] agree that the most important tasks of the first three years of human life are, first, establishing a close relationship with a caretaker—usually the mother—and, second, moving from that relationship through the process of separation and individuation. Separation means establishing a firm sense of differentiation from the mother, of possessing one's own physical and mental boundaries. Individuation means the development of a range of characteristics, skills, and personality traits that are uniquely one's own. Separation and individuation are the two "tracks" of development; they are not identical but they can reinforce or impede each other.

By the end of the third year of life, a "core identity" or a distorted one will have been established. Gender is a central element in this core identity. The child's sense of gender is firmly established by one and one-half to two years of age and has little to do with an understanding of sexuality or reproduction (cf. Money and Ehrhardt 1972, esp. pp. 176–194). What many therapists fail to analyze, although some

4. See Lillian Breslow Rubin (1976), pp. 114–133, for the impact of middle-class norms on the expectations working-class people have of marriage.

5. I will be following Margaret Mahler's theory most carefully. See Mahler, Pine, and Bergman (1975). Mahler's work is related to that of many others, especially the work of the "object relations" school and ego psychology. On object relations, see W. R. D. Fairbairn (1952). On ego psychology, see Gertrude and Rubin Blanck (1974).

note it, is that this sense of gender is not neutral.[6] Becoming aware of gender in a patriarchal system means recognizing that men and women are not valued equally, that, in fact, men are socially more esteemed than women. Learning about gender therefore entails a coming to awareness of and to some extent an internalizing of asymmetries of power and esteem.

Furthermore, the child's psychological development occurs within a socioeconomic system that also strongly affects the mother. The socioeconomic system, along with patriarchy, impinges on her ability to provide the emotional support needed by the child. Because her own psychological development occurred under patriarchy, it would have left an imprint upon her feelings about herself, about being a woman and being a mother. These feelings would in turn affect the type of mothering she would provide a child. It is my argument that mothering too is not gender neutral, and that women relate differently to male and female children. I am concerned in this paper with the consequences for women, both as children and adults, that result from the type of mothering they are likely to receive within contemporary families. By following through what is considered to be the normal process of psychological development while integrating into the account the impacts of patriarchy that are often left out, we can see the points at which developmental difficulties in women are likely to originate.

After the first few weeks of life (autism) in which the infant recovers from the birth experience and attempts to regain the physiological equilibrium it had in the womb, it enters into the period that Mahler calls "symbiosis," covering roughly the first six or seven months of life: "The infant behaves and functions as though he and his mother were an omnipotent system—a dual unity within one common boundary" (Mahler, Pine, and Bergman 1975, p. 44). The infant has no sense of its own body boundaries and is extremely sensitive to its mother's moods and feelings. In this state of fusion with the mother, I and not-I are not yet differentiated and inside and outside the self are only gradually distinguished. This phase is the "primal soil from which all subsequent human relationships form" (Mahler, Pine, and Bergman 1975, p. 48). The developmental task in this phase is to establish a strong bond with the mother. Later experiences cannot completely compensate for inadequacies in this period. The symbiotic bond provides grounding, the sense of ontological security, on which the infant can rely as it moves out of the symbiotic orbit into differentiation and exploration of the outside world.

In order for this phase to be adequate, the mother must be emotionally available to the child in a consistent, reasonably conflict-free way.

6. Important exceptions are Dinnerstein, Mitchell, and Chodorow (1974) and Harriet E. Lerner (1974).

The mother should be able to enjoy the sensual and emotional close-ness of the relationship without losing her own sense of separateness. She should be concerned about the child without smothering it. This appears to be more difficult for the mother of a girl to achieve. Al-though this cannot be proven definitively, it is a reasonable inference from the feelings of mothers, from the behavior of adult women in the transference relationship in therapy, and from the feelings they report about their own mothers.[7]

Mothers tend to identify more strongly with their girl babies (Din-nerstein, Mitchell, and Chodorow 1974, p. 48; Bowlby 1975, pp. 72, 75). They do not seem to have as clear a sense of physical boundaries between themselves and their girl children as do mothers of boys. Women in therapy have frequently said that they have no sense where they end and their mothers begin, even in a literal, physical way. The very fact of gender differences with boy babies enforces, on the moth-er's part, a sense that the child is "not me," is other than me.

Because women tend to identify more strongly with their girl chil-dren, more internal conflict is likely to be stimulated by their role as mother. Memories of unresolved wishes from their own infancy are more likely to be evoked. Women often admit that one motive for becoming a mother is to regain a sense of being mothered themselves. With girl children, the confusion over who is the child and who is the mother is intensified. Women patients have reported to me that they often felt pressure from their own mothers to provide the care the mothers themselves had lacked in their childhood. Women are less likely to have these confusions or expectations aroused with boy chil-dren because men are not seen as nurturers in our culture.

Furthermore, although women may be very physically affectionate with their girl children, they may be unconsciously more conflicted about this closeness. In a homophobic society, incestuous wishes toward daughters are far more forbidden and shameful than toward sons.[8] As adults, women must repress yearnings for physical closeness with other women so that once the mother's body is lost through dif-ferentiation, it is supposed to be forever lost; but a boy can replace his mother with another female.

As a therapist, I find that one of the hardest issues to discuss with female patients is their erotic feelings and fantasies about me. With men, while it is painful, it is also much more acceptable for them to acknowledge those feelings. Perhaps one of the motives for what is

7. I am accepting the psychoanalytic theory of transference. What is acted out in the relationship with the therapist has roots in the patient's past. Feelings reported in the present are traced back to the earliest possible roots.

8. Robert Stoller (1973, pp. 69–87) reports a case where these dynamics are especially evident.

diagnosed as "penis envy" is a desire for the object that makes it possible and acceptable to return to the fused state with the mother, for intercourse is not only sexual but a literal rejoining of two persons.

Finally, in a patriarchal society, it would be difficult for a woman not to feel conflicted, even if only unconsciously, about being female.[9] It is not only that the mother might value a son more, reflecting the higher social esteem enjoyed by men; but the mother, knowing the difficulties of being female in a man's world, might also wish that for the daughter's own sake she could have been born male. Yet because the mother identifies so strongly with a girl child, she also wants the child to be just like her.

As a result of all these conflicts, it is more difficult for the mother to be as emotionally available as her infant daughter needs her to be. Women are therefore more likely to retain a wish to return to the infantile state. This was demonstrated vividly to me by a female patient who started curling up in fetal position and refusing to talk every time she came to my office. After about three weeks of this behavior, she finally responded to my repeated question: "What are you angry about?" She had heard from someone that I wanted to have a child, and this evoked her own strong wish to be my baby. By curling up in the fetal position and returning to a preverbal state, she was attempting to get back within the symbiotic orbit that our relationship represented, the only place she felt "safe." This patient also had tremendous difficulty with separation and often the last part of a session would be spent preparing her to leave. After we analyzed the root of her behavior, it disappeared and did not recur. It is also possible that the fantasy women often have about male therapists—the wish to have a baby with them—is on a deeper level a wish to *be* their baby.

The feeling that women often report of not having had enough of something, of being cheated, is also related to the inadequacies of the symbiotic phase. It is not that women totally lack the experience of being nurtured; but it is rather that their experience takes place within a context in which the mother's conflicts render the experience less than optimal and, in some cases, profoundly inadequate. Developmental difficulties in boys are more likely to have roots in later stages. It is often observed that the preoedipal stage is more formative for girls than boys, although the explanation for this is not always understood.

If the symbiotic experience has not been adequate, the process of separation and individuation that follows is also more difficult for the female infant. She lacks to some degree the firm base from which to

9. Stoller (1973) stresses the importance of "the mother's capacity to accept femininity as a worthy quality in herself and other females, and her relatively unambivalent pleasure in her daughter's femaleness and femininity" (p. 316) to successful female development.

differentiate. Furthermore, because she is expected to be like the mother, both as a person and in terms of her adult roles, there is less need for her to differentiate. The mother will tend to be more conflicted about her girl infant's movement toward differentiation and will be less likely to give her the loving push that facilitates movement out of the symbiotic orbit. Differentiation, which begins at approximately six months and continues to about ten months, is the phase in which the infant starts to realize that it is a separate person from the mother and begins to explore the possibilities of being separate, developing the beginnings of an ego and becoming more physically mobile. If symbiosis has not been adequate, this phase will either be delayed or premature, as the infant desperately attempts to assert some autonomy without the inner resources to do so. In either case, the sense of self and ability to form relations with others are likely to be more fragile and impaired.

Differentiation overlaps with what Mahler calls "practicing"—the phase from about ten to twelve months to sixteen to eighteen months. In this phase, the child is developing pleasure in its own locomotor skills and developing a rudimentary autonomous ego. Again, this process works best when the mother expresses pleasure in the child's development and displays a sense of confidence in the child's abilities. Although the child takes increasing pleasure in its own achievements, it still needs to check back with the mother for reassurance and to use its relation with her as "home base." Mahler speaks of the "emotional refueling" the child receives from the mother. If the mother is ambivalent about giving up the symbiotic phase or if she is "parasitic," that is, reliving her own infancy through the child, then the child will find it more difficult to take pleasure in its own developing capacities. For the reasons previously stated, this is more likely to be true for the girl child.

It is in the third phase of separation-individuation, "rapprochement," that gender enters most explicitly into psychological development. The child is coming to full realization that it is a separate person from its mother and that it can never return to the symbiotic orbit. Some of the euphoria present in the practicing stage wears off, and the child discovers the limitations as well as the possibilities of its developing skills. The child learns that not only is it not omnipotent, but that the mother too is not all-powerful.

The girl child, because she is less likely to have successfully completed the earlier phases, will find these blows to her self-esteem harder to bear. In addition, because consciousness of gender and of some of its meanings develops at this point, the girl will suffer a gender-specific lessening of self-esteem as well.

Rapprochement (approximately fifteen to twenty-four months) is marked above all by ambivalence. The child both wants to return to the symbiotic state and fears being reengulfed by it. Fear of losing the love of the mother becomes increasingly evident: "One cannot emphasize too strongly the importance of the optimal availability of the mother during this subphase" (Mahler, Pine, and Bergman 1975, p. 77). At this point the father becomes a more important person in the child's world.

The mother's own ambivalence about being an adult may be intensely reexperienced during this period, especially in her relation with a daughter. The daughter is acting out the conflicts that the mother experiences unconsciously. Mahler notes that by the age of twenty-one months, there are significant developmental differences between boys and girls.

The boys, if given a reasonable chance, showed a tendency to disengage themselves from mother and to enjoy their functioning in the widening world. The girls, on the other hand, seemed to become more engrossed with mother in her presence; they demanded greater closeness and were more persistently enmeshed in the ambivalent aspects of the relationship. (Mahler, Pine, and Bergman 1975, p. 102)

Mahler attributes these differences to the child's discovery of the anatomical differences between boys and girls. Girls suffer a loss of self-esteem because they feel their mothers failed to give them something important; they cling to their mothers in the hope that she will settle this debt. Mahler also observed that girls tend to become more depressed during this period. Perhaps as they discover their imperfection, they fear that their mothers will also love them less.

I think this is an inadequate interpretation of the behavior that Mahler observed. She says the lack of a penis becomes important to the girl child because all children at this stage want everything the others have. Yet if this were the explanation, why would not boys develop "vagina envy"?

It is much more likely that this "penis envy" must be interpreted symbolically. As children become more aware of the social world, they would notice that for some reason, boys are esteemed more highly than girls. The conflicts that their mothers conveyed about being female now begin to make more sense. Boys can identify with their fathers as an alternative to the mother; girls cannot (Mahler, Pine, and Bergman 1975, p. 106). Furthermore, although both girls and boys become aware of the relationship between their mothers and fathers and realize that father has a claim on mother's affections that is special, it is easier for the girl to attribute the "loss" of exclusive possession to herself (lack of penis). Boys do not have to grapple fully with their fathers as rivals until later because at this point their "magic organ" seems unthreatened.

Thus although both boys and girls have to come to terms with the loss of their illusions about their own as well as their mothers' omnipotence, this discovery does not have the same consequences for boys as for girls. A girl is less likely to have the resources from the symbiotic period to develop an autonomous ego or to absorb blows to her self-esteem. Furthermore, it is easier for her to experience the loss of omnipotence and of the all-powerful mother as rooted in her own inadequacies. She is "only a girl," after all.

Instead of moving on to an identification with the powerful father, she is thrown back on the very person from whom she was unable to differentiate completely. Yet the mother too is now devalued—not only did she fail to give her daughter a penis, but she turned out to be "just a girl" as well. The girl cannot escape from infancy by becoming a "little man." She cannot through identification utilize the authority of the father to build her own sense of power and to protect herself from her mother and from regression to the helplessness of infancy.

The girl, unlike the boy, cannot repress the female part of herself and totally reject the mother, because it is precisely at this stage that she is coming to an awareness of her own femaleness, that is, her gender. The boy's repression of the female aspects of himself is one of the reasons men find it hard to be nurturant as adults. To be nurturant would threaten their sense of identity, which is in part built on being not like mother. Furthermore, it could revive the pain accompanying the boy's original acts of repression as well as the terror of the all-powerful infantile mother. Ironically, despite the inadequacies of her early infantile experience, because the girl is less differentiated from her mother she is more able to be nurturant as an adult. Her capacity to do so is of course reinforced by later socialization; the boy's capacity is not.

The girl is left in a painful bind. On the one hand, because she is less likely to have had an adequate symbiotic experience, her needs for a sense of fusion with a caring, reliable person remain strong. On the other hand, she may lack a sense of being rewarded for making moves toward autonomy. If she attempts to regain a sense of fusion, she will not be able to be autonomous. If she exerts autonomy, she must reject the infantile mother and give up her needs for fusion.

Her experience has shown her that her mother does not wish her to individuate, so perhaps she can please her mother by remaining in a more infantile state. In either case, she must choose between what feels like nurturance—the love of her mother, no matter how ambivalently expressed—and autonomy. Because very early preverbal experience is buried deep in the unconscious, it may seem to the girl that "it all began to go wrong" when she attempted to individuate from her mother. Autonomy, rather than being experienced as a way of pleasing the mother and being supported by her, is experienced as a rejection of the mother, for which the daughter in turn will be rejected. The bind is reinforced by her growing awareness that the world is divided up into male and female. Fathers are on the outside of the family, of the self, while mothers are defined by their role in the family. Fathers symbolize autonomy and independence; mothers symbolize nurturance and dependence.

As an adult, the daughter repeats the process by thwarting her daughter's moves toward autonomy. She makes herself powerful by overvaluing the son through whom she indirectly exerts power in the outside world. She thereby fulfills her own repressed wishes for autonomy and achievement. Her only source of emotional security is her daughter, whom she cannot allow to individuate. Thus her daughter ends up in the same situation as herself. Some mothers encourage daughters to escape; but often in the process they convey a double message of "be like me" but also "do not be like me."

There is a further cruel twist to the girl's development. The boy receives a promise of another mommy as a reward for the renunciation of his infantile wishes, but the girl receives nothing. She has to give up her infantile wishes much more completely, even though it is more difficult for her to do so. Under patriarchy, husbands are not expected to nurture their wives as wives nurture their husbands and children. To the extent that a woman devalues and mistrusts other women, she loses the possibility that they will nurture her. As women generally move far away from their families and are isolated in individual suburban homes, they forswear potentially affectionate female kinship networks. Only through relationships with other women can women heal the hurts suffered during their psychological development. The rift between identifying with the mother and being oneself can only be closed within a relationship in which one is nurtured for being one's autonomous self.

Women's unresolved wishes for the mother is the truth behind Freud's claim that what women wish for in a husband is their mother. The depth and intensity of these longings fill intimate female relationships with extraordinary powers to damage and gratify. Only women can enable us to experience ourselves as whole and to overcome the fear of punishment for the expression of autonomous selves. Our sense of self is bound up with other women in an intensity and depth simply not present in relations with men. When female relations fail to nurture our autonomous self, they create intense rage, hurt, and a feeling of betrayal. It is even more inappropriate when these needs have been transferred onto relations with men.

Much of what psychoanalysts have traditionally interpreted as oedipal wishes—for example, the wish to have a baby with the father and with the analyst as a symbol of the father—have deeper roots in the pre-oedipal relationship with the mother. The wish to have a baby is also a wish to *have* a mother. It is a wish for the therapist to be the good mother who can both bestow nurturance and reward autonomy. One wishes to regress to babyhood and redo the infantile development that is the ultimate source of one's troubles. These unconscious infantile wishes affect adult women's behavior in all aspects of their lives.

The feminist analysis of women's rage or depression that blames it all on external society, as in the slogan "Women are not mad, they are angry," overlooks the internal struggle. This view turns women into passive victims of social forces and ignores unconscious sources of self-defeating behavior. It is painful to understand the ways in which one's own conflicting wishes oppress oneself and other women. But however painful, the acknowledgment of how women oppress themselves and others is ultimately liberating. What is unconscious can be made conscious, with a corresponding increase in energy, sense of competence, and positive feelings. Once freed from unconscious complicity, one can more effectively deploy one's anger.

Women, especially those who wish to succeed in nontraditional ways, face a potentially paralyzing conflict. Success usually requires entering the world of men and adopting their behavior while rejecting or repressing the female within oneself. On an unconscious level, this may be experienced as treachery toward the mother. The successful woman in our society must choose between autonomy and self-fulfillment in the external world and her mother. Leaving the mother means leaving the world of childhood. This necessitates abandoning or repressing the hope that one's unsatisfied wishes for nurturance from the mother will ever be gratified.

Or one may become one's mother. This often means identifying primarily with the domestic sphere, even if one works outside the home. By becoming a mother herself, the woman can reexperience her own childhood, including the infantile feeling of merger with another person's identity. She can show solidarity with her own mother by joining that long chain of women who sacrificed themselves for the good of their children, their husbands, and the continuation of society as we know it.

Some mothers consciously encourage their daughters to succeed.

However, even they are likely to convey another covert message: to be a woman means to make compromises, to fail, to give up one's dreams, to settle for less than one wishes. Women who refuse to do this call into question the meaning of their mothers' lives and risk the hostility that arises from the mother's own anger at her situation.

The wish to fail is buried deep and is hard to retrieve from the unconscious. It does not cease to exist when women are able to identify the social forces that also pressure them toward failure or compromise. One may have a very sophisticated analysis of patriarchy and female socialization and still engage in self-defeating acts at work or in relations with others. The wish to fail may take more disguised forms, for instance, in a profound ambivalence toward work. A woman's desire to succeed may be undercut by a sense of being a "fake"— of being much less competent than people think, of not really belonging in this world, of marking time until her real fate arrives. It may be difficult for her to think of her work as a career, to work as single-mindedly as a man would. She may be profoundly troubled by questions about the ultimate worth and meaning of her efforts.

Given the organization of work in our society, men too may share some of these doubts. They are much less likely, however, to question whether they belong in the world of nondomestic work *at all*. Patriarchal ideology teaches that a woman's place is in the home; a man's place is in the factory or office. The man is expected both by his mother and by society as a whole to leave the family and to be somewhat autonomous at work. Men often feel something is wrong with them if they cannot exert some autonomy,[10] but women feel something is wrong if they do exert autonomy. At work, women also lack any female authority figures—not only as role models but as quasimaternal figures *outside* the home. For men this lack of female influence and power is one of the attractions of work. Their fear of returning to the mother's control may be an unconscious motive for keeping women out of the workplace, and especially out of positions of authority over men.

Nurturance does not lead to success in the outside world. For example, women professors who spend time with their students and become involved in their lives are less likely to have time for publishing, becoming known in their discipline, and being successful academic entrepreneurs. If they raise questions about the "scholarly" system, their male colleagues may suggest that it is only because they cannot do as well in male pursuits that they want to change the rules

10. See Richard Sennett and Jonathan Cobb (1973), pp. 53–79, for evidence of this among working-class men. Also Rubin (1976), pp. 155–184.

of the game. Women's ambivalence about male values and the unwillingness to give up the female identification of the self may lead to disabling conflicts about their work. Without a transformation in the character of work itself, including integration of noncompetitive, nurturant ways of relating and recognized time and support for child care for both men and women, these conflicts would remain.

Fear of failure has its roots in the infantile rage at the mother and terror at her power. As much as one wishes for nurturance, one is afraid of the vulnerability of the infantile state. The girl has a special grievance against the mother who is the model of what she must become. Father is a more realistic model for the boy. To the extent that the mother lacks the power and the esteem of others, she has already betrayed her daughter. The fear of failure is a fear of being a damaged person like the mother.

The wish to revert to infanthood and the mother and the fear of doing so may be equally strong, resulting in paralysis or self-defeating behavior. Inasmuch as society infantilizes and terrorizes women, for example, by rape and other forms of violence, the fear of losing one's autonomy may more easily be repressed. Once repressed, the urge for autonomy and the anger accompanying its repression may be expressed as depression, resentment of women who do succeed, and extreme conservatism about patriarchal values.

The character of mother-daughter relationships results in major difficulties in the relationships between adult women. Women are taught to devote themselves to their relationships with men, especially their husbands. Their relationships with women are often filled with conflict. Due to the unconscious roots of these difficulties, it is often difficult to work them through. Women may respond by abandoning intimate relations with women altogether, except for immediate family. This abandonment is encouraged by patriarchal ideology that devalues women, by men's jealousy and discomfort at strong female bonds, and by the economic structure that requires mobility and social fragmentation, as for example the subordination of personal needs to the demands of the man's career.

The lack of intimate female relations further weakens a woman's position. It reconfirms her devaluation of the female world, denies her a chance to mitigate the mother-daughter conflicts, and forces her to turn more exclusively to men. She becomes even more emotionally dependent on a lover or husband, often asking for something the nature of which neither he nor she can identify, that is, "motherly" nurturance. This emotional dependence complicates her financial dependence—whether on one man, on the male-dominated work world, or on the male-run state.

She may flee emotional intensity altogether by establishing intellectual relations with men. She confirms the split between irrationality (mother) and rationality (father) experienced in early childhood. She thus recreates the patriarchal ideology present in many cultures, including our own, which splits thought from feeling in order to maintain male dominance.[11]

She may complain that women, and thus ultimately she herself, are boring and trivial, confirming men's suspicion that only exceptional women—ones who think like men—can or should escape the domestic realm. These women, being exceptional, also offer no evidence as to the general capacities of women. Success for women once again comes as the betrayal or denial of her gender.

Conflict between women is further compounded by the intensely homophobic character of our society. Women who have intimate relations with and show physical affection for other women run the risk of being branded as lesbians—no matter who their actual sex partners may be. Not only is it difficult for women who are overwhelmingly weak economically and politically to risk another form of social discrimination, but such charges and such contact may also arouse deeply buried unconscious wishes and feelings. The mother is, after all, the first love object for the girl as well as the boy. All of us carry the memory of the experience of our mother's body—her softness, smell, comfort. These experiences have an erotic aspect. Girls must repress their desires for the mother as they transfer sexual allegiance to the father in the individuation process in our society. Without this transfer there can be no patriarchy. Yet without this transfer at the present time, there can be no female autonomy. The power of women's erotic memories and wishes for the mother may not be expressed in a directly sexual form. They may not even be available to consciousness. But their power is strong enough to frighten any woman in whom they are even semiconsciously aroused.

The fear of being a lesbian may be a powerful motive for avoiding intimate relations with women. Longing for the mother's body is also painful insofar as it is associated not only with the powerless yet gratifying state of infancy, but also because it has to be renounced. The pain may be dealt with by avoiding women or by defending the homophobic ideology prevalent in our society. A powerful source of women's sexuality—the memories of early infantile gratification—is denied. This correspondingly reduces sensuality as a whole.

Having sexual relations with women is no guarantee of the resolu-

11. For the persistence of this pattern, see Adrienne Rich (1976); Sherry B. Ortner (1972); Max Horkheimer and Theodor W. Adorno (1972), pp. 71–80.

tion of these problems, however, for inasmuch as their psychic roots remain unconscious, the conflicts may be acted out in destructive ways within lesbian relationships. Inasmuch as these wishes are attached to a fantasy mother, they need to be worked out, not acted out. This working out may take a variety of equally effective forms. The struggle against homophobia is part of the fight against patriarchy.

Antifeminism among women and our own antifemale behavior has left the feminist movement perplexed. Insights gained from analysis of mother-daughter relationships demonstrate certain problems of feminism and antifeminism and point the way to political solutions.

The women's liberation movement, especially in the early stages of "sisterhood is powerful," the "personal is political," and consciousness raising, aroused expectations among women that it simply could not fulfill. The psychic roots of these expectations are also the source of some of the opposition to feminism among certain women. In brief, the movement was unconsciously experienced by some women as a chance to attain both nurturance and reinforcement for autonomy. Other women viewed the attack on patriarchy—the system of domination associated with fatherhood—as an attack on motherhood. Without motherhood as currently practiced, they feared they would lose the potential for nurturance. They also feared the loss of the satisfaction they received as mothers. This was a denial of their female selves and of the sacrifices they had made to attain their present identity.

Women who joined the early women's liberation movement achieved euphoric pleasure in the company of women. "The personal is political" ideology allowed women to discuss their female experiences within a relatively safe context; consciousness-raising groups were considered both political (rational) and personal (emotional). Hence, some of the potentially threatening aspects of disclosing oneself to another woman were muted by the context. Nonetheless, feelings of anxiety, of competition, and of unmet needs often arose within these groups and were both unexpected and difficult to resolve. Some women felt that to uncover buried feelings and to reconstruct the meaning of life experiences was sufficient. Others argued that the groups should serve as preludes to more formal and political action or political study and analysis.

Although these disagreements reflect serious political differences, the sense of hurt went deeper. What occurred was a reenactment of the early childhood drama: The early euphoria, the sense of oneness and commonality, of self and others was breaking down. This sense of commonality stimulated longings for the early nurturant mother. Women who wished for a deepening of the "personal" aspect of the movement experienced the "political" women as not only differing with them, but, unconsciously, as invalidating nurturance needs that were so painful yet pleasurable to reexperience. Conversely, the "political" women felt punished and rejected for exerting their autonomy, by being criticized for being too intellectual, that is, male. Once again they were forced to experience the conflict between warmth and intimacy and connecting with the outside world of ideas and action.

Because the groups of women suffered from the same unconscious conflicts, both exhibited the characteristics of the domination of the unconscious: rigidity, inability to accept or discuss differences, dogmatism, absolute rejection of the other, inability to accept the authority of another, unrealistic idealization of certain models, anxiety, intellectual rationalization, and rage. Splits developed between gay and straight, radical and bourgeois, radical and Marxist-feminist, Third-world leadership versus defenders of women as a class, anti-imperialist and anti-patriarchal. These have material roots in class, race, and ideological differences; in differences in sexual preferences; and in differences in life experience. But there are also unconscious sources. The women's movement has never fully recovered from the discovery of the profound differences among women, nor has the movement developed adequate methods of discussing and mediating these differences. Feminism, however, has made it possible for many women to develop strong one-to-one intimate relationships with other women, sometimes for the first time in their lives.

Until the wishes and longings evoked by the movement can somehow be brought out and analyzed, this impasse will remain. The movement's failure to deal adequately with the issue of motherhood takes on new significance in this light. The highly abstracted forms in which the issue has been approached—through arguments about "mother-right," the relation between housework and surplus value, women as domestic workers, motherhood as patriarchal ideology, the social history of the family—reveals the anxiety that women experience around this issue. Furthermore, this anxiety is crippling not only because of internal relations but also because the movement is unable to comprehend and recruit antifeminist women.

Antifeminist women often view the women's liberation movement as a threat to a female identity forged out of compromises. The most vocal expression of antifeminist feelings is the antiabortion lobby and now, increasingly, the antihomosexual movement as well. Perhaps such women feel, unconsciously, that they are protecting the very existence of the symbolic mother. They could experience themselves as the guardians of nurturance, of the life-giving protective mother against the cold, calculating, self-absorbed, and autonomy-obsessed feminists. The language of the argument reveals the split. The "right to life" identifies woman as life giver and preserver. The "right to choose" is to exert control over one's body and one's life, to move out of the infantile state, but it is also to reject both the mother and identification in terms of that role. Another indication that feminism is seen as an assault on gender identity is the objection often voiced against the Equal Rights Amendment: that men and women would have to share the same bathrooms. By implication, genital differences would lose their meaning and protection.

The women's liberation movement has allowed the "right to life" and all it represents to be preempted by antifeminism because of its own ambivalence about motherhood and the traditional female condition. This is unfortunate, for the ambivalence prevents the movement from addressing what is progressive within antifeminism: an implicitly antipatriarchal stance, an assertion of the importance of caretaking and emotion that protect life, a refusal to accept equality if it means becoming like men. At the same time, the antifeminists are profoundly patriarchal in their insistence that nurturance can only be preserved at the expense of autonomy.

We once again encounter that paradox within female development: that an overidentification with the mother can mask a deep rage toward her and by extension toward all women—a rage that is expressed by extreme hostility to anyone who acts upon one's wishes to escape the traditional female condition. The hostility toward women results in an alliance with and a subordination to patriarchal authority itself. This can be seen in the alliance between antiabortion forces and the Catholic Church, historically one of the most oppressive and antifemale institutions. Women become the instruments of their own oppression, just as mothers unconsciously deny or repress their daughters' moves toward autonomy. "Love" is put into the service of oppression and the perpetuation of powerlessness. The life giver becomes the life denier.

The women's liberation movement is facing an awesome task. The split between nurturance and autonomy is carried by all of us as one of those archaic residues within the unconscious. The split is reinforced by powerful social forces such as the organization of production and reproduction. In order for women to become whole people, every social structure will have to be transformed. This is a terrifying thought. How reassuring to think all the contradictions will disappear when capitalism is smashed, or when we send all the men off to re-education camps, or when all women become lesbian-separatists and withdraw their energy from the patriarchal system.

If history teaches us anything, it is that such narrow solutions are no solutions at all (Rowbotham, 1974).[12] Indeed, the consequence of narrow "solutions" may be to diminish women's power. For example, women work both inside and outside the home without necessitating changes in men's relationship to children and without the creation of adequate child-care facilities.

Women may be forgiven a temporary failure of nerve in the face of the terrifying array of tasks ahead of us. The integration of work and play; new arrangements for human intimacy and child care; development of a technology that works with rather than exploits mother earth; the freeing of men from mastery and ourselves from participation in it; the integration of mind and body, feeling, and thought all lie before us. How ironic that in order to overcome the conflicts and ambivalence of the mother-daughter bond, we must take on the most traditional female role of all: the re-creation of life itself.

12. Rowbotham's (1974) study shows clearly that whenever women gave up demands for a total revolution—in production, modes of governance, sexuality, and the family—change was less than male leaders originally promised. She also shows that men were unable to act in women's interest or keep them in mind. Women frequently were urged to submerge their goals into the "larger" needs of the revolutionary, or reformist, movement. Whenever women agreed or were forced to accede to this demand, their struggles were lost. Women are perpetually seen as having special interests; men as representing humanity.

REFERENCES

Blanck, G., and Blanck, R. 1974. *Ego psychology: Theory and practice.* New York: Columbia University Press.

Bowlby, J. 1975. *Separation, anxiety and anger.* Middlesex, England: Penguin.

Dinnerstein, D. 1976. *The mermaid and the minotaur.* New York: Harper & Row.

_____, Mitchell, J., and Chodorow, N. 1974. Family structure and feminine personality. In *Women, culture and society,* ed. M. Z. Rosaldo and L. Lamphere, pp. 43–66. Stanford, Calif.: Stanford University Press.

Fairbairn, W. R. D. 1952. *An object-relations theory of the personality.* New York: Basic Books.

Freud, S. 1949. Femininity. In *New introductory lectures on psychoanalysis,* pp. 45–51. New York: Norton.

_____. 1974a. Female sexuality. In *Women and analysis,* ed. J. Strouse, pp. 53, 72. New York: Dell.

_____. 1974b. Some psychical consequences of the anatomical distinction between the sexes. In *Women and analysis,* ed. J. Strouse, pp. 27–38. New York: Dell.

Gordon, L. 1976. *Woman's body, woman's right.* New York: Grossman.

Hartmann, H. 1979. Capitalism, patriarchy, and job segregation by sex. In *Capitalist patriarchy and the case for socialist feminism,* ed. Z. R. Eisenstein. New York: Monthly Review Press.

Horkheimer, M., and Adorno, T. W. 1972. *The dialectic of enlightenment.* New York: Herder and Herder.

Horney, K. 1967. The flight from womanhood. In *Feminine psychology*, pp. 54–70. New York: Norton.

Lerner, H. E. 1974. Early origins of envy and devaluation of women: Implications for sex role stereotypes. *Bulletin of the Menninger Clinic* 38:538–553. [Reprinted herein chapter 2.]

Mahler, M. S., Pine, F., and Bergman, A. 1975. *The psychological birth of the human infant.* New York: Basic Books.

Mitchell, J. 1974. *Women and psychoanalysis.* New York: Random House.

Money, J., and Ehrhardt, A. A. 1972. *Man and woman, boy & girl.* Baltimore, Md.: Johns Hopkins University Press.

Ortner, S. B. 1972. Is female to male as nature is to culture? *Feminist Studies* 1(2): 5–31. Reprinted in *Women, culture and society*, ed. M. Z. Rosaldo and L. Lamphere. Stanford, Calif.: Stanford University Press.

Rich, A. 1976. *Of woman born.* New York: Norton.

Rowbotham, S. 1974. *Women, resistance and revolution.* New York: Random House.

Rubin, L. B. 1976. *Worlds of pain.* New York: Basic Books.

Sennett, R., and Cobb, J. 1973. *The hidden injuries of class.* New York: Vintage Books.

Stoller, R. 1973. *Splitting: A case of female masculinity.* New York: Delta.

Strouse, J. 1974. *Women and analysis.* New York: Dell.

Woolf, V. 1945. *A room of one's own.* Middlesex, England: Penguin.

Zilboorg, G. 1973. Masculine and feminine: Some biological and cultural aspects. In *Psychoanalysis and women*, ed. J. B. Miller. Baltimore, Md.: Penguin.

# 5

# Psychology of Women: Perspectives on Theory and Research for the Eighties

EMILIE F. SOBEL

The past decade has produced a plethora of psychological literature on sex differences, sex-role stereotypes, gender identity, and so forth. Both mental health professionals and the scientific community have been actively engaged in reassessing traditional views. This scholarly activity, prompted in part by the idea mongering of feminists, has provided a revision of Freudian orthodoxy and of the naive stereotypes that heretofore have pervaded experimental research in psychology. Many practicing clinicians have been struggling with these issues as well. While not comfortable functioning within traditional views, they are not prepared to abandon an intrapsychic orientation in favor of a sociocultural emphasis.

As a result of the research efforts of recent years, the view of the human female as passive, masochistic, and submissive has for the most part been debunked. Still, as the often-cited Broverman studies (Broverman et al. 1968, 1970) have indicated, the mental health professional has not escaped orthodoxy. Sex bias among male and female profes-

sionals still exists (Stricker 1977). At the same time new evidence is
emerging concerning a more active, assertive, and achievement-oriented woman.

Is this new woman an anomaly of nature and society or is she merely reemerging from the bonds of a patriarchal society that has castrated her socially? Has she lagged in accomplishment in the recent past
because of a performance or a competence (structural) decrement? An
examination of the biological, sociological, and psychological literature may provide an indication.

## Biological Determinants

The biological determinants of female behavior represent structural
givens that can provide clues as to the parameters of female behavior.
Gonadal steroids have been implicated in the formation of sex differences in mammals. Males, whose primary steroid is the androgen testosterone, have about ten times more of this substance than females.
Women have a complicated gonadal steroid pattern; they experience a
surge of testosterone production premenstrually and around the time
of ovulation, at which time estrogen levels are also increased, Masculine behavior is influenced by the effect of testosterone on the central
nervous system; similarly, female behavioral patterns are under the
influence of hormonal variables (Bardwick 1974).

Menstrual cycle and mood are interrelated (Benedek and Rubinstein
1942; Ivey and Bardwick 1968). While depression, irritability, anxiety,
and withdrawal are higher premenstrually, at midcycle women become more outer-directed, self-confident, and alert. Bardwick (1974),
who has reviewed the literature on the relationship between menstrual cycle and mood, cites one study that establishes a relationship between the menstrual cycle and aggression. Women using oral contraceptives, which stabilize steroid levels, display no significant
emotional fluctuations. One interesting finding by Oakes (1970) provides a physiological basis for the often-cited distinction between aggression and self-assertion. Oakes found that women who were not
taking oral contraceptives played more competitively midcycle than
premenstrually. Competitive behavior reflected the self-esteem of the
midcycle estrogen peak when these women scored high on personality measures of dominance and self-confidence.

Evidence in the literature on testosterone conclusively implicates a
hormonal basis for the surplus aggression found in genetic males and

premenstrual or androgenized females. The androgenized female monkey, for example, has increased play initiation as a juvenile, is more rough-and-tumble, makes playful threats, and mounts females in a masculine stance (Money and Ehrhardt 1976). In another study (Joslyn 1973), female monkeys were treated with male hormone at six and one-half months. Before treatment males were dominant; after treatment reverse behaviors ensued.

Bardwick (1974) raises the issue of whether socialization can influence physiology and suggests that there may be an interaction rather than an unidirectional physiological causality. Despite this admission, essentially Bardwick still adheres to the classical psychodynamic assumptions regarding the significance of biology and early experience (Mednick and Weissman 1975). Williams (1977), however, cites evidence that behavior can affect testosterone levels. Thus when single male monkeys were placed in an all-female group, their testosterone level was found later to have risen about four times its preexperimental level.

Stoller's work (1972, 1974) does much to further the general proposition that higher-level variables, rather than physiological status, mediate sexual identity. He emphasizes a point unknown in Freud's time: that mammalian tissue starts as female in fetal life regardless of chromosomal sexual identity. It is only through the intervention of the masculinizing hormone, an androgen, that the process of maleness progresses. Thus the penis is essentially an androgenized clitoris, rather than the clitoris being an inferior penis. On the brain level, the same condition for masculinization of behavior ensues: Without androgen at a critical period, masculine behavior will not occur. Intersexuality (a significant shift of one or more of the criteria for determining gender in the direction of the opposite sex) can be multidetermined. Thus Klinefelter's syndrome (too many sex chromosomes) or Turner's syndrome (too few), gonadal dysfunction, hermaphroditic genitalia, and disruption of normal sex hormone production are all distinct pathways that can determine sex.

Stoller contends that psychological forces, rather than physiological givens, are crucial in forming gender identity. He provides clinical evidence regarding two chromosomally male siblings who were born with normal male internal sexual apparatus and testes but had external female genitalia. Their internal apparatus and testes were missed at birth; they were assigned to a female sex and were unquestionably feminine psychologically. When the discrepancy was discovered at latency, the parents decided that the children would remain female. Through hormonal and surgical treatment, female anatomy was created, and there were no ensuing psychological problems. Stoller's work does not obviate the role of hormones, but it does cast serious doubt on the validity of extrapolations from biology to female behavior.

## Sociological and Psychological Factors

Parental attitudes, social dicta, and the like form what Hartmann, Kris, and Lowenstein (1949) have referred to as "institutional regulation" of behavior. These attitudes are internalized in the growing child and transmute ethological and biological givens. Although Whiting and Pope (1964) found that boys seek dominance more aggressively than girls in all countries, Mead's (1935) findings support the environmental hypothesis and question the uniformity of sex roles across cultures.

In a longitudinal study of early mother-child interactions, Moss (1976) found that mothers reacted to girl infants differently than to boy infants; that is, mothers reinforced verbal behavior in girls but responded physically to the greater irritability that boys displayed. Studies on neonatal sex differences (Maccoby and Jacklin 1974), however, found that two-thirds showed no sex difference. Yet one study (Lewis 1972) did demonstrate that mothers tended to encourage boys to separate, explore, and become autonomous while at the same time they maintained a closer interpersonal bond with daughters.

In recent years it has become fashionable to hold to an environmentalist point of view and attribute observed sex differences to differences in socialization pressures (Williams 1977). Bandura (1965), for example, found that boys produced more spontaneous imitations of an aggressive model but that girls produced a virtually equal number of imitations when the children were rewarded for their imitations. This casts doubt on the conclusions that can be drawn from such classical studies as that of Kagan and Moss (1962), who employed a longitudinal design to study eighty-nine white children from childhood to adulthood. They found that females maintained a high degree of passivity and dependence from birth to fourteen years; they also found a high correlation between childhood and adult passivity and dependency in females. However, sampling bias is an inherent feature of longitudinal research. The subjects of the Kagan-Moss study went through socialization in the 1950s, an era noted for aggressiveness in males and passivity in females.

The sex-role stereotypes that infiltrated the psychological literature of the 1950s and 1960s arose not from the fact that sex differences have been found (Maccoby and Jacklin 1974; Tietlebaum 1976; Williams 1977) but from the way in which these documented differences are dealt with. McClelland (1965), for example, draws fanciful assumptions from the literature on sex differences. From a complex body of data, he concludes that women are more "complexly interdependent" with the world, whereas men seek independent achievement. He makes use of a metaphor of bipolar opposition, in which masculinity and femininity are construed as opposing constellations of traits with enigmatic origins in the imagery of sex and reproduction.

Erikson (1974) is another psychological author whose conclusions display bipolar thinking unwarranted by the findings. In an observational study, he distributed to 150 boys and 150 girls such items as blocks, animals, people figures, and toy cars. Asked to construct a scene, girls constructed "peaceful" enclosed scenes, making use of "inner space," whereas boys constructed "aggressive" exteriors, such as scenes of street action. These "results" may merely reflect selective acculturation in the use of toys (cf. Marmor 1973).

Broverman and associates (1968) attempt to explain the sex differences in cognition by evoking a physiological explanation involving the sympathetic (or adrenergic) and the parasympathetic (or cholinergic) nervous systems. Both are sensitive to gonadal steroids. The male tendency to excel in problem solving and analytical behavior, which requires a suppression of an immediate response, is facilitated by the cholinergic system, which is an inhibiting system. Estrogen inhibits the parasympathetic transmitter while testosterone does not. Men therefore can do tasks requiring inhibition of impulses better than women because their parasympathetic activity is greater. In the neonatally androgenized rat, the masculinized female displays inhibitory spatial learning, such as occurs with normal male rats. Estrogen-injected male rats have increased activation and poorer spatial learning with more errors. This points to a biological substratum for the difference in cognition, as do cerebral lateralization and chromosomal factors. It does not, however, evaluate the role of higher-level processes in mediating these differences in humans. Women are increasingly becoming successful in areas that call for supposed "masculine" cognitive abilities.

The fact that women have not been successful in these areas in the past may have to do with selective acculturation for achievement orientation and aggressive activity in relation to it. Male socialization enhances options and encourages sex-role definitions that call for such direction. Women are discouraged in self-assertiveness, achievement orientation, and independence (Mednick and Weissman 1975). Hoffman (1972) has focused on the fact that women do not develop adequate mastery skills. They strive to please rather than to succeed.

Horner's (1970) "fear of success" construct is relevant in this regard and has stimulated an energetic research effort. Although the results of this literature are inconclusive at this time, some studies suggest that opposite-sex competition leads to a performance decrement for women. The expectancy literature (Mednick and Weissman 1975) clearly documents that females have higher expectations that they will fail at tasks involving intellectual mastery. They attribute their success at such tasks to good luck and hard work but not to ability.

From the 1930s to the 1950s, efforts were made to ferret out a range of sex differences and develop standard measures of masculinity and femininity on the assumption that there is a universe of stable and valid psychological differences between males and females (Lee 1976). Even in the 1970s, this kind of effort is reflected in the measures of Broverman and colleagues when they demonstrate that women are considered passive and dependent by mental health professionals. Stricker (1977) makes the well-taken point that the nature of the data does not warrant such sweeping conclusions but the language used in the initial stages of the project slanted the use of the scales. Thus, if males received a hypothetical score of 55 out of a possible 60 on the logical-illogical pole and females received 50, these authors labeled the male score as the "logical" and the female score as the "illogical" pole, even though the actual scores were not radically apart on the continuum. When Broverman and colleagues (1970) subsequently state that, relative to men, women are perceived to be dependent, subjective, passive, noncompetitive, and illogical, they again presuppose bipolar opposites rather than matters of degree.

Psychoanalytic literature represents an intrapsychic perspective on female development. Freud (1974) begins his essay on the distinction between the sexes with an apology for publishing speculative views on women. He felt that pure masculinity and femininity were theoretical constructions of uncertain content and would turn out to have general validity only when they came to be based upon more than the handful of cases upon which he drew. Later (1964) Freud hedged on an immutable biologically determined femininity with passive aims, and he acknowledged a social influence.

Feminist writers often tend to forget that psychoanalysis provides an anatomy of unconscious meanings based upon infantile psychosexual conflicts. It does not prescribe a life style or a phenomenology of female functioning. A promising kind of revisionism of the classical psychoanalytic position is provided by the ego psychological framework. While retaining an intrapsychic orientation, issues of autonomy vs. dependence and so forth can be considered as sex-role free aspects of ego functioning.

The psychological health of woman has not been furthered by a living out of cultural fantasy roles. The menopausal, depressive, agoraphobic housewife and the unassertive "fearful-of-success" woman have been cultural casualties produced by the repression of female independence and aggression. The work of Sandra Bem focuses on the concept of psychological "androgeny," wherein masculinity and femininity represent complementary domains of positive traits and behaviors. In principle, an individual can be both instrumental and expressive, integrated into a balanced androgynous personality. Bem's laboratory studies (Bem and Bem 1970; Bem 1974) demonstrate that "androgynous" individuals of both sexes are both independent and nurturing. Although Bem's work does depart from the bipolar thinking that has marred earlier research, it is not necessary to invent a new category, *androgynous*, to bypass the semantic difficulties of the connotative meanings of masculine and feminine. Instead one can conceive of a sphere of ego functioning that does not depend on sex role. It is only when this conflict-free sphere is instinctualized that an acting out of libidinal fantasies dominates the arena. The passive and submissive female "type" then appears, representing the personification of a neurotic conflict of a psychosexual nature. This "persona" is a stereotype that has pervaded Western culture but, despite its prevalence, it is essentially no less a characterological or neurotic problem than is the "macho" male with his surplus of aggression.

Human behavior is learned, motivated, and performed on the basis of complicated intrapsychic convolutions of simple biological and cultural facts. These facts interact to produce an ongoing dialectic of person and situation variables. As practitioners we must know that the kinds of expression that our female patients have the potential to produce is limited only by their organizing fantasy about what being female entails. A dialectical theory of human development focuses on simultaneous movements along at least the following four dimensions: inner biological, individual psychological, cultural sociological, and outer physical (Riegel 1976). At times, both in the history of the individual and that of the culture, development in any of these dimensions may not synchronize with that in the others. The development of a woman in the 1980s will not be the same as one in the 1960s or the 1970s or any other decade. Very early in development, biological "givens" —testosterone, earlier lateralization of the left hemisphere, estrogen peaks, less developed skeletal musculature—will interact with the sociolinguistic system, with the mother or other primary caretaker. Conscious and unconscious meanings will evolve and in turn interact with the outer environment. A dialectic of the development of the female, then, will progress as conflicts and contradictions are encountered, in vivo, during growth. Society, like our theories, has reached only a temporary equilibrium in its concept of female potential.

REFERENCES

Bandura, A. 1965. Influence of model's reinforcement contingencies on the acquisition of imitative responses. *Journal of Personality and Social Psychology* 1:589–595.

Bardwick, J. 1974. The sex hormones, the central nervous system and affect variability in humans. In *Women in therapy*, ed. V. Franks and V. Burtle, pp. 27–49. New York: Brunner/Mazel.

Bem, S. L. 1974. The measurement of psychological androgeny. *Journal of Consulting and Clinical Psychology* 42:155–162.

Bem, S. L., and Bem, D. J. 1970. Case study of a nonconscious ideology training the woman to know her place. In *Beliefs, attitudes and human affairs*, ed. D. J. Bem. Monterey, Calif.: Brooks/Cole.

Benedek, T., and Rubinstein, B. B. 1942. The sexual cycle in women: The relation between ovarian function and psychodynamic processes. *Psychonomic Medicine Monographs*, vol. 3, nos. 1 and 2.

Broverman, D. M., et al. 1968. Roles of activation and inhibition in sex differences in cognitive abilities. *Psychology Review* 75:23–50.

Broverman, I. K., et al. 1970. Sex-role stereotypes and clinical judgments of mental health. *Journal of Consulting and Clinical Psychology* 34:1–7. [Reprinted herein chapter 7.]

Deutsch, H. 1944. *The psychology of women: A psychoanalytic interpretation*, vol. 1. New York: Grune & Stratton.

Erikson, E. 1974. Womanhood and the inner space. In *Women and analysis*, ed. J. Strouse. New York: Grossman Publishers. [Originally published 1968.]

Freud, S. 1974. Some psychical consequences of the anatomical distinction between the sexes. In *Women and analysis*, ed. J. Strouse, pp. 291–319. New York: Grossman Publishers. [Originally published 1925.]

——— . 1964. New introductory lectures on psycho-analysis. In *The standard edition of the psychological works of Sigmund Freud*, ed J. Strachey, vol. 22, pp. 112–125. London: Hogarth Press. [Originally published 1933.]

Hartmann, H., Kris, E., and Lowenstein, R. 1949. Notes on the theory of aggression. *Psychoanalytic Study of the Child* 3:9–36. [Reprinted in *Papers on psychoanalytic psychology*, ed. H. Hartmann, E. Kris, and R. Lowenstein, vol. 4. New York: International Universities Press.]

Hoffman, L. W. 1972. Early childhood experiences and women's achievement motives. *Journal of Social Issues* 28:129–155.

Horner, M. 1970. Femininity and successful achievement: A basic inconsistency. In *Feminine personality and conflict*, ed. J. Bardwick, et al., Belmont, Calif.: Brooks/Cole.

Ivey, M. E., and Bardwick, J. M. 1968. Patterns of affective fluctuation in the menstrual cycle. *Psychosomatic Medicine* 30:336–345.

Joselyn, W. D. 1973. Androgen-induced social dominance in infant female rhesus monkeys. *Journal of Child Psychology and Psychiatry* 14:137–145.

Kagan, J., and Moss, H. A. 1962. *Birth to maturity: A study in psychological development*. New York: Wiley.

Lee, P. C. 1976. Psychology and sex differences. In *Sex differences*, ed. P. C. Lee and R. S. Stewart. New York: Urizen Books.

Lewis, M. 1972. Parents and children: Sex-role development. *School Review* 80:229–240.

McClelland, D. 1965. Wanted: A new self image for women. In *The woman in America,* ed. R. J. Lifton, pp. 173–192. Boston: Beacon Press.

Maccoby, E. E., and Jacklin, C. 1974. *The psychology of sex differences.* Stanford, Calif.: Stanford University Press.

Marmor, J. 1973. Changing patterns of femininity. In *Psychoanalysis and women,* ed. J. B. Miller, pp. 191–206. New York: Brunner/Mazel.

Mead, M. 1935. *Sex and temperament in three savage tribes.* New York: Morrow.

Mednick, M., and Weissman, H. 1975. The psychology of women, selected topics. In *Annual review of psychology,* ed. M. R. Rosensweig and L. W. Porter, vol. 26:1–18.

Money, J., and Ehrhardt, A. 1976. Fetal hormones and the brain: Effect on sexual dimorphism of behavior. In *Sex differences,* ed. P. C. Lee and R. S. Stewart. New York: Urizen Books. [Originally published in *Archives of Sexual Behavior* 1:241–262.]

Moss, H. 1976. Sex, age and state as determinants of mother-infant interactions. In *Sex differences,* ed. P. C. Lee and R. S. Stewart. New York: Urizen Books.

Oakes, M. 1970. Pills, periods and personality. Ph.D. dissertation, University of Michigan. Cited in J. Bardwick, 1974. The sex hormones, the central nervous system and affect variability in humans. In *Women in therapy,* ed. V. Franks and V. Burtle, p. 34. New York: Brunner/Mazel.

Riegel, K. 1976. The dialectic of human behavior. *American Psychologist* 34:689–700.

Stricker, G. 1977. Implications of research for psychotherapeutic treatment of women. *American Psychologist* 32:14–22.

Stoller, R. J. 1972. The bedrock of masculinity and femininity: Bisexuality. *Archives of General Psychiatry* 26:207–212.

―――――. 1974. Facts and fancies: An examination of Freud's concept of bisexuality. In *Women and analysis,* ed. J. Strouse, pp. 343–364. New York: Grossman Publishers.

Tietlebaum, M. S., ed. 1976. *Sex differences.* New York: Anchor.

Williams, J. 1977. *Psychology of women: Behavior in a biosocial context.* New York: Norton.

Whiting, B. B., and Pope, C. P. 1973. A cross-cultural analysis of sex differences in the behavior of children aged three through eleven. *Journal of Social Psychology* 91:171–188.

# PART I  Supplementary Readings

Chodorow, N. 1974. Family structure and feminine personality. In *Women, culture, and society*, ed. M. Z. Rosaldo and L. Lamphere, pp. 43–66. Stanford, Calif.: Stanford University Press.

Dinnerstein, D. 1976. *The mermaid and the minotaur: Sexual arrangements and human malaise.* New York: Harper & Row.

Fliess, Robert, ed. 1948. *The psycho-analytic reader. Part II: Theory, female and pre-oedipal sexuality*, pp. 159–258. [Contains key early papers by Deutsch, Lampl-de-Groot, and Brunswick.]

Freud, S. 1961. Some psychical consequences of the anatomical distinction between the sexes. *The standard edition of the complete psychological works of Sigmund Freud*, ed. J. Strachey (hereafter *Standard edition*), vol. 19, pp. 248–258. London: Hogarth Press. [Originally published 1925.]

————. 1963. Female sexuality. *Standard edition*, vol. 21, pp. 225–243. London: Hogarth Press. [Originally published 1931.]

————. 1964. Lecture 33: Femininity. *Standard edition*, vol. 22, pp. 112–135. London: Hogarth Press. [Originally published 1933.]

Hammer, S. 1975. *Daughters and mothers: Mothers and daughters.* New York: Quadrangle/New York Times Book Co.

Horney, K. 1973. *Feminine psychology.* New York: Norton.

Lewis, H. 1976. *Psychic war in men and women.* New York: New York University Press.

Manalis, S. A. 1976. The psychoanalytic concept of female passivity: A comparative study of psychoanalytic and feminist views. *Comprehensive Psychiatry* 17:241–247.

Miller, J. B. 1972. Sexual inequality: Men's dilemma. (A note on the oedipus complex, paranoia, and other psychological concepts.) *American Journal of Psychoanalysis* 32:147–155.

————. 1976. *Toward a new psychology of women.* Boston: Beacon Press. (See esp. pp. 2–12.)

Schafer, R. 1974. Problems in Freud's psychology of women. *Journal of the American Psychoanalytic Association* 22(3):459–485.

Strouse, J., ed. 1974. *Women and analysis, Dialogues on psychoanalytic views of femininity.* New York: Dell.

Thompson, C. 1964. *On women.* New York: Basic Books.

# PART II

# *General Issues of Sexism in Mental Health*

# 6

# The Prevalence of Gender-Role Bias in Mental Health Services

## MARJORIE BAYES

As we have seen, there is gender bias in the theories underlying the mental health field. How is this translated, what forms does it take in the actual delivery of mental health services, the therapist-patient relationship? We now look at evidence of frequent biases in the work of therapists, evidence gathered in different ways and under different circumstances, which independently verifies the gravity of discrimination against women.

We begin this section with two papers that may be regarded as classics, in that they are widely read and frequently cited. Chapter 7 is the 1970 study by Broverman and associates in which mental health professionals were asked to denote characteristics of the healthy female, the healthy male, and the healthy adult. It was discovered that clinicians held different standards of mental health for women than for men.

Chapter 8 is the report of a Task Force of the American Psychological Association that studied sex bias and sex-role stereotyping in thera-peutic practice. This Task Force identified four general areas of dis-crimination by therapists affecting women as clients, and strongly advocated educational efforts to overcome inequities.

Other studies, not included here, support the tenor and direction of these findings. Fabrikant (1974) found that male therapists and male patients agreed that women can be satisfied and fulfilled solely through the wife-and-mother role, while female therapists and female patients significantly disagreed with this contention. Similar findings of sex-role bias by counselors were found by Maslin and Davis (1975) and Abramowitz and associates (1973). From a questionnaire complet-ed by 177 therapists from several professions, Brown and Hellinger (1975) found that 50 percent of the therapists took a traditional, biased stance and that male therapists were significantly more biased than female therapists. This is particularly important since 90 percent of psychiatrists, 66 percent of clinical psychologists, and 40 percent of social workers in North America are male (Levine, Kamin, and Levine 1974).

Next in this section, chapter 9 by Stephenson and Walker covers a broad range of problems that arise for women as a result of therapist bias and stereotyped views of the "good woman."

Since the early 1970s, there have been several papers pointing to physician misuse of medication—particularly tranquilizers—with women patients and the tendency to overmedicate women to keep them more comfortable and less troublesome (e.g., Fidell 1973; Seiden-berg 1971). There is generally little attempt by clinicians to reinterpret women's individual distress as a product of social-psychological fac-tors related to role and gender stereotypes. Through medication, wom-en are induced to become accepting of the very conditions that give rise to their distress. A 1979 paper by Ruth Cooperstock, included as chapter 10, brings us up to date on the issues and the data.

And, in chapter 11, we confront the situation of sexual relations be-tween male therapist and female patient. Davidson's paper provides a discussion of the history of the issue of therapist-patient sex, its preva-lence, and its effects.

Women are becoming more aware of the biased services available to them. When clients as a group begin to voice concerns, service provid-ers must examine their theories, their methods, and the social systems they have built to support theory and method. Therapists may find that their training institutions teach and support sex discrimination, that their professional associations perpetuate male dominance, and that their day-to-day interchange with clients conveys a powerful mes-sage about how women should behave.

REFERENCES

Abramowitz, S., et al. 1973. The politics of clinical judgment. *Journal of Consulting and Clinical Psychology* 41:385–391.

Brown C., and Hellinger, M. 1975. Therapists' attitudes toward women. *Social Work* 20:266–270.

Fabrikant, B. 1974. The psychotherapist and the female patient: Perceptions, misperceptions and change. In *Women in therapy*, ed. V. Franks and V. Burtle, pp. 83–110. New York: Brunner/Mazel.

Fidell, L. 1973. Put her down on drugs: Prescribed drug usage in women. Paper presented at the Western Psychological Association Meeting, 12 April 1973, Anaheim, California.

Levine, S., Kamin, L., and Levine, E. 1974. Sexism and psychiatry. *American Journal of Orthopsychiatry* 44:327–336.

Maslin, A., and Davis, J. 1975. Sex-role stereotyping as a factor in mental health standards among counselors-in-training. *Journal of Counseling Psychology* 22:87–91.

Seidenberg, R. 1971. Drug advertising and perception of mental illness. *Mental Hygiene* 55:21–31.

# 7

# Sex-Role Stereotypes and Clinical Judgments of Mental Health

INGE K. BROVERMAN,
DONALD M. BROVERMAN,
FRANK E. CLARKSON,
PAUL S. ROSENKRANTZ,
AND SUSAN R. VOGEL

Evidence of the existence of sex-role stereotypes, that is, highly consensual norms and beliefs about the differing characteristics of men and women, is abundantly present in the literature (Anastasi and Foley 1949; Fernberger 1948; Komarovsky 1950; McKee and Sherriffs 1957; Seward 1946; Seward and Larson 1968; Wylie 1961; Rosenkrantz et al. 1968). Similarly, the differential valuations of behaviors and characteristics stereotypically ascribed to men and women are well established (Kitay 1940; Lynn 1959; McKee and Sherriffs 1959; Rosenkrantz et al. 1968; White 1950); that is, stereotypically masculine traits are more often perceived as socially desirable than are attributes that are stereotypically feminine. The literature also indicates that the social desirabilities of behaviors are positively related to the clinical ratings of these same behaviors in terms of "normality-abnormality" (Cowen 1961), "adjustment" (Wiener et al. 1959); and "health-sickness" (Kogan et al. 1957).

Given the relationships existing between masculine versus feminine characteristics and social desirability on the one hand, and between mental health and social desirability on the other, it seems reasonable to expect that clinicians will maintain parallel distinctions in their concepts of what, behaviorally, is healthy or pathological when considering men versus women. More specifically, particular behaviors and characteristics may be thought indicative of pathology in members of one sex, but not pathological in members of the opposite sex.

The present paper, then, tests the hypothesis that clinical judgments about the traits characterizing healthy, mature individuals will differ as a function of the sex of the person judged. Furthermore, these differences in clinical judgments are expected to parallel the stereotypic sex-role differences previously reported (Rosenkrantz et al. 1968).

Finally, the present paper hypothesizes that behavioral attributes that are regarded as healthy for an adult, sex unspecified, and thus presumably viewed from an ideal, absolute standpoint, will more often be considered by clinicians as healthy or appropriate for men than for women. This hypothesis derives from the assumption that abstract notions of health will tend to be more influenced by the greater social value of masculine stereotypic characteristics than by the lesser valued feminine stereotypic characteristics.

The authors are suggesting, then, that a double standard of health exists wherein ideal concepts of health for a mature adult, sex unspecified, are meant primarily for men, less so for women.

## Method

### Subjects

Seventy-nine clinically trained psychologists, psychiatrists, or social workers (forty-six men, thirty-three women) served as subjects (Ss). Of these, thirty-one men and eighteen women had Ph.D. or M.D. degrees. The Ss were all actively functioning in clinical settings. The ages varied between twenty-three and fifty-five years and experience ranged from internship to extensive professional experience.

### Instrument

The authors have developed a Stereotype Questionnaire, which is described in detail elsewhere (Rosenkrantz et al. 1968). Briefly, the

*87*

questionnaire consists of 122 bipolar items, each of which describes, with an adjective or a short phrase, a particular behavior trait or characteristic such as:

Very aggressive                                  Not at all aggressive
Doesn't hide emotions at all             Always hides emotions

One pole of each item can be characterized as typically masculine, the other as typically feminine (Rosenkrantz et al. 1968). On forty-one items, 70 percent or better agreement occurred as to which pole characterizes men or women, respectively, in both a sample of college men and a sample of college women (Rosenkrantz et al. 1968). These items have been classified as "stereotypic."

The questionnaire used in the present study differs slightly from the original questionnaire. Seven original items seemed to reflect adolescent concerns with sex, for example, "very proud of sexual ability . . . not at all concerned with sexual ability." These items were replaced by seven more general items. Since three of the discarded items were stereotypic, the present questionnaire contains only thirty-eight stereotypic items. These items are shown in table 7–1.

Finally, in a prior study, judgments have been obtained from samples of Ss as to which pole of each item represents the more socially desirable behavior or trait for an adult individual in general, regardless of sex. On twenty-seven of the thirty-eight stereotypic items, the masculine pole is more socially desirable (male-valued items), and on the remaining eleven stereotypic items, the feminine pole is the more socially desirable one (female-valued items).

*Instructions*

The clinicians were given the 122-item questionnaire with one of three sets of instructions, "male," "female," or "adult." Seventeen men and ten women were given the "male" instructions, which stated "think of normal, adult men and then indicate on each item the pole to which a mature, healthy, socially competent adult man would be closer." The Ss were asked to look at the opposing poles of each item in terms of directions rather than extremes of behavior. Another fourteen men and twelve women were given "female" instructions, that is, they were asked to describe a "mature, healthy, socially competent adult woman." Finally, fifteen men and eleven women were given "adult" instructions. These Ss were asked to describe a "healthy, mature, socially competent adult person" (sex unspecified). Responses to these "adult" instructions may be considered indicative of "ideal" health patterns, without respect to sex.

TABLE 7-1

*Male-valued and Female-valued Stereotypic Items*

| Feminine Pole | Masculine Pole |
|---|---|
| **Male-valued Items** | |
| Not at all aggressive | Very aggressive |
| Not at all independent | Very independent |
| Very emotional | Not at all emotional |
| Does not hide emotions at all | Almost always hides emotions |
| Very subjective | Very objective |
| Very easily influenced | Not at all easily influenced |
| Very submissive | Very dominant |
| Dislikes math and science very much | Likes math and science very much |
| Very excitable in a minor crisis | Not at all excitable in a minor crisis |
| Very passive | Very active |
| Not at all competitive | Very competitive |
| Very illogical | Very logical |
| Very home oriented | Very worldly |
| Not at all skilled in business | Very skilled in business |
| Very sneaky | Very direct |
| Does not know the way of the world | Knows the way of the world |
| Feelings easily hurt | Feelings not easily hurt |
| Not at all adventurous | Very adventurous |
| Has difficulty making decisions | Can make decisions easily |
| Cries very easily | Never cries |
| Almost never acts as a leader | Almost always acts as a leader |
| Not at all self-confident | Very self-confident |
| Very uncomfortable about being aggressive | Not at all uncomfortable about being aggressive |
| Not at all ambitious | Very ambitious |
| Unable to separate feelings from ideas | Easily able to separate feelings from ideas |
| Very dependent | Not at all dependent |
| Very conceited about appearance | Never conceited about appearance |
| **Female-valued Items** | |
| Very talkative | Not at all talkative |
| Very tactful | Very blunt |
| Very gentle | Very rough |
| Very aware of feelings of others | Not at all aware of feelings of others |
| Very religious | Not at all religious |
| Very interested in own appearance | Not at all interested in own apearance |
| Very neat in habits | Very sloppy in habits |
| Very quiet | Very loud |
| Very strong need for security | Very little need for security |
| Enjoys art and literature very much | Does not enjoy art and literature at all |
| Easily expresses tender feelings | Does not express tender feelings at all |

## Scores

Although Ss responded to all 122 items, only the stereotypic items that reflect highly consensual, clear distinctions between men and women, as perceived by lay people, were analyzed. The questionnaires were scored by counting the number of Ss that marked each pole of each stereotypic item within each set of instructions. Since some Ss occasionally left an item blank, the proportion of Ss marking each pole was computed for each item. Two types of scores were developed: "agreement" scores and "health" scores.

The agreement scores consisted of the proportion of Ss on that pole of each item that was marked by the majority of the Ss. Three agreement scores for each item were computed; namely, a "masculinity agreement score" based on Ss receiving the "male" instructions, a "femininity agreement score," and an "adult agreement score" derived from the Ss receiving the "female" and "adult" instructions, respectively.

The health scores are based on the assumption that the pole that the majority of the clinicians consider to be healthy for an adult, independent of sex, reflects an ideal standard of health. Hence, the proportion of Ss with either male or female instructions who marked that pole of an item that was most often designated as healthy for an adult was taken as a "health" score. Thus two health scores were computed for each of the stereotypic items: a "masculinity health score" from Ss with "male" instructions and a "femininity health score" from Ss with "female" instructions.

## Results

### Sex Differences in Subject Responses

The masculinity, femininity, and adult health and agreement scores of the male clinicians were first compared to the comparable scores of the female clinicians via $t$ tests. None of these $t$ tests were significant (the probability levels ranged from .25 to .90). Since the male and female Ss did not differ significantly in any way, all further analyses were performed with the samples of men and women combined.

### Agreement Scores

The means and sigmas of the adult, masculinity, and femininity agreement scores across the thirty-eight stereotypic items are shown in table 7-2. For each of these three scores, the average proportion of Ss agreeing as to which pole reflects the more healthy behavior or trait is significantly greater than the .50 agreement one would expect by chance. Thus, the average masculinity agreement score is .831 ($z =$

TABLE 7-2

*Means and Standard Deviations for Adult,*
*Masculinity, and Femininity Agreement*
*Scores on Thirty-Eight Stereotypic Items*

| Agreement Score | M | SD | Deviation from Chance | |
|---|---|---|---|---|
| | | | Z | p |
| Adult | .866 | .116 | 3.73 | < .001 |
| Masculinity | .831 | .122 | 3.15 | < .001 |
| Femininity | .763 | .164 | 2.68 | < .005 |

$3.15$, $p < .001$), the average femininity agreement score is .763 ($z = 2.68$, $p < .005$), and the average adult agreement score is .866 ($z = 3.73$, $p < .001$). These means indicate that on the stereotypic items clinicians strongly agree on the behaviors and attributes that characterize a healthy man, a healthy woman, or a healthy adult independent of sex, respectively.

## Relationship Between Clinical Judgments of Health and Student Judgments of Social Desirability

Other studies indicate that social desirability is related to clinical judgments of mental health (Cowen 1961; Kogan et al. 1957; Wiener et al. 1959). The relation between social desirability and clinical judgment was tested in the present data by comparing the previously established socially desirable poles of the stereotypic items (Rosenkrantz et al. 1968) to the poles of those items that the clinicians judged to be the healthier and more mature for an *adult*. Table 7-3 shows that the relationship is, as predicted, highly significant ($x^2 = 23.64$, $p < .001$). The present data, then, confirm the previously reported relationships

TABLE 7-3

*Chi-Square Analysis of Social Desirability*
*Versus Adult Health Scores on*
*Thirty-Eight Stereotypic Items*

| Item | Pole Elected by Majority of Clinicians for Healthy Adults |
|---|---|
| Socially desirable pole | 34 |
| Socially undesirable pole | 4 |

Note.—$\chi^2 = 23.64$, $p < .001$.

that social desirability, as perceived by nonprofessional *Ss*, is strongly related to professional concepts of mental health.

The four items on which there is disagreement between health and social desirability ratings are to be emotional; not to hide emotions; to be religious; to have a very strong need for security. The first two items are considered to be healthy for adults by clinicians but not by students; the second two items have the reverse pattern of ratings.

## Sex-Role Stereotype and Masculinity Versus Femininity Health Scores

On twenty-seven of the thirty-eight stereotypic items, the male pole is perceived as more socially desirable by a sample of college students (male-valued items); while on eleven items, the feminine pole is seen as more socially desirable (female-valued items). A hypothesis of this paper is that the masculinity health scores will tend to be greater than the femininity health scores on the male-valued items, while the femininity health scores will tend to be greater than the masculinity health scores on the female-valued items. In other words, the relationship of the clinicians' judgments of health for men and women is expected to parallel the relationship between stereotypic sex-role behaviors and social desirability. The data support the hypothesis. Thus on twenty-five of the twenty-seven male-valued items the masculinity health score exceeds the femininity health score; while seven of the eleven female-valued items have higher femininity health scores than masculinity health scores. On four of the female-valued items, the masculinity health score exceeds the femininity health score. The chi-square derived from these data is 10.73 ($df = 1$, $p < .001$). This result indicates that clinicians tend to consider socially desirable masculine characteristics more often as healthy for men than for women. On the other hand, only about half of the socially desirable feminine characteristics are considered more often as healthy for women rather than for men.

On the face of it, the finding that clinicians tend to ascribe male-valued stereotypic traits more often to healthy men than to healthy women may seem trite. However, an examination of the content of these items suggests that this trite-seeming phenomenon conceals a powerful, negative assessment of women. For instance, among these items, clinicians are more likely to suggest that healthy women differ from healthy men by being more submissive; less independent; less adventurous; more easily influenced; less aggressive; less competitive; more excitable in minor crises; having their feelings more easily hurt; being more emotional, more conceited about their appearance; less objective; and disliking math and science. This constellation seems a most unusual way of describing any mature, healthy individual.

## Mean Differences Between Masculinity Health Scores and Femininity Health Scores

The above chi-square analysis reports a significant pattern of differences between masculine and feminine health scores in relation to the stereotypic items. It is possible, however, that the differences, while in a consistent, predictable direction, actually are trivial in magnitude. A $t$ test, performed between the means of the masculinity and femininity health scores, yielded a $t$ of 2.16 ($p < .05$), indicating that the mean masculinity health score (.827) differed significantly from the mean femininity health score (.747). Thus despite massive agreement about the health dimension per se, men and women appear to be located at significantly different points along this well-defined dimension of health.

## Concepts of the Healthy Adult Versus Concepts of Healthy Men and Healthy Women

Another hypothesis of this paper is that the concepts of health for a sex-unspecified adult and for a man will not differ, but that the concepts of health for women will differ significantly from those of the adult.

This hypothesis was tested by performing $t$ tests between the adult agreement scores versus the masculinity and femininity health scores. Table 7–4 indicates, as predicted, that the adult and masculine concepts of health do not differ significantly ($t = 1.38$, $p > .10$), whereas a significant difference does exist between the concepts of health for adults versus females ($t = 3.33$, $p < .01$).

These results, then, confirm the hypothesis that a double standard of

TABLE 7–4

*Relation of Adult Health Scores to Masculinity Health Scores and to Femininity Health Scores on Thirty-Eight Stereotypic Items*

| Health Score | M | SD | |
|---|---|---|---|
| Masculinity | .827 | .130 | |
| | | | $t = 1.38^*$ |
| Adult | .866 | .115 | |
| | | | $t = 3.33\dagger$ |
| Femininity | .747 | .187 | |

$^*df = 74, p > .05.$
$\dagger df = 74, p < .01.$

health exists for men and women, that is, the general standard of health is actually applied only to men, while healthy women are perceived as significantly less healthy by adult standards.

# Discussion

The results of the present study indicate that high agreement exists among clinicians as to the attributes characterizing healthy adult men, healthy adult women, and healthy adults, sex unspecified. This agreement, furthermore, holds for both men and women clinicians. The results of this study also support the hypotheses that (1) clinicians have different concepts of health for men and women and (2) these differences parallel the sex-role stereotypes prevalent in our society.

Although no control for the theoretical orientation of the clinicians was attempted, it is unlikely that a particular theoretical orientation was disproportionately represented in the sample. A counterindication is that the clinicians' concepts of health for a mature adult are strongly related to the concepts of social desirability held by college students. This positive relationship between social desirability and concepts of health replicates findings by a number of other investigators (Cowen 1961; Kogan et al. 1957; Wiener et al. 1959).

The clinicians' concepts of a healthy, mature man do not differ significantly from their concepts of a healthy adult. However, the clinicians' concepts of a healthy, mature woman do differ significantly from their adult health concepts. Clinicians are significantly less likely to attribute traits that characterize healthy adults to a woman than they are likely to attribute these traits to a healthy man.

Speculation about the reasons for and the effects of this double standard of health and its ramifications seems appropriate. In the first place, men and women do differ biologically, and these biological differences appear to be reflected behaviorally, with each sex being more effective in certain behaviors (Broverman et al. 1968). However, we know of no evidence indicating that these biologically based behaviors are the basis of the attributes stereotypically attributed to men and to women. Even if biological factors did contribute to the formation of the sex-role stereotypes, enormous overlap undoubtedly exists between the sexes with respect to such traits as logical ability, objectivity, independence, and so forth; that is, a great many women undoubtedly possess these characteristics to a greater degree than do many men. In addition, variation in these traits within each sex is certainly great. In view of the within-sex variability and the overlap between sexes, it seems inappropriate to apply different standards of health to men compared to women on purely biological grounds.

More likely the double standard of health for men and women stems from the clinicians' acceptance of an "adjustment" notion of health, for example, health consists of a good adjustment to one's environment. In our society men and women are systematically trained, practically from birth on, to fulfill different social roles. An adjustment notion of health, plus the existence of differential norms of male and female behavior in our society, automatically leads to a double standard of health. Thus for a woman to be healthy from an adjustment viewpoint, she must adjust to and accept the behavioral norms for her sex, even though these behaviors are generally less socially desirable and considered to be less healthy for the generalized competent, mature adult.

By way of analogy, one could argue that a black person who conformed to the "precivil rights" southern Negro stereotype—that is, a docile, unambitious, childlike, and so forth, person—was well adjusted to his environment and, therefore, a healthy and mature adult. Our recent history testifies to the bankruptcy of this concept. Alternative definitions of mental health and maturity are implied by concepts of innate drives toward self-actualization, toward mastery of the environment, and toward fulfillment of one's potential (Allport 1955; Bühler 1959; Erikson 1950; Maslow 1954; Rogers 1951). Such innate drives, in both blacks and women, are certainly in conflict with becoming adjusted to a social environment with associated restrictive stereotypes. Acceptance of an adjustment notion of health, then, places women in the conflictual position of having to decide whether to exhibit those positive characteristics considered desirable for men and adults, and thus have their "femininity" questioned, that is, be deviant in terms of being a woman; or to behave in the prescribed feminine manner, accept second-class adult status, and possibly live a lie to boot.

Another problem with the adjustment notion of health lies in the conflict between the overt laws and ethics existing in our society versus the covert but real customs and mores that significantly shape an individual's behavior. Thus while American society continually emphasizes equality of opportunity and freedom of choice, social pressures toward conformity to the sex-role stereotypes tend to restrict the actual career choices open to women and, to a lesser extent, men. A girl who wants to become an engineer or business executive, or a boy who aspires to a career as a ballet dancer or a nurse, will at least encounter raised eyebrows. More likely considerable obstacles will be put in the path of each by parents, teachers, and counselors.

We are not suggesting that it is the clinicians who pose this dilemma for women. Rather we see the judgments of our sample of clinicians as merely reflecting the sex-role stereotypes, and the differing valuations of these stereotypes, prevalent in our society. It is the attitudes of our society that create the difficulty. However, the present study does provide evidence that clinicians do accept these sex-role stereotypes, at least implicitly, and, by so doing, help to perpetuate the stereotypes. Therapists should be concerned about whether the influence of the sex-role stereotypes on their professional activities acts to reinforce social and intrapsychic conflict. Clinicians undoubtedly exert an influence on social standards and attitudes beyond that of other groups. This influence arises not only from their effect on many individuals through conventional clinical functioning, but also out of their role as "expert" that leads to consultation to governmental and private agencies of all kinds, as well as guidance of the general public.

It may be worthwhile for clinicians to critically examine their attitudes concerning sex-role stereotypes, as well as their position with respect to an adjustment notion of health. The cause of mental health may be better served if both men and women are encouraged toward maximum realization of individual potential rather than to an adjustment to existing restrictive sex roles.

REFERENCES

Allport, G. W. 1955. *Becoming.* New Haven, Conn.: Yale University Press.
Anastasi, A., and Foley, J. P., Jr. 1949. *Differential psychology.* New York: Macmillan.
Broverman, D. M., et al. 1968. Roles of activation and inhibition in sex differences in cognitive abilities. *Psychological Review* 75:23–50.
Bühler, C. 1959. Theoretical observations about life's basic tendencies. *American Journal of Psychotherapy* 13:561–581.
Cowen, E. L. 1961. The social desirability of trait descriptive terms: Preliminary norms and sex differences. *Journal of Social Psychology* 53:225–233.
Erikson, E. H. 1950. *Childhood and society.* New York: Norton.
Fernberger, S. W. 1948. Persistence of stereotypes concerning sex differences. *Journal of Abnormal and Social Psychology* 43:97–101.
Kitay, P. M. 1940. A comparison of the sexes in their attitudes and beliefs about women. *Sociometry* 34:399–407.
Kogan, W. S., et al. 1957. Some methodological problems in the quantification of clinical assessment by Q array. *Journal of Consulting Psychology* 21:57–62.
Komarovsky, M. 1950. Functional analysis of sex roles. *American Sociological Review* 15:508–516.
Lynn, D. B. 1959. A note on sex differences in the development of masculine and feminine identification. *Psychological Review* 66:126–135.
McKee, J. P., and Sherriffs, A. C. 1957. The differential evaluation of males and females. *Journal of Personality* 25:366–371.

————— . 1959. Men's and women's beliefs, ideals, and self-concepts. *American Journal of Sociology* 64:356–363.

Maslow, A. H. 1954. *Motivation and personality.* New York: Harper.

Rogers, C. R. 1951. *Client-centered therapy: Its current practice, implications, and theory.* Boston: Houghton Mifflin.

Rosenkrantz, P., et al. 1968. Sex-role stereotypes and self-concepts in college students. *Journal of Consulting and Clinical Psychology* 32:287–295.

Seward, G. H. 1946. *Sex and the social order.* New York: McGraw-Hill.

————— , and Larson, W. R. 1968. Adolescent concepts of social sex roles in the United States and the two Germanies. *Human Development* 11:217–248.

White, L., Jr. 1950. *Educating our daughters.* New York: Harper & Row.

Wiener, M., et al. 1959. A judgment of adjustment by psychologists, psychiatric social workers, and college students, and its relationship to social desirability. *Journal of Abnormal Social Psychology* 59:315–321.

Wylie, R. 1961. *The self concept.* Lincoln, Neb.: University of Nebraska Press.

# 8

# Report of the Task Force on Sex Bias and Sex-Role Stereotyping in Psychotherapeutic Practice

ANNETTE M. BRODSKY
AND JEAN HOLROYD*
(*American Psychological Association*)

In July 1974, responding to requests by the American Psychological Association (APA) Committee on Women in Psychology, the Board of Professional Affairs established a task force to: (1) examine the extent and manner of sex bias and sex-role stereotyping in psychotherapeutic practice as they directly affect women as students, practitioners, and

* Task Force members included Annette Brodsky and Jean Holroyd, Cochairs, plus Carolyn Payton, Eli Rubinstein, Paul Rosenkrantz, Julia Sherman, and Freyda Zell. Tena Cummings was an ex-officio participant, and Carolyn Suber was APA staff liaison. Julia Sherman was responsible for the review of literature, and the initial data analysis was voluntarily donated by Gayle Janzen of the University of Alabama and Susan Pirhalla of Bryce State Hospital, Tuscaloosa, Alabama.

This study was authorized by the Board of Professional Affairs (BPA) of the American Psychological Association as an issue of sufficient concern to psychology at large to merit study; however, the report does not necessarily reflect the views of BPA or APA in general.

consumers; (2) recommend actions both within the formal structure of APA and to psychotherapists generally to reduce sex bias and sex-role stereotyping in psychotherapy; and (3) develop materials and methods of dissemination of relevant information to members of the APA and to related professionals and institutions providing psychotherapeutic services.

There are two problems central to sexism in psychotherapeutic practice with women: (1) the question of values in psychotherapy and (2) the therapist's knowledge of psychological processes in women.

At a minimum, the therapist must be aware of ter[1] own values and not impose them on the patient. Beyond that, tey has a responsibility for evaluating the mental health implications of those values. That psychologists expect women to be more passive and dependent than men while acknowledging that these traits are not ideal for mental health has been empirically demonstrated (Broverman et al. 1970; Broverman et al. 1972; Fabrikant 1974; Neulinger et al. 1970; Aslin 1974).

The therapist must also be aware of the ways in which conventional beliefs have biased theory, scientific research, and psychological assumptions (Levenson 1972; Bernard 1972). Tey will need to reevaluate theories about women, especially those theories of Freud.

Because female topics and females as subjects for research have been neglected (Carlson and Carlson 1960; Schwabacher 1972), therapists may find that they are ignorant of important aspects of female psychology. The female patient, for example, may be struggling with her fear of success (Horner 1972), yet the therapist may be totally unaware of the conflict. Seduction by her father may be overlooked because the therapist is fixated on Freud's oedipal theory of the child as the source of the sexual impulse. Psychosomatic reactions such as "frigidity," infertility, spontaneous abortion, or amenorrhea may be seen as pathological without awareness of the protective, constructive features of these reactions. Uninformed or misinformed, the therapist may mishandle questions of emotional changes accompanying the menstrual cycle, pregnancy, childbirth, and menopause.

The whole question of "masculinity," "femininity," and adaptation to sex role has been rife with unexamined value problems as well as conceptual and empirical difficulties (Constantinople 1973; Sherman 1971). For example, a woman may be told that she is "too aggressive" when her deficit in social skills is the result of anxiety about self-assertion. The psychological problems of "masculine" women have been found to relate more to the inconsistent quality of their "mascu-

---

1. Tey = he/she; ter = his/her; and tem = him/her. These neuter gender pronouns are substituted for the generic *he* throughout this report in order to raise the consciousness of the reader to the sexist effect of the structure of the English language.

linity," that is, unadaptive "feminine" traits, than to their masculinity (Sherman 1971). Rather than reporting a difficult transition for masculine women in middle age, Bart (1972) found that it was the excessively feminine woman who encountered trouble.

Biased treatment may occur differently for special groups of women, though little data are available. Intelligent women may have their intelligence unrecognized or in some manner discounted. There are certain prejudices about lower-class women. For example, a lower-class female client (bogus description) was seen by therapists as less self-confident, less well liked, less independent, less assertive, more conforming and submissive to authority, and less permissive and democratic with respect to the family than a middle-class female client (Briar 1961).

Black women are caught in a double bind. Swartz and Abramowitz (1974) found that white psychiatrists viewed black patients, especially female ones, as having a better prognosis than white patients. The authors suggest that the psychiatrists may attribute the psychopathology to external rather than internal sources, and therefore assign a better prognosis. The stereotyped attribution of inner strength to the black woman, sometimes exaggerated into a matriarchal and/or castrating caricature, is experienced by black women as a cruel farce and gross misinterpretation of their family role (Carkhuff 1972; Chesler 1972; Hare and Hare 1972; Hernandez 1974).

Lesbians are likely to be labeled as emotionally disturbed and to encounter the belief that a good heterosexual experience will solve their problems. Even fairly knowledgeable, well-intentioned therapists may find that their helpfulness is limited by a lack of knowledge of such experiences as "coming out" and the nuances of the social interactions of the gay and bisexual communities in the nexus with straight society (Chesler 1972; Reiss 1974).

Because most therapists are male and most patients are female, the problem of handling sexual attraction and sexual intimacy is of special concern. Many therapists are unprepared to handle these problems skillfully, thus contributing to antitherapeutic results, unnecessary marital discord, and even divorce. The most dramatic aspect of this problem is when a male therapist has sexual relations with his female patient. The percentage of therapists engaging in sexual relations with their patients is unknown but believed to be small (Kardener, Fuller, and Mensh 1973). However, numbers do not reflect the salience of the problem or the bitterness of many women who have had sexual relations with their therapists. Sexual relations between patient and therapist reflect sex bias in at least three ways: (1) Nearly all complaints are from women patients regarding male therapists; (2) stereotypic feminine qualities, especially passive dependence, are exploited;[2] and (3) the male therapist has considerably more power in the therapy situation than the female patient, a classic situation for the operation of sexual politics. In addition to the sex-bias consideration, sexual intimacy makes it difficult if not impossible for the therapist to remain objective and to conduct the course of therapy in a manner beneficial to the patient's interests.

The question has been raised as to whether sex between a female patient and male therapist can be assumed to be harmful. In one study, twenty-five women who had sexual relations with their therapists reported that they were nonorgasmic both before and after therapy with all men, including their therapists.[3] Thus far the literature review has failed to reveal even anecdotal cases in which sex with the therapist was reported as beneficial.

Some may argue that intercourse between a therapist and a patient that does not involve force or deceit is a private matter. The question of deceit is central because patients assume that therapists will act in the patient's best interests. However, the position that women who enter therapy are fully responsible for their behavior would at least require that we educate the female public so they may choose the kind of relationship they wish to pay for before a transference relationship obscures their objectivity.

Good process studies of sex bias and sex-role stereotyping during the therapy hour are lacking, but studies of clinical judgment are suggestive. Although two recent studies have found clinical judgments of women generally no different from those of men, in one of the studies the more conservative examiners found left-of-center political deviancy more indicative of maladjustment when the purported patient was female than male (Abramowitz et al. 1973; Swartz and Abramowitz 1974). Of course, left-of-center deviance is particularly associated with feminism. There is some evidence, too, that female therapists may be freer of bias, though findings are contradictory on this point (Delk and Ryan 1975; Fabrikant 1974; Aslin 1974; Abramowitz and Dokecki 1974).

Some indications of differential treatment were found by Fabrikant (1974), who reported that female patients were in therapy more than twice as long as male patients. Fabrikant concluded that "the overall results most strongly support the feminist viewpoint that females in therapy are victimized by a social structure and therapeutic philosophy that keeps them dependent for as long as possible" (p. 96).

2. B. Belote, personal communication, November 27, 1974.
3. Ibid.

Fabrikant also measured patients' perceptions of therapists' attitudes. Female patients perceived that therapists believe husbands should dominate the marital relationship, and both male and female patients perceived that therapists have a double standard of sexual behavior. While both male therapists and male patients agreed that the majority of women can be fulfilled by the wife-mother role and thought abortion should be a joint marital decision, neither female therapists nor female patients agreed with these views. Whether or not a patient perceives ter therapist's views correctly, these findings raise the question of whether a therapist may need to make ter values explicit in areas of rapidly changing social values.

Some additional insight into sex-biased and sex-role–stereotyped therapy can be gained by contrasting it with feminist therapy (Barrett et al. 1974; Brodsky 1973; Kirsch 1974; Rice and Rice 1973; Tennov 1973). Hannah Lerman (1974) characterizes feminist therapy as distinctly nonauthoritarian and claims that it denies the philosophical position of being an expert about the client. The personal is viewed as political, and the client must learn to differentiate between what are *her* problems and what are society's problems, what behaviors are considered socially appropriate and what may be appropriate for her. She is taught to be self-nurturing, is freed from the indiscriminate nurturing of others, and is shown that normal self-interest need not be viewed as "selfishness." Interestingly, making clients into feminists is not a goal of treatment, but rather helping tem "become the best person they can, within the limits of their personal circumstances and the patterns of society in general" (Lerman 1974).

Research that explicitly addresses the issues of sex bias and sex-role stereotyping in therapy is in its infancy. As a first step, and until more empirical data are amassed, the Task Force attempted to identify concern of female consumers and practitioners as gleaned from their own experiences.

## A Survey of Women Psychologists

An open-ended questionnaire was developed to elicit descriptions of incidents or circumstances that were perceived as indicative of sex bias or sex-role stereotyping in psychotherapy with women. The questionnaire was mailed to 2,000 women in APA Divisions 12, 17, 29, and 35[4]

4. Division 12 = Clinical Psychology; 17 = Counseling Psychology; 29 = Psychotherapy; 35 = Psychology of Women.

with the assumption that they had experience both as consumers and practitioners of psychotherapy and had a vested interest in responding in numbers.

Three hundred and twenty replies were received and categorized by themes involving issues of sexism affecting women as clients in psychotherapy.

Four general areas of perceived sex bias and sex-role stereotyping affecting women as clients of psychotherapy emerged: (1) fostering traditional sex roles; (2) bias in expectations and devaluations of women; (3) sexist use of psychoanalytic concepts; and (4) responding to women as sex objects, including seduction of female clients. The themes within these areas and selected verbatim responses are presented to illuminate the issues.

## Fostering of Traditional Sex Role

*Theme: The therapist assumes that problem resolution and self-actualization for women come from marriage or perfecting the role of wife.*

My therapist suggested that my identity problems would be solved by my marrying and having children; I was nineteen at the time and in no way ready for marriage. This stereotypic solution was unfortunately typical of the kind of response I later heard from my patients about their experiences with male therapists.

My woman therapist pushed for "adjustment of my marital problems"—exploration of major changes was quite hard—the message was "stay in the marriage." My male therapist teases "Just like a woman"—claims awareness, professes he will (should) stop it—and does not.

As a state hospital intern, I was appalled at the treatment given women—usually "go home and do more of what a wife should do—clean house, etc."—live lives of a kind that sent them to the hospital in the first place.

*Theme: The therapist lacks awareness and sensitivity to the woman client's career, work, and role diversity.*

I know of a therapist, seeing a married couple, who asked questions about the husband's work, then went on to other matters and never found out that the wife was an eminent biologist.

Spent six years in psychoanalysis. My major problem then as now, that is, the major source of my anxiety, was my sense of self-worth as a psychologist. I want to do a good job and enjoy status, prestige, money, etc., that comes from being a productive worker. Situational factors which thwart these ends such as sex discrimination are thus highly threatening and frustrating. In spite of the fact that my dreams, associations, day-to-day crises were job centered, my analyst never did accept this. It seemed impossible to him that a woman could place such high value on her competence, creativity, achievement. He considered my occupation a pesky, irrelevant resistance used to avoid facing early memories, "basic identity" problems, etc. "When are you going to quit talking about your job so that we can get down to the real trouble?"

Although I was encouraged to pursue my interests, I was at the same time made to feel less than adequate as a female because of my dissatisfaction with the role of "homemaker." The traditional role of a woman with respect to her husband and children was one I felt I had to deal with simultaneously with my career. I was never helped to see that there were viable alternatives.

*Theme: The female client's attitude toward childbearing and child rearing is viewed as a necessary index of her emotional maturity.*

My femininity was "questioned" by a male therapist colleague when I disagreed with him over marital and child-rearing principles.

My therapist, who was also a woman, argued strongly for me to have a child and not get my tubes tied. She finally conceded that maybe for me it was not necessary to have a child in order to be fulfilled as a woman.

*Theme: In family therapy or treatment of children, the therapist supports the idea that child rearing and thus the child's problems are solely the responsibility of the mother.*

Many of my friends have reported experiences . . . [in which] it will be the mother who is brought into therapy with the implication that it is her responsibility more than the responsibility of the father for whatever difficulties the child may be having . . . current practice tends to imply that the "blame" for a child's problems is attributable primarily to the mother.

Frequently the woman is scapegoated in family therapy. Implicit or explicit therapeutic goal often is strengthening husband's power in family constellation and weakening woman's power in family. Woman is "controlling" whereas man is "strong."

A family therapy case [juvenile delinquent] daughter, father a trained carpenter who had not sought employment for five years. Mother had gone out and gotten a job and had supported the family for most of that time. Interpretation—girl was disturbed because of sex-role reversal of family—father was exhorted to seek a job which he did and mother then described as hostile and castrating because she didn't quit her job.

*Theme: The therapist defers to the husband's needs in the conduct of the wife's treatment.*

Female psychiatrist asked me if I had my husband's agreement for me to see therapist twice a week. (I earn more money than he and am capable of making that decision with or without his agreement.)

I shouldn't work, I shouldn't go to school, all the problems in the marriage were mine. . . . I was not supposed to get angry or hurt my husband's feelings—In the meantime he was (always in private) threatening to kill my youngest kid—wouldn't have done it but plenty of things he did do. . . . First time I've ever mentioned it except to my female analyst—and still feel like I'm quite crazy for even putting it down on paper and no one will believe it.

I have had several women patients in therapy who complained that male therapists didn't understand them. One example was a woman whose alcoholic husband would leave the house for several days each time she disagreed with him. The male therapist told her that she was being too assertive, trying to be too dominant and rejecting her role as a woman.

## Bias in Expectations and Devaluation of Woman

*Theme: The therapist or colleague denies the adaptive and self-actualizing potential or assertiveness for female clients and fosters concepts of women as passive and dependent.*

I was in psychoanalytic therapy and was constantly reminded the man should run the home . . . that women were naturally bitchy and need to be controlled.

Three of the male psychologists . . . actually encouraged the client to continue to be "docile"—"passive"—"'seductive"—"nonassertive" and to stay in professions "open to women."

Whenever a female becomes active, assertive, and aggressive in group situations the label "castrating bitch" is applied to her.

*Theme: The therapist uses theoretical [terms and concepts] (e.g., masochism) to ignore or condone violence toward and victimization of women.*

Though my husband . . . was beating me periodically and we were in joint marital therapy with a well-known psychologist, he never questioned, probed, or interpreted the acting-out behavior. What passed for humanistic nonintervention therapy actually seemed to cover implicit acceptance of "lots of women are slapped around by their husbands in our society so it's nothing to be concerned with."

A psychoanalytically oriented male therapist, with some agreement from some of the other males [therapists], insisted that there was no such thing as rape—that the woman always "asked" for it in some way.

My co-therapist [male] and the male patients [in a psychoanalytically oriented group] made it clear that they assumed a woman patient had encouraged an unknown male to attempt to rape her. This was within one-half hour of the actual incident. The woman patient was extremely frightened and upset. Myself [female therapist] and other female patients saw the incident as potentially dangerous to the woman and having occurred without seductive motivation on the part of the patient. The male therapist interpreted my support . . . and view . . . as penis envy.

*Theme: Sexist jokes and off-hand comments by the therapist have the effect of demeaning women.*

If one assumes that how a male clinician talks about women and "women's lib" at parties reveals something of what happens in the office, we've got a *really* pervasive problem here!

In a recent staff conference to discuss the direction of therapy, I found my colleagues [male] chuckling over their decision that all a client needed was a "good man" banging her once in a while. When I disagreed, one psychologist said, "Don't give us any more of that liberation crap."

One of my major professors once bragged in my presence about how he had ridiculed a patient about her anxiety over her sexual functioning and then he made comments on her qualities as a sex object. I was more shocked than angry at the time, for this man had written several books about the importance of honest, mutually respectful communication. To this day I have no respect for him.

*Theme: The therapist employs inaccurate or demeaning labels (seductive, manipulative, histrionic, etc.) when describing female clients.*

I have merely noticed a tendency in psychiatry to apply the label "histrionic" and "manipulative" but especially "seductive"—much more frequently to women than to men patients—even when I personally have seen no clear evidence to justify the label.

A tendency among male therapists to attribute the anxiety of female patients stereotyping the women as "hysterical" and feeling very derogatory to them. Accompanied by frequent discussion of female patients "being controlling" of the therapist. Male therapists seldom talk about male patients being "controlling." If a woman is assertive this is viewed as a negative.

Disparaging attitudes about "hysterical" women and depressed women. Somehow, it's the idea that it's a woman with these symptoms who is obnoxious and unpleasant to treat. Taught that female psychiatric wards are more dangerous than male wards.

## Sexist Use of Psychoanalytic Concepts

*Theme: The therapist insists on Freudian interpretations.*

I underwent psychoanalysis because I was told that all psychologists should have the experience, and I was very Freudian at the time. After eight months of the effort, I began to realize that I was tailoring my responses to fit the Freudian concept of the female . . . and I realized that all of this had nothing to do with ME—either as an individual or a woman.

I picked my therapist very carefully with regard to attitudes toward women, but his Freudian "transference" training is a real problem. He feels this aspect of the therapy is not moving along quickly enough. I know if I say, "You're nice and you help me but you're twice my age and just *don't* turn me on," he'd say I was resisting. I don't think I can win!

In my own therapy with a male analyst, I often felt that interpretations were consistent with his value—that a woman *is* dependent, frightened, irrational. Particularly in the area of child rearing—his attitude was that he as a psychiatrist could better evaluate my infant's needs than I myself. . . . Dream occurring prior to first pregnancy (A kitten jumped on a table on which was standing a glass of milk). Despite my report of pleasant surprise as the major affect in the dream, the psychiatrist's interpretations focused on conflict over nursing a baby, fright, in the face of a dangerous and unpredictable animal.

*Theme: The therapist maintains that vaginal orgasm is a prerequisite for emotional maturity and thus a goal of therapy.*

I was told the need to have clitoral stimulation stuck out like a sore thumb in an otherwise well-integrated, feminine person.

Surprisingly many colleagues (male and female) still define maturity in women as the capacity for vaginal orgasm. My feeling is that women who do not experience or report this are seen (and therefore subtly treated) as emotionally limited.

Inordinately prolonged treatment aimed at achieving vaginal orgasm and contentment with motherhood as therapeutic goals (in the mind of the male therapist), with consubsequent guilt and frustration.

*Theme: The therapist labels assertiveness and ambition with the Freudian concept of "penis envy."*

Friends of mine in treatment experience the frustrations associated with therapists who interpret frustrations arising from the very real inequities that exist in our society as being nothing more than male envy or penis envy on the part of the female patient.

Everything was interpreted in terms of penis envy and my wanting to sleep with my father. My problems would decrease if only I would submit to the "male" society.

I had a classical analysis '61–66, four times per week. . . . I could write for hours on this: The interpretation of penis envy, questions regarding feeling that I was, in fact, a penis—honestly—when I reported my rapture on first standing on my toes in dancing as a child, "difficulties" accepting the "female" role, questioning me why I identified with male heroes primarily (although I pointed out that research indicated that women with female heroes were reported to have problems), implicit encouragement that now that I was divorced . . . I should look for another man, etc.

*Responding to Women as Sex Objects Including Seduction of Female Clients*

*Theme: The therapist seduces the client.*

I know of many abuses of women patients—hasty "termination" in order to have an affair with the patient, sexual seduction represented as "therapeutic," with disastrous consequences.

In my years as a psychotherapist, many women have come to me with stories of seduction and sexual intimacies with male therapists. In most instances the patients were deeply disturbed by these relationships, saw them as exploitative (although sometimes they justified the therapists' role and protected them), and sometimes resulted in psychotic breaks. This is the ultimate of sex-role bias: The rationalization of the therapist that his exploitation of the doctor-patient relationship for his gratification could be construed as therapeutic "for a woman."

Sorry to say it, but I know of too many cases of actual seduction of female clients by their male therapists usually justified by the view that frigidity is a fate worse than death which can be "cured" by the "right male" (the therapist). I know of *no* cases of young impotent males whose female therapists take the same stance. Also there is the tendency to think of lesbians not as a sexual choice but as inevitably "sick" . . . I know personally of two women (now both therapists themselves) who were seduced (one case) or propositioned (the other) by [name of therapist]. I have no reason to disbelieve their stories, but despite the anger which both of these women have now gotten in touch with (as a result of therapy and supervision) neither will formally complain or *consider* lodging a complaint with the ethics committee.

*Theme: Therapist has a double standard for male and female sexual activities.*

My husband and I separately saw a male marriage counselor . . . for one session each. The counselor dismissed my husband's extramarital affairs as "natural" extracurricular activities, yet he felt my having extramarital affairs was a sign that I was not happy in my marital relationship. My husband and I discussed the counselor's assessment and decided that we would not continue seeing him because we both felt he was "sexist."

Woman should not be promiscuous but have sex with love. My therapist (a woman) tried to make me regret an episode of sex without love or commitment.

At VA Hospital, as the only woman trainee, was told to be aware of my impact on patients because I was a woman, to dress discreetly, etc. I do not believe a male in an all-female installation would have been given these tips. Also, one male supervisor was interpreting my impact on patients because of my sex as if this was the only variable.

*Theme: The therapist heavily weighs physical appearance in the selection of patients or in setting therapeutic goals.*

We wasted an awful lot of time arguing about whether I should wear eye-shadow or not, misunderstanding each other grossly about what self-esteem means—until the women's movement came along and suddenly it became more acceptable to wear slacks and no makeup, as I had been doing for years.

The male counselors in the clinical area would reject the physically unat-tractive client who was female, in preference for her opposite.

My own therapist's concept of a woman was that she should be "femi-nine"—that is, slim, well dressed, good posture, soft voiced, etc.—a regular charm school or airlines image. The therapist, whom I later changed, was a woman also. She believed any woman who resisted such an image was there-fore "aggressive and unfeminine" (her own quotes).

# Other Aspects of the Survey

Respondents also provided information on treatment techniques they considered beneficial in particular for women clients and gave sugges-tions as to how professional psychology can respond to problems of sex bias and sex-role stereotyping in psychotherapy. They listed a vari-ety of circumstances as evidence of sex bias and sex-role stereotyping that influenced their training and employment as psychotherapists. They were actively discouraged from completing the Ph.D., directed away from (or into) clinical psychology because they were women, and accused of using graduate school or a job as a temporary stop gap until they got married (or if married, until they got pregnant). They were regarded as subordinate, overemotional, dependent, and decora-tive by some supervisors and colleagues. They were frequently expect-ed to assume a passive and nurturing role when doing cotherapy with a male, or else supervisors interpreted their therapeutic interactions in sexist terms, that is, that they would be automatically nurturant or would encourage dependency because they were women.

Sex-role stereotyping was cited particularly in the referral or case-assignment process. Women and children were preferentially referred or assigned to female therapists and men to male therapists. Extremely difficult or penniless cases were referred to women therapists for "mothering," while interesting or unusual cases were more likely to be assigned to male therapists.

The women reported that men often stated a preference for male therapists and were surprised or taken aback when their therapist turned out to be a woman, and also that some people in treatment responded negatively to a female therapist being unmarried.

Many respondents thought that there were no special techniques applicable to therapy with women. Indeed, some respondents indicated that the request for specific techniques that would be helpful with women was itself sexist. However, others mentioned specific techniques or areas of focus, such as encouraging independent and achievement-oriented behaviors, thus building self-esteem; accepting nonstereotypic feelings and behaviors; use of a female therapist as a role model and as a more adequate source of empathy; assertiveness training; use of consciousness-raising groups or all-female groups; and sexual reeducation. Many people advocated particular schools of therapy, though there was no consistency of response except a frequent rejection of the psychoanalytic approach.

The inquiry as to how professional psychology can respond to sex bias and sex-role stereotyping in psychotherapy provided the following three major groups of suggestions:

1. The main thrust was toward an educational effort primarily on graduate school level but also in the form of a variety of postgraduate workshops, lectures, and consciousness-raising sessions. A part of this effort would be reexamination of theories, texts, and so forth.

2. Another direction would be an ongoing effort to sensitize psychotherapists through a variety of group processes that, in the minds of the respondents, would help to change attitudes of psychotherapists.

3. Finally, many respondents urged sanctions within the profession and outside to compel modification of sexist behaviors on the part of the psychotherapists. A frequent message was one expressing frustration both with the state of affairs currently in the discipline and with the prospect of improvement. Most urged modification of the APA Code of Ethics to deal with this question. Others asked for public legal sanction.

## Task Force Recommendations

The following recommendations derive from an examination of the results and from the overall work of the Task Force.

The most immediate need is for consciousness raising, increased sensitivity, and greater awareness of the problems of sex bias and sex-role stereotyping in psychotherapeutic practice. This need must be responded to within APA at all levels, and by other organizations concerned with psychotherapy practices, as well as by therapists and clients. Specific activities should include: (1) workshops for therapists and therapists in training sponsored by relevant groups within APA, for example, by the Board of Social and Ethical Responsibility in Psychology and by the APA Ethics Committee with funds also made available to local and regional groups interested in running such workshops; (2) requesting relevant APA divisions (12, 17, 29, and 35) to develop programs directed toward problems of sex bias and sex-role stereotyping in psychotherapy; (3) convening of cross-disciplinary workshops and conferences among professionals in psychotherapy, psychiatry, social work, and other therapy professions to discuss sexism in psychotherapy; (4) developing training materials to sensitize therapists and therapists in training to sexism in psychotherapy.

A second important need is for development of guidelines for nonsexist psychotherapeutic practice. Funds have been requested for this project.

Third, formal criteria and procedures are needed to evaluate the education and training of psychotherapists in the psychology of women, sexism in psychotherapy, and related issues. This would include such things as presence of female role models as supervisors, training for increased competence in the handling of sexual attraction and seductive behavior by therapist and/or client, and sexist practices in psychological testing and diagnosis. The Education and Training Board should disseminate such training criteria.

Fourth, the Ethical Standards of Psychologists should include statements regarding sexism and the *Casebook on Ethical Standards of Psychologists* should provide illustrative case material.

Finally, the Task Force should be continued to carry out the following activities: (1) the development of guidelines for nonsexist psychotherapeutic practice; (2) the development of criteria for education and training; (3) the development of procedures for obtaining information from consumers about sexist practice in psychotherapy; and (4) the investigation of the ethical and therapeutic issues regarding sexual intimacy within psychotherapy.

REFERENCES

Abramowitz, C. B., and Dokecki, P. R. 1974. *The politics of clinical judgment: Early empirical returns.* Paper presented at the meeting of the American Psychological Association, New Orleans, September 1974.

Abramowitz, S., et al. 1973. The politics of clinical judgment: What nonliberal examiners infer about women who do not stifle themselves. *Journal of Consulting and Clinical Psychology* 41:385–391.

Aslin, A. L. 1974. Feminist and community mental health for women. Unpublished manuscript, University of Maryland.

Barrett, C., et al. 1974. Implications of women's liberation and the future of psychotherapy. *Psychotherapy: Theory, Research and Practice* 11:11–15.

Bart, P. 1972. Depression in middle-aged women. In *Readings on the psychology of women*, ed. J. Bardwick. New York: Harper & Row.

Bernard, J. 1972. Sex differences: An overview. Paper presented at the meeting of the American Association for the Advancement of Science, Washington, D.C., December 1972.

Briar, S. 1961. Use of theory in studying effects of client social class on students' judgments. *Social Work* 6:91–97.

Brodsky, A. 1973. The consciousness-raising group as a model for therapy with women. *Psychotherapy: Theory, Research and Practice* 10:24–29. [Reprinted herein chapter 47.]

Broverman, I. K., et al. 1970. Sex-role stereotypes and clinical judgments of mental health. *Journal of Consulting and Clinical Psychology* 34:1–7. [Reprinted herein chapter 7.]

———. 1972. Sex-role stereotypes: A current appraisal. *Journal of Social Issues* 28(2):58–78.

Carkhuff, R. R. 1972. Black and white in helping. *Professional Psychology* 3:18–22.

Carlson, E. R., and Carlson, R. 1960. Male and female subjects in personality research. *Journal of Abnormal and Social Psychology* 61:482–483.

Chesler, P. 1973. *Women and madness*. Garden City, N.Y.: Doubleday.

Constantinople, A. 1973. Masculinity-femininity: An exception to a famous dictum? *Psychological Bulletin* 80:389–407.

Delk, J. L., and Ryan, T. T. 1975. Sex role stereotyping and A-B therapist status: Who is more chauvinistic? *Journal of Consulting and Clinical Psychology* 43:589.

Fabrikant, B. 1974. The psychotherapist and the female patient: Perceptions and change. In *Women in therapy*, ed. V. Franks and V. Burtle, pp. 83–109. New York: Brunner/Mazel.

Hare, N., and Hare, J. 1972. Black women 1970. In *Readings on the psychology of women*, ed. J. Bardwick. New York: Harper & Row.

Hernandez, A. 1974. Small change for black women. *Ms.* August, pp. 16–18.

Horner, M. S. 1972. Toward an understanding of achievement related conflicts in women. *Journal of Social Issues* 28(2):157–176.

Kardener, S. H., Fuller, M., and Mensh, I. N. 1973. A survey of physicians' attitudes and practices regarding erotic and nonerotic contact with patients. *American Journal of Psychiatry* 10:1077–1081.

Kirsh, B. 1974. Consciousness-raising groups as therapy for women. In *Women in therapy*, ed. V. Franks and V. Burtle, pp. 326–354. New York: Brunner/Mazel.

Lerman, H. 1974. What happens in feminist therapy? In *Feminist therapy: In search of a theory*, chaired by A. Brodsky. Symposium presented at the meeting of the American Psychological Association, New Orleans, September 1974.

Levenson, E. A. 1972. *A fallacy of understanding*. New York: Basic Books.

Neulinger, J., et al. 1970. Perceptions of the optimally integrated person as a function of therapists' characteristics. *Perceptual and Motor Skills* 30:375–384.

Reiss, B. 1974. New viewpoints on the female homosexual. In *Women in therapy*, ed. V. Franks and V. Burtle, pp. 191–214. New York: Brunner/Mazel.

Rice, J., and Rice, D. 1973. Implications of the women's liberation movement for psychotherapy. *American Journal of Psychiatry* 130:191–196.

Schwabacher, S. 1972. Male versus female representation in psychological research: An examination of the *Journal of Personality and Social Psychology*, 1970, 1971. *JSAS Catalog of Selected Documents in Psychology* 2:20. (Ms. no. 82.)

Sherman, J. 1971. *On the psychology of women: A survey of empirical studies*. Springfield, Ill.: Charles C. Thomas.

———. In press. Social values, femininity and the development of female competence. *Journal of Social Issues.*

Swartz, J. M., and Abramowitz, S. I. 1974. Effects of psychiatrist values and patient race and sex on clinical judgment. Paper presented at the meeting of the American Psychological Association, New Orleans, September 1974.

Tennov, D. 1973. Feminism, psychotherapy and professionalism. *Journal of Contemporary Psychotherapy* 5:107–116.

# 9

# The Psychiatrist–Woman Patient Relationship

P. SUSAN STEPHENSON AND
GILLIAN A. WALKER

This paper draws attention to the place of psychiatrists in the medical and mental health systems—their attitudes, training, the theories they use, and the attributes and expectations of women patients that combine to produce a situation where psychiatric treatment at times merely patches up women in distress, rather than catalyzing their personal growth and positive coping skills. For a number of years critics have charged that, for women, psychotherapy is a dependency-engendering exercise that is based on adjustment to current circumstances. The superior-subordinate relationship of doctor and patient has been described as replicating middle-class marriage and reinforcing women's dependency on the authority and knowledge of males (Chesler 1972; Greer 1970; Levine, Kamin, and Levine 1974; Smith and David 1975).

Other issues that indicate the need for a reexamination of the psychiatric approach to women include:

1. *The overprescription of drugs for women.* Cooperstock (1976) states that women are prescribed two to two and one-half times as many psychotropic drugs as men. Community surveys suggest that 15 to 20 percent of women are cur-

This work was supported in part by Grant #1208–9–75 from the Non-Medical Use of Drugs Directorate, Department of Health and Welfare, Canada. Modified version of paper presented at the Canadian Psychiatric Association annual meeting, Saskatoon, Saskatchewan, September 1977.

rently on these drugs (Committee Concerned with Women's Health Issues, n.d.; Guse, Morier, and Ludwig 1976). Studying visually impaired children in Vancouver, Jan, Freeman, and Scott (1977) noted that, in both study and control groups, 17 percent of the mothers and 3 percent of the fathers were taking psychoactive drugs.

2. *The woman as an alcoholic.* Alcoholism in women is frequently missed (Lindbeck 1972); they may be given a psychiatric diagnosis and put on tranquilizers with resulting multiple addiction (Kerr 1974).

3. *Unidimensional approaches to family violence.* Child abuse is perceived as resulting from parental psychopathology (Bell 1973; Steele and Pollock 1968). Other instances of family violence such as wife battering are rarely recognized by clinicians (Munson and Hilberman 1977), who tend to treat the women as psychiatric patients.

4. *The scapegoating of mothers.* Psychiatric theory and practice has blamed mothers for their children's problems (Chess 1964). This tendency persists (Thomas and Chess 1977).

To understand these issues as they relate to the psychiatrist and the woman patient, we need to look at the medical and mental health systems within which psychiatrists work; the psychiatrists themselves—attitudes, training, theoretical backgrounds; and the women patients who, as a result of their socialization, bring certain attitudes and expectations to the interaction.

## The Medical and Mental Health Systems

Illich (1975) and Szasz (1970) have stated that during this century, medicine has tended to replace religion in people's lives and to become a powerful force of social control. The widened jurisdiction of medicine is described by Zola (1972), who notes that pregnancy and old age, previously thought to be stages of development, are now considered medical problems, and that alcoholism and drug addiction, hitherto regarded as human foibles and weaknesses, are now referred to as diseases.

When a problem of living, a difficulty, or a habit is defined as disease, the definition is perpetuated by the organization of the medical system, its referral methods, diagnostic practices, billing procedures, report writing, statistic collection, and overall policies. In addition, physicians fear being criticized for failure to diagnose and treat, and must beware of the pressure of media forces that suggest that every minor pain needs an analgesic, every day-to-day problem a tranquilizer (Cooperman 1977).

This process of "medicalization" allows some women's problems, which may actually be social, economic, ethical, or legal, to be misidentified or erroneously regarded as psychiatric disturbances. Such a definition means that there is no need for physician or patient to look at the social structure within which women live in order to locate causes or solutions.

The four issues identified initially are ones in which this process can be clearly illustrated.

### Overprescription of Drugs for Women

Women who exhibit signs of disturbance or distress are often treated with drugs to restore their functioning as wives or mothers, or help them compensate for their supposed painful deviance as single, divorced, separated, widowed, or elderly women. Doctors, whose training presents women in these ways (Howell 1974), are also bombarded by material from the pharmaceutical industry that promotes the universality of symptoms of emotional distress. This is illustrated by the advertising pages of journals where, for instance, a pretty, tear-streaked young woman is depicted as needing an antidepressant for her "copelessness," and "N" is pictured as the answer for an astounding variety of symptoms in women of varying ages. As Muller (1974) has stressed, the doctor's use of drugs may appear practical, problem oriented, and compassionate. Those who actually benefit may be the pharmaceutical industry and society in general, rather than the woman herself.

### The Woman as an Alcoholic

The "disease concept" of alcoholism became a major focus about twenty years ago (Hershon 1974). Before 1920 drinking tended to be viewed as a moral problem. During the twenties, as Allen (1971) has documented, the church and other reform groups engaged in an internal controversy about moral versus social explanations for behavior. It is beyond the scope of this paper to discuss whether alcoholism is a moral, social, or medical problem, or a complex and multidimensional issue. The "disease concept," however, has allowed the emergence of various medical and psychiatric theories that hold the alcoholic, or his physiology, responsible for the problem and help to obscure the fact that another network of pressures are designed to promote drinking as a way to gain popularity, get ahead, and be desirable, sophisticated, and attractive (Whitehead and Ferrence 1976). While alcoholism rates rise yearly, and related health care costs are soaring, industry and government benefit from flourishing liquor sales that are aided by increasingly sophisticated marketing techniques.

## *Unidimensional Approaches to Family Violence*

Family violence is an area in which psychiatric theories are often misapplied to problems that have social, legal, economic, or ethical roots. Although child abuse has been prevalent for centuries (DeMause 1975), it did not come into the province of medicine, and was rarely recognized by doctors, until the 1960s (Kempe et al. 1962). The discovery of this new syndrome was accompanied by theories about the diseases of the parents' psyches that would allow them to perpetrate such horrific acts. A review of psychodynamic theories of child abuse yields an abundance of speculations (Bell 1973; Ounsted, Oppenheimer, and Lindsay 1974; Steele and Pollock 1968); in one instance based on a series of two cases (Smoller and Lewis 1977), Gelles (1973) has decried the narrowness and inconsistency of the psychopathological model, while Gil (1977) lays bare the social policies that sustain different levels of rights for children from different social and economic backgrounds. Newberger and Hyde (1975) have pointed out that implicit concepts of parental fault underlie both narrow and broad definitions of child abuse, and that medical and legal practices have often held the parents responsible, regardless of all the pressures in their lives. At a recent symposium on Violence in the Family, Newberger and Bourne (1977) contended that "legalization" and "medicalization" allows child abuse to be viewed as a sickness, an individual problem that is managed by doctors and lawyers and their respective institutions. Looking at class differences, they stress that the poor are more likely to be perceived as abusive. In this regard Kempe (1973) suggests that it is only the poor who are expected to be perfect mothers twenty-four hours a day, seven days a week, all year long.

It seems likely that theories about wife abuse, more recently recognized as a prevalent practice, may follow a similar process of evolution, initially being missed, minimized, or denied and later coming to be defined as a medical or psychiatric problem. Munson and Hilberman (1977), in a study of 120 women referred to them for psychiatric assessment by the medical staff of a rural health clinic, found that wife battering was missed in 56 out of 60 women who were abused. These women had been seen frequently by physicians for problems ranging from somatic complaints to suicidal behavior. Most had been treated with psychoactive drugs. Even when the battering is overt and recognized, women get little support for leaving their violent husbands if this is the only recourse. Mental health and social services offer therapy or marital counseling and usually view preservation of the marriage as their goal (Martin 1976). Still-prevalent beliefs that women are innately masochistic (Bonaparte 1965; Deutsch 1945; Robinson 1959) facilitate the common assumption that the wife is responsible for her own abuse and that she needs therapy. These beliefs hide enormous pressures from social structures, the institution of marriage, and women's economic dependency that may make leaving the marriage an impossibility.

Psychiatric theories that hold the child or mother responsible for incest may allow fathers to avoid responsibility and serve to cloud issues in this multidimensional problem. Freud's theory of infantile sexuality led to the assumption that incestuous feelings arose within the child and influenced adults (Rosenfeld 1977). Children have been described as active participants—precocious and charming (Abraham 1942; Bender and Blau 1937), or aggressive and seductive (Revitch and Weiss 1962). Incest may be attributed to the child's deprivation by an unloving mother (Rosenfeld et al. 1977), to the mother's unconscious desire to put a daughter in a maternal role (Kaufman, Peck, and Taguiri 1954), or to her conscious or unconscious collusion with the father (Brant and Tisza 1977). While we are trying to prevent or treat incest, other elements in society are cashing in on incest and the sexual exploitation of children. A *Penthouse* article (Nobile 1977), describing recent books, films, and TV shows with an incest theme, comments: "Just as we seem to be 'running low on marketable taboos, the unspeakable predictably popped up." Child pornography is a growing industry.

## The Scapegoating of Mothers

During this century women's reproductive processes, from menstruation through menopause, have become the province of medicine (Corea 1977). While the "medicalization" of childbirth has been thoroughly criticized (Arms 1975; Newton and Newton 1972), the medicalization of motherhood has received little attention. During this century, psychiatric theories stemming from Freud's work have made mothers responsible for the psychological health of their offspring. "Maternal deprivation" is felt to cause a wide range of conditions, including delinquency, mental retardation, dwarfism, depression, and affectionless psychopathy (Ainsworth 1962; Bowlby 1951). Spitz (1965) views the early mother-child relationship as a closed dyad, and his influential book, *The First Year of Life*, contains only one paragraph about fathers! Norms have been developed for "natural motherliness" (Deutsch 1945; Erikson 1968) and for a mother's role in the family. Traditional families with dominant fathers and subservient mothers are felt to be optimal and most likely to produce mentally healthy children (Ackerman 1958; Westley and Epstein 1969). The latest addition to the "scapegoating literature" assumes that the "liberated mother" has castrated her family (Voth 1977). This attack can be seen as the exact opposite of Wylie's (1942) campaign of three decades ago, when American "moms," nonworking wives and mothers, were accused of ruining their menfolk. This concept of "momism" was echoed by Erikson (1962).

## The Psychiatrist

Within this structure the psychiatrist operates according to his or her own personality, training, and experience. Delineating patterns of selection, Light (1975) notes that medical schools indirectly give preference to characteristics that are associated with a strong premedical record. These include intellectual narrowness, intense compulsiveness, and, at times, difficulties in relating to other people. He describes the highly technical training of medical students and their inability to integrate psyche and soma, and goes on to conclude: "By insisting on a medical degree, psychiatry finds itself in the awkward position of letting another profession select its pool of candidates on different, if not counterproductive, grounds." Howell (1974) has highlighted the process by which medical schools teach demeaning and derogatory attitudes to women, both as patients and students. Physicians are taught that women's illnesses are not worth understanding, are unimportant, and are of emotional origin. The woman patient is objectified and fun is made of her. Howell goes on to ascribe these attitudes to assumptions about women that are part of the fabric of our society.

Thus the neophyte psychiatrist may bring with him or her a rigid and inflexible personality structure, in addition to sets of beliefs about the medical model, the scientific validity of medicine, and women patients. Offer and Sabshin (1975) emphasize that psychiatric training produces a "trained incapacity." Because he or she is trained to recognize abnormal behavior, the psychiatrist has problems with recognizing, let alone conceptualizing, normal behavior. These authors comment further that the majority of theories of normality have been derived from studies of clinical populations or of white, middle-class males. Definitions of normality for women are closely linked with stereotypes that are derived from archetypal ideas.

Understanding of archetypes is crucial to the task of beginning to unravel knowledge and ideology when we examine psychiatric theories about women. The myths, legends and folk tales, and the philosophic and theological literature that are part of our cultural heritage abound with images of women as they have been seen through the ages (Hays 1964; Lederer 1968). In our male-dominated culture they amount to men's perceptions of women. Recurrent themes can be loosely grouped into two categories. The evil woman or temptress has two sides: One is strong, powerful, and destructive; the other is weak, untrustworthy, and unreliable. Similarly the good woman has two sides. She is seen as earth mother, civilizer, symbol of moral inspiration, the "power behind the throne." Her fragile side consists of innocence, chastity, and a need for protection. Ambivalence toward women is illustrated by opposing themes—strength-weakness and good-evil. Sometimes these qualities are seen in a single figure, such as the Hindu goddess Kali, who represents both life and death, fertility and destruction. The Virgin Mary combines the ideals of motherhood and sexual purity.

From the archetypes we can derive a summary of common qualities that are attributed to, or required of, women. The bad woman is, or should be, licentious, unfaithful, immodest, stinking, diseased, barren or fecund, shrewish, greedy, exploitive, manipulative, vain, self-centered, cold, destructive, murderous, untrustworthy, seductive, gossiping, irrational, emotional, weak-willed. The good woman is, or should be, obedient, submissive, pleasing, gentle, chaste, pure, clean, nurturant, diligent, hardworking, selfless, self-effacing, self-sacrificing, altruistic, enduring, serene, intuitive, tender, feeling, delicate, fertile (if married, and preferably with sons).

Modern-day feminine stereotypes are derived from this list, with a weeding out of the more overwhelming elements. Medical and psychiatric understanding of women is colored by, or even based on, these stereotypes. The menopausal woman, no longer fertile, is assigned some of the "bad" characteristics and depicted as diseased, shrewish, irrational, emotional, weak-willed. She is usually given tranquilizers for her depression or estrogens to restore her lost youth rather than helped to reorder priorities in her life, which has previously been defined as sex object and childbearer (Corea 1977). Physicians' attitudes to women with venereal disease often contain the assumption that women are licentious, disease distributors, and a source of embarrassment as they have fallen from grace and failed to be chaste, pure, and clean. Historically, medical treatment of venereal disease has been aimed at men, while ignoring the fact that it is harder to detect and has more disastrous effects in women (Corea 1977).

Broverman's work (1970) indicates that therapists' attitudes embrace these stereotypical views of women as contained within psychiatric theory. In this study clinicians held that healthy mature women differed from healthy mature men (and healthy mature adults) by being more submissive, less independent, less adventurous, more easily influenced, less aggressive, less competitive, more excitable in minor crises, more easily hurt, more emotional, more conceited about their appearance, less objective, and less interested in mathematics and science. Rather than attempting to tease out archetypes and stereotypes in psychiatric theory as a whole, we will return to the more concrete examples provided by the four issues raised initially.

Drug advertisements are aimed at bad-woman characteristics, with the goal of returning her to good-woman status. Women are depicted as irrational, emotional, weak-willed, self-centered, unable to fulfill their duties as wife or mother, and shrewish. Seidenberg (1974) has emphasized that drug companies realize that they can sell their products most effectively by presenting physicians with a derogatory and demeaning image of women who are portrayed as bad tempered, nagging, vain and selfish, and "irrationally" unhappy with their role in life.

Both societal and medical attitudes to the alcoholic woman appear to contain the moral stance that a drunken woman is disgusting. Lindbeck (1972) notes that alcoholism in women "while it is labelled an illness, is treated as a disgrace." Feminist critiques of treatment centers stress the double censure of the female alcoholic patient (Frazer 1973). It seems likely that good-woman images underlie the conviction that "ladies" do not get drunk and the typical denial or minimization of the emergence of a drinking problem, in which a woman, her relatives, and doctors all collude. If she is kept on a pedestal no one needs to look at what is happening in her life. When alcoholism can be concealed no longer, attitudes switch suddenly and she is viewed with disgust and disdain. There is a fascinating contrast between attitudes to spouses of alcoholic men and women, in which archetypes clearly play a part. Psychiatric theories about male alcoholics have often appeared to contain the popular assumption "she drove him to drink" (Baker 1941; Boggs 1944; Futterman 1953), and Beckman (1976) feels that many clinicians continue to espouse this view. On the other hand, the spouse of the alcoholic woman is likely to be treated with sympathy (Lindbeck 1972).

Descriptions of the child-abusing mother reflect bad-women characteristics. She is described as immature, impulsive, and depressed (Bennie and Sclare 1969), pervasively angry (Kempe et al. 1962), dependent, egocentric, narcissistic, demanding, and insecure (Zalba 1971). Treatment often centers around restoring or unleashing her nurturant capabilities (Kempe and Helfer 1972); that is, turning her into a good woman.

Attitudes toward the abused wife tie in with long-held opinions about beating one's wife (Davis 1971): "A woman, a dog, and a walnut tree, the more they're beaten, the better they be." Both good-woman and bad-woman traits appear in theories. The contention that an abused woman is masochistic (Shore et al. 1971), thus bringing the abuse on herself, appears to be buttressed by perceptions of women as self-sacrificing, enduring, choosing martyrdom. On the other hand, she may be depicted as angry, provocative (Whitehurst 1975), and emasculating (Lederer 1968) or rejecting of her husband's need for nurturing (Schultz 1960).

Bad-woman characteristics appear in theories about incest. The little girl is portrayed as seductive and aggressive (Revitch and Weiss 1962), manipulative (Abraham 1942; Bender and Blau 1937), lying (Goodwin and Sahd, 1977; MacDonald 1971). The mother is depicted as sick (Lustig, Dresser, and Spellman 1966), childish (Kaufman, Peck, and Taguiri 1954), self-centered and cold (Rosenfeld et al. 1977), failing to protect the child (Brand and Tisza 1977), and sexually frigid (Weiner 1963). An archetypal prototype of incest is illustrated by the Biblical story of Lot. His wife, who had become a pillar of salt, was unavailable, and his daughters got him drunk and seduced him.

The most blatant examples of bad-woman archetypes are seen in theories about the schizophrenogenic mother who is set forth as domineering, nagging, and hostile (Arieti 1955), ill (Bateson et al. 1956), destructive, and engulfing (Wolman 1972). Similarly, mothers of autistic children are described as self-centered and cold (Despert 1951; Kanner 1943), annihilating (Bettelheim 1967), and totally uncaring (Mahler 1952).

Mothers are expected to have good-woman characteristics: submissive (Westley and Epstein 1969), pleasing, nurturant (Bowlby 1951), hardworking, selfless, self-sacrificing (Deutsch 1945), intuitive (Erikson 1968). Any deviation from this bodes ill for their children, and perhaps for society as a whole. Rheingold (1964) contends that a good life and a stable world can only be attained if women accept their reproductive functions, avoid contamination by feminist doctrines, and become fulfilled and altruistic mothers. Furthermore, he claims (1967) "the syndrome of decay, the evil tendency in man is basically rooted in the mother-child relationship."

Brownmiller's (1976) account of the imaginative profile of the Boston strangler, constructed by a Medical-Psychiatric Committee, shows without doubt the influence of archetypes. The committee, noting that one of the victims was a seventy-five-year-old woman, postulated that the killer was a conservative, tidy, orderly fellow, who was quite likely to be middle aged, impotent, and homosexual. They felt that, consumed by hatred for his overwhelming, seductive, punitive, sweet, orderly, neat, and compulsive mother, the strangler was driven to mutilate and murder old women in a manner that revealed both love and hate. When caught, the strangler "single-handedly smashed every cherished psychiatric concept of a sex murderer. . . . He proved to be genuinely attached to his mother, who was still alive, and not particularly sweet, neat or overwhelming."

## Women

Almost all women believe in the archetypes and stereotypes that represent how they can be good women. So deep is women's socialization that even the committed feminist is subject to doubts and indecision about possible deviance. A woman's socialization is reinforced on a day-to-day basis by the way people relate to her, as detailed by Jan Morris in *Conundrum* (1974). She found that people and social structures treated her in a totally different way after her change-of-sex operation. Smith (1975) points out that women are trained to invalidate their own experiences, understanding, and feelings and to look to men to tell them how to view themselves. Ideas, concepts, images, and vocabularies available to women to think about their experiences have been formulated from the male viewpoint by universities, professions, industries, and other organizations. These are reinforced by images of women in the media: women's magazines, women's novels, women as depicted in advertisements, in children's stories, movies, as well as in the social sciences. How, she goes on to ask, can women understand their situation? Psychiatric ideologies, she emphasizes, teach women to see their resentment and despair about their place in the social structure as an individual problem, an emotional disorder.

These perceptions gain support from the findings of a Vancouver study (Boulter and Campbell 1977) that questioned groups of women about their understanding of the uses of minor tranquilizers. They appeared to mirror the opinion of the clinicians in the Broverman study (1970). Women felt that tranquilizers were sometimes needed to help them cope. Coping, for them, meant the management of their role as housewife and mother. One woman felt that her doctor transmitted the expectation "that all I was expected to do was get on with being who I was, which was a woman with two children and a husband." Some women felt that a general practitioner does not have the time, understanding, or experience to talk about their problems, and talked knowledgeably about other professional helpers that they could turn to. They perceived a hierarchy of people with the psychiatrist at the top as someone who was most able to give the best help or work with the most acute problems. It appeared clear that when a crisis occurred in a woman's life, she readily construed it as something for which she personally needed professional help in order to cope, to maintain her functioning. In retrospect, reflecting upon the situation, a few women expressed doubts about the sick role that they had accepted and wondered about other options. One woman said, "I feel that, essentially, when a doctor prescribes a pill for me, it's to put him out of my misery." Another commented that a prescription for baby-sitters would have been much more useful than a prescription for diazepam.

Looked at in a historical perspective, there have been massive changes in women's role and status in the family over the last 200 years. Women used to have an enormously important and valued role in creating and maintaining the family and the home. Gardening, baking, preserving, making clothes, mending, caring for children, often under the most arduous conditions, their input was an immediate, vital, and necessary service (Corrective Collective 1974). In this century, no longer intimately connected with family subsistence, made less challenging by the advent of prepared foods, ready-to-wear clothes, and technology, women's work in the home has become trivialized (Smith 1973) and taken less and less seriously. Galbraith (1973) says that the rise of industrialism led to the need for a class of cryptoservants to maintain the households of men, who were then seen as the family breadwinners. He emphasizes that the concept of "convenient social virtue" is important in inducing people to do unpleasant tasks, and that its ultimate success has been in converting women to menial personal service.

Looked at in this way, one can begin to see the masses of contradictions that a woman attempts to deal with in her life. She apologizes for being "just a homemaker," while feeling desperately and frantically overwhelmed by the care of several preschool children. She boosts her husband's self-esteem, nurturing him and preparing him for another day at work, while dimly aware, perhaps, of her own resentment and lack of stimulation and recognition. She attempts, particularly when all the children are in school, to fill her days with ceramics, weaving, and pottery and justify her existence by being a "good little shopper" and preparer of gourmet meals. She may press her husband and children to achieve, thus vicariously gaining something that she has given up herself.

While many women manage to live with these contradictions and develop compromises and compensations, many others become aware of increasing dissatisfaction and unhappiness. Because of the way life is constructed for them, they look for the cause in themselves. In the words of one patient who eventually entered a treatment center because of alcoholism and addiction to tranquilizers, "I had everything I wanted. A beautiful house, three nice children, a successful husband, club memberships, three holidays a year. Yet I became more and more unhappy. I felt, my family felt, and my husband felt that there must be something wrong with me."

## Implications for Therapy

We have delineated three interacting sets of factors: the medical and mental health systems and the process of medicalization; the psychiatrist, his or her training, attitude, and theoretical background; and the woman patient and her socialization. As a result of these factors, any woman referred to a psychiatrist is likely to fall within a diagnostic category and be viewed as a psychiatric patient. A psychiatric model may be used to treat women who need other resources such as job counseling, legal aid, and women's self-help groups (Stephenson 1973). Women's problems may be seen as individual and intrapsychic without awareness of the massive societal obstacles that women face.

Lack of awareness of these social structures causes problems, for instance those between spouses, to escalate into a vicious, bitter interpersonal battle with neither recognizing the part played by socialization and social pressures. The woman may feel oppressed, put upon, unsatisfied, emotionally drained, inadequate, yet still responsible for satisfying all the needs of her husband and family. Her husband cannot understand her feeling of oppression. It is likely that he feels tied down himself by his family's dependency, tired and overwhelmed himself by the pressures and expectations of the male role.

A therapist who acknowledges historical perspectives, understands social structures, is aware of archetypes and stereotypes, and understands how theories and concepts are constructed and used can appreciate how women have been forced into a secondhand understanding of the world. There is a disjunction between women's actual experience and how they are told to interpret it. As concepts like femininity and women's second-class status in the world have a very long history of being perceived as the natural order of things (Mell 1970), grasping and holding onto alternative ways of analyzing situations presents a repeated challenge. The realization that "feminine" characteristics can, in fact, be seen as those of any oppressed group of people (Miller 1976) tends to be astounding to the psychiatrist, when first encountered.

There is much to change! Realization of the need for a new medical model is appearing (Engel 1977), and the supposed scientific foundation of psychiatry has been greatly criticized (Halleck 1971; Torrey 1974). Psychiatrists are beginning to allude to sexism as a barrier to our understanding of the family (Rae-Grant 1977) and to acknowledge that "much patriarchal rhetoric has masqueraded as theory" (Adams 1977).

Hopefully, the inclusion of a chapter "Gender and Psychiatry" in the Residents Training Guide will catalyze teaching about these issues in training programs. Meanwhile both theoretical and practical alternatives are emerging that approach women's problems in ways that are more closely connected with women's life experiences. Feminist therapy is developing to such a degree that Seiden (1976) suggests it has some of the characteristics of a school of psychotherapy. She underscores the increased egalitarianism between patient and therapist, the main focus on environmental interpretations, the disregard for sex-role prescriptions, and the role modeling provided by a competent woman therapist as its principal features.

Alternatives to traditional psychotherapy are available in many urban centers. Wyckoff (1977) has provided a practical guide for women's self-help groups. She sees demystification as crucial to the growth process. Women in groups can come to realize that cultural values they had accepted unquestioningly, such as material success, full-time motherhood, and consumerism, are a major source of their tensions and dissatisfactions.

Rape Relief centers supply women with practical help, enabling them to get in touch with their anger and avoid chronic and disabling shame and embarrassment, and advising them on possible legal action and its implications. Transition houses for battered women, modeled on Pizzey's (1974) original center in Chiswick, England, function as shelters for battered women and their children and have served to alert the community to the enormity of this problem.

A range of other resources, where available, provide support that reduces the isolation of women in nuclear families. These include day care, family centers, women's resource centers, job counseling, assertiveness training, and legal clinics. Some communities have a range of vocational, educational, and volunteer possibilities that can provide a starting point for a woman who wants to make changes in her life. It is vital that these services be encouraged and recognized as viable sources of help for women who have hitherto all too often been seen as needing psychiatric treatment.

## Conclusion

In this paper we have attempted to highlight the interacting factors that affect the psychiatrist–woman patient relationship. Additionally, it is contended, they may exert a powerful pressure and must be understood in order to avoid negative implications. There are many implications for change in both theory and practice.

## Summary

This paper contends that the psychiatrist–woman patient relationship is affected by a number of powerful, yet often subtle, pressures. There are three major interacting sets of factors: the medical and mental health systems and the process of medicalization of life that has taken place over the last century; the psychiatrist, his or her training, attitude, and theoretical background; and the woman patient, her socialization and view of the world, which is based on perspectives formulated from a male viewpoint. As a result of these factors, any woman referred to a psychiatrist is likely to be given a psychiatric diagnosis, her problems viewed as individual and intrapsychic, the societal obstacles she faces ignored or minimized, and treatment probably geared to helping her adapt to traditional expectations.

The implications for therapy are discussed, with emphasis on the need to appreciate how women have been forced into a secondhand understanding of the world. Alternatives to traditional psychotherapy are discussed briefly, stressing the need for recognition and use of these resources.

REFERENCES

Abraham, K. 1942. The experiencing of sexual traumas as a form of sexual activity. In *Selected papers on psychoanalysis,* ed. K. Abraham, pp. 47–63. London: Hogarth Press.
Ackerman, N. W. 1958. *The psychodynamics of family life.* New York: Basic Books.
Adams, P. 1977. Fatherlessness: Policy suggestions. Paper presented at the North American Seminar on The Impact of Change on Mental Health and Child and Family Development, Val David, Quebec, 7 June 1977.

Ainsworth, M. D. 1962. The effects of maternal deprivation: A review of findings and controversy in the context of research strategy. In *Deprivation of maternal care: A reassessment of its effects.* Geneva: World Health Organization.

Allen, R. 1971. *The social passion: Religion and reform in Canada 1914-1918.* Toronto: University of Toronto Press.

Arieti, S. 1955. *Interpretation of schizophrenia.* New York: Brunner/Mazel.

Arms, S. 1975. *The immaculate deception: A new look at women and childbirth in America.* Boston: Houghton Mifflin.

Baker, H. M. 1941. Observations on prisoners. *Journal of Criminal Psychopathology* 2:367-375.

Bateson, G., et al. 1956. Toward a theory of schizophrenia. *Behavioral Sciences* 1:251-264.

Beckman, L. J. 1976. Alcoholism problems in women: An overview. In *Alcoholism problems in women and children,* ed. M. Greenblatt and M. A. Schuckit. New York: Grune & Stratton.

Bell, G. 1973. Parents who abuse their children. *Canadian Psychiatric Association Journal* 18:223-228.

Bender, L., and Blau, A. 1937. The reaction of children to sexual relations with adults. *American Journal of Orthopsychiatry* 7:500-518.

Bennie, E., and Sclare, A. 1969. The battered child syndrome. *American Journal of Psychiatry* 125:975-979.

Bettelheim, B. 1967. *Infantile autism and the birth of the self.* New York: Free Press.

Boggs, M. H. 1944. The role of social work in the treatment of inebriates. *Quarterly Journal of Studies on Alcohol* 4:557-567.

Bonaparte, M. 1965. *Female sexuality.* New York: Gore Press.

Boulter, A., and Campbell, M. 1977. An ethnography of minor tranquilizer use in selected women's groups in Vancouver. Report prepared for the *Non-Medical Use of Drugs Directorate,* 1 September 1977.

Bowlby, J. 1951. *Maternal care and mental health.* Geneva: World Health Organization.

Brant, R. S. T., and Tisza, V. G. 1977. The sexually misused child. *American Journal of Orthopsychiatry* 47:80-90.

Broverman, K., et al. 1970. Sex-role stereotypes and clinical judgments of mental health. *Journal of Consulting and Clinical Psychology* 34:1-7. [Reprinted herein chapter 7.]

Brownmiller, S. 1976. *Against our will: Men, women and rape.* New York: Bantam Books.

Chesler, P. 1972. *Women and madness.* Garden City, N.Y.: Doubleday.

Chess, S. 1964. Editorial: Mal de mere. *American Journal of Orthopsychiatry* 34:613-614.

Committee Concerned with Women's Health Issues in Etobicoke, Ontario. The use of prescription medicine by women 18 years and over in Etobicoke. Study in progress.

Cooperman, E. M. 1977. Editorial: Antibiotics: No panacea. *Canadian Medical Association Journal* 116:229-230.

Cooperstock, R. 1976. Psychotropic drug use among women. *Canadian Medical Association Journal* 115:760-763.

Corea, G. 1977. *The hidden malpractice: How American medicine treats women as patients and professionals.* New York: Morrow.

Corrective Collective. 1974. *Never done: Three centuries of women's work in Canada.* Toronto: Canadian Women's Educational Press.

DeMause, L. 1975. *The history of childhood.* New York: Harper Torchbooks, Harper & Row.

Despert, J. L. 1951. Some considerations relating to the genesis of autistic behavior in children. *American Journal of Orthopsychiatry* 21:335-350.

Deutsch, H. 1945. *The psychology of women: A psychoanalytic interpretation.* New York: Grune & Stratton.

Engel, G. L. 1977. The need for a new medical model: A challenge for biomedicine. *Science* 196:129-136.

Erikson, E. H. 1962. *Childhood and society.* New York: Norton.

————. 1968. *Identity, youth and crisis.* New York: Norton.

Frazer, J. 1973. The female alcoholic. *Addictions* 20:64-80.

Futterman, S. 1953. Personality trends in wives of alcoholics. *Journal of Psychiatric Social Work* 23:37-41.

Galbraith, J. K. 1973. *Economics and the public purpose.* Boston: Houghton Mifflin.

Gelles, R. J. 1973. Child abuse as psychopathology: A sociological critique and reformulation. *American Journal of Orthopsychiatry* 43:611–621.

Gil, D. G. 1977. Child abuse: Levels of manifestation, causal dimensions and primary prevention. *Victimology* 2:186–194.

Goodwin, J., and Sahd, D. 1977. Incest hoax: False accusations and false denials. Paper presented at the American Psychiatric Association annual meeting. Toronto, 4 May 1977.

Greer, G. 1970. *The female eunuch.* London: MacGibbon & Kee.

Guse, L., Morier, G., and Ludwig, J. 1976. *Winnipeg survey of prescription (mood-altering) use among women.* Technical report, NMUDD, Manitoba Alcoholism Foundation, October 1976.

Halleck S. L. 1971. *The politics of therapy.* New York: Science House.

Hays, H. R. 1964. *The dangerous sex: The myth of feminine evil.* New York: Putnam.

Hershon, H. 1974. Alcoholism and the concept of disease. *British Journal of Addiction* 69:123–131.

Howell, M. C. 1974. What medical schools teach about women. *New England Journal of Medicine* 291:304–307.

Illich, I. 1975. *Medical nemesis: The expropriation of health.* Toronto: McClelland & Stewart.

Jan, J. E., Freeman, R. D., and Scott, E. P. 1977. *Visual impairment of children and adolescents.* New York: Grune & Stratton.

Kanner, L. 1943. Autistic disturbances of affective contact. *Nervous Disorders of the Child* 2:217–250.

Kaufman, I., Peck, A. L., and Taguiri, C. K. 1954. The family constellation and overt incestuous relationships between father and daughter. *American Journal of Orthopsychiatry* 24:266–279.

Kempe, C. H. 1973. A practical approach to the protection of the abused child and rehabilitation of the abusing parent. *Pediatrics* 51:804–809.

————, and Helfer, R. E. 1972. *Helping the battered child and his family.* Philadelphia: Lippincott.

Kempe, C. H., et al. 1962. The battered child syndrome. *Journal of the American Medical Association* 181:17–24.

Kerr, B. 1974. *Strong at broken places: Women who have survived drugs.* Chicago: Follett.

Lederer, W. 1968. *The fear of women.* New York: Harcourt.

Levine, S. V., Kamin, L. E., and Levine, E. L. 1974. Sexism and psychiatry. *American Journal of Orthopsychiatry* 44:327–336.

Light, D. 1975. The impact of medical school on future psychiatrists. *American Journal of Psychiatry* 132: 607–610.

Lindbeck, V. L. 1972. The woman alcoholic: A review of the literature. *International Journal of Addiction* 7:567–580.

Lustig, N., Dresser, J. W., and Spellman, S. W. 1966. Incest: A family group survival pattern. *Archives of General Psychiatry* 14:31–40.

MacDonald, J. M. 1971. *Rape: Offenders and their victims.* Springfield, Ill.: Charles C. Thomas.

Mahler, M. S. 1952. *On child psychosis and schizophrenia: Autistic and symbolic infantile psychoses in the psychoanalytic study of the child,* vol. 7. New York: International Universities Press.

Martin, D. 1976. *Battered wives.* San Francisco: Glide Publications.

Mill, J. S. 1970. *The subjection of women.* Cambridge, Mass.: M.I.T. Press. [Originally published 1869.]

Miller, J. B. 1976. *Towards a new psychology of women.* Boston: Beacon Press.

Morris, J. 1974. *Conundrum.* New York: Harcourt.

Muller, C. 1974. Economic aspects of the medical use of psychotropic drugs. In *Social aspects of the medical use of psychotropic drugs,* ed. R. Cooperstock. Toronto: Addiction Research Foundation of Ontario.

Munson, K., and Hilberman, E. 1977. Sixty battered women: A preliminary survey. Paper presented at the American Psychiatric Association annual meeting. Toronto, 5 May 1977.

Newberger, E. H., and Bourne, R. 1977. The medicalization and legalization of child abuse. Paper presented at Symposium on Violence in the Family. Second World Conference of the International Society on Family Law. Montreal, 13 June 1977.

Newberger, E. H., and Hyde, J. N. 1975. Child abuse: Principles and implications of current pediatric practice. *Pediatric Clinics of North America* 22:695-715.

Newton, N., and Newton, M. 1972. Childbirth in crosscultural perspective. In *Modern perspectives in psycho-obstetrics,* ed. J. G. Howells. New York: Brunner/Mazel.

Nobile, P. 1977. The last taboo. *Penthouse,* December 1977.

Offer, D., and Sabshin, M. 1975. Normality. In *Comprehensive textbook of psychiatry II,* ed A. M. Freedman, H. I. Kaplan, and B. J. Sadock, pp. 459-464. Baltimore: Williams & Wilkins.

Ounsted, C., Oppenheimer, R., and Lindsay, J. 1974. Aspects of bonding failure: Psychopathology and psychotherapeutic treatment of families of battered children. *Developmental Medicine and Child Neurology* 16:447-456.

Pizzey, E. 1974. *Scream quietly or the neighbors will hear.* Middlesex, England: Penguin.

Rae-Grant, Q. 1977. Influence of individual, social and cultural differences on child development. Paper presented at the North American seminar on The Impact of Change on Mental Health and Child and Family Development. Val David, Quebec, 6 June 1977.

Revitch, R., and Weiss, R. 1962. The pedophiliac offender. *Diseases of the Nervous System* 23:73-78.

Rheingold, J. C. 1964. *The fear of being a woman.* New York: Grune & Stratton.

————. 1967. *The mother, anxiety, death and the catastrophic death complex.* London: J. & A. Churchill.

Robinson, M. N. 1959. *The power of sexual surrender.* Garden City, N.Y.: Doubleday.

Rosenfeld, A. A. 1977. Sexual misuse and the family. *Victimology* 2:226-235.

————, et al. 1977. Incest and sexual abuse of children. *Journal of the American Academy of Child Psychiatry* 16 (2) :327-339.

Schultz, L. G. 1960. The wife assaulter. *Journal of Social Therapy* 6:103-112.

Seiden, A. M. 1976. Overview: Research on the psychology of women. II. Women in families, work, and psychotherapy. *American Journal of Psychiatry* 133:1111-1123.

Seidenberg, R. 1974. Images of health, illness and women in drug advertising. *Journal of Drug Issues* 4:264-267.

Shore, M. F., et al. 1971. Patterns of masochism: An empirical study. *British Journal of Medical Psychology* 44:59-65.

Smith, D. E. 1975. Women and psychiatry. In *Women look at psychiatry,* ed. D. E. Smith, and S. J. David. Vancouver: Press Gang Publishers.

————. 1973. Women, the family and corporate capitalism. In *Women in Canada,* ed. M. Stephenson. Toronto: New Press.

————, and David, S. J., eds. 1975. *Women look at psychiatry.* Vancouver: Press Gang Publishers.

Smoller, B., and Lewis, A. B. 1977. A psychological theory of child abuse. *Psychiatric Quarterly* 49:38-44.

Spitz, R. A. 1965. *The first year of life: A psychoanalytic study of normal and deviant development.* New York: International Universities Press.

Steele, B. F., and Pollock, C. B. 1968. Psychiatric study of parents who abuse infants and small children. In *The battered child,* ed. R. E. Helfer, and C. M. Kempe, pp. 89-133. Chicago: University of Chicago Press.

Stephenson, P. S. 1973. Modern woman: Implications for psychotherapy. *Canadian Psychiatric Association Journal* 18:79-82.

Szasz, T. S. 1970, *The manufacture of madness.* New York: Harper & Row.

Thomas, A., and Chess, S. 1977. *Temperament and development.* New York: Brunner/Mazel.

Torrey, E. F. 1974. *The death of psychiatry.* Radnor, Pa.: Chilton Book Co.

Voth, H. 1977. *The castrated family.* Kansas City: Universal Press.

Weiner, I. B. 1962. Father-daughter incest: A clinical report. *Psychiatric Quarterly* 36:605-632.

Westley, W. A., and Epstein, N. B. 1969. *The silent majority.* New York: Jossey-Bass.

Whitehead, P. C., and Ferrence, R. G. 1976. Women and children last: Implications of trends in consumption for women and young people. In *Alcoholism problems in women and children,* ed. M. Greenblatt and M. A. Shuckit. New York: Grune & Stratton.

Whitehurst, R. N. 1975. Violence in husband-wife interaction. In *Violence in the family,* ed. S. K. Steinmetz and M. K. Strauss, pp. 75–82. New York: Dodd, Mead.

Wolman, B. B. 1972. Schizophrenia in childhood. In *Manual of child psychopathology,* ed. B. B. Wolman. New York: McGraw-Hill.

Wyckoff, H. 1977. *Solving women's problems: Through awareness, action and contact.* New York: Grove Press.

Wylie, P. 1942. *Generation of vipers.* New York: Rinehart.

Zalba, S. 1971. Battered children. *Transaction* 8:68–71.

Zola, K. 1972. Medicine as an institution of social control. *Social Review* 20:487–504.

# 10

# A Review of Women's Psychotropic Drug Use

## RUTH COOPERSTOCK

Some of the factors readily identified by epidemiologists and medical sociologists as contributing to the higher consumption of psychotropic drugs by women is that women frequently define their symptoms poorly, and the physicians' frustrated responses to these vague symptoms cause them to view these symptoms as "trivia" (Mechanic 1970). Additionally, the number of prescriptions per physician visit has been increasing, so that currently one prescription is written per physician visit (Coleman and Patrick 1970). Also, the vague, poorly defined complaint makes it likely that the prescribed medication will be equally nonspecific—that is, a tranquilizer.

This paper reviews the state of our knowledge regarding the consumption of psychotropic drugs by women, the characteristics of high-use groups within this population, and attempts to understand differences between the sexes in help-seeking behavior and pathways to the health care system that can explain these data.

## Consumption Patterns in Canada

It has been consistently demonstrated (Chaiton et al. 1976; Dunnell and Cartwright 1972; Guse, Morier, and Ludwig 1976; Skegg, Doll, and Perry 1977) that females receive more prescriptions for all drugs than males—the Department of Health (1975–1976), Saskatchewan, for example, reported 62.9 percent for females and 37.9 percent for males. The difference in the proportions of psychotropics dispensed is, in all studies examined (Balter, Levine, and Manheimer 1974; Cooperstock 1976; Cooperstock and Sims 1971; Parish 1971; Parry 1973), greater than that in all other drug classes, with between 67 and 72 percent of psychotropics going to women.

Table 10–1 presents data on consumption patterns in Canada from 1970 to 1978. The ratios of male-to-female use are more consistent between studies than the total quantities reported by either sex. Variations in the amounts reported may well be an artifact of the different methods employed, including prescription studies (Cooperstock 1976; Guse, Morier, and Ludwig 1976), mail questionnaires (Guse, Morier, and Ludwig 1976), personal interviews (Chaiton et al. 1976; Committee Concerned with Women's Health Issues, n.d.; Fejer and Smart 1973; Smart and Goodstadt 1976), and regional differences in consumption. The time period asked about also varied (it is generally agreed that inquiring about consumption over periods longer than two weeks leads to memory problems and hence to underreporting).

For tranquilizer drugs in particular there is a consistency in the findings. The Etobicoke Committee (n.d.) and Guse, Morier, and Ludwig (1976) asked the most detailed questions and reported the highest consumption. In Winnipeg, 20 percent of the women reported use in the previous two weeks, while in Etobicoke, 15 percent of a sample of adult women claimed they had used a tranquilizer in the previous two days.

The Gallup data (Provisional Results of Gallup Survey 1977), in which people were asked about their use over three time periods, illustrate the findings of other studies (Bass and Paul 1977; Dunnell and Cartwright 1972); that while more women reported use of these drugs in a one- or two-day period, the difference in consumption between men and women widens the longer the period studied. A study of a southern Ontario insurance plan (Cooperstock 1976) found that more females than males received multiple tranquilizer prescriptions during the year. More than twice the number of females as males received ten or more prescriptions, indicating steady use, while only slightly more females than males (6.3 percent versus 4.5 percent) received only one

## TABLE 10-1
### Canadian Data (1970–1978) on Sex Differences in Psychotropic Drug Use

| Place | Date | Time Frame | Sedatives Total | Sedatives M | Sedatives F | Tranquilizers Total | Tranquilizers M | Tranquilizers F | Sedatives and Tranquilizers | All Psych. Drugs |
|---|---|---|---|---|---|---|---|---|---|---|
| Chaiton et al. Small Ontario Community | 1971 | 0-2 days | | | | | | | Use 2.2 more frequent among F. than M. | |
| Etobicoke Comm. | | | | | | | | | | |
| Etobicoke, Ont. | 1977 | 0-2 days | | | | | | 15% | | |
| GALLUP NMUDD | | 0-2 days | 2.1% | 1.3% | 3.0% | 3.9% | 3.2% | 4.6% | | |
| | | 0-14 days | 2.9 | 1.7 | 4.2 | 5.7 | 4.7 | 7.2 | | |
| Nat. Sample | 1977 | 0-2 mons. | 3.5 | 1.9 | 5.2 | 7.2 | 5.2 | 9.2 | | |
| Guse et al. Winnipeg | 1976 | 0-14 days | | | | | | 20% | | |
| Fejer and Smart Metro. Toronto | 1972 | Past Year | | | | 12.7% | 7.2% | 16.3% | | |
| Smart and Goodstadt Ontario | 1976 | Past Year | 8.6% | 8.1% | 11.1% | 13.7% | 8.2% | 19.3% | | |
| Cooperstock Greenshield S.W. Ontario | 1973/4 | One Year | | 4.9% | 7.1% | | 9.0% | 15.3% | | |
| Guse et al. Winnipeg | 1975 | One Year | | 31% | 69% | | 28% | 72% | | Ratio of 2.32:1 |

prescription over the year studied. Skegg, Doll, and Perry (1977), in a similar study in the United Kingdom, reported the same phenomena.

## Characteristics of Consumers

Since a very small proportion of consumers of psychotropic drugs obtain them illegally, the most obvious characteristic of consumers of these drugs is that they consult physicians. This helps identify psychotropic drug users in a crude fashion, although the difference in physician visits between the sexes does not account for all of the excess in prescriptions to women (Cooperstock 1971).

A number of studies have examined the age at which men and women are prescribed psychotropics (Balter, Levine, and Manheimer 1974; Committee Concerned with Women's Health Issues, n.d.; Guse, Morier, and Ludwig 1976; Hemminki 1974; Bellinger, Balter, and Manheimer 1971; Parish 1971; Parry et al. 1973; Skegg, Doll, and Perry 1977; Westerholm 1976). Typically, male consumption rises steadily with increasing age, reaching its highest point in the middle years or in the oldest age group.

Although some surveys of psychotropic drug use found peak use of minor tranquilizers among young women in the United States (Bellinger, Balter, and Manheimer 1971), most studies have found peak use in the middle years (Committee Concerned with Women's Health Issues, n.d.; Guse, Morier, and Ludwig 1976; Hemminki 1974; Parish 1971; Parry et al. 1973; Westerholm 1976). When sedatives and hypnotics are combined with minor tranquilizers, the peak age tends to rise.

In one of the few recent large-scale studies of prescriptions that examined age and type of psychotropic drug (Skegg, Doll, and Perry 1977), the highest frequency of use of antidepressant medications among males was in those over 75 years of age (7.2 percent), while the peak age among females was 45 to 59 (11.2 percent).

Because of the limitations of the existing data base, especially because of differences in linking prescription data to other demographic information, there are no clear links between psychotropic drug use and marital status, economic status, or class.

One variable, that of work status (Pflanz, Basler, and Schwoon 1977), remains consistent in its relationship with psychotropic drug use among both sexes. Those who are retired, unemployed, or not in the labor force are the highest consumers of psychotropic drugs (Chambers, Inciardi, and Siegal 1974; Guse, Morier, and Ludwig 1976). These findings require careful examination since they could be largely due to age. Guse, Morier, and Ludwig (1976), however, found that at each age level women who worked outside their homes reported lower psychotropic drug use than those who did not. They also found a statistically significant correlation between the amount of time spent in working outside the home and drug use; 11 percent of those in full-time jobs, 19 percent of those with part-time jobs, and 25 percent of those at home full time reported use in the previous two weeks.

The same study inquired about social activities outside the home such as club participation, sports, and visits to friends. Relating this "activity level" to psychotropic drug use, it was found that as activity decreases psychotropic drug use increases.

A possible intervening variable between work status, activity level, and drug use is general health. Again holding age constant, Guse and associates found that use of psychotropics increased as the women's subjective health rating became more negative. The Etobicoke study (Committee Concerned with Women's Health Issues, n.d.) also found higher use among those reporting a poorer health rating.

These data do not distinguish between actual illness and perceptions of illness in relation to drug use. Two studies (Greenblatt, Shader, and Koch-Weser 1975; Pflanz, Basler, and Schwoon 1977) did examine drug use and diagnosed illness, but because their methods differed the evidence is inconclusive.

Twenty percent of patients entering medical and surgical wards in Boston hospitals reported use of a psychotropic drug in the previous three months, with differences between diagnostic groups. The highest frequency of use was among those with neurological disorders (25 percent). The male-female differences were still striking, with 25 percent of women and 15 percent of men reporting use (Greenblatt, Shader, and Koch-Weser 1975).

In a study of fifty-year-olds in Hanover, Germany, Pflanz and associates (1977) assessed the medical status of their sample and found no differences between users and nonusers of psychotropics in the prevalence of hypertension, rheumatic diseases, angina, dyspnea, and chronic bronchitis. Among males only there was a difference in the prevalence of peptic ulcer. There were, however, differences between users and nonusers in indices of health-related behavior. Users were significantly more likely to have visited a physician in the previous two months, to be concerned about their weight (males only), and to report their health as poor.

To summarize our findings to date:

1. Females receive more prescriptions than males in all classes of drugs, but the greatest difference is in psychotropics.

2. Females are more likely than males to be frequent and steady users of psychotropics.

3. Frequency of use increases with age in both sexes, although the peak use of minor tranquilizers for women is in the middle years.

4. Use is highly correlated with work status in both sexes.

5. Use is also highly correlated with use of physician services (though this factor alone cannot explain the excess of prescriptions to women).

6. Use is related to subjective ratings of poor health, but not necessarily to actual ill health.

## Help-Seeking Behavior

To date there is little conclusive evidence that any major biological differences between the sexes explains these findings. Thus we must postulate other explanations. One factor is the difference in reporting of symptoms by men and women. Women consistently report more distress, anxiety, and depression than men. Whether this greater awareness stems from role strains in contemporary society or from the greater cultural freedom of expression given to females, one must still ask about the translation of this greater awareness into help-seeking behavior. Our concern is primarily with the use of health services, but it is important to examine the whole range of help-seeking.

Horwitz (1977), in a recent study of psychiatric patients in a community mental health facility, tested two hypotheses: that women would be more likely than men to recognize the existence of their problems, and that before seeking psychiatric help, women would be more likely to look to members of their intimate networks. In this respect, 44 percent of men as opposed to 14 percent of women reported themselves friendless. Men discussed their problems with only 1 person outside their nuclear family, on the average, while women spoke to 4.5 such people. Men typically reported speaking to their spouse, while women spoke to husbands and other family members, friends, and workmates. While both sexes were equally likely to attend a physician for help, women consulted clergymen, marriage counselors, and other social agencies more than men, as has been shown elsewhere (Coates 1972). This study found that women accept the self-label of psychiatric illness; that having spoken to more intimates about their problem they enter treatment more willingly; and that they accept the role of patient more readily than men, who are more typically coerced into treatment.

## Paths to the Health Care System

Ideally, one should do a prospective study of the help-seeking behavior of a large population to examine the development of awareness of distress, the number and types of people approached for help, and how these are related to the use of physician services. As Horwitz's study has the limitation of using a population already in the health care system, the sexes are similar in their use of physician services.

Coleman and Patrick (1977) studied attendance at a prepaid primary care facility and found that patients with "chronic emotional problems" (85 percent of whom were said to be neurotic or suffering situational disorders) made over four times the number of visits during the year as did patients without emotional disorders. A group with nonchronic emotional problems made three times the number of visits as did those without emotional complaints. In both groups with emotional problems, the number of prescriptions corresponded with the number of visits.

Also relevant to help-seeking behavior and attendance at physicians' offices, and lending further support to the sociocultural explanation of excess female psychotropic use, is the finding that the more severe the symptoms or the more problems reported, the fewer sociocultural or sex differences appear, though they continue to exist (Pflanz, Basler, and Schwoon 1977; Scheff 1966). Again, analyses of sex differences in psychiatric diagnoses show gross sex differences in the least serious and most poorly defined diagnoses: neurosis and psychosomatic illness (Dohrenwend 1976).

At all ages, females attend physicians' offices more than males (Drury 1977; Wadsworth, Butterfield, and Blaney 1971). Increasing age, lack of employment outside the home, and the existence of chronic illness predispose to more frequent visits (Chaiton et al. 1976; Nathanson 1975). This parallels our findings on drug use. But after entering the health care system, are there differences between the sexes in requests for psychotropic drugs and, more important, do men and women who present with the same symptoms receive the same number of these drugs?

There has been little documentation for the common clinical impression that females request drugs more often than males. Winstead and associates (1974) studied the drug-seeking behavior of psychiatric inpatients by offering diazepam on demand up to four times daily over six months. Women sought and used more drugs than males. Interestingly, high demand correlated significantly with a patient's self-rating of anxiety but not with the diagnosis. Particularly relevant was the finding that patients requested tranquilizers on average only every three days in contrast to the typical physician's pattern of prescribing daily use. The crucial question is whether physicians prescribe differently to males and females with the same symptoms or complaints. Of two recent studies (Bass and Paul 1977; Milliren 1977), one examined tranquilizer prescribing in a family-practice setting in a teaching hospital and the other studied major tranquilizers dispensed within a long-term care facility for the elderly. The latter study (Milliren 1977) found more women than men defined by the staff as anxious; but with the anxiety level held constant, significantly more women than men were given drugs.

Since almost 70 percent of tranquilizer prescriptions in Canada are written by general practitioners, it seems appropriate to examine prescribing patterns in a family-practice clinic (Bass and Paul 1977). All patients with the following complaints were included in the study: (1) unhappy, crying, depressed; (2) nervous; and (3) worried, restless, and tense. At first contact no differences existed between sexes in the proportion counseled or receiving a drug other than a minor tranquilizer; however, the latter were more often prescribed to females. Males received slightly more physical therapies and laboratory tests. Six months later, investigators found that the prescribing differential to these same patients had increased. Prescriptions for tranquilizers increased in proportion to total female visits, but this was not so for male visits.

## Conclusion

Women are more willing to discuss their problems with their network of intimates, to attend physicians because of these problems, and to request drugs. At the same time the situation seems to be compounded by the fact that physicians are more likely to offer tranquilizers to women than to men presenting with the same complaints.

## Summary

This paper reviews current knowledge regarding the use of psychotropic drugs by women, who are more likely than males to be frequent and, particularly, steady users. Age and work status are also correlated with use in both sexes. Differences between the sexes in help-seeking behavior, paths to the health care system, and physician prescribing practices are also examined.

## REFERENCES

Balter, M. B., Levine, J., and Manheimer, D. I. 1974. Cross-national study of the extent of antianxiety sedative drug use. *New England Journal of Medicine* 290:769–774.

Bass, M., and Paul, D. 1977. The influence of sex on tranquilizer prescribing. Paper presented at the North American Primary Care Research Group Meeting. Williamsburg, Virginia, March 1977.

Bellinger, G. B., Balter, M. B., and Manheimer, D. I. 1971. Patterns of psychotherapeutic drug use among adults in San Francisco. *Archives of General Psychiatry* 25:385–394.

Chaiton, A., et al. 1976. Patterns of medical drug use—a community focus. *Canadian Medical Association Journal* 114 (1) :33–37.

Chambers, C. D., Inciardi, J. A., and Siegal, H. A. 1974. *Chemical coping: The extent of non-addicting drug use in the United States.* New York: Spectrum Publications.

Coates, D. B. 1972. On the edge of a nervous breakdown. Unpublished paper from the Yorklea Project, December 1972.

Coleman, J. V., and Patrick, D. L. 1977. Psychiatry and general health care. Paper presented at the 130th Annual Meeting of the American Psychiatric Association. Toronto, May 1977.

Committee Concerned with Women's Health Issues in Etobicoke. The use of prescription medication by women 18 years and over in Etobicoke. Study in progress.

Cooperstock, R. 1971. Sex differences in the use of mood-modifying drugs: An explanatory model. *Journal of Health and Social Behavior* 12 (5):238–244.

————. 1976. Psychotropic drug use among women. *Canadian Medical Association Journal* 115:760–763.

————, and Sims, M. 1971. Mood-modifying drugs prescribed in a Canadian city: Hidden problems. *American Journal of Public Health* 6 (5) :1007–1016.

Dohrenwend, B. P., and Dohrenwend, B. S. 1976. Sex differences and psychiatric disorders. *American Journal of Sociology* 81 (6) :1447–1454.

Drury, T. F. 1977. *Current estimates from the health interview survey—United States—1975.* U.S. Department of Health, Education, and Welfare. National Health Survey, series 10, no. 115, March 1977.

Dunnell, K., and Cartwright, A. 1972. *Medicine takers, prescribers and hoarders.* London: Routledge & Kegan Paul.

Fejer, D., and Smart, R. 1973. The use of psychoactive drugs by adults. *Canadian Psychiatric Association Journal* 18 (4) :313–320.

Greenblatt, D. J., Shader, R. U., and Koch-Weser, J. 1975. Psychotropic drug use in the Boston area. *Archives of General Psychiatry* 32 (4) :518–521.

Guse, L., Morier, G., and Ludwig, J. 1976. Winnipeg survey of prescription (mood-altering) use among women. Technical Report, NMUDD. Manitoba Alcoholism Foundation, October 1976.

Hemminki, E. 1974. General practitioners' indications for psychotropic drugs. *Scandinavian Journal of Social Medicine* 2:79–85.

Horwitz, A. 1977. The pathways into psychiatric treatment: Some differences between men and women. *Journal of Health and Social Behavior* 18 (2) :169–178.

Mechanic, D. 1970. Correlates of frustration among British general practitioners. *Journal of Health and Social Behavior* 11 (2) :87–104.

Milliren, J. W. 1977. Some contingencies affecting the utilization of tranquilizers in long-term care of the elderly. *Journal of Health and Social Behavior* 18 (2) :206–216.

Nathanson, C. A. 1975. Illness and the feminine role: A theoretical review. *Social Sci Med* 9 (2) :57–62.

Parish, P. A. 1976. The prescribing of psychotropic drugs in general practice. *Journal of the Royal College of London Physicians*. Supplement no. 4, 21 (92) :1–77.

Parry, H. J., et al. 1973. National patterns of psychotherapeutic drug use. *Archives of General Psychiatry* 28 (6) :760–783.

Pflanz, M., Basler, H., and Schwoon, D. 1977. Use of tranquilizing drugs by a middle-aged population in a West German city. *Journal of Health and Social Behavior* 18 (2) :194–205.

Provisional Results of Gallup Survey, 1977. Commissioned by Non-Medical Use of Drugs Directorate, Department of National Health and Welfare, Ottawa.

Saskatchewan Department of Health, Saskatchewan Prescription Drug Plan. Annual Report, 1975–1976.

Scheff, T. J. 1966. Users and non-users of a student psychiatric clinic. *Journal of Health and Social Behavior* 7:114–121.

Skegg, D. C. G., Doll, R., and Perry, J. 1977. Use of medicines in general practice. *British Medical Journal* 1:1561–1563.

Smart, R. G., and Goodstadt, M. S. 1976. Alcohol and drug use among Ontario adults: Report of a household survey, 1976. Addiction Research Foundation, Substudy no. 798.

Waldworth, M. E. J., Butterfield, W. J. H., and Blaney, R. 1971. *Health and sickness: The choice of treatment*. London: Tavistock.

Westerholm, B. 1976. Sources of information on drug usage in Sweden. *Clin Pharmacol Ther* 19 (5) :644–650.

Wilder, C. S. 1976. *Health characteristics of persons with chronic activity limitation—United States—1974*. Washington, D.C.: U.S. Department of Health, Education, and Welfare, National Health Survey, series 10, no. 112, October 1976.

Winstead, D., et al. 1974. Diazepam on demand: Drug seeking behaviour in anxious in-patients. *Archives of General Psychiatry* 30:349–351.

# 11

---

# Psychiatry's Problem with No Name: Therapist-Patient Sex

---

## VIRGINIA DAVIDSON

---

The inclusion in the Hippocratic oath of a specific injunction against a physician's having sexual relationships with patients indicates that this concern has a venerable history among physicians. Elaboration of these same ethical proscriptions in the current annotated version of medical ethics applicable to psychiatrists confirms that this concern exists into the present (Official Actions of the American Psychiatric Association, 1973). Moral outrage is regularly expressed by physicians toward those physicians who, in spite of the ethical restraints imposed by the above-mentioned codes, nonetheless indulge themselves sexually with their patients. Yet the force and sincerity of the call for integrity among physicians (Masters and Johnson 1970, pp. 388–391; Demac 1975; Macklin 1976) does not appear to have much deterrent effect on that segment of the profession that chooses to have sex with their patients.

How can this ethical stance be reconciled with the increasing evidence that indicates therapist-patient sex may be far more prevalent than previously thought? Writers who have dealt with this topic have comforted themselves and their audiences with the hopeful observation that serious forms of unethical behavior—such as having sex with one's patients—exists only among a few practitioners (Stone 1975; Braceland 1979; West 1969). One writer, finding the idea "absurd" that any well-qualified analyst could not refrain from being carried away by physical contact with an attractive patient, commented that such an impulse-ridden person would scarcely be safe on a dance floor (Mintz 1969). The more serious question is whether there are a considerable number of male therapists who are not safe, with women patients, in the consulting room.

The idea that women patients may develop intense sexual feelings toward their male therapists during treatment for psychological illness did not originate with psychoanalysis, although it has been during the past seventy-five years that this relationship, in the metaphor of transference-countertransference, has been extensively studied. Before that, the magnetizers of the eighteenth century were well aware of the erotic component in the therapeutic encounter; the possibility that sexual seduction might occur between male magnetizer and female magnetized was recognized; the fact that the female patient was "passive" and that the male magnetizer was "active" was considered likely to increase the possibility that seduction might occur. An eighteenth-century Viennese physician and magnetist, Anton Mesmer, introduced the term "rapport" into our psychological language. He was well aware of the importance of his own charisma in the therapeutic relationship and of its importance in treatment outcome. Mesmer's most famous patient was a blind woman pianist who developed a strong attraction to him during the course of treatment, and he similarly to her. During the period in which she was his patient, Mesmer became permanently estranged from his wife (Ellenberger 1970, pp. 891–893).

Approximately 100 years later another Viennese physician, Josef Breuer, came into difficulty in his marriage because of the erotic attachment an attractive female patient had toward him. The importance of this relationship in the history of psychoanalysis is well known; alongside many other hysterical women patients, Breuer's Anna O. took her place in psychotherapeutic history. Little attention has been paid to the role women patients have played in the development of dynamic psychiatry, although their names, when paired with their famous male physicians, are familiar: Mesmer's Maria Paradis, Janet's Leonie and Madeleine, Charcot's Blanche Wittman, and Freud's Elizabeth von R. Still less attention has been paid to the effects these therapeutic relationships have had on the marriages of the physicians themselves; for example, during the treatment of Anna O., Mrs. Breuer became jealous and, finally, morose. When Mrs. Freud heard about the situation, she immediately identified with Mrs. Breuer and required reassurance from Dr. Freud that their marriage would not be complicated by therapeutic relationships of that sort (Jones 1953a, pp. 224–

225). So wives of psychiatrists have had a long history of concern and understandable interest in the animal magnetism, rapport, and erotic transferences and countertransferences that characterize a part of their husband's working role. For the most part, these women have formed a silent population, yet we know that the effects these therapeutic relationships have on marriages of psychiatrists are considerable.

Within psychoanalysis the development of therapist-patient sexual relationships inside or outside the therapeutic hour has always posed a problem for discipline. Freud's position on therapist-patient sex was clear (Freud 1958, pp. 159–171; Jones 1953b, pp. 163–165,) yet his warnings that therapists should never gratify their patients' erotic demands did not prevent some of his followers from marrying their patients (Roazen 1969; Marmor 1972). Analysts maintain that therapy must always be carried out for the best interests of the patient (as opposed to the analyst) and that an atmosphere of basic trust is crucial for treatment, yet they have demonstrated little interest in reconciling lapses in the conduct of their practitioners with the basic rules of analytic practice. Even when presenting the case histories that document the existence of the problem within psychoanalysis, the issue is not raised as an ethical dilemma for the profession but tends to be seen as a complicating feature of treatment (Voth 1972). Emphasis on the transference is probably related to the greater degree of comfort that is maintained when the "problem" of therapist-patient sex is seen as a manifestation of the patient's—rather than the analyst's—illness.

Marmor (1972) is one of the few writers who has seriously suggested that the therapist could be seductive and could exhibit "countertransference acting-out" within the context of therapist-patient sex. While this is a refreshing departure from the time-worn saw of "transference acting-out," Marmor comes to a disappointing conclusion. For therapists who cannot master their countertransference feelings, he recommends termination of therapy; then, marriage to a patient under these circumstances is seen as an "honorable end-point" of the seductive therapeutic relationship. Several interesting questions come to mind about this approach.

What is to be done with the therapist's current wife?

What is to be done when the therapist enters into the same situation with another patient in the future? For if the same rules of human conduct apply to therapists as to patients, we can assume that this particular kind of acting-out in the service of the repetition compulsion will recur in time.

Are male therapists licensed to choose from their female patients which ones they prefer as marital partners, so long as they verbally terminate the doctor-patient relationship before marriage?

Is it possible for the psychiatrist ever to terminate his moral and ethical obligations to the patient, or do these endure for an indefinite amount of time after the termination of the fee-for-service relationship? There is some legal precedent for believing that duties of a physician toward a patient continue after termination of the contractual agreement (Dawidoff 1973). Aside from the legal question, it seems unlikely that the patient can ever erase the import of the therapist-patient relationship (Finney 1975).

That the doctor-patient relationship (male doctor/female patient) is a subject of much attention in the popular press, the cinema, and medical advertising need hardly be called to attention—everyone knows that already. Yet when note is taken of this fact, it is more often discounted than investigated (Siassi 1973). Rather than discount these sources of popular culture that reveal much about how the male doctor/female patient relationship is seen in larger society (as well as within the medical community), it might be well to examine the portrayal of this relationship. One recent example (October 1975) is a cover from *Esquire* magazine, which is an excerpt from a short story about a woman whose relationship with her analyst included sex on the couch. Although written by Truman Capote, the vignette has much in common with the clinical histories reported by Chesler (1972), Belote (1974), and Dahlberg (1970). From the cinema is a scene from Ingmar Bergman's *Scenes from a Marriage*, shown at the 1975 annual meeting of the American Psychiatric Association; in it the estranged husband asks his wife if she is having sex with her psychiatrist. She matter-of-factly replies that they have gone to bed a couple of times, but that it was a dead loss (Bergman 1974). In that, too, there is a parallel with the clinical literature. Seductive male therapists have unenviable track records as lovers, suffering frequently from impotence and premature ejaculation (Belote 1974; Dahlberg 1970; Bergman 1974; Boas 1966). Finally, the view of women patients that is afforded us from the cartoons and advertising printed in our medical journals suggests that the idea of women's sexual availability is closely intertwined with the male physician's image of himself with female patients. Young, attractive women are frequently pictured in various stages of undress to draw attention to ad copy designed with the male physician in mind. One recently published survey of medical journals found that obstetrical and gynecological journals contained the highest percentage of advertising that was unflattering and degrading to women (Moyer 1975).

Before the 1970s, there were few published series of cases describing therapist-patient sex, although the history of dynamic psychiatry has been punctuated with famous therapist-patient marriages and love affairs. Not much has been written about them for obvious reasons, and they belong more to the oral history of psychiatry than to the published accounts of relationships. Masters and Johnson noted in 1970 that an "unfortunately large" number of their patients had had sex with prior therapists. This was the first time to my knowledge that any data had been published that suggested that therapist-patient sex was not limited to a small number of ill-trained quasiprofessionals. Dahlberg's article, also published in 1970, reported on nine patients who had had sex with their therapists. Dahlberg had collected the data over a twenty-year period, and he noted the difficulty he had getting his paper accepted among organizations since it was "too controversial." It is possible that there have been other such case reports over the years that have been collected but suppressed at publication because of the nature of the material. Chesler (1972) reports on eleven women who had had sex with their therapists. Belote (1974) advertised in a San Francisco newspaper and obtained twenty-five cases of women who had had sex with their male therapists during treatment.

The Kardener and associates study (1973) revealed that 10 percent of the psychiatrists in the sample acknowledged that they engaged in erotic activities with their patients; 5 percent acknowledged that they engaged in sexual intercourse. The most interesting aspect of this study is that Kardener clearly implies that there are kinds of kissing, touching, and affectionate hugging between patient and psychiatrist that are *non*erotic. More than 50 percent of the psychiatrists in the sample acknowledge that they engaged in such nonerotic behavior with patients. How kissing, hugging, and touching (however affectionately labeled) within the context of the psychiatrist-patient relationship can be considered nonerotic requires a certain amount of imagination—or a determined lack of it.

In a recent article, Michael Stone (1975) reported on unethical behavior among psychiatric residents, including two examples of sexual affairs with female patients. He describes the sloth with which the senior psychiatrists responded administratively, when they responded at all, to the residents' behavior. In one case, the errant resident was referred for psychoanalysis; in the other, the resident was dismissed. But it seems that he was dismissed only from that training program; presumably he continued training elsewhere. In all cases that have been reported in the literature, not one raises the question of what to do with the psychiatrist who seduces patients in the course of therapy—whether it is called transference or countertransference love or acting-out (or up), incest, or rape. Whether some therapists involve themselves in serial affairs with patients is suggested by some of the case reports, but even the question of how to deal with this phenomenon is not raised. No one asks whether such a therapist is fit to continue the practice of psychotherapy, for example, while he is being treated for professional misconduct.

Other more difficult data sources to tap include the inevitable knowledge that every practicing psychiatrist has about the community in which he or she practices. The fact that the history of the community most likely includes a certain number of therapist-patient marriages is an indicator of the extent to which the practice of marrying patients is accepted by one's peers. Conversations with colleagues may reveal that certain psychiatrists (sometimes with their patients) are in treatment for the complications related to therapist-patient sex. Treatment, then, may be little more than a convenient way for the seductive psychiatrist to escape censure. By becoming a patient himself, he binds the treating psychiatrist to all the rules of confidentiality and ethical practice and at the same time secures for himself a certain protection and immunity. I have no solution to offer to this practice; I mention it only to indicate the enormity of the ethical question involved.

The available evidence indicates that erotic practices with patients may be quite widespread and that they involve practitioners at all levels of training, from psychiatric resident to training analyst. The therapist who engages in sex with patients or who marries patients may be quite acceptable in his community. If he is to marry a patient, it is hoped that proper—even if somewhat hasty—termination of the therapist-patient relationship precedes the assumption of the therapist-wife one. But even in cases where the niceties of conventional practice are not observed (the "honorable end-points" of relationships), no real risks are run by the psychiatrist who engages in such practices. If he is an academician, he will lose no rank; if he is in analytic training or aspires to enter it, such behavior will not prejudice his candidacy, for he will himself be in treatment with a competent analyst whose training has prepared him for dealing with such difficult cases; he risks little censure from his community peers and no risk of unfavorable action from the local ethics or grievance committees— composed as they are likely to be of men more like himself than otherwise.

While these studies do not discuss the existence of female-therapist/ male-patient sex, it is likely that this phenomenon exists as well, although certainly to a much lesser degree (Perry 1976). Whether women therapists are less involved on account of their fewer numbers in the profession, or because of the greater societal barriers that operate against a woman's expressing her sexual feelings, or because of different cultural expectations that define the sexual role of the woman therapist cannot be said at this time.

In attempting to understand the phenomena of therapist-patient sex, several important questions beg for answers:

Is this particular form of patient exploitation related to sexism within the profession? Does it represent the covert sanctioning by male practitioners of behavior that degrades all women? The image of women patients as available sex objects for their male physicians pervades our popular culture and is rampant in our medical advertising.

Do male therapists who themselves do not engage in sexual activity with patients lend subtle support to the practice by protecting their errant male colleagues with silence or with treatment? Do they allow to go unchallenged facile notions that place the blame for seductive psychotherapy on the woman patient?

Is therapist-patient sex a form of rape? Do women victims of seductive therapy need special forms of therapeutic intervention when they decide to reveal to friend, family, or another therapist that prior therapy has included sex? Women victims in both instances experience considerable guilt, risk loss of love and self-esteem, and often feel that they may have done something to "cause" the seduction. As with rape victims, women patients can expect to be blamed for the event and will have difficulty finding a sympathetic audience for their complaint. Added to these difficulties is the reality that each woman has consulted a therapist, thereby giving some evidence of psychological disequilibrium prior to the seduction. How the therapist may use this information after the woman decides to discuss the situation with someone else can surely dissuade many women from revealing these experiences.

Do women patients need women advocates within the profession, especially on the ethics and grievance committees to insure that their complaints are not dismissed out of hand, much as rape victims have needed advocates within the health care system to obtain proper medical and psychiatric attention?

Women therapists are increasingly interested in the phenomenon of therapist-patient sex (Minutes 1975–1976; American Psychological Association 1975 [reprinted herein chapter 8]) and in the questions it poses for the ethical practice of psychiatry. They readily identify with women patients and with wives of psychiatrists as well—the two groups of women most affected by this practice. Since it is generally agreed that therapist-patient sex is psychologically deleterious for the involved woman patient and is unethical practice for the male practitioner, it remains to be explained why such an unhealthful practice continues to flourish within the profession.

REFERENCES

American Psychological Association. 1975. Report of the task force on sex bias and sex-role stereotyping in psychotherapeutic practice. American Psychological Association, April 1975. [Reprinted herein chapter 8.]

Belote, B. 1974. Sexual intimacy between female clients and male psychotherapists: Masochistic sabotage. Ph.D. dissertation, California School of Professional Psychology.

Bergman, I. 1974. *Scenes from a marriage*, trans. A. Blair. New York: Pantheon Books.

Boas, C. V. E. 1966. The doctor-patient relationship. *Journal of Sex Research* 2:215–218.

Braceland, F. 1969. Historical perspectives of the ethical practice of psychiatry. *American Journal of Psychiatry* 126:230–237.

Chesler, P. 1972. *Women and madness*. Garden City, N.Y.: Doubleday.

Dahlberg, C. 1970. Sexual contact between patient and therapist. *Contemporary Psychoanalysis* 6:107–124.

Dawidoff, D. 1973. *The malpractice of psychiatrists*. Springfield, Ill.: Charles C. Thomas.

Demac, D. 1975. Masters blasts innumerable patient rapes. *Hospital Tribune* 9 (13):1.

Ellenberger, H. 1970. *The discovery of the unconscious*. New York: Basic Books.

Finney, J. C. 1975. Therapist and patient after hours. *American Journal of Psychotherapy* 29:593–602.

Freud, S. 1958. Observations on transference-love. In *The standard edition of the complete psychological works of Sigmund Freud*, ed. J. Strachey, vol. 12, pp. 159–171. London: Hogarth Press.

Jones, E. 1953a. *The life and work of Sigmund Freud*, vol. 1. New York: Basic Books.

———. 1953b. *The life and work of Sigmund Freud*, vol. 3. New York: Basic Books.

Kardener, S., Fuller, M., and Mensh, I. 1973. A survey of physician's attitudes and practices regarding erotic and non-erotic contact with patients. *American Journal of Psychiatry* 130:1077–1081.

Macklin, R. 1976. *Ethics, sex research and sex therapy*. The Hastings Center Report 6:5–7.

Marmor, J. 1972. Sexual acting-out in psychotherapy. *American Journal of Psychoanalysis* 32:3–8.

Masters, W. H., and Johnson, V. E. 1970. *Human sexual inadequacy*. Boston: Little, Brown.

Mintz, E. 1969. Touch and psychoanalytic tradition. *Psychoanalytic Review* 56:365–376.

Minutes of Northern California Psychiatric Society on Women, 1975–1976.

Moyer, L. 1975. What obstetrical journal advertising tells about doctors and women. *Birth and the Family Journal* 2:111–116.

Official Actions of the American Psychiatric Association. 1973. The principles of medical ethics with annotations especially applicable to psychiatry. *American Journal of Psychiatry* 130:1061.

Perry, J. A. 1976. Physicians' erotic and nonerotic physical involvement with patients. *American Journal of Psychiatry* 133:838–840.

Roazen, P. 1969. *Brother animal*. New York: Alfred A. Knopf.

Siassi, I., and Thomas, M. 1973. Physicians and the new sexual freedom. *American Journal of Psychiatry* 130:1256–1257.

Stone, M. 1975. Management of unethical behavior in a psychiatric hospital staff. *American Journal of Psychotherapy* 29:391–401.

Voth, H. M. 1972. Love affair between doctor and patient. *American Journal of Psychotherapy* 29:394–400.

West, L. J. 1969. Ethical psychiatry and biosocial humanism. *American Journal of Psychiatry* 126:226–230.

# PART II / Supplementary Readings

American Psychological Association. 1978. Task force on sex bias and sex-role stereotyping in psychotherapeutic practice, guidelines for therapy with women. *American Psychologist* 33:1122–1123.

Chesler, P. 1972. *Women and madness.* Garden City, N.Y.: Doubleday.

Dahlberg, C. C. 1970. Sexual contact between patient and therapist. *Contemporary Psychoanalysis* 6:107–124.

Lewis, H. B. 1976. *Psychic war in men and women.* New York. New York University Press.

Rice, J. K., and Rice, D. G. 1973. Implications of the women's liberation movement for psychotherapy. *American Journal of Psychiatry* 130:191–196.

Seidenberg, R. 1971. Drug advertising and perception of mental illness. *Mental Hygiene* 55:21–31.

# PART III

# Diagnosis
# and Psychopathology

# 12

---

# The Influence of Gender
# on Diagnosis and
# Psychopathology

---

## ELIZABETH HOWELL

---

The topic of Part III is diagnosis and psychopathology as they are influenced by gender. Before beginning an examination of the specific syndromes that the papers in this section address, a general discussion of the influence of gender on diagnosis and psychopathology will provide a useful backdrop. Diagnosis and psychopathology are differentiated here because diagnosis refers to our labeling practices that may or may not be meaningful or accurate, whereas psychopathology refers to the presence of an actual disorder that may or may not be specified by a diagnosis. Gender influences each of these. First, gender bias in the mental health profession is reflected in diagnostic labeling practices and in the descriptive terminology used therein, calling into question the meaningfulness of certain diagnoses. Second, gender influences psychopathology; there are differences in the numbers of men and women who develop psychiatric disorders and in the types of disorders they are more prone to develop. This chapter will examine problems with our diagnostic terminology and issues of psychopathology among men and women, including the rates of disorders and the types of disorders.

## Problems with Diagnostic Terminology

While our diagnostic system is still to some extent a general conceptual jungle, this is particularly true of diagnostic practices regarding women. When there is uncertainty as to the rules of proper procedure, there are no criteria for the elimination of subtle and unintentional prejudice. Perhaps it is precisely this kind of unclarity that has allowed the antiwoman bias of our culture to become part of our operating diagnostic system in ways that are so familiar to most of us that we often cannot see them. For example, the diagnoses of hysteria and depression are often misunderstood and misused.

Beginning students of diagnosis and psychopathology often observe that more women are diagnosed as hysterics and more men are diagnosed as obsessives. Students then wonder if there are experiential and/or constitutional factors that predispose men and women to these or if the diagnoses themselves are gender-biased.

Consider the question of gender bias. The term hysteria is often inappropriately applied to any disturbed, but not psychotic, woman who presents herself for psychiatric treatment. There has been vast confusion and disagreement as to what actually constitutes a hysterical disorder. Two things, however, remain certain: (1) the descriptive terms are often pejorative and (2) the diagnosis of hysteria often denotes characteristics that are simply a caricature of feminine styles (e.g., emotional responsivity, naïveté, dependency, childishness) (Lerner 1974; Chodoff and Lyons 1958; and Wolowitz 1972).

Lerner (1974) argues that when the diagnosis of hysteria is made strictly on the basis of symptomatology, it may accomplish little more than paste a label on someone who has learned the feminine role very well. This has raised an issue of confusion within our diagnostic system—not only as to the definition of hysteria, but also as to the criteria for making diagnoses. Diagnosis on the basis of surface characteristics and symptoms, which some advocate and many follow without examining its implications, breeds the above sorts of difficulty. According to Lerner, when we pay attention to structural and genetic-dynamic considerations, we are in a better position to accurately diagnose a hysterical personality, which now becomes a meaningful category from which men are no longer excluded.

Depression is another category into which psychiatrically disturbed women frequently fall. There is no dispute that many women really are depressed. Neither is there much dispute that women's experience in this culture predisposes them to this type of disorder (Lewis 1976; Weissman and Klerman 1977). However, because of the particular constellation of environmental circumstances that rather universally characterizes married[1] women in this culture, we are often to some extent diagnosing a *situation* rather than a *person* when we diagnose a woman as depressed. This constellation of circumstances includes the following:

1. Without outside employment, women who are housewives and mothers are usually both financially and emotionally dependent on their husbands, while the husbands themselves have gained independence as well as a major source of gratification—work. In addition, mothers of young children are likely to be tied down, often isolated in the home, and overburdened with barely gratifying chores.

2. If a woman is employed, it is generally in addition to household and child-care responsibilities—so that physical fatigue is not uncommon. In addition, the complexity of multiple roles may lead to role stress and an increase in symptomatic outlets.

3. Family moves tend to follow the husband's employment, not the wife's, so that she may be uprooted from her own employment and friends, becoming temporarily unemployed and isolated. When she does find employment, it is likely that it will be something other than what she wanted and that her pay will be a little more than half her husband's.[2]

## Psychopathology Among Men and Women

The question of which sex is characterized by the higher rate of psychopathology in Western society today is certainly a complicated one. Differences in the researchers' methods and definitions give different meanings to their varying results. In a recent large epidemiological study encompassing community surveys, first admissions to mental hospitals, psychiatric admissions to general hospitals, psychiatric care in outpatient clinics, psychiatric care in private practice, and psychiatric disorders among the general practice of physicians in the year 1967, Gove and Tudor (1973) found more mental illness among women than men from every data source. Furthermore, the ratio of disorders among females to disorders among males varied from 1.4 to 1 to

1. Gove and Tudor (1973), who viewed studies of the relationship between marital status and mental disorder, found that married women had higher rates of disorder than married men, while the reverse was true of unmarried men and women. It must be remembered, however, that such statistics do not imply causality. For instance, not only do they suggest the possibility that marriage as presently organized in a male-dominated society is an institution that benefits men at women's expense, but they could also be used to suggest that mental disorder is more characteristic of men who don't marry and/or women who do.

2. Weissman (1973, 1977) has studied extensively depression in women.

1.89 to 1 across the sources of data. In a mammoth epidemiological literature search of over eighty studies conducted since the turn of the century, Dohrenwend and Dohrenwend (1976) found a shift toward the current higher rates among women. Chesler's (1972) extensive and frequently cited statistics also indicate higher rates among women than men. Gove (1980) cites a recent study by Kramer (1977) which tallies according to gender the treatment rates across the various settings and facilities for the year 1971. These data indicate that if we equate psychiatric treatment with mental illness, women do not have higher rates of mental illness than men.

Before accepting statistics such as these at face value, it is important to understand those issues of measurement involved in their generation. For instance, Dohrenwend and Dohrenwend point out that before 1950, the available evidence indicated that the rates of mental illness were higher among men. The reason for this shift, they say, is more methodological than substantive: prior to 1950 statistics tended more often to be generated by reliance on key informants and official records, whereas later investigations tended to rely on direct interviews. The former procedures best identified antisocial behavior and addictions, more prevalent among men, and were not as likely to identify private suffering and other kinds of disturbed behavior that do not come to public attention. In addition, the later studies tend to focus more on symptoms of depression, anxiety, and psychophysiologic disorders that are more prevalent among women. Thus the methodology biased the rates of psychiatric disorder toward greater incidence in men before 1950 and toward greater incidence in women after 1950.

Another methodological issue of concern is the inclusion or exclusion of certain psychiatric categories within one's definition of "mental illness." For example, Gove and Tudor excluded the category of personality disorders from their analysis, while Dohrenwend and Dohrenwend included it in theirs. This is a predominantly male category, and as Dohrenwend and Dohrenwend point out, excluding it biases the results in favor of higher rates among females. Including it, however, illustrates the blurred boundary between the respective domains of psychiatric nosology and the criminal justice system. Furthermore, it is not necessarily correct to equate treatment rates with psychopathology rates (Gove 1980), for not everyone in treatment is necessarily afflicted by psychopathology, nor are all of the mentally ill in treatment.

Other kinds of methodological defects have been noted by Lewis (1976) in the statistics presented by Chesler. One defect has to do with the failure to consistently calculate the statistics as rates—that is, numbers of disorders per 100,000. Since women tend to live longer than men, failure to calculate per 100,000 artificially inflates the apparent incidence of mental illness in women. Another defect, according to Lewis, is that Chesler's statistics overrepresent the better psychiatric facilities (where there are more women) and underrepresent the state hospitals (where the ratio of men to women is approximately equal or where there are more men). After analyzing the interrelationships between socioeconomic class, severity of disorders, and sex, Lewis concludes that Chesler's figures may be more indicative of higher treatment rates of less severe disturbances at higher economic levels than of a true difference between numbers of men and women in treatment.

However, it must be noted that the statistics from the public inpatient institutions may be misleading as well. Housewives and housewife/mothers usually perform their duties in relative isolation, and often the state of their mental health is of little concern to those around them unless their functioning is impaired. Partly because child rearing and housework tend to be devalued, a high level of functioning is not generally required. Further, an overt breakdown among such women may occasion a total breakdown in the functioning of the households they maintain. Often women who are married, mothers, and poor cannot afford to take the time off for a breakdown—until it is beyond their control. In contrast, the quality of men's work "out in the world" is generally more open to scrutiny and is of more concern to those around them. Thus there may be many women whose severe emotional distress is hidden from the statistics-takers. In consonance with this suggestion and by extension from the Broverman (1970, reprinted in this volume as chapter 7) study and others, Gove (1980) observes that standards of appropriate behavior appear to be more stringent for males than for females.

In sum, statistics regarding overall rates of mental illness among men and women vary with time and place as well as with researchers' methodology and concepts. The important distinction between "incidence" and "prevalence" is not always made. "Incidence" refers to data such as first admissions to hospitals or the available statistics on outpatient treatment and does not necessarily reflect "prevalence," or the actual number of people, not all of whom may have been counted, suffering from the disorder. Thus, depending on the data, there may be overrepresentation in some categories of disorder and underrepresentation in others.

Because methods can exert such a powerful influence on reported statistics, Dohrenwend and Dohrenwend (1976) suggest that a comparison of general rates of psychiatric disorder among men and women is relatively meaningless. In contrast, they observe that consistent relationships between sex and different *types* of disorders are meaningful. In their research they did find such relationships that were consistent over time and place. Their results are as follows:

(1) There are no consistent sex differences in rates of functional psychoses in general (34 studies) or one of the two major subtypes, schizophrenia (26 studies), in particular; rates of the other subtype, manic-depressive psychosis, are generally higher among women (18 out of 24 studies). (2) Rates of neurosis are consistently higher for women regardless of time and place (28 out of 32 studies). (3) By contrast, rates of personality disorder are consistently higher for men regardless of time and place (22 out of 26 studies). (p. 1453).

Results of this sort, they feel, make the question of whether women or men are more prone to mental illness less pressing; rather the more important question becomes "What is there in the endowments and experiences of men and women that pushes them in these different deviant directions?" (p. 1453).

Lewis, who has studied this question extensively, suggests that the differences arise primarily from the respective roles of men and women in our exploitative society.

About the dilemma of men she says:

Men are expected to "get over" their childhood affectionateness and their "childish" craving for affection. They are expected to become aggressive and competitive, especially in earning a livelihood. But our exploitative society also hypocritically disavows aggressive behavior, presents men with moral dilemmas about just how aggressive they ought to be. So after renouncing their own intrinsically affectionate natures and cultivating aggression, men must make still another adaptive compromise with their cultivated aggressions. No wonder their mental illness is more bizarre than women's, and no wonder it so often seems to present them with an insoluble dilemma of guilt. No wonder they often try to solve the dilemma by turning off their feelings altogether. (1976, pp. 267–278)

According to Lewis, largely because undischarged guilt has a triggering effect on obsessions and compulsions, socialization such as that previously described predisposes men to obsessional neurosis, schizophrenia, alcoholism, drug addiction, and deviant sexual compulsions such as child molesting, rape fetishisms, exhibitionism, voyeurism, transvestism, sadism, and masochism.

In contrast, she says, women are encouraged to keep and cultivate their affectionateness. Their problem is that such affectionateness is devalued by our society. Thus women's psychiatric disorders, in particular depression and hysteria, though they can be extremely painful and debilitating, are more understandable in human terms and more often people-oriented, frequently involving attempts to deal with disappointment in a relationship.

The readings that follow address some of these issues in more specificity and depth, in particular the diagnoses of hysteria and depression. In addition, other female-linked disorders, such as anorexia and phobias, are examined, and the gender-related aspects of other diagnoses common to men and women, such as sexual dysfunction, drug addiction, and alcoholism, are presented.

REFERENCES

Chesler, P. 1972. *Women and madness.* New York: Avon Books.

Chodoff, P., and Lyons, H. 1958. Hysteria, the hysterical personality and hysterical conversion. *American Journal of Psychiatry* 114:734.

Dohrenwend, B., and Dohrenwend, B. 1976. Sex differences and psychiatric disorders. *American Journal of Sociology* 81:1447–1454.

Gove, W. 1980. Mental illness and psychiatric treatment among women. *Psychology of Women Quarterly* 4:345–362.

————, and Tudor, J. 1973. Adult sex roles and mental illness. *American Journal of Sociology* 78:812–835.

Lerner, H. 1974. The hysterical personality: A "women's disease." *Comprehensive Psychiatry* 15:157–164. [Reprinted herein chapter 14.]

Lewis, H. 1976. *Psychic war in men and women.* New York: New York University Press.

Weissman, M., and Klerman, G. 1977. Sex differences in the epidemiology of depression. *Archives of General Psychiatry* 34:98–111. [Reprinted herein chapter 13.]

Weissman, M., et al. 1973. The educated housewife: Mild depression and the search for work. *American Journal of Orthopsychiatry* 4:565–573.

Wolowitz, H. 1972. Hysterical character and feminine identity. In *Readings on the psychology of women,* ed. J. Bardwick, pp. 307–314. New York: Harper & Row.

# 13

# Sex Differences
# and the Epidemiology
# of Depression

MYRNA M. WEISSMAN AND
GERALD L. KLERMAN

A frequent observation in epidemiologic studies of depression is that women preponderate. Observations of a sex difference in the frequency of any disease attracts attention and stimulates explanations. Depression has recently gained the attention of biologists, sociologists, feminists, and the educated public. Is it a "true" finding that women are more prone to depression? Or are the observations the result of confounding factors in case reporting or the organization of the health care system? If the finding is "real," what processes, biological or psychosocial, can best explain the differences?

The topic is timely for a number of reasons. All aspects of women's roles are currently under scrutiny. Demographic changes in the past century have increased longevity for women more than for men. However, while these changes have resulted in a larger population of

This research was supported in part by Public Health Service grant 1 RO1 MH25712 from the Center for Epidemiologic Studies, National Institute of Mental Health, Rockville, Maryland.

Kenneth Kidd, Ph.D., assisted in the preparation of the section on genetics. Ben Locke, M.P.H., reviewed this manuscript.

women in the sixth to eighth decades, the aging of the female population in itself cannot account for the predominance of women in epidemiologic studies. For one thing, the preponderance of women is not just in absolute numbers of depressed patients but, more significantly, in rates per population group adjusted for age. At every age group rates of depression are higher for women. If anything there is evidence for a shift in the peak age of onset of depression. Whereas pre-World War II textbooks characterized the onset of depression as rising after the fourth decade of life, recent reports emphasize depressions in young adults, again with a predominance of females.

A number of explanations for the female preponderance have been offered. One set of explanations questions whether the findings are "real" and hypothesizes that they are more likely an artifact accounted for by women's perceptions of stress-coping responses, their willingness to express affective symptoms, and the high frequency with which they seek medical help. Alternately, the finding is considered a real phenomenon and attributed to female biological susceptibility or to social causes. In this article, we first review the evidence for differing rates of depression between the sexes and then critically analyze the various explanations offered.

## Methodological Issues

In any discussion of epidemiological issues, it is customary to express cautions about the methodologic problems in gathering data and the consequent difficulties in comparing findings across studies. A detailed discussion of these issues can be found in several recent reviews (Silverman 1968; Winokur 1969; Kramer 1969; Klerman and Barrett 1973).

One major source of discrepancy is that of case definition. There are at least three meanings to the term depression—a mood, a symptom, a syndrome.

Although the boundaries between mood, symptom, and syndrome are not always clear, in this article we will be interested in the depressive syndrome of primary affective disorders (Weissman, Pincus, and Prusoff 1975; Katz 1971). We will not be focusing on normal mood states or demoralization as reported, for example, in the studies on happiness (Bradburn and Caplowitz 1965), or on secondary depressions associated with medical or psychiatric disorders.

Some of the variations in rates can be explained by variations in methodology, particularly case definition. The problems in methodological difficulties notwithstanding, it is striking that the findings show amazing consistency—that females predominate among depressives.

## Evidence That Women Preponderate Among Depressives

The available evidence for the preponderance of females among depressives comes from four sources: (1) clinical observations of patients coming for treatment; (2) surveys of persons not under treatment; (3) studies of suicide and suicide attempters; (4) studies of grief and bereavement. These sources, from which a number of trends have emerged, are reviewed in tables 13–1 through 3. The data are arranged by place and time of reporting.

### Most Diagnosed Depressives Are Women

Rates of treated depressions are underestimates, subject to the availability of treatment facilities, the individual's willingness to seek and ability to afford care, and other factors related to utilization of health care. Therefore, such rates do not represent true estimates of the prevalence of the disorder.

Table 13–1 summarizes reported findings of the sex ratios for treated depressives for the United States and elsewhere, between 1936 and 1973. Looking first at the United States, a two-to-one sex ratio is fairly consistent over the time period. When a specific diagnosis is given, the ratios are lower for manic-depressives (1.2:1) and higher for neurotic depressives. Countries other than the United States report similar preponderances of females, with the exception of a number of developing countries such as India, Iraq, New Guinea, and Rhodesia. Interesting exceptions to the sex ratios among highly industrialized countries are Finland in 1965, and Norway in 1969, where reports describe nearly equal sex ratios.

### Do More Women Get Depressed?

Since rates of treated cases do not represent true prevalence, epidemiologic analysis requires data from community surveys. Such surveys usually involve a random sample drawn from a total community, and

TABLE 13–1
*Sex Ratios in Depression: Treated Cases*

| Place and Time | Sex Ratios (Female-Male) | Reference |
|---|---|---|
| **United States**<br>Baltimore | 2:1 (psychoneurosis, including depression and manic-depression) | Cooper, Lemkau, and Tietze (1942) |
| Boston,<br>1945, 1955, 1965 | Marked increase in young females with diagnosis of depressive reaction | Rosenthal (1966) |
| Pittsfield, Mass.,<br>1946–1968 | 2.4:1 (patients treated with electroconvulsive therapy) | Tarnower and Humphries (1969) |
| New York State,<br>1949 | 1.7:1 | Lehmann (1971) |
| Massachusetts,<br>1957–1958 | 2.5:1 (all depressives) | Weschler (1961) |
| Ohio,<br>1958–1961 | First admissions:<br>1.9:1 (white)<br>2.7:1 (nonwhite) | Duvall, Kramer, and Locke (1966) |
| Madison, Wisc.,<br>1958–1969 | Increase in depression for women over decade (patients referred for psychological testing) | Rice and Kepecs (1970) |
| Monroe County, New York,<br>1960 | 2.1:1 (affective psychosis) | Gardner et al. (1963) |
| United States,<br>1961 | Outpatient admissions:<br>1.4:1 (psychotic depression)<br>1.2:1 (manic depression)<br>1.8:1 (involutional psychosis)<br>1.6:1 (depressive reactions) | Rosen, Bahn, and Kramer (1964) |
| Monroe County, New York,<br>1961–1962 | 1.6:1 (prevalence)<br>1.3:1 (incidence) | Pedersen, Barry, and Babigian (1972) |
| New Haven, Conn.,<br>1966 | 3:1 (all depressions) | Paykel and Dienelt (1971) |
| United States,<br>1970 | Admissions to all psychiatric facilities:<br>2.1:1 (all depressive disorders) | Cannon and Redick (1973) |
| **Outside United States**<br>Amsterdam,<br>1916–1940 | 2.3:1 (Ashkenazim Jews)<br>2.4:1 (Gentiles) | Crewel (1967) |

TABLE 13-1 (continued)
Sex Ratios in Depression: Treated Cases

| Place and Time | Sex Ratios (Female-Male) | | | | | Reference |
|---|---|---|---|---|---|---|
| Gaustad, Norway, 1926–1955 | Lifetime risk of first admission: 1.37:1 (1926–1935) 1.36:1 (1946–1950) 1.33:1 (1951–1955) | | | | | Odegaard (1961) |
| Buckinghamshire, England, 1931–1947 | 1.8:1 (1931–1933) 1.9:1 (1945–1947) | | | | | Lehmann (1971) |
| Basel, Switzerland, 1945–1957 | 1.5:1 (approximately) | | | | | Kielholz (1959) |
| 1965–1971 | First admissions of manic-depressives; involutional melancholia and affective psychosis | | | | | N. Sartorious, written communication, 1974 (World Health Organization data) |
| | 1965 | 1967 | 1969 | 1971 | | |
| Canada | 1.8:1 | 1.7:1 | 1.8:1 | 1.7:1 | | |
| Czechoslovakia | 2.1:1 | … | … | 2.1:1 | | |
| Denmark | 2.4:1 | 1.9:1 | 1.8:1 | 1.8:1 | | |
| Finland[a] | 1:1 | 1.3:1 | … | … | | |
| France | … | … | 1.7:1 | 1.6:1 | | |
| Norway | 1.2:1 | 1.2:1 | 0.9:1 | 1.5:1 | | |
| Poland[a] | 1.4:1 | 1.4:1 | 1.4:1 | … | | |
| Sweden[b] | 1.8:1 | 1.8:1 | … | … | | |
| Switzerland[a] | 1.6:1 | 1.3:1 | 1.4:1 | … | | |
| England and Wales | 1.9:1 | 1.9:1 | 1.8:1 | … | | |
| New Zealand | 1.5:1 | 2.2:1 | 1.8:1 | … | | |
| London, 1947–1949 | 2:1 | | | | | Lehmann (1971) |
| Scania, Sweden, 1947, 1957 | 1.8:1 (Lifetime prevalence of severe depression) | | | | | Essen-Moller and Hagnell (1961) |
| England and Wales, 1952, 1960 | 1.6:1 (1952) 1.7:1 (1960) | | | | | Lehmann (1971) |

Sex Ratios in Depression: Treated Cases

| Place and Time | Sex Ratios (Female-Male) | Reference |
| --- | --- | --- |
| Aarhus County, Denmark, 1958 | 2:1 (endogenous depression) 4:1 (psychogenic depression) 3:1 (depressive neurosis) | Juel-Nielsen et al. (1961) |
| Salford, England, 1959–1963 | 1.9:1 (Depressive psychosis) | Adelstein et al. (1964) |
| Dakar, Guinea, 1960–1961 | 0.5:1 | Collomb and Zwingelstein (1961) |
| Madras and Madurai, India, 1961–1963 | 0.2:1 | Venkoba Rao (1966) |
| Tokyo and Taiwan, 1963–1964 | Women have more depressive symptoms | Rin, Schooler, and Caudill (1973) |
| Madurai, India, 1964–1966 | 0.56:1 (endogenous depression) | Venkoba Rao (1970) |
| Bulaways, Rhodesia, 1965–1967 | 1.1:1 (N = 76) | Buchan (1969) |
| Baghdad, Iraq, 1966–1967 | 1.1:1 | Bazzoui (1970) |
| Honduras, 1967 | 1.6:1 (admissions) 6.7:1 (outpatients) | Hudgens, deCastro, and deZuniga (1970) |
| New Delhi, 1968 | 0.55:1 | Teja, Aggarwal, and Narang (1971) |
| Jerusalem, 1969–1972 | 2.1:1 (affective disorders) | Gershon and Liebowitz (1975) |
| Papua, New Guinea, 1970–1973 | 0.4:1 (based on a few cases) | Torrey (1973) |
| Denmark, 1973 | 1.9:1 (first admissions for manic depression) | Dupont, Videbech, and Weeke (1974) |
| Bangkok, Thailand (time not indicated) | 1.3:1 (Far East Orientals) 0.8:1 (Occidentals) | Tongyonk (1971) |

[a] Manic-depressives only.
[b] Discharges only.

therefore provide information on many persons who have the disorder but have not received treatment.

Table 13-2 summarizes data from community surveys in the United States and elsewhere. In clinical studies of diagnosed cases, the sex ratios show minor variations, but in the community surveys there are no variations, with the exception of bereaved widows (which will be discussed separately). Women preponderate in all countries and over all time periods.

## Suicide and Suicide Attempters

Since Stengel's work (1964) it is conventional to distinguish between persons who die from suicide (completers) and those who make attempts (suicide attempters). Suicide attempters tend to be young females while completers are older males. Rates of suicide attempts are an indirect index of depression since many suicide attempters are depressed.

The sex ratios reported for suicide attempters in recent years are especially interesting because of the rise in rates among youthful adults (mostly under thirty years of age), a consistent trend reported internationally. All countries report an increase in suicide attempts over the last decade, which persists even after correcting for population growth or changes in reporting. Reviewing the figures (table 13-3) from Australia, Great Britain, the United States, Israel, and India, the sex ratio in suicide attempts is about two to one. The only exception is India, where the sex ratios are reversed. This reversal is consistent with the ratios of treated cases of depression but not with data from community surveys, suggesting that this may be due to a national pattern of help seeking. In Poland the sex ratios are nearly equal for suicide attempts, but this is consistent with the data from first admissions (table 13-1); no survey data could be found.

## The Depression of Bereavement: Is It Normal?

The data on the bereaved spouse from community surveys deserve special mention since the sex ratios found in studies of bereavement are different from those found in clinical depression. The naturally occurring depression accompanying bereavement, usually called grief, has been universally noted in almost all societies, and unlike depression is considered normal and adaptive (Clayton, Halikas, and Maurice 1971; Klerman and Izen, forthcoming; Lindemann 1944; Engel 1961).

The fact that there are few differences between men and women in frequency or types of depressive symptoms in the first year following bereavement lends support to the view that regards grief as qualita-

TABLE 13-2

*Sex Differences in Depression: Community Surveys*

| Place and Time | Sex Ratios (Female-Male) | Reference |
|---|---|---|
| **United States** | | |
| Brooklyn and Queens, N.Y., 1960 | Women were more depressed | Benfari et al. (1972) |
| Baltimore, Md., 1968 | 1.6:1 (Includes wives of blue-collar workers only) | Siessi, Crocetti, and Spiro (1974) |
| Northern Florida, 1968 | 1.8:1 | Schwab, McGinnis, and Warheit (1973) |
| Carroll County, Md., 1968 | Women were more nervous, helpless, anxious | Hogarty and Katz (1971) |
| New Haven, Conn., 1969 | 2:1 (suicidal feelings) | Paykel et al. (1974) |
| St. Louis, Mo., 1968–1969 | No significant sex differences in depression in bereaved spouse | Clayton, Halikas, and Maurice (1972) |
| New York City, 20-year period | More referrals for minor depression in female employees in one company | Hinkle et al. (1960) |
| **Outside United States** | | |
| Iceland, 1910–1957 | 1.6:1 (all depressions) | Juel-Nielsen et al. (1961) |
| Samso, Denmark, 1960 | 3.5:1 (all depressions) | Sorenson and Stromgren (1961) |
| Ghiraz, Iran, 1964 | 3.6:1 (N = 23) | Bach and Bash-Liechti (1969, 1974) |
| Luchnow, India, 1969–1971 | 2:1 | B.B. Sethi, MD, written communication, March 1974 |
| Herfordshire, England, 1949–1954 | 2.4:1 | Martin, Brotherston, and Chave (1957) |
| Agra, India (time not indicated) | 1.6:1 (manic depression) | Dube and Kumar (1973) |
| Aarhus County, Denmark, 1960–1964 | 1.6:1 (manic depression) 3.8:1 (psychogenic depression) 2.9:1 (neurotic depression) | Weeke et al. (1975) |

TABLE 13-3
*Sex Ratios in Suicide Attempts*

| Place and Time | Sex Ratios (Female-Male) | Reference |
|---|---|---|
| **United States** | | |
| New York, 1960 | 3:1 | Hirsh, Zauder, and Drolette (1961) |
| Window Rock, Ariz., 1968 | 2:1 | Miller and Schoenfeld (1971) |
| St. Louis, Mo., 1968–1969 | 2:1 | Clendenin and Murphy (1971) |
| Providence, R.I., 1968 | 3:1 | Ianzito (1970) |
| New Haven, Conn., 1970 | 2:1 | Weissman et al. (1973) |
| **Outside United States** | | |
| Israel, 1962–1963 | 1.5:1 | Modan, Nissenkorn, and Lewkowski (1970) |
| Jerusalem, Israel, 1967–1969 | 2.1:1 | Gershon and Liebowitz (1975) |
| New Delhi, India, 1967–1969 | 0.8:1 | Venkoba Rao (1965) |
| Madurai, India, 1964 | 0.8:1 | Venkoba Rao (1971) |
| Krakow, Poland, 1960–1969 | 1.5:1 (1960) 0.6:1 (1962) 1.0:1 (1966) 1.2:1 (1967) 0.8:1 (1969) | Weissman (1974) |
| Poznania, Poland, 1970 | 1.1:1 | Weissman (1974) |
| Western Australia, 1961 | 2:1 | James, Derham, and Scott-Orr (1963) |
| Northeast Tasmania, Australia, 1961–1963 | 1.7:1 | Gold (1966) |

| | | |
|---|---|---|
| Victoria, Australia, 1963 | 1.3:1 | Krupinski, Stoller, and Polke (1966) |
| Melbourne, Australia, 1963–1968 | 2.4:1 | Hetzel (1971) |
| Brisbane, Australia, 1965–1966 | 2.5:1 | Edwards and Whitlock (1968) |
| Southern Tasmania, Australia, 1968–1969 | 2.5:1 | Freeman, Ryan, and Beattie (1970) |
| Melbourne, Australia, 1970 | 2.2:1 | Oliver et al. (1971) |
| Glasgow, Scotland, 1960–1962 | 1.3:1 | Sclare and Hamilton (1963) |
| Sheffield, England, 1960–1961 | 1.7:1 | Parkin and Stengel (1965) |
| Edinburgh, Scotland, 1962, 1967 | 2.1 (1962) 1.6 (1967) | Aitken, Buglass, and Kreitman (1969) |
| Leicester, England, 1961 | 2.4:1 | Ellis, Comish, and Hewer (1966) |
| London, England, 1963 | 2.1:1 | Bridges and Koller (1966) |
| Bristol, England, 1964–1965 | 2:1 | Roberts and Hooper (1969) |
| Shropshire, Montgomeryshire, England, 1965–1966 | 2.3:1 | Hershon (1968) |
| Brighton, England, 1967 | 2:1 | Jacobson and Tribe (1972) |
| Newcastle-upon-Tyne, England, 1962–1964, 1966–1969 | 2.5:1 | Smith and Davison (1971) |
| Glasgow, Scotland, 1970 | 1.4:1 | Patel, Roy, and Wilson (1972) |

tively different from clinical depression. Longer-term studies are required to determine possible delayed consequences of bereavement per se, or whether absent, delayed, or atypical grief predisposes to psychosomatic, medical, or psychiatric illness. Such studies may show male-female differences, but the current evidence is that there are no differences between the sexes in the frequency of depressive symptoms following bereavements.

### Summary of Evidence for Female Preponderance

To summarize, the evidence from international comparisons of diagnosed and treated depressed patients and from community surveys that include both treated and untreated "cases" is consistent. Women preponderate in the rates of depression.

## Is the Preponderance of Female Depressives an Artifact of Sex Differences in Reporting Stress and Distress?

The "artifact" hypothesis proposes that women perceive, acknowledge, report, and seek help for stress and symptoms differently than men and that these factors account for the sex-ratio findings. Put another way, the "artifact" hypothesis would hold that response set and labeling processes serve to overestimate the number of female depressives.

### Are Women Under More Stress?

Before the sex differences in rates of depression can be regarded as an artifact, the possibility must be considered that women are under more stressful life events and therefore are at greater risk for depression. There is an extensive research literature concerning the relationship between stress and general illness.

Many clinicians have observed stressful events occurring before the onset of clinical depression and, therefore, concluded that these events serve as precipitating events. In spite of this clinical conviction relating stress to depression, until recently there had been relatively little systematic research testing of these hypotheses. Holmes and Rahe (1967) provided great impetus to these studies by developing a simple quantitative scale for assessing life events that have been used in epidemiologic and clinical studies. The results support the hypothesized relationship between stressful life events and the onset and severity of numerous medical illnesses and psychiatric disorders, particularly depression. No consistent sex differences in stress reports have appeared (Horowitz 1975).

Uhlenhuth and Paykel and colleagues (1973a, b) have conducted elegant studies to examine the relationship between actual or perceived stress, using newer life events scales and the report of symptoms among patients in both psychiatric settings and normal populations in community studies. They found a direct relationship between stress and symptom intensity, but did not find that women reported more stressful life events. At the same levels of stress, women reported symptom intensities about 25 percent higher than men. This study was repeated in a probability sample of all households in Oakland, California, with similar results (Uhlenhuth et al., 1974).

One possible criticism of these studies is that most stress scales emphasize discrete life events and acute changes in life conditions. They are relatively insensitive to certain chronic conditions, such as poverty, the impact of large family size, or health problems, that might differentially impact to a greater extent on women than men. However, pending empirical research, the available evidence is that women do not experience or report more stressful events.

## Do Women Weigh Events as More Stressful?

While women may not report more stressful life events, they may evaluate events as more stressful. To study the weighing given to stress, Paykel, Prusoff, and Uhlenhuth (1971) asked patients and their relatives to judge the degree to which various life events were upsetting; they found no sex differences. Men and women do not appear to evaluate the standard lists of life events as having different impacts on their lives.

## Women Report More Symptoms, Especially Affective Distress

One hypothesis proposed to account for the excess of symptoms among women is that women respond to stress with affective distress because they feel freer to acknowledge symptoms (Blumenthal 1975). Clancy and Gove (1974) examined the possible role of social disapproval in affecting the reporting of symptoms, and they found no significant sex difference. Women did not report more desire for social approval and did not judge having psychiatric symptoms as less undesirable. They concluded that sex differences in symptom reporting appear to reflect actual differences and are not an artifact of response bias. Women experienced more symptoms.

Women cope with problems by visiting doctors and, by every measure of utilization of the general health care system, women preponderate. They have increased rates of use of outpatient facilities, of visiting physicians, of prescriptions, and of psychotropic drug use (Mazer 1974; Parry et al. 1973). Hinkle and associates (1960) in a twenty-five-year study of over 200 telephone company employees in New York City, found that women had more visits to the doctor and were away from work for health reasons more frequently, but these differences were accounted for almost entirely by minor illnesses. On the other hand, life-endangering illness occurred [more] among men. Analysis of the risk of death based on expected case fatality rates led to an estimate that, over a twenty-year period, men experienced a greater risk of death from illness than did women, in a ratio of about four to three. On the basis of this evidence, Hinkle inferred that men and women probably experience a similar variety of minor illnesses, but men do not seek medical attention.

There is a consistency in the findings for help seeking. Women come for help for minor complaints, and mortalities show that men die sooner. For depression, women seek treatment more often and men have a higher suicide rate (Silverman 1968). In our society the public assumption of the sick role is interpreted by men as a sign of weakness. Moreover, the health care system is organized in ways that make it difficult for most men to come for treatment, that is, office hours usually conflict with hours of employment.

Help-seeking patterns alone cannot account for the preponderance of depressed women in community surveys. The majority of persons judged depressed in community surveys have not been treated in psychiatric clinics. Therefore, they have not been included in any official treatment rates. Consequently, health care–seeking behavior cannot account for the female preponderance.

*Men Use More Alcohol*

While depression is more common in women, alcohol use and abuse are considerably more common in men (Gomberg 1974). It has been hypothesized that depression and alcoholism are different but equivalent disorders. Women get depressed; men are reluctant to admit being depressed or to seek treatment and mitigate this by drinking. Thus, men self-prescribe alcohol as a psychopharmacological treatment for depression.

Winokur and Clayton (1967) noted that environmental factors may render it difficult for women to drink excessively. In families that discourage drinking by women, the same "illness" might manifest itself as depression rather than alcoholism. This hypothesis holds that alcoholism and depression are different manifestations of the same familial-genetic disorder.

While alcohol in moderate to high amounts is a central nervous system pharmacologic depressant (Mayfield and Coleman 1968; Mayfield 1968), in small amounts it is a psychic relaxant. Moreover, the social context of the consumption can provide support. The working-class man seeks the local pub, while middle- and upper-class men seek the country clubs or cocktail lounges; all settings provide a group atmosphere for psychopharmacological self-treatment. The psychosocial supports provided by these group situations should not be overlooked as powerful reinforcers for participation, synergistically reinforcing the pharmacological actions of alcohol itself on mood and self-esteem.

Many treated alcoholics have symptoms of depression. Tyndel (1974) in a study of 1,000 alcoholic patients, found serious depressive symptoms either at interview or in the past history of approximately 35 percent of alcoholics. Studies of outpatients coming for treatment of alcoholism in New Haven, Connecticut, found that over 50 percent had depressive disorders of sufficient magnitude to require antidepressant treatment. These results are consistent with earlier reports by Winokur (1972). However, studies of frequency of depression among alcoholics coming for treatment are not suitable for assessing the true incidence of depression among alcoholics, since people with two serious conditions (in this case, alcoholism and depression) have a greater probability of coming for treatment (Lilienfeld, Pedersen, and Dowd 1967).

As further evidence for an association between alcoholism and depression, excessive alcohol use has been reported in patients with bipolar illness (Reich, Davies, and Himmelhoch 1967). Female depressed patients who have an early onset of depression have an increased rate of alcoholism in their first-degree relatives (Winokur and Clayton 1968). Suicide and suicide attempts frequently occur in the context of alcohol abuse. Depression is associated with alcohol postwithdrawal states (Butterworth 1971), and antidepressants and other psychotropic drugs have suggested therapeutic value in the treatment of detoxified alcoholics (Mayfield 1968; Overall et al. 1973; Rosenberg 1974; Wren et al. 1974).

These studies have not successfully sorted out causes from consequences. Two processes certainly operate. Alcohol is used by men to mitigate their symptoms of depression. For others, chronic alcohol abuse and the consequent social impairment can lead to depression.

Whether cause (primary) or effect (secondary), the hypothesis that a substantial portion of depressed men appear under the diagnostic rubric of alcoholism cannot be ruled out.

## Males Preponderate in Law Enforcement and Correctional Systems

In most industrial nations, women preponderate in the health care system and men in the law enforcement system and correctional institutions. It is hypothesized, therefore, that depressed men may show up in the courts rather than in the clinics; for example, a depressed man may get drunk, get into a fight, and end up in court. This hypothesis has been supported by Mazer's studies in Martha's Vineyard (Mazer 1974).

If these hypotheses are verified, epidemiological studies of rates of depression must include more extensive case reporting from correctional institutions. Where this has been done in studies ascertaining rates of suicide attempts, a higher number of male attempters than is usually reported has been found (Clendenin and Murphy 1971; Whitehead, Johnson, and Ferrence 1973).

## Summary of Evidence for Female Preponderance

Women do not have more stressful life events and do not judge life events as more stressful. While women acknowledge having symptoms and affective distress more frequently, this does not seem to be because they feel less stigma or because they wish to win approval. Women and men have different help-seeking patterns. However, increased female utilization of health care would not account for the preponderance of depressed women in community surveys, since most survey "cases" are not in psychiatric treatment either at the time of the interview or in the past.

There is no question that more males than females have alcohol abuse problems, so that some unknown proportion of depressed men appear in the alcoholism rates and are not identified as depressed. It could be debatable, however, as to whether or not these men are really depressed. Accurate diagnostic assessments are required to determine the morbid risk of depression and the time sequence of onset in relationship to alcoholism. Similar considerations apply to the possibility that the depressed men are to be found in the law enforcement system. Pending further research to test this possibility, it remains an interesting, but unproven, hypothesis. When all these possibilities are considered, our conclusion is that the female preponderance is not an artifact.

## The Female Preponderance Is Real

We must regard the sex differences as real findings and examine the possible explanations. These include hypotheses involving biological susceptibility and others involving social discrimination and its psychological consequences. Among the biological hypotheses, possible genetic transmission and female endocrine physiological processes have been investigated.

### Is There a Genetic Transmission for Depression?

The possibility of a genetic factor in the etiology of depression has regularly attracted attention. There are mainly four sources of evidence for the genetic hypothesis: family aggregation studies that compare illness rates within and between generations of a particular family on the basis of the fact that members of the same family share the same genes to varying degrees; studies of twins comparing illness rates in monozygotic twins with those of dizygotic twins; cross-rearing studies; and linkage studies in which known genetic markers are used to follow other traits through several generations or in siblings. The majority of genetic studies in depression are concerned with evidence from the first two types of studies.

The available evidence summarized by several investigators (Klerman and Barrett 1973; Gershon, Dunner, and Goodwin 1971; Slater and Cowie 1971) shows an increased morbid risk of affective disorder in the first-degree relatives of diagnosed depressives as compared with the general population, and a higher concordance rate for affective disorders in monozygotic than dizygotic twins. Taking all the studies, there is reasonable evidence for a genetic factor operating in depressive illness.

A greater frequency of a disorder in one sex is a genetically interesting phenomenon. One possible explanation is X=linkage, that is, the location of the relevant locus on the X chromosome. For an X-linked locus, if the trait is dominant, females (with two X chromosomes) will be affected more commonly. A rare X-linked recessive trait will seldom appear in the parents of children of an affected male but will always be found in both the father and all sons of an affected female. A rare X-linked dominant trait will usually appear in the mother and all of the daughters of an affected male and will occur in at least one parent and at least half of the children of an affected female. The exact frequencies with which first-degree relatives are affected is also a function of the allele frequency in the population and of the mating pattern. Based on assumptions of random mating and an X-linked dominant trait, Slater and Cowie (1971) calculated that for every affected male sibling of an affected female there would be three affected female siblings.

The examination of possible X-linkage in depression has been accelerated by the identification of at least two groups of affective disorders: unipolar, which includes persons only with a major depressive illness, usually of a recurring nature (although the definition varies); and bipolar, which includes persons with episodes of both mania and depression (Leonhard 1957; Leonhard, Korff, and Schulz 1962; Winokur and Clayton 1967; Perris 1966; Goodwin and Ebert 1973). The results of family studies investigating X-linkage are conflicting. Perris (1971) has reported data consistent with X-linked transmission for unipolar but not for bipolar depression. However, Helzer and Winokur (1974) and Reich, Clayton, and Winokur (1969) found data suggesting X-linkage for bipolar but not for unipolar depression. The inconsistency of studies has continued into recent work as well. Gershon and associates (in press) have found no evidence for X-linkage of bipolar affective disorder in a study in Jerusalem; Goetzl and associates (1974) had similar results in a study conducted in New Hampshire.

Another possible explanation of the different incidences in the two sexes is a differential interaction of genotype and environment depending on sex. Kidd and colleagues, in published (1973) and unpublished studies, have shown that a sex effect can be treated as a differential threshold, with the less commonly affected sex having a higher threshold. The underlying liability is determined by a combination of genetic and environmental factors. They have considered two types of inheritance: a polygenic model and a single major autosomal locus. While they have not applied these models to data on depression, they have shown that many of the commonly observed aspects of the sex effect could be explained by these models. The results of Uhlenhuth and Paykel (1973a, b) suggest that at the same level of stress females have more symptoms than males, which is consistent with the concept of females having a lower threshold.

At this stage the findings are in need of further examination. The samples studied are small, and family data on depressives who may not fit either the unipolar or bipolar classification are not available. Currently the evidence from genetic studies is insufficient to draw conclusions about the mode of transmission or to explain the sex differences.

## Can Female Endocrine Physiology Cause Depression?

Interest in the possible relationships between female sex hormones and affective states derives from observations that clinical depression tends to occur in association with events in the reproductive cycle. Included are the menstrual cycle, use of contraceptive drugs, the postpartum period, and the menopause. Four questions are raised for each event: (1) Are depressive symptoms more likely to be associated with these events; (2) do they occur with sufficient frequency to account for the excess of depressed women; (3) is there a specific clinical syndrome associated with the event; and (4) is any specific female hormone implicated as mediating the depression?

### Premenstrual Tension

Mood changes associated with hormonal fluctuation during the normal menstrual cycle have received much attention (Neu and DiMascio 1974; Shader and Ohly 1970; Sommer 1973; Bardwick 1974; Tonks 1968). The syndrome, called premenstrual tension, includes irritability, depression, bloated feelings, and headaches during the four to five days before the onset of the menses. If a substantial number of women undergo such changes on a regular monthly basis, this could account for some of the excess of female depressives. Moreover, it would suggest that some aspect of female hormonal balance plays a role in pathogenesis of depression.

The frequency of premenstrual tension as a real phenomenon has received systematic study, and a few careful clinical studies are available. Sommer (1973), in a critical review, has identified the major methodologic problem inherent in these studies, including variations in the cycle phase and response bias, and notes that studies asking the subject to report behavior changes associated with the menses are positive, whereas studies using actual objective performance measures generally fail to demonstrate menstrual cycle–related changes. Morton and associates noted premenstrual tension in 80 percent of a volunteer sample of women prisoners, 5 percent of whom reported severe symptoms (Tonks 1968). Lamb and associates found such symptoms in 73 percent of a sample of student nurses (Tonks 1968). McCance, on the other hand, in a study of 167 women who gave daily information about mood, found great discrepancies between what they claimed were their symptoms related to menstruation and what was actually reported on the forms (Tonks 1968).

Numerous etiological hypotheses, both physiological and psychological, have been offered to explain premenstrual tension. These hypotheses have been reviewed by Tonks (1968), with no definitive conclusions, and no one sex hormone can be implicated.

## Oral Contraceptive Use

The use of oral contraceptives, which provide exogenous gonadal steroids, is believed to be associated with increased depression. This hypothesis is supported by findings from case reports, uncontrolled studies, and overall side-effect incidence rates. Adequately controlled studies are lacking because of the problems inherent in their design. For example, ideal control groups are difficult to establish because contraceptives cannot easily be randomly assigned or compared to placebos. Moreover, the suggestability attendant to use of all medication requires placebo controls to differentiate the psychological from the pharmacologic effects of oral contraceptives.

Weissman and Slaby (1973) have reviewed the evidence and conclude that there is insufficient data to justify the conclusion that oral contraceptives cause depressive symptoms on a pharmacologic basis. There is evidence that women with a prior psychiatric history and those with an expectation of adverse side effects tend to develop more depressive symptoms while taking oral contraceptives. Weissman and Slaby's well-controlled study showed that mild psychiatric disturbances may develop during the first four weeks of use with high estrogen preparations. These symptoms, however, gradually disappear.

While these studies do not exclude the hypothesized physiological basis to psychiatric symptoms associated with oral contraceptive use, such an association is probably of low incidence. For example, Adams and associates (1973) and Winston (1973) have suggested that a small number of women taking steroid hormones may become depressed because of the inhibition of the synthesis of biogenic amines in the central nervous system. This is the result of a functional pyridoxine deficiency caused by the estrogens in the oral contraceptive and may be alleviated or prevented by supplementary vitamin $B_6$ administration. Both studies agree that this occurs in a small number of women.

Evidence based on experiences with oral contraceptive use, like that from premenstrual tension, is not conclusive. In summary, the amount of female depression that could be attributed to the possible psychopharmacologic effects of oral contraceptives is small.

## Postpartum Depression

In the postpartum period, significant hormonal changes occur and depressive mood changes have been described. Transient emotional disturbances in the first weeks following delivery, the "new baby blues," occur with such frequency as to be considered normal and resolve without treatment (Yalom et al. 1968). However, there is overwhelming evidence that the longer postpartum period (up to six months) carries an excess risk for more serious psychiatric disorders (Thuwe 1974; Brown and Shereshefsky 1972; Butts 1969; Gordon and Gordon 1959; Asch and Rubin 1974). The most comprehensive studies on the risk of mental illness in the prepartum and postpartum periods were reported by Paffenberger and McCabe (1966) and by Pugh and associates (1963) Paffenberger and McCabe studied the medical records of all women in Cincinnati during a two-year period, aged fifteen through forty-four, who were inpatients on any psychiatric service. They found that age-adjusted rates of mental illness were low for married women in general, but they were higher for women in the postpartum period and lowest for pregnant women. The peak rates of mental illness occurred in the first months following delivery. Moreover, about half of the women who suffered a postpartum illness had a recurrence in one-third of their subsequent pregnancies.

Paffenberger and McCabe's results were very similar to those of Pugh and associates, who studied all females, aged fifteen to forty-four, who were first admissions to Massachusetts mental hospitals during 1950. Pugh and colleagues also found an excess of psychosis, especially the manic-depressive type, during the first three months postpartum. While all authors agree that endocrine changes are involved in the postpartum psychiatric illness, in a previous era many acute psychotic states, including delirium, may have been related to infections, fevers, dehydration, and hemorrhage following childbirth. However, with better medical care, these are rare occurrences in industrialized countries. Currently the severe psychiatric reactions of postpartum are almost all of a depressive nature. It must be concluded that women are at greater risk for psychiatric disorders, particularly depression, in the postpartum period, although, if any specific endocrine abnormality is involved, the mechanism is not understood.

## Menopause

The menopausal period is presumed to produce an increased risk of depression, and depressions occurring in this period are supposed to have a distinct clinical entity. It is believed that women who are normally symptom-free experience depressive changes during this period. Moreover, the depression occurring in the menopause is described as a separate entity, and involutional melancholia appears in the official American Psychiatric Association diagnostic classification.

In regard to the supposedly characteristic clinical picture, Rosenthal reviewed thirty years of studies and concluded that involutional melancholia never existed as a separate entity. The early clinical studies were poorly controlled and contained small samples, and the recent studies find few patients with the characteristic symptom pattern. If such an entity existed in the past, its relative absence now may have to do with the availability of better case finding and effective treatments, so that depressed patients are seen earlier, before the full-blown "involutional" syndrome emerges (Rosenthal 1968).

In regard to the possible increased risk of depression around the menopause, Winokur (1973) found that there was no greater risk for depression during the menopause than during other times of the life span. Similar findings have been noted by others (Silverman 1968; Juel-Nielsen et al. 1961; Adelstein et al. 1964; Sorenson and Stromgren 1961; Juel-Nielsen and Stromgren 1965). McKinley and Jeffreys (1974) conducted a community survey of over 600 women in the premenopausal and menopausal age range to ascertain the prevalence of depressive symptoms. They found that hot flashes occurred more frequently in women whose menstrual flow showed evidence of change or cessation, but few of the women sought treatment for this symptom. There was no direct relationship between depression and menopausal status. Moreover, the majority of respondents did not experience any difficulties at menopause and only 10 percent expressed regret at the cessation of menses. These conclusions have also been reported by Neugarten (1968), although this may vary in rural cultures, and by Hallstrom (1973).

The most definitive epidemiologic study of mental disorders in the climacteric was recently completed in Sweden (Hallstrom 1973). Between 1968 and 1970, more than 800 women, aged thirty-eight to sixty, were surveyed to determine possible changes in mental health status during the climacteric. No significant differences were observed in the incidence rates for mental illness, depressive states, or psychiatric morbidity in the different age strata as a function of menopause. Moreover, there was no evidence that characteristic personality or emotional changes took place.

The psychologic impact of the menopause has also been implicated along with the hypothesized hormonal changes. Deykin and associates (1966), Bart (1970), and others have pointed out that the period coinciding with the menopause may be associated with other life events such as departure of children from the home. These psychosocial changes may have more of an impact on women than the cessation of the menses itself.

In summary, there is no evidence that women are at greater risk for depression during the menopausal period or that depressions occurring in this period have a distinct clinical pattern.

## Summary of the Endocrine Evidence

The pattern of the relationship of endocrine to clinical states is inconsistent. There is good evidence that premenstrual tension and use of oral contraceptives have an effect to increase rates, but these effects are probably of small magnitude. There is excellent evidence that the postpartum period does induce an increase in depression. Contrary to widely held views, there is good evidence that the menopause has no effect to increase rates of depression.

There is little evidence to relate these mood changes and clinical states to altered endocrine balance or specific hormones. However, it must be emphasized that no study could be located that correlated clinical state with female endocrines, utilizing modern endocrinological methods or sensitive quantitative hormonal assays. Here is an area for fruitful collaboration between endocrinology and psychiatry. While some portion of the sex differences in depression, probably during the child-rearing years, may be explained endocrinologically, this factor is not sufficient to account for the large differences.


# Psychosocial Explanations

Sociologists, psychologists, feminists, and others concerned with women have become increasingly occupied with explaining why more women become depressed. The conventional wisdom is that the long-standing disadvantaged social status of women has psychological consequences that are depressing, and the persistence of social status discrimination is proposed to explain the long-term trends of female preponderance in depression. In addition to this hypothesis based on social status differences, there are explanations offered based on psychoanalytic theories of female personality and historical changes associated with rapid social stress.

## Psychological Disadvantages of Women's Social Status

Various hypotheses have been proposed specifying the pathways whereby women's disadvantaged status might contribute to clinical depression. Our review of these hypotheses indicates two main proposed pathways. One emphasizes the low social status, legal, and economic discrimination of women; the other emphasizes women's internalization of role expectations, which results in a state of learned helplessness.

The first pathway, which we call the *social status hypothesis*, is widely accepted in the recent discussions on social discrimination against women. Many women find their situation depressing because the real social discriminations make it difficult for them to achieve mastery by direct action and self-assertion, further contributing to their psychological distress. Applied to depression, it is hypothesized that these inequities lead to legal and economic helplessness, dependency on others, chronically low self-esteem, low aspirations, and, ultimately, clinical depression.

The second pathway, which we call the *learned helplessness hypothesis*, proposes that socially conditioned, stereotypical images produce in women a cognitive set against assertion, which is reinforced by societal expectations. In this hypothesis, the classic "femininity" values are redefined as a variant of "learned helplessness," characteristic of depression (Seligman 1974). Young girls learn to be helpless during their socialization and thus develop a limited response repertoire when under stress. These self-images and expectations are internalized in childhood, so that the young girl comes to believe that the stereotype of femininity is expected, valued, and normative (Cole, Pennington, and Buckley, in press; Menaker 1974; Beck and Greenberg 1974; Maccoby and Jacklin 1975; Friedman, Richart, and Vande Wiele 1975; Keller 1974; Bart 1975; Chesler 1972; Gove and Tudor 1973; Broverman et al. 1970; Gove and Lester 1974).

## Marriage and Depression

In the few attempts to test this hypothesis that the high rates of depression are related to the disadvantages of the woman's social status, particular attention has been given to differential rates of mental illness among married and unmarried women. If this hypothesis is correct, marriage should be of greater disadvantage to the woman than to the man, since married women are likely to embody the traditional stereotyped role and should, therefore, have higher rates of depression. Gove, in particular, has focused his research on examining whether rates of mental illness among married women compare to those of other women and married men. Gove and associates found that the higher overall rates of many mental illnesses for females are largely accounted for by higher rates for married women. In each marital status category, single, divorced, and widowed women have lower rates of mental illness than men. He concludes that being married has a protective effect for males but a detrimental effect for females (Gove 1972, 1973). Similar conclusions were reached by Radloff

(1975) from data from a community survey of depressive symptoms conducted in Kansas City, Missouri, and Washington County, Maryland; by Porter in a study of depressive illness in a Surrey, England, general practice (Bachrach 1975); by a National Health Survey of psychological distress (Bachrach 1975); and by Manheimer and associates in a California survey of factors related to psychotropic drug use (Bachrach 1975).

Gove and others attribute the disadvantages of the married female to several factors: role restriction (most men occupy two roles, as household head and worker, and therefore have two sources of gratification whereas women have only one); housekeeping being frustrating and of low prestige; the unstructured role of housewife, allowing time for brooding; and even if the married woman works, her position is usually less favorable than a working man's.

Additional, but indirect, support for the hypothesized disadvantage of the female role comes from experimental research on boredom in humans. Ramsey (1974) presented evidence for the negative effect of boredom, which characterized the lives of many married women. In one experiment human subjects were exposed to a uniformly uninteresting environment; reaction time, sensory acuity, power of abstract reasoning, verbal ability, space visualization, and internal motivation to move, to daydream, or to think all decreased.

Boredom and role restriction may not be the major or only risk factors in marriage; other intervening factors such as family size and financial resources must also be taken into account. An elegant study of the interaction of some of these factors was recently reported by Brown, Bhrolchain, and Harris (1975). Using data collected from a community survey in London, they examined the relationship between psychosocial stress and subsequent affective disorders and found that working-class married women with young children living at home had the highest rates of depression. Subject to equivalent levels of stress, working-class women were five times more likely to become depressed than middle-class women. Four factors were found to contribute to this class difference: loss of a mother in childhood; three or more children under age fourteen living at home; absence of an intimate and confiding relationship with husband or boyfriend; lack of full- or part-time employment outside of home. The first three factors were more frequent among working-class women. Confidants other than spouse or boyfriend did not have a protective effect. Rather, the general levels of satisfaction and intimacy in the relationship with the husband or boyfriend and the amount of emotional support he gave the woman in her role was the important factor in preventing against depression in the face of life stress. Employment outside the home, it was suggested, provided a protective effect by alleviating

*183*

boredom, increasing self-esteem, improving economic circumstances, and increasing social contacts.

The association of poor interpersonal relations within the marriage and clinical depression is further supported by studies of depressed women during psychiatric treatment. The New Haven group found that marital discord was the most common event in the previous six months reported by depressed patients compared to normals (Paykel et al. 1969). Weissman and Paykel (1974) found that acutely depressed women as compared to matched normal controls reported considerably more problems in marital intimacy, especially ability to communicate with the spouse. Moreover, these marital problems often were enduring and did not completely subside with symptomatic remission of the acute depression. Furthermore, the data that unmarried women have lower rates of mental illness than unmarried men, but that married women have higher rates than married men, are cited as evidence that the excess of symptoms noted currently are not entirely due to biological factors intrinsic to being female, but are contributed to by the conflicts generated by the traditional female role.

## Psychoanalytic Explanations

Among mental health clinicians, a widely held explanation for the high rates of depression among women locates the cause in female intrapsychic conflicts. It is of interest that two parallel psychoanalytic theories related to this issue were developed in the early decades of this century but were not linked together until recently with the emergence of the feminist critique. These two theories are: (1) the psychoanalytic theory of female psychological development and (2) the psychodynamic theory of the psychogenesis of depression.

As regards the psychoanalytic theory of the psychology of women, Freud and others proposed that the personality of adult women, normal and neurotic, is characterized by narcissism, masochism, low self-esteem, dependency, and inhibited hostility as a consequence of the young girl's special resolution of her oedipal complex. As is widely known, this theory has been extensively criticized, recently by Kate Millett (1970) but earlier by Clara Thompson and Karen Horney.

In parallel with the theory of femininity, the classic psychodynamic theory of depression emphasized that individuals prone to depression were characterized by difficulties in close relationships, excess dependency, early childhood deprivation, excessive guilt, and tendency to turn hostility against themselves. The immediate precipitant for the overt clinical depression was hypothesized to be a loss, either actual or symbolic.

Interestingly, these two theories developed in parallel with each other for almost fifty years. Few psychoanalysts attempted to deal with the epidemiologic fact that women preponderate among depressives by linking the predisposition to depression among women to their presumed characteristic psychic conflicts related to childhood experiences of penis envy, narcissism, low self-esteem, dependency, etc.

Although these two theories in one form or another have been widely accepted among clinicians, empirical evidence in their support has been meager (Chodoff 1972).

## The Mental Health System's Contribution

The predominance of these psychodynamic views among clinicians has contributed to criticism of the mental health system by feminists. It is claimed that women find difficulty in freeing themselves from the feminine stereotype because it has been consistently reinforced in public by "experts" on child development and psychology.

Keller (1974), Kirsh (1974), and others state that psychotherapeutic treatment too often reinforces the negative self-image of women and perpetuates the problems of women who suffer symptoms from their life situation. Psychotherapy, it is claimed, promotes dependency by reinforcing stereotypical roles.

The most pertinent work supporting the existence of sex-role stereotype among mental health professionals is that of Broverman and associates (1970), who asked mental health clinicians what behaviors they considered healthy in men, women, and adults with sex unspecified. These researchers found a powerful negative assessment of women. The standard for a healthy adult was the same for a healthy man, but *not* for a healthy woman. Healthy women were seen as differing from healthy men in that the healthy women were supposed to be submissive, dependent, subjective, emotional, and easily hurt. Thus, a double standard of mental health was found that parallels the sex-role stereotypes in our society. Moreover, both sexes incorporated the better or worse aspects of the stereotypical role in their image of themselves and women tended to have a more negative self-concept than men (Broverman et al. 1970).

Feminist critics have been intense in their assertions that psychiatry is a male-oriented profession that has perpetuated male-dominated theories. Attempts have been made to encourage women to seek female therapists and to join groups for consciousness raising. Before these assertions can be accepted, the results of some recent studies on the attitudes and views of female mental health practitioners need to be appraised (Schwartz and Abramovitz 1975). In response to various case histories, male psychotherapists actually judged protocols of female patients less stringently than did female counselors. Male mental health professionals were not necessarily bound by their ideology to discriminate against women.

## Historical Change, Rising Expectations, and Changing Rates of Depression

Any attempt to understand the female preponderance in depression must explain both the long-term and the short-term trends. Conventional explanations have assumed that the female preponderance in depression has been a long-term trend. Most of the studies do support this, and the data that exist from the nineteenth century indicate a female preponderance of depression. These enduring trends can be interpreted as supporting either the biological or the social status theories.

On the other hand, recent evidence suggests short-term trends. There has been an increase in the rates of depression (Secunda et al. 1973), especially among young women, manifested by rising suicide attempt rates among young women (Weissman 1974) and by high attendance by women at psychiatric outpatient clinics (Zonana, Henisz, and Levine 1973). This has prompted speculation about the possible role of recent historical changes, especially the presumed pathogenic pressures of modern life.

Rising expectations, increased life events, separations, and loss of attachment bonds are all risk factors of depression that have been suggested as mechanisms by which social change can be psychic stressors (Klerman 1974). These stressors are proposed to have a greater impact on women because of their more vulnerable social position.

Rate increases in depression have been reported to have occurred during earlier periods of rapid social change. Schwab (1970) has pointed to possible historical parallels to the current era in late Elizabethan and early seventeenth-century England, when depression was described to have reached epidemic proportions. Similarly, Rosen (1959), citing the example of late eighteenth-century England, quotes Edgar Shepherd (1773) who, attributing the rise in mental illness to the "wear and tear of a civilization," speculated on the reasons for the differential prevalences of mental disorder between the sexes.

Rising expectations, access to new opportunities, and efforts to redress the social inequalities of women have been suggested as further explanation for the recent increase in depression among women. Depressions may occur not when things are at their worse, but when there is a possibility of improvement and a discrepancy between one's rising aspirations and the likelihood of fulfilling these wishes. The women's movement, governmental legislation, and efforts to improve educational and employment opportunities for women have created higher expectations. Social and economic achievement often have not kept pace with the promises, especially in a decreasing job market and where long-standing discriminatory practices perpetuate unequal opportunities.

These new role expectations may also create intrapsychic personal conflicts, particularly for those women involved in traditional family tasks but who also desire employment and recognition outside the family. While the women's movement has mainly involved middle- and upper-class and educated women, it has had an impact on women from other social classes where opportunities for work outside the home, management of money, dominance in the marriage, and so forth, may be crucial. Even for the educated and economically comfortable women, ambivalence and conflict continue about careers not conventionally seen as feminine (Horner 1972; Weissman et al. 1973). The documented increase in suicides and suicide attempts among women suggests that social changes may be exacting psychological costs for many young women. In this regard, Gove and Tudor (1973) note that communities that are extremely close-knit, stable, traditionally family-oriented, and culturally isolated have lower rates of mental illness in general, with the women having even lower rates than the men. Although support can be adduced for the hypothesis that participation in the women's movement is associated with psychological distress, it is unlikely that this is the major factor for the excess of depression among women. The differing rates substantially predate the women's movement. The short-term changes may be disruptive, but in the long term a new equilibrium may be reached and the high female rates may begin to decrease. Such a reduction in rate of depression would be indirect confirmation of the hypothesis that the female excess of depression is due to psychological disadvantages of the female role. As behaviors become more similar between the sexes, females may begin to employ modes of coping with stress that are similar to men. There are some indications that this may be occurring in that the female rates of alcoholism, suicide, and crime (predominantly male behaviors) have begun to rise. Alternatively, the sex ratios for depression could become equal because of an increase in depression among men due to the stress produced by the change in the roles of women and by the uncertainty of the male role. In this regard, it would be interesting to determine the rates of depression among educated and emancipated women. Similarly, are the rates of depression equalized between the sexes in cultural subgroups whose sex-role allocations are less rigid or nonconventional?

*Summary of the Psychosocial Explanations*

The most convincing evidence that social role plays an important role in the vulnerability of women to depression is the data that suggest that marriage has a protective effect for males but a detrimental effect for women. This supports the view that elements of the traditional female role may contribute to depression. Further understanding of social stress and its interactions with components of the female vulnerability in the traditional role is a promising area of research. This research would need to take into account intervening variables such as women's employment and the quality of the marriage. Any comprehensive theory, including biological ones proposed to account for the preponderance of depression among women, must explain both long-term rates and recent changes in rates.

# Conclusions

The male-female differences in rates of depression are real. The evidence in support of these differential rates is best established in Western industrialized societies. Further studies in non-Western countries, particularly in Africa and Asia, are necessary before any conclusions can be drawn as to the universality of this differential rate.

There is little doubt, however, that the sex differences found in depression are a promising lead that requires considerably broader-based inquiry in epidemiology. It is highly unlikely that any one of the explanations already described will be the sole factor accounting for the phenomena, or that all types of depressions will be associated with the same risk factors. As was shown, the explanations cross such a wide variety of disciplines that rarely are all interactions entertained by any one group of investigators. There has been an unfortunate tendency for fragmentation, so that the investigators in genetics, social psychology, or endocrinology are not specifically aware of attempts by their scientific colleagues to deal with similar phenomena. The purpose of this review has been to assess different positions and, hopefully, to guide further research. The salient areas include: (1) broad community-based epidemiologic studies that use consistent and operationalized diagnostic criteria and overcome the problem of reporting and response set; (2) further research on the genetics of depression, including the nonbipolar and less severe forms of the disorder, and examination of the rates of depression in first-degree relatives of depressed patients to see if they fit frequencies and patterns consistent with a particular mode of inheritance; (3) endocrine studies on the relationship between hormones and mood; (4) cross-cultural epidemiologic studies, using consistent and similar diagnostic criteria, that examine the suggestion that depression may be less frequent in females in nonindustrialized countries; (5) longitudinal studies of the help-seeking pattern and rates of depression of women who do not assume the traditional female roles, especially in countries where women have achieved increased emancipation; and (6) close surveillance of changes in rates by sex and marital status.

In summary, we have reviewed the evidence critically and believe that the sex differences in depression in Western society are, in fact, real and not an artifact of reporting or health care behavior.

REFERENCES

Adams, P. W., et al. 1973. Effect of pyridoxine hydrochloride (vitamin B₆) upon depression associated with oral contraception. *Lancet* 1:897–904.

Adelstein, A. M., et al. 1964. The epidemiology of mental illness in an English city: Inceptions recognized by Salford Psychiatric Services. *Social Psychiatry* 3:455–468.

Aitken, R. C. B., Buglass, D., and Kreitman, N. 1969. The changing pattern of attempted suicide in Edinburgh, 1962–1967. *British Journal of Preventive and Social Medicine* 23:111–115.

Asch, S. S., and Rubin, L. J. 1974. Postpartum reactions: Some unrecognized variations. *American Journal of Psychiatry* 131:870–874.

Bachrach, L. 1975. *Marital status and mental disorder: An analytical review*. Publication (ADM) 75–217. Washington, D. C.: U. S. Department of Health, Education, and Welfare.

Bardwick, J. M. 1974. The sex hormones, the central nervous system and affect variability in humans. In *Women in therapy*, ed. V. Frank and V. Burtle. New York: Brunner/Mazel.

Bart, P. 1970. Mother Portnoy's complaints. *Trans-Action*. November–December 1970, pp. 69–74.

————. 1975. Unalienating abortion, demystifying depression, and restoring rape victims. Paper presented to the American Psychiatric Association, Anaheim, California, 7 May 1975.

Bash, K. W., and Bash-Liechti, J. 1969. Studies on the epidemiology of neuropsychiatric disorders among the rural population of the province of Khuzestran, Iran. *Social Psychiatry* 4:137–143.

————. 1974. Studies on the epidemiology of neuropsychiatric disorders among the population of the city of Shiraz, Iran. *Social Psychiatry* 9:163–171.

Bazzoui, W. 1970. Affective disorders in Iraq. *British Journal of Psychiatry* 117:195–203.

Beck, A. T., and Greenberg, R. L. 1974. Cognitive therapy with depressed women. In *Women in therapy*, ed. V. Frank and V. Burtle. New York: Brunner/Mazel.

Benfari, R. C., et al. 1972. Some dimensions of psychoneurotic behavior in an urban sample. *Journal of Nervous and Mental Disease* 155:77–90.

Blumenthal, M. D. 1975. Measuring depressive symptomatology in a general population. *Archives of General Psychiatry* 32:971–978.

Bradburn, N., and Caplowitz, A. 1965. *Reports on happiness: A pilot study on four small towns.* Chicago: Aldine.

Bridges, P. K., and Koller, K. M. 1966. Attempted suicide: A comparative study. *Comprehensive Psychiatry* 7:240–247.

Broverman, I. K., et al. 1970. Sex-role stereotypes and clinical judgments of mental health. *Journal of Consulting and Clinical Psychology* 34:1–7. [Reprinted herein chapter 7.]

Brown, G., Bhrolchain, M., and Harris, T. 1975. Social class and psychiatric disturbance among women in an urban population. *Sociology* 9:225–254.

Brown, W. A., and Shereshefsky, P. 1972. Seven women: A prospective study of postpartum psychiatric disorders. *Psychiatry* 35:139–159.

Buchan, T. 1969. Depression in African patients. *South African Medical Journal* 43:1055–1058.

Butterworth, A. T. 1971. Depression associated with alcohol withdrawal: Imipramine therapy compared with placebo. *Quarterly Journal of Studies on Alcohol* 32:343–348.

Butts, H. F. 1969. Postpartum psychiatric problems. *Journal of the National Medical Association* 61:136–139.

Cannon, M., and Redick, R. 1973. *Differential utilization of psychiatric facilities by men and women: U.S. 1970.* Statistical note 81. Surveys and Reports Section, U.S. Department of Health, Education, and Welfare, June 1973.

Chesler, P. 1972. *Women and madness.* Garden City, N.Y.: Doubleday.

Chodoff, P. 1972. The depressive personality: A critical review. *Archives of General Psychiatry* 27:666–673.

Clancy, K., and Gove, W. 1974. Sex differences in mental illness: An analysis of response bias in self reports. *American Journal of Sociology* 80:205–216.

Clayton, P. J., Halikas, J. A., and Maurice, W. L. 1971. The bereavement of the widowed. *Diseases of the Nervous System* 32:597–604.

————. 1972. The depression of widowhood. *British Journal of Psychiatry* 120:71–77.

Clendenin, W. W., and Murphy, G. E. 1971. Wrist cutting: New epidemiological findings. *Archives of General Psychiatry* 25:465–469.

Cole, J. D., Pennington, B. F., and Buckley, H. H. In press. Effects of situational stress and sex roles on the attribution of psychological disorder. *Journal of Consulting and Clinical Psychology.*

Collomb, H., and Zwingelstein, J. 1961. Depressive states in an African community. In First Pan-African Psychiatric Conference Report, ed. J. Lamba. Adeokuta, Nigeria.

Cooper, M., Lemkau, P., and Tietze, C. 1942. Complaint of nervousness and the psychoneuroses: An epidemiological viewpoint. *American Journal of Orthopsychiatry* 12:214–223.

Crewel, F. 1967. Psychiatric differences in Ashkenazim and Sephardim. *Psychiatr Neurol Neurochir* 70:339–347.

Deykin, E. Y., et al. 1966. The empty nest: Psychosocial aspects of conflict between depressed women and their grown children. *American Journal of Psychiatry* 122:1422–1426.

Dube, K. C., and Kumar, N. 1973. An epidemiological study of manic-depressive psychosis. *Acta Psychiatrica Scandinavica* 49:691–697.

Dupont, A., Videbech, T., and Weeke, A. 1974. A cumulative national psychiatric register: Its structure and application. *Acta Psychiatrica Scandinavica* 50:161–173.

Duvall, H. J., Kramer, M., and Locke, B. Z. 1966. Psychoneuroses among first admissions to psychiatric facilities in Ohio, 1958–1961. *Community Mental Health Journal* 2:237–243.

Edwards, J. E., and Whitlock, F. A. 1968. Suicide and attempted suicide in Brisbane: I. *Medical Journal of Australia* 1:932–938.

Ellis, G. G., Comish, K. A., and Hewer, R. L. 1966. Attempted suicide in Leicester. *Practitioner* 196:557–561.

Engel, G. 1961. Is grief a disease? *Psychosomatic Medicine* 23:18–22.

Essen-Moller, E., and Hagnell, O. 1961. The frequency and risk of depression within a rural population in Scania. *Acta Psychiatrica Scandinavica* 162 (suppl):28–32.

Freeman, J. W., Ryan, C. A., and Beattie, R. R. 1970. Epidemiology of drug overdosage in Southern Tasmania. *Medical Journal of Australia* 57:1168–1172.

Friedman, R. C., Richart, R. M., and Vande Wiele, R. L., eds. 1975. *Sex differences in behavior.* New York: Wiley.

Gardner, E. A., et al. 1963. All psychiatric experience in a community. *Archives of General Psychiatry* 9:365–378.

Gershon, E. S., Dunner, D. L., and Goodwin, F. K. 1971. Toward a biology of affective disorders. *Archives of General Psychiatry.* 25:1–15.

Gershon, E. S., and Liebowitz, J. H. 1975. Sociocultural and demographic correlates of affective disorders in Jerusalem. *Journal of Psychiatric Research* 12:37–50.

Gershon, E. S., et al. In press. The inheritance of affective disorders: A review of data and of hypotheses. *Behavioral Genetics.*

Goetzl, U., et al. 1974. X linkage revisited. *Archives of General Psychiatry* 31:665–672.

Gold, N. 1966. Attempted suicide with chlorpromazine. *Medical Journal of Australia* 1:492–493.

Gomberg, E. S. 1974. Women and alcoholism. In *Women in therapy,* ed. V. Franks and V. Burtle. New York: Brunner/Mazel.

Goodwin, F. K., and Ebert, M. H. 1973. Lithium in mania: Clinical trials and controlled studies. In *Lithium: Its role in psychiatric research and treatment,* ed. S. Gershon and B. Shopsin. New York: Plenum.

Gordon, R., and Gordon, K. 1959. Social factors in the prediction and treatment of emotional disorders of pregnancy. *American Journal of Obstetrics and Gynecology* 77:1074–1083.

Gove, W. R. 1972. The relationship between sex roles, marital status, and mental illness. *Social Forces* 51:34–44.

––––––––. 1973. Sex, marital status, and morality. *American Journal of Sociology* 79:45–67.

––––––––, and Tudor, F. J. 1973. Adult sex roles and mental illness. *American Journal of Sociology* 78:812–835.

Gove, W. R., and Lester, B. J. 1974. Social position and self-evaluation: A reanalysis of the Yancy, Rigsby, and McCarthy data. *American Journal of Sociology* 79:1308–1314.

Hallstrom, T. 1973. *Mental disorder and sexuality in the climacteric.* Goteberg, Sweden: Orstadius Biktryckeri AB.

Helzer, J. E., and Winokur, G. 1974. A family interview study of male manic depressives. *Archives of General Psychiatry* 31:73–77.

Hershon, H. I. 1968. Attempted suicide in a largely rural area during an eight year period. *British Journal of Psychology.* 114:279–284.

Hetzel, B. S. 1971. The epidemiology of suicidal behavior in Australia. *Australia New Zealand Journal of Psychiatry* 5:156–166.

Hinkle, L. E., et al. 1960. II. An explanation of the relation between symptoms, disability, and serious illness in two homogeneous groups of men and women. *Journal of Public Health* 50:1327–1336.

Hirsh, J., Zauder, H. L., and Drolette, B. M. 1961. Suicide attempts with ingestants. *Archives of Environmental Health* 3:94–98.

Hogarty, G. E., and Katz, M. M. 1971. Norms of adjustment and social behavior. *Archives of General Psychiatry* 25:470–480.

Holmes, T. H., and Rahe, R. H. 1967. The social readjustment rating scale. *Journal of Psychosomatic Research* 11:213–218.

Horner, M. 1972. Towards an understanding of achievement related conflicts in women. *Journal of Social Issues* 28:157–175.

Horowitz, M. 1975. New directions in epidemiology. *Science* 188:850–851.

Hudgens, R., deCastro, M. I., and deZuniga, E. A. 1970. Psychiatric illness in a developing country: A clinical study. *American Journal of Psychiatry* 60:1788–1805.

Ianzito, B. M. 1970. Attempted suicide by drug ingestion. *Diseases of the Nervous System* 31:453–458.

Jacobson, S., and Tribe, P. 1972. Deliberate self-injury (attempted suicide) in patients admitted to hospital in Mid-Sussex. *British Journal of Psychiatry* 121:379–386.

James, I. P., Derham, S. P., and Scott-Orr, D. N. 1963. Attempted suicide: A study of 100 patients referred to a general hospital. *Medical Journal of Australia* 1:375–380.

Juel-Nielsen, N., and Stromgren, E. 1965. A five-year survey of a psychiatric service in a geographically delimited rural population given easy access to this service. *Comprehensive Psychiatry* 6:139–165.

Juel-Nielson, N., et al. 1961. Frequency of depressive states within geographically delimited population groups. *Acta Psychiatrica Scandinavica* 152:69–80.

Katz, M. M. 1971. The classification of depression: Normal, clinical and ethnocultural. In *Depression in the 70s*, ed. R. R. Fieve. The Hague: Excerpta Medica.

Keller, S. 1974. The female role: Constants and change. In *Women in therapy*, ed. V. Franks and V. Burtle. New York: Brunner/Mazel.

Kidd, K. K., Reich, T., and Kessler, S. 1973. A genetic analysis of stuttering suggesting a single major locus, abstracted. *Genetics* 74:s137.

Kielholz, P. 1959. Drug treatment of depressive states. *Canadian Psychiatric Association Journal* 4:S129–137.

Kirsh, B. 1974. Consciousness-raising groups as therapy for women. In *Women in therapy*, ed. V. Franks and V. Burtle. New York: Brunner/Mazel.

Klerman, G. L. 1974. Depression and adaptation. In *The psychology of depression: Contemporary theory and research*, ed. R. Friedman and M. Katz. Washington, D.C.: V. H. Winston.

———, and Barrett, J. E. 1973. The affective disorders: Clinical and epidemiological aspects. In *Lithium: Its role in psychiatric research and treatment*, ed. S. Gershon and B. Shopsin. New York: Plenum.

Klerman, G., and Izen, J. Forthcoming. The effects of grief and bereavement on physical health and general well being. In *Advances in psychosomatic medicine: Epidemiologic studies in psychosomatic medicine*, ed. F. Reicksman. Basel, Switzerland: S. Karger.

Kramer, M. 1969. Cross-national study of diagnosis of the mental disorders: Origin of the problem. *American Journal of Psychiatry* 125 (suppl 10):1–11.

Krupinski, J., Stoller, A., and Polke, P. 1966. Attempted suicides admitted to the mental health department, Victoria, Australia: A sociodemiological study. *International Journal of Social Psychiatry* 13:5–13.

Lehmann, H. E. 1971. The epidemiology of depressive disorders. In *Depression in the 70s*, ed., R. R. Fieve. The Hague: Excerpta Medica.

Leonhard, K. 1957. *Aufteilung der Endogenen Psychosen.* Berlin: Akademieverlag.

———, Korff, I., and Schulz, H. 1962. Die temperamente in den familien der monopolaren and bipolaren phasischen psychosen. *Psychiatr Neurol* 143:416–434.

Lilienfeld, A., Pedersen, E., and Dowd, J. E. 1967. *Cancer epidemiology: Methods of study.* Baltimore: Johns Hopkins Press.

Lindemann, E. 1944. The symptomatology and management of acute grief. *American Journal of Psychiatry* 101:141–148.

Maccoby, E. E., and Jacklin, C. N. 1975. *Psychology of sex differences.* Palo Alto, Calif.: Stanford University Press.

McKinley, S. M., and Jeffreys, M. 1974. The menopausal syndrome. *British Journal of Preventive Social Medicine* 28:108–115.

Martin, F. F. Brotherston, J. H. F., and Chave, S. P. W. 1957. *British Journal of Preventive Social Medicine* 11:196–202.

Mayfield, D. G. 1968. Psychopharmacology of alcohol: I. Affective change with intoxication, drinking, behavior and affective state. *Journal of Nervous and Mental Disease* 146:314–321.

———, and Coleman, L. L. 1968. Alcohol use and affective disorder. *Diseases of the Nervous System* 29:467–474.

Mazer, M. 1974. People in predicament: A study in psychiatric and psychosocial epidemiology. *Social Psychiatry* 9:85–90.

Menaker, E. 1974. The therapy of women in the light of psychoanalytic theory and the emergence of a new view. In *Women in therapy*, ed. V. Franks and V. Burtle. New York: Brunner/Mazel.

Miller, S. I., and Schoenfeld, L. S. 1971. Suicide attempt patterns among the Navajo Indians. *International Journal of Social Psychiatry* 17:180–193.

Millett, K. 1970. *Sexual Politics.* New York: Doubleday.

Modan, B., Nissenkorn, I., and Lewkowski, S. R. 1970. Comparative epidemiologic aspects of suicide and attempted suicide in Israel. *American Journal of Epidemiology* 91:393–399.

Neu, C., and DiMascio, A. 1974. Variations in the menstrual cycle. *Medical Aspects of Human Sexuality*, February 1974. Pp. 164–180.

Neugarten, B. 1968. *Middle age and aging.* Chicago: University of Chicago Press.

Odegaard, O. 1961. The epidemiology of depressive psychoses. *Acta Psychiatrica Scandinavica* 162:33–38.

Oliver, R. G., et al. 1971. The epidemiology of attempted suicide as seen in the casualty department, Alfred Hospital, Melbourne. *Medical Journal of Australia* 1:833–839.

Overall, J. E., et al. 1973. Drug treatment of anxiety and depression in detoxified alcoholic patients. *Archives of General Psychiatry* 29:218–221.

Paffenberger, R. S., and McCabe, L. J. 1966. The effect of obstetric and perinatal events on risk of mental illness in women of childbearing age. *American Journal of Public Health* 56:400–407.

Parkin, D., and Stengel, E. 1965. Incidence of suicidal attempts in an urban community. *British Medical Journal* 2:133–138.

Parry, H. J., et al. 1973. National patterns of psychotherapeutic drug use. *Archives of General Psychiatry* 28:769–783.

Patel, A. R., Roy, M., and Wilson, G. M. 1972. Self-poisoning and alcohol. *Lancet* 2:1099–1102.

Paykel, E. S., and Dienelt, M. N. 1971. Suicide attempts following acute depression. *Journal of Nervous and Mental Disease* 153:234–243.

Paykel, E. S., Prusoff, B. A., and Uhlenhuth, E. H. 1971. Scaling of life events. *Archives of General Psychiatry* 25:340–347.

Paykel, E. S., et al. 1969. Life events and depression: A controlled study. *Archives of General Psychiatry* 21:753–760.

Paykel, E. S., et al. 1974. Suicidal feelings in the general population: A prevalence study. *British Journal of Psychiatry* 124:1–10.

Pederson, A. M., Barry, D. J., and Babigian, H. M. 1972. Epidemiological considerations of psychotic depression. *Archives of General Psychiatry* 27:193–197.

Perris, C. 1966. A study of bipolar (manic-depressive) and unipolar recurrent depressive psychoses. *Acta Psychiatrica Scandinavica* 42 (suppl 194):1–89.

————. 1971. Abnormality on paternal and maternal sides: Observations in bipolar (manic-depressive) and unipolar depressive psychoses. *British Journal of Psychiatry* 118:207–210.

Pugh, T. F., et al. 1963. Rates of mental disease related to childbearing. *New England Journal of Medicine* 268:1224–1228.

Radloff, L. 1975. Sex differences in depression: The effects of occupation and marital status. *Sex Roles* 1:249–269.

Ramsey, E. R. 1974. Boredom: The most prevalent American disease. *Harpers* 249:12–22, November 1974.

Reich, L. H., Davies, R. K., and Himmelhoch, J. M. 1974. Excessive alcohol use in manic-depressive illness. *American Journal of Psychiatry* 131:83–86.

Reich, T., Clayton, P., and Winokur, G. 1969. Family history studies: V. The genetics of mania. *American Journal of Psychiatry* 125:1358–1369.

Rice, D. G., and Kepecs, J. G. 1970. Patient sex differences and MMPI changes—1958 to 1969. *Archives of General Psychiatry* 23:185–192.

Rin, H., Schooler, C., and Caudill, W. 1973. Symptomatology and hospitalization: Culture, social structure and psychopathology in Taiwan and Japan. *Journal of Nervous and Mental Disease* 157:296–312.

Roberts, J., and Hooper, D. 1969. The natural history of attempted suicide in Bristol. *British Journal of Medical Psychology* 42:303–312.

Rosen, B. F., Bahn, A. K., and Kramer, M. 1964. Demographic and diagnostic characteristics of psychiatric clinic outpatients in the U.S.A., 1961. *American Journal of Orthopsychiatry* 34:455–468.

Rosen, G. 1959. Social stress and mental disease from the 18th century to the present: Some origins of social psychiatry. *Milbank Memorial Fund Quarterly* 37:5–32.

Rosenberg, C. 1974. Drug maintenance in the outpatient treatment of chronic alcoholism. *Archives of General Psychiatry* 30:373–377.

Rosenthal, S. H. 1966. Changes in a population of hospitalized patients with affective disorders, 1945–1965. *American Journal of Psychiatry* 123:671–681.

————. 1968. The involutional depressive syndrome. *American Journal of Psychiatry* 124 (suppl):21–35.

Schwab, J. 1970. Coming in the 70's—An epidemic of depression. *Attitude* 1:2–6.

Schwab, J. J., McGinnis, N. H., and Warheit, G. J. 1973. Social psychiatric impairment: Racial comparisons. *American Journal of Psychiatry* 130:183–187.

Schwartz, J. M., and Abramovitz, S. I. 1975. Value-related effects on psychiatric judgment. *Archives of General Psychiatry* 32:1525–1529.

Sclare, A. B., and Hamilton, C. M. 1963. Attempted suicide in Glasgow. *British Journal of Psychiatry* 109:609–615.

Secunda, S., et al. 1973. *The depressive disorders.* Washington, D.C.: U.S. Department of Health, Education, and Welfare.

Seligman, M. E. 1974. Depression and learned helplessness. In *The psychology of depression: Contemporary theory and research,* ed. R. J. Friedman and M. M. Katz. Washington, D.C.: V. H. Winston.

Shader, R. I., and Ohly, J. I. 1970. Premenstrual tension, femininity, and sexual drive. *Medical Aspects of Human Sexuality,* April 1970. Pp. 42–49.

Siessi, I., Crocetti, G., and Spiro, H. 1974. Loneliness and dissatisfaction in a blue-collar population. *Archives of General Psychiatry* 30:261–265.

Silverman, C. 1968. *The epidemiology of depression.* Baltimore: Johns Hopkins Press.

Slater, E., and Cowie, V. 1971. *The genetics of mental disorders.* Oxford Monographs on Medical Genetics. London: Oxford University Press.

Smith, J. S., and Davison, K. 1971. Changes in the pattern of admissions for attempted suicide in Newcastle-upon-Tyne during the 1960s. *British Medical Journal* 4:412–415.

Sommer, T. 1973. The effect of menstruation on cognitive and perceptual-motor behavior: A review. *Psychosomatic Medicine* 35:515–534.

Sorenson, A., and Stromgren, E. 1961. Frequency of depressive states within geographically delimited population groups. *Acta Psychiatrica Scandinavia* 37:32–68.

Stengel, E. 1964. *Suicide and attempted suicide.* Middlesex, England: Penguin.

Tarnower, S. M., and Humphries, M. 1969. Depression: A recurring, genetic illness more common in females. *Diseases of the Nervous System* 30:601–604.

Teja, J., Aggarwal, A. K., and Narang, R. L. 1971. Depression across cultures. *British Journal of Psychiatry* 119:253–260.

Thuwe, I. 1974. Genetic factors in puerperal psychosis. *British Journal of Psychiatry* 125:378–385.

Tongyonk, J. 1971. Depression in Thailand in the perspective of comparative-transcultural psychiatry. *Journal of the Psychiatric Association of Thailand* 16:337–354.

Tonks, C. 1968. Premenstrual tension. *British Journal of Hospital Medicine* 7:383–387.

Torrey, E. F. 1973. Is schizophrenia universal? An open question. *Schizophrenia Bulletin* 7:53–59.

Tyndel, M. 1974. Psychiatric study of 1,000 alcoholic patients. *Canadian Psychiatric Association Journal* 19:21–24.

Uhlenhuth, E. H., and Paykel, E. S. 1973a. Symptom intensity and life events. *Archives of General Psychiatry* 28:473–477.

————. 1973b. Symptom configuration and life events. *Archives of General Psychiatry* 28:744–748.

Uhlenhuth, E. H., et al. 1974. Symptom intensity and life stress in the city. *Archives of General Psychiatry* 31:759–764.

Venkoba Rao, A. 1965. Attempted suicide (an analysis of 114 medical admissions into the Erskine Hospital, Madurai). *Indian Journal of Psychiatry* 7:253–264.

————. 1966. *Depression in Southern India.* International Congress Series 150. The Hague: Excerpta Medica.

————. 1970. A study of depression as prevalent in South India. *Transcultural Psychiatric Research* 7:166–168.

————. 1971. Suicide attempters in Madurai. *Journal of the Indian Medical Association* 57:278–284.

Weeke, A. B., et al. 1975. The incidence of depressive syndromes in a Danish county. *Acta Psychiatrica Scandinavia* 51:28–41.

Weissman, M. M. 1974. The epidemiology of suicide attempts. *Archives of General Psychiatry* 30:737–746.

Weissman, M. M., and Slaby, A. E. 1973. Oral contraceptives and psychiatric disturbance: Evidence from research. *British Journal of Psychiatry* 123:513–518.

Weissman, M. M., and Paykel, E. S. 1974. *The depressed woman: A study of social relationships.* Chicago: University of Chicago Press.

Weissman, M. M., Pincus, C., and Prusoff, B. 1975. Symptom patterns in depressed patients and depressed normals. *Journal of Nervous and Mental Disease* 160:15–23.

Weissman, M. M., et al. 1973a. The educated housewife: Mild depression and the search for work. *American Journal of Orthopsychiatry* 43:565–573.

Weissman, M. M., et al. 1973b. Suicide attempts in an urban community, 1955 and 1970. *Social Psychiatry* 8:82–91.

Weschler, H. 1961 Community growth, depressive disorders, and suicide. *American Journal of Sociology* 67:9–16.

Whitehead, P. C., Johnson, F. G., and Ferrence, R. 1973. Measuring the incidence of self-injury: Some methodological and design considerations. *American Journal of Orthopsychiatry* 43:142–148.

Winokur, G. 1972. Family history studies: VIII. "Secondary depression is alive and well, and . . ." *Diseases of the Nervous System* 33:94–99.

————. 1973. Depression in the menopause. *American Journal of Psychiatry* 130:92–93.

————, and Clayton, P. 1967a. Family history studies: I. Two types of affective disorders separated according to genetic and clinical factors. In *Recent advances in biological psychiatry,* ed. I. J. Wartis. New York: Plenum.

————. 1967b. Family history studies: II. Sex differences and alcoholism in primary affective illness. *British Journal of Psychiatry* 113:973–979.

————. 1968. Family history studies: IV. Comparison of male and female alcoholics. *Quarterly Journal of Studies on Alcohol* 29:885–891.

————, and Reich, T. 1969. *Manic depressive illness.* St. Louis: C.V. Mosby.

Winston, F. 1973. Oral contraceptives, pyridoxine, and depression. *American Journal of Psychiatry* 130:1217–1221.

Wren J. C., et al. 1974. Evaluation of lithium therapy in chronic alcoholism. *Clinical Medicine* 81:33–36.

Yalom, I. D., et al. 1968. Postpartum blues syndrome. *Archives of General Psychiatry* 18:16–27.

Zonana, H., Henisz, J., and Levine, M. 1973. Psychiatric emergency service a decade later. *Psychiatry and Medicine* 4:273–290.

# 14

# The Hysterical Personality: A "Woman's Disease"

## HARRIET E. LERNER

It is widely recognized that the diagnosis of hysteria is infrequently applied to male patients and very commonly to female ones. A paper by Robins and associates (1952) suggests that hysteria in men is extremely rare, if indeed it occurs at all, and there is general agreement that an initial diagnosis of hysteria in males is somewhat of a clinical anomaly (Berger 1971). It should be noted that grave hysterical symptoms (e.g., conversion reactions, dissociative phenomena) have been observed in male patients, but these individuals tend not to manifest the type of cognitive and personality organization that is characteristic of the hysterical individual (Chodoff and Lyons 1958). It is especially in regard to the hysterical personality, character, or "style" that the male patient is a rarity, and it is in this sense that the word hysteria will be used in the present paper.

In explaining the preponderance of female hysterics, psychoanalytic theorists have focused on differences in preoedipal and oedipal developmental tasks that the two sexes must master (Zetzel 1968). It is my opinion, however, that theories of libidinal development offer only a partial explanation of the sex difference in hysteria and that social and cultural factors play a major role. Although the importance of such extrapsychic factors has not been fully appreciated, neither have these

The author wishes to thank Dr. Leonard Horwitz and Dr. Paul Pruyser of the Menninger Foundation for their helpful suggestions and criticisms.

factors been entirely ignored. Marmor (1953), for example, has noted that the traits characteristic of the hysterical personality are feminine ones and are thus more acceptable in women than in men. Chodoff and Lyons (1958) have commented that the hysterical personality "is a picture of women in the words of men and . . . what the description sounds like amounts to a caricature of femininity!" But beyond noting that the concept of hysteria involves a description of traditionally feminine qualities, the theoretical and diagnostic significance of this observation has not been explored.

The plan of the present paper is first to review the diagnostic indications and behavioral characteristics of this patient group in order to outline with some specificity the criteria that will lead to a diagnosis of hysterical personality. Next it will be demonstrated how a girl's immediate social environment puts enormous pressure on her to develop a style of cognition and personality that will lend itself to this diagnosis on the clinical test battery or diagnostic interview. In this regard, it will be noted how the ego-constricting effects of a feminine socialization process may too readily be confused with the effects of massive repression. Finally, certain conceptual tangles that have resulted from the overlap between the hysterical character and the feminine character will be outlined.

## Diagnostic Indications of Hysteria

Although psychological tests and diagnostic interviews may be informative in determining the nature of psychosexual development, neuroses are diagnosed primarily in terms of their characteristic defense mechanisms and styles of adaptation (Rappaport, Gill, and Schafer 1968). The diagnosis of hysteria is frequently inferred from excessive use of repression, with only secondary concern for the hypothetical reconstruction of the fate of the Oedipus complex and the interplay of various drives (Rappaport, Gill, and Schafer 1968; Schafer 1954). Because a repressive style of defense has clearly defined effects on cognition and personality, the diagnostic assessment of hysteria should present no special problems. As Shapiro (1965) points out, "In our current understanding of the operation of various neuroses . . . the picture of hysterical neurosis is relatively clear-cut . . . and, among neuroses, none has been more definitely or clearly associated with the operation of a specific defense mechanism than has hysteria with repression" (p. 108).

In regard to the diagnostic test indications of hysteria, Schafer (1948) has made the following summary statement:

This diagnostic term [hysteria] covers those persons who rigidly and pervasively resort to the defense of repression in their efforts to cope with their impulses and the demands of the world about them. Excessive reliance on this defense appears to hamper the development of broad intellectual, cultural interests, to impair the ability for independent and creative thinking, and to make for striking emotional lability and naiveté. One or another of these characteristics will color a large part of the thought processes elicited by the test items. (p. 32)

An example of a hysterical mode of responding on the Rorschach test is offered by Shapiro (1965):

Where the compulsive person may list and actively organize relations between varieties of botanical or marine specimens, the hysterical person says, "A beautiful bouquet" or "It's Paris! . . . like in the French Line posters." (p. 112)

Purportedly as a result of pervasive reliance on repression, the cognitive style of the hysteric is a dramatically nonintellectual one characterized by a lack of concern with intellectual achievement, productivity, and mastery (Shapiro 1965; Schafer 1948). There is little investment in abstract and complex ideas, a flippant disregard for factual and technical information, and an inability to perform effectively on tasks demanding these skills. Independent and critical thinking is impaired, and the general mode of cognition is fuzzy, global, and undifferentiated. Hunch and intuition may replace active, effortful thought and concentration. Because intellectual activity and mastery are continuously avoided, the hysteric's thinking has been described as naive, egocentric, unreflective, affect-laden, and cliché-ridden.

In contrast to their lack of a technical–factual apprehension of the world, hysterical persons have a heightened involvement in interpersonal relationships and a direct and active engagement with the human world (Shapiro 1965; Easser and Lesser 1965). It is not unusual for these people to do superior work on a task of social judgment on the Wechsler intelligence test or to demonstrate an excellent understanding of conventional and proper social behavior. Similarly, hysterics are often vivid and likable social companions, and personality descriptions of them frequently include such adjectives as buoyant, sprightly, lively, colorful, and feminine (Easser and Lesser 1965).

At the same time, one sees dependent, demanding behavior and a heightened concern with receiving approval, admiration, and attention from others (Easser and Lesser 1965). Flirtatious and seductive behavior is frequently apparent, often accompanied by complaints of frigidity. Although Freud (1931) did not conceptualize a hysterical personality, he did suggest that the "erotic" type of person who is largely preoccupied with loving and being loved is predisposed to the development of hysteria. It should be noted that the romanticism of hysterics, although pervasive, is also shallow and superficial. Shapiro (1965) has described the Prince-Charming-will-come-and-everything-will-turn-out-all-right view of life that is characteristic of these individuals, and a naively romantic view of life is frequently conspicuous in Thematic Apperception Test (TAT) productions.

Emotional lability is a term that is ubiquitous in descriptions of hysterical individuals, and it speaks to their inability to adequately modulate affective experience as well as to a stylistic tendency to utilize feelings rather than thought in dealing with crises and conflicts (Schafer 1954; Shapiro 1965). In keeping with an emotional and somewhat impulsive approach to life, childlike features are noteworthy. Easser and Lesser (1965) have described the little-girl qualities of a group of hysterical patients and noted that their families regarded these women as juvenile, dependent, cute, and lovable, one patient keeping the nickname Baby until marriage. In regard to diagnostic testing, Schafer (1954) has noted that hysterics' childlike qualities make them appear like "babes in the woods" or "bunnies" (p. 197).

## Hysterical Character Versus Feminine Character

When I was teaching a graduate seminar in diagnostic testing, one student responded to the above summary with the confused protest, "But you're not describing a neurosis—you're just describing a woman!" There is, indeed, much truth to the observation that the diagnostic indicators of hysteria are very much in keeping with the media presentation of the female sex. We are all familiar with the stereotype of the giggling, blushing woman whose head is filled with Hollywood romance and trivia, who prefers people to ideas, who is unconcerned with technical or abstract intellectual problems, who prefers hunch and intuition to effortful concentration, who is childlike and dependent in the presence of men, who is emotional and impulsive in her behavior. In fact, many of the diagnostic indicators of hysteria are related to essential aspects of femininity and female attractiveness.

One might speculate that the female sex en masse suffers from a hysterical personality and that the media are merely portraying woman's true nature. Even so, a vicious cycle is created by the fact that the role models for young girls are almost exclusively hysterical ones. (I cannot, for example, recall seeing a television program in which a group of women struggled effectively to solve a technical or scientific problem, while the men concerned themselves with social trivialities.) But the problem is not simply one of role models, for if we examine societal notions of masculinity and femininity we find that the pressures on women to adopt a hysterical style are intense and continue throughout a lifetime. I wish to examine this point in greater detail.

It is widely believed that a woman should find her true sense of fulfillment (and identity) in wifehood and motherhood (Chesler 1972). From her earliest years the young girl is taught to spend her major efforts in preparation for these roles, and the task of learning to be attractive to men, with the hope of eventually finding a husband, frequently becomes consuming. There is little doubt that this state of affairs may be conducive to the development of good social judgment and a heightened sensitivity to pleasing (as well as manipulating) other people. Colloquial language suggesting that women catch, snare, or hook their men speaks to the notion that highly developed social skills are an important asset for females. There is much truth to Firestone's (1970) statement that "more real brilliance goes into a one-hour coed telephone dialogue about men than into that same coed's four years of college study" (p. 21).

But if the cultivation of female attractiveness is conducive to the development of social skills, it is inimical to intellectual development. Females are taught in a variety of ways that an independent and masterful intellectual style is unattractive, and women who develop an aggressive and critical intellect are often considered castrating or masculine. A growing body of literature documents the remorseless stifling of a young girl's creative intelligence as she learns to be feminine and attractive to men (Lynn 1972; Lerner 1973). Since femininity is based on a model of intellectual dependence and docility, it is not surprising that women tend to develop what appears to be a hysterical mode of cognition. It is perhaps more surprising that certain women escape it.

In this regard, an examination of popular teenage literature is especially enlightening. I have recently surveyed a wide selection of books and magazines written for teenage girls on issues of femininity and popularity, from which it is evident that girls are encouraged to adopt a mode of personality and intellect in keeping with the hysterical characteristics described earlier. The recurring theme in this literature is that girls must be clever enough to catch a man, but never to outsmart him, or as Arlene Dahl (1965) puts it in her book *Always Ask a Man*, a woman must "never let her competence compete with her femininity" (p. 8). Young women are encouraged to be intellectually docile and to cultivate childlike dependent qualities and social manipulative skills. In many ways the "feminine character" and the "hysterical character" are synonymous. A comment by Kreps (1970) on the traditional female role is relevant:

She is exhorted to play out the role of Cinderella, expecting fortune and happiness from some Prince Charming, rather than to venture out by herself. Be pretty, be pleasant, use mouthwash and deodorant, never have an intellectual thought, and Prince Charming will sweep you off to his castle where you will live happily ever after. (p. 98)

In contrast, the qualities cherished in masculinity are not in keeping with the hysterical picture. For the male sex, intellectual achievement, production, efficiency, and assertion are important values, and an interest in abstract and technical problems is encouraged. Male heroes chart the stars, cure diseases, create masterpieces, and actively build, shape, and destroy the world around them. Male children are encouraged to be logical (rather than intuitive), practical (rather than romantic), intellectually aggressive and forceful (rather than passive and conforming), self-reliant (rather than dependent and childlike), and intellectual (rather than emotional). Interpersonal sensitivity is not considered a priority for men, and a certain amount of social brutality, self-interest, and toughness may be considered attractive.

It seems then that the diagnostic indications of the hysterical character as presently conceptualized define a style of cognition and personality that runs dramatically counter to traditional notions of masculinity. Should a male begin to develop a hysterical style, he will be discouraged from giving expression to it. Our current notions of masculine attractiveness do not allow for expressions of childishness, naïveté, fearfulness, dependency, intellectual ineptness, or emotional (rather than intellectual) wisdom. For this reason a diagnosis of hysteria in a male patient involves very serious difficulties in sexual identification. This has indeed been borne out by the clinical literature (Berger 1971; Chodoff and Lyons 1958).

## Hysterical Personality: Repression or Role Pressure

The literature regarding the hysterical personality is perhaps more replete with contradictions than any other (Easser and Lesser 1965), and the confusion between femininity and hysteria has undoubtedly contributed much to this state of affairs. For one thing, it has too readily been assumed that the style of personality and cognition described earlier results from defensive reliance on repression against the potential awareness of or expression of instinctual impulses and their derivatives. I suggest, however, that the same diagnostic indications may instead reflect a lifelong history of suppression (rather than repression) of intellectual skills and the adoption of a personality style that has been most linked to success in social situations. For certain women it may indeed by anxiety-arousing to relinquish a flirtatious, childlike, sexualized style of interacting and assume instead a critical, independent, and intellectually "phallic" one. However, their anxiety may be related to a long socialization process regarding what is acceptable and desirable feminine behavior. When the diagnosis of hysteria reflects the effect of role pressures on women, the individuals so labeled will constitute a markedly heterogeneous group, for an exaggerated feminine style may exist with varying types and degrees of pathology. It is not surprising then that there are many clinical reports of women who initially "look hysterical" and later prove to be characterized by far more serious emotional disturbances (Zetzel 1968; Easser and Lesser 1965).

I also have some doubt regarding the widely held notion that women rely more heavily on the defensive use of repression than do men. Rather, an additional theory suggests that the socialization of women leads to a style of personality and cognition that in its observable outcome is not dissimilar to the effect of repression. A related point of considerable importance is that men who do in fact rely on a repressive style of defense will tend not to be diagnosed as hysterical, for our present stereotype of the hysterical character runs dramatically counter to the male socialization process and to acceptable masculine behavior. Of interest is Berger's (1971) statement that "the proclamation that hysteria can occur in males appears to be an attempt to appear objective. One gets the impression that a male hysteric is one who behaves 'like a woman.' "

## Recent Trends in Diagnosis

Recent trends in diagnosis of the hysterical personality have gravely compounded the problems that are posed by the overlapping of the feminine character and the hysterical character. Certain diagnosticians are suggesting that we move away from psychodynamics and etiologic speculations and confine ourselves to surface manifestations and observable behavior in diagnosing this particular character disorder

(Chodoff and Lyons 1958; Lazare and Klerman 1968). This descriptive approach is epitomized by the work of Chodoff and Lyons (1958), who have consulted a representative group of publications and abstracted certain behavioral characteristics of hysterics that were agreed upon by most or all of the authors involved. They have suggested that six behavioral characteristics (e.g., vanity, sexual provocativeness, dependency) be generally agreed criteria for a diagnosis of hysterical personality and that underlying factors be ignored. Similarly, Lazare and Klerman (1968) state that hysteria can be defined and diagnosed only by searching the literature for clinical descriptions of these patients and abstracting out the common elements. These authors have defined hysteria by seven traits: egocentricity, exhibitionism, emotionalism, dependency, provocativeness, fear of sexuality, suggestibility.

If this descriptive approach is adopted, then we may do well to discard the diagnostic category of hysterical personality (with all its rich structural and dynamic implications) and simply speak of a feminine personality style that does not purport to be more than a description of certain female characteristics in the eyes of male diagnosticians. It is puzzling to me that Chodoff and Lyons (1958), who champion this descriptive approach, have at the same time concluded their discussion of the historical development of hysteria with the following comment:

A situation analogous to the one described might be imagined if women psychiatrists spent some generations coolly and rather inimically observing the less attractive foibles of males, and then put them together as the manifestations of a kind of personality characteristic of men!

What is perhaps more puzzling is that psychiatry still remains mystified over the sex difference in hysteria and has invoked some rather esoteric theorizing in the service of partial explanation.

## Where Do We Go from Here?

In a recent paper Berger (1971) suggests that the hysterical personality does not exist in the patient, but rather in the observer. He states that the best definition of hysteria is "behavior or symptoms which arouse unconscious sexual feelings in the observer," and he argues that this clinical entity should be defined and understood in terms of its countertransference effect. While I do not support Berger's proposed conceptualization of hysteria, I do believe there is a danger that the hysterical personality will be reduced to a description of a particular type of feminine behavior that has a certain effect on a male observer. To define hysteria in this manner, however, seems like a singularly nihilistic approach that is hardly a step forward from the descriptive method described earlier. Hopefully we can adopt a more constructive approach and apply ourselves to untangling the confusions that presently exist between the hysterical character and the feminine character.

Clearly this task is not a simple one, particularly in an interview situation where the diagnostician is male and the evaluation procedure is limited in time. For one must ask: Is the patient's dependent and childlike behavior the regressive defense against genital fears of the hysteric or is it a learned aspect of feminine behavior? Is emotional lability a defensive operation reinforcing repression or is it rather the patient's attempt to be a vivid and exciting companion? Are sexual provocativeness and flirtatiousness reflective of oedipal conflicts or are they the behavior of a woman who feels she has little else to offer the male psychiatrist? These distinctions, which are not mutually exclusive, may be difficult ones to make in a brief diagnostic workup, and the stereotype of the hysterical female is so deeply ingrained that women are often carelessly and prematurely diagnosed.

In the midst of this conceptual muddle it is easy to lose sight of the fact that a rather impressive body of clinical and theoretical literature has accumulated for this group of patients. Kernberg's (1967, 1970) summary of the hysterical personality, for example, is very much in keeping with the work of other psychoanalytic theorists who have noted that hysterical patients (as compared to those with lower-level character disorders) manifest better integration of ego and superego, a predominance of genital oedipal conflicts over oral and pregenital ones (although oral conflicts are often present), and a wider range of conflict-free ego functions and structures. Further, there is an absence of severe pathology of internalized object relations, and the hysterical individual is capable of fairly deep and stable relationships involving a variety of affective responses. Repression is the main defensive operation of the ego, and there is little instinctual infiltration into defensive character traits. We may note that none of the above diagnostic criteria is inherently feminine as opposed to masculine. The challenge for diagnosticians is to refine their ability to evaluate the above structural and genetic–dynamic considerations in a manner that will extricate them from the present confusion between hysteria and femininity. To do this we must put minimal diagnostic emphasis on the behavioral indices that overlap with traditional aspects of femininity, and we must also attempt to identify the observable effects of a repressive style of defense in men. In this regard, psychological testing can be an invaluable research and diagnostic tool, especially if clinical psychologists apply themselves to identifying formal test indications of hysteria that are independent of feminine and masculine role stereotypes.

In discussing the hysterical personality, I have not directed attention to the variety of clinical symptoms that have been associated with severe hysterical disorders, such as dissociative phenomena and disordered thinking. It seems evident that such symptomatology is not the result of cultural pressures, and in these cases the conceptual tangle posed by the overlapping of femininity and hysteria hardly seems relevant. In fact, such grave symptoms are by no means limited to female patients, and here at the Menninger Clinic we have seen male patients in hysterical fits, complete with arching backs, Charcot-style. But the diagnosis of hysterical personality is very infrequently made on the basis of such symptomatology. Rather, it typically refers to the style of personality and cognitive organization described earlier, and it is here that the failure to account for social factors has led to a lack of conceptual clarity and diagnostic precision. Hopefully the present paper will encourage clinicians to reformulate the diagnostic criteria of the hysterical personality so that this entity does not in fact become what Chodoff and Lyons have labeled "a caricature of femininity."

REFERENCES

Berger, D. M. 1971. Hysteria: In search of the animus. *Comprehensive Psychiatry* 12:277.
Chesler, P. 1972. *Women and madness.* Garden City, N.Y.: Doubleday.
Chodoff, P., and Lyons, H. 1958. Hysteria, the hysterical personality and "hysterical conversion." *American Journal of Psychiatry* 114: 734–740.
Dahl, A. 1965. *Always ask a man.* Englewood Cliffs, N.J.: Prentice-Hall.
Easser, B. R., and Lesser, S. R. 1965. Hysterical personality: A re-evaluation. *Psychoanalytic Quarterly* 34:390–405.
Firestone, S. 1970. Love. In *Notes from the second year: Women's liberation,* ed. S. Firestone. New York: Radical Feminism.
Freud, S. 1931. Libidinal types. In *The standard edition of the complete psychological works of Sigmund Freud,* ed. J. Strachey, vol. 21. London: Hogarth Press.
Kernberg, O. 1967. Borderline personality organization. *Journal of the American Psychoanalytic Association* 15:641–685.
―――――― . 1970. A psychoanalytic classification of character pathology. *Journal of the American Psychoanalytic Association* 18:800.
Kreps, B. 1970. The new feminist analysis. In *Notes from the second year: Women's liberation,* ed. S. Firestone. New York: Radical Feminism.
Lazare, A., and Klerman, G. L. 1968. Hysteria and depression: The frequency and significance of hysterical personality features in hospitalized depressed women. *American Journal of Psychiatry* 124:48–56.
Lerner, H. 1973. Women's liberation. *Menninger Perspective* 4:10.

Lynn, D. B. 1972. Determinants of intellectual growth in women. *University of Chicago Review* 80:161.

Marmor, J. 1953. Orality in the hysterical personality. *Journal of the American Psychoanalytic Association* 1:656–671.

Rappaport, D., Gill, M., and Schafer, R. 1968. *Diagnostic psychological testing.* New York: International Universities Press.

Robins, I., et al. 1952. Hysteria in men. *New England Journal of Medicine* 246:677–685.

Schafer, R. 1948. *Clinical application of psychological tests.* New York: International Universities Press.

———. 1954. *Psychoanalytic interpretation in Rorschach testing.* New York: Grune & Stratton.

Shapiro, D. 1965. *Neurotic styles.* New York: Basic Books.

Zetzel, E. 1968. The so called good hysteric. *International Journal of Psychoanalysis* 49:256–260.

# 15

## Madness in Women

### HELEN B. LEWIS

### Depression

To fall ill of depression is more often women's lot than men's. Depression in everyday life is, as everyone knows, a temporary experience that can range from mild dejection to profound despair. Depression becomes an illness when the person cannot throw off a state of deep sadness that paralyzes the self. Even then, the symptoms of depression are understandable to the lay person. As one expert puts it: "Affective disorders . . . strike the student of psychiatry for the facility with which their clinical concepts are grasped even by the beginner" (Arieti 1974, p. 449).

The only other major mental illness that claims more women than men is hysteria. "Hysteria" is a more recondite label than "depression," but its symptoms are equally mundane. In one kind, called "conversion hysteria," the person is afflicted with physical symptoms with no discernible organic base. The other kind of hysteria involves massive anxiety, sometimes to the point of "fugue" or amnesia. In other instances the anxiety takes a specific form and the person is phobic about some particular thing: for example, snakes, heights, airplane travel, and so forth. Such cases are given the name "anxiety hysteria" or "phobia." In other cases a massive anxiety occurs "for no reason," and the person who has once experienced it dreads a recurrence.

In this section we shall be concerned mainly with women's proneness to depression. Discussion of women's proneness to hysteria is being postponed to the next section. But before concentrating on depression, it is useful to consider what depression and hysteria have in common besides claiming more women than men as victims. For one thing, symptoms of depression and hysteria often occur together. The experience of unutterable sadness feels literally like a weight on one's insides, so depressed patients often worry that something is wrong with them physically. Individuals plagued with unaccountable ("hysterical") pain or body symptoms tend to be depressed because of their inability to shake their symptoms. There are thus few cases of depression without increased physical awareness of the self, or of hysteria without some depression because the anxiety is so debilitating.

The close link between depression and body symptoms is well known. One authority describes for us how easy it is to be led astray by the depressive patient whose complaints are often about "physical pain, a feeling of discomfort, digestive difficulties, lack of appetite and insomnia . . . [which seem like] simple psychosomatic dysfunctions" (Arieti 1974, p. 456). The link between hysteria and depression is less well known. A psychiatric stereotype about hystericals is that they are *not* depressed, but rather show a *"la belle indifférence"* to their illness. Hystericals are often described as dramatic, exhibitionistic, narcissistic, and seductive. As we shall see later, these stereotypes about hystericals were developed by male psychiatrists who have had a particularly hard time understanding women. Hystericals do suffer depression over their physical symptoms or their uncontrollable anxiety.

In both depression and hysteria, a plague has descended upon the experience of the *self*, literally including the body. The self dominates the patient's awareness, with a resulting magnification of body sensations. It is interesting that depression and hysteria do not involve dramatic or bizarre disturbances of sexual identity. The symptoms of depression and hysteria are exaggerations of ordinary feelings: Sadness, ache or pain, or anxiety (fear) are all everyday experiences. In this respect, women's more frequent mental illnesses are very different from the sexual perversions, obsessional neurosis, and schizophrenia—men's more frequent illnesses. These latter illnesses sometimes involve elaborate transformations of the self and bizarre ideas of transforming the world. Underlying this bizarreness is a profound loss of emotional connection to other people. Women's illnesses are not bizarre, only an exaggeration of ordinary feelings. Women's more frequent mental illnesses are cast in common human terms, perhaps because women have not given up their affectionateness, only devalued it. Paradoxically, women, who are trained to be "selfless"—to be more concerned with others than with themselves—fall victim to mental illness in which the malfunctioning *self* takes over their lives.

Although the self is carrying this burden of bad experience, it is also clear that both depressives and hystericals are very much and very openly involved with significant other people. Often the patient is accompanied to the doctor by a devoted husband, parent, or child. Often something has gone wrong with a close relationship and the depressive or hysterical patient is trying to cope with the resulting disappointment. Symptoms arise that could have the effect of disturbing the significant other's well-being. For this the patient feels guilty. The observer (and often the patient) cannot escape the idea that the symptoms are "put on" to plague the other person. It is easy for an observer (and sometimes even for the patient) to see that the plague that has descended upon the self is some kind of protest against the self's close involvement with an "important" other person. So depressive and hysterical patients, while they are coping with some awful experience being borne by the *self*, are also defending themselves against the fact that their symptoms are transparently "other-connected."

Of course, men also fall ill of depression and the hysterias. But as we shall see, considering why women are more frequently afflicted in these ways helps to illuminate one kind of insoluable conflict between affectionateness and exploitative values. Women are not pushed by cultural expectations to give up their affectionateness. On the contrary, as childbearers they are expected to cultivate it, only to discover that affectionateness is actually devalued by our society, however much it is hypocritically praised. Women thus become ashamed of their own loving feelings, which actually do not count for much in the marketplace. And, by a process that is not altogether clear, the chronic state of shame is transformed into depressive illness or into one of the hysterias.

The statistics that tell the story of women's greater proneness to depression and the hysterias are themselves fascinating. For one thing, they come from many different sources; sometimes they were entirely unexpected by the researchers themselves. For another thing, the statistics all speak the same answer. Usually, when one is trying to evaluate the evidence on a particular point, some studies give one answer, while others say the opposite. It becomes a hard job to evaluate whether the evidence says yes when on the other hand it is saying no. But in the case of women suffering from depression and the hysterias more often than men, all the statistics say yes. Studies that say that women are more "people-oriented" than men are also practically unanimous, as are the studies that say that men are more aggressive than women. Women's greater proneness to depression and the hysterias has a great deal to do with their greater degree of people-orientation and their lesser aggressiveness as well as with their greater shame-proneness.

Let us turn now to depressive illness and look first at the statistics on its frequency in men and women. One authority has estimated that about 70 percent of patients with manic-depressive psychosis are women (Arieti 1974, p. 456).

More precise evidence comes from statistics on "first admissions to state hospitals." (See table 15-1.) These figures apply more to poor people who cannot afford private hospitals or private individual treatment. They apply to quite sick people since people with less severe symptoms of depression can usually stay out of hospitals. The statistics show that, from 1910 on, year by year, women were at least twice as often afflicted with depression as men (Malzberg 1940, 1959).

The reader will note that there has been a decline in the diagnosis of manic-depressive psychosis over the years. This decline is not understood: A guess is that it reflects an increasing tendency in recent

TABLE 15-1

*First Admissions to New York
State Hospitals 1910–50
Per 100,000 Population for
Manic-Depressive Psychosis\**
*(Adapted from B. Malzberg.)*

| Year | Men | Women | Total |
|------|-----|-------|-------|
| 1910 | 4.5 | 7.4 | 6.0 |
| 1912 | 5.7 | 8.6 | 7.1 |
| 1914 | 5.7 | 8.4 | 7.0 |
| 1916 | 5.8 | 9.9 | 7.8 |
| 1918 | 6.6 | 12.0 | 9.3 |
| 1920 | 6.4 | 12.1 | 9.2 |
| 1922 | 6.8 | 12.1 | 9.4 |
| 1924 | 6.7 | 11.8 | 9.2 |
| 1926 | 6.7 | 11.6 | 9.2 |
| 1928 | 7.1 | 12.3 | 9.7 |
| 1930 | 7.4 | 11.7 | 9.5 |
| 1932 | 8.3 | 12.4 | 10.4 |
| 1934 | 7.6 | 12.2 | 9.9 |
| 1936 | 5.8 | 10.4 | 8.2 |
| 1938 | 5.0 | 9.8 | 7.4 |
| 1940 | 4.4 | 8.2 | 6.3 |
| 1942 | 3.7 | 6.8 | 5.3 |
| 1944 | 2.7 | 7.0 | 4.9 |
| 1946 | 2.6 | 6.0 | 4.4 |
| 1948 | 2.4 | 4.3 | 3.3 |
| 1950 | 1.9 | 3.1 | 2.5 |

\* Rates are based on the average annual number of first admissions during three years: that is, the rate for 1910 is the average for 1909–1911, inclusive.

years to diagnose schizophrenia in cases of severe mental disturbance.

Evidence that women are more often depressed than men comes not only from statistics on first admissions to state hospitals but from private, middle-class hospitals as well (Tarnower and Humphries 1969; Chesler 1972). Middle-class women, as well as poor women, are more prone to depression than men. In fact, women's greater tendency to depression is so pervasive that they are more often depressed whatever the official diagnosis with which they are admitted to a mental hospital. Not only among patients officially diagnosed as depressed, but among all patients in mental hospitals, whatever the diagnosis, the women are more depressed than the men (Zigler and Phillips 1960; Beck 1967; Blaser, Löw, and Schäublin 1968).

Not only in hospitals, but among less sick patients in outpatient clinics as well, women come to psychiatry for depression more often than men. Women are more depressed than men in both rural and urban areas. A study of 400 new cases seen between 1963 and 1967 in an outpatient clinic in rural England showed that women were more often depressed than men (Mitchell-Heggs 1971). A study of more than 2,000 patients who applied for treatment to a midtown New York mental health center also showed that women patients came for depression more often than men patients.[1]

When a finding is unexpected because it comes as an incidental result of looking into some other problem, it is even more dramatic and to some extent more persuasive because it cannot be the product of the investigators' unconscious bias in favor of their own hypothesis. One investigator conducted a follow-up study of 500 juvenile delinquents who grew to adulthood. She came upon the finding that depression was the more frequent diagnosis for the women who had been juvenile delinquents than for the men who had. She also found that depression occurred more often in women than in men among the "normals," that is, nondelinquent cases she had assembled as her "controls" (Robins 1966).

A very recent dissertation at Yale asked the question whether the depressive experience is different for blacks and whites. In a population of "normal" residents of New Haven, with socioeconomic factors controlled, there were no significant differences between blacks and whites in their report of depressive experience. Across both blacks and whites, however, the women, as usual, were more depressed than the men.[2] Thus whether the question is studied among the poor or middle class, in hospitals, outpatient clinics, or among "normals," in cities or in rural areas, women are more prone to depression than men.

1. Jeanne Safer, Postgraduate Center for Mental Health, New York City, personal communication.
2. Robert Steele, personal communication.

Among depressed men and women, the women report that they *feel* worse than the men (Sedivec 1969). Another study observed the frequency of episodes of actual crying among hospitalized depressed patients. About one-third of the women patients cried; *none* of the men patients was ever seen to cry (Davis, Lamberti, and Ajans 1969). Even when their feelings have got so out of hand as to warrant hospitalization for depression, men still have less overt feeling than women! Women are thus not only more often depressed than men but more deeply depressed.

These findings have often been interpreted to be the results of some hormonal factors that are different for women than they are for men. Women's tendency to go into a depression at menopause is cited as an example of the hormonal factor. The relatively good success that psychiatry has recently had in treating depression with mood-elevating and mood-stabilizing drugs is cited as further evidence of a chemical factor. Many women (and others) who hear this factor mentioned are likely to bristle, because it is often cited in an effort to deny the importance of psychological conflicts. The idea is that women are helpless victims of their hereditary hormones. But if we disregard this false quarrel between heredity and internalized social forces, there may indeed be a hormonal factor in women's falling ill of depression. This hormonal factor would only add an extra factor to an already existing set of psychological conflicts.

Let us look for a moment at what psychological effects hormones are known to have. Estrogen, the hormone females have more of than men is, among other things, a "gentling" secretion. Estrogen fosters maternal behavior, that is, caring for another life. Androgen, the hormone males have more of, is an "activity-inducing" secretion. Depression (and the hysterias) are mental illnesses that more often afflict the less aggressive people, women, who are "gentled" not only by their hormones but by cultural expectations that they absorb at their mother's breast.

Now that we have looked at some statistics on depression in men and women, let us look at what depression is like as an experience. Depression is an experiential state like the grief or sadness that ordinarily accompanies bereavement. There is a loss of interest in the world, a sense of dullness about the self, and a feeling as if there were an intolerable "weight" on the self. But depression is unlike real bereavement because there has not been any visible or tangible loss. There is no good reason in reality why the patient should be feeling as if someone he or she loved had died. No one knows this better than the patient, but the knowledge is useless against the weight of depressed feeling that descends upon the self. When the state is so overwhelming that the patient cannot manage to hold on to a wish for life, we call it psychotic depression and suggest hospitalization. But even when depression is acute, we understand the quality if not the intensity of suffering.

One of the most faithful investigators of depressive illness, Dr. Aaron Beck, has developed a Depression Inventory, a questionnaire that tries to measure the state (1967). The topics covered under the headings of the questionnaire give us a vivid picture of what assorted miseries are assembled to plague the self of a patient in depression. Here is a list of the headings and a brief sample of the statements under one heading. The other headings also have five appropriate statements under each.

A. Sadness

I do not feel sad.
I feel blue or sad.
I am blue or sad all the time and I can't snap out of it.
I am so sad or unhappy that it is quite painful.
I am so sad or unhappy that I can't stand it.

B. Pessimism
C. Sense of Failure
D. Dissatisfaction
E. Guilt
F. Expectation of Punishment
G. Self-Dislike
H. Self-Accusations
I. Suicidal Ideas
J. Crying
K. Irritability
L. Social Withdrawal
M. Indecisiveness
N. Body-Image Change
O. Work Retardation
P. Insomnia
Q. Fatiguability
R. Loss of Appetite
S. Weight Loss
T. Body Worries
U. Loss of Libido (Sex Interest)

These are twenty-one assorted ways of being miserable, readily understandable to us all, that descend much more frequently on women than on men. And in a comparable group of men and women patients, women get a higher score on Beck's Depression Inventory (1967).

What is hard for the observer of depression to take is that there is no visible reason for it and that the depressed state does not seem to go away. Depressive people are monotonous to us in their misery (as well as to themselves). They evoke our scorn for their endless suffering and thus put us into a state of guilt toward them—which in turn makes us tend to be impatient with them. So we suppress as long as we can the impulse to tell them to "snap out of it," or "stop pitying themselves," and to "get interested in *something*." The depressive patient of course agrees with us, because he or she also sees no reason to be depressed and would desperately like to get interested in something. So the depressive patient is all the more ashamed of failure to "straighten up and fly right," and becomes even more depressed and more ashamed of being depressed, in a vicious cycle.

Before they fall ill, depressed patients are generally affectionate, warmhearted people who have little difficulty in being close to people. If anything, they tend to be overinvolved with other people rather than detached from them. Above all, their feelings are easily evoked, so that although they may be rather shy of initiating relationships, once the initial barrier is overcome, it is easy for them to form close friendships. Depressive people do little to give offense to others; correspondingly, they are relatively unaccustomed to take up arms when they are put down. Depressive people are noted for their lack of aggressivity. One study, for example, showed that a group of paranoid women projected more hostility than a comparable group of depressed women (Caine 1960). Another study showed that depressive women patients are much less hostile verbally than nondepressed "controls" (Friedman 1970).

When they fall ill, depressed patients have no idea what has made such a change in their customary well-being. That they have fallen into a state of unremitting sadness as if they had suffered some profound loss makes sense to them descriptively. But who or what has been lost? Little children often deal with the loss of a beloved person by yelling and screaming about it sometimes for days on end. Only after they become aware that their rage is ineffectual do they settle into a depressed mood, which also expresses their helplessness. Their rage is directed exactly against the person who is beloved and who has deserted them. Very often these children begin to behave as if they were somehow defective or unworthy (Bowlby 1969). They are no longer enraged, or even grieving, but rather they seem easily made ashamed of themselves. Depressed patients are in a state of chronic grief and are also easily humiliated, as if they were bereaved children. But why should they more often be women than men?

The theory has been put forward that depressed patients may actually have suffered the childhood loss of a parent and are still, because of their emotional scars, subject to a renewal of their childhood grief in adulthood. Ever since Freud's fundamental discovery that much of mental illness is of emotional origin and based in childhood experience, it has been taken for granted that such a profound emotional upheaval as losing a parent in childhood would increase the chances of later mental illness. But have women depressives actually suffered more often from childhood bereavement than other kinds of psychiatric patients? Or than other adults from the same general environment who do not become ill? Or than men?

The answer to these questions requires putting together the results of several studies. In general, psychiatric patients (of all kinds) have suffered more often from bereavement in childhood than ordinary individuals living in the same region who do not fall ill (Dennehy 1966). And women psychiatric patients (all diagnoses) have suffered childhood bereavement even more often than men (Birtchnell 1971). This same study showed that there were more women psychiatric patients who had lost their mothers and been left with younger siblings to take care of than there were men patients in the same circumstance. And, in fact, there is some evidence that *depressed* women are more likely to have suffered from being orphaned before adulthood than depressed men (Beck 1967). Losing a parent in childhood does make women more vulnerable to later illness than men. Depressives who seem to be mourning a loss may actually be reliving a childhood bereavement—and the chances that this is so are even greater for women than for men.

The most important dynamics of the depressive illness thus come from an internalized conflict resulting from closeness to other people. Women are even more vulnerable to bereavement in the course of growing up than men. Their greater vulnerability to bereavement fits with the fact that they have a self that attaches itself to mother during infancy earlier than boy infants. But women are scorned, and scorn themselves, for this emotional closeness that makes them emotionally dependent.

Insight into the dynamics of depression becomes clearer if we go with a therapist through some of the steps in treating a depressed patient. When we first meet them depressed patients are obviously very dependent on the people around them for support. This "dependency" of depressed patients is not just a widespread clinical observation. In fact, depressed patients are more likely than other psychiatric patients to be field-dependent perceivers (Lewis 1971). And field-dependent patients are likely to be shame prone (Lewis 1971). Depressed patients are in a chronic state of shame proneness, if only because they are depressed and helpless to get out of it. But although they are in a humiliated state—a state, incidentally, usually accompanied by quick fury—they are not at all *conscious* of being angry at anyone. Of course, they are angry at their own helplessness, but what sense is there in being angry at anyone for that? Of course, they are envious of the close persons who are not depressed, but what justice is there in hating them? Especially when they are just the people most needed and most helpful?

One of the first discoveries to be made by these patients in therapy is that their envy of the important "other" people in their lives who are "healthy" is perfectly natural, in fact, an inescapable feeling. And the humiliated fury—the hatred—that is the inevitable accompaniment of envy is also inescapable. At the same time, however, humiliated fury—shame fury—is an unacceptable, in fact, a demeaning state. To hate someone you need and love not only involves you in a profound disloyalty, but it is a state of fury allowable only to helpless children, not to self-sufficient adults. Humiliated fury is a feeling trap; it feeds upon itself because it is such an unacceptable and "illogical" feeling that it cannot be expressed.

The release of these feelings within the confines of therapy sessions is very relieving. Release usually comes with the understanding that the person who is in a humiliated fury is an inevitable "loser" compared to the "calm," unhumiliated therapist. This puts some distance between the state of humiliated fury and the sufferer. The solution to a depressive state, however, is not just the freedom to feel and express humiliated fury without shame. Some understanding is also needed that proneness to humiliated fury itself does not occur without one's having embraced a very high standard of affectionateness and closeness to others: a most oppressive ego-ideal.

This ego-ideal of affectionateness and closeness not only makes it intolerable to hate and envy others, but it makes it difficult always to keep the internal image of the self distinct from the image of the other. To love someone deeply means that he or she becomes a "part" of yourself, as we all know when we actually suffer bereavement. It takes some time and is the work of mourning during actual bereavement to divest oneself of a lost person, to stop feeling lost without his (or her) presence. In neurotic or psychotic depression, the person needs to stop feeling lost without the important (living) person with whom he or she is "overinvolved," and on whom the ego-ideal has been projected.

Women in our society are trained to devote their lives to others. The biological and cultural expectation that they will be mothers makes it appear natural that they should spend their lives devoted to others— husband and children. But our society also scorns people who are not self-sufficient and independent of others. Women thus learn early that they should be ashamed of the very set of qualities that are particularly theirs. Ironically, at the same time, they are constantly threatened by the prospect that if they are not affectionate enough and as close and loving to others as they ought to be, they will have failed in their own and others' eyes. They are ashamed of themselves if they are close to others and guilty and ashamed of themselves if they are not.

Within this profound conflict, the chances for throttled humiliated fury are great. Any disturbance in their relationship to others—either the cooling of husband's ardor in marriage, or the failure to get a husband, or the arrival of a new baby that seems to demand more nurturance than can be given, or the departure of a child who was once so close—any of these circumstances in a woman's life can throw her into a state of unconscious fury at the way her self has been torn. But at whom is she furious—herself or the beloved, admired other with whom she is so close? This is the same confusion she faced when first she experienced rivalrous hatred of her mother. Then, also, it was hard to separate the hatred of herself from the hatred of her first caretaker, in emulation of whom her self had been developed. In adulthood, humiliated fury is deflected by women from the "other," who is its "unjust" target, back upon the self. The resulting experience is depression.

## The Hysterias

"Hysteria," writes an authority on the subject, "is a term loosely applied to a wide variety of sensory, motor, and psychic disturbances which may appear in the absence of any known organic pathology" (Abse 1974, p. 155). I have chosen to speak of the "hysterias" precisely because the range of symptoms covered is so broad. In the hysterias there can be body dysfunction or a dissociated state of consciousness, such as "fugue," amnesia, or some acute, unbearable, irrational anxiety. When there is a body dysfunction without known organic base, the patient is diagnosed as having "conversion hysteria." The assumption is that an underlying emotional conflict that threatens anxiety has been "converted" into a physical symptom. These range in severity from ordinary pains and aches to paralyses, convulsions, or even blindness.

Dissociated states of consciousness are another kind of flight from anxiety, and they are given the following diagnosis: hysteria, dissociated state. These are the most dramatic of the hysterias, as, for example, the patient described so vividly in *The Three Faces of Eve* (Thigpen and Cleckley 1957). These cases are relatively rare—too rare for statistics. The general impression is they occur more often among women, except when there are men on the battlefield.

When there is strong, conscious anxiety about encountering some specific event, the patient is said to have "anxiety hysteria" (Freud's term), for which the more usual term now is phobia. Anxiety hysteria also refers to cases of sudden, acute anxiety states that come unexpectedly "out of the blue" and for no apparent reason. In cases where there is more generalized, pervasive anxiety, without specific content, the patient is said to be suffering from anxiety neurosis, a category in-between hysteria and obsessional neurosis. The hysterias thus cover physical conversions, dissociated states, phobias, and other acute anxiety states. Although the overt anxiety states and phobias are often sharply distinguished diagnostically from hysteria, I prefer to classify them with the other hysterias, not only because anxiety is so prominent, but because their dynamics involve the other-connected super-ego mode, shame.

Why hysterical symptoms should be to the fore of some people's experience, while depression is to the fore in others', is a puzzling question. There is some specific connection between forbidden sexual excitement and hysterical symptoms. Depressive patients seem to have no interest at all in sex, at least while they are depressed, unlike hysterical patients whose struggles against forbidden sexuality are often pathetically clear to an observer, as well as to themselves.

Hysterical symptoms were the symptoms that first aroused the attention of psychiatrists during the nineteenth century. The history of the hysterias is, in fact, a reminder that the era when people were treated as if possessed of the devil was not so long ago. The crazy people who showed hysterical symptoms were mostly women. Aldous Huxley's *The Devils of Loudon* (1971) is a magnificent reconstruction of the terrible suffering of hysterical women accused as witches and the terrible fate of the priest who had trifled with them sexually. A very recent study of the persecution of witches during the fifteenth to the seventeenth centuries tells us, furthermore, that the fantasy of a clandestine society of women practicing "wholly abominable" rites originated not in the minds of the poor and unlettered, but with the learned and those in authority: "monks, bishops and popes, great nobles, orthodox theologians and inquisitors and magistrates." Needless to say, these authorities were all men (Cohn 1975).

The early modern psychiatrists, who were the enlightened French, approached hysterical symptoms as if they sprang from natural causes instead of the machinations of witchcraft. They had made the discovery that they could make the symptoms disappear at least temporarily by putting the patients into a hypnotic trance. The fact that the symptoms were so malleable led some psychiatrists (who were, of course, all men) to believe that the symptoms were "put on" (an attitude still with us today). Others accepted that the symptoms were not under voluntary control, but hypothesized that they were the result of some kind of failure in the level of brain functioning (Janet 1920).

Because so many of the patients suffering from hysteria were women, it was also supposed that their symptoms had something to do with the functioning of the uterus, and accordingly the term "hysteria" was derived from the Greek word for the uterus, *hysteron*. "Hysteria" thus reflects a tradition of observations about the connection between mental illness and frustrated sexuality going back to ancient Greece. Plato (91 B.C.) for example, writes about the "lust for generation" as a cause of mental illness. He writes:

In the male the genitals are mutinous and self-willed, and, like a beast deaf to the voice of reason, attempt to have all their will because of their frenzied passion; while in women what is called the matrix or womb, a living creature within them longing for childbearing, when remaining unfruitful long beyond its proper time, becomes discontented and, wandering about through the body, closes up the passages of the breath, and obstructs respiration, thus provoking extreme disorientation, and all sorts of other diseases (from *Timaeus*).

Plato is here clearly describing the symptoms of anxiety, which ancient theories linked to frustrated sexuality.

In more modern times, it was the French psychiatrist Charcot, Freud's teacher, who believed that hysterical symptoms have something to do with women's unfulfilled and deeply forbidden sexual desires. It took Freud's courage, however, to say that openly and by saying it, to put forward the basic assumption that hysteria as well as other mental illness is of emotional origin.

Most often the body dysfunction in conversion hysteria is not so extreme as a seizure, blindness, or paralysis. Rather there is some plaguing pain or discomfort in some (vaguely localized) part of the body. The pain does not correspond to the pattern it ought to take if it followed the anatomy of the nervous system. It is not totally incapacitating but is nevertheless a decided interference with the patient's ability to follow normal activities mostly because, as it appears to the observer, she is so preoccupied with her symptoms. The patient is also likely to be quite depressed at having such a puzzling symptom. Confronted with a "sad sack" patient, who is emotionally involved in a set of peculiar physical symptoms that need not incapacitate her but do, the physician-observer is likely to develop the angry suspicion that he is the victim of a "put-on." As one medical authority, speaking gently, put it, "the term 'hysterical' is often used as a defamatory colloquialism and . . . this usage is to a varying extent carried over into the medical sphere" (Abse 1974, p. 106).

In recent years the knowledge that physical illness often accompanies times of emotional stress has made the term "psychosomatic illness" household words. This term is used to cover not only physical illnesses with a possible emotional component, like asthma or ulcers, but hypochondriacal symptoms and any illness that physicians cannot diagnose. Thus the understanding of hysteria, which increased our knowledge of a close tie between emotional stress and physical illness has, paradoxically, tended to obscure the fact that hysterical symptoms need to be taken seriously and that they require therapy.

It also sometimes happens that today's patients have to insist on a thorough physical examination because their illness, if at all mysterious, is all too easy to diagnose as "psychosomatic." And this diagnosis, although an elegant term, is often used hypocritically, as a fancy way of saying that the patient is faking. It is a diagnosis that carries with it a powerful threat of "put-down." And since hysterical symptoms more often afflict women than men, women are more often caught in this bind. On the one hand, they have a physical symptom that is worrisome and debilitating; on the other hand, it threatens them with the mortification of being thought a fake. As to the latter possibility, the women themselves are not always sure.

There is an amusing instance of sexism in the history of the way hysteria has figured in psychoanalytic theory. This example of sexism has to do with the concept that different mental illnesses represent fixations at different levels of infantile sexuality. An important part of Freud's theory was the idea that sexual life begins in infancy and develops on different levels as the person matures. So, early in life when nursing at its mother's breast is most important, infantile sexuality is at the oral level; later on, when toilet training is to the fore, sexuality is anal, and still later, when children identify their own sexual organs, sexuality is more specifically sexual or "phallic." The earlier the level of infantile sexuality at which the mentally ill person is fixated in his mental illness—oral, anal, or "phallic"—the more "regressed" or severely ill he or she is thought to be.

It was clear early on that hysterical mental illness has a strong overt phallic sexual component in its dynamics. On this basis, then, it represents a later level of personal development than obsessional neurosis, which is clearly "anal" in its dynamics. But somehow the statement that women's more frequent mental illness is at a "higher level" than men's is hardly to be found in psychoanalytic literature. This in spite of the fact that obsessional neurosis is a more stubborn illness than hysteria, which often disappears for long periods of time. On the contrary, hysteria is said to reflect an orally regressed personality (Marmor 1954).

The way the concept of hysterical personality has been used in psychiatry is another instance of sexism. One subcategory of hysteria in the official American Psychiatric Association nomenclature is called "hysterical personality, histrionic style." Such personalities are, in the words of a pair of experts, "vain, egocentric individuals, displaying labile and excitable but shallow affectivity. Their attention-seeking and histrionic behavior may encompass lying and pseudolgia phantastica. They are conscious of sex and appear provocative. . . . Histrionic character features occur frequently . . . among women. They are considered feminine by our societal standard . . . (Brody and Sata 1967).

The reader can surely discern the heavy disapproval between the lines of this psychiatric personality description. And indeed such malformed characters do occur among women (as well as men). The point is that if such people come to psychiatrists for help in reforming their characters, then the psychiatric description ought at least to allow points for self-awareness. If not, and, as is more likely, they come for conversion hysteria or some other painful symptoms, then the defamatory personality description hardly augurs a sympathetic listener in the psychiatrist.

Amusingly enough, one study of conversion hystericals demonstrated that their symptoms did *not* occur within the context of a hysterical personality (Chodoff and Lyons 1958). Careful examination of case material suggested that conversion hysteria occurred in a variety of personalities, a finding that ran contrary to Wilhelm Reich's (and other post-Freudians') view that hysterical symptoms were reflections of hysterical personality (Reich 1972). (Freud himself was careful not to confuse hysterical personality with hysterical symptom.) Another careful study of hysterical personalities in psychoanalysis failed to observe the "provocative, seductive, exhibitionistic" behavior commonly ascribed to these patients (Easser and Lesser 1965). A sensible solution might have been to drop the category of hysterical personality at least from the official American Psychiatric Association list. Instead, the diagnosis of hysterical personality continues to be "promiscuously used" (Easser and Lesser 1965). The myth of Eve's wickedness dies hard, especially in male-dominated psychiatry.

An important study by Pauline Bart (1968) tells us, further, that it is poor and ignorant women who are more likely to be diagnosed hysterical more often than their more affluent sisters. Hollingshead and Redlich (in Janet 1920) had observed that hysteria occurs more often in the lowest social class; the poor expect "pills and needles" as their treatment. Following up on this observation by Hollingshead and Redlich, Bart studied women between the ages of forty and fifty-nine who were admitted to the *neurological* service of UCLA Neuropsychiatric Institute and who emerged with a psychiatric diagnosis, usually hysteria. These women tended to come from poor, rural areas where, as Bart puts it, they did not have available the "psychiatric vocabulary of discomfort." They experienced themselves as physically ill—their vocabulary of psychic distress. A comparable group of women who entered the psychiatric service, that is, volunteering psychiatric reasons for their distress, were of higher social status and urban residents.

Bart's results remind us that, in the nineteenth century, sexual mores were cruelly restrictive against women of all classes, so that even the most cultivated and educated women were liable to hysteria. In modern times sexual enlightenment is more widespread; hysteria has become the lot of poor, uneducated women. And it is these women who have the least sexual pleasure.

Bart's study also makes it easier to understand how conversion hystericals originally came to be thought of as displaying *"la belle indifférence"* to their own sufferings. In the absence of a "psychiatric vocabulary," women patients in the last century naively described physical symptoms without the slightest awareness of their symbolic meaning. Even though a "spasm" might perfectly describe motions suggestive of intercourse, the women were not aware of what they were "saying." Even though Janet, who first used the term *"la belle indifférence,"* specifically described it as a façade covering profound anxiety, this part of Janet's description tended to be lost. A sexist climate in psychiatry transmuted *"la belle indifférence"* into a sign that the women really did not suffer.

Hysteria, women's more frequent illness, is an inarticulate body language in which women protest their emotional distress. More direct expression of their protest would involve them in too much anxiety. Because their symptoms are so "primitive" and so transparently emotional in origin, women patients are likely to evoke the scorn of their more intellectual, articulate (male) psychiatrists. "It is remarkable" says one authority, "with what contempt these [hysterical] symptoms may be treated by some physicians . . ." (Abse 1974, p. 174).

It is instructive to note in this connection that in contrast to hysteria, obsessional neurosis is a much more solidly defined and well-understood illness. It has been suggested that "intellectualized, scientific, methodologically bound investigators have been more at ease in the study of patients characterized by rigid, intellectual and definitive ego maneuvers, namely obsessionals" (Easser and Lesser 1965, p. 391). To which we might add that *male* psychiatrists may find it easier to understand patients more like themselves.

Now let us briefly look at the statistics on the hysterias. At a general hospital in Wisconsin during 1963 about 1 percent of the patients were discharged with a diagnosis of conversion hysteria. This is the diagnosis that is given when no organic basis can be found for the patient's complaints. Within this group of patients there were four women for every one man (Lewis and Berman 1965). In an outpatient clinic in New York, a survey showed women diagnosed as "hysterical" significantly more often than men.[3] Not only in our own country, but in a recent study in India, a preponderance of women was found among those patients diagnosed as hysterical (Dube 1968).

Another kind of evidence that makes the same point comes from making a comparison between the number of "medical symptoms" and the number of actual physical illnesses. If more "medical symptoms" are complained of by patients than there are physical illnesses diagnosed, the difference represents "conversion symptoms." In two separate studies done in general hospitals, women reported more "medical symptoms" than men, although the two sexes were equal in the number of physical illnesses (Brodman et al. 1953; Phillips and Segal 1969). The inference drawn by the researchers is that the greater number of complaints by women represents a greater frequency of conversion hysteria. In another study, the number of "medical symptoms" was compared to the number of "psychiatric symptoms" reported by the two sexes (Matarazzo, Matarazzo, and Saslow 1961). In general, the number of psychiatric symptoms varies in the same way as the number of "medical symptoms." When people are complaining of pains and aches they are also likely to be complaining of anxiety or worry or depression. But in this study, women did *not* report more psychiatric symptoms than men, only more *medical* symptoms. Again, the researchers drew the inference that the women were reporting more conversion-hysterical symptoms.

With respect to anxiety hysteria, the evidence is also that women are more prone to it than men. A recent study done at a famous mental hospital in New York (Hillside) found that anxiety attacks were the reason why 4 percent of the patients had been admitted. These anxiety attacks were so terrifying that the patients had become afraid to leave their homes for fear of a recurrence. And there was a decided preponderance of women among these terrified patients (Mendel and Klein 1969).

One investigator, reporting from England, tells us that two-thirds of agoraphobic patients seen by psychiatrists are women (Marks 1969). An epidemiological study done in the United States also showed that women suffer from anxiety states about twice as often as men (Leighton et al. 1963). These figures coincide with others that show women reporting more symptoms of nervousness, nightmares, and other anxiety experiences than men. Among "normal" people, women also report more anxiety than men (Maccoby and Jacklin 1974).

Freud's first insight into mental illness was his realization that hys-

3. Jeanne Safer, Postgraduate Center for Mental Health, New York City, personal communication.

terical symptoms are the products of unconscious conflicts. He was able to unravel the salient sexual experiences which had been kept unconscious by guilt and shame. "Strangulated affect," as he called it, was released and the symptoms relieved. The conflicts were over sexual longings—longings to be loved, of which the women patients were dreadfully ashamed.

Lucy R., an English governess in a Viennese widower's household, was another of Freud's hysterical patients. She suffered from chronic nose and throat symptoms, and from experiences of smelling cigar smoke that she thought were hallucinatory. She was also quite depressed. Freud offered her the interpretation that these symptoms resulted from her being in love with her employer. He suggested that she had had the secret hope of marrying him. Lucy answered in her usual "laconic" fashion: "Yes, I think that's true." When Freud asked her why she hadn't told him this before, she said: "I didn't know, or rather I didn't want to know. I wanted to drive it out of my head and not think of it again. I believe latterly I have succeeded. . . ." "Were you ashamed of loving a man?" Freud asked. "No," came the answer from Lucy, "I'm not unreasonably prudish. We are not responsible for our feelings. But," she went on, "it was so distressing to me because he is my employer and I am in service and live in his house. I don't feel the same independence toward him that I could toward anyone else. I am a poor girl and he is a rich man. People would laugh at me if they had any idea of it."

So Lucy tells us explicitly that she was not "responsible" for, that is, not *guilty* of her sexual thoughts or feelings and that she was not "unreasonably prudish." In her own good judgment, therefore, she ought to have been able to put the feelings she had out of her head. And she thought she had succeeded in forcing her feelings underground. But there came instead a chronic running nose and cough and the cigar smell and an awful feeling of depression. In some way that still is not exactly clear, the feelings she had were converted into physical sensations which gave her no rest. Lucy R. is a classic case of conversion hysteria.

That she was ashamed of her unrequited love, even though she didn't think she ought to be, is a perfect description of her conflict. That she had no "good reason" to feel humiliated fury toward her employer is also the force that would automatically throttle her humiliated fury at her unrequited love. What was left in her experience was depression and a running nose—as if she had been crying. And— you've guessed it—the smell of cigar smoke, which, although she was not aware of it, was a symbol of the man she loved. Women are all too frequently ashamed of themselves if they are in a fury, if, that is, they are *not* loving enough, and at the same time ashamed of themselves if they *are* in love.

This profound conflict is all the more difficult to grasp because it is not "rational" and because the person is so deeply involved in loving. Hysterical patients are said to have "love-craving" characters (Fitzgerald 1948) or "erotic" personalities (Freud). This is pretty much what women are trained to expect themselves to be. When they fall ill of it, especially from disappointments in loving, they themselves do not feel entitled to anger, because their "demands" were "inappropriate" in their own eyes. Their humiliated fury is repressed and transformed into the body language of self-hatred.

Since it is repressed humiliated fury which is causing the trouble, the answer often held out to women patients is that they should become more aggressive. The implication is that if they did, they would be less terrified, less afflicted with body symptoms, and less depressed. There is a kind of easy rightness about this answer since the observer senses what a price women patients pay for their affectionateness. Patients are often urged to cultivate anger during therapy—sometimes they even "put it on" in the vain hope that they will experience a catharsis. Usually the only result is that they feel even more defeated because they are too "chicken" to be properly angry.

Another answer often held out to depressed and hysterical patients is to "get interested in something," some cause larger than themselves. This is excellent advice, except that detaching the self from its closeness to others and attaching it to more important causes is not so easily done. Depression and hysteria are not so easily treated. They are not "put on" or a result of self-indulgence. In short, they are not so easily exhorted away. That was the way exhortations used to be made to witches to dispossess themselves of the devil.

Taking on men's role as exploiters, adopting their pattern and level of aggression is also not the answer. The conflict which produces depressive and hysterical symptoms, like the conflict which produces obsessional neurosis and schizophrenia, is unconscious. Women's symptoms originate in and reflect a profound contradiction between their natural affectionateness, which has also become an ego-ideal, and the internalized cultural scorn of it as weakness.

REFERENCES

Abse, W. 1974. Hysterical conversions and dissociative syndromes and the hysterical character. In *American handbook of psychiatry*, 2nd ed., ed. S. Arieti, vol. 3, pp. 155–194. New York: Basic Books.

Arieti, S. 1974. Affective disorders. In *American handbook of psychiatry*, 2nd ed., ed. S. Arieti, vol. 3, pp. 449–490. New York: Basic Books.

Bart, P. 1968. Social structure and the vocabularies of discomfort: What happened to female hysteria? *Journal of Health and Social Behavior* 9:188–193.

Beck, A. 1967. *Depression: Clinical, experimental and theoretical aspects.* New York: Harper & Row.

Birtchnell, J. 1971. Case-register study of bereavement. *Proceedings of the Royal Society of Medicine* 64:279–282.

Blaser, P., Löw, D., and Schäublin, A. 1968. Die Messung der Depressionstyle mit einem Fragebogen. *Psychiatrica Clinica* 1:299–319.

Bowlby, J. 1969. *Attachment and loss*, vol. 1. New York: Basic Books.

Brodman, K., et al. 1953. The Cornell medical index-health questionnaire. VI. The relation of patients' complaints to age, sex, race and education. *Journal of Gerontology* 8:339–342.

Brody, E. B., and Sata, L. S. 1967. Personality disorders. I. Trait and patterns disturbances. In *Comprehensive textbook of psychiatry*, 2nd ed., ed. Alfred M. Freedman, et al., vol. 2, chap. 25. Baltimore, Md.: Williams and Wilkins.

Caine, T. M. 1960. The expression of hostility and guilt in melancholic and paranoid women. *Journal of Consulting Psychology* 24:18–22.

Chesler, P. 1972. *Women and madness.* Garden City, N.Y.: Doubleday.

Chodoff, P., and Lyons, H. 1958. Hysteria, the hysterical personality and "hysterical conversion." *American Journal of Psychiatry* 114:734.

Cohn, N. 1975. *Europe's inner demons: An enquiry inspired by the great witch-hunt.* New York: Basic Books.

Davis, D., Lamberti, J., and Ajans, Z. 1969. Crying in depression. *British Journal of Psychiatry* 115:597–598.

Dennehy, C. M. 1966. Childhood bereavement and psychiatric illness. *British Journal of Psychiatry* 112:1049–1069.

Dube, K. C. 1968. Mental disorders in Agra. *Social Psychiatry* 3:139–143.

Easser, B., and Lesser, S. 1965. Hysterical personality: A re-evaluation. *Psychoanalytic Quarterly* 34:390–405.

Fitzgerald, O. 1948. Love deprivation and the hysterical personality. *Journal of Mental Science* 94:701.

Freud, S. 1933. On libidinal types. In *The standard edition of the complete psychological works of Sigmund Freud*, ed. J. Strachey, vol. 21. London: Hogarth Press (S.E. published 1964).

Friedman, A. 1970. Hostility factors and clinical improvement in depressed patients. *Archives of General Psychiatry* 23(6):524–537.

Huxley, A. 1971. *The devils of Loudon.* New York: Harper & Row.

Janet, P. 1920. *The major symptoms of hysteria*, 2nd ed. New York: Macmillan.

Leighton, D. C., et al. 1963. *The character of danger.* New York: Basic Books.

Lewis, C., and Berman, M. 1965. Studies of conversion hysteria. *Archives of General Psychiatry* 13:275–282.

Lewis, H. B. 1971. *Shame and guilt in neurosis.* New York: International Universities Press.

Maccoby, E., and Jacklin, C. 1974. *The psychology of sex differences.* Stanford, Calif.: Stanford University Press.

Malzberg, B. 1940. *Social and biological aspects of mental disease.* Utica, N.Y.: State Hospitals Press.

————. 1959. Important statistical data about mental illness. In *American handbook of psychiatry*, 1st ed., ed. S. Arieti, vol. 1, pp. 161–174. New York: Basic Books.

Marks, I. M. 1969. *Fears and phobias.* London: Heinemann Medical Co.

Marmor, J. 1954. Orality in the hysterical personality. *Journal of the American Psychoanalytic Association* 1:656–671.

Matarazzo, R., Matarazzo, J., and Saslow, G. 1961. The relationship between medical and psychiatric symptoms. *Journal of Abnormal and Social Psychology* 62:55–61.

Mendel, J., and Klein, D. 1969. Anxiety attacks with subsequent agoraphobia. *Comprehensive Psychiatry* 10:190–195.

Mitchell-Heggs, N. 1971. Aspects of natural history and clinical presentation of depression. *Proceedings of the Royal Society of Medicine* 64:1174.

Phillips, L., and Segal, B. 1969. Sexual status and psychiatric symptoms. *American Sociological Review* 34:58–72.

Reich, W. 1972. *Character analysis.* New York: Farrar, Straus.

Robins, L. 1966. *Deviant children grow up.* Baltimore, Md.: Williams & Wilkins.

Sedivec, V. 1969. Manic phases of manic-melancholy and its forms during the course of illness. *Czekoslovanska Psychiatrica* 65:85–91 (abstract).

Tarnower, S., and Humphries, M. 1969. Depression: A recurring genetic illness more common among females. *Diseases of the Nervous System* 30:601–604.

Thigpen, H., and Cleckley, H. M. 1957. *The three faces of Eve.* New York: McGraw-Hill.

Zigler, E., and Phillips, L. 1960. Social effectiveness and symptomatic behaviors. *Journal of Abnormal and Social Psychology* 61:231–238.

# 16

# Phobias After Marriage: Women's Declaration of Dependence

## ALEXANDRA SYMONDS

For many years I have been interested in a specific clinical problem that occurs when a young woman, who was apparently independent, self-sufficient, and capable, changes after marriage and develops phobias or other signs of constriction of self. These changes invariably cause her to become excessively dependent and helpless. This sometimes occurs suddenly and dramatically, as in the development of phobias, or it may occur gradually and insidiously over a period of years. Either way, her entire way of life is changed. Where before marriage she was an active, apparently self-sufficient young woman who traveled, drove a car, had many interests, held a responsible job, and went many places alone, now all these activities are sharply curtailed, or completely impossible. She becomes fearful of traveling, especially by plane or subway. She may be afraid to be alone even for a moment. She usually can no longer drive a car herself, and in extreme cases may not be able to travel in a car at all, even as a passenger. In the less dramatic cases where this change occurs without specific phobias, she becomes fearful of making any decision or of taking any sort of responsibility on her own. She clings to her husband for constant support, apparently changing from a capable, "strong" person into a classically "helpless female."

Many of these women give up all their previous interests and activities that had represented independence of action, or expression of self, such as in the field of creativity. One of my patients, who had gone to art school and had done excellent paintings as a young woman, gave up art entirely. Another young woman who had begun to develop a promising career in the opera dropped singing and never sang at all, even for pleasure.

These changes do not necessarily occur suddenly. Often it is a gradual process, and it takes place without conscious decision. In fact, these patients do not usually mention their former interests, enthusiasms, or involvements and may refer to them only in passing as though they were not important. References to their life of activity and responsibility before marriage are often elicited by me in the course of treatment and seem to represent no contradiction to the patient.

I want to make it clear that I am not referring to those young women who shift their interests and energies after getting married from outside activities to the home and family, as many young women do. These women continue to grow and develop, although in a different sphere. I am referring to the small but significant number who seem to shrivel up after getting married, who seem to lose all interest and involvements, who constrict their inner life, and who become depressed, anxious, and excessively dependent. Very often these patients have psychosomatic problems and make the rounds of internists and gynecologists. I had one patient of this type who had glaucoma, and another had a thyroidectomy. Several suffer from various gastrointestinal symptoms, insomnia, and other evidences of chronic unresolved conflict. Phobias are only one of the psychiatric symptoms that may develop, and are likely to attract attention because they are dramatic. However, we also see many other signs of this process. All these patients are depressed to some degree, sometimes severely.

While phobias and other signs of constriction are not remarkable in themselves, what attracted my interest was the fact that they occurred after marriage. Instead of marriage representing a broadening and enriching experience, it caused the reverse effect. Incidentally, these patients do not usually complain about their husbands, nor do they feel they have made a bad marriage. On the contrary, they portray their husbands as kind and helpful and they earnestly desire to stay married to them.

I have wondered about this apparent paradox ever since I first came across it about twenty years ago. At that time I saw a very successful professional woman in her thirties who seemed to be quite accomplished, yet she suffered from intense fear of traveling and of being alone. It seemed such a contradiction to me. She told me that these fears had developed suddenly about a year after she had gotten married, eight years previously. She was very ashamed of her "weakness," as she called it, and tried to master it by willpower. Unfortunately, I saw her only briefly and I was not able to learn more about her personal dynamics, but it remained in back of my mind for many years as a puzzle that interested me. Since that time, however, I have had the opportunity to work with similar patients in greater detail, and I have found that it is not an unusual syndrome. It is frequently reported in the literature on phobias. For example, Frederick C. Redlich and Daniel X. Freedman, in their chapter on phobias in *The Theory and Practice of Psychiatry*, give a lengthy case report of a professional woman who fits into the same category as I am describing.

In preparing my material for this presentation, I went over my records for the past twenty years. I have seen ten to twelve patients who fall into this category, some for consultation only and others for prolonged treatment. I treated four of these patients in analysis for several years at least two or three times a week. I have also had contact with many others of similar type through my work with various hospitals and agencies as a consultant, and on occasion I have met such women socially. I have selected three patients who will be described in some detail to bring out the features they have in common. (Names and identities have been disguised.)

Mrs. A. was a woman of about thirty-eight who was referred to me by an internist to whom she had gone because she felt weak and rundown. The internist recognized that she was quite depressed and sent her for psychiatric treatment. She was a tall, thin woman who looked malnourished, neglected her appearance, and was seriously depressed. She cried profusely during our sessions.

There were certain marked discrepancies in her manner that were quite apparent. She was a well-educated woman, who spoke with authority when discussing impersonal matters. However, when talking of more personal things, such as her feelings and her life at home, she became uncertain, wispy, and vague. Her appearance also showed marked contrasts. She was rather tall and gangly and she appeared her age or older, yet she wore the clothing of a schoolgirl, with knee-high socks, skirt or jumper, and had a plain straight haircut with bangs. It was obvious that there were tremendous extremes in her personality. Intellectually she was developed and mature, while emotionally she was still childlike.

She stated in the very first session that her marriage was a failure because she felt that she was a total failure as a wife and mother. She was married for eight years and had two children. Since getting married, she had sex very rarely, perhaps once or twice a year, because her husband was usually impotent. However, he had convinced her that this was her fault, although he would never tell her just what she was doing that was at fault. He told her repeatedly that she was an aggressive, castrating woman and all their difficulties were because of her. They did not argue often. She accepted his accusations and was overwhelmed with feelings of guilt and hopelessness.

Mrs. A.'s accepting all the blame and her lack of criticism of her husband are characteristic of these patients. On the conscious level they express no resentment, or even the ordinary griping typical of most married people. They never complain openly about their husbands (or anyone else for that matter). However, they are involved in the special sort of interpersonal dynamic that is characteristic of the dependent personality with the "appeal of helplessness" as described by Karen Horney. While these individuals do not allow themselves to express any open hostility or criticism, they describe to the analyst or listener such outrageously provocative behavior on the part of their husbands that the listener may be impelled to come to their defense and even to become angry at the husband. For example, the material I have just presented about this patient's husband may have made you annoyed at the husband. In this type of communication, the analyst or the observer becomes more upset about the partner's behavior than the patient seems to be. They describe outlandish and extreme behavior on the part of their husbands with no affect—and with no visible protest, presenting a picture of a weak, helpless woman being pushed around at home by an inconsiderate and aggressive husband. This particular message, the appeal of helplessness in a woman, often comes across as seductiveness. In therapy or in analysis, a male analyst is especially vulnerable to this and may be drawn into a very sticky and confusing countertransference where he finds himself constantly coming to the aid of his patient against the husband. As a woman, I am not affected in the same way by these patients.

Superficial therapy, such as marriage counseling or direct intervention, is also a frequent occurrence because the patient externalizes to such an extent that it appears as though all her troubles would be over if only she had a different husband or if only someone else would get her husband to change. It may be tempting, but it does not usually bring any lasting benefit, since the problem lies not in the marriage or in the husband, but within the patient herself. I think we have all seen instances where people get a divorce and then remarry the same sort of individual as before. We must recognize that these women are caught in a state of chronic, unresolved conflict of a profound nature that paralyzes them, and it may take years of analysis before they develop enough of a sense of self to handle their lives effectively. However, unless they do it themselves, it will not work out.

The need to avoid criticism of their husbands often leads to outlandish situations at home, since the husband goes blithely about his business doing as he pleases, while the wife builds up an explosive rage, all unknown to both of them. The many psychosomatic symptoms are an expression of this repressed anger. Mrs. S., for example, only mentioned in passing that her husband's hobby was collecting antique automobiles. He insisted on keeping an automobile motor disassembled on the living-room floor for months while he tinkered with it. At other times he would bring in all sorts of assorted junk and clutter up the entire house with it. Mrs. S. said that occasionally she felt annoyed, but she never complained because she felt that she should be more understanding.

A few words about the third patient, Mrs. M. She also came into treatment by way of a medical referral. She had been suffering from severe anxiety for three or four years, with headaches, palpitations, insomnia, gastrointestinal distress, and tremendous feelings of tension. These symptoms were becoming so severe that she was afraid she was losing her mind. She was in her thirties, had been married for ten years, and had a child of two. She expressed no criticism or dissatisfaction with her husband, stating that he was extremely helpful and sympathetic to her distress. He did all he could to help out. In the course of the first few sessions, however, she gave numerous examples that described him as an extremely difficult man to live with. He had a fear of germs, and had insisted that they wear masks until the baby was eighteen months. He would not allow anyone to baby-sit for the child, so they were forced to take him everywhere. He did not trust restaurants and would never eat out, or allow the child to. However, in spite of many, many peculiarities on his part that differed from her point of view, Mrs. M. said that she deferred to his opinion because she felt he was very thorough, and he must know. And besides, if she insisted on her way and anything happened to the child, she would not be able to endure it.

In each case the patient tries to build up rationalizations for herself so that she can avoid direct confrontation with her husband's peculiarities, and thus avoid awareness of her own hostile or aggressive feelings. It is not that the husbands are so peculiar or different (although in certain instances this may be true), but the problem is rather in the wives' inability to handle even the ordinary friction that occurs between two people who live together.

The attempt to avoid open friction by retreating results in an enormous personal restriction in their lives. For example, Mrs. A.'s phobias developed gradually, within the last few years. She did not recall any abrupt event or sudden onset (this is frequently the case). However, she could not use an elevator, subway, drive a car, or travel by plane. Any attempt to do so produced panic and unbearable anxiety. When she was single she had her own car and had enjoyed traveling. She often flew to distant places on her vacations. However, now she had become practically housebound. Interestingly, while the inability to use the subways and elevators hampered her activities, she did not give it any special emphasis in telling me about it, and it wasn't mentioned in the first few sessions. She also seemed untroubled by other evidences of this constriction that had occurred since getting married. Her husband did not particularly like to socialize or to go out, so they rarely did. They seemed to have few friends and few interests in common, and they spent most of their time at home, reading or listening to music (in separate rooms) because this was his preference. All this she apparently accepted as natural because she was married, reiterating that she loved her husband and had always wanted to be married and have a family. While this may sound on the surface like an ordinary, contended domestic scene, keep in mind that there was very little display of affection or love between them. Mr. A. frequently spent the entire evening alone in his room, and Mrs. A. felt miserably neglected by him most of the time that they were together. If she ever tried to approach him affectionately he would freeze up.

Mrs. M. also had many phobias that restricted her; however, she was more overtly troubled by them. She was angry at herself for being so "stupid," as she called it, and she desperately tried to get to the bottom of them by direct assault. Occasionally she would force herself to travel even though it made her have vomiting spells. She would frequently come into the sessions and start the hour with a very precise statement such as, "I still can't think of any reason why I should be afraid of subways." She was a highly intelligent women, a college graduate (as were all three patients), and was exceptionally intellectualized. She stressed the control of feelings, and talked of "arranging her feelings" so that they would not betray her. She had many dreams where people wore masks—usually the mask was benign and friendly while, underneath, the real face was frightening. She was terrified of her own hostility, and it was only with great difficulty that she came to accept some of it. Of these three patients, Mrs. M. had the most subjective anxiety and the most distressing physical symptoms. Sleep was very difficult for her—often she would awake in a panic, without remembering her dreams or having any clue as to what was disturbing her. When she did recall her dreams, they were filled with emotion— usually rage, anger, anxiety, and apprehension. There were also many sexual dreams. In telling them she seemed disconnected from the feeling, but her face showed the extreme tension and inner pressure she was under.

Mrs. M. was the only one of the three who remembered a sudden onset of her phobias. They had occurred about eight years ago while she and her husband were on a tour. She recalled the details of this with great difficulty, only after many years of treatment. The essential factor was that Mrs. M. had insisted on the trip over her husband's reluctance. To her this represented a very aggressive act, and when he expressed some dissatisfaction with the trip, she remembers only a mild feeling that he was dampening her enthusiasm. The next day she was frightened of the plane they took, and the remainder of the trip was a nightmare. Insisting on the trip in the first place had a special significance to Mrs. M. It was one of the only times that she can remember where she persisted in actualizing a very personal desire of hers. She had always yearned to travel and especially looked forward to this after getting married. The awareness that her husband did not share her enthusiasm was catastrophic for her, although she only realized that after years of therapy.

All three patients had the same sort of relationship with their husbands. Whenever any area of difference developed that would ordinarily have caused friction between man and wife, they avoided it at all costs. Rather than differ and perhaps fight, or at least argue, they would automatically and unconsciously drop their point of view, their need, or their desire—and go along with the husband's. The phobias were one of the ways to handle their repressed feeling. It seemed to immobilize them and prevent them from any act that might be interpreted as aggressive or self-assertive; in fact, it was a statement very much to the contrary, since it made them helpless and harmless.

I was always struck by the price these patients were willing to pay in order to avoid the faintest possibility of expressing anger or hostility openly. And they were doing all of this silently and without their husbands' being aware of what was happening. Thus they became more like villains as time went on. Part of the problem is their inability to communicate clearly to their partner. To do this would require a stronger sense of self and a willingness to accept the consequences of their acts. They would have to consider their wishes worth fighting for. However, since these are people who consider ordinary assertion to be the equivalent of hostility, they have an exaggerated fear of this type of encounter. They do not express their needs directly, yet they feel angry and hurt because the partner does not perceive them. All of these feelings are pushed out of awareness. One of the patients had a dream where she was hanging outside a fifth-floor window, just barely holding on, and her husband passed by without seeing her. She was only able to whisper in a very low voice—"help."

This is what interested me from the very beginning. Why do certain women respond to marriage with such extreme suppression of self, especially when it occurs in those who seemed to have been so different in their life before marriage? Without making a conscious decision, ruthlessly they choke off their inner self; in Horney's terms, they give up their real self. One of these patients expressed this brutal deadening of self in a dream that she had when she thought she was pregnant. In the dream she strangled several baby birds. She often dreamed of birds as a symbol of herself, sometimes as a canary in a cage. The canary was especially significant since Mrs. S. had a particular joy in singing and when she was a young girl she had been quite involved in it.

We must come to the conclusion that people who so readily give up their own genuine growth are either desperately in need of what they get in return, or value themselves so little that it does not seem to matter—or both. If this is true, then what sustained them earlier in life? And what was happening in marriage that triggered such a negative reaction?

As I got to know these patients, I began to understand more about them. They all had some similar experiences in background. All came from families where self-reliance, independence, and control of feelings were necessary, either because they were highly prized and encouraged (as with the first two) or because they were necessary for survival. Not only was control of feelings necessary, but in their background there was very little respect for childlike interests. As a result, they had to grow up in a hurry. For example, Mrs. S.'s parents would not allow any conversation at the dinner table unless it was of interest to the adults. The children could not speak to each other. She recalls that most of her meals were spent in silence. Mrs. M.'s parents were totally ineffectual and immature, and unable to respond to their children's needs. Mrs. M. was the eldest and had to take care of the younger children as well as herself. She felt from an early age that she could not trust her parents if she needed their help.

This early need for control of feelings and self-reliance was important in understanding their later predicament. From early childhood they developed skills and qualities that gave the illusion of strength. They all chose work or education that seemed to bear out the illusion, and that gave others the feeling that they were strong and self-sufficient. They repressed their healthy needs to be taken care of and repressed the child in them as well. They only did "important" things. For example, when Mrs. A. was a child she loved gardening, but she recalls that she raised only vegetables because these were useful and she could sell them whereas flowers were only to look at. As teenagers and young women all these patients acted cool, capable, and self-reliant. They remember themselves as fearless, and several were known as tomboys or daredevils. Mrs. A. said that she had always loved the ocean and had been an active swimmer as a young woman, although now she was afraid to swim anywhere except in a pool. They had no conscious plan to be different after getting married, yet each of them underwent a profound change. Mrs. M. had been a nurse before she was married. She had been in charge of a large ward in a busy hospital and had no difficulties in handling her job. It was only in analysis that she realized that she had been secretly yearning for marriage so that she would no longer have to be a responsible person and maintain the façade of strength. Then she would be able to put down a tremendous burden, which she had been carrying all her life, and be the dependent little girl she had never been before. But she would only allow herself this luxury in marriage, because there it was socially acceptable and no one could criticize her for it.

Many women freely admit their dependency needs, and they are not ashamed to say that they are looking forward to marriage so they can quit work and be taken care of. Healthy needs are not insatiable and do not cause difficulties. On the other hand, those who deny these needs all their life, who repress and feel ashamed of these feelings, and who have not had their ordinary needs gratified as they are growing up often have secret expectations of marriage that make them vulnerable and cause them many difficulties. Marriage for them represents their opportunity to be dependent without self-criticism and self-hate. Marriage then becomes their "declaration of dependence." If for any reason this is questioned, or the marriage does not seem to be all they expected, they are in a panic and they cling even more. Their rage at being frustrated is immediately suppressed and cannot be acknowledged by them since it seems so destructive.

We often see the first stages of this process when an apparently capable, highly educated young woman—perhaps even a professional such as a doctor—gives up her work and her education as soon as she marries, and seems to settle for very little other than the mere structure of a marriage. This may be the first indication that she is trying to utilize the marriage relationship to fulfill an enormous neurotic need to be taken care of. Marriage for these women reveals an aspect of themselves that was not obvious before. They have exaggerated and idealized expectations of what marriage is to be, and what a strong man will be. No matter how sophisticated or broadminded they were before marriage as to the role of men and women, they tend to become the paragons of Victorian femininity—helpless, housebound, and ineffectual.

I borrowed the term "declaration of dependence" from Dr. Carl Binger, who used it in an article entitled "Emotional Disturbances among College Women." In the college population he found that many women's reaction to any crisis was a tendency to become depressed, apathetic, and excessively dependent, suddenly losing their former self-sufficiency. He does not mention this, but I have found that women often get married as an alternative to continued growth and as a retreat from life. When they are faced with a difficult problem in their own development, they may seek marriage as a refuge.

Many women, and men too, equate morbid dependency and helplessness with femininity. My patients all had some confusion and uncertainty about their femininity and saw marriage as a confirmation of their feminine identity. This proved that they were really women. They were willing, in fact eager, to avoid any evidence of self-assertion, since they consider such impulses as masculine. Healthy impulses and feelings of growth and self-assertion were rejected by them as too aggressive, and too masculine. When they were single, they could develop expansively to some extent since they were not attached to a man, and there would be no question of coming into conflict with a man and perhaps winning out. However, once they become involved with men, they tend to suppress all their assertive impulses for fear it would endanger their much-needed partnership.

Treatment for these patients is painstakingly slow and prolonged. Underlying the anger, the frustration, and the fear of conflict is a profound resignation. I found that marriage had represented to them the only acceptable way for them to have significance and for the deeply repressed and denied self to have an opportunity to live. They tenaciously refuse to accept the concept of separateness. For example, one patient who liked art and theater at first would not consider going anywhere alone or with another woman even though she had done this often when she was single. She felt that she would be pitied or ridiculed as unmarried. As treatment progressed, she did begin to go places without her husband, and to enjoy things on her own. She even went on a few vacations with her children.

It is not too difficult for these patients to recognize that they are angry, and this awareness relieves much of the depression. However, though they are less depressed, for a long period of time there may be no essential change in their life. They have so successfully compartmentalized their feelings that they often achieve intellectual understanding without true insight. We know that phobias represent isolation and compartmentalization of feeling, and are of necessity difficult to treat. Perhaps the prolonged analysis that all three of these patients had was necessary so that by way of the analytic relationship they could allow themselves to be taken care of by the analyst. This was brought out in one of the first dreams of Mrs. A., where she saw me as a pediatrician.

A word about the significance of the phobias in these patients. They expressed the typical fears that patients have who fear closed spaces or who fear travel. They described their fears as fear of being closed in, a fear of being trapped, a fear that they would not be able to leave any time they wanted to (as on a turnpike or in a plane). Mrs. M. said that once she was in a plane she would have to give control over to the pilot. Mrs. S. could not drive a car anymore (although she did at one time) because she feared that the car would do something that she did not want it to do. One patient became terrified if she had the slightest stuffiness of her nose, because she was afraid she might not be able to breathe and she would die. All these fears that the patients described, the fear of being closed in, trapped, helpless, and without control, are symbolic repressions of how the individual closes herself in, keeps down her impulses, and imprisons herself. However, direct interpretation of this nature is usually not understood early in therapy.

The traditional explanation for phobias is related to the fear of loss of control. Freud felt it was loss of control of sexual or aggressive impulses. Others, such as Leon Salzman in his book *The Obsessive Personality*, broaden it to be a fear of loss of control of any impulses that would be considered a threat to the integrity of the personality or, as Horney would say, to the pride system. This would include tender impulses, power drives, needs for detachment or closeness, and so on. The fear of humiliation is closely tied up to the anxiety involved.

I would like to add another dimension to the understanding of the function that these phobias played in this type of patient. These women were actually afraid to be *in* control. They feared the consequences of taking their life into their own hands, of setting their own direction (as driving a car), of movement on their own, of exploring, of enjoying, of discovering. They feared dealing with the unknown, they feared the ordinary aggression and assertiveness that accompanies growth and involvement. Many years ago, Otto Rank referred to this when he said that more people have a "fear of life" than a "fear of death." The existentialists call it fear of being. Kierkegaard stated in speaking of anxiety "the alarming possibility of being able causes dizziness."

This problem has nothing to do with femininity or masculinity. These are only convenient catchwords for the people I am describing. They may attach their anxiety to these concepts, and may find ready acceptance in others. But their problem is a deeper and more basic one. It is a fear that many people have who are unable to actualize their own growth and development. Unfortunately, many women suffer from this because of ancient cultural prejudices that have barred them from full participation and growth, and that make it easy for them to defer their own development and to live vicariously in others.

Such people express their fears of self-realization in terms of fear that by their growth they will hurt others. Thus it comes easy for them to accept any accusation such as being "a castrating female" or "too aggressive."

In my therapy with such patients I focus on themselves—not on the marriage or the husbands. Slowly and painstakingly they discover islands in themselves that they have ignored, discarded, and minimized. Gradually they acquire enough feeling of self to make their needs known to themselves and their husbands, to stand behind themselves and not abandon themselves (as they accuse others of doing). This requires prolonged treatment, often with only partial success.

In conclusion, what sort of people have I been talking about? These are women who came from an atmosphere where they had to grow up in a hurry. They had little opportunity for genuine self-expression, especially of warmer feelings. They may have had great compassion for the suffering of others, but very little sympathy for their own. As girls they were capable and self-reliant, but were not really whole. They saw marriage as an absolute necessity for them to achieve status and significance, and minimized or completely ignored any achievements or interests prior to marriage. Once married, then all their unexpressed needs would be allowable. When faced with the ordinary difficulties in marriage, when faced with the necessity for friction and for self-expression, they reacted with enormous rage and, underlying this, a profound despair. For these women, the phobias and other signs of constriction of self were the end result of the tremendous emotional turmoil that lies within.

REFERENCES

Binger, C. A. L. 1961. Emotional disturbances among college women. In *Emotional problems of the student*, ed. G. B. Baline, Jr. New York: Doubleday.

Horney, K. 1945. *Our inner conflicts.* New York: Norton.

————. 1950. *Neurosis and human growth.* New York: Norton.

Redlich, F. C., and Freedman, D. X. 1966. *The theory and practice of psychiatry.* New York: Basic Books.

Salzman, L. 1968. *The obsessive personality.* New York: Science House.

# 17

# A Starving Family:
# An Interactional View
# of Anorexia Nervosa

## DOROTHY CONRAD MAZUR

### Introduction

Primary or true anorexia nervosa is the relentless pursuit of being thin. This pursuit differentiates this disorder from emaciation associated with various other psychiatric conditions. It is vital to understand the development of anorexia nervosa within the context of the total family because the anoretic child seems to be the spokesman for the emotional deprivation and starvation of her parents. Such transgenerational deprivation leads to a dysfunction of the total family.

### Historical Review

In recent years the longstanding debate over whether the environmental or intrapsychic dynamics were most responsible for emotional conflict seems to have waned. The current literature now describes personality as an interplay of both factors, leaving the original argument an antiquated one.

Since William Gull in 1868 first identified anorexia nervosa as a distinct entity, clinicians worldwide have been trying to untangle the personality dynamics of adolescents with this disorder. In the 1940s, Masserman (1941), Moulton (1942), and others described anorexia in terms of intrapsychic conflicts of oral ambivalence, oral aggression, and fear of oral impregnation. In the 1950s psychoanalytic practitioners like Grinker (1953) focused more specifically on the development of object relations within the anoretic child. In this regard, the classically defined Kleinian depressive position provides insight into orality and oedipal strivings that aids in further dynamic understanding of anorexia. However, with all the varied theoretical contributions toward understanding the intrapsychic phenomena, the experts seemed to be pessimistic about whether traditional analytic techniques were effective in the treatment of primary anorexia nervosa. This frustration stimulated an even more relentless pursuit by clinicians to understand what might increase the probability of a successful outcome of treatment.

In the 1960s Selvini (1965) arrived at a broader conceptual base describing the anoretic's use of the body as a tool in a personal struggle for existence. At that time Bruch (1966), probably the leading authority on eating disorders, also began to redefine and expand her descriptions of adolescents with anorexia. She defined three primary characteristics of this eating disorder: (1) a disturbance in body image of delusional proportion; (2) a disturbance of the accuracy of perception or cognitive interpretation of stimuli arising in the body; and (3) a paralyzing sense of ineffectiveness that pervades all thinking and activities. This ineffectiveness results from early problematic interactions with the parents. In identifying this dynamic, Bruch highlights the interactional aspects of the illness. The feeling of ineffectiveness she describes was previously masked by the negativism commonly observed by clinicians.

Blitzer and associates (1961), Dally (1969), Bruch (1973), and others have attempted to document observable characteristics of parents of anoretic adolescents. They describe the parents of anoretic patients as upwardly mobile, middle class, with strict moralistic values who often place emphasis on appearance, conformity, and obedience. High expectations and rigid attitudes are the norm. Bruch (1973) more specifically has found these parents to be out of tune with their children. Expressions of affect emanating from the child are routinely ignored as parents respond instead in a manner that gratifies their own needs. Thus anoretic children learn to respond to externally initiated cues rather than learning to recognize their own somatic sensations, such as hunger and anxiety. This type of interaction with its concomitant sense of ineffectiveness sets the stage for symptomatic emaciation to develop and be denied by the child.

As therapists have become increasingly aware of the interactional patterns that characterize this self-starvation, they have systematically stressed the importance of family involvement in treatment (see, e.g., Aponte and Hoffman 1973; Blitzer et al. 1961; Bruch 1971, 1973; Galdston 1974; Liebman et al. 1974). Structural family therapy as described by Minuchin (1974) and his co-workers (Liebman et al. 1974; Rosman et al. 1975) has increasingly been recognized as one of the most effective and efficient means of treating primary nervosa. A technique developed by Minuchin, the family therapy lunch session, has been used at the Philadelphia Child Guidance Clinic "to initiate the anoretic's family into treatment" (Rosman et al. 1975, p. 846). This technique frequently promotes immediate symptom extinction in the anoretic child.

## Case Material

Recently in the treatment of a family with an anoretic child, the mother recalled certain aspects of her own development—loneliness, isolation, and deprivation—which she hastily minimized. Describing her family origin, she pulled from her purse a family reunion booklet containing a photograph of eleven sullen faces, which shockingly resembled a funeral pamphlet.

The father, on the other hand, described an insatiable yearning for attention, care, and recognition that was partially fulfilled in his early years by his doting mother. After his marriage, his mother continued to live close to the family and to provide nurturance and support for both parents as well as for their four adolescent children. Nevertheless, another "feeder" had been produced by this family, the child with anorexia nervosa.

The development of the family seemed to predispose the child to become the starving nurturer. A hungry, needy man married an empty, deprived woman. The script for this couple was one in which the husband said, "I want," and the wife responded, "I don't have." This dialogue became a ritual, both spouses asking each other to give and to receive but their interaction only maintained the status quo. Children were born with the hope that they would add something to the family as givers of love and nurturance and symbols of change and growth.

The anoretic child was the third of four children: Her brother was two years older, one sister was a year older, the other sister was two years younger.

The first years of this anoretic child's life spent in close relationship with the mother were ungratifying for both mother and daughter. Something in the combination of mother and this particular infant led to a mismatch. The mother, because of her own faulty emotional development, was unable to give consistently to her child, thus contributing to the child's perception of her as a rejecting mother. Once aware of the extreme need for the mother, the infant's fear of losing her made her intensely anxious. Hence a precarious relationship was established between the mother and her child.

With difficulty, this mother continued to give to her child. The father, feeling deprived and envious, moved into the mother-daughter relationship competing with mother for the daughter's affection and nurturance. Angrily he assumed the mothering role, negating his wife and spiting her inability to give to him. This arrangement appeared satisfactory until the child attempted to resolve the oedipal issues. With such an overinvolved father, the girl's oedipal anxieties were multiplied, creating an obstacle to their resolution. When the father became drained of his ability to give to his child, his own needs intensified. Hence he began to take a rigid stance, transmitting the message to his family that they could have so much from him but no more and that what they did get was a conditional tradeoff. The father's emptiness was also translated by him into highly prized value statements and moralizing attitudes, both communicating his unmet needs, first as a child himself and second as a spouse and parent. The mother's attempts to give constructive attention and care to the children were drastically hampered. She continued as a peripheral yet enmeshed parent.

This anoretic child seemed to translate the emotional deprivation she experienced through her parents into physical starvation.[1] In a primitive manner, food became the interactional commodity of the family. A double bind developed in which the parents demanded that the child eat and become autonomous, yet conveyed to her that to do so would lead to the emotional emaciation of her parents, their abandonment, and their loss of a defense that helped them avoid the conflicts in their marriage.

A mutual dependence developed between the child and her parents, making it impossible to accomplish constructively separation and individuation. The child had a pathological but necessary function to fill

---

1. Hinsie (1945) notes that "The stomach is a favorite locus for the psychology of deprivation" (p. 103).

in the family, that of taking care of the father for mother and keeping the parents apart because of their fear of intimacy. This role reversal between mother and daughter represented a blurring of generational boundaries (Minuchin 1974). With envy and jealousy, the anoretic child's siblings sustained the dysfunction and avoided assuming the anoretic's role due to their own need to become independent (and not get devoured).

In order to continue her development, the anoretic child would have had to break out of the powerful family arrangement that was established to keep the family together. To accomplish the emancipation would be difficult if not hazardous for the child. Unless the family structure was altered, the child could not or did not dare risk change or development (Mandelbaum 1977). At this point, the child, unable to free herself to mature both because of her extreme dependency needs and the pervasive family dynamics, began to lose weight. Her self-starvation began after her only brother left home for a month, merely leaving a note explaining his absence. His abrupt departure seemed to dramatize for the patient her own grave enmeshment.[2]

In this family, and in other documented cases of anorexia nervosa, a paradox exists. The child prepared and served food to her family yet starved herself. She collected recipes, planned menus, and took an interest in shopping for food. At the same time she did not ingest a sufficient amount to sustain her own life. For this girl food became an issue not so much of physiologic maintenance, but rather of developing a method to cope with the emotional deprivation of the entire family. Themes of control and rage were prominent, but they seemed to conceal the emotional hunger that prevailed in the anoretic child, her parents, and her siblings. Why, though, did this child starve herself while others ate?

On an archaic level, the child perceived the food she received from her parents during infancy as "bad" or "poisonous." She reacted to the perceived emptiness of herself by giving tasty and appealing nurturance to others while she maintained her dysfunctional role in the family. From a more Kleinian position, the mother was experienced as both a good and bad object. To eat would symbolically have meant to destroy the gratifying as well as the depriving mother. With one dramatic maneuver, the child expressed her oral rage and oedipal envy through starvation without the fear that she would destroy mother.

Food became a battleground, a symbol of self-control. Mock independence was expressed in negativistic and manipulative ways. The

---

2. Weight loss can often be triggered by an interpersonal loss of some kind. Grinker (1953) notes that the loss of a significant person can lead to a regression and a resurfacing of issues that had been previously hidden. Often this regression is expressed psychosomatically.

child acted as if the only control she could maintain over her life was through regulating her food intake. This self-starvation became a ritual in the family interaction and was held to with fanatic control. The realistic struggle which ensued over the issue of physical life or death was symbolic of the emotional fight for autonomy and self-control. The child's pseudoindependence around food revealed the depth of her dependent ambivalence.

The family initially reacted with bewilderment and became more protective and intrusive. Thus they increased and perpetuated the dynamics which had seemingly promoted the problem. Moreover, the parents' fear turned into anger and an increased ambivalence as the humiliating illness continued to insult their parenting abilities. After a time it became difficult for them not to view their child's death as a solution to the agony of her self-starvation. The child was hopelessly locked into her dysfunctional role in the family, keeping the system barely afloat. Not being able to accomplish all the functions she assumed, the anoretic child withered away in her effort and inevitably brought her family into treatment.

## Therapeutic Implications

Many therapeutic inferences can be drawn from this case. In working with the family of an anoretic patient, the anoretic's starvation needs to be understood not only intrapsychically but also in the light of interactional and systems phenomena. The child needs to stop feeding and parenting her family in order to resume eating herself. The family needs to be realigned to permit the parents to look toward each other as the major sources of support and gratification, thus freeing the anoretic patient from her dysfunctional position. Other family members are likely to become enmeshed in this dysfunction if the relationships are not altered carefully. For example, in this case, when the family structure began to shift, moving the anoretic child out of her role, the older brother became psychotic with delusions that the devil had left the body of his anoretic sister and had entered his. This delusion revealed the family myth that someone had to remain ill in order to sustain the parents. Hence the therapist must be careful to help the family establish more appropriate roles and alliances while discouraging the dysfunctional ones.

Even though the therapist intervenes in a careful, patient, and deliberate manner, family resistance to treatment, that is, change, is likely to increase. Such resistance results from the family's wish to deal with food rather than with the underlying dysfunctional family patterns that would shift the focus from the anoretic child and emphasize the marital discord.

Involving the extended families of the parents to deal with issues of deprivation, gratification, and dependency may help resolve the marital conflict as it emerges. Through the parents' awareness of their own "hunger," they may be able to differentiate between their needs and those of their anoretic daughter. In this way, the parents may be able to achieve some separation and individuation from their families of origin. In so doing, they may begin a reconstructive nurturing process with the child that will help her separate and individuate from them and their projective use of her. Thus the therapist will begin to help the family address the generations of nurturing and dependency deficits that have set the stage for the anorexia nervosa.

A transference paradigm may develop during family treatment in which the therapist becomes the feeder and displaces the anoretic child. With such a hungry family, the therapist may easily become enmeshed in rather severe countertransference reactions. Systematically, the therapist needs to turn the nurturing responsibilities back to the family members in a manner which will lead to greater growth and development rather than to another dysfunctional family pattern.

## Summary

This case was one in which starvation and deprivation pervaded the whole family system and dominated the family interactions in a rigid pattern. The anoretic child was the spokesman for two generations of family deprivation. Her symptom paradoxically provided the nurturance for her parents. She translated the family's emotional deprivation into physical starvation, with food becoming the interactional commodity of the family. A double bind was created: The child's eating and becoming autonomous would result in the emotional emaciation of her parents, their abandonment, and the loss of a defense against the marital conflict. The anoretic child's rage concealed the emotional hunger within herself, her parents, and her siblings.

Anorexia nervosa needs to be understood in terms of interactional and systems theory as well as through intrapsychic phenomena. The diagnostic and treatment issues are many, but they seem to resolve around understanding and working with a particular type of family— a starving one.

REFERENCES

Aponte, H., and Hoffman, L. 1973. The open door: A structural approach to a family with an anorectic child. *Family Process* 12(1):1–44.

Blitzer, J. R., et al. 1961. Children who starve themselves: Anorexia nervosa. *Psychosomatic Medicine* 23(5):369–383.

Bruch, H. 1966. Anorexia nervosa and its differential diagnosis. *Journal of Nervous and Mental Disease* 141(5):555–566.

————. 1971. Family transactions in eating disorders. *Comprehensive Psychiatry* 12(3):238–248.

————. 1973. *Eating disorders: Obesity, anorexia nervosa, and the person within.* New York: Basic Books.

Dally, P. J. 1969. *Anorexia nervosa.* New York: Grune & Stratton.

Galdston, R. 1974. Mind over matter: Observations on 50 patients hospitalized with anorexia nervosa. *Journal of the American Academy of Child Psychiatry* 13(2): 246–263.

Grinker, R. R. 1953. *Psychosomatic concepts.* New York: Norton.

Hinsie, L. E. 1945. *The person in the body: An introduction to psychosomatic medicine.* New York: Norton.

Liebman, R., et al. 1974. The role of the family in the treatment of anorexia nervosa. *Journal of the American Academy of Child Psychiatry* 13(2):264–274.

Mandelbaum, A. 1977. The family treatment of the borderline patient. In *Borderline personality disorders,* ed. P. Hartocollis, pp. 423–438. New York: International Universities Press.

Minuchin, S. 1975. *Families and family therapy.* Cambridge, Mass.: Harvard University Press.

Rosman, B. L., et al. 1975. Family lunch session: An introduction to family therapy in anorexia nervosa. *American Journal of Orthopsychiatry* 45(5):846–853.

Rowland, C. V., Jr. 1970. Anorexia nervosa: A survey of the literature and review of 30 cases. In *Anorexia and obesity* [International Psychiatry Clinics, vol. 7, no. 1], ed. C. V. Rowland, Jr., pp. 37–137. Boston: Little, Brown.

# 18

# Cinderella's Stepsisters: A Feminist Perspective on Anorexia Nervosa and Bulimia

## MARLENE BOSKIND-LODAHL

> Reading the literature on female socialization reminds one of the familiar image of Cinderella's stepsisters industriously lopping off their toes and heels so as to fit into the glass slipper (key to the somewhat enigmatic heart of the prince)—when of course it was never intended for them anyway.
>
> —Judith Long Laws

During my early months of internship in 1974 in the mental health section of a university clinic, I encountered Anne, a lively, attractive, and slim young woman of eighteen. For three years she had been on a cycle of gorging and starving that had continued without relief. She felt desperate and out of control.

Anne was the first in a series of 138 binger-starvers that I was to

This paper is dedicated to my original group of patients, for me the first of Cinderella's stepsisters.

treat. It became clear that the exaggerated gorging and purging reported by these patients was part of a self-perpetuating syndrome that was
primarily a problem of women.[1] The women I interviewed were consumed by constant but self-defeating attempts to change their bodies
so that they might each fit into the glass slipper. Anne was well informed about her symptoms. She even recommended books for me to
read. I searched the traditional literature for insights into her problem.
Bruch, who has written extensively on eating disorders, has most
clearly diagnosed the starvation or anorexic aspect of this syndrome.
According to her, characteristics of primary anorexia nervosa are: (1)
severe weight loss; (2) a disturbance of body image and body concept,
which Bruch calls "delusional"; (3) a disturbance of cognitive interpretation of body stimuli, combined with the failure to recognize signs of
nutritional need; (4) hyperactivity and denial of fatigue; (5) a paralyzing sense of ineffectiveness; (6) a family life in which (a) self-expression was neither encouraged nor reinforced, (b) the mother was frustrated in career aspirations, subservient to her husband, and generally
conscientious and overprotective, (c) the father was preoccupied with
outer appearances, admired fitness and beauty, and expected proper
behavior and measurable achievements from his children (Bruch 1973,
pp. 251–254). Little else, however, was helpful. Most writers treated
the starvation and the binge-ing (bulimia) as separate and distinct diseases, although several researchers had noted in passing the compulsion of the self-starver to binge.

This paper is intended to provide the nucleus of a new approach.
Relating anorexia to bulimia, it may also help to stimulate successful
therapies for the young women whom I shall describe as
"bulimarexics."

1. Four men who reported the binge-ing–starving behavior were also treated. I saw
three of these men in individual therapy. Since the writing of this paper I have been
engaged in therapeutic interventions and research designed to test some of these theoretical arguments. Taking advantage of a new philosophical and innovative movement
within our mental health clinic, I attempted an outreach program designed to break
through the isolation and shame experienced by women who are food bingers. In September 1974 an ad was placed in our university newspaper describing the symptom and
offering a group experience with a feminist orientation that would utilize Gestalt and
behaviorist techniques. Sixty women responded; fifteen were admitted to the group.
Some of the before, after, and follow-up measurements administered were: questionnaires specifically dealing with the binge-fast behavior and early childhood training; a
body cathexis test (Secord and Jourard 1953); and the Sixteen Personality Factor questionnaire (Cattell 1972). Based on the success of this initial group, two subsequent
groups have been run and data collected. Our outreach program, designed as a preventive intervention, revealed a much larger population manifesting this behavior than had
been suspected. After seeing 138 women and 4 men in two years at our clinic and systematically studying 80 of these with a variety of tests and other measurements, we are
now working on developing an operational definition of the bulimarexic syndrome,
analyzing our data for publication, and outlining a new therapeutic approach to this
problem.

## Psychoanalytic Interpretation of Anorexia and Bulimia

The view of anorexia as a rejection of femininity that often manifests itself as a fear of oral impregnation is widely held. (See figure 18-1.) Szyrynski (1973) observes:

They appear to be afraid of growing and maturation and they find it difficult to accept their respective sexual identity. In the case of girls, fear of pregnancy often dominates the picture; pregnancy being symbolized by food, getting fat means becoming pregnant. Such fantasies are also quite often formulated as oral impregnation. The girl, after kissing a boy for the first time, gets panicky lest pregnancy should follow. She pays particular attention to her gaining weight, and not infrequently a casual remark of a visitor, a relative, or a friend that she is looking well and probably gained some weight will unleash the disastrous ritual of self-starvation. (p. 497)

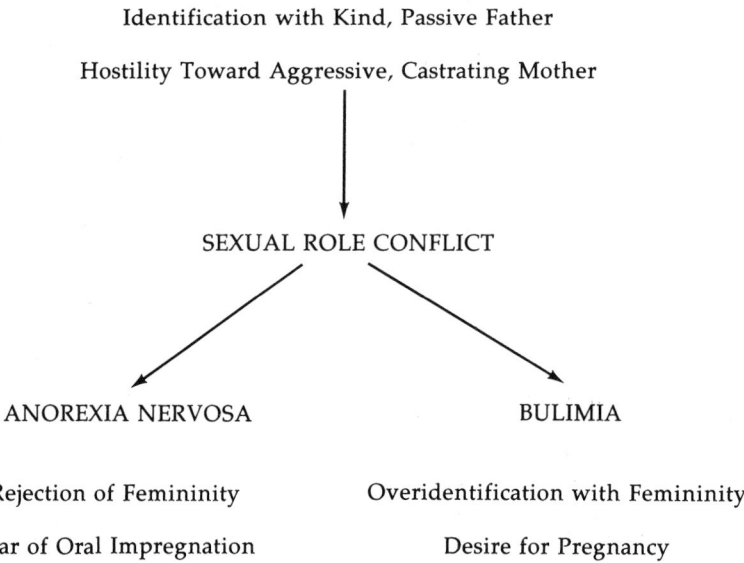

PREOEDIPAL RIVALRIES AND ORAL SADISTIC DRIVES

Identification with Kind, Passive Father

Hostility Toward Aggressive, Castrating Mother

SEXUAL ROLE CONFLICT

ANOREXIA NERVOSA                    BULIMIA

Rejection of Femininity        Overidentification with Femininity

Fear of Oral Impregnation              Desire for Pregnancy

Figure 18-1 Psychoanalytic Model of Anorexia Nervosa and Bulimia

Behind such fears is said to be an unconscious hatred of the mother, who is ineffective and discontent but castrating. Wulff (1945), writing in the early 1930s, describes such psychodynamics.

This neurosis is characterized by the person's fight against her sexuality which, through previous repression, has become greedy and insatiable. . . .

This sexuality is pregenitally oriented and sexual satisfaction is perceived as a "dirty meal." Periods of depression in which patients stuff themselves and feel themselves "fat," ... "dirty," or "pregnant," ... alternate with "good" periods in which they behave ascetically, feel slim and conduct themselves normally.... Psychoanalysis discloses that the unconscious content of the syndrome is a preoedipal mother conflict, which may be covered by an oral-sadistic Oedipus conflict. The patients have an intense unconscious hatred against their mothers and against femininity. (p. 241)

Lindner (1955), describing the case of Laura in *The Fifty-Minute Hour*, is a more modern proponent of traditional theory. His patient, Laura, complained of the same gorging-fasting symptoms as my patient, Anne, but his interpretation of these symptoms diverges sharply from mine. He fits Laura neatly into a stereotyped feminine role, maintaining that her symptoms show a neurotic, unhealthy resistance to that role. His cure involves putting an end to that hatred of femininity by helping the woman learn to accept and to act out the traditional female role, often described as accommodating, receptive, or passive. What Lindner's Laura "really wanted" was to become pregnant. He observes Laura's desperate desire for a man, but presupposes that it is healthy for a woman to feel desperate without a man and likewise to feel completely fulfilled once she is in a relationship.

Bruch (1973) writes more critically on the oral impregnation interpretation. She states that "modern psychoanalytic thinking has turned away from this merely symbolic, often analogistic etiological approach and focuses now on the nature of the parent-child relationship from the beginning." However, she confirms that "even today fear of oral impregnation is the one psychodynamic issue most consistently looked for" (p. 217). The fact that most anorexic women suffer from amenorrhea, interruption of the menstrual cycle, is seen as further evidence that these women are rejecting their "femininity" (Waller, Kaufman, and Deutsch 1940). Medical evidence has shown, however, that amenorrhea is consistently observed in women with abnormally low body weight who do not have symptoms of primary anorexia. This suggests that it is low body weight that is the key factor in initiating hormonal changes associated with amenorrhea (Boyer et al. 1974).

## Women Who Become Bulimarexic

My experience with bulimarexics contradicts standard psychoanalytic theory. (See figure 18-2.) Far from rejecting the stereotype of femininity—that of the accommodating, passive, dependent woman—these

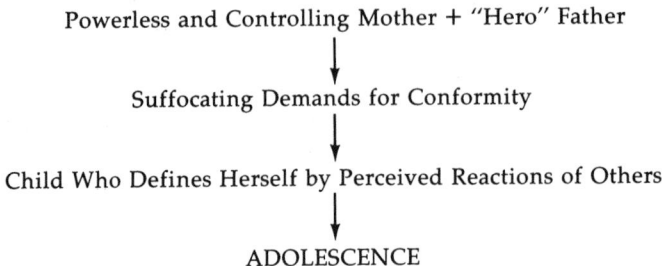

CHILDHOOD

Powerless and Controlling Mother + "Hero" Father

Suffocating Demands for Conformity

Child Who Defines Herself by Perceived Reactions of Others

ADOLESCENCE

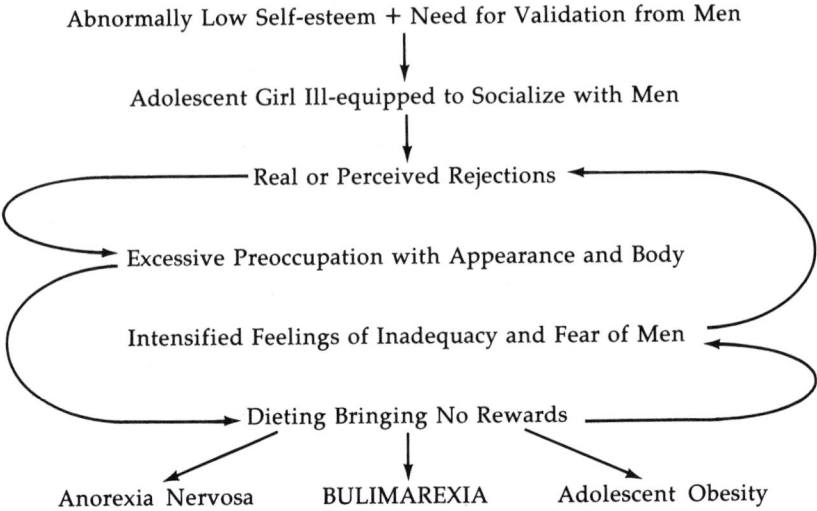

Abnormally Low Self-esteem + Need for Validation from Men

Adolescent Girl Ill-equipped to Socialize with Men

Real or Perceived Rejections

Excessive Preoccupation with Appearance and Body

Intensified Feelings of Inadequacy and Fear of Men

Dieting Bringing No Rewards

Anorexia Nervosa          BULIMAREXIA          Adolescent Obesity

Figure 18–2 Development of Bulimarexic Behavior

young women have never questioned their assumptions that wifehood, motherhood, and intimacy with men are the fundamental components of femininity. I came to understand that their obsessive pursuit of thinness constitutes not only an acceptance of this ideal but an
exaggerated striving to achieve it.[2] Their attempts to control their
physical appearance demonstrate a disproportionate concern with
pleasing others, particularly men—a reliance on others to validate
their sense of worth.[3] They have devoted their lives to fulfilling the

2. I am indebted to Dr. Ronald Leifer for his insights into the implication of bulimarexic behavior and to Janet Snoyer and Holly Bailey for their assistance.
3. The four male bingers I interviewed exhibited the following striking commonal-

feminine *role* rather than the individual person. None has developed a basic sense of personal power or of self-worth.

Bruch (1974) says that these women have a basic *delusion* "of not having an identity of their own, of not even owning their body and its sensations, with the specific inability of recognizing hunger as a sign of nutritional needs." She attributes this to, among other things, "the mother's superimposing on the child her own concept of the child's needs." Thus the child, believing that she is hungry because her mother says so, has little sense of what hunger is about internally. In my experience with these women, the feeling of not having any identity is not a delusion or a misperception but a reality that need not be caused solely by the stereotyped protective mother but by other cultural, social, and psychological pressures as well.

Anne, for example, was a good, generally submissive child. She had lived her life the way "she was supposed to"—precisely her problem. She had been socialized by her parents to believe that society would reward her good looks: "Some day the boys are going to go crazy over you." "What a face! With your good looks you'll never have to worry about getting a job." Clinging and dependent, she could not see herself as a separate person. Our early sessions had an unreal quality. I searched for a glimpse of unique character, but Anne had no identifiable sense of self from which to project a real person. Her dependency on others prevented any development of self. Most of the women in my study had been rewarded for their physical attractiveness and submissive "goodness," while characteristics such as independence, self-reliance, and assertiveness were generally punished by parents, grandparents, teachers, and peers. Peggy said, "I was always a tomboy. In fact at the age of ten to twelve I was stronger and faster than any of the boys. After I won a race against a boy, I was given the cold shoulder by the rest of the boys in my class. The girls teased me and my parents put pressure on me to 'start acting like a girl should.' I did, and stopped having as much fun."

Wulff refers to an intense, unconscious mother hate in these wom-

---

ities with the women in the study: (1) all complained of feelings of inadequacy and helplessness and exhibited abnormally low self-esteem; (2) all were extremely dependent and passive individuals who worked very hard at pleasing their parents through academic achievement; (3) all expressed feeling inadequate because they had never been able to sustain relationships with women, and, indeed, all had suffered female rejection in adolescence, which left them fearful of women and further encouraged their isolation; (4) all described their parents as excessively repressive. Unlike the women in the study, the men strongly identified with their mothers and expressed hostility toward their fathers, whom they experienced as demanding and authoritarian. All had been pushed into athletics at an early age by their fathers. Although none were overweight as children and some were, in fact, slight of build, they became preoccupied with weight because of their desire to maintain slim and athletic bodies.

en. In my experience they were, on the contrary, painfully conscious of despising their mothers, most of whom they described as weak and unhappy, women who had abandoned careers in order to raise children. "My mother wanted to be a lawyer but gave it all up when she married my father." Though the mothers are painted as generally ineffectual, they do exercise power in one limited realm: over their children. There, as if they are compensating for their misery elsewhere, they are often suffocating, dominating, and manipulative. Rather than rejecting the passive-aggressive behavior of their mothers and with it the more destructive results of such behavior, the women to whom I listened described their struggle for a social acceptance that would allow them to enact their mother's role. Most of them also strongly identified with their fathers, despite the fact that many fathers spent little time with their families. Instead, they concentrated on interests outside the home. Some of the women reported that the fathers were more persistent in their demands for prettiness and feminine behavior than the mothers. Fathers were objects of hero worship, even though they were preoccupied, distant, or emotionally rejecting.

A distorted concept of body size, a characteristic of the anorexics described by Bruch and the bulimarexics I have studied, is related to the parental and societal expectations that emphasize physical appearance. At the first session with Anne, I was struck by the utter distortion of her body size. She complained frequently of how fat she was; I saw her as exceedingly thin.

M.B.-L.: Why don't you stand up and point out to me where you experience yourself as fat.
ANNE: Here . . . here . . . everywhere. [She jabbed and pulled.]

I noted at this session that Anne's "distorted body image" was linked to a complete lack of confidence in her own ability to control her behavior. She reported that she felt inadequate as a woman and that she had never been able to sustain a loving relationship with a man.

As well as striving to perfect and control their physical appearance, the bulimarexics displayed a need for achievement. All the women were high achievers academically and above average in intellect. However, in most cases the drive to achieve had as its goal pleasing parents and marrying "well." Continued success in academe was essential to feelings of self-worth, but the pressure to achieve, with its rewards, was expected to be forgotten and tucked away in exchange for the fulfillments that marriage and childbearing could bring. These women saw achievement mainly in terms of what rewards it could provoke from others. For example, a doctor is more likely to meet and desire for a mate a woman who is educated; a woman is most likely to meet this man in a university. Achievement was not seen in terms of intrinsic rewards to the self.

Obviously, women who grew up struggling to perfect the female role expect that perfection to be rewarded by fulfillment. Their expectations are founded on what they perceive to be the expectations and standards of the rest of the world for them. It is expectation that has left the women I interviewed sadly vulnerable to rejection. In adolescence they begin to look eagerly for their reward, for the men who will see them as they have struggled to be seen. But rather than being offered rows of handsome princes waiting to court, many women suffer male rejection about this time. For others the rejection was *perceived* rather than actual (i.e., these adolescent girls felt rejected if they were not pursued by males and socially active). The experience of male rejection often precipitates dieting. The girl somehow believes that the appearance of her body must be related to the reason for her rejection. Bruch (1973) describes a young woman who could trace the beginning of her anorexic behavior to an incident she experienced as a rejection.

Celia (No. 12) had begun her noneating regimen during her second year in college, when her boyfriend commented that she weighed nearly as much as he. He was of slight build weighing only 130 lbs. and was sensitive about this, feeling that his manliness was at stake. He expressed the desire that she lose a few pounds and she went on a diet in an effort to please him. However she resented that he had "fixed" their relationship at a certain weight. When she first talked about this she said, "I completely lost my appetite"; later she added that she had been continuously preoccupied with food but denied it to herself. . . . As she began to lose weight she experienced a great sense of strength and independence. (p. 268)

Some women reported that they were, in fact, chubby at this time, but others described themselves as slim but not slim enough, according to their ideal image of what they believed a beautiful body should look like. Along with these slimming efforts, other attempts were sometimes made to beautify the body; three women reported having their noses straightened. However, these dieting attempts also do not produce anticipated rewards (i.e., male attentiveness).

When the expectations of these women of being desired and pursued by men did not materialize, they believed themselves to be undesirable, unattractive, and unworthy. These beliefs reinforced their already existing pervasive sense of inadequacy. Fear of rejection then became a crucial motivating force in their behavior. A rejection, real or perceived, shatters the self-image of the person who has constructed that image around the expectations of others. The person adopts a behavior that will protect her against future rejection. Lee (1973) supports this view: "There was an overwhelming preoccupation with weight and a tendency to view others according to their weight as a way of defending against feelings of inadequacy and fear of rejection by others. The struggle consists of a 'relentless pursuit of thinness.' "

A fear of rejection as a source of Anne's symptoms appeared rather dramatically one day. After three months, she had not been able to recall her first food binge or the circumstances that had led to it. This day she was describing a binge she had had the night before. Using Gestalt techniques, I suggested she try a role-playing fantasy, something with which she was familiar.

M. B.-L: Okay—in that chair is your *body*. The chair you are sitting in is *the food*. Now *be the "food"* and tell your body what you are doing and why.

ANNE: I'm your food and I'm going into you now ... stuffing you ... making you disgusting ... fat. I'm your shame and I'm making you untouchable. No one will ever touch you now. That's what you want ... that no one will touch you. [She looked up in surprise.]

M. B.-L.: Are you surprised about something you just said?

ANNE: Yes. About not being touched ... [silence].

M. B.-L.: Is that something you feel you could get into talking about now?

ANNE: Yes, I guess it might be important.... When I was fifteen [three years ago] I was on a cruise down the Snake River. I impulsively decided I didn't want to be a virgin anymore and since I liked the boat man, I decided to let him make love to me. The only thing is I got drunk, passed out, and that's when he did it to me. I didn't remember anything the next day except feeling miserable and disgusted with myself. And the worst part was this guy didn't want anything to do with me after that. After this happened I lost some weight because I felt maybe I was too fat and that this is what had turned him off. Shortly after I lost weight I had my first binge, and it's gone on ever since.

The first rejection often becomes a pattern. Many women revert to dependent behavior, which assures the repetition of the rejection. Anne would meet a man, "fall in love," and eventually drive him away by growing increasingly possessive and clinging. She then tried to compensate for what she perceived as a failure, attempting to alter herself through fasting in order to accommodate to some mysterious standard of perfection men held. Other women become supercritical of most men they encounter, thereby eliminating the possibility of warm and loving relationships.

Another of my patients, Linda, petite, soft-spoken, and lovely, says of her first binge:

Well, my mother thinks it all started after I was rejected by a boy in my junior year of high school ... [silence] ... he was my first boyfriend, and I was really crazy about him. One day he just dropped me without any explanation.... I never did find out what I had done. It was so confusing.... I was really depressed. Shortly after I had my nose fixed and began to diet. I wasn't fat, but it was the Twiggy era, and I can't remember exactly, but I started to binge somewhere around that time, but I don't really know if there's any connection.

## The Psychodynamics of the Binge and Purge

The cycle the bulimarexic endures can be physically damaging. (See figure 18–3.) The women report fasting, habitual forced vomiting, and amphetamine and laxative abuse as means to counteract a binge. However, for these young women who have been "good" girls and who are afraid of parental disapproval and the rejection that might result from sexual activity, food is one of the few elements in their tightly regulated lives that they can choose to indulge excessively. For the person who is struggling to meet unrealistic goals by imposing severe and ascetic control over herself, the binge is a release.

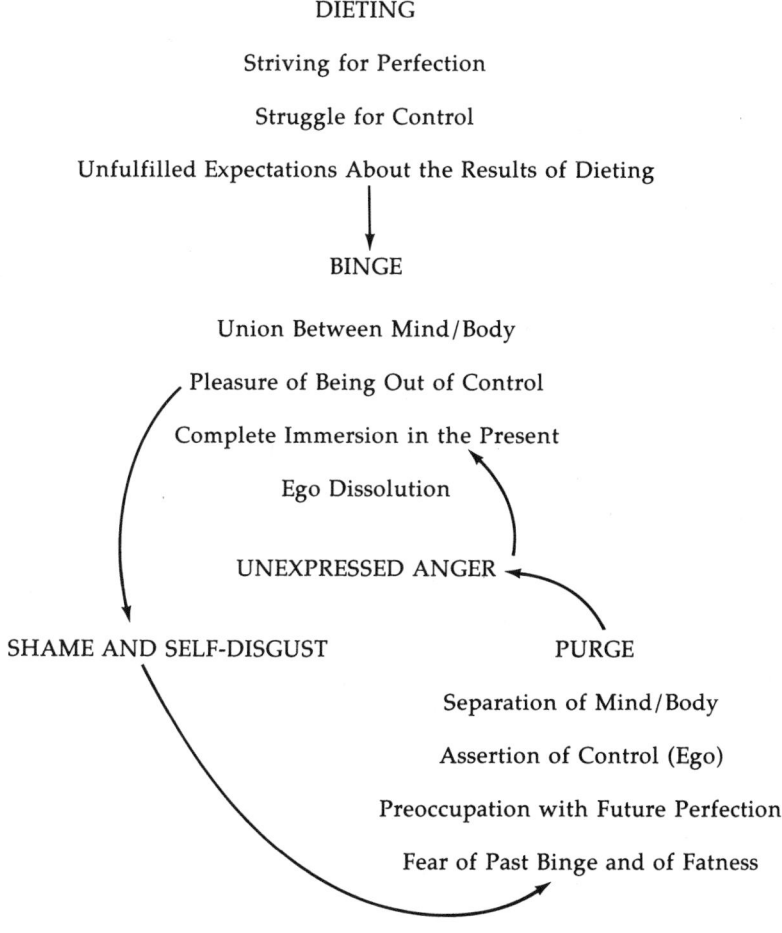

DIETING

Striving for Perfection

Struggle for Control

Unfulfilled Expectations About the Results of Dieting

BINGE

Union Between Mind/Body

Pleasure of Being Out of Control

Complete Immersion in the Present

Ego Dissolution

UNEXPRESSED ANGER

SHAME AND SELF-DISGUST

PURGE

Separation of Mind/Body

Assertion of Control (Ego)

Preoccupation with Future Perfection

Fear of Past Binge and of Fatness

Figure 18–3 The Psychodynamics of Bulimarexia

ANNE: When I am into a binge it doesn't matter if I have just eaten . . . I just go crazy . . . completely out of control. Whatever is around I eat . . . candy . . . four or five bars . . . a whole quart of ice cream. If I am in the cafeteria, I fill my plate with everything. I then go back for seconds, thirds, and even more. I eat until I feel sick. After I binge I feel disgusted with myself and start my fast. I don't eat anything except liquids for a few days. I usually stick to this for as long as a week.

Moreover, the binge brings about a union between the mind and body. One gives one's self to the food, to the moment completely. There is a complete loss of control (ego). It is an absolute here-and-now experience, a kind of ecstasy.

However, the giving over of one's self to this kind of experience leads to shame and guilt. Socialization and cultural pressures intrude to initiate the purification rites, purging or fasting. The purging represents a concentration on past and future. In reliving the past, the self is a helpless child, rewarded for beauty and feminine passivity, punished for being assertive and rebellious. In anticipating the future, the self preoccupies itself with the repercussions of having a fat body in American culture, which will bring about male rejection. For the bulimarexic, ego manifests itself in social symbols (i.e., beautiful body = male approval = self-validation). Because the binge will bring about an ugly body, it carries with it the threat of ego dissolution and social humiliation. In purging, the mind separates itself from the body by focusing on the shame of being out of control.

A feature of fasting that feeds the persistence of the syndrome is the false sense of power that the faster derives from her starvation. The woman feels "good," "in control," and "disciplined" when her life has narrowed to self-denial. Bruch (1973) refers to anorexia as a "struggle for control for a sense of identity, competence, and effectiveness." She writes that many of these youngsters "had struggled for years to make themselves over and to be perfect in the eyes of others" (p. 251). What her otherwise reasonable interpretation of the syndrome overlooks is the fact that the fasting behavior in this syndrome also strives for power and control over the bulimic behavior. Thus the bulimarexic is involved in a struggle against a part of the self rather than a struggle toward a self. In the early stages of the syndrome, the adolescent girl may be asserting ownership rights over her body. She also may be using this behavior as a passive-aggressive reaction to her mother, whom she perceives as controlling and suffocating. The refusal of food—along with compulsive masturbation, nailbiting, and so forth— are all behaviors that the parents cannot completely control. The child chooses privacy and isolation for her acting out. However, when bulimia first occurs the nature of the syndrome undergoes a transformation. The underlying beliefs about one's self ("I am unlovable, unattractive, and inadequate") are pervasive and make the woman extraordinarily sensitive to the reactions of other people toward her. The most minor or insignificant slight is exaggerated and distorted, creating massive self-loathing, and is used as an *excuse* for binge-ing. The anger the woman feels toward her imagined rejector is not acknowledged, and this unexpressed anger is turned inward, adding to the fury of the binge.

The fast-binge cycle of the bulimarexic is confining. It consumes enough energy to prevent the woman from looking beyond it or outgrowing it. It serves to keep her socially isolated. Binge-ing wards off people with a "wall of [perceived] fat." It is a way of "filling up" without needing others. A fairly typical example from Anne's case supports this hypothesis. Anne was invited to go out to dinner by a boy she really liked; she wanted to go but was on the fasting part of her cycle. She feared the temptation and thus worked herself into a high state of anxiety, fearing a binge and vacillating between going and staying home. On the date, she ate moderately and had an enjoyable time. When the man dropped her off, she proceeded to binge grotesquely.

The fact that the behavior is a secret one, carried out in private, further isolates the bulimarexic. For her food becomes a *fetish*, as Becker uses the term in "Fetishism as Low Self-Esteem" (1969).

"General inactivity," "low self-esteem," and "sense of inadequacy" indicate that the fetishist is a person who has sentenced himself (herself) to live in a certain kind of object world. It will be shallow in terms of the complexity and richness of its objects; it will represent a narrow commitment instead of a broad and flexible one; yet it will be a segment of the world which has to bear a full load of life meaning. In other words, the fetishist will be a behaviorally poor person, who has the resourceful task of creating a rich world. As we said, the record of that resourceful contriving is the fetish behavior itself. (pp. 18–19)

## A Feminist Perspective

None of the women in this study had ever experienced a satisfying love relationship in spite of their attractiveness and high intelligence. All longed for one. Most were virgins. Others froze up when sexual overtures were made or developed severe anxiety or depression during or after sex. The sexual conflicts that are evident in these women do not reflect a rejection of femininity or a bizarre fear of oral impregnation.[4] Rather, these women have already learned a passive and accommodating approach to life from their parents and their culture. This accommodation is combined with two opposing tensions: the desperate desire for self-validation from a man and an inordinate *fear of men* and their power to reject. Since most of the women have already experienced a real or perceived rejection by a male or males, this perpetuates the already larger-than-life belief in the power and importance of men. The sexual fears of these women are often associated with intercourse, which is viewed as an act of surrender exposing their vulnerability to rejection. Rather than finding an obsession with bizarre fantasies (oral impregnation), I found a preoccupation with the fear of rejection in sex, of not being good enough to please a man.

If the woman is able to find a male companion who loves her, in spite of the obstacles her behavior presents to the relationship, a remission of symptoms might occur. This relationship, while relieving the surface of the bulimarexic's problem, can be more ultimately destructive. If the woman has not strengthened her sense of self and self-worth, the future of the relationship can be at best uncertain; failure of the relationship can be devastating.

Why is it that the bulimarexic gives men the power to reject her? Why does she give up her own power and make men larger than life? A reasonable answer, one more direct than that found in a theory of the innate psychology of women, lies in our heritage of sexual inequality. Between the ages of thirteen to seventeen, some adolescent girls find that society in general and men in particular do not reward them as they have been socialized by both their parents and their culture to *expect*. Obviously this image of men affects a woman not only as a daughter but as a mother. It is my conviction that the mothers of these women became what they are for the same reasons that their daughters became bulimarexics. Most women are socialized to dependency to some degree. Laws (1979) has summarized ways in which this affects women:

Social dependence, as a habit of responding, has a number of consequences. . . . First, the reliance on rewards coming from others makes the individual very flexible and adaptable, ready to alter her behavior (or herself) in response to words and threats. Second, she is limited to others as a source of rewards, including self-esteem, for two reasons: (1) the necessity of being accommodating and responsive works against the development of a sense of self which

---

4. Normal adolescent girls often express a fear of oral impregnation. These fears occur between the ages of ten and thirteen and usually are connected with inaccurate sexual information and imagined parental disapproval. Since such fears are so often experienced by normal women, I can see no basis for assuming that these fears foster anorexic behavior.

might oppose the demands of others, and (2) any evidence of the development of the self as a source of approval or of alternative directions is punished by others. The "responsiveness" and the sole reliance on social support make the women extraordinarily vulnerable to rejection (meaning failure).

Many traditional approaches to therapy with women see men as solutions to problems of low self-esteem. Szyrynski (1973) exaggerates these assumptions when he suggests that "since a great majority of such patients are adolescent girls, a male therapist may be probably more effective than a woman. He can replace for the girl her inadequate father figure; on the other hand, he will not be identified by the patient with her hostile mother" (p. 502).[5] I believe, on the contrary, that female therapists can provide positive female role models for these women that are a marked contrast to the negative experiences they recount in relationships with their mothers. In addition, it is unrealistic to expect that the presence of a man, or any other person, can compensate for a nonexistent sense of self. It is equally unrealistic to expect a man to want to serve this function. I can only offer a pessimistic prognosis for the woman who looks at the accession of an approving man as the solution to her psychological conflicts.[6] Since anorexia nervosa and bulimarexia are appearing with greater frequency,[7] I can only hope that the increasing number of women suffering from these syndromes can avail themselves of a humane therapy to help alleviate the low self-esteem that is at the root of their problems.

5. In the cases of the three men I saw in individual therapy, the same Gestalt-behaviorist approach used with women was utilized. It emphasized awareness, responsibility, assertiveness training, and male consciousness raising. In all cases, at a particular stage in the therapy it was decided that a male therapist would be useful to deal with issues of sexuality, and these patients were then referred to a male counselor with a similar therapeutic orientation. All eventually gave up the bulimarexic behavior and reported many positive changes in their attitudes toward themselves, women, and their parents.

6. The extent to which such attitudes prevail in our culture is indicated by the account of a "cured" anorexic. "I fell in love. By no means do I want to suggest that love is the answer to everything. For me, loving someone shifted my attention away from the compulsive, convoluted world of self I had created inside me, toward another person. Finally, I felt some self-esteem because I had been found worthy by someone else" (Lynch 1974, p. 107).

7. With a few exceptions, most of the literature on these behaviors has not acknowledged this upward trend. One exception is the British study by Duddle (1973). Most of the food bingers I have encountered know of other women who binge. I suspect that most cases are seen in a high-school guidance office or college mental health service. Many more women probably suffer secretly from this compulsion and do not seek help because of inordinate shame about their behaviors.

REFERENCES

Becker, E. 1969. *Angel in armor.* New York: Free Press.

Boyer, R. M., et al. 1974. Anorexia nervosa: Immaturity of the 24-hour luteinizing hormone secretory pattern. *New England Journal of Medicine* 291:861–865.

Bruch, H. 1973. *Eating disorders.* New York: Basic Books.

————. Children who starve themselves. *The New York Times Magazine,* November 10, 1974, p. 70.

Cattell, R. B. 1972. *The 16 P-F.* Champaign, Ill.: Institute for Personality and Ability Testing.

Duddle, M. 1973. An increase of anorexia nervosa in a university population. *British Journal of Psychiatry* 123:711–712.

Laws, J. L. 1979. Woman as object. In *The second X.* New York: Elsevier.

Lee, A. O. 1973. Disturbance of body image in obesity and anorexia nervosa. *Smith College Studies in Social Work* 44:33–34.

Lindner, R. 1955. The case of Laura. *The fifty-minute hour.* New York: Holt.

Lynch, K. 1974. Danger! You can overdo dieting. *Seventeen* 24 (March):107.

Miller, J. B. 1972. Sexual in-equality: Men's dilemma; a note on the Oedipus complex, paranoia, and other psychological concepts. *American Journal of Psychoanalysis* 32(2):140–155.

Secord, P., and Jourard, S. 1953. The appraisal of body-cathexis: Body cathexis and the self. *Journal of Consulting Psychology* 17:343–347.

Szyrynski, V. 1973. Anorexia nervosa and psychotherapy. *American Journal of Psychotherapy* 27(2):492–505.

Waller, J. V., Kaufman, R. M., and Deutsch, F. 1940. Anorexia nervosa: A psychosomatic entity. *Psychosomatic Medicine* 2:3–16.

Wulff, M. 1945. Ueber einen interessanten oralen Symptomenkomplex und seine Beziehung zur sucht. In *The psychoanalytic theory of neuroses,* ed. O. Fenichel, p. 241. New York: Norton.

# 19

# Group Process for Women with Orgasmic Difficulties

## LONNIE GARFIELD BARBACH
## AND TONI AYRES

It is well known that many women have difficulty experiencing orgasm. According to the research of Kinsey and his associates (1953) and the more recent survey of Hunt (1974), about 10 to 15 percent of the married women studied have never experienced orgasm by any method, and approximately 40 to 50 percent rarely or never experience orgasm during intercourse. For the sexually active unmarried female population, the percentage is even higher. Because of its prevalence, people often discuss this concern with counselors.

In November 1972, at the University of California—Berkeley, Lonnie Barbach and Nancy Carlson began the development of a group treatment program for women who complained of orgasmic difficulties but who were deemed inappropriate candidates for traditional couple sex therapy (Masters and Johnson 1970) due to the lack of a steady sexual partner, partner unwillingness to attend conjoint therapy, unwillingness to tell the partner that a problem exists, or the expense of conjoint sex therapy.

The women included in the program had never experienced an orgasm by any means. The group members decided to label themselves "preorgasmic," since they viewed themselves as not yet having the proper information and experience to enable them to achieve orgasm. At present the preorgasmic group program generally consists of six women meeting together as a group with two female cofacilitators. These groups meet for two weekly sessions of an hour and a half each for five weeks.

## The Group Process

Groups have proven to be an efficient treatment modality in general, and we have found women's groups to be more effective for preorgasmic women than either one-to-one or couple counseling for several reasons. First, most women have been brought up in a tradition of not discussing sexuality. The group process provides a forum for open, detailed, and honest discussion. This helps eliminate the sense of isolation as the women find that they share similar experiences and concerns. One woman noted that just meeting five other women with the same problem helped her feel less "abnormal." In addition, participants begin to realize that there are no "norms" and that each woman is as unique sexually as she is in every other way. This becomes obvious as the six women discuss their likes, dislikes, areas of sensitivity, and turn-ons in the process of talking about their experiences with the at-home exercises.

Second, since sex has been an unrewarding and anxiety-producing area for most of these women, the group setting provides peer-group support that motivates the women to explore their sexuality and complete the at-home exercises. Each woman's progress serves as a stimulus for the others. The feedback from peers is often more powerful than interventions made by the facilitators, particularly as far as attaining orgasm is concerned. The fact that one member of the group, one who was like the others just the session before, has been able to experience orgasm and have none of her worst fears realized offers the kind of encouragement an already orgasmic group leader cannot possibly offer.

## Homework

In addition to the time spent in group sessions, an important part of the process is the concept of homework. The women are required to spend one hour each day practicing their assignments. These at-home

264

exercises follow a modified version of LoPiccolo and Lobitz's (1972) nine-step masturbation program. The exercises assigned progress as the women's sexual responsiveness progresses.

The women begin their homework hour by getting into a relaxed frame of mind. This may include a bath, a shower, soft music, erotic literature, and so on. For the first few sessions, the women generally receive identical assignments. They are taught the Kagel (1952) exercises. They are expected to spend an hour exploring their own bodies visually and tactually in great detail just to learn to be more accepting of their bodies. They are given important information about the anatomy of their genitals and information pertaining to the sexual response cycle, and then they are instructed to examine their genitals carefully with a hand mirror. Before being given instructions about masturbation, the women are shown a film entitled "Reaching Orgasm," which was developed by the Human Sexuality Program at the University of California Medical Center.

Later, assignments vary as each woman takes greater responsibility for assigning herself the appropriate at-home exercises that will help her attain orgasm. For example, some women fantasize while they masturbate, some use a vibrator, others change to positions that facilitate the buildup of muscle tension, some hold their breath as they reach high levels of arousal, others do breathing exercises to aid them in relaxing. The appropriate homework is decided by the women and leaders as the result of each woman's analysis of her progress as she relates her experience with the assigned at-home exercise during the subsequent group session.

After a woman has become proficient at experiencing orgasm through masturbation, her at-home exercises stress the development of specific, direct sexual communication with her partner, if she has one and wants to be orgasmic with the partner. These exercises often entail such tasks as setting aside time for listening to one another or for communicating grievances and appreciations to one another. Specifically sexual homework includes touching and massage exercises, visual and tactual exploration of the man's and the woman's genitals, masturbation in front of the partner, and intercourse with additional manual clitoral stimulation. The most important aspect of the exercises is the couples' verbal and nonverbal communication throughout the process of the exercise, particularly a rehashing afterward about what was learned by the woman and her partner. In this way the couple can learn to adapt their sexual practices to fit the specific needs of the two people involved. For more extensive descriptions of the at-home exercises, see Barbach (1974, 1975) and Ayres and associates (1975).

## Breaking Through the Barriers

The women in these groups learn to gain control not only over their sexuality but also over other aspects of their lives. Breaking through the barriers to orgasmic response is accompanied by enhanced self-esteem and increased body acceptance. The women also feel better able to communicate with a partner and express their feelings more openly and directly (Wallace and Barbach 1974).

Over 600 women have completed the preorgasmic group program. In a small research sample of 17 women, 100 percent of the women attained orgasm through masturbation by the end of the five-week program. Within eight months afterward and with no additional treatment, 86 percent of the sample could achieve orgasm with a partner, and 68 percent could achieve orgasm with a partner more than 75 percent of the time (Wallace and Barbach 1974).

Orgasm *with a partner* rather than orgasm during intercourse is the goal. This creates a climate in which orgasms through manual stimulation by the partner, mutual masturbation, oral sex, or vibrator stimulation are all seen as equally valid routes to orgasmic release. In this way the pressure on the woman to respond only in certain ways is relieved and the burden is taken off the male partner to produce and maintain an erection. Sexual experiences may then be approached as a much more varied and open means of physical and emotional expression.

The group members' ability to continue sexual growth with a partner after the group program had ended encouraged the development of group programs for women who could experience orgasm with masturbation but not with a partner. These groups are labeled secondary groups, since they represent a second stage in the educational process.

## Secondary Groups

The secondary groups, which meet once a week for ten weeks, are divided into two categories: those for women with willing partners and those for women without partners. In both types of groups the goal of the process is to enable each woman to experience orgasm in at least one new way with her partner, if she has one, or to give her the tools to make this possible when she finds a partner.

Since women who can have orgasms through masturbation are considered sexually functional, the group takes an educational rather than a therapeutic approach. Most of these women discount their masturbatory orgasms and masturbate quickly and surreptitiously. With an emphasis on the validity of masturbatory orgasms from the outset, the women rapidly gain confidence in their ability to communicate to a partner the sexual likes and dislikes they have learned while masturbating.

Each woman who has a partner is required to bring her partner to an initial session, where both the women and the men receive the same information regarding female sexual functioning. This enables both partners to share the same goals and expectations of the program. More important, this procedure provides an opportunity for the male partners to meet the counselors and discuss with them their fears and concerns. An experienced male counselor attends this session and facilitates the sharing of the men's concerns in a nonjudgmental atmosphere.

The homework assignments for the secondary group include both self-stimulation exercises and partner exercises (Barbach 1975). Again, the group setting provides a supportive, validating, and permission-giving environment for women to discuss sex, to experiment, and to learn from one another's experiences. The women report experiencing the same kinds of nonsexual changes as do the preorgasmic women in terms of increased assertiveness, emotional expressiveness, body acceptance, and enhanced partner communication. In addition, approximately 85 percent of the women with willing partners begin to have orgasms in new ways with their partner by the end of the ten-week program. The success of the program, however, frequently depends on the strength of the couple's relationship.

The women without partners will have to be followed up to see if they develop more steady relationships and if they become orgasmic in these relationships.

## Conclusion

We have concluded through our work that the direct treatment of only the female partner in a group situation is a viable and effective form of sex counseling. The results of a recently developed group treatment program for men who have no sexual partners (Zilbergeld 1975) indicates that group process also has positive results for men with sexual concerns.

REFERENCES

Ayres, T., et al. 1975. *SAR guide for a better sex life*. San Francisco: National Sex Forum.

Barbach, L. G. 1974. Group treatment of preorgasmic women. *Journal of Sex and Marital Therapy* 1:139–145.

————. 1975. *For yourself: The fulfillment of female sexuality*. Garden City, N.Y.: Doubleday.

Hunt, M. 1974. *Sexual behavior in the 1970's*. Chicago: Playboy Press.

Kagel, A. H. 1952. Sexual functions of the pubococcygeus muscle. *Western Journal of Surgery* 60:521–524.

Kinsey, A. C., et al. 1953. *Sexual behavior in the human female*. Philadelphia: Saunders.

LoPiccolo, J., and Lobitz, W. C. 1972. The role of masturbation in the treatment of primary orgasmic dysfunction. *Archives of Sexual Behavior* 2:163–172.

Masters, W., and Johnson, V. 1970. *Human sexual inadequacy*. Boston: Little, Brown.

Wallace, D., and Barbach, L. G. 1974. Preorgasmic group treatment. *Journal of Sex and Marital Therapy* 1:146–154.

Zilbergeld, B. 1975. Group treatment of sexual dysfunction in men without partners. *Journal of Sex and Marital Therapy* 1:204–214.

# 20

# Issues in the Treatment of Female Addiction: A Review and Critique of the Literature

WALTER R. CUSKEY, LISA H. BERGER, AND JUDIANNE DENSEN-GERBER

In 1968 a Special Subcommittee on Alcoholism and Narcotics estimated that there were 110,000 heroin addicts in the United States; in 1971 a Special Study Mission of the House of Representatives placed the figure at 250,000 (Cuskey, Premkumar, and Ligel 1972). The National Institute on Drug Abuse (NIDA) estimated that in 1973, 415,200 addicts were concentrated in twenty-four standard metropolitan statistical areas (SMSA's); in 1974 a prevalence rate of 399,000 was presented and in 1975 the number was approximately 391,300 (Person, Retka, and Woodward 1977).

These reports did not provide statistics on the number of female addicts included, but estimates have ranged from 20 percent (Cuskey, Premkumar, and Ligel 1972; Mandell, Goldschmidt, and Drover 1973) to over 30 percent (National Institute on Drug Abuse [NIDA] 1976a; New York City Narcotics Register 1973). The conservative estimates indicate that in 1968 there were approximately 22,000 female heroin addicts, with comparable figures of 50,000 in 1971, 83,000 in 1973 and 78,200 in 1975. From these figures we can conclude that female addiction runs to about .3 to .4 percent of each urban population.

Concentration on prevalence rates for these large urban areas seems justified when one notes that heroin use, among both males and females, is increasingly becoming an urban phenomenon (Cuskey, Premkumar, and Ligel 1972). Major points of entry for heroin are seaports, including Chicago and, increasingly, along the Mexican border. Modern transportation makes all areas vulnerable, with highest concentrations in cities closest to the point of entry.

The largest concentrations of heroin users are in the SMSA's of New York (69,600), Los Angeles (60,000), Detroit (33,200), and Chicago (47,700), according to 1975 NIDA estimates (Person, Retka, and Woodward 1977). New York City addiction statistics are of particular import as the number of heroin addicts located in that city constitutes the largest concentration of addicts in any U.S. urban environment. Of the estimated 415,200 urban addicts in 1973, NIDA reported that 80,000 were living in the New York City area (Person, Retka, and Woodward 1977), although other sources placed the figure between 100,000 and 125,000 (New York City Narcotics Register 1973). According to NIDA, the proportion of addicts in that locale in 1974 was 91,000 (Person, Retka, and Woodward 1977). Thus, extrapolating from the most conservative estimates (specifically the male/female ratio of 20 percent [Cuskey, Premkumar, and Ligel 1972; Mandell, Goldschmidt, and Drover 1973] and the above-reported NIDA statistics [Person, Retka, and Woodward 1977]), the number of female addicts in the SMSA of New York City is less than 18,200.

Another major consideration is the fact that the majority of addicted females are of childbearing age, about two-thirds being between the ages of eighteen and thirty and 93 percent between fifteen and thirty-five (Demaree, Kee, and Sells 1975; Drug Enforcement Administration and NIDA 1975; NIDA 1976a). In New York City the problem seems to be equally severe: The Addiction Services Agency (ASA) reports that 86 percent of the female addicts are between the ages of eighteen and thirty; 90 percent within the range of fifteen to thirty-five years (Burt and Glynn 1976). Thus, in consideration of the above-mentioned prevalence estimates, over 74,000 female addicts in 1975 were of childbearing age, and over 16,000 in New York City.

With numbers of this magnitude it is surprising that so little attention has been paid to pregnant addicts, and/or addicts with children and neonatal addiction, both on national and citywide levels. From the few studies that have been conducted to date, it appears that the number of pregnant addicts is increasing (Zelson 1975). In 1970, Philadelphia General Hospital reported that 1 out of 71 deliveries was to an addicted woman. In 1971 this number increased to 1 in 21 and in 1972 the figure was 1 in 16 (Finnegan, Connaughton, and Schutt 1975). The same phenomenon has been noted in New York City: In 1963 only 1 out of 164 admissions to New York City College Metropolitan Hospital Center was an addicted female; in 1973 the ratio was 1 in 47 (Nathenson 1974). It might also be noted that due to the unwillingness of females to be identified as addicts, or fear of reprisals from the courts, it is probable that many pregnant addicts escape detection. In addition, it is suspected that a significant number may self-deliver or deliver at home without a physician in attendance (Finnegan, Connaughton, and Schutt 1975); thus it may well be that the incidence of pregnancies among addicted females has been underestimated.

In addition, it appears that female addicts are having more children: In 1944 Pescor reported that the typical female addict had one child; in 1966 Ellinwood and associates estimated that the median was two children. Extrapolating from these figures, it can be estimated that over 234,000 children in the U.S. have mothers who are addicted to heroin, with more than 43,000 such children in New York City.

What is even more striking is that many of these children were sentenced at birth—either stillborn, born addicted, or dead soon after birth due to withdrawal. In 1960, 300 cases of neonatal narcotism were reported by the New York Hospital Committee (Sussman 1963); in 1972, 550 cases were noted, and in 1973 this figure rose to over 911 (National Clearinghouse for Drug Abuse Information [NCDAI] 1974). Since addicted mothers are often reluctant to confide in medical personnel as to their drug habits, many infants are not monitored for withdrawal symptoms. Many women go off drugs when pregnant; an estimated 50 percent of the children born to addicts show no withdrawal symptoms (Carr 1975), and symptoms are frequently confused with meningitis, hypoglycemia, central nervous system infection, and respiratory problems (NCDAI 1974). Thus the 911 reported cases of neonatal narcotism in 1973 may only represent one-half of the total.

Estimates of neonatal mortality have ranged from 7 to 20 percent. Stern reported in 1966 that 7 percent of the babies in his sample of 66 addict mothers were stillborn and in 1967 Perlmutter found a perinatal mortality rate of 17.4 percent compared to a figure of 2.2 percent among nonaddicted mothers. Another study showed that of 40 infants, 10 percent died soon after birth and about one-quarter were critically ill, but survived after therapy (Stoffer 1968). Hill and Desmond (1963) estimated the mortality rate for infants who show symptoms and are treated at 9 percent.

Of course, the female addicts themselves often end up as statistics in the medical examiners' reports. A study at Lexington Hospital indicated that observed deaths for female addicts exceed nonaddict norms 3 to 1, compared to 2.5 to 1 for male addicts (O'Donnell 1969). In 1973 mortality rates for female addicts were given as 4 per 1,000 per year; among black females aged eighteen to twenty the figure was as high as 26 per 1,000 (Helpern 1972). In 1973 alone a total of 409 females died heroin-related deaths (Drug Enforcement Administration and NIDA 1975). Since addicts frequently ingest heroin in combination with other substances, the attribution of cause of death at autopsy is often subsumed under other headings. It is therefore suspected that incidences of mortality are probably underestimated (Baden 1972).

With female addiction becoming more and more prominent, it is important to examine the proportion of such women who are receiving help, either on an outpatient or residential basis. In 1975 only 21.8 percent of the estimated female addict population received treatment;[1] by the end of that year a total of only 3,000 women had been treated in therapeutic community (TC) facilities (DeLeon and Beschner 1977). In examining prevalence statistics as compared to rates of entry into traditional treatment, Burt and associates (1977a) concluded that females were vastly underrepresented in federally funded drug treatment programs. Thus along with evidence that more females are becoming addicted to heroin is the fact that a very small percentage are receiving help.


## Barriers to Recruitment


### Admission Criteria

A significant proportion of women may be discouraged from entering treatment because of certain restrictions placed on enrollment. A great many programs do not admit pregnant addicts or addicted mothers. Thus, as increasing numbers of addicts are becoming pregnant and having children, it would seem that a larger percentage are being automatically barred from treatment because of their maternal status. As centers seldom include day-care facilities or programs for children, it may be that mothers would be more inclined to stay out of treat-

---

1. This percentage was computed as the number of female addicts receiving residential or outpatient care in 1974 (information supplied by the Drug Enforcement Administration and NIDA [1975] and NIDA [1974]) compared to the derived prevalence estimates for female addiction reported earlier (Person, Retka, and Woodward 1977; Cuskey, Premkumar, and Ligel 1972; Mandell, Goldschmidt, and Drover 1973).

ment than to seek help and relinquish their children to relatives or the courts (Bauman et al. 1976).

Other programs require that every addicted person with whom the addict lives enter treatment. It has been noted that many female addicts are involved in relationships with addicted or otherwise deviant males, and that there is a greater tendency for the men to make deviants of their nondeviant female partners than vice versa (Cuskey 1977; Cuskey, Premkumar, and Ligel 1972; O'Donnell, Besteman, and Jones 1967; Tucker 1977). This would point to a stronger position of dominance among the males, which seems to agree with findings of lower levels of assertiveness and excessive dependency needs among female addicts (Colten 1977; Tucker 1977). Thus female addicts may be less able to induce their mates to enter treatment than their male counterparts.

## Mixed-Sex Program

Female addicts have serious problems relating to men, including frigidity, feelings of victimization and conflicting protection needs, severe mistrust, hostility, in addition to suffering from the greater stigma accorded to female drug addicts and prostitutes by equally deviant males (Colten 1977; DeLeon 1974; Ellinwood, Smith, and Vaillant 1966; Soler, Ponsor, and Abod 1976). Thus, as the majority of programs include mixed-sex therapeutic modalities, women might be less likely to enroll in a program where perpetuation of these problems and continuation of sexist street role values and societal bias seems inevitable. In addition, lesbian addicts, many of whom "perceive and praise their homosexuality as the ultimate escape from male domination" (White 1976) would be obviously less inclined to enter a program that includes male clients.

## Use of Male-Oriented Treatment Models

Despite the fact that female addiction has become a problem large enough to warrant national attention, very little is known as to the process and implications of addiction among women. The literature devoted to female addicts has been sparse compared to that dealing with men and the increased attention in research efforts over the past decade has provided little insight into the problem. The majority of studies have focused on medical concerns, particularly health problems of the newborn contracted through maternal drug taking. Even in areas where a sizable amount of research has been conducted, the findings are often inconsistent and limited due to a number of methodological flaws, including problems in conceptualization, definition of terms, research design, instrumentation, sampling, and data analysis techniques.

Little is known about the forces that combine to produce a female addict, and what little there is has been extrapolated from research on male addicts. As a model of female addiction has not as yet been developed, most programs operate from the perspective of male-oriented treatment models, which are inappropriate to the needs and problems of female addicts and which probably discourage a significant proportion from entering treatment.

One of the currently popular treatment approaches derives from what may be called the physiological model, where addiction is viewed as a metabolic disorder caused by continued narcotics use (Dole and Nyswander 1967; Goldstein 1972). Treatment methods employing methadone maintenance operate from this perspective; however, it has been suggested that low recruitment of female addicts into these types of programs is because the programs offer them fewer alternatives (Levy and Doyle 1976).

The functionality or social competence model views addiction as a chronic condition unresponsive to "curative" treatment such as methadone maintenance, and modalities operating from this position focus on the amelioration of different kinds of functional or adaptational problems such as unemployment and crime (Brotman, Meyer, and Freedman 1965). However, Arnon and associates (1974) have suggested that addicted women turn to heroin as a means of resolving intrapsychic conflict, so that it is conceivable that fewer of these females would enter a program that did not provide therapy for psychological or emotional problems.

On the other hand, the personality model, which explains addictive behavior by the users' immature and inadequate personality development and growth (Braucht et al. 1973; Fracchia et al. 1975), and the sociocultural model, focusing on aspects of the addicts' social environment (Eldred and Brown 1974; Seldin 1972) (i.e., antecedent family factors, social development and support networks, etc.) are typically employed in drug-free highly structured inpatient environments, such as TC's, where the goal of therapy is resocialization (Densen-Gerber 1973; Waldorf 1971). But as in methadone maintenance programs, these approaches seemingly discourage female enrollment, as they provide restrictive and undesirable alternatives to their current life style. For women who have already "broken out of the bounds of acceptability" (Maglin 1973), such goals do not provide sufficient attraction to motivate a complete change in patterns of living.

Females may also be disinclined to enter TC's because of the strict regime of punishment and confrontation. As mentioned earlier, many female addicts lack assertiveness and may have lower levels of self-esteem than their male counterparts (Colten 1977; Cuskey 1977; Ross and Berzins 1974), possibly due to their participation in a male-dominated deviant subculture where female deviancy is more severely stigmatized. Thus many women, feeling extremely vulnerable to punishment or to the effects of radical "tearing down" sessions (especially where males will be present), may be discouraged from entering treatment programs that employ such seemingly harsh regimens.

## Characteristics of Female Addicts

Several characteristics, found among a large proportion of female addicts, could act to impede their enrollment in currently conceived treatment programs. For example, methadone maintenance programs assume that elimination of the drug craving will allow the addict to concentrate on rehabilitative activities. However, this emphasis on self-reliance might discourage females from entering, as extreme dependency has been found to be characteristic of addicted women (Colten 1977).

Many TC's require a strong motivation to change as a prerequisite for admission. As female addicts have been found by some researchers to be more depressed and to have lower levels of self-esteem than males (DeLeon 1974; Colten 1977; Cuskey 1977; Ross and Berzins 1974), it seems unlikely that they would take any positive measures to improve their condition. Densen-Gerber and associates (1972) refer to "a reluctance to change without significant pressure to do so." Furthermore, females have also been found to display a high degree of "externality" on psychological tests (Arnon, Kleinman, and Kissin 1974; Coughlan and Gold 1974; DeLeon 1974), attributing control of their lives to fate or destiny, and thus are less likely to view any actions they might take as steps that could significantly influence their future.

This is not to say that female addicts are inherently more pathological than males, but that they might be disposed to more severe depression and have a poorer self-concept as a result of their maltreatment by society and by male addicts, and because "the data on their social relationships and on their life problems indicate that they have more about which to complain" (Colten 1977). Similarly, female addicts may appear more "external," as females in general have not been socialized to take active control of their lives (Marsh and Neely 1977) and addicted women may feel a greater degree of victimization by virtue of their existence as a "deviant subsection of a male-dominated deviant subculture" (Maglin 1973).

In addition, the literature indicates a trend toward a greater number of marriages (Campbell and Freeland 1974; Cuskey, Moffet, and Clifford 1971; Ellinwood, Smith, and Vaillant 1966; O'Donnell, Besteman, and Jones 1967), and also toward a greater number of these marriages ending in divorce or separation (Cuskey, Premkumar, and Ligel 1972; Cuskey, Moffet, and Clifford 1971; Marsh and Neely 1977; O'Donnell, Besteman, and Jones 1977). Other reports have shown that the majority of female subjects had never been married (Cuskey 1977; Douvan 1977); thus it would appear that the greater proportion of these women are either single, separated, or divorced from their husbands, and thus less likely to receive partner encouragement to enter treatment.

Even those females who are involved in relationships are not likely to be prompted by their mates to seek help as they tend to be involved with deviant partners (Cuskey 1977; Cuskey, Premkumar, and Ligel 1972; O'Donnell, Besteman, and Jones 1967; Tucker 1977) and are more likely than males to interact in "non-supportive milieu" social groups (Eldred and Washington 1976). Furthermore, addicted females, both married and single, have been found to have inadequate social support structures, leading relatively isolated existences (Eldred and Washington 1976; Marsh and Neely 1977; Tucker 1977). Without a great deal of self-motivation or encouragement from others, the incentive for change seems minimal.

Several studies have indicated that female addicts are extremely dependent on others, especially males (Tucker 1972; Wallace 1977), so that women who are involved in such relationships might refuse to enter treatment for fear of separation. In this same vein, the high incidence of homosexuality among female addicts (Ellinwood, Smith, and Vaillant 1966; Waldorf 1973; Willis 1970) may preclude the possibility of a significant proportion of these women entering TC's where homosexuality is barred or discouraged.

Another reason why a large number of female addicts are not likely to enter treatment relates to the discussion of criminal behavior associated with a deviant life style. Several researchers have noted that the majority of addicted females are involved in illegal activities, including prostitution, narcotics violations such as dealing or "bag following," property crimes and, to a lesser extent, more violent crimes such as assault (Cuskey 1977; Ellinwood, Smith, and Vaillant 1966; Rosenbaum 1973; NIDA 1976b). However, females are arrested, convicted, and sentenced less frequently than males (Burt et al. 1977), and, therefore, are less often given the option of entering treatment in lieu of an extended sentence.

Prostitution, which is a common method of support for a significant proportion of female addicts (File, McCahill, and Savitz 1974), provides a sure and steady source of income. Once this security has been established, "there is less reason to see rehabilitation from the drug world as an attractive alternative" (Maglin 1973). Additionally, addict prostitutes may be less inclined to enter treatment because of the lack of a satisfactory posttreatment image. As female deviancy is stigmatized to a greater extent than that of males, the reputation the women had established will most likely persist after treatment. Few males want to marry and few employers want to hire ex-prostitutes; and it might be enormously difficult for these women to reestablish ties with their friends and families.

## Entry into Treatment

To account for the small percentage of women entering treatment, we must learn how those who seek help differ from those who do not. First, those who enter programs may be distinguished by the maternal condition (i.e., they are not pregnant and do not have children). Regarding criminal activity, it is conceivable that those who utilize methods of support that provide more sporadic incomes than prostitution (for example, drug dealing or theft) might be more likely candidates for enrollment. With the characteristic of extreme dependency and a tendency to follow their partners' wishes (Bauman et at. 1976), it may also be suggested that encouragement from a mate among the minority who are involved in "supportive milieu" social groups could have considerable impact on their decision to enroll.

Females who enter treatment might also be distinguished from those who do not by their existing needs. Although several authors have noted that the majority of female addicts suffer from some kind of psychological disturbance (Cuskey 1977; Hall 1968; NIDA 1976b), the varied findings regarding the prevalence of specific kinds of disorders suggest that different kinds of females are entering treatment with different types of emotional difficulties, and thus for different reasons. Females who are highly anxious (Colten 1977; DeLeon 1974; Kilmann 1974), might be more likely to seek help for their problems, as may be true with those who are hypochrondriacal (Ross and Berzins 1974).

Finally, females who enter programs may be distinguished by length of drug use. Ellinwood and associates (1966) found that about half of the women in their sample enrolled because they were "tired of the life" or concerned about their health—the majority had been using heroin for well over five years upon admission. The studies reviewed have indicated a national average age of between seventeen and twenty years for beginning heroin use (Binion 1977; Campbell and Freeland 1974; NIDA 1976*b*). The majority of females entering treatment are between ages twenty-one and twenty-five (Demaree, Kee, and Sells 1975; Drug Enforcement Administration and NIDA 1975; NIDA 1976*a*), and, therefore, a delay of four years seems the rule. Those involved in heroin abuse for shorter periods of time may not yet have become dissatisfied with the deviant life style; a subgroup of those involved for longer time spans may have had more disheartening experiences (or were more sensitive to them) or had different perceptions and feelings relating to rehabilitation, or differed by any of the above-mentioned factors accounting for entry into treatment.

## Barriers to Retention

Given that a very small proportion of addicted women come into treatment, the prominence of female addiction becomes even more serious by virtue of the fact that the rate of attrition is enormously high; almost 50 percent of those entering residential programs drop out regardless of age, race, or modality (detoxification, maintenance, or drug-free settings) (Burt et al, 1977*b*).

### Use of Male-Oriented Treatment Models

The reasons behind these early terminations may be the same as those behind the low rates of entry into treatment. The use of therapeutic techniques based on male-oriented models constitutes a central problem, most likely decreasing the likelihood that female addicts will complete the full course of treatment.

For example, the philosophy of Odyssey House assumes that the perception by the addict that his or her deviant behavior will no longer be rewarded by the group is instrumental in therapeutic change. However, female addicts, who have been severely stigmatized by their male comrades and by society in general, have also been found to disparage other female abusers to a greater extent than do males (Colten 1977). Thus it seems presumptuous to assume that equality and/or acceptance will suddenly be achieved without specific attention to correcting these prejudices. It has, in fact, been noted that street-type sexist thinking is reinforced in TC settings (Levy and Doyle 1974) (see pp. 000 to 000).

The addict in Daytop Village is provided with role models, presumably to encourage identification with healthier ways of behaving. In TC's the goal for females is to "bring out the feminine instincts of the women—as the mother instinct" (Calof 1969), or to establish a stable relationship with the opposite sex (Soler, Ponsor, and Abod 1976). But women who have already broken the bonds of socially accepted norms may view such goals as confining and unattractive alternatives to their former life style or deviancy. Furthermore, female addicts have been found to conform to traditional sex role ideology to a greater extent than nonaddicted females (Colten 1977). However, since their deviant life style is at odds with what society deems acceptable feminine behavior, it is probable that considerable guilt and confusion blur their concept of female identity. Treatment emphasis on reversion to roles that had formerly been rejected and to which a great amount of anxiety had been attached would most likely seem unsatisfactory. Kirsh (1974) has stated that such an approach "forces the person to deny her perceptions of dissatisfaction and discomfort. She is urged to continue using male standards of herself as the criteria of her behavior rather than attempting to display whatever urges she feels. . . ." It would seem that the problem of an inadequate female identity (Colten 1977; Densen-Gerber, Wiener, and Hochstedler 1972; Escamilla-Mondanaro 1976) would not disappear with the assumption of "feminine" roles, but that marital relationships and child-caring practices (Lief 1977; Stryker 1977; Wilson 1977) are likely to continue to be hazardous. Furthermore, the emphasis on social conformity for female addicts in treatment creates a severe conflict between "culturally bound expectations of women's behavior and the goals of therapy" (Soler, Ponsor, and Abod 1976): They are expected to be autonomous, self-reliant individuals while fulfilling the needs of others at the same time.

Thus two important components of TC approaches, founded on a male model of addiction, are strikingly inappropriate to the treatment of females and probably contribute significantly to their low rates of retention.

## Mixed-Sex Group Therapy

Several TC's employ "encounter" sessions as an intrinsic part of the treatment regimen. The rationale for this technique is to strip the addict of his or her former pretenses and attack antisocial behavior in an effort to institute healthier ways of reacting and behaving. However, many addicted females expect to be hurt, used, and abused by men (Colten 1977), and the use of such radical "tearing down" techniques may exacerbate their feelings of victimization and encourage departure from the program.

Addicted men have been found to be more manipulative and less concerned with the feelings of others than their female counterparts, and addicted women participating in mixed-sexed therapy groups or those being treated by male therapists could be at a severe disadvantage since it has also been found that "individuals high in Machiavellianism almost come out ahead . . . at the expense of those lower in Machiavellianism" (Colten 1977). This is supported by the findings of Aries (1974), where mixed group settings "benefitted men more than women by allowing them more variation in their interpersonal style while for women it brings more restrictions in style."

Soler and associates (1976) found that mixed groups generally averaged three men to one woman. Females consistently expressed the view that the discussions were not helpful in providing supportive and constructive feedback, creating an environment for change, or in minimalizing isolation. Rather the groups became settings for displays of power on the part of the males, who bonded together to form positions of dominance, and this drastically reduced the women's chances to be heard. When attention was directed toward the women it was in the form of recriminations and sexist attacks.

As the disadvantages of mixed-sex groups seem to outweigh the benefits, and since mixed-sex techniques are employed in TC's, methadone maintenance programs, low-level intervention programs, screening units, and in storefronts, it would seem that the inclination to remain in treatment will be radically reduced by the use of this technique.

*Sexism*

Not only are the above-mentioned features of drug rehabilitation programs inadequate or inappropriate for female addicts, but discrimination against women seems to be common and pervasive in most treatment settings.

Part of this bias has developed because of exclusive use of male-oriented treatment models; the staff even has difficulty in identifying the problems of females and recognizing their differing and prejudicial perceptions of male/female needs. Women are viewed as implicitly "sicker" than men, and their main problems are thought to revolve around interpersonal and intrapersonal sensitivities. Male problems, on the other hand, are believed to be centered around an absence of job training and/or a lack of desire to improve themselves (Levy and Doyle 1974).

These biased views naturally have repercussions on the female's prognosis for treatment. Several programs utilize house jobs organized in a hierarchy of responsibility as part of the therapeutic regimen (for example, Daytop Village). But since staff members view female addiction as a function of sexual or interpersonal problems, women are not supported in expanding their skills or developing competence in new areas. Men and women do not get the same job assignments—women are placed in traditional "female" jobs such as cooking and secretarial positions and are usually discouraged from learning "male" household skills such as painting or carpentry. In addition, promotion to a position of status, where the female can take more direct control of herself and of her treatment experience, is made more difficult and is more easily revoked (Levy and Doyle 1974; Soler, Ponsor, and Abod 1976).

Job achievement is not felt to be an important area of concern and staff have lowered expectations of females' employment capacities. Consequently, females have restricted access to vocational placement services and are seldom encouraged to pursue educational or vocational upgrading (Edwards and Jackson 1975). Thus the resulting frustration or disappointment in the possibility of changing to an independent, self-reliant, and socially acceptable life style may be reason enough to terminate treatment prematurely.

Bias also exists in the dominance of male staff members, both in numbers and in positions of authority, who allow their personal feelings toward women to enter the treatment setting. The double standard that was present on the street is reinforced, and both male staff and residents become instigators of a significant barrier to retention. For example, it has been pointed out that ex-prostitutes carry the stigma with them throughout the treatment experience, and even those who were not "sluts" or "whores" are often treated as such. On the other hand, males are admired for pimping and playing the playboy role, "as a sign of masculinity." Other typologies applied to female addicts include "intellectual junkie, bad mother, and hypochondriac" (Soler, Ponsor, and Abod 1976).

In addition, Soler and associates (1976) reported that women's sensitivities and vulnerabilities relating to their sexual practices are frequently abused, often becoming a focus of morbid curiosity in group therapy sessions. Rules for obtaining "sex privileges" are often applied to, or created for, females. Criticism of the program is either ignored or labeled as manipulation; oftentimes it is met with arbitrary and harsh forms of punishment that usually cannot be appealed.

Furthermore, this same study found that half of the women interviewed had been propositioned by male staff members and often were forced by circumstances to submit to their demands. Thus while prostitution is severely stigmatized and program goals are supposedly directed toward developing "acceptable" behavior for women, sex is used as a commodity of exchange by the very persons responsible for these females' therapeutic progress. Female addicts, who might not have developed an adequate sexual identity, are not likely to be helped by these practices and may opt to return to life on the street, where the rules (although still sexist) are known, and where such attitudes may be forgotten under the influence of heroin.

Finally, homosexual women seem more than likely to drop out of treatment, as they suffer from even harsher discriminatory practices and attitudes. For one, staff members view homosexuality as a sickness derived from psychological or developmental catastrophes, and thus treatment focuses on changing the individual's sexual orientation. However, the taboo of homosexuality seems unfairly applied to females, since it has been suggested that men feel threatened by homosexual women and perceive them both as rivals and sources of rejection—the call for sexual favors from female residents on behalf of male staff members has been noted. In practice, homosexual females in treatment are frequently humiliated and lovers are denied participation in the same therapeutic groups. Many lesbians already have troubled feelings about their sexual activities, and although the recommended focus has been on alleviating any resulting guilt, anxiety, self-hatred, or self-doubt, current approaches do more to reinforce these anxieties than to relieve them (Soler, Ponsor, and Abod 1976; White 1976).

### Lack of Attention to Female Needs

Another contributory factor in attrition relates to the lack of attention to problems particular to female addicts. Females come into treatment with a range of needs that programs are either unwilling to identify and/or treat.

Some of the most noticeable problems specific to females and that they perceive as major concerns involve medical complications (Levy and Doyle 1976). The major difficulties include venereal disease, menstrual irregularities, infertility, and other gynecologic problems (Blinick 1971; Perlmutter 1967; Stoffer 1968; NIDA 1976b).[2] Moreover, females have been found to have greater medical needs in a number of areas, including thyroid, hypertension, dental care, and tetanus (Cherubin 1968; Cuskey 1977; Ellinwood, Smith, and Vaillant 1966; Yablonsky 1965).

However, one analysis of practices in treatment programs found that medical complaints are usually ignored or go untreated, rationalized by the view that these females cannot endure any level of pain, cannot distinguish between real pain and minor physical discomfort, or create symptoms to attract attention. Women on methadone and narcotic antagonists, many of whom suffered severe side effects, were initially

2. G. Beschner, personal communication, July 29, 1977.

not informed as to potential symptom development. Later, symptoms were treated as manifestations of their psychological problems and were treated ineffectively, if at all. Women who frequently suffer from menstrual cramps due to withdrawal are seldom excused from strenuous activities; in drug-free programs needed medication after dental surgery has been denied, whereas prescriptions for the relief of anxiety have been provided (Soler, Ponsor, and Abod 1976).

In programs where pregnant addicts or addict mothers are admitted, additional difficulties arise. Some of the medical problems seen during pregnancy include venereal disease, anemia, pelvic disorders and malnutrition, hepatitis, toxemia, hypertension, and a variety of infections (Blinick 1971; Naeye et al. 1973; Stoffer 1968; Stone et al. 1971). At the time of delivery, addicts typically experience obstetrical complications (Blinick, Jerez, and Wallach 1973; Finnegan 1977), particularly premature rupture and/or separation of the membranes, precipitous births, preeclampsia, meconium, and hemorrhaging (Statzer and Wardell 1972; Strauss et al. 1974; Zarin-Ackerman 1977).

The use of heroin will have effects on the health of the newborn. The incidence of breech births and prematurity has been found to be abnormally high among addicted mothers (NCDAI 1974; Perlmutter 1967; Stern 1966; Zelson, Rubio, and Wasserman 1972). Furthermore, prematurity has been associated with light birth weight and its concomitant complications, neonatal mortality and infections in the amniotic fluid (Bauman and Teisan 1976; Rosenthal, Patrick and Krug 1964).

Several studies have indicated that birth weights of babies born to addicted mothers are lighter than those born to drug-free women (Davis, Brown, and Glendinning 1973; Finnegan, Connaughton, and Schutt 1975; Perlmutter 1967; Zelson, Rubio, and Wasserman 1972). Snyder (1949) pointed out that the infants are light even for their own stage of development and that even full-term babies are lighter than normal. The importance of these findings is underlined by Finnegan and associates (1975):

The death rate of the low weight neonate is 40 times that of the full size infant born at term. Moreover the incidence of cerebral palsy, associated with prematurity, may be as high as 10 times; mental deficiency five times; and lethal malformations in undersized infants, 7 times that of a full size infant. Emotional disturbances, social maladjustments, and visual and hearing deficits are also multiplied.... The medical and custodial cost for these individuals is incalculable. (p. 22)

Medical complications seen among newborns include congenital anomolies, toxemia, jaundice, pneumonia, hypocalcemia, sepsis, asphyxia, hypoglycemia, congenital syphilis, convulsive disorders, and central nervous system hemorrhaging (Bauman and Teisan 1976; Finnegan, Connaughton, and Schutt 1975; Perlmutter 1967, Stone et al. 1971; Zelson, Rubio, and Wasserman 1972). Neonatal abstinence symptoms may persist for up to six months after birth, involving patterns of hyperactivity, hyperaphagia, hyperacusis, irritability, disturbed sleep, and diarrhea (Wilson, Desmond, and Verniaud 1973). Maturation during the first few years of life may be impeded by deficits in cognitive, perceptual, and language abilities and by limitations in social and emotional responsiveness (Cuskey 1977; Lief 1977; Lodge 1977; Nathenson 1974; Strauss et al. 1976; Zarin-Ackerman 1977).

The life style of the addict, involving malnutrition, infections from prostituting, and hepatitis from dirty needles, may also produce complications at birth. Neonatal mortality, which is becoming an increasingly significant problem (Davis, Brown, and Glendinning 1973; Naeye et al. 1973; Strauss et al. 1974), has been attributed to "dehydration from diarrhea, lack of food intake, multiple congenital anomolies, pneumonia, incomplete expansion of the lungs at birth and intracranial hemorrhage" (NCDAI 1974).

Likewise, the probability of the infant contracting passive drug dependency, which also has increased in recent years (Finnegan, Connaughton, and Schutt 1975; Perlmutter 1974; Rajegowda et al. 1972), and the dangers of unsupervised withdrawal emphasize the importance of attending to the needs of the newborn, although current treatment approaches are felt to be inadequate in this respect. The use of methadone during pregnancy may be even more harmful to the fetus and may involve more severe withdrawal symptoms than maternal heroin use (Escamilla-Mondanaro 1976; Rajegowda et al. 1972; Whittaker 1973). Detoxification likewise may be inappropriate, as abrupt withdrawal has been associated with intrauterine deaths (Bauman and Teisan 1976).

Similarly, the importance of attending to the emotional needs of pregnant addicts is underlined by the fact that groups receiving psychosocial support have higher treatment retention records at the time of delivery and lower incidences of medical/obstetrical complications, neonatal morbidity, and perinatal loss than those who do not receive such support. Additionally, these services impact positively on childcare practices, offset the complications of neonatal narcotism, and promote normal physical and psychological development in the offspring (Blinick, Jerez, and Wallach 1973; Davis, Brown, and Glendinning 1973; Finnegan, Connaughton, and Schutt 1975; Statzer and Wardell 1972). However, treatment programs seldom go as far as to secure hospital attention for their pregnant addicts.

Not only do addicted females and their children come into treatment with particular and serious types of medical concerns, but they also present psychological problems of differing types and to differing degrees than do males; many of whom are not attended to in currently conceived treatment programs. TC approaches and methadone maintenance programs emphasize resocialization and/or functionality as the goal of therapy. Whereas retention among males has been associated with sociological concerns, that of women has been significantly correlated with psychological issues (Aron and Daily 1976).

Females in both types of programs have a greater number of problems than do males, specifically relating to bad feelings about their body, suicide attempts, physical health, inability to express their feelings, and insecurities about their intelligence. Staff perceptions of clients' problems have either indicated no differences between those of males and females, or expressed the view that the central problem of female addicts is related to interpersonal and intrapersonal sensitivities (Levy and Doyle 1974, 1976).

However, these views are problematic, not only because they ignore a large proportion of female difficulties, but also because the perceived problems of female clients are inadequately handled. Although females have expressed concern over opposite-sex relationships, the therapeutic solution of social conformity to the role of wife and/or mother does not eliminate other needs and problems that might be important in female addiction; nor does it satisfactorily handle the problem of inadequate female identity (Schultz 1975). What appears to be more important is the elimination of the destructive use of sex to solve identity conflicts, although practices instituted on behalf of males in the treatment settings most likely exacerbate these difficulties. Likewise, the typology of the "bad mother," while often unjustly and inordinately applied, is not considered in therapeutic programs. Some female addicts do seem to have problems in successful parenting (Cuskey 1977; Lief 1977; Stryker 1977; Wilson 1977), but more attention has been given to destructive criticism than to constructive development of adequate mothering practices (Soler, Ponsor, and Abod 1976).

Even the emphasis on employment to fulfill perceived "male" needs has not been successfully applied to female addicts in treatment. Burt and associates (1977) found that approximately 97 percent of the females in federally funded residential settings did not develop any skills and about nine-tenths completed less than one year of schooling (only about 40 percent had completed high school before entry), regardless of level at intake. Those aged eighteen to twenty had less education than their male counterparts, and females in drug-free settings (i.e., TC's) developed fewer skills. Therefore, resocialization methods do not appear to be appropriate to the treatment of women, and where they are instituted the females fare worse than the males.

The perception by staff members that females are more disturbed than males and thus less amenable to treatment (Levy and Doyle 1974) may actually be a reflection of their treatment experience. Females have been found to be suffering from extreme anxiety and low levels of self-esteem (DeLeon 1974; Colten 1977; Cuskey 1977; Ross and Berzins 1974). With the use of therapeutic techniques that contribute little to the female's rehabilitative progress, her condition could worsen as she compares improvement in her male comrades with her own stagnated position. As some females have probably internalized some of the pressures operating against them in the outside world as part of their self-image (Maglin 1973), responsibility for their unsatisfactory improvement might be taken on themselves and thus self-esteem may drop even lower, and anxiety become more acute. With a seemingly constricted prognosis for emotional adjustment and future self-reliance, it is not surprising that a significant number terminate treatment prematurely.

## Long-term Prognosis

Vaillant (1966) suggested that abstinence seems to depend more on the addict's ability to discover satisfying alternatives to addiction than on methods of treatment. Without the prerequisites for an independent, socially acceptable life style, and without the emotional strength to cope with the problems and stresses of day-to-day living, reversion to a life style of deviancy would probably constitute the most likely alternative to the extremely difficult and unfamiliar life style of a drug-free existence. It might also be noted that addiction in females has been viewed as a means of creating a sense of self-control, of preventing the ego from being overwhelmed by anxiety, and of attempting to prevent the self from lapsing into psychosis (Coughlan and Gold 1974). Thus leaving treatment with the same set of central psychological disturbances with which they entered, recourse to the pattern that formerly provided a familiar and adequate method of handling these problems would seem to be a logical development—"they are essentially left out on the street corners from which the treatment programs pretend to rescue them" (Soler, Ponsor, and Abod 1976).

These suggestions are supported by reports documenting previous treatment experiences. Ellinwood and associates (1966) found that almost one-half of their females had been hospitalized for drug problems one or more times before entering the studied program. Chambers, Hinesley, and Moldestad (1970) reported almost 60 percent and Aron and Daily (1976) over 90 percent for their mixed-sex sample of TC residents.

However, the discussion of recidivism is complicated by a lack of information regarding the fate of these women after leaving treatment. How rapidly both dropouts and graduates become reimmersed in a deviant subculture remains an unknown, as the few follow-up studies that have been conducted to date tend to focus on discrete units of time, instead of employing longitudinal type designs that might yield more valid information regarding individual changes over time.

But even without specific data on the long-term prognosis of female addicts who have been exposed to or have completed treatment, from the preceding discussion it follows that for females the ultimate TC goals of resocialization and personality reorientation probably will not be realized. The current structure of these modalities does not adequately equip the female with the survival skills necessary for a new drug-free existence and does not significantly alter her basic psychological problems. Even in instances where female ex-addicts remain drug-free for an extended period of time, it seems that treatment has served to detoxify the addict but has been less than successful in preparing her for reentry into the community (Pittel 1971).

*Aftercare*

Females leaving treatment are likely to have limited financial resources; no credit; criminal and civil legal problems; few nonaddict friends; a scattered or unsympathetic family; no housing, car, or proper clothing; and generally poor health (Marsh and Neely 1977). While the deficiencies of current treatment models offer few benefits for females in the way of psychological growth and resocialization, the lack of attention to problems they present upon discharge is another reason behind the high rate of recidivism and inadequate adjustments even where detoxification has been achieved. If any strengths have been gained from the treatment experience at all, the women are not given the knowledge of how to apply them in community adjustment.

The concept of aftercare is often overlooked, as it is commonly believed that community agencies providing such services already exist or that the ex-addict's problems should be treated at psychiatric facilities. However, the huge listings of community agencies are often outdated; getting services is usually difficult because staff is less inclined to devote time to ex-drug addicts (especially females); budget problems necessarily limit the number of clients, and where services exist they are frequently inadequate. Furthermore, services are neither comprehensive nor interrelated, so that obtaining help in different areas becomes a time-consuming and frustrating process. Moreover, even if services in the community are available, the female in treatment is often not told what services exist, nor does she know how to go about securing help.

Nevertheless, aftercare is an extremely important issue in reentry planning. At the present time, however, it is not known what services are needed, which ones are provided, or which ones will ultimately deliver what they profess to offer to female ex-addicts. The focus on aftercare has been limited to vocational placement, which has not been adequately implemented for females. Emphasis on preoccupational training and the development of employable job skills, encouraging those who are interested in educational and/or vocational upgrading, unique job placement, the constructive utilization of street survival skills, education in financial management, the handling of employers and/or vocational service agencies who are less inclined to consider females, especially female addicts, should meet with success (Edwards and Jackson 1975). Women should be made aware of what vocational services, educational programs, and welfare agencies exist, as well as be alerted to the proper procedures for securing these services.

Although the area of employment is, as noted previously, extremely important to future independent functioning, other problem areas including housing, clothing, transportation, health and nutrition, medical and dental troubles, and legal matters must be assessed and referrals made where deficiencies exist. In addition, "feminine" needs often ignored or considered trivial or vain by program staff but of demonstrated importance to female self-regard, such as lessons in appearance, dress, makeup, diet, and so on, should also be considered (DeLeon and Beschner 1977).

Accessibility to mental health agencies is an equally significant aspect of aftercare for these women. For one, many psychosocial problems they present upon entry into treatment are not likely to improve under current therapeutic methods. Family and peer relationships that will be resumed upon reentry must be assessed, so that absence of sufficient or positive social support structures can be met by referrals to community-based social clubs or organizations, implementation of some sort of "friendship" program, or services providing marital or psychiatric counseling. Similarly, information on recreational interests or hobbies should be gathered so that constructive and satisfying means of relaxation can be encouraged or developed.

The general picture regarding the background of heroin use indicates that the majority of females did not purchase their first heroin, but most tried the substance the first time it was offered (Binion 1977; Burt et al. 1977b; Marsh and Neely 1977). Two patterns of heroin abuse have emerged from the literature: The "southern" addict is typified as white and living in a small town; introduced to drugs (usually psychoactive substances such as barbiturates, sedatives, and minor tranquilizers) by her physician; securing the drugs legally, most often listing medical or quasi-medical reasons for first drug use, and becoming addicted at a later age. The "modern" addict, on the other hand, is likely to be nonwhite, young, and from urban, slum areas in the North Central or Middle Atlantic regions of the country; introduced to heroin by her peers; obtaining the substance illegally, and most often beginning drug use for kicks or curiosity (Cuskey, Premkumar, and Ligel 1972).

The findings indicate that the trend toward the more modern pattern is accelerating: Greater numbers of female addicts come from large metropolitan areas, and larger proportions of inner city drug users are taking to heroin (Cuskey, Premkumar, and Ligel 1972; Ellinwood, Smith, and Vaillant 1966). Most often these females are introduced to heroin by an already addicted person, and it has been noted that "the greatest predisposing factor for female addiction, at least in an illicit opiate market, is the addicted male associate" (Binion 1977; Cuskey 1975, 1977; Eldred and Washington 1976).

Research regarding reasons for continuation of drug use has generally been divided into two currents of thought: (1) avoidance of withdrawal symptoms (Brown et al. 1971; Cuskey, Premkumar, and Ligel 1972; Drug Enforcement Administration and NIDA 1975) and (2) search for euphoria (MacDonald and LeBlanc 1973). To this may be added a motivation to escape a painful reality, to aid in the forgetting of one's problems, to resolve psychic conflict (Aron and Daily 1974; Binion 1977; Carr 1975; Arnon, Kleinman, and Kissin 1974) or as a form of "chronic suicide" (Cuskey 1977; Drug Enforcement Administration and NIDA 1975).

With the onset of drug addiction the female becomes immersed in a deviant subculture, beginning a life style including other forms of deviancy and a host of physical, social, psychological, and practical problems. As noted earlier, the majority of addicted females are unemployed, illegally employed, or dependent on others for their support (Cuskey 1977; Cuskey, Moffet, and Clifford 1971; Marsh and Neely 1977; NIDA 1976a; Demaree, Kee, and Sells 1975; Drug Enforcement Administration and NIDA 1975). Many have no job skills and poor employment records (Demaree, Kee, and Sells 1975; Ellinwood, Smith, and Vaillant 1966; NIDA 1976b; Escamilla-Mondanaro 1976; Marsh and Neely 1977; NIDA 1976; Drug Enforcement Administration and NIDA 1975). Impaired functioning due to vacillation between euphoria and withdrawal and the all-consuming orientation toward drug procurement usually precludes the possibility of steady employment.

The literature indicates that the majority of addicted women have been arrested or are engaged in illegal activities (Cuskey 1977; Driscoll and Barr 1972; Ellinwood, Smith, and Vaillant 1966). A large proportion are involved in prostitution (Ellinwood, Smith, and Vaillant 1966; File, McCahill, and Savitz 1974; Waldorf 1973) and, to a lesser extent, in property crimes (NIDA 1976b) and the more violent forms of criminal behavior such as assault (Marsh and Neely 1977). It appears that most are arrested at least once (Cuskey 1977; Ellinwood, Smith, and Vaillant 1966; Marsh and Neely 1977) with an average of two to four convictions (Cuskey 1977; Rosenthal and Biase 1969).

The deviant life style associated with addiction is accompanied by a set of psychological and emotional problems, some of which are rooted in reactions to early childhood disturbances; others are the result of existing as a "deviant subsection of a male-dominated deviant subculture" (Maglin 1973). Since research in this area has evolved from treatment populations, it is not known which problems were present before the onset of addiction or which were intensified by its concomitant life style, nor can it be determined what factors precipitated or exacerbated these disturbances.

Nevertheless, it is generally agreed that the majority of addicted females suffer from emotional and/or psychological problems (Ellinwood, Smith, and Vaillant 1966; Hall 1968; NIDA 1976b) as evidenced by their repeated contacts with adult psychiatric centers (Climent et al. 1974; Cuskey 1977; Eldred and Washington 1976). Personality or character disorders seem to be the most common diagnoses, followed by neurosis, psychosis, and sociopathy (Chein et al. 1964; Densen-Gerber 1972; Ellinwood, Smith, and Vaillant 1966; Hall 1968; Escamilla-Mondanaro 1976; Ross and Berzins 1974). Female addicts have been found to exhibit a high degree of externality (DeLeon 1974), although some studies have reported an elevated level of internality (Berzins and Ross 1973). These women appear to be highly anxious, overly hostile, and a significant proportion have been found to be suffering from depression (Colten 1977; DeLeon 1974; Kilmann 1974).

REFERENCES

Aries, E. 1974. Interaction patterns and themes of male, female and mixed groups. Paper presented at the American Psychological Association Convention, New Orleans, Louisiana, 30 August–3 September 1974.

Arnon, D., Kleinman, M., and Kissin, B. 1974. Psychological differentiation in heroin addicts. *International Journal of the Addictions* 9:151–159.

Aron, W. E., and Daily, D. 1974. Short and long-term therapeutic communities: A follow-up and cost-effectiveness comparison. *International Journal of the Addictions* 9:619–636.

———. 1976. Graduates and splittees from therapeutic community drug treatment programs: A comparison. *International Journal of the Addictions* 11:1–18.

Baden, M. 1972. Homicide, suicide and accidental deaths among narcotic addicts. *Human Pathology* 3:91–95.

Bauman, A., and Teisan, M. 1976. Pregnancy and Drugs. In *Women in treatment: Issues and approaches*, ed. A. Bauman et al. Arlington, Va.: National Drug Abuse Center for Training and Resource Development.

Bauman, A., et al., eds. 1976. Interview with a Chicana ex-addict. In *Women in treatment: Issues and approaches*. Arlington, Va.: National Drug Abuse Center for Training and Resource Development.

Berzins, J., and Ross, W. 1973. Locus of control among opiate addicts. *Journal of Consulting and Clinical Psychology* 40:84–91.

Binion, V. 1977. A descriptive comparison of the family of origin of women heroin users and non-users. In *Report on comparative analyses of psycho-social variables: Self perceptions and attitudes, social supports, and family backgrounds of heroin addicted women, Women's Drug Research Project, 1977*. Rockville, Md.: National Institute on Drug Abuse.

Blinick, G. 1971. Fertility of narcotic addicts and effects of addiction on the offspring. *Social Biology* 18:534–539.

———, Jerez, E., and Wallach, R. 1973. Methadone maintenance, pregnancy and progeny. *Journal of the American Medical Association* 225:447–479.

Braucht, G., et al. 1973. Deviant drug use in adolescence: A review of psychosocial correlates. *Psychological Bulletin* 79:92–106.

Brotman, R., Meyer, A., and Freedman, A. 1965. An approach to treatment of narcotic addicts based on a community mental health diagnosis. *Comprehensive Psychiatry* 6:99–114.

Brown, B., et al. 1971. In their own words: Addicts' reasons for initiating and withdrawing from heroin. *International Journal of the Addictions* 6:635–645.

Burt, M., and Glynn, T. 1976. *A follow-up study of former clients of New York City's addiction services agency: Volume II*. Bethesda, Md. Burt Associates.

Burt, M., et al. 1977a. *An investigation of outcomes of traditional drug treatment/service programs*. Bethesda, Md.: Burt Associates.

Burt, M., et al. 1977b. *An investigation into the characteristics of drug-abusing women*. Bethesda, Md.: Burt Associates.

Campbell, R., and Freeland, J. 1974. Patterns of drug abuse. *International Journal of the Addictions* 9:289–300.

Carr, J. 1975. Drug patterns among drug-addicted mothers: Incidence, variance in use, and effects on children. *Pediatric Annals* 4:408–417.

Chalof, J. 1969. *A study of voluntary treatment programs for narcotic addicts, part III: Lifeline to tomorrow*. New York: Department of Public Affairs of the Community Service Society of New York.

Chambers, C., Hinesley, R., and Moldestad, M. 1970. Narcotic addiction in females: A race comparison. *International Journal of the Addictions* 5:257–278.

Chein, I., et al. 1964. *The road to H: Narcotics, delinquency and social policy*. New York: Basic Books.

Cherubin, C. 1968. Review of the medical complications of heroin addiction. *International Journal of the Addictions* 3:163–175.

Climent, C., et al. 1974. Epidemiological studies of female prisoners, II. *International Journal of the Addictions* 9:345–350.

Colten, M. 1977. A descriptive and comparative analysis of self-perceptions and attitudes of heroin addicted women. In *Report on the comparative analyses of psycho-social variables: Self-perceptions and attitudes, social supports, and family backgrounds of heroin addicted women, women's drug research project, 1977*. Rockville, Md.: National Institute on Drug Abuse.

Coughlan, A., and Gold, R. 1974. Self destructive behavior in female adolescent addicts. *American Journal of Orthopsychiatry* 44:252–253.

Cuskey, W. R. 1975. Drug abuse as self-destructive behavior. In *Self-destructive behavior*, ed. A. Roberts. Springfield, Ill.: Charles C Thomas.

————. 1977. An assessment of the clinical efficacy of the Mabon parents demonstration program. Report prepared for Odyssey Institute.

————, Moffet, A., and Clifford, H. 1971. Comparison of female opiate addicts admitted to Lexington Hospital in 1961 and 1967. *HSMHA Health Reports* 86:332–340.

Cuskey, W. R., Premkumar, T., and Ligel, L. 1972. Survey of opiate addiction among females in the U.S. between 1850 and 1870. *Public Health Reviews* 1:8–39.

Davis, M., Brown, B., and Glendinning, S. 1973 (March). Neonatal effects of heroin addiction and methadone treated pregnancies: Preliminary report on 70 live births. In Proceedings of the Fifth National Conference on Methadone Treatments, pp. 17–19. Washington, D.C.

DeLeon, G. 1974. Phoenix House: Psychopathological signs among male and female drug-free residents. *Addictive Diseases* 1:135–152.

————, and Beschner, G., eds. 1977. *The therapeutic community: Proceedings of therapeutic communities of American planning conference, January 29–30, 1976*. Rockville, Md.: Department of Health, Education, and Welfare and the National Institute on Drug Abuse.

Demaree, R., Kee, C., and Sells, S. 1975. *Effectiveness measures of treatment programs: Drug abuse reporting program (DARP) admission, 1969–1973*. Fort Worth, Tex.: Texas Christian University, Institute for Behavioral Research.

Densen-Gerber, J. 1973. *We mainline dreams*. Baltimore, Md.: Penguin Books.

————, Wiener, J., and Hochstedler, R. 1972. Sexual behavior, abortion and birth control in heroin addicts: Legal and psychiatric considerations. *Contemporary Drug Problems* 1:783–793.

Dole, V. P., and Nyswander, M. E. 1967. Heroin addiction—a metabolic disease. *Archives of Internal Medicine* 120:19–24.

Douvan, E. 1977. Overview. In *Report on comparative analyses of psycho-social variables: Self perceptions and attitudes, social supports, and family backgrounds of addicted women, Women's Drug Research Project, 1977*. Rockville, Md.: National Institute on Drug Abuse.

Driscoll, G., and Barr, H. 1972. Comparative study of drug dependent and alcoholic women. Paper presented at the 23rd annual meeting of the Alcohol and Drug Problems of North America, Atlanta, September 1972.

Drug Enforcement Administration and the National Institute on Drug Abuse (NIDA). 1975. *Drug abuse warning network (DAWN) statistical summary, October, 1975*. Ambler, Pa.: IMS Americ.

Edwards, E., and Jackson, J. 1975. Rehabilitative services provided by women versus men in a substance abuse treatment program. In *Developments in the field of drug abuse—1974 proceedings of the National Association for the Prevention of Addiction to Narcotics*, ed. V. Shorty and H. Alksne. Cambridge, Mass.: Schenkman Publishing Co.

Eldred, C., and Brown, B. 1974. Heroin addict clients' descriptions of their families of origin. *International Journal of the Addictions* 9:315–320.

————, and Washington, M. 1976. Interpersonal relationships in heroin use by men and women and their role in treatment outcome. *International Journal of the Addictions* 11:117–130.

Ellinwood, E., Smith, W., and Vaillant, G. 1966. Narcotic addiction in males and females: A comparison. *International Journal of the Addictions* 1:33–45.

Escamilla-Mondanaro, J. 1976. Women: Pregnancy, children and addiction. In *Women in treatment: Issues and approaches*, ed. A. Bauman et al. Arlington, Va.: National Drug Abuse Center for Training and Resource Development.

File, K., McCahill, T., and Savitz, L. 1974. Narcotics involvement and female criminality. *Addictive Diseases* 1:177–188.

Finnegan, L. P., Connaughton, J. F., and Schutt, J. 1975. Infants of drug dependent women: Practical approaches for management. Paper presented at the 37th annual scientific meeting of the Committee on Problems of Drug Dependence of the National Research Council, May 21, 1975.

Finnegon, L. 1977. Management of the drug dependent pregnancy and effects on neonatal outcome. In *Symposium on comprehensive health care for addicted families and their children, May 20–21, 1976*, ed. G. Beschner and R. Brotman. Department of Health, Education, and Welfare and the National Institute on Drug Abuse.

Fracchia, J., et al. 1975. Manifest psychological needs of heroin addicts. *Comprehensive Psychiatry* 16:133–136.

Goldstein, A. 1972. Heroin addiction and the role of methadone in its treatment. *Archives of General Psychiatry* 26:291–297.

Hall, M. 1968. Mental and physical efficiency of women drug addicts. *Journal of Abnormal and Social Psychology* 33:332–345.

Helpern, M. 1972. Fatalities from narcotic addiction in New York City: Incidence, circumstances and pathologic findings. *Human Pathology* 3:13–21.

Hill, R., and Desmond, M. 1963. Management of the narcotic withdrawal syndrome in the neonate. *Pediatric Clinics of North America* 10:67–86.

Kilmann, P. 1974. Personality characteristics of female narcotic addicts. *Psychological Reports* 35:485–486.

Kirsh, B. 1974. Consciousness-raising groups as therapy for women. In *Women in therapy*, ed. V. Franks and V. Burtle. New York: Brunner/Mazel.

Levy, S., and Doyle, K. 1976. Attitudes towards women in a methadone maintenance program. In *Women in treatment: Issues and approaches*, ed. A. Bauman et al. Arlington, Va.: National Drug Abuse Center for Training and Resource Development.

Lief, N. 1977. Some measures of parenting behavior for addicted and nonaddicted mothers. In *Symposium on comprehensive health care for addicted families and their children, May 20–21, 1976*, ed. G. Beschner and R. Brotman. Washington, D.C.: Department of Health, Education, and Welfare and the National Institute on Drug Abuse.

Lodge, A. 1977. Developmental findings with infants born to mothers on methadone maintenance: A preliminary report. In *Symposium on comprehensive health care for addicted families and their children, May 20–21, 1976*, ed. G. Beschner and R. Brotman. Washington, D.C.: Department of Health, Education, and Welfare and the National Institute on Drug Abuse.

MacDonald, A., Walls, R., and LeBlanc, R. 1973. College female drug users. *Adolescence* 8:189–196.

Maglin, A. 1973. Sex role differentiation in heroin addiction. *Social Casework* 55:189–196.

Mandell, W., Goldschmidt, P., and Drover, P. 1973. *Interdrug—final report. An evaluation of treatment programs for drug abusers*. Baltimore, Md.: Johns Hopkins University School of Hygiene and Public Health.

Marsh, J., and Neely, B. 1977. *Women helping women: The W.O.M.A.N. Center evaluation report: Year three*. Rockville, Md.: National Institute on Drug Abuse.

Naeye, R., et al. 1973. Fetal complications of maternal heroin addiction: Abnormal growth, infections and episodes of stress. *Journal of Pediatrics* 83:1055–1061.

Nathenson, G. 1974. Neonatal addiction in 1973. *Journal of the National Medical Association* 66:19–22.

National Clearinghouse for Drug Abuse Information (NCDAI). 1974. Neonatal narcotic dependence. *NCDAI Report Series* 29.

National Institute on Drug Abuse (NIDA). 1976a. *1976 client oriented data acquisition process (CODAP) national management handbook*. Rockville, Md.: National Institute on Drug Abuse.

NIDA, 1976b. Women's treatment demonstration project: Report I. Report prepared for the National Institute on Drug Abuse.

New York City Narcotics Register. 1973. *Analysis of narcotic addiction trends through June, 1973*. New York: New York City Narcotics Register.

O'Donnell, J. 1969. Narcotic addicts in Kentucky. *Public Health Service Publication*. 1886.

————, Besteman, K., and Jones, J. 1967. Marital history of narcotic addicts. *International Journal of the Addictions* 2:21–38.

Perlmutter, J. 1967. Drug addiction in pregnant women. *American Journal of Obstetrics and Gynecology* 99(4):569–572.

_____ . 1974. Heroin addiction during pregnancy. *Obstetrical and Gynecological Survey* 29:439–446.

Person, P., Retka, R., and Woodward, J. 1977. *A method for estimating heroin use prevalence.* Rockville, Md.: National Institute on Drug Abuse.

Pescor, M. 1944. A comparative statistical study of male and female drug addicts. *American Journal of Psychology* 100:771–774.

Pittel, S. 1971. Psychological aspects of heroin and other drug dependence. *Journal of Psychedelic Drugs* 4:40–45.

Rajegowda, B., et al. 1972. Methadone withdrawal in newborn infants. *Journal of Pediatrics* 81:532–534.

Rosenbaum, M. 1973. The world and career of women heroin addicts. Report prepared for the National Institute on Drug Abuse.

Rosenthal, M., and Biase, V. 1969. Phoenix Houses: Therapeutic communities for drug addicts. *Hospital and Community Psychiatry* 20.

Rosenthal, T., Patrick, S., and Krug, D. 1964. Congenital anomolies neonatal narcotics addiction: A natural history. *American Journal of Public Health* 54:1252.

Ross, F., and Berzins, J. 1974. Personality characteristics of female addicts on the MMPI. *Psychological Reports* 35:779–784.

Schultz, A. 1975. Radical feminism: A treatment modality for addicted women. In *Developments in the field of drug abuse,* ed. E. Seray, V. Shorty, and H. Alksne. Cambridge, Mass.: Schenkman Publishing.

Seldin, N. 1972. The family of the addict: A review of the literature. *International Journal of the Addictions* 7:97–107.

Snyder, F. 1949. *Obstetrical analgesia and anesthesia: Their effects upon labour and the child.* Philadelphia: W.B. Saunders.

Soler, E., Ponsor, L., and Abod, J. 1976. Women in treatment: Client self-report. In *Women in treatment: Issues and approaches,* ed. A. Bauman et al. Arlington, Va.: National Drug Abuse Center for Training and Resource Development.

Statzer, D., and Wardell, J. 1972. Heroin addiction during pregnancy. *American Journal of Obstetrics and Gynecology* 113:273–278.

Stern, R. 1966. The pregnant addict: A study of 66 case histories, 1950–1959. *American Journal of Obstetrics and Gynecology* 94:253–257.

Stoffer, S. 1968. A gynecological study of drug addicts. *American Journal of Obstetrics and Gynecology* 101:779–783.

Stone, M., et al. 1971. Narcotic addiction in pregnancy. *American Journal of Obstetrics and Gynecology*

Strauss, M., et al. 1974. Methadone maintenance during pregnancy: Pregnancy, birth and neonate characteristics. *American Journal of Obstetrics and Gynecology* 120:895–900.

Strauss, M., et al. 1976. Behavioral characteristics of prenatal addiction to narcotics. *Journal of Pediatrics* 89:842–846.

Stryker, J. 1977. A unique situation—two people must be considered: An overview of the Hutzel Hospital program. In *Symposium on comprehensive health care for addicted families and their children, May 20–21, 1976,* ed. G. Beschner and R. Brotman. Washington, D.C.: Department of Health, Education, and Welfare and the National Institute on Drug Abuse.

Sussman, S. 1963. Narcotic and methamphetamine use during pregnancy: Effect on newborn infants. *American Journal of Diseases of Children* 106:125–130.

Tucker, B. 1977. A descriptive and comparative analysis of the social support structure of heroin addicted women. In *Report on comparative analyses of psycho-social variables: Self-perceptions and attitudes, social supports, and family backgrounds of heroin addicted women, women's drug research project, 1977.* Rockville, Md.: National Institute on Drug Abuse.

Vaillant, G. 1966. A twelve year follow-up of New York narcotic addicts. *Archives of General Psychiatry* 15(6):599–609.

Waldorf, D. 1971. Social control in therapeutic communities for the treatment of drug addicts. *International Journal of the Addictions* 6:29–43.

_____ . 1973. *Careers in dope.* Englewood Cliffs, N.J.: Prentice-Hall.

Wallace, N. 1977. Support networks among drug addicted men and women. In *Women helping women: The W.O.M.A.N. Center evaluation report: Year three,* by J. Marsh and B. Neely. Rockville, Md.: National Institute on Drug Abuse.

White, L. 1976. It isn't easy being gay. In *Women in treatment: Issues and approaches,* ed. A. Bauman et al. Arlington, Va.: National Drug Abuse Center for Training and Resource Development.

Whittaker, F. 1973. Drug dependence in newborns. *Southern Hospitals* (September).

Willis, J. 1970. Drug dependence: Some demographic and psychological characteristics in United Kingdom and United States subjects. *British Journal of the Addictions* 64:135.

Wilson, G. 1977. Management of pediatric medical problems in the addicted household. In *Symposium on comprehensive health care for addicted families and their children, May 20–21, 1976,* ed. G. Beschner and R. Brotman. Washington, D.C.: Department of Health, Education, and Welfare and the National Institute on Drug Abuse.

————, Desmond, M., and Verniaud, W. 1973. Early development of infants of heroin-addicted mothers. *American Journal of Diseases in Children* 126:457.

Yablonsky, L. 1965. *The tunnel back: Synanon.* New York: Macmillan.

Zarin-Ackerman, J. 1977. Developmental assessment of all infants born to the family care program, 1975–76. In *Symposium on comprehensive health care for addicted families and their children, May 20–21, 1976,* ed. G. Beschner and R. Brotman. Washington, D.C.: Department of Health, Education, and Welfare and the National Institute on Drug Abuse.

Zelson, C. 1975. Acute management of neonatal addiction. *Addictive Diseases* 2:159–168.

————, Rubio, E., and Wasserman, E. 1972. Neonatal narcotic addiction: 10 year observation. *Journal of Pediatrics* 48:178–189.

# 21

---

# The Female Alcoholic

---

## JUDY FRASER*

---

The mass movement by women to redefine their place in Western civilization has been called the most significant social change to evolve from the sixties, a decade of rapid-fire attacks on status quo so altered now that few can accurately recall it. In relinquishing her centuries-old state of grace for a modern bill of rights, today's woman faces a challenge of uncharted dimensions. The aftertaste of the revolution may be bitter; it should be sweet. For the female alcoholic it may have special meaning.

By loosening the ties that bind her to the traditional wife-mother role and permitting her full self-realization without guilt, society may effectively deal with the frustration, boredom, and loneliness that have long nourished problem drinking among women. By ruling out self-sacrifice as a prerequisite for womanly happiness and encouraging the development of confidence in herself and all her abilities, society may nurture in her the kind of self-image that will not turn upon itself with liquid hate.

At the same time there are those who suggest that women's liberation, which forces woman to perform not only at home but also in the larger world of work, will create alcoholism. By entering the male-dominated battleground that has yielded such ironic spoils as heavier alcoholism and early mortality, she may be subject to the pressure to conform to the same code of behavior as her brothers. This is the de-

---

*This article originally appeared in *Addictions*, Fall '73. It was updated in May, 1976 by Lavada Pinder of the Addiction Research Foundation.

bate. On the side of liberation is the work of researcher Elaine Cumming of the University of Victoria. Her studies show that the greatest protection for women against suicide is employment outside the home. Social relationships gained on the job are the preventive features. Perhaps this is true for alcoholism.

Historically, men have been bigger drinkers. Boozing long ago achieved a questionable but real virility score. Men drink more and sooner, and alcohol often acts as a social bond between them. Only in recent years have women even been granted the right to drink in public bars without a male escort. Men outnumber women in hospital, clinic, and detoxication admissions, and in alcohol-related arrests and convictions. But the gap could close. And there is little at this point to preclude the possibility that women may one day earn equal representation among alcohol statistics.

One prominent expert in the treatment field is not entirely convinced that in spite of lack of supportive data this dubiously desired equality hasn't already been achieved. R. Gordon Bell, founder and president of Toronto's Donwood Institute, a public alcoholism hospital and day clinic, feels the ability of women to manipulate their environments to accommodate their drinking may be an important factor in obscuring an accurate ratio, particularly in middle and upper social circles.

It is not that one less woman than man drinks dangerously, it is simply that society still effectively protects so many women from a full reckoning.

In 1975 Donwood admitted 828 patients, of which one-quarter were women. This 3 to 1 ratio, which has been consistent from 1970 to 1976, is considerably lower than other facilities report. Dr. Bell firmly believes it is also "a far more realistic reflection" of the full extent of alcoholism than the 6 to 1 average currently proffered by detoxication units. Serious drinking problems are much more prevalent among women than any figures have yet shown, says Dr. Bell, but most of it remains unrecognized and untreated.

While one factor remains consistent in the demography of alcoholism—that women are outnumbered by men—the statistical picture of women alcoholics, indicated by deaths caused by liver cirrhosis, is showing a marked increase. In the Ontario female population between the ages of fifteen and seventy during the years 1962 to 1973, deaths from liver cirrhosis increased by 120 percent. The female population increased by only 35 percent in the same period. And yet they remain a small minority wherever problem drinkers show up. Admissions to hospitals, clinics, and detoxication centers generally vary between 3 to 1 and a skid-row high of 8 to 1. Alcoholics Anonymous estimates one-quarter of its membership to be women.

The margin of difference between the incidence of alcoholism among men and women is explained as the result of stronger social forces inhibiting women from excessive drinking. Women have historically worked double-duty in the preservation of social mores. They risk society's censure by bucking the prevailing code of acceptable behavior, and they risk the added disgrace of being women who faltered. As Joseph Hirsh wrote in "Women and Alcoholism": "Woman represents important social and moral symbols that are the bedrock of society. And when angels fall, they fall disturbingly far. We would rather have them in their place, which is another way of saying that they define and make our own place possible and even more comfortable."

We are a society that largely condemns heavy drinking and is only beginning to come to terms with the insidious "double standard." In spite of the vast and profound changes our social attitudes are undergoing, including a new tolerance for many practices weighted by sanction and taboo, the negative social value of excessive drinking remains. We have always come down hard on alcoholics. We have always come down harder on alcoholic women.

The pressure exerts itself at two levels, but need only act at one to prevent a woman from becoming a statistic, something real to deal with. Should the existing negative forces not be sufficient to dissuade a woman from the excess consumption of alcohol, she may yet be effectively dissuaded from confronting her problem. Society may not succeed in discouraging her illness, but in discouraging instead her acknowledgment of it. Either way, we are spared another tarnished angel, and the question of the accountability of a whole body of women with hidden drinking problems remains strictly a social issue.

Our social attitudes, in fact, have created and nourished a great number of irregularities in our perceptions of the female alcoholic and our subsequent interactions with her. She appears to be so threatening a digression from the current cultural ideal that she throws us into fits and starts of confusion. We challenge her simultaneously with strong inhibitions and notable latitude. She is punished and protected, both because she is an alcoholic and because she is a woman. Relationships with family, physician, police, and employers, which typically present opportunities for identifying the problem and helping, are made impotent by these attitudes.

Studies have shown convincingly that the woman who drinks is more highly criticized than any drinking man. Her assault on the bottle represents the breaking of a more rigid taboo, the shattering of a deeply divined image of femininity. Regardless of her social or economic status, the woman alcoholic faces greater castigation and rejection from a less tolerant society.

Our reluctance to deal effectively—even honestly—with the female alcoholic is supported by a multitude of social nuances. Many are designed to postpone the crucial labeling process, to delay the truth of her distress, and drive her further into her foggy underground. It is a cruel measure of our collective reluctance to humanize our concept of woman, even to save her.

Social researcher Gus Oki has noted the deliberate action of skid-row social agencies to exclude, or at least seriously restrict, temporary accommodations and services for deviant women drinkers. "Some contend that there are no more services than are necessary," says Oki. "And some, ignoring the evidence, believe society only creates deviance by providing accommodation for it." The reasoning is somewhat naive—that female alcoholism will be blockaded absolutely by denying women the facilities available to men—but no different from that called up to rationalize our discomfort in a variety of similar situations.

Women alcoholics also receive special consideration, or camouflage again, from male police officers, notes Oki. These men often appear either shaken by her loss of control or charitable in view of her lapsed femininity. Their attitude is generally pro-release and they may choose to pack her off home in a cab or notify a friend or relative instead of booking her. This favored state is indeed threatened, however, if she becomes an habitual concern.

A crown attorney in Toronto's women's court, who rarely sees a day pass without at least one appearance on public drunkenness, notes the court's rather perfunctory demeanor: "We're generally very lenient with women. They just plead guilty and walk out. Drunks very seldom have lawyers. The court won't afford them legal aid. The judge grants a suspended sentence in most cases. Usually it's enough punishment that she's spent a night in jail."

Figures on public drunkenness convictions for Ontario during 1972 support observations of police protectionism. Only 7 percent of the arrests for public drunkenness were women, while it is estimated that 17 percent of the alcoholic population is female. Conversely, 93 percent of those arrested for public drunkenness were male, while in fact it is estimated that only 83 percent of the alcoholic population is male.

A woman receives differential treatment at both the arrest and disposition stage of an offense and men, clearly, take up the slack. Her position is compounded further by considerations of social status. Class, money, and reputation are the most precious associates of the public inebriate. They regularly frustrate the alcoholic's reckoning. The higher a woman's socioeconomic class, the greater society's will to protect itself from her. She is less likely to be picked up, jailed, charged, or convicted if she has any of these additional bargaining agents.

Tolerance of women alcoholics is highest on skid row, where even abusive drinking behavior is less frowned upon. Thus it is this woman who accounts for the vast majority of public drunkenness arrests. She is more vulnerable to police action because of all women she is both less likely and less able to hide her problem.

With fifteen years behind her as director of the Salvation Army's Homestead, a twenty-four-bed home for women with alcohol problems, Major Betty Peacock would agree that these women are more vulnerable. She says: "They simply go where night finds them. They are specially lonely, afraid of the unknown, afraid of trying, needing special support and understanding."

A rather vital measure of our inadequate concern for the woman alcoholic is the manner in which our understanding of her has been effectively delayed by a lack of real knowledge, research, and education. For decades studies have tended either to ignore her completely or to assume her alcoholic experience is precisely the same as a man's. A Washington University medical school psychiatrist, Dr. Marc Schuckit, conducted an extensive search and review of the literature on women alcoholics in 1972 and uncovered only twenty-eight studies published in the English language between 1929 and 1970. Data drawn from alcoholic studies of men and applied to women are of questionable significance, stated Schuckit, and so the new interest in research and treatment for the alcoholic woman is long overdue.

There have been several unfortunate outgrowths of this situation. Most existing treatment facilities have been designed with only men, or primarily men, in mind. This was the opinion of twenty-seven Ontario women who met in October 1975 for a three-day consultation in Ottawa concerning women, alcohol, and drugs. They focused on the need for training professionals and developing services for women alcoholics. "There's a lack of teaching about alcoholism in all curriculums," said one experienced alcoholism worker, "but it is most apparent where women are concerned. The medical profession, in particular, seems to define female patients as nervous, menopausal, or hypochondriacal when actually they could be alcoholic." The prescriptions that follow lead to the state of cross-addiction.

Alcoholism workers from across the province agree that women enter their programs with "a fist full of pills." Diane Hobbs, coordinator of Detoxication and Rehabilitation Programs for ARF, observes that women admitted to the 15 available beds for detox in the province (227 for men) tend to be younger, but use more tranquilizers and are less likely to accept referral.

Ms. Hobbs, formerly a professional development consultant with the ARF, traveled widely in an effort to effect the kind of communication between her fellow nurses and their female alcoholic patients that will benefit both. "We're very concerned about our communications on a woman-to-woman basis," she remarks. "Nurses sometimes associate the female alcoholic with promiscuity, personal failure, being a poor wife and mother. We see ourselves in her and we're repulsed. We have to try to establish trust between us, and women aren't used to trusting each other."

Emphasis on women helping women and on sensitive staffing of services are two themes that permeate all discussions with those committed to services for the female alcoholic. The Donwood Institute has taken leadership in these areas. Doreen Birchmore and Rodeen Walderman of the Donwood note that, in their institute, there is a large number of female staff members and therapists, some of whom are sympathetic to feminist theories of emotional stress among women. Perhaps this has some bearing on the high rate of recovery of many female Donwood patients. Whatever the case, it seems advisable that female alcoholics should be treated by individuals who are concerned and informed about sex-role conflicts of women in today's society. Marguerite O'Rourke, director of a program in Hamilton, puts it simply "I choose staff who have good feelings about themselves as women. This is what must be transmitted."

Most would agree that where treatment for female alcoholics is concerned it is a pioneering experience. Myrtle Deschamps opened a recovery home for women in North Bay, Ontario, in 1976. She says: "It's a learning process. The women are prouder, more uptight, and not as amiable as men who have been through the network of services. But this means that they have a lot of energy to devote to their recovery if we can only be flexible and listen carefully to their ideas about what they need."

Women drink differently than men. And they drink for different reasons. In any discriminating consideration of alcoholism these distinctions are important.

Most women do the majority of their drinking at home and alone. This is perhaps the single most discerning factor in a comparison of the consumer behavior of men and women. It is also one of the clearest indicators of the type of environment that begets and fosters alcoholism among women. Housewives swell the ranks of female alcoholism and indeed constitute the greater proportion of heavy drinkers. They have more opportunity to drink than any other women, and in the case of affluent social classes, they have more money to buy more and better booze, time, and recuperative aids.

An enterprising Don Mills, Ontario, man has probably met more of these women in the past few years than many career workers in the alcoholism field. He started an independent delivery service called Dial-a-Bottle. For a minimum $2 fee, he picks up liquor from an Ontario Liquor Control Board outlet and delivers it—legally—to telephone customers. He boasts that many of his orders come from "little old ladies who don't want their neighbors to see them headed for the liquor store."

Why such women drink is a question for Dr. Bell, whose thirty years' experience in the alcoholism field makes his observations both accurate and insightful:

Most women today seem to drink to relieve boredom, loneliness, and frustration. A great many women in our society have been educated to expect more out of life than merely being a good wife, mother, and homemaker. One woman can be all these things and still feel unfulfilled, while for other women it's enough.

There are so many reasons a woman deserves to be able to be more than the traditional wife-mother. Women see a wide range of life beyond motherhood and being a good wife. They want life, and we at Donwood support them. We feel that a woman, as a man, needs the opportunity for personal fulfillment. It's so simple. It's common sense. Some people are partially enslaved by the definitions of what is man's and woman's role. I say dump these old ideas, they're dated!

If there's a chance for the fulfillment of a woman's education and her identity, then the likelihood of her ever turning to a drug is reduced to begin with, and certainly reduced should later problems arise.

Aside from this, there's been such a dramatic change in the relative stability of life's institutions in the past quarter century—there are so many broken marriages that marriage itself has become a seedbed for planting alcohol and other drugs to alleviate boredom, frustration, and the lack of a sense of personal identity.

Few women regularly get drunk on beer; they prefer—in the beginning, at least—the more "feminine" sherries and fine wines. The beer-drinking female is nonetheless an increasingly frequent discovery now that taverns have been opened to unescorted women and the drinking age has been lowered to eighteen in many constituencies. Indeed, women are drinking more openly today than at any time in the past and on many more occasions. Alcohol, rather than tea or coffee, in now the beverage that accompanies many traditional activities such as showers and coffee klatches. It is this factor, coupled with a new awareness of women in general, that has created the appearance in recent years of an upswing in alcoholism among women.

In considering this openness Dr. Bell offers the qualification that the hidden alcoholic may not wish to expose herself on such an occasion. "They're not necessarily the ones who get sloshed at cocktail parties. Women who don't want anyone to know they drink heavily are frequently careful to avoid disclosure."

At the ARF Dundas Street West detoxication center, where five of the nineteen beds are reserved for women, most have been classified as lower-class drunks, with a high representation from skid row. And while the occasion is rare when at least one female resident isn't a skid-row type, it is not so rare any more to find her in company with a middle-class working woman. She may be a single young professional who got too drunk in a bar to get home, or a divorced middle-aged secretary found stumbling home from an office party.

A persistent misconception is that the only women with serious drinking problems are bored losers at either end of the social scale— the down-and-out street drinkers and the charity workers of the upper income brackets. While alcoholism may well be concentrated among these women, a new curiosity and concern seems to be developing for heavy drinkers in another identifiable group.

The unattached middle-aged working woman, an almost invisible and inconsiderable entity to alcohol experts at one time, is causing many to look again. Not only are her numbers increasing—as a result of reduced social pressure to marry and the availability of divorce— but apparently so is her alcohol consumption. She, too, drinks at home and alone, but she lacks the cloistering of the housewife.

While housewives may feel isolated in an emotional sense, working women are often isolated both emotionally and physically. Self-supporting, they are independent and able to drink unhampered by husbands and children but also without the support that families have the potential to offer.

One of the ways in which alcoholic working women can be reached is through their places of employment. Large corporations such as Bell Canada, Ontario Hydro, Eaton's, Simpson's, The Royal Bank, Imperial Oil, and some departments in the civil service, all of which employ a great number of women, have taken the initiative to detect drinking problems and refer employees to industrial treatment projects. A Manual for Supervisors developed by Ann St. Louis, personnel counselor for the Department of National Revenue, has received considerable attention from employers in both public and private sectors.

The problems, however, in using industrial programs to assist alcoholics are many, particularly for early intervention. Industrial alcoholism counselors are well aware of the procrastination on the part of employers and supervisors when it comes to confronting their employees. This hesitation is even more pronounced where female employees are concerned. The difficulties are compounded as the employer is usually male, and not necessarily any more enlightened about women with alcohol problems than the rest of society. The ARF's May Street Clinic, which takes referrals from cooperating businesses, sees about one woman for every twenty men in its rehabilitation program. Most of these are clerks, secretaries, and nurses committed to treatment by their respective supervisors who then become major participants in their recovery.

Women, as a rule, encounter drinking difficulties later in life than men. The average woman alcoholic begins abusing alcohol between the ages of twenty-eight and thirty-three. And unlike men, in whom the progression of the illness normally occurs over a period extending up to fifteen years or more, the onset of symptoms is rapid, telescoped into only a few years. A woman's first hospital admission for alcoholic complications occurs on the average about the age of forty and by then her physical health and appearance have usually deteriorated strikingly. If she escapes treatment at this point—as she often succeeds in doing—the rate of impairment only accelerates.

It has been noted that women often begin their dependence on alcohol in response to a specific stressful situation. Dr. Martha Sanchez-Craig, who directs the Spadina Project, a co-ed recovery home in Toronto for twenty-two men and seventeen women, finds that most of the women who enter the home report that their heavy drinking started after a loss, either by death or separation, of someone close—usually a friend, child, or husband. Statistics have shown that as many as two-thirds of alcoholic women are divorced, a rate not matched by the male segment of the alcoholic population. It is a common belief that for every ten wives who see an alcoholic husband through, only one husband remains with an alcoholic wife. After years of denying the problem and fearing disclosure, he leaves her.

A vast body of literature has been accumulated about the nonalcoholic wife of an alcoholic man, much of which seemed to indicate that the wife contributed to her husband's illness. This literature has not stood the test of time. However, Vera L. Lindbech points out in her 1972 review of the literature that there still remains a difference of attitude toward the spouse of the alcoholic depending on whether the inebriate is male or female. Generally, the nonalcoholic husband of the alcoholic woman has been given more sympathy although relatively little research effort.

Researchers have, however, demonstrated that the incidence of alcoholism in the immediate families of women alcoholics is often notably high, particularly among male members. A cross-section of such studies confirms that at least one-third have alcoholic fathers or brothers, and, in some cases, as many as one-half.

Until recently the single most repeated statement about women alcoholics was in relation to their having a high incidence of psychological disorders. This is now being seriously questioned within the context of women's role and the way they are perceived by our society. Linda J. Beckman, in her 1975 analysis of the research, says that perhaps what appears to be greater pathology in women could be a result of their alcoholism and the greater social disapproval and rejection of it. A 1976 Donwood Institute study compared 100 women alcoholics with a matched group of 100 nonalcoholic women. They shared common attitudes with nonalcoholic women with regard to current thinking about working outside the home, husbands and wives sharing tasks, and the women's liberation movement. But where feelings of worth and confidence in attaining goals were concerned the alcoholics viewed themselves as inadequate. So side by side with contemporary aspirations are found doubts about ability to achieve. Here are the indicators for designing education and treatment programs.

As women better understand themselves, their hopes and aspirations, both our conception of womanhood and our understanding of her lapse into alcohol dependency are undergoing profound changes. What problems the revolution in women's thinking might create among experts in the alcoholism field, who are just beginning to deal with her in terms of current attitudes, is unknown. But it is clear that by recognizing her potential for developing a strong individual self-image and acting on it, they will be at an immediate advantage.

# PART III   Supplementary Readings

Dohrenwend, B., and Dohrenwend, B. 1976. Sex differences and psychiatric disorders. *American Journal of Sociology* 81:1447–1454.

Gove, W., and Tudor, J. 1973. Adult sex roles and mental illness. *American Journal of Sociology* 78:812–835.

Lewis, H. 1971. *Shame and guilt in neurosis.* New York: International Universities Press.

——— . 1976. *Psychic war in men and women.* New York: New York University Press.

McMullen, S., and Rosen, R. 1979. Self-administered masturbation training in the treatment of primary orgasmic dysfunction. *Journal of Consulting and Clinical Psychology* 47:912–918.

Symonds, A. 1979. Violence against women, the myth of masochism. *American Journal of Psychotherapy* 33:161–173.

Weissman, M., and Paykel, E. 1974. *The depressed woman: A study of social relationships.* Chicago: University of Chicago Press.

Weissman, M., et al. 1973. The educated housewife: Mild depression and the search for work. *American Journal of Orthopsychiatry* 4:565–573.

Wolowitz, H. 1972. Hysterical character and feminine identity. In *Readings on the Psychology of Women,* ed. J. Bardwick, pp. 307–314. New York: Harper & Row.

# PART IV

# *Women's Particular Treatment Needs*

# 22

---

# Women's Treatment Needs

---

ELIZABETH HOWELL AND MARJORIE BAYES

---

In North America today there are more women than men with diagnosed psychiatric disorders. In clinics and private psychiatric care women predominate, equaling 60 to 75 percent of the patients (Levine, Kamin, and Levine 1974). Outside of the formal psychiatric world we find a multitude of programs, activities, and treatments designed for women. The complexities and informal nature of most of these activities provide little in the way of data, but evidence suggests that, for women, alternate forms of treatment aimed at special needs have proliferated in the past ten years and are not likely to decrease in the future. A few examples are consciousness-raising groups, abortion counseling, family planning, and counseling for the rape victim.

Why do women have special treatment needs? The answers fall into two categories.

First, women must confront particular developmental and sociopsychological issues that are different in some ways from the issues of men. There are aspects of living in which men as well as women may experience difficulty; however, often for women such difficulty has a different etiology, different repercussions, or a different recommended treatment than that of men. Treatment without regard to gender may not address women's particular issues—for example, problematic aspects of menstruation, pregnancy, the mothering role, the midlife transition—and may in other ways be skewed so as to limit intended outcome. Second, women are vulnerable to certain kinds of traumata. As a result of their childbearing capacity, they may need help such as abortion counseling or postmastectomy counseling. As a result of their special role as wife, they may have to deal with diverse issues at times of divorce or widowhood. Still another kind of trauma results when women are the victims of physical violence by men. Treatment must respond to psychological as well as physical damage. Examples are treatment for rape, battering, and father-daughter incest.[1]

This section of the book is divided into two subsections, one with papers covering several developmental issues and the second presenting papers on traumatic events to which women are vulnerable. Many therapists have not been trained in these areas. While general therapeutic skills will serve in many situations, clear knowledge of specific problems is essential in order to work competently and compassionately with particular needs of our women clients.

1. We do not wish to perpetuate victim blaming here. It is important to remember that many of the women in this group, in particular victims of rape and to a lesser and more complicated extent of battering, are first and primarily victims of violence, not psychiatric patients.

REFERENCE

Levine, S., Kamin, L., and Levine, E. 1974. Sexism and psychiatry. *American Journal of Orthopsychiatry* 44:327–336.

# DEVELOPMENTAL ISSUES

# 23

# A Study of Attitudes Toward Menarche in White Middle-Class American Adolescent Girls

## LYNN WHISNANT AND LEONARD ZEGANS

In many societies the menarche is recognized as a crucial time in a girl's physiological, psychological, and social development. It is openly acknowledged, publicly marking her entry into the adult world (Henderson 1967; Brown 1969).

The authors wish to acknowledge the contributions of Elizabeth Brett, Ph.D.

Biologically, menarche is an important life event for a girl. It regularly follows the year of her maximum growth spurt and comes at a time of changes in her physiology. It follows the development of breasts, pubic hair growth, and beginning changes in body contour (Tanner 1962; Lewis 1958; Group for the Advancement of Psychiatry 1968). It is a visible reminder of the establishment of rhythmic cycles of hormonal secretion (Hellman et al. 1974; Boyar et al. 1972).

In our culture, however, little formal recognition has been granted the occurrence of this event. The lack of explicit social recognition of the changes in a girl, coexisting with acute tacit awareness, has been well described by Mead (1930) as follows:

We prescribe no ritual, the girl continues on a round of school or work, but she is constantly confronted by a mysterious apprehensiveness on the part of her parents and guardians. . . . The society in which she lives has all the tension of a room full of people who expect the latest arrival to throw a bomb. (Mead in Caplan 1969, p. 57)

Educators and parents have puzzled over how best to help a girl deal with this happening, which in our society may create tension since it signals her inauguration into physiological maturity at a time when she will still be regarded socially as a juvenile.

Educationally, the subject of menarche has been approached principally from the viewpoint of hygiene (Lewin 1930; Thompson 1971). Behavioral scientists discuss menarche as a normative crisis in terms of castration anxiety and of achieving an identity with the "reproductive prototype" (Blos 1962, p. 109). Most experts have relied on their own memories, imagination, or reports of adult women who are undergoing psychotherapy for information about menarche (Bardwick 1941; Deutsch 1944; Shainess 1961; Sherfy 1973; Greenacre 1950).

The chief drawback of this approach has been the inaccessibility to the investigator of the emotional components of the adolescent's experiences (Deutsch 1967; Freud 1958; Lampl-de Groot 1960). Few reports have been based on interviews with young girls themselves (Kestenberg 1961).

Just how is the experience of menarche perceived by a young girl in this culture, and what is its emotional significance for her? What does she know about what is happening or has happened to her, and where has she learned it? Does she feel or act differently afterward? How do family members influence her reaction to menarche, and how does this event change her view of her position in the family and her relationships to peers?

We sought the answers to these questions by interviewing twenty-five girls aged twelve through fifteen and ten girls aged seventeen through twenty-one. This was a naturalistic, empirical survey seeking to identify phenomena by direct observation, to generate new hypotheses, and to evaluate these adolescents' attitudes and feelings concerning menarche in light of the theoretical formulations that psychotherapists have derived from their treatment of older women.

## Review of the Literature

Psychoanalysts have written of menarche as an important time in woman's identity formation, emphasizing the role of this event in precipitating an accelerated period of psychological work for the adolescent as she moves toward acceptance of herself as a female and as a future mother.

Menstruation is thought to be closely associated with a girl's relationship to her mother and mothering. After menarche she may experience herself as more womanly, more like her mother (Benedek 1959). The mother-daughter relationship is seen to be critical to the outcome of the crisis of menarche. If the identification is not overly charged with hostility, it is expected that a girl should be able to accept heterosexual desires without undue anxiety and regard motherhood as a desired goal. Deutsch (1944) emphasized the strong emotional connection between menstruation and reproduction, suggesting that each period is an occasion for some disappointment at not being pregnant. She felt that the first appearance of blood at menarche may provoke ideas of genital injury and reactivate old childhood sexual conflicts, fears, and anxieties, including masturbatory guilt and castration anxiety. Menarche may also evoke fears associated with anticipation of pain during defloration and childbirth (Benedek 1959). The girl is forced by menstruation to confront a perception of her vagina and internal sexual organs, stimulating acceptance of the uterus as an integral part of her body (Fliess 1957). Kestenberg (1961) felt that this may have a positive organizing effect on a girl's perception of herself and her world.

Much of the earlier writing about menarche emphasized the traumatic nature of the event, attributing this to the lack of preparation in terms of factual knowledge.

Several studies have attempted to survey the effect of menarche upon normal subjects. Stone and Barker (1939) made an effort to determine, through a questionnaire survey of a large number of schoolgirls, in what ways premenarcheal girls were different from postmenarcheal girls. The study did not elicit responses concerning the girls' experiences of menarche. More recently, Haft (1973) attempted to differentiate the two groups through the use of psychological tests and questionnaires. Both studies yielded inconclusive results. Shainess (1961) has interviewed adult women—asking them to recall their menarche—in an effort to elucidate their attitudes toward menarche with an emphasis on their subsequent feelings about their femininity and sexuality. We have found no studies that directly addressed the experience of the young girl herself as she anticipates menarche and as she reacts and assimilates the experience in subsequent years.

## Method

Data were obtained during August 1973 from interviews with campers and counselors at an overnight nondenominational girls' camp in mid-New England. The camp attracts white middle-class girls from nearby suburban areas. In the population of the camp, about 40 percent of the girls listed their religious affiliation as Protestant, about 25 percent as Jewish, and 25 percent Catholic, with the rest unaffiliated.

The girls lived in cabins to which they were assigned by age and grade in school. Four cabins with girls in the appropriate age categories were selected by the order in which they were listed on the camp roster. Girls from these cabins were interviewed consecutively as they became free from scheduled camp activities. There was no preselection of subjects by menstrual status. None of the girls refused to participate, although one did not wish to discuss some specific topics. All of the girls were interviewed by the same female psychiatrist (L.W.). The interviews, which were tape-recorded, were flexibly structured. The following three different groups emerged: ten premenarcheal girls aged twelve to thirteen (average age, 12.5 years), fifteen postmenarcheal girls aged twelve to fifteen (average age, 13.2 years), and ten counselors aged seventeen to twenty-one (average age, 19.7 years). The counselors were a self-selected group; the first ten counselors to volunteer were interviewed.

Initially the campers approached the interview as an assignment that interrupted their day's activities. As news of the focus of the interviews spread, girls began joking about which one would be the next to be called. Counselors reported that the presence of "the period lady" at the camp had for the first time introduced menstruation as an open topic for discussion. Counselors began to volunteer to be interviewed. The following is a summary of some of the concerns and feelings that emerged in interviews with the 35 premenarcheal, postmenarcheal, and late postmenarcheal girls. Certain trends emerged that touched on current patterns of education about menstruation and the girls' attitudes toward and reactions to the experience of menarche.

This was a naturalistic study based on semistructured interviews without forced answers. The text gives representative samples of responses. Table 23-1 presents an approximate distribution of the frequency of important comments and feelings.

# Results

## Education

The girls interviewed had been exposed to much material about menstruation. They had learned about their bodies and menstruation from friends, commercial booklets, school, and parents, especially their mothers. Friends were an important source of information. Several girls made the following statements: "[I] didn't really learn anything from my mother; [I] picked it up from friends." "I would sit in a corner with my girl friends, talk about it while boys are in gym." "[I] knew it before the school movies—a person reads advertisements, picks it up from other kids. In kindergarten they know everything."

Most of the girls had seen commercially prepared films about menstruation, and many had also had health or hygiene lectures in school prior to menarche. Pamphlets and "starter kits" from the makers of sanitary napkins were widely available. Many of the girls reported discussing menstruation with their mothers (only seven in this sample talked about it with their fathers). One girl discussed menstruation prior to menarche with her sisters. Often the talk with the mother occurred as part of the "facts of life talk," which the girls reported as having when they were quite small, or in conjunction with their mother's giving them a starter kit of sanitary products or commercial pamphlets. Girls intimated that they felt their parents assumed that the education of a girl about her body and menstruation was primarily the task of the school. They said, "Mother didn't talk about what to do—she figured I'd learn it at school," or "mother's a nurse—she didn't talk about it—she signed permission for the film."

## TABLE 23-1
### The Frequency of Important Comments and Feelings About Menstruation

| Item | 10 Premenarcheal Campers | 15 Postmenarcheal Campers | 10 Late Postmenarcheal Counselors |
|---|---|---|---|
| **EDUCATION** | | | |
| Before menarche, discussed menstruation with | | | |
| Mother | 10 | 13 | 9 |
| Father | 4 | 1 | 2 |
| Sister | 1 | 2 | 0 |
| Friends | 10 | 14 | 9 |
| School personnel | 9 | 12 | 10 |
| Others | 1 | 3 | 1 |
| **ANNOUNCING THE FIRST PERIOD** | | | |
| Planned to tell about first period immediately | | | |
| Mother | 10 | — | — |
| Father | 2 | — | — |
| Sister | 2 | — | — |
| Friend | 6 | — | — |
| Did tell about first period immediately | | | |
| Mother | — | 14 | 10 |
| Father | — | 0 | 1 |
| Sister | — | 1 | 1 |
| Friend | — | 2 | 0 |
| Identified with mother in expecting first period at same age | 3 | 2 | 2 |
| **KNOWLEDGE ABOUT MENSTRUATION** | | | |
| Described menstruation as being "like a sickness" | 8 | 9 | 10 |
| **THE MEANING OF MENSTRUATION** | | | |
| Expected to act differently, more like a girl | 7 | — | — |
| Reported acting or feeling significantly different | — | 10 | 5 |
| Different relationship to father | 0 | 2 | 2 |
| Different relationship to mother | 5 | 8 | 7 |
| Daydreamed about becoming a mother | — | 4 | 5 |
| **THE FIRST PERIOD** | | | |
| Had concrete plans for managing first period | 7 | — | — |
| Anticipated being scared | 3 | — | — |
| Reported being scared or upset | — | 12 | 7 |

## Knowledge About Menstruation

Both premenarcheal and postmenarcheal girls perceived themselves as very knowledgeable about menstruation.

The girls were initially quite facile in describing the anatomy and physiology of menstruation and gave a superficial impression of being well informed. They described their bodies in terms of "uterus," "ovary," and "fallopian tube"; however, when they were questioned further it became evident that most had little conception of what the inside of the body was like or how it functioned. They were especially inept in articulating their conceptualizations of their external genitalia, for which they lacked even vocabulary—they referred to "my bottom," "down there," "it," "the hole," or "my vagina" (meaning everything outside). "Clitoris," "labia," and "vulva" were unfamiliar words.

The girls' ideas about why women menstruated included the following: "It's waste blood from your body," "I have no idea what's going on inside," "Periods are stuff to have a baby with that wasn't used by whatever you call it—comes out with blood and junk," "Blood is there to protect the womb from the baby," "The egg inside doesn't get fertilized so it drops down—turns to blood." They described the uterus as "a sack maybe," "a bag," "all messy," and "Can't say in words, but I have a picture in my mind from the film where the egg drops down." Despite their access to factual information about menstruation, the girls seemed unable to assimilate the education material about anatomy and physiology. Most were well informed about the hygienic aspects of menstruation. There were a few misconceptions about the duration of the flow ("fifteen minutes"), amount of flow ("only a teaspoonful"), and the nature of the flow ("bright red blood"). A postmenarcheal girl commented, "I expected bright red blood—I thought something was really wrong."

Their concern did not center about the psychological meaning of menstruation, why it takes place, or about the anatomy involved, but on the practical issue of "What do I do when I get my period?" The girls focused their conscious attention on preparation for this event. They expressed worry that they would not know what to do, even though they had mentally rehearsed strategies for almost any occasion; this suggests the presence of underlying anxiety.

## Announcing the First Period

The premenarcheal girls anticipated that they would not be ashamed to have their family and friends know that they had begun to menstruate. One planned to announce, "Guess what, everybody, something new happened to me today." All of them specifically said that they would first tell their mothers. Most had talked about menstruation with their friends and planned to share this event with their best friends. Several premenarcheal girls gave strong evidence of identification with their mothers in predicting that they would get their period at the same age as the mothers did and would experience the same symptoms. The girls thought their mothers would be interested and pleased. They said, "She'd be happy," and "She'd be excited" and felt that their mothers would take charge and teach them what to do.

All but one of the postmenarcheal girls interviewed had told their mothers as soon as possible about their first period; the remaining girl stated that her mother had been "depressed and screwed up" and she waited three days to tell her.

Contrary to the openness that the premenarcheal girls anticipated, the postmenarcheal girls had actually been quite secretive! Few of them had told anyone except their mothers about beginning to menstruate. They stated that they had expected their mothers to tell their fathers or that they had preferred that their fathers did not find out. Even the girls whose fathers had been the parent who provided most of the early education about menstruation chose to tell only their mothers. They reported that they had not, in fact, told their best friends but expected them to figure it out. Several girls who matured later than their friends described themselves as hurt and confused by their friends' unwillingness to share information about menstruation, which, prior to the friends' menarche, they had planned to discuss freely. Thus there was a marked difference between how these girls anticipated sharing their experience of menarche with others and their willingness to do so when the time came. Cognitive awareness did not prove to be strong enough to neutralize the conflict; despite the availability of knowledge, the girls reacted privately.

### The First Period

Premenarcheal girls were asked to describe what they felt their first period might be like. Often they first expressed nonchalance, as follows: "It wouldn't make any difference," "I can't do anything about it anyway," "Why think about it," "No big deal." Then they admitted that in fact they thought about it a lot and worried about it. Almost all of the girls thought that they would be scared but were unable to articulate or formulate for themselves the source of fear. A few felt that "I'd be happy." Most seemed to view their period as a kind of illness and felt that with their periods they would feel tired and less energetic and that they would be in a "bad mood." They expected to have cramps, which they described as being like "gas pains" or "an upset stomach." All expressed concern at being "normal" and starting "on time." Many of the girls assumed that menstruation would be a new type of excretory function. When asked how they thought menstruation would feel, they explained that it might be "like going to the bathroom, except not, because you couldn't stop it—like dripping." One spoke of menstruation as being like a wound, "like you cut yourself somewhere only it doesn't hurt."

The postmenarcheal girls were asked to recall their first period. While one emphatically denied remembering the circumstances of the event even though it had happened less than a year before, the others clearly described the day, circumstances, and emotions surrounding the event. Every girl starting her period recognized it as such almost immediately (one girl thought for a few minutes that she had been cut). Most of these girls described themselves as being scared, angry, upset, or tearful, although they were unable to account for these feelings, maintaining that menstruation was "just another thing" to them. One recalled that "I was really scared—you knew what was happening but it came as a surprise. You thought you'd know but you didn't. The blood was scary." The camp director said that a girl experiencing her first period at camp is often distraught and inconsolably tearful.

Most of the premenarcheal girls had already planned what to do. The mother often provided the first supplies. In one family where the parents were divorced and the daughter lived with the father, the mother bought the supplies and brought them to the daughter. The mother instructed the daughter in how to wear the pad or tampon, and in one instance inserted the tampon for the girl.

## The Meaning of Menarche

The girls looking forward to menarche sensed that it would signal "being really grown up." They saw menarche as meaning "you can have children" but were not clear about how that related to their lives. They expected that they should act differently. They felt they would "act more ladylike" but were vague about what that entailed. One girl expressed it as acting "less crazy—sometimes I do nutty things." Another said that it meant being more careful of yourself, "not taking risks—like climbing up cliffs." However, they denied that others, except their mothers, would view them or treat them differently. They believed that their mothers would see them as "more grown up." Their mothers might expect them to be more responsible and "more ladylike" but might grant more privileges. They would be more careful about their daughters "messing around with boys."

The postmenarcheal girls emphasized that they were "the same person" after menarche. Some did report feeling closer to their mothers since menarche. A few said that they had started to think more about what to do with their lives, about having babies, or about what kind of mothers they would be compared to their own mothers. With several girls it was evident that around the time of the menarche they had become more private, introspective, and concerned with their relationships to other people. One reported, "I wasn't a little girl anymore. . . . Mother said things wouldn't be so easy—things get rougher, more complicated." Several girls reported being worried that their relationships to their fathers had changed and that their fathers felt differently about them. This was especially true of those girls who felt that they had a special relationship with their fathers, but they could not articulate just what might be different in their fathers' feelings toward them.

The postmenarcheal girls emphasized that a menstrual period should be "no great thing." They were quite fatalistic, saying, "There's nothing you can do about it, anyway. You're stuck with it." They spoke of feeling tired, nauseated, and irritable during their period and of being slowed down and dragged down. Most of these girls attempted to deal with menstruation by strict adherence to "the rules" given in health texts, especially commercial pamphlets. For example, they stated, "I really follow the instructions, I change my pad every three hours whether I need to or not," "I usually shower every other day, but the book says to shower every day during your period, so I do." They stressed the importance of "acting natural" and appearing "cool" and agreed that menstruation ought to be kept secret and that symptoms could and should be concealed by willpower. One girl summarized these feelings as follows: "Life won't change if you handle it right; if you start shooting off your mouth or yelling at them, they'll know."

The need to be natural and casual is so successfully met at this age that most cabinmates did not know when the others were having their periods. One girl strongly preferred not to know "when others are having their periods." Another said, "When a girl blabs it around, you really feel sick. I feel like saying, 'Oh, shut up.'"

## Discussion

Menarche has been described as "a puberty rite cast upon woman by nature itself" (Benedek 1959). Ritual serves as a cultural means of identifying significant transitions in the individual's life cycle, interpreting new emotional meanings, and redefining the person's role and status within the society. Our interviews with young adolescents confirm our belief that today's culture tends to ignore the affective importance of menarche. There are no formal customs to mark it, and no obvious change in the girl's social status follows it. Most of the people around her will not even be aware that menarche has occurred, and the mother often does not respond to the daughter's needs for working through the experience.

The prevalent view that menstruation is like a sickness is conveyed through advertisements for "women's medications" and "feminine products." Preparation for menarche involves assembling a suitable array of products, which are conveniently packaged and available by mail order. Menarche is then portrayed as a hygienic rather than a maturational crisis.

However, our interviews suggest that menarche is, in fact, experienced by a girl as an affectively charged event related to her emerging identity as an adult woman, her newly acquired ability to reproduce, and her changing relationship to her mother. Regardless of the quality of the past relationship, the girls in our study turned to their mothers for instruction about this task of becoming a woman. However, many of the mothers were uninformed or unable or unwilling to discuss the broader significance of menarche with them. The girls spoke of being more aware of themselves as "young ladies" after menarche, of giving more thought to their future, and of wondering more about having babies and being a mother. Often the girl was alone in dealing with this crisis of turning toward womanhood and motherhood. For a time, postmenarcheal girls stopped discussing their bodies with their peers. They stated that menarche was "no big thing." They had learned that menarche is something that happens and is best ignored.

This study supports, by direct interviews with adolescent girls, several hypotheses that have been advanced about the significance of menarche. It demonstrates that the significant emotional responses of girls to the experience of puberty are accessible for study in a one-to-one interview situation in a nonclinical setting.

This group of girls did seem to experience menarche as a disturbing event; they were frightened and ashamed in spite of their stated belief that they should not be. Their response was not primarily due to a lack of available factual information prior to menarche but to more fundamental issues. It was apparently difficult for these girls to assimilate the educational material they did receive. This was evident in their responses to questions about their anatomy. A similar observation has been made by Deutsch (1944), who commented that the girls' own emotional contribution to menarche stemmed from unresolved conflicts about menstruation.

The girls strongly associated the menses with excretory soiling, as hypothesized by Lewin (1930). This association is evident both in the description of menstruation given by the premenarcheal girls and in the emphasis by the postmenarcheal girls on maintaining cleanliness and freshness during the menstrual period. The education provided them, in particular by commercial companies, focuses on this aspect. This association is in accord with Lewin's position that some of the shame experienced by these girls has to do with the recall of loss of sphincter control evoked by the experience of menstruation.

Several girls spoke spontaneously of menarche being like a cut or wound. This imagery is reminiscent of earlier speculations about the intrapsychic meaning of menarche as a symbol of castration. Certainly menarche is anticipated as a time for giving up an active stance, whether for part of the month or altogether, and assuming a more stereotyped feminine role with emphasis on ladylike clothing and a more protected life style. This conflict is reflected in the emphatic denial by the older girls that anything had changed, which contrasted with their description of menstruation as being "like a sickness" and of themselves as different.

The focus on the girls' relationship to their mothers centers on the mothers' role as caretaker and arbiter of excretory functions. These feelings emphasize the girls' wishes to return to a more dependent relationship with their mothers. This common wish of young adolescent girls has been discussed by Blos (1962). However, the girls also related to their mothers by struggling to identify with them, thus moving toward assuming a more adult female role. The regressive pull is reflected in the girls' turning toward their mothers for support at the time of menarche and is most striking in those girls who had not previously been close to their mothers or discussed menstruation with them. Identification is reflected in the postmenarcheal girls' description of themselves as spending time thinking about what kind of a mother they would like to be, often specifically comparing themselves with their own mothers.

Equally notable is the girls' avoidance of their fathers at the time of menarche, especially when contrasted with the expectations of the premenarcheal girls.

The cultural denial of the importance of menarche is compounded by the secretiveness of the girls themselves with regard to discussing this event with others. The girls seemed more able to ignore the cultural mandates to "be discreet" before rather than after they began to menstruate. It is tempting to hypothesize in light of these observations that the function of public ritual at the time of menarche in primitive cultures is to reduce the sense of secret shame over loss of excretory control and fears of mutilation and to counter the regressive movement toward relating to the mother in a dependent, infantile fashion.

By ritually acknowledging this change as a valued developmental landmark, these cultures may strengthen a girl's perception of her mother as a positive figure for identification.

Much more needs to be understood about the relative contributions of biological, psychological, and social variables in determining a particular girl's response to the onset of menstruation.

Our mores concerning menarche emphasize intellectual understanding on the part of the young adolescent and the proper use of sanitary devices to reduce fear of excretory soiling. However, even if a cognitive mastery of the facts about menstruation is achieved, it may not be sufficient to neutralize the conflicts that arise in conjunction with this event. This knowledge does not assist a girl in trying to integrate the emotional and sociological implications of this change into her altered self-image. Didactic schoolroom presentations and commercial booklets cannot substitute for familial and cultural traditions needed to mark and work through this transition from childhood to maturity through identification with the mother and her adult role.

We are not suggesting the artificial creation of a new ritual but rather the development of a more socially and culturally appropriate substitute to serve the emotional function that more primitive societies have met with familial and social rituals.

Our culture has acted as if there were a social and professional blind spot in regard to the psychological impact of menarche, seeming to assure that teaching girls how to keep clean is sufficient. There is a need for a data base of empirical observations in order to develop a rational basis for meeting the psychological needs of the young adolescent girl.

REFERENCES

Bardwick, J. M. 1971. *Psychology of women.* New York: Harper & Row.

Benedek, T. 1959. Sexual functions in women and their disturbance. In *American handbook of psychiatry,* ed. S. Arieti, vol. 1, pp. 727–748. New York: Basic Books.

Blos, P. 1962. *On adolescence.* New York: Free Press.

Boyar, R., et al. 1972. Synchronization of LH secretion with sleep during puberty. *New England Journal of Medicine* 287:582–586.

Brown, J. 1969. Adolescent initiation rites among preliterate peoples. In *Studies in adolescence,* ed. R. E. Grinder, pp. 59–68. New York: Macmillan.

Deutsch, H. 1944. *The psychology of women,* vol. 1. New York: Grune & Stratton.

————. 1967. Selected problems of adolescence. In *The psychoanalytic study of the child,* ed. R. S. Eissler et al., vol. 3, pp. 19–24, 93–130.

Fliess, R. 1957. *Erogeneity and libido: Addenda to the theory of the psychosexual development of the human.* New York: International Universities Press.

Freud, A. 1953. Adolescence. In *The psychoanalytic study of the child*, ed. R. S. Eissler et al., vol. 13, pp. 255–278.

Greenacre, P. 1950. The prepuberty trauma in girls. *Psychoanalytic Quarterly* 19:298–317.

Group for the Advancement of Psychiatry. 1968. *Normal adolescence: Its dynamics and impact*. Report 68. New York: Group for the Advancement of Psychiatry.

Haft, M. S. 1973. An exploratory study of early adolescent girls: Body image, self-acceptance, acceptance of "traditional female role," and response to menstruation. Ph.D. dissertation, Columbia University.

Hellman, I., et al. 1974. Anorexia nervosa: Immaturity of the circadian secretory program for plasma luteinizing hormone. Paper presented at the 31st annual meeting of the American Psychosomatic Society, Philadelphia, Pennsylvania, 29–31 March 1974.

Henderson, J. L. 1967. *Thresholds of initiation*. Middletown, Conn.: Wesleyan University Press.

Kestenberg, J. 1961. *Menarche in adolescents—psychoanalytic approach to problems and therapy*, ed. S. Lorand and H. I. Schneer, pp. 19–50. New York: Harper & Row.

Lampl-de Groot, J. 1960. On adolescence. In *The psychoanalytic study of the child*, ed. R. S. Eissler et al., vol. 15, pp. 95–103.

Lewin, B. 1930. Kotschmieren, menses und weibliches uber-ich. *Internationale Zeitschrift für Psychoanalyse* 16:43–56.

Lewis, E. C. 1958. *Developing woman's potential*. Ames, Iowa: University of Iowa Press.

Mead, M. 1930. Adolescence in primitive and modern society. In *The new generation*, ed. V. F. Calverton and S. Schmalhausen, pp. 169–188. New York: Macaulay. Cited in G. Caplan and S. Lebovic, 1969. *Adolescence*. New York: Basic Books.

Shainess, N. 1961. A re-evaluation of some aspects of femininity through a study of menstruation: A preliminary report. *Comprehensive Psychiatry* 2:20–26.

Sherfy, M. 1973. *The nature and evolution of female sexuality*. New York: Vintage Books.

Stone, C. P., and Barker, R. G. 1939. Attitudes and interests of premenarchial girls. *Journal of Genetic Psychology* 54:27–73.

Tanner, J. M. 1962. *Growth at adolescence*, 2nd ed. Oxford, England: Basil, Blackwell & Mott.

Thompson, C. 1971. *On women*. New York: New American Library.

# 24

# Teenage Pregnancy: A Research Review

## CATHERINE S. CHILMAN

Although a general impression exists that the nation is currently undergoing an epidemic of births to adolescents, this is hardly the case. As table 24-1 shows, the rate of births to teenagers aged sixteen to nineteen has actually decreased, although until recently there has been an increase in the birth rate for mothers under the age of sixteen. It is true, however, that since the mid-1960s there has been an increase in the proportion of babies born to adolescents *outside marriage*. Among

TABLE 24-1
*Births Per 1,000 Women,*
*14–19 Years of Age, 1960–1976*

| Year | Age of Women | | | | | |
|------|------|------|------|------|------|------|
|      | 14   | 15   | 16   | 17   | 18   | 19   |
| 1960 | 5.4  | 17.8 | 40.2 | 75.8 | 122.7 | 169.2 |
| 1965 | 5.2  | 16.5 | 36.0 | 66.4 | 105.4 | 142.4 |
| 1970 | 6.6  | 19.2 | 38.8 | 66.6 | 98.3 | 126.0 |
| 1975 | 7.1  | 19.4 | 36.4 | 57.3 | 77.5 | 92.7 |
| 1976 | 6.8  | 18.6 | 34.6 | 54.2 | 73.3 | 88.7 |

Source: Report of Task Force on Adolescent Pregnancy (Chicago: American College of Obstetricians and Gynecologists, forthcoming).

unmarried women aged fifteen to nineteen, the birth rate increased from approximately 16 per 1,000 in 1960 to 25 per 1,000 in 1975 (Sklar and Berkov 1974; and National Center for Health Statistics 1976).

Among both married and unmarried adolescents, the *number* of births—not the rate of births—rose during the 1960s and early 1970s because the adolescent population was so large during those years, a result of the 1948–58 "baby boom." During 1976 about 1.2 percent of white teenage girls and 9.2 percent of black teenage girls gave birth outside marriage. More striking, about one-fourth of the babies born to white adolescents and 80 percent of those born to black adolescents in 1976 were born out of wedlock (National Center for Health Statistics 1978). Since about 90 percent of unmarried teenage mothers today decide to keep their babies rather than surrender them for adoption, teenage single parenthood is a growing phenomenon in this society.

Ideally, public policy must rest upon a sound knowledge base. Therefore, before considering existing and needed policies concerning adolescent childbearing, it is important to look at what research has revealed about its apparent causes and consequences.

## Causes

The late 1960s brought to this country enormous changes, one of which was the sexual revolution. It was characterized by a sharp increase in premarital intercourse among adolescents—about half today's youth are sexually active by the time they reach age eighteen and about 75 percent by age twenty-one (Kantner and Zelnik 1972; Zelnik and Kantner 1977; Chilman 1978)—the upsurge of the feminist movement and a push toward equality in sexual behavior; a rapid rise in divorce rates; a growing acceptance of "alternative life styles"; and a generally free and open sexual climate. These trends have continued into the late 1970s.

Adolescents who have grown up during this period have had a vastly different developmental experience with respect to their sexuality than those who matured in earlier, more sedate times. By the early 1970s, premarital intercourse by age eighteen was almost normative for both males and females, and the double standard of sexual behavior had almost disappeared (Kantner and Zelnik 1972; Zelnik and Kantner 1977; Jessor and Jessor 1975; Cvetkovich and Grote 1975; Vener and Stewart 1974; Chilman 1978; Gagnon and Simon 1973). Adequate research is lacking concerning the sexual behavior of older men and women during the 1960s and 1970s, but it seems highly probable that their behavior became much more "liberated" during this period and that many adolescents lived in families in which their parents were having nonmarital affairs.

Table 24-2 summarizes other factors that seem to be associated with participation in coitus outside marriage before the age of eighteen. Although no well-designed nationwide study of adolescents has adequately examined variables associated with early nonmarital coitus, a

TABLE 24-2

*Summary of Major Factors Apparently Associated with Premarital Intercourse Among Adolescents*

| Factors | Males | Females |
|---|---|---|
| *Social Situation* | | |
| Father having less than a college education | unknown | yes, for blacks |
| Low level of religiousness | yes | yes |
| Norms favoring equality between the sexes | probably | yes |
| Permissive sexual norms of the larger society | yes | yes |
| Racism and poverty | yes | yes |
| Migration from rural to urban area | unknown | yes |
| Peer-group pressure | yes | not clear |
| Lower social class | yes (probably) | yes (probably) |
| Sexually permissive friends | unknown | yes |
| Single-parent (probably low-income) family | unknown | yes |
| *Psychological* | | |
| Use of drugs and alcohol | yes | yes |
| Low self-esteem | no[a] | yes[a] |
| Desire for affection | no[a] | yes[a] |
| Low educational goals and poor educational achievement | yes | yes |
| Alienation | no[a] | yes[a] |
| Deviant attitudes | yes | yes |
| High social criticism | no[a] | yes[a] |
| Permissive attitudes of parents | yes | yes |
| Strained parent-child relationships and little parent-child communication | yes | yes |
| Going steady; being in love | yes | yes |
| Risk-taking attitudes | yes[a] | yes[a] |
| Passivity and dependence | no[a] | yes[a] |
| Aggression, high levels of activity | yes[a] | no[a] |
| High degree of interpersonal skills with opposite sex | yes[a] | no[a] |
| Lack of self-assessment of psychological readiness | no[a] | yes[a] |
| *Biological* | | |
| Older than 16 | yes | yes |
| Early puberty | yes | yes (probably, for blacks) |

[a] Variables supported by only one or two small studies. Other variables are supported by a number of investigations.

number of studies (Kantner and Zelnik 1972; Jessor and Jessor 1975; Cvetkovich and Grote 1975; Chilman 1978) have produced sufficiently similar results to inspire a certain amount of confidence in their findings. These findings lead to a number of speculations. Along with the effects of changing norms about sex, the influence of racism, poverty, low levels of educational achievement, and low goals is clearly important. The effects of poor family relationships and limited communication between parents and youths also seem evident.

A few well-designed local studies (Jessor and Jessor 1975; Cvetkovich and Grote 1976) suggest that, particularly for some girls, strong dependency needs and the desire for affection and self-esteem lead to early participation in coitus. For what is probably a different group of girls, belief in equality between the sexes, criticism of society, attitudes that deviate from the norm, and alienation seem to be highly influential. Boys appear to be affected more than girls by peer-group pressure, attitudes favoring risk taking, and generally aggressive and active modes of behavior.

The evidence is conflicting about whether use of drugs and alcohol causes readier participation in coitus by adolescents or whether the same cluster of social and psychological characteristics that leads to adolescent sexual activity also increases the likelihood of drug and alcohol use. Similar alternatives might be presented regarding the effects of having sexually permissive friends. Such friends might encourage sexual activity, or sexually active adolescents might seek similar friends.

### Use of Contraceptives

A number of recent studies show that only about 50 percent of sexually active women of high-school and college age use contraceptives at their first intercourse. No national data are available for males, but a few local studies indicate that about 90 percent of sexually experienced black males of high school age and 70 percent of white ones report having had unprotected intercourse at least once (Cvetkovich and Grote 1975; Finkel and Finkel 1975).

In 1971 young white women were about twice as likely as young black women to use contraceptives at each intercourse (Shah, Zelnik, and Kantner 1975). Only about one-fourth of teenage women under age eighteen used the pill. When Zelnik and Kantner repeated their 1971 national survey of young women between ages fifteen and nineteen in 1976, they found that in some ways use of contraceptives had improved for both races (Shah, Zelnik, and Kantner 1975; Zelnik and Kantner 1977). Thirty percent of the single sexually active women in their study reported that they "always" used contraception, compared to only 18 percent in 1971. However, 25 percent said that they "never" used contraceptives. This was a greater proportion than in 1971 and thus indicates a decline in use of contraception. Among married teenagers, in 1973 only about half said they were using contraceptives (Zelnik and Kantner 1977).

A group of studies, one national and the remainder local (e.g., Shah, Zelnik, and Kantner 1975; Kantner and Zelnik 1972; Rosen, Martindale, and Griselda 1976; Lindemann 1974; Cvetkovich and Grote 1975; Luker 1975; Presser 1974), sought to learn what those factors are that differentiate young women who use contraceptives from those who do not. According to currently available research, adolescent women with the following characteristics are less likely to use contraceptives or to use effective ones consistently:

*Demographic Variables*
   Age less than 18
   Single status
   Low socioeconomic status
   Minority-group member
   Not planning to attend college
   Fundamentalist Protestant

*Situational Variables*
   Not in a steady, committed relationship
   Never pregnant
   Having intercourse sporadically
   Being in a stressful situation
   Lack of access to a free, confidential, personally reassuring family planning
      service that does not require parental consent
   Lack of communication with parents about sexuality and contraceptives
   Lack of friends who use contraceptives with satisfaction
   Recent initiation into coitus

*Psychological Variables*
   Desire for pregnancy; high value placed on fertility
   Ignorance of risks of pregnancy and of family planning services
   Feelings of fatalism, powerlessness, alienation, incompetence, and trusting
      to luck
   Passivity, dependence; traditional attitudes toward female role
   High levels of anxiety; low ego strength
   Lack of acceptance of reality of sexual behavior
   Attitudes favoring the taking of risks and the seeking of pleasure
   Fear of side effects and possible infertility from contraception
   Low educational and vocational goals
   Low level of interpersonal communication skills

Only a brief discussion of these variables is possible here. A number of researchers observe that young adolescents who have only recently begun to engage in intercourse are especially unlikely to use contraceptives (Lindemann 1974; Gabrielson et al. 1971; Reichelt 1976; Zabin,

Kantner, and Zelnik 1979). In fact, it is common for teenage girls to be sexually active for a year or more before they seek help in obtaining contraceptives—an indicator that the availability of contraceptives does not stimulate adolescents to participate in coitus.

The part played by demographic variables, including socioeconomic status, race, and ethnicity, is not shown with sufficient clarity by this list. However, research on adolescent sexuality and other aspects of behavior strongly suggests that poverty often breeds attitudes of fatalism, powerlessness, alienation, a sense of personal incompetence, and hopelessness with respect to striving for high, long-range educational and occupational goals (Stack 1974; Ladner 1971; Rainwater 1970; Rubin 1976). This is especially apt to be true when racism combines with poverty to reduce an individual's options in life. All these characteristics are associated with poor use of contraceptives.

The many situational and psychological factors that contribute to poor contraceptive practice lead to the conclusion that a multifactor approach is necessary if ultimately pregnancies among teenagers are to be prevented. This point will be discussed later at greater length.

## Trends in Abortion

A series of Supreme Court decisions and resultant changes in federal policy in the early 1970s made free, legalized abortions available to adolescents. However, in 1978, as a result of pressure by "right-to-life" groups, federal funds for abortion were withdrawn except in cases of rape, incest, or serious threats to the mother's physical health. Between 1973 and 1976, the abortion rate for both black and white teenagers rose rapidly, and this played a large part in the reduction of the adolescent birth rate (Baldwin 1976). It is too early to know whether the loss of federal funding for abortion will lead to a rise in the rate of adolescent childbearing.

Only a few recent studies are available on the effects of abortion on adolescents and the characteristics of teenagers who have had abortions. Evans, Selstad, and Welcher (1976) showed that pregnant teenagers who chose abortion were likely to have been doing well in school before pregnancy and to have come from intact, non-Catholic families that were not dependent on welfare. Those who underwent abortion but later regretted their decision were more likely to be Catholic, be from low socioeconomic origins, do poor work in school, and feel that the abortion was forced on them by their parents. Clues from research (Osofsky and Osofsky 1972; Perez-Reyes and Falk 1973; Monsour and Stewart 1973) also indicate that relief is the most usual reaction immediately following an abortion. Later adverse emotional reactions appear to be relatively rare and are more likely to occur among women with a previous history of depression and anxiety. Findings also point to the positive contribution to the adolescents' morale of support from friends, parents, and boyfriends at the time the abortion is performed (Cobliner, Schulman, and Romney 1973).

# EFFECTS

## Effects on Parents

A number of studies (e.g., Moore and Hofferth 1978; Moore and Caldwell 1977; Furstenberg 1976) show that young women who have their first child before the age of eighteen or nineteen are more likely to have certain characteristics at the time of their first pregnancy or in subsequent years than those who have their first child later in life. These characteristics include lower levels of educational achievement, lower earnings from employment, a greater tendency to be dependent on public assistance, a stronger tendency toward having a large number of children, a higher incidence of births outside of marriage, higher rates of both early marriage and separation or divorce, and a greater likelihood of having male partners of low educational and occupational status.

However, these findings need to be qualified. A careful analysis of research that looks at the characteristics of young people before as well as after pregnancy strongly suggests that many of the supposed consequences of teenage childbearing are interwoven with its underlying causes. This was already indicated in the discussions of factors influencing premarital intercourse and such use of contraceptives. Many of these youngsters would be likely to experience educational, vocational, familial, and financial problems in the future whether or not they became adolescent parents. In many instances, becoming teenage parents merely adds further difficulties for youngsters who have been burdened throughout their developmental years by such factors as racism, poverty, poor family relationships, and low levels of achievement in school. Preventing early pregnancies would not solve every problem for such young people, but it would reduce the difficulties that many face in attempting to finish high school, find employment, establish satisfying and stable families, and control the size of their families.

*Effects on Children*

It has been frequently claimed that early childbearing poses severe risks for the health of both mother and baby. However, observed health problems such as higher rates of infant mortality, premature births, and childbirth complications for the mother may be related more to the greater incidence of poverty, poor nutrition, and lack of adequate prenatal care among pregnant adolescents than to age (Menken 1975). Recent experiments indicate that when special efforts are made to provide first-rate medical care to pregnant teenagers, differences in maternal and infant health associated with the mother's age disappear (Report of Task Force on Adolescent Pregnancy, forthcoming).

It is also frequently claimed that adolescents are inadequate as parents. This claim is yet to be proved by careful research. The few studies that do exist (Furstenberg 1976; Dreyfoos and Belmont 1978) fail to confirm this assumption, especially when the adverse effects of the adolescents' low socioeconomic status, rather than their age per se, are taken into account.

*Effects of Unmarried Parenthood*

Little systematic knowledge exists about the effects of unwed parenthood on young mothers and fathers or their children. Earlier norms that proscribed premarital coitus for women and condemned unmarried mothers and their youngsters as social outcasts have faded in recent years. However, human service professionals tend to view unmarried mothers (unmarried fathers are rarely considered) as presenting especially complex psychological and social problems. This is partly because of age-old, sexist cultural myths and prohibitions and partly because these professionals generally see only those young women who do have problems. This subject is far too complex for adequate discussion here, but it can be briefly pointed out that the adverse effects of unmarried parenthood are generally much less severe than they were earlier. This is largely a result of more permissive sexual norms, increased social acceptance of unmarried parenthood, growing equality between the sexes, and greater availability of jobs for women.

Although it is frequently claimed that adolescents have babies in order to go on welfare, sophisticated analysis of large bodies of data casts doubts on this assumption. For example, adolescent illegitimacy rates are not higher in states with liberal policies for granting Aid to Families with Dependent Children (AFDC) or with more generous benefits (Moore and Caldwell 1977). The availability of public assistance to young mothers apparently does not cause them to seek pregnancy but increases their options. Once pregnant, they can choose to carry the child to term rather than seek an abortion, to stay single rather than enter a possibly poor marriage, and to keep the child rather than release her or him for adoption. The poor employment opportunities for many young men today—over 50 percent of inner-city youth are unemployed (Keniston and Carnegie Council on Children 1977)—plus restrictive AFDC policies in many states for married couples mean that young mothers and their children may be better off financially if they opt for single status and welfare rather than marriage (Ross and Sawhill 1975).

The far higher rates of out-of-wedlock births found among black teenagers compared to whites deserves comment. Analysis of research shows that these differences are associated with a number of factors: Black teenagers tend to initiate intercourse at an earlier age, are twice as likely to have coitus outside marriage, more frequently place high value on fertility, are less apt to use effective contraceptives consistently, resort less often to marriage in order to legitimate a child, and until recently, were less likely to obtain an abortion. There are numerous clues from research that recent migration from rural to urban areas, lower socioeconomic origins, discrimination, and blocked educational and occupational opportunities are the chief reasons for these attitudes and behaviors, rather than race per se (Kantner and Zelnik 1972; Billingsley 1970; Stack 1974; Ladner 1971; Chilman 1978).

Although it is sometimes assumed that black families, especially those of lower socioeconomic status, readily accept childbirth out of wedlock, this is not true. Childbearing within marriage is greatly preferred. However, the strong value placed on family support supersedes this preference, so that more black families than white tend to provide assistance to unmarried adolescent parents and their children (Ladner 1971; Rainwater 1970; Stack 1974). As the individualistic, achievement-oriented norms and bureaucratic arrangements of the larger society impinge more heavily on black families, such help may well become less available (Chilman 1978).

# Implications for Policy

A number of policies to prevent adolescent childbearing are induced by the research that has been briefly sketched here. The following summary of primary prevention strategies applies both to the adolescents' families of origin and to the adolescents themselves:

- Reduction of poverty through adequate income maintenance, job training and placement, and creation of needed jobs.
- Welfare reform, in particular (1) making public assistance equally available to one- and two-parent families, couples without children, and childless single persons and (2) subsidy of inadequate wages.
- Provision of child care for children of parents employed outside the home.
- Increased affirmative action in regard to equal jobs and wage opportunities for women and members of minority groups and in regard to housing for minority groups.
- Increased attention to school integration: enriched education for children and adolescents who have learning problems; increased participation of parents in the schools; and improved staffing for such student services as school social work, guidance counseling, school psychology, and school health services, in elementary schools as well as the higher grades.
- Increased access to high-quality health care financed by comprehensive health insurance.
- Support of social and psychological services to families and their members, especially services addressed to poor family communication, overly lenient or overly restrictive behavior on the part of parents, problems of single parents, and conflicts between parents and children and parents and adolescents.

These strategies constitute a familiar list of recommended public policies aimed at preventing or ameliorating a wide range of social problems in addition to adolescent pregnancy, including the breakdown of the family, poor physical and mental health, dropping out of school, crime and delinquency, and substance abuse. The reason this familiar policy prescription is offered is that adolescent sexual behavior, like all human behavior, has its strongest roots in the family and community environment in which the person develops. The earlier discussions of the factors influencing such behavior have already illustrated this point. Genuine efforts to prevent adolescent childbearing and its alleged consequences of dropping out of school, unemployment, dependence on welfare, poor health of mother and child, marital problems, and inadequate parenting must change the social and economic situations that are the primary cause of these problems.

## Specific Programs

At the more immediate level, a number of specific programs are called for. Some of these programs are already in existence but need further strengthening and enlightened community support. These policies for secondary prevention of untimely adolescent childbearing include the following:

1. Federal and state funding of family planning services for low-income persons regardless of age, marital status, or parity (having borne children). This funding became available primarily through the Family Planning and Services Act of 1970. Such funds are also available through Title VI (Maternal and Child Health), Title XIX (Medicaid), and Title XX (Social Services) of the Social Security Act. However, availability of such funding does not necessarily mean that family planning programs, especially those for adolescents, are implemented locally. This requires community initiatives that may well be lacking, particularly in rural areas.

2. Readily available, high-quality family planning services geared to special needs of male and female adolescents. These needs include free or low-cost services without the requirement of parental consent; confidentiality; services open during after-school hours and within easy reach of teenagers; staff members who are sensitive to the physical, social, and psychological characteristics of a wide variety of adolescents; and counseling, educational, and referral services in addition to more strictly medical services. The Planned Parenthood Federation of America and its affiliates have taken leadership in developing these kinds of programs for adolescents, but further federal funding is needed to support the counseling and educational aspects of these programs.

3. Continued support and further implementation of the 1972 federal legislation prohibiting schools that receive public funding from excluding pregnant girls.

4. Training and program support for personnel in schools, youth organizations (including religious ones), and health and social service agencies to provide a range of educational, counseling, advocacy, and referral services for adolescents in regard to all aspects of their sexuality. This would include the use of contraceptives for those who are sexually active as well as support for those who choose not to become sexually involved.

5. Further public and private funding for knowledgeable, skilled teaching about human sexuality, including adolescent sexuality. In recent years, federal grants for projects that include sex education have been made to such organizations as the Parent-Teacher Association, Boy Scouts, Girl Scouts, Boys Clubs, 4-H Clubs, Salvation Army, and National Federation of Settlements. Of special interest is a grant to the School of Social Work of the University of Hawaii in Honolulu to train faculty members of various schools of social work to teach courses in human sexuality.

Recent surveys show that sex education is offered in about one-third of the nation's public schools, but details about contraception are rarely mentioned (Scales 1978). To date, studies (e.g., Miller 1976; Cvetkovich and Grote 1975; Gabrielson et al. 1971; Finkel and Finkel 1975; Monsour and Stewart 1973) have failed to show that improved knowledge about human sexuality results in changes in sexual behavior and contraceptive use. Despite this, high-quality sex education, placed in the context of broader aspects of interpersonal relations and life goals, is clearly called for. This is especially true in a society that has changed its values and norms so radically in the past ten years and in which parents and children have such difficulty in communicating about sexual topics. Furthermore, recent experimental projects suggest the usefulness of specially designed educational programs in promoting more effective contraceptive behaviors among sexually active adolescents (Schinke 1978). These programs deal with sexuality in the context of the individual's life and include specific information about the high risk of unprotected coitus, training and practice in contraceptive use and in communication about sexual relationships between two people, and information about the various kinds of contraceptives. Further education and counseling for parents regarding their own sexuality and that of their children is also strongly indicated.

6. Free or low-cost legal abortion services for teenagers, including skillful counseling about problem pregnancies, without the requirement of parental consent. Because of the strong anti-abortion feelings in this country, it is difficult enough to support such a radical measure as abortion itself, let alone abortion without parental consent. However, advocacy of this policy seems essential under current conditions.

Policies to reduce problems associated with adolescent childbearing are also needed for teenagers who become parents. Family and child welfare services delivered by skilled personnel should be available for adolescent parents, preferably before the birth of the child, to help the young prospective parents and their families examine carefully and realistically the options open to them. These options include adoption, marriage, continued single status for the mother, establishment of a separate residence, or living with the parents of either the young father or mother. Emphasis should be placed on permanent planning for the child so that the number of children "adrift" can be reduced.

Further development of resources is needed for young parents who decide to keep their babies. This includes income maintenance, job training and job development, day-care provisions, and support for health and social services, as described in the primary policy recommendations.

Legislation passed in 1978 (the Adolescent Health Services and Pregnancy Care Act) purports to provide for

comprehensive health, educational, and social services to teen-agers so as to prevent unwanted pregnancies and to provide these services to young parents and their children, especially for those parents who are under age 18.

According to this act, grants will be made available to local public or nonprofit agencies to coordinate available community resources, including those from a variety of state and federal programs. Critics cite many problems with this legislation. It is not clear how funds will be allocated between direct service and linkage of services. Emphasis is placed on providing services to adolescents who are already pregnant or who are parents, not on preventing pregnancy. Providers of services are required to offer counseling about maternity and adoption but need only inform the teenager of the possible availability of abortion. Furthermore, studies of the outcomes of comprehensive service programs for adolescent parents have failed to show that they are particularly effective in accomplishing such stated goals as high school graduation and financial independence (Jekel 1975; Furstenberg 1976).

## Conclusions

In general, existing programs seem to place too much emphasis on providing services for pregnant adolescents as a special group. Improved provision of comprehensive services and enhanced life opportunities for all children, adolescents, and parents would probably be a far more effective approach to preventing and dealing with adolescent childbearing as well as preventing and treating a host of other problems that affect youths. It appears that minimal attention is paid to the needs of adolescents until they get into serious trouble.

Another difficulty with focusing services on adolescent childbearing is that the needs of older parents with social, psychological, physical, economic, and employment problems are overlooked. Are problems of parenting somehow magically solved when fathers and mothers are over the ages of eighteen or twenty? In actuality, both childbearing and illegitimacy rates are higher for people in their twenties than for those in their teens (National Center for Health Statistics 1976). It is easier to mobilize public concern for adolescent parents than for older ones. This is but one example of an unfortunate contemporary trend toward "single issue" political activity that results in "Band-Aid" legislation for special groups.

REFERENCES

Baldwin, W. 1976. *Adolescent pregnancy and childbearing—growing concerns for Americans.* Washington, D.C.: Population Reference Bureau, September 1976.

Billingsley, A. 1970. Illegitimacy and the black community. In *Illegitimacy: Changing services for changing times,* pp. 70–85. New York: National Council on Illegitimacy.

Chilman, C. 1978. *Adolescent sexuality in a changing American society: Social and psychological perspectives.* Washington, D.C.: U.S. Department of Health, Education, and Welfare.

Cobliner, G., Shulman, H., and Romney, S. 1973. The termination of adolescent out-of-wedlock pregnancies and the prospects for their primary prevention. *American Journal of Obstetrics and Gynecology* 115:432–444.

Cvetkovich, G., and Grote, B. 1975. Antecedents of responsible family formation. Paper presented at the National Institute of Child Health and Human Development, Bethesda, Md.

————. 1976. Psychological factors associated with adolescent premarital coitus. Paper presented at the National Institute of Child Health and Human Development, Bethesda, Md., May 1976.

Dreyfoos, J., and Belmont, L. 1976. The intellectual and behavioral status of infants born to adolescent mothers. Fourth Progress Report to the Center for Population Research, National Institute of Child Health and Human Development. Washington, D.C.: U.S. Department of Health, Education, and Welfare.

Evans, J., Selstad, G., and Welcher, W. 1976. Teenagers: Fertility control behavior and attitudes before and after abortion, childbearing or negative pregnancy test. *Family Planning Perspectives* 8:192–200.

Finkel, M., and Finkel, D. 1975. Sexual and contraceptive knowledge, attitudes and behaviors of male adolescents. *Family Planning Perspectives* 7:256–260.

Furstenberg, F. 1976. *Unplanned parenthood: The social consequences of teenage childbearing.* New York: Free Press.

Gabrielson, I., et al. 1971. Adolescent attitudes towards abortion: Effects of contraceptive practice. *American Journal of Public Health* 61:730–738.

Gagnon, J., and Simon, W. 1973. Youth, sex and the future. In *Youth in contemporary society*, ed. Gottlieb, pp. 211–250. Beverly Hills, Calif.: Sage Publications.

Jekel, J. 1975. The past decade of special programs for school-age parents. *National Alliance Concerned with School-Age Parents Newsletter* 3 (Spring).

Jessor, S., and Jessor, R. 1975. Transition from virginity to nonvirginity among youth: A social-psychological study over time. *Developmental Psychology* 11:473–484.

Kantner, J., and Zelnik, M. 1972. Sexual experiences of young unmarried women in the U.S. *Family Planning Perspectives* 4:9–17.

Keniston, K., and the Carnegie Council on Children. 1977. *All our children: The American family under pressure.* New York: Harcourt.

Ladner, J. A. 1971. *Tomorrow's tomorrow: The black woman.* Garden City, N.Y.: Doubleday.

Lindemann, C. 1974. *Birth control and unmarried young women.* New York: Springer.

Luker, K. 1975. *Taking chances: Abortion and the decision not to contracept.* Berkeley: University of California Press.

Menken, J. 1975. Health consequences of early childbearing. Paper presented at the Conference on Consequences of Adolescent Pregnancy. Washington, D.C., October 1975.

Miller, W. 1976. Some psychological factors predictive of undergraduate sexual and contraceptive behavior. Paper presented at the 84th Annual Convention of the American Psychological Association. Washington, D.C., September 1976.

Monsour, K., and Stewart, B. 1973. Abortion and sexual behavior in college women. *American Journal of Orthopsychiatry* 43:804–814.

Moore, K., and Caldwell, S. B. 1977. Out of wedlock childbearing. Mimeographed. Washington, D.C.: Urban Institute.

Moore, K., and Hofferth, S. 1978. The consequences of age of first birth. Mimeographed. Washington, D.C.: Urban Institute.

National Center for Health Statistics. 1976. *Advance report: Final natality statistics 1975.* Supplement to *Monthly vital statistics report.* (Series 25, no. 10.) Hyattsville, Md.: U.S. Department of Health, Education, and Welfare.

————. 1978. *Advance report: Final natality statistics, 1976.* Supplement to *Monthly vital statistics report.* (Series 26, no. 10.) Hyattsville, Md.: U.S. Department of Health, Education, and Welfare.

Osofsky, J., and Osofsky, H. 1972. The psychological reactions of patients to legalized abortions. *American Journal of Orthopsychiatry* 42:48–60.

Perez-Reyes, M., and Falk, R. 1973. Follow-up after therapeutic abortion in early adolescence. *Archives of General Psychiatry* 28:120–126.

Presser, H. 1974. Early motherhood: Ignorance or bliss? *Family Planning Perspectives* 6:8–14.

Rainwater, L. 1970. *Behind ghetto walls: Black families in a federal slum*. Chicago: Aldine.

Reichelt, P. 1976. Psychosexual background of female adolescents seeking contraceptive assistance. Paper presented at the 84th Annual Convention of the American Psychological Association, Washington, D.C., September 1976.

Report of Task Force on Adolescent Pregnancy. Chicago: American College of Obstetricians and Gynecologists, forthcoming.

Rosen. R. A., Martindale, L., and Griselda, M. 1976. Pregnancy study report. Mimeographed. Detroit, Mich.: Wayne State University.

Ross, H., and Sawhill, I. 1975. *Time of transition: The growth of families headed by women*. Washington, D.C.: Urban Institute.

Rubin, L. 1976. *Worlds of pain*. New York: Basic Books.

Scales, P. 1978. A survey of sex education programs for adolescents in the United States. Paper presented at the Family Impact Seminar on Adolescent Pregnancy. Washington, D.C., 1978.

Schinke, S. 1978. Adolescent pregnancy: An interpersonal skill training approach to prevention. *Social Work in Health Care* 3:159–167.

Shah, F., Zelnik, M., and Kantner, J. 1975. Unprotected intercourse among unwed teenagers. *Family Planning Perspectives* 7.

Sklar, J., and Berkov, B. 1974. Teenage family formation in postwar America. *Family Planning Perspectives* 6:80–90.

Stack, C. 1974. *All our kin: Strategies for survival in a black community*. New York: Harper & Row.

Vener, A., and Stewart, C. 1974. Adolescent sexual behavior in Middle America, revisited: 1970–1973. *Journal of Marriage and the Family* 36:728–735.

Zabin, L., Kantner, J., and Zelnik, M. 1979. The risk of adolescent pregnancy in the first months of intercourse. *Family Planning Perspectives* 11:215–222.

Zelnik, M., and Kantner, J. 1977. Sexual and contraceptive experiences of young women in the United States, 1971–1976. *Family Planning Perspectives* 9:55–73.

# 25

# Psychological Reactions of Postpartum Women

### ELIZABETH HOWELL

Probably most women in this culture experience some feelings of helplessness, depression, and/or emotional disorganization in the first few months after giving birth. Other symptoms that often occur during this period are restlessness, confusion, insomnia, and episodic crying. While estimates of the actual prevalence of postpartum psychological reactions vary considerably, one recent estimate indicates that four-fifths of the total of new mothers experience some psychological distress postpartum while one-sixth of the total experience distress serious enough to require professional care (Della Quadri and Breckenridge, n.d.). In the first three months postpartum, women experience a four- to fivefold increase in the risk of emotional disorder, particularly of psychosis (Melges 1968; Pugh et al. 1963).

Surprisingly, the milder postpartum reactions have received relatively little attention in the psychiatric literature. Until quite recently, the literature has focused on postpartum psychosis or severe depression and the effect on the infant of maternal behavior (Grossman et al., 1980). Even more surprising in consideration of their relatively common occurrence, there is currently no classification in DSM-III of non-psychotic postpartum distress. Indeed, "The transient mild depression occurring postpartum (the postpartum blues) is so ubiquitous and ostensibly benign that it has not often been deemed worthy of serious study" (Yalom et al., 1968, p. 16). Of course, postpartum psychological reactions can be quite severe and are not always transient. Even if this were not the case, the distress of varying intensity that is experienced by so many women warrants serious consideration and study. Ironically, many women who experience postpartum distress feel not only unhappy but "abnormal" and are at a loss as to how to understand and cope with this new constellation of feelings.

Since the fourth century B.C. postpartum disturbances have been noted and described. Hippocrates speculated that the cause was that lochial discharge had been carried to the head, causing symptoms of agitation and delirium. And, according to one current research team, "Today we are not much closer to understanding the interaction between experience, physiology, and psychopathology in the postpartum period" (Brown and Shereshefsky 1972, p. 139).

There is evidence that some portion of the postpartum psychological reactions may arise from the abrupt change in hormonal activity. For instance, menopausal women on replacement estrogen often report a surge of feeling of well-being, while postpartum women who are rapidly losing estrogen report a loss of this feeling (Panter and Linde 1976). However, this viewpoint does not provide sufficient explanation for the fact that adoptive mothers (Melges 1968) as well as fathers and grandmothers (Asch and Rubin 1974) have exhibited symptoms of depression and confusion, which are typical of the psychological reactions often observed in postpartum mothers.

Within the limited research that exists on postpartum syndromes, some of the correlational findings can be briefly summarized. Postpartum reactions tend to recur with subsequent pregnancies (Melges 1968). Despite this, the earlier pregnancies, in particular the first one, appear to be most frequently followed by postpartum distress (Yalom 1968; Paffenberger and McCabe 1966; Gordon and Gordon 1959). Grossman and associates (1980) found major differences in postpartum adjustment between first-time and experienced mothers. Experienced mothers were more concerned about issues external to themselves and their immediate families. A longer interval since the last pregnancy (Yalom 1968; Paffenberger and McCabe 1966), shorter gestation, and greater age have been associated with postpartum reactions. In addition, infections, as well as the length and difficulty of labor and amount of blood loss, have been linked to postpartum depression (Yalom 1968).

The research, although scant (Oakley 1979), that exists on the relationship of exhaustion, sleep loss and sleep disturbance, social isolation, and work overload to postpartum symptoms is indicative of the importance of these factors. According to Larsen and associates (1968), cited in Boston Women's Health Book Collective (1971), when women are asked what experiences connected with childbearing they found most stressful, many mentioned fatigue—and this fatigue was more often during postpartum than during pregnancy. The fatigue factor appears to be of particular importance in the early postpartum period as a result of the greater vulnerability of many women to sleep loss in late pregnancy. Williams (1967), cited in the Boston Women's Health Book Collective (1971), found that in the last few weeks of pregnancy, women tend to lose REM[1] sleep.

Rossi (1968, 1978) suggests that one cause of postpartum depression is the work overload and isolation that most women in this culture experience upon returning home from the hospital. She notes that in earlier periods of human history, extended kinship systems provided support for the mother and supplemental care to the infant. She speculatively relates this information to the scant evidence of postpartum depression in ethnographic accounts of these societies. Rossi states that the kinship system made up for the discrepancy between the child's need for mothering, which, as Benedek[2] observed, is absolute and the mother's need to mother, which is relative. Rossi continues:

Yet what has been seen as a failure or inadequacy of individual women may in fact be a failure of the society to provide institutionalized substitutes for the extended kin to assist in the care of infants and young children. It may be that the role requirements of maternity in the American family system extract too high a price of deprivation for young adult women reared with highly diversified interests and social expectations concerning adult life. (1968, p. 27)

In the light of this, Le Masters's (1957) finding, cited in Oakley (1979), that professional women who give up their work tend to be vulnerable to especially severe postpartum reactions, is not surprising.

In an early (1959) study, Gordon and Gordon found that the number of stressful situational social variables (including background and current environment) in a woman's life correlated highly with her postpartum emotional reactions. They later developed a list of fourteen stress factors predictive of postpartum difficulties. These were as follows:

1. Primapara (woman having first baby)
2. No relatives available for help with baby care
3. Complications of pregnancy in family history
4. Husband's father dead
5. Wife's mother dead
6. Wife ill apart from pregnancy
7. Wife ill during pregnancy
8. Wife's education higher than her parents'

1. Rapid-eye-movement sleep, which is associated with dreaming, is considered to be the most important part of the sleep cycle for physiological and psychological replenishment.

2. Cited in Rossi.

9. Husband's education higher than his parents'
10. Wife's education incomplete
11. Husband's occupation higher than his parents'
12. Husband's occupation higher than his wife's parents
13. Husband often away from home
14. Wife has had no previous experience with babies

(Gordon et al. 1965)

Forty percent of the women with scores above five (five of the fourteen factors) experienced postnatal difficulties, while only 6 percent of those women with scores under four experienced these.

Later studies have strengthened some of the initial findings of Gordon and Gordon. Liakos and associates (1972), as cited in Oakley (1979), found in a sample of Greek women that the likelihood of postpartum blues was lessened if the mother had either her own mother or mother-in-law to help. Shereshefsky and Yarrow (1973) found the help of the husband in taking over some of the child-care responsibilities to be extremely important in the postpartum woman's adaptation. Furthermore, the husband's attendance at prenatal classes during pregnancy has been found to be predictive of better adaptation (Chertok 1969). Conversely, aggression and hostility on the part of the husband have been found to have a precipitating effect on postpartum psychiatric syndromes (Kaplan and Blackman 1969; Ketal and Brandwin 1979). Cohen (1966) and her co-workers found that the quality of the husband's collaboration had a crucial impact on his wife's well-being during pregnancy and the postpartum period. A more recent study by Grossman and others (1980) indicates that a husband's ability to be supportive to his wife through pregnancy and childbirth was highly predictive of her postpartum adjustment.

The current relative isolation of the nuclear family frequently forces the mother and father to rely exclusively upon each other despite the other pressures and burdens that impinge on both. At the time immediately following delivery, the new mother's dependency needs, often sheer physical needs, increase; and the pressure for the satisfaction of these needs often falls squarely on the new father's shoulders. As noted earlier, fathers have psychological reactions to the birth of their children too. Yet the father's vulnerability in this respect is generally not considered worthy of attention, much less treatment. In the light of these considerations, it would probably be more accurate in most cases to speak of disturbances in the "postpartum family" than in the postpartum mother.

While, after examination, it seems obvious that the postpartum family, not just the mother, warrants our attention, an assumption persists in the clinical literature that the mother alone, as a *psychological* entity, is the source of the difficulties she experiences postnatally; and, of course, a further assumption is that the psychodynamic source of the postpartum mother's conflicts is her unfulfilled and ambivalent relationship with her own mother. Without denying that the postnatal woman's feelings about herself and her new infant are bound to be in many ways powerfully derivative of her early experiences with her own mother, to focus on this relationship exclusively would be just one more instance of the continuing assumption of pathogenesis via "Mom."

While they indicate stress and distress, postpartum reactions are not necessarily pathological. In many ways they constitute a functional adjustment to a momentous life change. Reorganization of family structure and, for first-time mothers (Grossman 1980), enlargement of their sense of identity, must occur. Panter and Linde (1977) see some feelings of helplessness and dependency as useful, for some identification with the baby is required in order that the mother be able to relate to the child. These same authors suggest that postpartum depression is a feeling of mourning for the person the mother used to be.

Given the nature of the postnatal woman's task of simultaneous identification with her own mother and with her infant via her own early experience, a regressive "pull" is to be expected. Indeed, it might be more harmful than not if the unsettling aspects of this situation were given no attention at all, however unconsciously. Interestingly, Markam (1965), cited in Oakley (1979), followed a group of patients who had been classified as suffering from postpartum depression and a group of controls. She found that the controls, while they had been chosen because they had been classified as *not* suffering from depression, gave evidence of a depressive reaction also. What differentiated them from the pathological group was that they employed a vast arsenal of defenses to ward off the depressed feelings.

Very little research has been devoted to the treatment of postpartum syndromes. In their study, Gordon and Gordon (1959) found that therapists who actively pointed out the social strains in the postpartum client's life and recommended procedures for their improvement were more successful than those using a more passive, analytic approach. Of course, neither should the importance of the intrapsychic dynamics be overlooked. For instance, Melges (1968) found conflicts over mothering to be a paramount issue in the etiology of postpartum reactions. He estimates that almost all of the patients (88 percent) in his study suffered from ambivalent identification with their mothers. Although they repudiated their own mothers, the experience of suddenly becoming mothers themselves thrust them back upon their experience with their own mothers as a reference point. This caused identity diffusion and subjective confusion.

In the context of long-term individual psychotherapy and keeping in mind the importance of other variables, it can be most helpful to focus on the client's relationship to her mother, exploring, among other things, the sources of feelings of frustration and deprivation in this relationship. An important conflict that may emerge, in addition to the one described by Melges, is that between the client's feelings of frustration, deprivation, and damage via her mother and the cultural stereotype of perfect selfless and all-loving motherhood, internalized as an aspect of the client's superego. (The very existence of this split-off "good" part of the image of motherhood as our cultural mandate reveals the difficulties with images and expectations of "mother" inherent in our culture.) A thorough examination of this cultural image which fits no real person, can result in a greater appreciation of its absurdity and can thereby be conducive to the client's development of a sense of absolution for both herself and her mother. This can help reduce the conflict concerning the simultaneously held demand for perfect mothering and guilt and anger held toward herself and her mother respectively.

The therapist must judge the appropriateness of various interventions in the context of the needs of the individual client. Family therapy may be appropriate. A preventive approach or an approach designed to promote optimal family development (Flapan and Schoenfeld 1972) appears promising. Flapan and Schoenfeld (1972) have designed a set of procedures to help women assess their readiness for parenthood and to enhance their maternal role development.

In sum, it is paradoxical that postpartum distress is usually a fairly normal response that involves the display of what in other contexts could be considered psychiatric symptoms. The postpartum period is one of massive biological change for the mother and one of tremendous emotional and environmental upheaval for all members of the family. Cultural stereotypes concerning the joyfulness of the occasion can serve to minimize the realistic stresses of the new situation and burden the new parents in their assessment of their success or failure in adaptation. On the positive side, this period of transitional adjustment offers opportunities for productive reorganization and growth. Until recently, scant research attention has been paid to the important topic of mothers' and fathers' emotional adjustments to the birth of a new baby. Perhaps some of this neglect arises from the confusing sets of expectations commonly held about this period.

REFERENCES

Asch, S., and Rubin, L. 1974. Postpartum reactions: Some unrecognized variations. *American Journal of Psychiatry* 131(8):870–974.

Boston Women's Health Book Collective, ed. 1971. Postpartum: After the baby is born. In *Our bodies, ourselves,* pp. 207–225. New York: Simon and Schuster.

Brown, W., and Shereshefsky, P. 1972. Seven women: A prospective study of postpartum psychiatric disorders. *Psychiatry* 35:139–159.

Chertok, L. 1969. *Motherhood and Personality.* Philadelphia: Lippincott. Cited in Our bodies, ourselves (1971), Boston Women's Health Book Collective, ed. New York: Simon and Schuster.

Cohen, M. B. 1966. Personal identity and sexual identity. *Psychiatry* 29:1–14.

Della Quadri, and Breckenridge, K. n.d. *Mothercare.* Los Angeles: J. P. Tarcher.

Flapan, M., and Schoenfeld, H. 1972. Procedures for exploring women's childbearing motivations, alleviating childbearing conflicts and enhancing maternal role development. *American Journal of Orthopsychiatry* 42:389–397.

Gordon, R., and Gordon, K. 1959. Social factors in the prediction and treatment of emotional disorders of pregnancy. *American Journal of Obstetrics and Gynecology* 77:1074–1083.

Gordon, R., et al. 1965. Factors in postpartum emotional adjustment. *Obstetrics and Gynecology* 25:158–166.

Grossman, F., et al. 1980. *Pregnancy, birth, and parenthood.* San Francisco: Jossey-Bass, Inc.

Kaplan, E., and Blackman, L. 1969. The husband's role in psychiatric illness associated with childbearing. *Psychiatric Quarterly* 43:396–409.

Ketal, R., and Brandwin, M. 1979. Childbirth-related psychosis and familial symbiotic conflict. *American Journal of Psychiatry* 136:190–193.

Melges, F. 1968. Postpartum psychiatric syndromes. *Psychosomatic Medicine* 30:95–108.

Oakley, A. 1979. A case of maternity: Paradigms of women as maternity cases. *Signs* 4:607–631.

Paffenburger, R., and McCabe, L. 1966. The effect of obstetrical and perinatal events on risk of mental illness in women of childbearing age. *American Journal of Public Health* 56(3):400–407.

Panter, G., and Linde, S. 1977. *Now that you've had your baby.* New York: Spectrum Books.

Pugh, T., et al. 1963. Rates of mental disease related to childbearing. *New England Journal of Medicine* 268:1224–1228.

Rossi, A. 1968. Transition to parenthood. *Journal of Marriage and Family* 30:26–39.

————. 1978. A biosocial perspective on parenting. In *The family,* ed. A. Rossi et al., New York: Norton.

Shereshefsky, P., and Yarrow, L. 1973. *Psychological aspects of a first pregnancy and early postnatal adaptation.* New York: Raven Press. Cited in A case of maternity: Paradigms of women as maternity cases, by A. Oakley. *Signs* (1979) 4:607–631.

Yalom, et al. 1968. Postpartum blues syndrome. *Archives of General Psychiatry* 18:16–27.

# 26

# Attitudes Toward Parenting
# in Dual-Career Families

COLLEEN LEAHY JOHNSON AND
FRANK ARVID JOHNSON

As the women's liberation movement has expanded opportunities for qualified women, increasing numbers of middle-class women with children have been turning to careers, in contrast to jobs, for personal satisfaction and self-enrichment rather than simply for supplemental income. This situation has created an interesting variant in the conjugal family, namely, the dual-career family. The purpose of this paper is to review current research on this family type and to present findings from a pilot study of young dual-career families in an upstate New York college community.

We are primarily concerned with the patterns of adaptation used by families in which both the husband and wife engage in careers involving a high degree of emotional commitment and time involvement while they are rearing young children. In a recent paper (Johnson and Johnson 1976) the authors suggested that career women are less able than men to resolve role strain stemming from the two-career situation because of specific gender-linked social-psychological and psychodynamic factors. There are also innumerable practical difficulties

The authors wish to thank the graduate students in the Department of Child and Family Studies, Syracuse University, for their invaluable assistance in conducting this research.

connected with attempts to delegate domestic and child-rearing duties as well as impressive normative sanctions against such delegation.

Although the two-career families are frequently admired as futuristically oriented, we feel that they face the same pressures and consequences of social change as do all families in American society. Therefore, it is worthwhile to examine these pressures and illustrate some of the responses evolved by the two-career family, particularly in terms of child-rearing patterns.

Almost by definition, those families in which both partners have careers (rather than jobs) are from the middle or upper-middle class. Logically, one would expect certain characteristics of middle-class family ideology to influence the adaptation of the two-career family. Like other American families, the two-career family has become an increasingly nucleated and specialized unit of interacting personalities in which the primary functions center on fulfilling the emotional needs of its members (Parsons 1949). As the middle-class nuclear family has become more isolated from kin and other primary relationships, increased expectations have been placed on the marital relationship for satisfaction of intellectual, sexual, emotional, and social needs. Rostow (1965) commented that focusing such expectations within the marriage makes the union considerably more emotionally charged and vulnerable, since there are few other acceptable alternatives available to fulfill primary emotional needs. Hence the marriage is expected to maintain its primacy and durability in the face of the entrance and exit of children from the nuclear family. It is not that children are unimportant, but that their position in the family is transitory. According to Hill and Rodgers (1964) the closer spacing of children, reduction of family size, and earlier separation from the family have compacted child-rearing functions into fewer and fewer years.

In addition to the expanded emotional component in family relationships, some popularizers of psychoanalytic theory have significantly changed the mother's attitude toward the developing child (Wolfenstein 1955; Slater 1970; Storr 1972). This change particularly affects the educated mother who is likely to turn to her own college training, the opinions of professionals, or the child-rearing manuals. However beneficial this intellectual approach to child rearing has been, it is important to consider how it has enlarged and complicated the content of the mother's role.

Mead and Wolfenstein (1955) pointed out that the conception of the child's nature has changed radically during the past 100 years, from the view of "infant depravity" of the nineteenth century, through the turn-of-the-century view of the child as a "bundle of impulses" needing control, to the current emphasis on children as "reservoirs of rich potential." Hence, if the modern mother adopts this view, she faces the complex task of molding and developing these "bundles of potential" into future presidents, scientists, and above all happy, well-adjusted adults. In order to accomplish this, many women feel that their maternal role must be a full-time job demanding high commitment and total investment. Hypothetically, the mother's reward consists of producing "outstanding" offspring of the next generation; however, producing less than outstanding children may be associated with personal failure that cannot be assigned to outside forces or some uncontrollable fault of nature. Instead, the blame is placed squarely on the mother's shoulders, and she must bear the guilt. It seems unlikely that the career woman who is also a mother can escape or ignore the expectations and pressures imposed by the current child-rearing philosophy (Wolfenstein 1955).

Although some present ideology has promulgated the importance of fathers' sharing in the vicissitudes of child rearing, motherhood, in most segments of society, remains a sacred task that demands high dedication and commitment and specifically involves the mother rather than the father. Irrespective of the father's supportiveness in two-career families, such "experiments" face the gradient of strong, gender-linked psychological differences. McClelland (1964) summarized some of the psychological research documenting the theory that women in general display a heightened capacity for perceptiveness to the social environment and a greater sensitivity to interpersonal relations. If a career woman is more aware of what goes on around her both on the job and at home, and is less able to ignore it, she will have more difficulty than her husband in insulating her career role from the complex family environment in which children are socialized.

The intensification of relationships in today's nuclear family along with the guilt-tinged results of socialization practices may be assumed to be salient factors that motivate the middle-class mother to fulfill her needs for self-enrichment outside the traditional arena of domesticity. If these women respond to these pressures by leaving the home, it is important to examine how they have adapted—particularly in regard to whether they have escaped the "costs" of such a family system or remain its "victim."

The literature on two-career families directly documents the additive nature of the mother's role, that is, the assumption of a career role in addition to her domestic roles rather than an orderly transition from one role to the other (Holmstrom 1972; Rapaport and Rapaport 1971). Hoffman (1974) pointed out that the effects on children of the mother's working depend on the nature of her employment, her family circumstance, social class, the age and sex of the children, and the kinds of child-care arrangements that are made. She suggests that the working mother provides a largely positive role model for her children. However, other researchers (Hoffman 1963; Birnbaum 1971) suggest that working mothers experience considerable guilt and anxiety. One result of this guilt—at least among mothers who like their work—is that they make increased efforts to compensate for their employment and may in fact overcompensate. Despite the popular myths regarding maternal deprivation in families where mothers work, there is no solid evidence that the mother's employment status, in itself, leads to juvenile delinquency or other forms of social or psychological problems, at least for school-age children.

## Method

Our random sample was composed of twenty-eight dual-career families. Each family had at least one child under the age of twelve, and most of the children were considerably younger. Their mean age was 5.6, and the mean number of children was 1.7. All parents had a college degree, and approximately half of the wives were in high-commitment careers (e.g., medicine, law, and college teaching). The remainder of the wives held such occupations as nursing, school teaching, and administrative positions in businesses.

Husband and wife were interviewed separately for approximately two hours. A combination of open-ended and forced-choice questions was asked in the areas of career activities, power and task allocations in the marriage, attitudes and behaviors toward child rearing, and the patterns of family activities.

Questions concerning career activities were designed to elicit the objective occupational investment as well as to illuminate the qualitative aspects regarding degree of emotional commitment, job stresses, and rewards. Questions dealing with marital power looked into the nature of decision making and the extent of flexibility and/or reciprocity in the character of the marriage. Task allocations between the marital partners were itemized in order to objectively examine the workload distribution both inside and outside the home in regard to marketing, home maintenance, food preparation, cleaning, and so forth. The distribution of child-rearing activity was carefully investigated in regard to both the quantitative distribution of care and the responsibility and emotional stresses connected with child care. Additional questions were designed to quantify and qualify the activities of husband and wife in their relations to kin, friends, and colleagues—particularly in terms of how such relationships functioned to verify or deny their operations as a dual-career family.[1]

# Results

## General Characteristics and Marital Power

An attempt to generalize on the characteristics of these families revealed that they were distinctive in their flexibility and role interchangability. All respondents gave evidence of some degree of jointly solving problems that arose in the areas of child care, scheduling, and domestic responsibilities. Although only one husband had only minimal participation in these domestic functions, all the wives retained the major responsibility in most areas of child rearing.

In response to questions on power distribution in the marriage, eleven marriages were categorized as egalitarian, nine as husband-dominated, and six as wife-dominated. An examination of the wife-dominated families revealed that all of these wives showed high scores of role strain. This finding suggests that a reversal of marital roles that contradicts societal expectations might involve some costs for the wife. Paloma's data (1972) lend support to this conclusion; in some cases of unresolved role strain, the wife had assumed the major breadwinner role against her own preferences. Nevertheless, a relatively high marital adjustment was typical in the study group. Only two families gave responses that indicated sufficient marital conflict to interfere with the mutually supportive relationship.

## Parental Adaptation to Role Strain

Despite the prevalence of supportive husbands, all wives reported major concerns over the conflict between their career and their children. Role strain is a useful concept to describe these worries; it has

---

1. The statements and answers to questions in these six categories were scaled and scored by two raters. Some rudimentary statistical procedures (e.g., chi-square analyses) were carried out in an effort to look at possible significant differences between men and women, numbers of children in family, quality of occupations, and so forth. Since this current research was a pilot study utilizing a nonrandom sample of fifty-six subjects, the results will not be reported in this form. Both the original questionnaire as well as some tabulated results are available from the first author.

been defined by Goode as a "felt difficulty in fulfilling role obliga-tions" (1960). The role strain for the wives involved fatigue, emotional depletion, and in some cases guilt. One woman physician reported frequent fatigue in the following terms: "I come home and I just don't have anything to give to Paul—that is a terrible feeling. I feel it's not worth it—I resent my job. Then I resent myself for being so damned conscientious—to give so much at work and have to be reserved at home." Other mothers reported similar feelings: "being drained," "emotionally leeched," "overwhelmed," "guilty." Of the 116 reports of role strain, 64 percent centered on the child-rearing problems main-ly in terms of their own guilt and fatigue. Major concerns centered on the expressive aspects of the parent-child relationship—the idea of missing out on watching the child grow or not being around to handle the child's emotional needs. Most mothers felt that they had the child's physical needs well under control. Marital or financial prob-lems accounted for less than 15 percent of the reports of strain.

The highest degree of strain was reported by six wives who were under situational pressures that created unusual tension: being in a medical residency, finishing a dissertation, temporary high demands of an incapacitated parent, marital conflict (apparently unrelated to career), or adjustment as new residents in the community. The remain-der of the interviews indicated that excessive strain could be resolved when the situational pressures were alleviated, although a role strain at a lower level remained omnipresent.

The statements concerning role strain in the wives are in sharp con-trast to the husbands' reports of role strain. When husbands did make such statements they were either vague or unemotional. For example, characteristic responses were "Well, occasionally it gets a bit busy, but we manage to work it out"; "My wife is happier when working, so any disadvantages are evened out." In most cases, the husband resolved any perceived role strain by using denial or minimizing its effects; for example, if a wife reported that their child was unhappy, her husband would reply that it was "just a stage he's going through" and thus reassure the wife that her worries were groundless. Such processes were found irrespective of the amount of support the husbands were giving their wives in both emotional and practical areas, which was impressive in the majority of families.

Our findings resemble Paloma's research, which was limited to ca-reer women in law, medicine, and college teaching (1972). This simi-larity suggests that the sources of role strain can be identified in the family situation as well as the career and can equally affect the woman physician, teacher, or nurse. The fact that there is a high level of mari-tal adjustment and some support from the husbands in our sample further supports the conclusion that the source of strain can be identified with child rearing, not the marriage relationship.

## Techniques for Modifying Role Strain

These interviews revealed that role strain was pervasive among the wives but not the husbands. Role strain, however, was generally kept within tolerable limits by the following techniques of tension management (Paloma 1972).

1. The most common technique, used by at least half of the wives, was through the assignment of priority to domestic roles. By temporarily lowering their career ambitions, these wives reallocated their time toward greater involvement with their children. Two families with the lowest level of role strain had recently chosen this means of tension management. This process, technically termed "role cycling," has been suggested by some feminists as a convenient facilitation for the two-career family (Holmstrom 1972). In our sample there were numerous husbands who accommodated reasonably well to their wives' careers, although none had temporarily lowered his own career strivings to accommodate to his wife's career.

2. The second technique used by these families to control conflict involved subjective systems of rationalization. Almost all wives used the time-tried phrase "It's the quality of the time spent with children that counts—not the quantity." In other words, most respondents felt that, compared with nonworking mothers, they put more of themselves into the time they spent with their children, thus providing a richer and more meaningful interaction. Thus, in their own eyes, they were better mothers because they worked.

3. Such subjective control over role strain generally was translatable into patterns of compensation through objective activities enhancing the environment of the children both within the home and in educational settings (this can be colloquialized as "making every moment count"). Structured family activities such as skiing, camping trips, bedtime stories, or dinners and movies out as a family were commonly reported. In addition, mothers of school-age children participated as parents in their children's school and uniformly expressed high achievement goals. Such compensation for the competing loyalty to their careers is compatible with the characteristics of high-achievement women in general, for example, high energy levels, high aspirations for self, career, and other family members, as well as a commitment to the arts, education, and self-actualization.

4. This mode of managing role strain involves the patterns of child rearing that were geared to techniques that eventually could alleviate

some role strain. Through two separate measures, the norms and behaviors in child rearing were consistently directed toward training children to be self-reliant and independent, qualities that would adapt well to the two-career family. Using Kohn's parental values index (1969), we found that parents consistently chose those values that lead to self-direction. In response to open-ended questions, both mothers and fathers chose both independence values and a cluster of values involving sensitivity to others, compassion, receptivity, and extroversion. Discipline techniques were nonpunitive and love-oriented (Brofenbrenner 1952). Essentially these families espouse child-rearing techniques commonly identified with the middle class, techniques that concentrate on the internal dynamics of the child. This pattern of child rearing focuses on internal standards of control by the use of indirect discipline techniques such as reasoning and isolation. These techniques can be contrasted to those used by working-class mothers, who give high priority to behavioral conformity, obedience, and respect, which are instilled through direct techniques of physical punishment.

The point of the finding that the two-career families express the values of their class centers on the impact these patterns of child rearing have on the career mother. The patterns, which emphasize the internal world of the child and attempt to instill sensitivity along with independence and achievement through more indirect discipline techniques, obviously make child rearing more time consuming. Additionally, these patterns involve a higher degree of reflection and sensitivity on the mother's part than if she were using more traditional values instilled directly by the "back of the hand." Furthermore, most mothers espoused the high societal expectations for dedicated mothering along with the assumption of responsibility for the child's success or failure. Therefore, we tentatively conclude that the career mother has not devised new child-rearing techniques that are more compatible with her busy schedule and competing commitments. Essentially, these mothers have not escaped the burdens and costs connected with current child-rearing ideology among well-educated parents.

5. In contrast to the wives' concentration on the emotional costs of the career-motherhood demands, the husbands were more likely to suggest the techniques involving the management principles of optimization and efficiency; that is, problems that arise should be considered immediately (as they are at the office). One must identify the problem, examine various options, incorporate all levels of management (including the children), and arrive at the most acceptable solution. One businessman stated this most explicitly: "Raising children is management." How much these efficiency principles of optimum use of time and energy reduced the role strain on the wives is question-

able, for their pervasive mention of strain would suggest that the techniques were not totally effective.

6. The last process evidenced in these families, the exclusion of competing norms, is not specifically related to child rearing but has an important influence on the total family process. In examining the social network of the families, the majority had minimal contact with kin and predominantly chose friends from two-career families. Hence they associated with individuals who most likely have a consensus on norms regarding careers, marriage, and child rearing. Conflicting norms usually were introduced by grandparents who expressed concern for the possible neglect of the children. The adaptive maneuvers usually used were to dismiss criticism and increase the mutual supportive activities within the marriage. In other words, there was a tendency to tighten the boundaries around the nuclear family to the exclusion of kin, essentially making it more isolated from the support that traditionally stems from the kinship system.

## Conclusions

The foregoing responses have illustrated the pressures imposed on the two-career family, particularly in the area of child rearing. Our research indicates that these families do not differ greatly from other middle-class families in the psychologically complex family environment in which children are raised. Child rearing among middle-class Americans focuses on fostering the development of an internal locus of control and uses indirect and verbal discipline techniques. However beneficial to the developing child, such techniques make raising children time consuming and not without some propensity for generating guilt and anxiety. Such a family system imposes a larger burden on the wife and mother because of her greater sensitivity to her social environment. The career mother is particularly vulnerable because the demands on her time and her absence from the home preclude extensive attention to these diffuse needs.

Clinicians might benefit from investigating the social dynamics of these strains, which may be quite separate and different from the psychogenetic history of the individual. If the career mother, like her husband, were more successful in compartmentalizing her career role from her mothering role (through insulating the expressive-emotional content of her role at home from her work role), she would be resolving role strain with the usual male techniques her husband uses. The therapeutic setting might be a productive place to work at such resolutions. As consciousness raising has accomplished some heightening in women's self-esteem, individual psychotherapy that is goal-directed toward the resolution of role strain could possibly alleviate some pressures on the career wife and mother.

REFERENCES

Birnbaum, J. A. 1971. Life patterns, personality style and self-esteem in gifted family oriented and career committed women. Ph.D. dissertation, University of Michigan.

Brofenbrenner, U. 1952. Socialization and social class through time and space. In *Readings in social psychology*, ed. E. E. Maccoby, J. Newcomb, and E. Hartley, pp. 400–425. New York: Holt.

Goode, W. 1960. A theory of role strain. *American Sociological Review* 25:483–499.

Hill, R., and Rodgers, R. 1964. The development approach. In *Handbook of marriage and the family*, ed. H. Christensen. Chicago: Rand McNally.

Hoffman, L. 1963. The decision to work. In *The employed mother in America*, ed. F. I. Nye and L. Hoffman, pp. 126–166. Chicago: Rand McNally.

————. 1974. Effects on children. In *Working mothers*, ed. F. I. Nye and L. Hoffman. San Francisco: Jossey-Bass.

Holmstrom, L. 1972. *The two-career family*. Cambridge, Mass.: Schenkeman Publishing Co.

Johnson, F. A., and Johnson, C. L. 1976. Role strain in high-commitment career women. *Journal of the American Academy of Psychoanalysis* 4:13–36.

Kohn, M. 1969. *Class and conformity*. Homewood, Ill.: Dorsey Press.

McClelland, D. 1965. Wanted: A new self image. In *The woman in America*, ed. R. Lifton, pp. 173–192. Boston: Beacon Press.

Parsons, T. 1949. The social structure of the family. In *The family: Its function and destiny*, ed. R. Anshen, pp. 173–201. New York: Harper & Row.

Paloma, M. M. 1972. Role conflicts and married professional woman. In *Toward a sociology of women*, ed. C. Safilios-Rothschild, pp. 187–198. Lexington, Mass.: Xerox College Publishing.

Rapaport, R., and Rapaport, R. 1971. *Dual career families*. London: Penguin.

Rostow, E. 1965. Conflict and accommodation. In *The woman in America*, ed. R. Lifton, pp. 211–235. Boston: Beacon Press.

Slater, P. 1970. *The pursuit of loneliness*. Boston: Beacon Press.

Storr, C. 1972. Freud and the concept of parental guilt. In *Freud: The man, his world, his influence*, ed. J. Miller, pp. 98–110. Boston: Little, Brown.

Wolfenstein, M. 1955. Fun morality: An analysis of recent American child-training literature. In *Childhood in contemporary cultures*, ed. M. Mead and M. Wolfenstein, pp. 168–178. Chicago: University of Chicago Press.

356

# 27

# Female-Headed Families: Trends and Implications

ESTHER WATTENBERG AND
HAZEL REINHARDT

The decline of the archetypal family dramatically challenges the concept of what is "normative" in the United States. Only 6 percent of all American families fit the traditional definition of a working husband, a wife who is a full-time homemaker, and two young children (Norwood 1977, p. 31). Certainly dynamic trends are reshaping American families, and evidence of new family formations is emerging in the national demographic data that follow.

1. *A shift in the timing of marriage.* The proportion of women between ages twenty and twenty-four who remain single has almost doubled since 1960, increasing from 28 to 48 percent (Glick and Norton 1977, p. 6).

2. *A rise in the rate of women who have never married.* For women aged twenty-five to twenty-nine, in 1970, 11 percent were single; in 1978, 18 percent were single (U.S. Bureau of the Census 1978a, p. 4).

3. *A rise in the rate of out-of-wedlock births.* In 1960, 5 percent of all births were out of wedlock; by 1975, the percentage had risen to 14 (Glick and Norton 1977, p. 6).

4. *A dramatic growth in the number of households.* Since 1970 the number of households has increased by 20 percent. In addition, for the first time in the history of the United States, more than half (53 percent) of all households consists of just one or two people. This reflects a propensity for individuals to maintain independent households at all stages of life. Separate households include those now maintained by widowed men and women, by young cou-

ples no longer "doubling up" with relatives, and by single-parent families (U.S. Bureau of the Census 1978a, p. 1).

5. *A change in the rates of marriage, divorce, and remarriage.* First marriages per 1,000 single women aged fourteen to forty-four and remarriages per 1,000 widowed and divorced women aged fourteen to fifty-four have decreased since 1972. Divorces per 1,000 married women aged fourteen to forty-four have increased since 1972 (Glick and Norton 1977, p. 5).

6. *The steady increase in the number of families with older members.* This category includes households with an aging parent with aging children. Fifteen percent of the females who head families are sixty-five years old or more. Five percent of female-headed families have at least two members over sixty-five years of age, in some cases representing two generations (U.S. Bureau of the Census 1977, pp. 9, 17).

7. *The growth of two-income families.* In 1970, 51 percent of the families had both spouses working; by 1976 this figure rose to 57 percent (U.S. Bureau of the Census 1978b, p. 115).

8. *The increasing number of female-headed families.* Between 1970 and 1978 female-headed families increased by 46 percent (U.S. Bureau of the Census 1978a, p. 1). Families headed by teenage mothers are a subgroup in this category.

## Female-Headed Families

Perhaps the most dramatic statistic is the unprecedented increase in the number of female-headed households with children. Of all American families, 13 percent are headed by single, separated, divorced, or widowed women (U.S. Bureau of the Census 1978a, p. 3). Children living with only one parent rose from 12 percent in 1970 to 17 percent in 1977. One of every six children in the United States is living in a family in which, because of death, divorce, separation, or an out-of-wedlock birth, the father is absent (U.S. Bureau of the Census 1978c, p. 24). Moreover, the trend is accelerating. Since 1960 families headed by a mother living alone with her children have increased by 81 percent.[1] It should be noted that male-headed families without a wife present currently represent only 3 percent of all families. Many of these may include families headed by elderly siblings or comprising three generations. Although becoming more common, the single-parent male-headed family with children under eighteen currently represents such a small proportion of all families that it cannot be accurately measured.

1. For a detailed discussion of essential trends in the growth of families headed by women, see Ross and Sawhill (1975).

Female-headed families now represent the single largest subgroup of the population that lives below the poverty level. More than half of these families depend on welfare payments as a source of income (U.S. Bureau of the Census 1978b, p. 127). Concern for their economic welfare has prompted a number of studies and analyses, and continued research of the trend is clearly indicated to understand its impact on public expenditures, as well as on the social consequences of this major alteration in the formation of the family (cf. Ross 1973 and Subcommittee on Fiscal Policy 1973). Study should be made, for example, of the effect of a father's absence on a child's development (Ross and Sawhill 1975).

One striking characteristic is the transient nature of female-headed families. It is inaccurate to think of women who head families simply as women "between husbands," and recent studies reveal dynamic changes in their lives.[2] They move on and off the welfare rolls, in and out of marriage, in and out of poverty, and in and out of the labor market. Data on female-headed families are more like "snapshots." Major events such as marriage, separation, divorce, widowhood, remarriage, and the birth of children create life-shaping circumstances that determine whether women can control their economic and social fate. The multiplicity of these events in the lives of female heads of families contributes to a constantly shifting array of living arrangements.

Although individual women may appear and disappear in the statistical constellation of female-headed families, the total number is expanding. Why families headed by females between the ages of fifteen and forty-four are increasing has been examined by Glick and Norton (1977) as well as Cutright (1974). Glick and Norton note that the 1970s is the decade in which the baby-boom generation has come of age; therefore the number of adult females in the population is larger. Furthermore, although the tendency to form female-headed families has been particularly pronounced among younger women and among those who are black, the growth of such households is substantial among all segments of the population. Cutright, however, after examining census data from 1940 to 1970, asserts that the current number of such families may be no greater than in the past. He contends that living arrangements in past decades obscured the dimensions of this particular family formation; for example, the tendency of mothers to live with relatives as subfamilies distorted the count of the actual number of female-headed families. Cutright concludes that the contemporary propensity for both white and nonwhite women aged fif-

2. A rich source of information concerning the various events through which female-headed families appear and disappear is presented in Morgan (1974).

teen to forty-four who have children to form separate households, along with the increase in population, contributes to the statistical rise in the number of these families. He contends that changes in marital stability over the past three decades for both white and nonwhite families contribute only minimally to the rising statistics. Whether this analysis will hold for the seventies must await the 1980 census data.

## Marital Instability

Marital instability, nevertheless, is an important factor in demographic data. It is predicted that almost one of every three marriages among younger couples will end in divorce. Several factors are involved in the increasing number of marital dissolutions: readjustment to peacetime after the disruptive Vietnam War, the women's movement, the increased participation of women in the labor force, a general cultural expectation emphasizing self-fulfillment and consequently a lower tolerance for an unhappy marriage, and a general shift in attitudes toward divorce that is reflected in the more liberal attitudes of the churches and in the legislative introduction of "no-fault" divorce.

Although complex factors in personal and cultural circumstances influence marital behavior, three demographic elements appear to have decisive effect: income, age, and mobility.

### Income

Examination of the effect of income on marital stability involves such factors as absolute level of income, earning stability, sources of income, income relative to peers, socioeconomic effects of occupational status, length of marriage, race, and region of the country.[3] The issue is further complicated by the observation that a wife's income may affect the stability of a marriage differently than a husband's income. Although positive correlation has been found between a husband's or family's income and the stability of a marriage, the effect of a wife's income may provide her a degree of independence that offsets this.

Income maintenance experiments in Denver and Seattle indicate that short-term changes in socioeconomic conditions affect marital decisions in low-income populations (Hannan, Tuma, and Groeneveld

3. For an excellent summary of recent studies that explore the relationship between marital stability and income, see Sawhill et al. (1975).

1977). Overall, income maintenance increases the rate of marital dissolution. For black, white, and Chicano women, the greatest increase occurs at the lowest levels of support. Income maintenance also affects remarriage, but these statistics vary by race and ethnicity. For Chicanos, the rate of remarriage decreases as the level of support increases. For blacks and whites, income maintenance has no discernible impact on the rate of remarriage.

Apparently, given a slight boost in economic resources, poor women no longer feel compelled to remain in unhappy marriages. Given feasible options, they will make rational decisions to improve the quality of their lives.

Sawhill and associates (1975, pp. 34–41), examining data from a longitudinal study of 5,000 families in Michigan, found that each $1,000 increase in the earnings of wives led to a 1 percent increase in the separation rate. Evidence also exists that two spouses earning high incomes have a much lower rate of marital dissolution than lower income groups. Undeniably, however, a source of income enables women and children to form families on their own if they choose or are required to do so. In Levinger's (1976) study of couples who had applied for divorce, the critical variable between those who reconciled and those who did not was the wife's level of income. The lower her income, the more likely it was she and her husband would reconcile.

Wolf and MacDonald (1978), however, examined a range of variables and concluded that it is the wife's evaluation of her husband's role as breadwinner and the stability of his income, rather than the absolute level of income, that influenced marital disruption. Sawhill and associates' examination of the Michigan data extends the point by concluding that the level of a family's income does not assure greater marital stability.

An associated issue concerns the degree to which unemployment rates relate to marital dissolution. Several studies affirm the finding from the Michigan data that men who have experienced substantial job instability are about twice as likely to separate from their wives as those who have not. It is not clear whether unemployment per se with its loss of self-respect and family respect or the loss of income contributes more to separation. Sawhill and associates (1975, pp. 44–45) tentatively conclude, however, that it is *employment* rather than income that is critical to the stability of the family.

Another question is whether Aid to Families with Dependent Children (AFDC) plays a role in the increase of female-headed families by providing resources to women who have separated and their children. Honig (1974) found that a 10-percent increase in the level of welfare benefits increased the proportion of female-headed families by 3 or 4 percent. Is it the *amount* or *availability* of welfare that affects separation? Are welfare payments simply higher than a male's earnings? Do AFDC benefits precipitate or facilitate the dissolution of an intolerable marriage? In a sample of 451 welfare mothers in New York City, Bernstein and Meezan (1975) reported that the most important reasons the women gave for the dissolution of their marriages concerned their husbands' involvement with drugs, alcohol, and other women and physical abuse. Only 12 percent cited "financial problems" as a primary reason for dissolution.

In summary, the relationship of income to marital stability poses a serious challenge for further investigation. The conceptual framework for these studies involves at least two hypotheses. One, the family can be viewed as an economic unit. The research hypothesis is that the transfer of income within the family affects its stability. Studies then involve how resources are transferred from family members who work in the marketplace to those who do not (most often women and children), the effect of the wife's working, and the effect of resources available outside the family. Two, the family can be viewed as a source of status for its members, the research hypothesis being that family stability is associated with fulfillment of self-esteem. Studies involve the influence of income on role performance. An individual's satisfaction with the role of breadwinner or additional earner (as in the case of women who work outside of the home in a two-income family) is measured and correlated with factors such as education, social class, occupation, and income.

## Age

The highest rate of separation, desertion, and divorce is experienced by individuals between the ages of twenty and twenty-nine. The correlation between early marriage and marital instability is affirmed by recent findings that teenagers are twice as likely to get divorced as are those who marry in their twenties. Furthermore, the proportion of women divorced in their early twenties has more than doubled in little over a generation. Norton and Glick (1976) estimate that twenty-five to thirty percent of the women currently in the early stage of marriage (in their late twenties) will end this first marriage in divorce.[4] It is estimated that for each year of a person's life in which getting married is delayed, the annual separation rate is reduced by 0.1 percent (Sawhill et al. 1975, p. 42).

Age is also related to the rate of out-of-wedlock births. The propor-

4. For a careful review of trends in the age composition of marriage dissolution, see Norton and Glick (1976), p. 7.

tion of children born to unmarried women has steadily risen. In 1960, 5 percent of all births were out of wedlock; by 1975 the proportion was 15 percent. Although birth rates are declining for older unmarried women, the out-of-wedlock birth rates for women aged fifteen to nineteen are rising. Two factors are involved in the alarming number of "children giving birth to children." One is the proportion of young women "at risk" in the population as the tail end of the postwar baby boom comes of age; the second factor involves behavior that arises from social forces not yet understood. It is projected that by 1980 the number of unwed mothers will have increased by almost a third from the 1965 level.[5]

Examination of the population receiving AFDC reveals that in 1975 over 50 percent of the women were under the age of twenty-nine (U.S. Social Security Administration 1977, table 37). The age of heads of families is also related to a family's economic status. During the 1970s a clear shift in the ranks of the poor occurred. The number of elderly poor diminished while families headed by females aged fourteen to twenty-four became the majority of poor families (Women's Bureau 1977). Young people receive the lowest income, experience the highest rate of unemployment, and obtain the fewest benefits associated with a job, yet these same youngsters must deal with the high costs of raising families. This economic "squeeze" combines with the unseasoned abilities of younger people to cope with the stresses of early marriage and, perhaps, explains the frequency of marital disruptions among the young.

## Mobility

Although data are scattered and partial, emerging trends indicate that mobility is also a factor in marital instability. Interstate migration is dominated by individuals aged twenty to twenty-nine (Grumm 1972). Residential stability is measured by the length of time one lives in the same house. Recent census data reveal that the mean income of female-headed households decreases as geographical mobility increases. This is especially apparent for households headed by black females (Jackson 1979, p. 20). Grumm (1972) examined the relationship of interstate migration to recipients of AFDC and found that interstate migration had a destabilizing influence on families. Although the effect of moving within states, counties, and neighborhoods is not documented clearly, it is possible to speculate on its impact. Leaving a supportive network of relatives and friends, facing economic insecur-

5. For a fuller discussion of the data mentioned here, see Glick and Norton (1977).

ity in the search for a new and better job, and adjusting to an unfamiliar environment all contribute to marital stress, dissolution, and subsequent pressure on the resulting female-headed families.

## Remarriage

Although the data indicate an increase in the rate of divorce, 60 percent of all marriages are expected to last. Moreover, although basic transformations in the institution of marriage are underway, strong evidence exists that society's preference for individuals is still a married state. This does not necessarily mean, however, one marriage to the same partner throughout life. A high rate of remarriage accompanies American society's high rate of divorce.

Essential data on marriage reveal that 67 percent of divorced women subsequently remarry, the highest rate or remarriage occurs during the first year after a divorce, only 40 percent of widowers remarry, only 15 percent of women whose marriages terminate after age forty remarry, the average woman spends about six years as a divorcee, and black widows over forty who are on welfare are least likely to remarry (Norton and Glick 1976, p. 6; Ross and Sawhill 1975, pp. 18–31). The increasing rate of remarriage has not kept pace with the mushrooming rate of divorce, however, and the number of female-headed families has grown. It is estimated that 33 percent of divorced women will remain on their own. Furthermore, remarriage does not guarantee stability: demographers predict that 44 percent of second marriages will also fail. A woman's decision to remarry is influenced by the availability of eligible men and by such variables as her previous marital status, the time elapsed since her last marriage, the number of dependent children, and her present economic situation. Race and age are also factors. Being nonwhite and older both have negative effects on remarriage possibilities.

Important evidence shows that welfare recipients have a lower rate of remarriage (Sawhill et al. 1975, p. 46). In the Michigan study, nonrecipients of AFDC were three times as likely to remarry as were recipients. No clear reason for this has emerged, but speculations include the small pool of available men whose economic resources equal those of the AFDC payments as well as personal characteristics associated with dependence on welfare.

In contrast, it should be noted that a small, discernible trend has been emerging since the last decade, that is, women who choose to remain unmarried mothers. Twenty-five percent of participants receiving AFDC are women who have never married and who have children (U.S. Social Security Administration 1977). Although this trend has not been studied extensively, current research is examining the relationship of women's economic opportunities to their single marital status and to the postponement of marriage by young women seeking advanced education and careers. In addition, studies concern young women born at the beginning of the baby boom coming of age who choose single parenthood because, through fluctuations in the birth rate, they are confronted by a scarcity of traditionally preferred slightly older men.[6] This trend presents challenging questions for research and analysis.

# Analysis

As Cutright (1974) reported, in one generation the number of female-headed families maintaining independent households increased by almost 40 percent. Undeniably, then, large numbers of women with children are facing a series of dramatic changes in their lives. Their precarious economic position may lead them into marriage, separation, divorce, and possibly remarriage. The question is, then, do national institutions acknowledge this situation?

The economic status of female-headed families has attracted considerable attention. It is paradoxical that, at a time when other trends suggest the improving status of women, female heads of households account for the largest proportion of economically disadvantaged persons. (See table 27-1.) (From 1970 to 1974, the number of *poor* families headed by women rose 21 percent; at the same time those headed by men declined 17 percent [McEaddy 1976, p. 3].) This country's economic and social welfare institutions have failed these women.

The issue of child support is a harsh reminder of the economic dislocation of divorce. Studies of child support and alimony reveal that women simply do not receive adequate economic support for child rearing.[7] Furthermore, only 14 percent of divorced women are granted alimony and fewer than half collect it regularly. Court judgments bear little relationship to the father's ability to pay and vary dramatically from judge to judge. Awards are not revised to keep pace with infla-

6. For a discussion of the "marriage squeeze," see Glick (1979), p. 2.
7. For a review of these studies, see Urban Institute (1978).

TABLE 27–1

*Primary Source of Income*
*for Female-Headed Families*

| Income | Percentage Female-Headed Families |
|---|---|
| Alimony and child support | 7 |
| Employment | 28 |
| Social security payments | 12 |
| Other income transfer programs | 2 |
| AFDC | 51 |

Source: Compiled by the authors from Beverly Johnson McEaddy, "Women Who Head Families: A Socioeconomic Analysis," *Monthly Labor Review*, 99 (June 1976), p. 3; and U.S. Bureau of the Census, "Money Income in 1976 of Families and Persons in the United States," *Current Population Reports*, Series P-60, No. 114 (Washington, D.C.: U.S. Government Printing Office, 1978), pp. 125–127.

tion and the changing needs of children. In 1975, with the passage of Title IV-D of the Social Security Act, the government became formidably involved in the issue of child support. That law requires that three steps must be completed when an individual with dependent children applies for public assistance. The absent or noncustodial parent must be identified and located, a program of support based on the ability of the noncustodial parent to pay must be established, and the arrangements for support must be implemented. Despite this rigorous attempt to enforce child support, it is estimated that some form of compliance is obtained in only 33 percent of the cases followed up by the AFDC program. In December 1975, after a year of increased effort, the AFDC program closed only 1 percent of its cases because child support from the noncustodial parent had been initiated. The average amount received per month was $6 per recipient. It appears that in almost every circumstance the plight of the single mother worsens after divorce, and at the same time the father enjoys a higher standard of living. A man's remarriage complicates the situation. To whom do support payments belong? To his first or second family? The data are indeed grim. Almost one-half of court-ordered payments are delinquent and in one-half the cases, the absent father has not even been located.

The extent to which the government can and should strengthen enforcement of child support is debated vigorously. One position is that, when the father is poor, coercive support procedures erode the informal network of support that does in fact exist in families with very low income. It is argued that it may be more valuable for a father to retain this relationship than contribute a negligible amount of child support. Others argue that children have a right to their father's economic support regardless of the amount and that both parents—not just the mother—should bear financial and social responsibilities for children. It is clear that research that attempts to measure the costs and benefits of vigorous child-support enforcement needs to be developed. Such research should examine the effect of enforcement on the father's relationship with his children.

Discrimination in women's employment has received extensive scrutiny, including examination of disparities in the wages of men and women, occupational segregation, unemployment, the dual labor market (high wage, stable job market versus low wage, part-time, seasonal job market), and the role of human capital (attributes of education, skills, and experience of individual and worker).[8] These studies generally conclude that even great effort on the part of female heads of families does not help to reduce poverty and dependence. Their situation will not change as long as these women face a labor market that regards them as a source of cheap labor (Garfinkel and Haveman 1977).

To the extent that AFDC supplements the poor wages that women workers earn, the possibility exists that the government is institutionalizing a permanent underclass of cheap labor. By alternating between employment and welfare and sometimes by combining both, almost half of the population receiving AFDC retains some attachment to the labor market. Is AFDC the least expensive and most effective way of supporting a low-skilled labor supply? Is the mandatory work requirement under AFDC guidelines simply a harassment for women who cannot manage the rigors of a job *and* parenting? How long can discrimination so clearly based on gender be tolerated in the labor market? For women who rely on AFDC as a sole source of income, in almost half the states payments are below the state's own determination of need. As table 27–1 shows, only a small portion of female-headed households can rely on spouse-related benefits.

Unemployment figures also show that female-headed families are economically disfavored. Of the unemployed men who headed families in the first quarter of 1977, nearly half had a family member with a job. Of the unemployed women heading families, only 18 percent had a family member with a job (Watts and Skidmore 1978, p. 11). Watts and Skidmore conclude, "If a breadwinner is defined as someone with dependents who is the only family member in the labor market, a higher proportion of working women who head families now fill that role than working husbands" (1978, p. 12).

The economic status of women is inferior, whether they are work-

8. For a summary of these issues and a bibliography, see Pearce (1978), pp. 24–36.

ing or not. Women are discriminated against by the economic institutions that control their lives. To reverse the pauperization of female-headed households will require sustained attention to discrimination in the labor market and will require a redefinition of unemployment in recognition that women's work within the home is essential.

## Ideological Debate

In 1975 one in four parents under age twenty-five was the head of a household without a spouse. Most were women. For the mother who must manage a household alone, the responsibilities of being both provider and homemaker are overwhelming. It is frequently argued that the loss of a father is not the only drastic change for children after divorce, but also the loss of the mother's presence as she spreads herself between work and home. The need to restructure work with flexible hours and family sick leave is being recognized. It is clear that the demands of work and family must be integrated more successfully for single-parent families to survive.

The data suggest that single-parent households exist in isolation. This presents a significant challenge to social work. Are there, for example, informal supportive networks between separate households? If so, can they be reinforced? If not, can a variety of support systems be initiated at the neighborhood level? For social workers, the development of neighborhood resources for these families is critical. In almost every study of female-headed households, women mention their loneliness, isolation, and overwhelming responsibilities.

Statistical data must be interpreted within a social context. It is a struggle to make relationships, the family, and its legal institution—marriage—fit the changing times and serve the best interests of society. Polarized interpretations of the statistical data showing the increasing number of single-parent families are not surprising.[9]

At one end of the spectrum, the public views data on marital instability as an American tragedy.[10] They believe the growth of single-parent families is a fundamental threat to the traditional roles of men

9. For a range of opinions on what is happening to the American family, see the testimony of Urie Bronfenbrenner, Margaret Mead, and Edward Zigler in Hearings Before U.S. Senate Subcommittee on Children and Youth (1974).

10. See, for example, in an article reporting on the results of the Seattle minimum income experiment, the following statement: "These findings [high rates of marital dissolution] have been widely taken as spelling doom for the minimum income concept" (Reinhold 1979, p. A1).

*368*

and women and to the traditional family. "Family integrity" has become a political issue. Coalitions, identifying themselves as "pro-family," attack social policies that range from family-planning services to equal rights for women. Well-organized groups are attempting to reverse no-fault divorce legislation, to resist the pursuit of legal equality for women, and to hinder policies and practices to reduce sex-role stereotyping.

The ideology that supports these actions views individuals who divorce as "adulterous, criminal, neurotic, immature, or at best frivolous and unfortunate" (Gettleman and Markowitz 1974, p. 15). Although the severity of these indictments appears to be waning, evidence still exists that for female-headed households, the community traditionally values the widow most highly, the divorced or separated woman with less regard, the never-married mother as immoral, and the lesbian mother with contempt. The antidivorce position relies on studies, fragmented and partial as they are, that purport to show that children are damaged in one-parent families and that the single parent suffers abandonment, rejection, and catastrophe.

At the other end of the spectrum are the humanists and feminists who view the growth of single-parent families not as an index of decline and decay but as a necessary adaptation to a postindustrial society that creates rising expectations of personal fulfillment. Separation or divorce is perceived as a temporary disruption, providing the opportunity to repair a faulty marital arrangement and leading to a more satisfying family formation. From this perspective, higher divorce rates mean fewer individuals are in unhappy marriages. The preservation of a marriage at any cost is considered too high a price to pay for the injuries inflicted on parents and children in unstable relationships. This position asserts that young women and men should have every option to pursue the ideal: to love and be loved equally. Furthermore, it is argued that a psychologically strong parent who is empathic and supportive can provide loving care for children apart from the environment of a traditional marriage. The decision to separate from an unsatisfying relationship is seen as a strong, independent, and self-reviewing choice. Publicly, adherents of this position support various living arrangements for families, marital dissolutions that minimize penalties for both partners, and child-care arrangements such as joint custody that distribute responsibilities more equitably.

## Conclusion

The eighties will be a transitional decade.[11] The traditional family with a mother and father is still predominant. However, the single-parent family is a unit in its own right. It also may be a stage, preceding a reconstituted or "blended" family. It is clear that demographic data point to vivid realities in changing family composition, and individuals vary in their capacity to cope with these changes.

Traditional female socialization does not prepare women never to marry, or for the loss of their role as wife, the demands of raising children alone, or the stress of "single again" identities. When women separate, they show classic symptoms of distress compounded by economic helplessness. Women are slowly adapting to this reality, however. There is a new woman emerging on the social landscape. Encouraged by the egalitarian ideology of the women's movement, having realistic expectations of themselves, and valuing their own independence, single mothers may live with confidence and even zest.

There appears to be an irresistible urge to rush to judgment on national family policy. The impact of single-parent families on child development, however, is complex and ambiguous. Studies have not been able to recommend a single direction for social policy. Beginning research has been good (cf. Brandwein, Brown, and Fox 1974; Herzog and Sudia 1970). But the consequences for children in changing family formations require sustained attention.

Further studies should involve the following: the impact of mobility on family instability; the problems of youthful marriages; the effect of economic opportunities on never-married, married, and remarried women; and an examination of individuals who live with nonrelatives in a single household. (For example, it is estimated that the number of unmarried couples living together has skyrocketed by more than 800 percent in the past decade.) Race is also a complex factor in changing family formations. Women of color are disproportionately represented among poor women. Nowhere is racism more vicious: A formidable barrier to the success of two-parent families is the paucity of men employed with stable income.

Demographic data clearly indicate a trend toward single-parent families. Further research should be undertaken to understand not the pathology of "deviant" families but rather how institutions and policies can be altered to meet the changing needs of individuals in this society. It is clear that economic policies must expand the earning and nonearning sources of income for single-parent families. The direction

11. For a thorough discussion of changes in and predictions for family formations, see Bane (1976).

that national social policies should take is less clear. Variables that influence marital behavior are not understood well enough to recommend specific policies on the family. Demographic trends provide the broad outlines. The details for enlarging our understanding must be left to social workers, and their contribution, pooled in an ultimate knowledge of how and why single-parent families endure, is indispensable.

REFERENCES

Bane, M. J. 1976. *Here to stay: American families in the twentieth century.* New York: Basic Books.

Bernstein, B., and Meezan, W. 1975. *The impact of welfare on family stability.* New York: New School for Social Research, Center for New York City Affairs.

Brandwein, R. A., Brown, C. A., and Fox, E. M. 1974. Women and children last: The social situation of divorced mothers and their families. *Journal of Marriage and the Family* 33.

Cutright, P. 1974. Components of change in the number of female family heads aged 15–44: United States 1940–1970. *Journal of Marriage and the Family* 36:714–721.

Garfinkel, I., and Haveman, R. H. 1977. *Earnings capacity, poverty and inequality.* New York: Academic Press.

Gettleman, S., and Markowitz, J. 1974. *The courage to divorce.* New York: Simon & Schuster. In Aslin, A. L. Counseling "single-again" divorced and widowed women, in Harmon, L., et al. *Counseling women,* p. 230. Monterey, Calif.: Brooks/Cole Publishing Co.

Glick, P. C. 1979. The future of the American family. *Current Population Reports,* series P-23, no. 78. Washington, D.C.: U.S. Government Printing Office.

Glick, P. C., and Norton, A. J. 1977. Marrying, divorcing, and living together in the U.S. today. *Population Bulletin* 32:6.

Grumm, J. G. 1972. Population change and state government policy. In *Governance and population: The governmental implications of population change,* ed. Keir Nash, A. E. Washington, D.C.: Commission on Population Growth and the American Future.

Hannan, M. T., Tuma, N. B., and Groeneveld, L. P. 1977. Income and marital events: Evidence from an income maintenance experiment. *American Journal of Sociology* 82:1186–1210.

Herzog, E., and Sudia, C. E. 1970. *Boys in fatherless families.* Washington, D.C.: Children's Bureau, U.S. Department of Health, Education, and Welfare.

Honig, M. 1974. The impact of welfare payment levels on family stability. In *The family, poverty, and welfare programs: Factors influencing family stability,* Studies in Public Welfare, paper no. 12, part I, pp. 37–53. Prepared for the use of the Subcommittee on Fiscal Policy, Joint Economic Committee, U.S. Congress. Washington, D.C.: U.S. Government Printing Office.

Jackson, J. J. 1970. Changes in the American family. *Public Welfare* 36:20.

Levinger, G. 1976. A social psychological perspective on marital dissolution. *Journal of Social Issues* 32:30.

McEaddy, B. J. 1976. Women who head families: A socioeconomic analysis. *Monthly Labor Review* 99:3.

Morgan, J. N., et al., eds. 1974. *Five thousand American families: Patterns of economic progress, vol. 1.* Ann Arbor, Mich.: University of Michigan, Survey Research Center.

Norton, A. J., and Glick, P. C. 1976. Marital instability: Past, present, and future. *Journal of Social Issues* 32:7.

Norwood, J. L. 1977. New approaches to statistics on the family. *Monthly Labor Review* 100:31.

Pearce, D. 1978. The feminization of poverty: Women, work and welfare. *Urban and Social Change* 2:24–36.

Reinhold, R. 1979. Test in Seattle challenges minimum-income plan. *New York Times*, 5 February 1979, p. A1.

Ross, H. L. 1973. *Poverty: Women and children last.* Urban Institute Working Paper 971–08–02. Washington, D.C.: Urban Institute.

Ross, H. L., and Sawhill, I. V. 1975. *Time of transition: The growth of families headed by women.* Washington, D.C.: Urban Institute.

Sawhill, I. V., et al. 1975. *Income transfers and family structure.* Urban Institute Working Paper 179–03. Washington, D.C.: Urban Institute.

Subcommittee on Fiscal Policy. *The family, poverty, and welfare programs.* Studies in Public Welfare, paper no. 12. Prepared for the use of the Subcommittee on Fiscal Policy, Joint Economic Committee, U.S. Congress. Washington, D.C.: U.S. Government Printing Office.

U.S. Bureau of the Census. 1977. Household and family characteristics: March 1976. *Current Population Reports,* series P-20, no. 311. Washington, D.C.: U.S. Government Printing Office.

———. 1978a. Households and families by type: March 1978. *Current Population Reports,* series P-20, no. 327. Washington, D.C.: U.S. Government Printing Office.

———. 1978b. Money income in 1976 of families and persons in the United States. *Current Population Reports,* series P-60, no. 114. Washington, D.C.: U.S. Government Printing Office.

———. 1978c. Characteristics of American children and youth: 1976. *Current Population Reports,* series P-23, no. 66. Washington, D.C.: U.S. Government Printing Office.

U.S. Senate Subcommittee on Children and Youth. 1974. *American families: Trends and pressures.* Washington, D.C.: U.S Government Printing Office.

U.S. Social Security Administration. 1977. *1975 Recipient characteristics study, part I.* Washington, D.C.: U.S. Social Security Administration, Office of Research and Statistics.

Urban Institute. 1978. *Child support payments in the United States.* Washington, D.C.: Urban Institute.

Watts, H.W., and Skidmore, F. 1978. *The implications of changing family patterns and behavior for labor force and hardship measurement.* Special Report Series, no. 21. Madison, Wisc.: University of Wisconsin, Institute for Research on Poverty.

Wolf, W. C., and MacDonald, M. 1978. The earnings of males and marital disruption. Center for Demography and Ecology Working Paper 78–14. Mimeographed. Madison: University of Wisconsin.

Women's Bureau. 1977. *Women with low incomes.* Washington, D.C.: Women's Bureau, U.S. Department of Labor.

372

# 28

---

# Lesbian Families: Cultural
# and Clinical Issues

---

## MARNY HALL

---

As the traditional nuclear family declines as the norm in this country—in numbers if not in influence—members of alternative families
are appearing with greater frequency in the agency offices and clinical
practice of social workers. Parenthood for same-sex couples and single
gay people, most often lesbians, is currently under scrutiny as an alternative life style. Social workers are finding themselves in the roles of
experts about the viability of such alternatives, and as such their influence can be profound. For example, their testimony in cases in which
lesbian mothers seek to retain custody of their children may weigh
heavily in judges' final decisions about placement of the disputed children. The growing number of occasions for social workers to take
stands on such critical issues requires a professional community that is
informed about problems unique to lesbian families. These issues,
which social workers face in their contacts with lesbian clients as family members and as couples, are the focus of this article.

The issues for the practitioner, as the case examples in the article
demonstrate, are two tiered. The first level of feelings and attitudes
involves the social worker's own degree of comfort with the client's
life style. Is the practitioner comfortable with the spectrum of her own
sexuality? Does she have questions about the validity of a lesbian's life

The author wishes to acknowledge the help of Katherine Fengler, Nan Golub, Janis
Janus X, Kathy Gauen, Marilyn Mehr, and Willyce Kim.

choice? Are her cognitive and emotional responses to her lesbian client divergent? Does she, for example, find her client's life style acceptable as an abstraction, but become distressed to imagine her actually involved in "those activities"? Or does she genuinely like and accept her lesbian client, but find the concept of lesbianism unacceptable? These questions, not easily answered, require self-exploration over time and in different contexts—alone, with friends and colleagues, in workshops, and, perhaps, by reading works by lesbian authors and becoming more aware of the lesbian subculture.

The second level of issues to consider is conceptual. Damage to self-esteem resulting from the stigmatizing process of our culture is always an explicit or implicit part of lesbians' presenting problems. At the same time, women who are lesbians may occupy a number of roles in which their lesbianism is incidental. As a parent experiencing difficulties with her child, the lesbian mother may share more with her heterosexual counterpart than with a lesbian who is not a parent. An interracial lesbian couple may identify more with the problems of a black man and white woman living together than with those of a racially homogeneous lesbian couple. Is the practitioner able to see the ways in which the client's presenting problem is both affected by and separate from her sexual orientation? Such a dual focus is an indispensable clinical tool.

Equally important is the clinician's familiarity with a variety of functional lesbian life styles—models on which she can base her judgments about ego strength and other intrapsychic dimensions of her client. Ideally, the practitioner will have assimilated such models through some contact with lesbians who are not clients and will have experience enough of the lesbian subculture to know about lesbian support networks and other resources that may be useful to lesbian clients.

## Changing Climate

Another factor that will enable the practitioner to work more effectively with lesbian families is her awareness of the dominant culture's impact on the lesbian subculture. Particularly important is the clinician's knowledge of the regional and political variables affecting her client. The sociopolitical climate in which a woman first identified herself as a lesbian, as well as the differences between urban and rural values, have profound impact on lesbian life styles.

Lesbians who identified themselves as gay before the women's movement have adjusted—often after periods of self-denial and doubt—to isolation and very guarded, underground modes of making contact. Suddenly their need for secrecy seems obsolete and their way of living anachronistic. Lesbians, particularly in urban areas, are no longer invisible. They are sexually in vogue, "coming out" amid the sisterly support, even fanfare, generated by the women's movement. A recent random survey taken of gynecological patients waiting for checkups at the University of California Medical School in San Francisco showed a dramatic increase in bisexuality compared with a similar survey taken a few years ago. Almost 30 percent of those questioned have tried or would consider having sex with a woman (Petit 1977, p. 1). A recent *New York Times* article attributed the falling enrollment at Sarah Lawrence to the growing number of self-identified lesbian students on campus (Roiphe 1977, p. 21). As the following case illustrates, more traditional lesbian relationships that did not form in the socially tolerant climate of the women's movement reflect the stress of this shift.

Sandy and Marie met in the WAVES nine years before, when they were both training to be nurses. The beginning of the relationship was marked by emotional and circumstantial obstacles. The Navy often placed them in different cities; and when they were housed in the same hospital, the risk of discovery was a powerful deterrent to intimacy. Marie was Catholic, and after visits home and talks with her priest, she endured months of torment and guilt about her lesbianism. Nevertheless, the relationship endured through and beyond military service.

When they came to therapy, both women were in their mid-thirties, had good jobs, and had bought a house with a pool in a California suburb. Sandy complained about feelings of suffocation and boredom. She felt they had sequestered themselves for years, long beyond the need for such isolation, and wanted to go out and meet people. Marie was afraid that Sandy would easily meet someone new, fall in love, and dissolve their relationship.

The social worker catalogued the positive aspects she saw in the relationship, and acknowledged her bias in wanting to maintain the family, a continuing theme in her work with the couple. Within this context, she also acknowledged the fears associated with the apparent need for change in the relationship. She anticipated with Marie the pain and the perceived risk of letting go and explored Sandy's fear of losing the relationship by making major demands on Marie for freedom that were so vague they could not be met. The worker began to model and rehearse negotiation skills with both partners. With practice, Sandy was able to make a specific request for time away from Marie. Both negotiated about the amount of time and when during the week it should be.

On her first free night, Sandy asked out a lesbian she knew from work. In the following session, she chose to share her disappointment with the evening. After that, although Sandy did not usually exercise her free-night-out option, her feelings of boredom dissolved, and both partners felt a renewed commitment to the relationship.

Traditional masculine and feminine role delineations in heterosexual relationships have been challenged by the women's movement. As a result, turbulence, pain, and disorientation are common among male-female couples attempting to behave in less role-bound ways. Similarly, as the following case shows, lesbians who have assumed traditionally masculine, or "butch," roles and traditionally feminine, or "femme," roles in relationships experience the same sort of turbulence and disorientation when confronted abruptly with a more egalitarian mode of relating.

Lee and Natalie, both in their mid-forties, came into therapy because Natalie was dissatisfied with their sexual relationship. Since the beginning of their relationship, seven years before, Lee had never taken her underpants off in bed and said she never would. Natalie, who had been satisfied before, now wanted a more sexually reciprocal arrangement.

The social worker supported and validated Lee's values and began to form a solid, trustful relationship with her. The social worker then felt comfortable pointing out to Lee that she was missing some potentially pleasurable experiences and gave her some home assignments that included permission for fantasy and sensual self-exploration. To avoid the possibility of Lee's refusal, the therapist didn't tell Lee to take her pants off during the home exercises; she did, however, instruct her to put them on halfway through the exercise, "just to feel the difference." Gradually the therapist began to incorporate Natalie into the exercises. The struggle over underpants was avoided, Lee began to talk about her feelings of vulnerability, and both partners began to make other shifts in their relationship.

## Political Correctness

Less traditional lesbians, who have "come out" through the women's movement, may live in communities in which "politically correct" behavior is tightly circumscribed. The result is a sameness in manner, behavior, and political doctrine. Resources, as well as political struggle against social oppression, are shared. Monogamous relationships are judged politically incorrect because they duplicate the nuclear family, viewed as the foundation of a capitalist power structure in which women are owned and exploited. Monogamy, therefore, is considered a form of ownership and exploitation, and political struggle is seen as vital to individual and social growth. As the following case shows, however, the transposition of sociopolitical norms and values into intimate relationships creates problems.

Janet and Carol, both students in their early twenties, had been lovers for two years, ever since they had come out together in their consciousness-raising group. They lived together and shared a car. Although they both agreed that each was free to relate to other people sexually, neither had acted on that option. They belonged to several feminist and lesbian political organizations together, shared friends, and pooled money. They looked and dressed alike and, in therapy, frequently talked for each other.

They were vaguely unhappy with the relationship, but the only problem they could pinpoint was a discrepancy in their needs for sexual contact. Janet often wanted sex, and Carol often refused. In the first session the social worker asked them to sit facing each other and use the phrase "I disagree" several times. She also questioned their assumption that they would split the therapy fee equally.

When Janet began to talk about dreams toward the end of the session, the social worker acknowledged the importance of the material, and asked if they could have a session alone together. Although Janet refused, she brought a written record of her recent dreams to the next conjoint session and talked at length about parts of her life that were separate from her relationship with Carol. Janet enjoyed the session but expressed the fear that Carol might be angry with her for not sharing the therapy time equally. Carol acknowledged feelings of jealousy and irritation.

At the next session, Janet and Carol talked about differences and disagreements between them. They looked different, acted differently, and said with amazement that they had agreed about sex that week and had had a pleasurable time together. As therapy went on, the social worker continued to support the positive aspects of their differences.

For various reasons, such as discrepancies in expectations, values, and life experiences, certain lesbian couples experience much pain and discord in their relationships, just as their gay male and heterosexual counterparts do. Because lesbians have been socialized as women to "make it work," to attach and nurture, they may never have initiated a process of letting go.

Sharon and Sue, both in their mid-twenties, had fallen passionately in love two years before, exchanged vows of life-long commitment, and bought a house together. Though they were originally students together, in the intervening time their career paths had diverged dramatically. Sharon was a law student who spent long hours studying. She described herself as a sedentary person, academic and single-minded. Sue was a drummer and had recently started playing for a rock group that was on the road touring for weeks at a time. When she was home, she spent much of her time practicing with the group.

They came to therapy because they found themselves bickering constantly, over household chores, schedules, and Sue's affairs with women when she was on the road. Both acknowledged that the relationship was not working on any level for either of them. Because of shared property and commitment, because of Sharon's ideal of an enduring relationship, and because of Sue's feeling that it would be her fault if the relationship ended, neither woman could initiate the process of letting go.

In the first session, the social worker made the unspoken explicit: Separation was a possible outcome of therapy. In the following sessions she explored the women's fears of loss and what it would be like to let go. With the therapist's guidance, the two women imagined the first minute, week, and month of separation. Sue's feeling of "badness" for disappointing Sharon alternated as a focus with Sharon's despair. The social worker encouraged this process, continuing to evoke fears of loss and talk about practical ways of handling it.

During the six months that therapy lasted, both partners acknowledged the possibility of separation many times—and each time quickly moved more tightly together. Each time, the imagined separation seemed both more painful and more bearable. Eventually Sharon and Sue agreed that after her next long tour, Sue would simply not move back into the house. When Sue was gone, Sharon came alone to therapy. She expressed a great deal of pain over a number of months. Eventually she began to see other women and became involved with one whose values coincided more closely with her own.

## Lesbians as Parents

The normal problems associated with parenthood, whether as a single parent, as a couple, or as communal parents, are compounded by lesbianism. Several issues emerge from publications and interviews with lesbians, as a growing number of lesbians give themselves permission to be parents. One avenue to accomplishing this is adoption or foster placement. Such placements are rarely made, however, if the investigating worker is aware that the prospective parent is a lesbian. Resolutions affirming the right of gay people to be considered as prospective foster and adoptive parents have been supported by a substantial portion of the memberships of both the National Association of Social Workers and the American Psychological Association; however, these professional endorsements have yet to be translated into general practice. Another route to parenthood is artificial insemination. It is an unreliable method, however, and physicians are afraid of future legal entanglements, paternity claims, and denials of paternity.

For lesbians who are biological parents, custody battles are always a threat. If lesbians are not covert—and sometimes even if they are—they risk losing custody of their children. Though lesbianism per se is ostensibly not grounds for loss of custody, it frequently shows up as the real reason, thinly disguised by judges' concerns about "the best interests of the child" (Basile 1974, p. 11). Typical of judicial comments is the following excerpt from a court transcript.

Frankly, Ma'am, you should take therapy, as the doctor suggested, if you are going to overcome your, beat your psychological problem. And the Court—we are dealing with a four-year-old child on the threshold of its development—

just cannot take the chance that something untoward should happen to it. . . . I'm sincere in saying that I want this child protected, and if the lady takes therapeutics and the psychiatrist can assure me, then I will look for unrestrained visitation. It would depend on the factors. Right now, I just can't take the chance. (Klaich 1976, p. 6)

Behind the judicial evaluation that having a lesbian parent is detrimental to the best interests of the child are three fears. The first is fear of sexual molestation of the child by the parent or the parent's friends. This fear persists in spite of the high incidence of heterosexual assaults involving underage females and the absence in court records of any such incidents between lesbians and minor female children. The second fear influencing court decisions is the dread that the child of a lesbian mother is more likely to become homosexual. Aside from the court's prejudicial stance about the undesirability of such a developmental outcome, several experts in the field of psychiatry and pediatrics concur that such a conclusion is unfounded. Judd Marmor, past president of the American Psychiatric Association, and Benjamin Spock agree that most homosexuals are children of heterosexual parents (Klaich 1976, p. 37). After testing two children of opposite-sexed single homosexual parents, Weeks and Derdeyn (1975, pp. 26–32) concluded:

The manifestation of sexual conflict in these homosexual parents expressed in attitudes and behavior toward the child is not unique and does not differ significantly from that of the heterosexual parent who has sexual conflicts.

In current research on gender identity being conducted at the University of California at Los Angeles, Kirkpatrick* compared a group of children from single-parent homosexual households with children from single-parent heterosexual households. In both groups the parents were divorced. Preliminary findings show both groups of children experiencing reactions to the loss of the other parent, most frequently in the form of a disturbance, such as separation anxiety. The two groups do not differ with regard to gender orientation.

The final fear of the courts is that the child will be harmed by the stigmatizing process that inevitably surrounds deviants. However, in analogous court cases in which the issue was the possible stigmatizing effect on the child of having interracial parents, courts have commonly found that making such a decision constitutes an abuse of the court's discretion or that the interracial relationship of the parents is irrelevant to a determination of the child's best interests (Basile 1974, pp. 14–15).

* Martha Kirkpatrick, University of California, Los Angeles, personal communication, June 16, 1978.

Currently, lesbians have a substantial chance of maintaining custody of their children if they are not political activists and if they lead conventional lives in other respects, and if the children are female and under five years of age (Basile 1974, p. 12). Judges commonly append restrictions when they award custody to lesbians. If she wants to maintain custody, the mother may not be able to live with her lover and may have to stop seeing her in the presence of the children or perhaps completely. Parents who lose or are unsatisfied with a decision often appeal, and families are often embroiled in bitter, financially draining court battles for years.

## Children and Lovers

The relationship she and her children have with her lover is another difficult area for a lesbian mother. How will the lover relate to the children or to the biological male parent of the children? In lesbian rap groups, a complaint frequently expressed by mothers is that the new lover, perhaps because of her socialization as a woman, expects herself to be an "instant parent." She may come on like "supermom" and feel shocked and rejected when she is regarded ambivalently by the child. The child, who has experienced loss of a parent before, may feel threatened by losing the attention that the remaining parent is now directing toward the new lover. When the expected idyllic relationship between the new parent and the child never materializes, the new parent may feel shocked and disoriented.

After this phase, the biological parent and the new parent may begin to clash over disciplining the child. Mothers may be caught in a cycle of compensating for the loss and stigma to which she feels she has exposed her child by abandoning limits, neglecting her own needs, and attending meticulously to her child. In an effort to balance what seems like a mother-child system run amok, the new parent may start setting severe limits and become the villain in both the child's and parent's eyes, as the following case illustrates.

After three months of regular contact with Betty, and irregular contact with her nine-year-old daughter Lonni, Deb decided to move in with the family. She felt from the beginning of the new living arrangement that Lonni got whatever she asked for from her mother, took no responsibility for herself, and constantly invaded the physical and emotional space that Deb felt was reserved for her relationship with Betty. More upsetting for Deb was Betty's refusal to curb Lonni's behavior and Betty's anger when Deb tried to assume the role of disciplinarian.

They came to therapy because the problem was affecting all parts of their relationship and seemed unresolvable. In sessions that included her, Lonni clung to her mother, commented that Deb was "mean," and said she had liked it better when Deb hadn't lived with them. In conjoint sessions, Betty acknowledged doubt about her decision to adopt a lesbian life style, depriving Lonni of a father and conventional home life, and expressed doubts about Deb's competency as a parent.

The social worker explored Betty's feelings and Deb's sense of exclusion and emphasized both women's good intentions. She conjectured that Lonni probably had two sets of feelings: She wanted her mother all to herself but felt worried that that might happen and that she would have the sole responsibility for filling her mother's needs. The social worker helped Betty reconcile the notion of being a good parent with setting limits and allowing Lonni to experience some anger and loss at the addition of someone new to the family.

Betty began to spend specific time alone with Lonni and also set aside time for herself alone and with Deb. She started to include Lonni in family chore expectations, which often had Lonni and Deb paired in a work crew. Deb, no longer feeling the need to play the "heavy," began to enjoy Lonni, and Lonni reciprocated her feelings.

## Male Children

Male children pose another dilemma for lesbian mothers. Lesbians who identify themselves as feminists are concerned about bringing up their male children in a nonsexist way and wonder how they can manage this when older nonsexist role models are scarce or nonexistent. If a boy exists in an all-female, woman-affirming environment, can he like himself? Lesbian mothers of male children are often not supported within their communities. At a planning session in Berkeley of a "playshop" for lesbian mothers and children celebrating Mother's Day, a participant raised the question of including male children. Several planners felt reluctant to allow them to participate and yet chose not to exclude them. This ambivalent attitude toward male children often characterizes the community networks that usually support lesbian mothers. As the following case demonstrates, the problem intensifies as boys grow older, become adolescent, and reflect the attitudes of their peers.

Karen left her husband because he was an alcoholic and abusive. Her son, Greg, was three at the time. Two years later, she became attracted to a female co-worker at the factory where she worked. It was the first lesbian experience for both of them. The relationship continued, but Karen chose not to live with her lover because she felt Greg was her first responsibility, and she worried about the impact a woman lover living with them might have on him.

Although Greg's father lived in the area, he was not interested in pursuing a relationship with his son and did not contribute financial support. When Greg was fourteen he began to take drugs and was caught dealing them at school. At the court hearing, it emerged that Greg had secretly sought out his father six months before, had been seeing him, and wanted to move in with him. His father was amenable, and Greg made the switch.

Karen came into therapy depressed, angry, and self-punishing. The social worker's approach combined education and support. Karen had not been exposed to feminist ideas and had not placed the troubles with Greg in any larger social context. The social worker gave her some literature and put her in touch with a feminist group. She acknowledged Karen's feeling of personal failure and introduced her to the notion that women are devalued in this culture. Rather than get closer to his mother and perhaps come in for a share of that devaluation, Greg chose to align himself with the more culturally valued group. The pressing need for such a choice showed Greg's preoccupation with his identification as a male and with the approval of his peers—both common adolescent concerns. As the social worker continued to explain Greg's move in terms of cultural components and his individual needs as an adolescent, Karen's loss remained acute, but her self-depreciation diminished.

"Coming out of the closet" to children is another concern of lesbian mothers. They may reveal their sexual orientation to friends and colleagues long before telling close family members. As the following case examples show, parents, for various reasons, may misjudge children's degree of comfort with their mothers' sexual orientation.

Mark was going away to college. Colleen and Margaret had always been discreet, and, in fact, had gone to great pains to disguise their life style. Both concurred Mark was old enough to handle the information about their sexual orientation. They sat down together before his departure and told him tremulously about their relationship. He was quite casual, saying that he had known about it for years and was glad they had finally gotten around to trusting him.

Celeste and Jean were political activists and frequently talked about lesbian motherhood in front of groups. They had always been open with their children and had long ago discussed lesbianism with them. When a brick was thrown through their front window and the word "dyke" spray-painted in their driveway, they explained to their children that lesbianism is perceived by many people as bad, sick, and immoral and that people will show in various ways that they disapprove of their way of living. The children received the information attentively and asked clarifying questions from time to time.

However, the oldest girl, Jan, who was thirteen, reacted dramatically another time when her girl friend's mother refused to let her daughter stay overnight with Jan after seeing Celeste speak about lesbianism on a local educational television program. Jan came home in tears and demanded to know why they had to be "queers." Despite their experience and ease with hostile audiences, Celeste and Jean were not able to respond to her.

Clinical interventions in such situations are palliative at best. The pain, perhaps damage, inflicted by negative stereotypes operating both outside and inside family boundaries, is evident. Because the membrane that separates the dominant homophobic culture from the lesbian subculture is so permeable, effective social work with lesbian families must include cultural, as well as clinical work.

## Steps for Social Work

What steps can social workers take to assist these families? The first is to acknowledge the existence of the lesbian family and recognize it as a special group with a special identity and special needs. Second, social workers can continue the process of self-exploration and dialogue with lesbians and nonlesbians, clients, and colleagues about the issues that have been raised in this article: parenting, self-disclosure, stigma, and formation and maintenance of lesbian families within the inimical context of the dominant culture's fear of homosexuality.

Finally, social workers can support lesbian families directly. They can serve as experts in court custody cases, as foster and adoption placement workers, and as marriage and family counselors. They can legitimize lesbian families by endorsing the validity of the lesbian's choice of life style in individual work with lesbian clients and collectively with peers and colleagues in professional organizations (cf. Clark 1977, p. 172).

Much of the damage to lesbians' self-esteem comes from the struggle to maintain relationships in an unsupportive culture. Steps such as these taken by social workers and other professionals help lessen the damage and begin the critical and painful process of cultural change.

REFERENCES

Basile, R. A. 1974. Lesbian mothers I. *Women's Rights Law Reporter* 2:11.
Clark, D. 1977. *Loving someone gay*. Millbrae, Calif.: Celestial Arts.
Fengler, K. 1977. Ten interviews with lesbian mothers. Unpublished research paper, April 1977.

Janus X, J. 1976. *Lesbians and kids* (newsletter). Oakland, Calif.: October 1976.

Klaich, D. 1976. Parents who are gay. *New Times* 6:37.

Lesbian Mothers' National Defense Fund Newsletter. 1977. *Mom's Apple Pie.* Seattle, Wash., January 1977.

Petit, C. 1977. Sex survey's big surprise. *San Francisco Chronicle,* 8 February 1977, p. 1.

Roiphe, A. 1977. The trouble at Sarah Lawrence. *New York Times Magazine,* 20 March 1977, p. 21.

Weeks, R., and Deredyn, A. 1975. Two cases of children of homosexuals. *Child Psychiatry and Human Development* 6:26–32.

# 29

# Midlife Concerns of Women: Implications of the Menopause

## MALKAH T. NOTMAN

Except for the adult stages described by Erikson, adult development has received little attention until the past few years. Recent work by Neugarten (1968, 1975), Levinson and associates (1978), Gould (1972), Barnett and Baruch (1978), and others has focused attention on the middle years as a time of development and change rather than a static period or one whose major dynamic is toward aging and death.

## Defining Midlife

Midlife for women has in the past been defined in relation to the menopause, often in terms of loss. A closer look at actual midlife concerns for women as well as at the menopause and its implications indicates that this is highly questionable.

Most studies of development, including those of the middle years, have had male subjects and have been based on a male model, where development is seen as proceeding linearly through a series of stages, more or less clearly described. Neugarten (1979) and others have challenged this "staircase" view of life.

This conceptualization of universally applicable stages has been criticized further as not adequately reflecting differences in social class and historical circumstances. It is particularly inappropriate for women (Barnett and Baruch 1978; Notman [forthcoming]), who may be in different role patterns and phases at different times because of changing combinations of children, work, and marriage. Further, women's identity and autonomy issues may be resolved only partially in early adult years, then combined with the developmental experiences of motherhood, and then returned to when children are grown. Thus the Eriksonian sequence of autonomy, identity, intimacy, and generativity does not hold in quite the same way for women, for whom a more simultaneous development through these phases has been postulated by Gilligan and myself (1978).

Chronological age as a basis for developmental stages has also received considerable criticism (Neugarten 1975; Butler 1963). For instance, Neugarten (1968), in a study on "the awareness of midlife," found that in a sample of 100 middle-aged "well placed men and women" chronological age was a less important marker for this group than for young or old people. The author noted that the women in this group but not the men defined their age status "in terms of timing of events within the family cycle. For married women, middle age is closely tied to the launching of children into the adult world, and even unmarried career women often discuss middle age in terms of the family they might have had." However, these concepts may be changing in the light of current developments in family patterns.

Levinson and associates' conceptualization of life stages observed in their studies of men (1978) give central importance to the role of work in establishing oneself in the world. Although the importance of family relationships for the adult man is acknowledged, they are not the organizing theme of his life. Separation from the family of origin is placed more centrally in a man's development than is the birth of his first child.

Defining middle age is a complex problem. The central theme in the awareness of midlife for each person seems to be connected with the sense of the finiteness of time left to live in contrast to the infinite perspective of youth (Neugarten 1968; Neugarten and Datan 1974). For women this awareness is also closely related to their reproductive potential, and because their lives do take place within the limitations of this biological timetable, the reproductive milestones have been stereotyped as being the central and dominant ones. Although hormonal and physical changes mark the major periods of a woman's life, the characteristics and experiences of these periods may be less related to the actual biological changes and more to social and psychological events than has been assumed.

It is important here to distinguish a woman's concerns about her potential for having children as a framework for her sense of life phase from the idea that her fulfillment and self-realization is limited to childbearing or dominated by children. In reality many women have not found their children or their role as mothers predominantly gratifying. Children may be draining, stressful, and conflict producing. However, the finiteness of the period during which pregnancy is possible makes the choice an issue that cannot be ignored.

The separation of the biological and social life cycles in recent years has meant that the time of childbearing corresponds less to the span of fertility than in the past and may end earlier or start later than is biologically possible. With the advent of reliable fertility control and the increasing availability of work and careers for women, the birth rate has declined markedly. Many women have waited to have children until their careers are established, or have chosen not to have children. The increasing spread in maternal age at childbirth—from teenage pregnancy to the growing number of primiparas who are in their thirties and even forties—means that age and life phases correspond even less (Price 1977).

Neugarten and Datan's idea that middle age in women corresponds to the point of launching children into the adult world (1974) and Rossi's definition of middle age as beginning with the ending of the parental role (1968) may be less applicable if children are born later in the woman's life or if their birth is spread over a wide maternal age range.

For women who have not had children, there is an age-related crisis of a sort at about thirty (Notman [forthcoming]). For many women this age symbolizes the transition from youth to middle age and evokes concern about whether they will ever have children. If this seems unlikely, or if a woman chooses not to have children, contemplation of the finiteness of reproductive possibility creates an early confrontation with what is actually a midlife issue.

## Menopause

In this context we come to a consideration of the menopause. Menopause is defined as the cessation of menses for one year and thus is a retrospective diagnosis. A more appropriate term for this period would be the "perimenopausal years." During this time there is a gradual diminution of ovarian function and a gradual change in endocrine status (Perlmutter 1978). Menopause has been considered a dominant factor in the midlife phase of women and blamed for much symptomatology. In clinical discussions of women with depression or other problems, there has been a tendency to focus automatically on the menstrual history as if it constituted an adequate explanation of the symptoms. In fact, the relationships are neither inevitable nor clear (Bart and Grossman 1978; McKinlay, Jeffreys, and Thompson 1972). Many misconceptions have existed about the nature and extent of menopausal symptoms, and research in this area has been both sparse and poor. McKinlay and McKinlay (1973), in a review of the menopause literature in 1974, and Parlee in 1975 (1976) pointed to the lack of attention to menopause in the medical literature and criticized the research that does exist. They cited methodologic problems such as the failure to develop consistent objective definitions of menopause and of menopausal symptomatology; the use of retrospective data, case histories, and clinical impressions; and the selection of samples from populations of women who are under the care of gynecologists or psychiatrists. The more reliable studies show that "psychosomatic and psychological complaints were not reported more frequently by so called 'menopausal' than by younger women" (McKinlay, Jeffreys, and Thompson 1972).

This lack of correspondence between symptomatology and endocrine status has been cited also by Perlmutter (1978), who concluded, "There are multiple disorders that have been ascribed to the changing hormonal balance and are equated with menopause. In reality, not all of those changes that are noted are due to hormonal imbalances." Some are the consequences of aging and others have a basis in psychological factors and life patterns (Perlmutter 1978).

Age at menopause ranges from the late thirties to the middle or even late fifties. This variation supports the tendency to assign a variety of symptoms occurring during these years to a woman's menopausal status. In a study of age at menopause, McKinlay and associates found that:

the median age at menopause in industrial societies now occurs at about fifty years of age and there is no firm evidence that this age has increased at least in the last century, nor any indication of any close relationships between the age at menopause and the age at menarche or socioeconomic status. . . . There is some evidence that marital status and parity are related to the age at menopause, independently of each other. (1972, p. 171)

## Midlife and Menopausal Symptoms: Undoing Stereotypes

What symptomatology is directly attributable to the menopause? Vasomotor instability, manifested as hot flashes, sometimes called flushes, and episodes of perspiration, sometimes particularly noted at night, is one of the most consistent symptoms accompanying menopause (Reynolds 1962) and is present in up to 75 percent of women who report some degree of symptomatology. McKinlay and associates (1974), in a review of symptoms of women aged forty-five to fifty-four in the London area, found that hot flashes and night sweats are "clearly associated with the onset of a natural menopause and that they occur in a majority of women." The other symptoms investigated, "namely headaches, dizzy spells, palpitations, sleeplessness, depressions, and weight increase, showed no direct relationship to the menopause but tended to occur together." The length of time a woman experiences hot flashes is variable. They may originate several years before actual menopause and can be considered a sign of waning estrogen levels. Hot flashes reach a peak at about the time of the actual cessation of the menses and persist for as long as five years (Reynolds 1962).

The etiology of the hot flashes is unclear; they appear to be related to hormonal imbalance rather than simple estrogen deficit. Psychological factors such as anger, anxiety, and excitement are considered important in precipitating flashes in susceptible women, as are activities giving rise to excess heat production or retention, such as a warm environment, muscular work, and eating hot food (Reynolds 1962). However, the symptoms may arise without any clear psychological or heat-stimulating mechanism.

Many other midlife symptoms have been attributed to menopause, and many menopausal symptoms have been attributed to estrogen deficiency or hormonal changes. The symptoms have included insomnia, irritability, depression, diminished sexual interest, headaches, dizzy spells, and palpitations. Neugarten and Kraines (1965) studied 100 women aged forty-three to fifty-three by using menstrual histories as an index of menopausal status. They found "climacteric (menopausal) status to be unrelated to a wide array of personality measures." They also found there were few important and consistent relationships between the severity of somatic or psychosomatic symptoms and personality or test scores. Kraines (in Bart and Grossman 1978) found that menopausal status did not contribute significantly to self-assessments of middle-aged women. She also found, as one might expect, that women who had had low self-esteem and life satisfaction were likely to have difficulties with menopause. This supports understanding menopause as one of the important experiences for women but one best understood in the context of their entire lives.

Benedek (1950) and Deutsch (1945) held that a woman's reaction to menopause was similar to her reactions to puberty and pregnancy, although they and others conceptualized menopause being a loss rather than a change. Deutsch (1945) spoke of the menopause as constituting a "narcissistic mortification that is difficult to overcome" and noted that the woman at menopause "loses all she received during puberty." She wrote that mastery of the psychological reactions to this organic decline is one of the most difficult tasks of a woman's life. Deutsch saw increased postmenopausal activity of women as a "struggle to preserve femininity." Femininity in turn was closely tied to sexual attractiveness and reproductive possibilities, according to Deutsch.

This is an expression of a defensive view of femininity, held by many earlier theorists, based on the view that feminine identity is derived from and associated with compensation for something which is missing or "different" about women. In this view, when reproductive possibility is gone a woman must compensate for the loss rather than progress to a developmental stage that is normal for a later period in life. The postmenopausal decreases in estrogen levels can be considered normal for this age, just as low estrogen levels are appropriate for the prepubertal girl.

Benedek (1950) believed menopause was a difficult time of complex and demanding personal and social tasks in adapting to grown and more independent children, changing sexual relations with the husband, and changing responses to the woman's life. She believed that women experienced different levels of stress and thought that women who had not borne and mothered children and who were less "feminine" had greater problems. However, she thought that the energy released by the ending of reproductive tasks gave women with flexible egos impetus for learning and socialization.

## Depression and Menopause

Depression has been linked with menopause but appears to be more clearly associated with psychosocial variables than with endocrine changes, although depression does constitute an important clinical entity (Winokur 1973). Weisman and Klerman (1977) concluded that the pattern of relationship between endocrine levels and clinical status is consistent and that there is good statistical evidence that menopause does not increase rates of depression. Other authors agree (McKinlay, Jeffreys, and Thompson 1974; Winokur 1973; Osofsky 1970) and cite the lack of studies using modern endocrinologic methods that have shown correlations between clinical state and endocrine state.

Data from a study by Bart and Grossman (1978) indicate that women who have had children, who have "high motherliness" scores on psychological scales, and who have invested heavily in their childbearing and rearing are more likely to experience depression. These findings are opposite to the predictions of both Deutsch and Benedek. Actually, women who have not had children do not always have the most difficulties at menopause. My clinical experience indicates that many women have come to terms with their childlessness before the biological menopause and have found other ways of organizing their lives. The menopause then represents a less critical event. Childlessness may represent the expression of underlying ambivalence about motherhood, which is more readily acted upon in contemporary society with less conflict than was possible earlier and can be better implemented with effective contraception and abortion.

Social class is an important variable in the experience of menopause. Middle-class and upper-class women appear to find the cessation of childbearing more liberating because more alternatives are open to them than to women of lower social status. Neugarten and Kraines (1965) reported that upper- and middle-class women tend to minimize their reactions compared with lower-class women. In this relatively advantaged group younger women anticipating menopause were more concerned than women who were actually menopausal. Postmenopausal women generally took a more positive view than premenopausal women, with greater numbers stating that the menopause created no major discontinuity in their lives. Those women who thought they had a relative degree of control over their symptoms felt they did not inevitably have difficulties.

Other studies (in Bart and Grossman 1978) confirm that middle-class women are less anxious about the menopause than lower-class women, but found that across classes menopausal status generally is not associated with measurable anxiety (Reynolds 1962). Bart and Grossman (1978) stressed the role of cultural factors in determining the importance of menstruation, child rearing, and mothering in the self-esteem and status of women, as well as in determining their alternatives. Cross-cultural studies indicate that in those cultures where there is improved status at middle age and a clear role for the middle-aged woman there are greater feelings of well-being in the menopausal years. In our society, women whose lives have not been child-centered and who are still married and women whose children remain close and gratifying have an easier time at middle age and menopause. A woman who has given all her life to her children and then feels useless when they are gone is more likely to become depressed.

## Family Experiences and Relationships

Family experiences are important in determining the outcome of this period. The midlife transition for men, many of whom are married to menopausal women, is accompanied by new stresses and often by sexual problems, which can lead to affairs, marital disruption, and abandonment of wives. Adolescent children may be sexually and aggressively provocative, challenging, or disappointing. Children leaving home for school or marriage change the family balance in a way that has been described generally as loss. However, some women view this as an extension and expansion of parenting to include the wider interests and loci of their children. Change and transition do cause stress and require new adaptations, which are sometimes accompanied by symptoms. Studies of marriage (Bernard 1972) indicate that at least in some dimensions marital satisfactions increase as children leave the home; thus the "empty nest syndrome" does not seem universal (Bernard 1972). Separation, for example, the ability to separate from children as they move out of the family, is an important developmental task at this time. These moves may revive separations in the woman's own past and prove difficult if these separations are unresolved. Occasionally separation fails and children return, or do not leave. This too can lead to depression.

Thus menopause itself does not appear to be the inevitable source of symptomatology it once was thought to be. However, midlife strains and midlife depression are real clinical entities, and attention must be paid to the social and psychological issues involved. Stereotyping with the automatic conclusions that symptoms are menopausal leads to ignoring the possible help that might be offered and to inappropriate if not dangerous estrogen treatment on the basis of the conceptualization that menopause is a "deficiency disease" rather than a normal progression leading to the next phase of life. There may indeed be some psychological work and even some mourning required before one can move on.

Some women experience this period as being "restored to themselves" and to their own development. This does not mean being alone. Women depend much more than men on maintaining relationships for their development, not only for their emotional comfort and security but also for expressing fulfillment.

The period of midlife has been compared to adolescence. The importance of separation, the change in relationship to family, and the potential for further development of one's own interests are common to both periods. However, the differences are highly significant (Gilligan and Notman 1978). At adolescence the separation is from parents, who are incestuous object choices. At midlife the separation is from children, and the experience often revives some sense of loss. The adolescent perspective of infinite time and choices to be made differs from the midlife sense of the finite and the reassessment of choices that have been made. The reality is that time is limited and that although choices do exist or even increase, there is also a limited range and variety of careers, new physical pursuits, and new relationships.

## Conclusions

The possibilities for expansion do exist. The potential for greater autonomy, changes in relationships, and the development of occupational skills, interpersonal contacts, and an expanded self-image may receive a major impetus after childbearing is over.

Further research is needed about adult development in women in a variety of life circumstances, with fewer preformed assumptions about the phases they are experiencing but with adequate attention to the implications of their reproductive life stage.

REFERENCES

Barnett, R., and Baruch, G., 1979. Women in the middle years: A critique of research and theory. *Psychology of Women Quarterly* 3:187–197.

Bart, P., and Grossman, M. 1978. The menopause: A gynecologist's view: In *The woman patient: Medical and psychological interfaces,* ed. M. Notman and C. Nadelson, pp. 337–354. New York: Plenum Press.

Benedek, T. 1950. Climacterium: A developmental phase. *Psychosomatic Quarterly* 19:1–27.

Bernard, J. 1972. *The future of marriage.* New York: World.

Butler, R. 1963. The facade of chronological age: An interpretive summary. *American Journal of Psychiatry* 119:721–728.

Deutsch, H. 1945. *Motherhood: The psychology of women,* vol. 2. New York: Grune & Stratton.

Gilligan, C., and Notman, M. 1978. The recurrent theme in women's lives: The integration of autonomy and care. Paper presented at the Eastern Sociological Meetings, Philadelphia, Pennsylvania, 27 February–2 March 1978.

Gould, R. L. 1972. The phases of adult life: A study in developmental psychology. *American Journal of Psychiatry* 129:521–531.

Levinson, D., et al. 1978. *The seasons of a man's life.* New York: Alfred A. Knopf.

McKinlay, S., and McKinlay, J. 1973. Selected studies on the menopause. *Journal of Biosocial Science* 5:533–555.

McKinlay, S., Jeffreys, M., and Thompson, B. 1972. An investigation of the age at menopause. *Journal of Biosocial Science* 4:161–173.

_____ . 1974. An investigation of the age at menopause. *British Journal of Preventive and Social Medicine* 28:16–17.

Neugarten, B. 1968. The awareness of middle age. In *Middle age and aging,* ed. B. Neugarten, pp. 93–98. Chicago: University of Chicago Press.

_____ . 1975. Adult personality: Towards a psychology of the life cycle. In *Human life cycle,* ed. W. Sze, pp. 379–394. New York: Jason Aronson.

_____ . 1979. Time, age, and the life cycle. *American Journal of Psychiatry* 136:887–894.

_____ , and N. Datan. 1974. The middle years. In *American handbook of psychiatry,* ed. S. Arieti, 2nd ed., vol. 1, pp. 592–608. New York: Basic Books.

Neugarten, B., and Kraines, R. J. 1965. Menopausal symptoms in women of various ages. *Psychosomatic Medicine* 27:266–273.

Notman, M. Forthcoming. Adult life cycles: Changing roles and changing hormones. In *Gender roles: A dialectical biopsychological perspective,* ed. J. Parsons. Washington, D.C.: Hemisphere Publishing Corporation.

Osofsky, H. J., and Seidenberg, R. 1970. Is female menopausal depression inevitable? *Obstetrics and Gynecology* 36:611–615.

Parlee, M. 1976. Social factors in the psychology of menstruation, birth and menopause. *Primary Care* 3:477–490.

Perlmutter, J. 1978. The menopause: A gynecologist's view. In *The woman patient: Medical and psychological interfaces,* ed. M. Notman, and C. Nadelson. New York: Plenum Press.

Price, J. 1977. *You're not too old to have a baby.* New York: Farrar, Strauss.

Reynolds, S. 1962. Physiological and psychogenic factors in the menopausal flush syndrome. In *Psychosomatic obstetrics, gynecology and endocrinology,* ed. W. Kroger. Springfield, Ill.: Charles C. Thomas.

Rossi, A. 1968. Transition to parenthood. *Journal of Marriage and the Family* 38:26–39.

Weisman, M., and Klerman, G. 1977. Sex differences and the epidemiology of depression. *Archives of General Psychiatry* 34:98–111.

Winokur, G. 1973. Depression in the menopause. *American Journal of Psychiatry* 130:92–93.

# TRAUMA

# 30

## Abortion Counseling

### MARLA KAHN-EDRINGTON

When a woman finds herself unexpectedly pregnant, the continuation of pregnancy may cause a greal deal of grief to the woman, the child, family members, and society. Women are often unprepared, unable, or unwilling to include a child in their lives. Although abortion may be a better alternative for a variety of reasons, it is a difficult decision for most women to reach. Feelings of shame, guilt, fear, and moral ambivalence concerning both the pregnancy and abortion are common. Unwanted pregnancy often precipitates a state of agitated reactive depression; the woman may be withdrawn, have difficulty sleeping, be preoccupied with death and dying, and be preoccupied with the pregnancy and abortion (Leiter 1972). An unwanted pregnancy and its termination thus constitute a crisis situation for most women.

The crisis nature of an unplanned pregnancy may be precipitated or aggravated by social aspects. The social situation of aborting women is consistently more strained than that of women who continue their pregnancy to term. "They are either very young or rather old from an obstetric point of view, they are more often alone, are studying or unemployed, have more children, are often pregnant without a stable relationship, and their economic situation is less favorable . . . the prevailing social situation seems to be the most important reason for wanting a legal abortion" (Jacobsson, von Schoultz, and Solheim 1976, p. 84). Women are often unable to support a child; are unwilling to marry, or interrupt schooling and careers; or feel that their existing family is large enough. Older women may be unwilling to begin a new family now that their present children are grown. Shusterman (1976) concluded that

women who carry their pregnancy to term seem to have relatively stable family situations into which to bring children, while abortion tends to be chosen by women who do not have those family conditions . . . the reasons women give for choosing abortion appear to reflect a fair appraisal of their capacity to provide a satisfactory home for a child. (p. 89)

The majority of abortion counseling is done in abortion clinics, in family planning centers, and by individual physicians. Anywhere pregnancy testing is done, personnel should be prepared to deal with the abortion issue. Counseling will often include emotional reactions to the pregnancy, discussion of available procedures and alternatives, and issues surrounding a decision to abort. Many clergymen are confronted with women who are struggling with the difficult moral aspects of an abortion decision. Any counselor in any capacity may have to deal with this problem. Every female client is a potential candidate for an unwanted pregnancy. Couples may seek help if opposing views are straining their relationship. Parents may become involved in teenage pregnancy. Counselors who see these diverse cases will likely be dealing with ambivalence in decision making and peripheral issues aggravated by the pregnancy and its termination.

The abortion counselor's goal is to mobilize each woman's coping skills, deal with the many complex aspects of each individual's situation, and to provide information and support throughout the crisis. Mobilization of coping skills depends on where each woman is in the decision-making process, and the dynamics and vulnerabilities of her particular situation. Scott (1971) described the stages of the decision-making process for abortion, and how the counselor can react at each stage to facilitate movement toward a final, fully integrated decision. Discussion of the following areas may facilitate decision making: the woman's total life picture, social and economic situation, plans for the future, role expectations for her age and background; attitudes toward the pregnancy, the abortion, the fetus, and contraception; her relationship with the man, other children, and family members; the reactions of others; subconscious desires to be pregnant; issues of self-control; alternatives and possible outcomes; motivation for abortion; and fears or misconceptions regarding abortion.

Fear of the procedure itself, of permanent damage, or of later complications are common concerns. Because abortion involves a medical procedure, many women fear an invasion of their bodies. The counselor can greatly reduce fear by giving a detailed description of the procedure including information about sensations that might be felt and discussing possible risks. *Our Bodies, Ourselves* (Boston Women's Health Book Collective 1976) describes available abortion procedures and the possible risks of each method.

Different groups of women may have special problems. Teenage pregnancy may indicate difficulties in choosing, obtaining, or effectively using contraceptives. On the other hand, these young women may be using sexual acting-out in an attempt to bring attention to personal or family problems (Grover and Tinkham 1975). They may need to prove their independence, femininity, maturity, or fertility to themselves and others. They may be testing ongoing relationships with boyfriends or parents. The possible effects of pregnancy, as they see it, may be unrealistic and overromanticized (i.e., marriage or a child to love and care for who will love them in return). Although any woman may react with pregnancy to the real or anticipated loss of a significant other, the reaction is often seen in teenage dynamics (Grover and Tinkham 1975; Gedan 1974).

Second trimester aborters may have felt helpless or unable to make a decision during their first trimester, and the decision becomes increasingly more difficult to make. By the second trimester there is an increased sense of "baby." The decision is more emotionally laden, and ambivalence is higher. The abortion itself is more frightening and painful. Because the sense of "baby" is stronger and the procedure essentially involves labor and delivery, there is a stronger sense of loss and a greater need to mourn (Kaltreider 1973). Special attention to ambivalence and additional support are necessary.

Repeat aborters tend to be in poorer general health, have less favorable personality structures, have more pronounced problems in their psychosocial backgrounds, have more sexual partners and have tried more types of birth control (Jacobsson, von Schoultz, and Solheim 1976). For some of these women repeated abortion is a symptom of their inability to effectively use birth control measures. For others, unconscious motivations to become pregnant must be explored. The counselor should help repeat aborters find effective methods of birth control, explore unconscious motivations, and point out the possible risks of repeated abortion.

Abortion counseling involves emotionally laden decisions that must be made quickly. To effectively provide the information and support clients need during this crisis requires special attitudes and skills of the counselor. The counselor must have worked out his or her own feelings regarding abortion and birth. A belief in the client's right and responsibility to make her own decision is essential. In addition, knowledge of the value systems of other cultures and religions will help the counselor understand decisions made by those with different backgrounds. Because the decision must be made quickly, crisis intervention and problem-solving skills will help the counselor spot and deal with problematic areas quickly and effectively. To summarize, the following knowledge, skills, and attitudes are recommended for effective abortion counseling.

## Recommended Principles

Knowledge: 1. Counselors/therapists are aware of the definition, prevalence, myths, types of procedures, risks, and sequels of abortion.
2. Counselors/therapists are aware of alternatives to problem pregnancy: abortion, adoption, marriage.
3. Counselors/therapists have information about sexuality, contraception, and community resources.
4. Counselors/therapists have knowledge of value systems of other cultures and religions.

Skills: 1. Counselors/therapists have crisis intervention and problem-solving skills.

Attitudes: 1. Counselors/therapists evaluate personal attitudes toward birth and abortion.
2. Counselors/therapists believe that the client has the right and responsibility to make her own decisions regarding abortion.

REFERENCES

Boston Women's Health Book Collective. 1976. *Our bodies, ourselves* (rev. ed.). New York: Simon & Schuster.
Gedan, S. 1974. Abortion counseling with adolescents. *American Journal of Nursing* 74:1856–1858. [Reprinted herein chapter 31.]

Grover, J., and Tinkham, C. 1975. Abortion in teenagers—positive intervention at a negative time. *Psychiatric Opinion* 12:13–22.

Jacobsson, I., von Schoultz, B., and Solheim, F. 1976. Repeat aborters—first aborters, a social-psychiatric comparison. *Social Psychiatry* 11:75–86.

Kaltreider, N. 1973. Psychological factors in mid-trimester abortion. *Psychiatry in Medicine* 4:129–134.

Leiter, N. 1972. Elective abortion. *New York State Journal of Medicine* 1972:2908–2910.

Scott, L. 1971. Possible guidelines for problem pregnancy counseling. *Pastoral Psychology* 23:41–49.

Shusterman, L. 1976. The psychosocial factors of the abortion experience: A critical review. *Psychology of Women Quarterly* 1:79–106.

# 31

# Abortion Counseling
# with Adolescents

## SHARON GEDAN

Emotional counseling is an essential part of care for the woman who elects to terminate her pregnancy. In my experience with counseling over 400 women since abortion became legalized in Hawaii, I am convinced that helping a woman express her feelings about abortion can make it a more comfortable event and, in some cases, can help the woman grow emotionally. Recent studies done since abortion became legal indicate that there are no serious emotional consequences that can be attributed to abortion, but it is still a significant event in the patient's life (Gedan 1973).

Approximately 25 percent of my patients were teenagers, and I came to realize that in addition to having an accepting attitude toward these women, the counselor must also be willing to freely disclose her own feelings and experiences. I have found that patients of all ages resist doing all the revealing and appreciate the involvement of their therapist. An adolescent, in particular, may feel she is being interrogated and resent the intrusion of an authority figure into sensitive areas.

If the counselor takes some initiative in exposing her thoughts and feelings particularly in the beginning of the interview, the adolescent is likely to follow her example. Openness on the part of the counselor makes the tone of the interview a conversation between equals.

When an adolescent girl comes to a health agency, she brings with her memories of her former experiences with physicians, nurses, other health workers, and authority figures. She may project onto the abortion counselor feelings and perceptions from these prior relationships. This can happen with any patient, but because adolescents may have negative feelings toward authority figures the likelihood of projection is higher and may be troublesome. If the counselor is aware of this possibility she will not take hostile remarks personally and can provide the adolescent with a positive experience with authority.

In such a counseling session, the abortion counselor brings her own expectations, perceptions, and feelings about teenagers. These need to be sorted out in the counselor's mind so that she can see each teenager as an individual. It is well to remember that "adolescence is a time of striving to achieve social and emotional maturity and is characterized by the capacity for change" (Lore 1973).

During adolescence the physiological and maturational changes that occur lead to extremely strong emotional reactions. Teenage love is felt deeply and is a highly sensitive area of the teenager's life. Feelings about children, although often romantic and unrealistic, are strong. Anger, jealousy, and sadness are often new experiences. Because the teenager is unused to these feelings, she may be frightened or embarrassed about them and attempt to deny them. Preabortion counseling is effective if the counselor can help the girl identify and express her current emotional reactions. However, encouraging emotional expression in an adolescent must be handled with care because she lacks experience with her feelings and does not have the emotional control of an adult.

Her fantasies about her feelings may be quite dramatic and frightening. She may think she will not be able to stop crying once she starts or she may believe she'll hurt someone irreparably with her anger. Fantasies about her parents' feelings may be exaggerated. Adolescents who are feeling particularly guilty may expect severe retaliation from parents. About 20 percent of my patients have expressed fears of beating or being struck and, although there was a history of physical violence in a few of the families involved, such fears have proven unfounded.

The patient's attitude toward her own behavior needs to be explored in the preabortion interview. During adolescence attitudes are still being formed and are influenced by peers and idols. Young adolescent girls often choose to emulate movie actresses. In the areas of dress and hairdos, such emulation is harmless, perhaps useful, and usually is altered as the adolescent girl matures. However, in attitudes toward sex, contraception, and motherhood, the matter is more complicated. In the past few years a number of single actresses have kept out-of-wedlock babies and expressed joy in raising them, without having a stable relationship with a man. The adolescent girl who has identified with these actresses may become sexually active and shun birth control, or may become pregnant and be unable to see any alternative to her pregnancy except raising her baby alone. Adolescents do not realize that their attitudes may change drastically in years to come and that teenage idols are temporary gods. This subject must be handled with great sensitivity because the teenager's loyalty is usually strong and emotionally charged.

## Counseling the Family

Significant people in the adolescent's family must be included in some way in the counseling. These may be parents, relatives, or members of a communal living unit. In my practice I interview the patient's parents. This interview has a dual focus: helping their daughter and helping them. A daughter's pregnancy often will create a family crisis and, in any case, all members of the family will have some reaction to the pregnancy and how it is handled. During a crisis, "changes may be made toward increased health and maturity, in which case the crisis was a period of opportunity" (Caplan 1974). Skilled counseling can help the family grow and change.

During a family interview the counselor should encourage expression of both parents' feelings about the pregnancy and support of these feelings. She should question a judgmental attitude toward the daughter's behavior, if such exists. Information about the alternatives to pregnancy should be shared and reassurance given about the effects of abortion if this is the alternative of choice. The counselor needs to explore the parents' information about sex and contraception, and assist with planning for their daughter's future use of contraception.

Abortion on demand has been legal in Hawaii for four years so we have had time to begin making observations about patients who have repeat abortions. One characteristic of some "repeat patients" is that they abdicate personal responsibility for selecting abortion as an alternative to pregnancy. If a patient does not accept responsibility for terminating her pregnancy she may likewise give up responsibility for her future sexual behavior and for her contraception. This may lead her to have negative feelings about herself, to adopt dependent rather than independent behavior, and possibly conceive again. In such a case an adolescent girl might say, "I want to have the baby but my parents are making me get rid of it." I believe it is extremely important for all patients having abortions to accept some responsibility for their decision to abort. Accepting responsibility is one characteristic of a mature person and expecting adolescent patients to act maturely is one part of respecting them and helping them to grow.

Helping adolescent patients to accept responsibility for the decision to abort can become complicated because under the law parents can, in fact, either force a daughter to abort or prevent her from doing so. Parents who impose their will on daughters usually are well-intentioned but ignorant of the potential hazardous consequences of their actions. My counseling with such parents has two goals: to educate them as to what probably will occur if they continue to make decisions for their daughter, and to help them understand how they learned to be authoritarian. Frequently they adopted the posture of their own authoritarian parents. The second goal helps to alleviate guilt in parents who feel they are failures because of their daughter's pregnancy.

## Game Playing

Because adolescents can be forced to terminate their pregnancies, some get involved in destructive game playing with their parents. I have found one way of testing whether or not such a game is going on. When the adolescent protests her parents' decision and insists she wants to have the baby, I explore with her the reality of her caring for an infant. Some girls have highly romantic ideas about motherhood and I gently challenge these with facts about an infant's dependency and demanding schedule. With a nongame-playing patient this kind of discussion is often enough for her to see that, although she likes the idea of having a baby, at this point in her life she cannot realistically care for one. Other girls will continue to insist they want a baby and their parents are not being fair. At this point I take a very strong stand in support of my patient. My words might be: "Okay. I have some influence with your parents and your doctor. I'll support you all the way and fight for your right to have this baby." The purpose of this tactic is to break up the alignment of patient versus authority figures. Because this fight with authority is a common maturational task in adolescence, it may be interfering with the girl's rational decision about abortion. At this point a look of surprise and fear will come to the girl's face and she will quickly reconsider. It is then important to support the girl's change in thinking and avoid any remarks that indicate you've "caught her" playing a game. Breaking up such a game can assist the family members to relate to each other genuinely rather than as hostile opposing forces.

## Contraceptive Counseling

All abortion counseling should include contraceptive counseling. Many women are concerned about putting anything "unnatural" into their bodies, such as birth control pills or intrauterine devices. In my practice, such thoughts and feelings are expressed frequently by adolescents. I believe that when an adolescent has a negative attitude, based on fact, toward a contraceptive method, her feeling should be respected. Some of these women may eventually be instrumental in pushing for the development of better contraceptive methods for women and men, and I believe their efforts should be supported.

I believe it is my responsibility to dispel myths where they exist and to discuss the physiological toll of pregnancy and of abortion if these facts are being omitted from the patient's thinking. Also frankness and honesty about side effects, discomforts, and unknown factors about contraceptive methods should be shared freely if the adolescent asks questions about them. We may think it essential that she accept a birth control method. However, I believe it is most important that we present information honestly and not slant our presentation to force her choice. Some adolescents ask questions to which they know the answers in order to test us. Completely honest answers will encourage trust.

On the other hand, some adolescent patients expect to be judged if they want contraceptives and will refuse them in order to "look good." They might say, "This experience has taught me a lesson and I won't be having sex again until I'm married." Such an answer may be appealing if the counselor thinks the girl is too young or immature to handle sexual experiences. However, I believe such a comment should be challenged because once the adolescent girl is sexually active it is likely that she will continue. An expression of disbelief may allow the girl to express her expectations more realistically and often will lead to a fuller, more open discussion of birth control.

An adolescent girl may need some assistance in letting her physician know that she wants a contraceptive method prescribed. She may expect a physician to judge her, preach to her, or refuse to give her a birth control method until she is "of age." If she is already sensitive about her sexual behavior, she will not want to risk the embarrassment of requesting birth control from a physician who may refuse her. I believe it is very important for adolescent girls to have positive experiences in seeking birth control. This will help them in developing positive attitudes toward themselves as sexual persons and in relating to health workers as helping rather than judgmental persons. I believe it is important for anyone who counsels adolescents to be aware of family planning clinics and private physicians who are sensitive to the needs of adolescents so she can help patients find them. Within our nurse community in Honolulu we freely share such information so that we can make appropriate referrals. I also think that nurses who are aware of mental health nursing principles and who are interested in helping adolescents can perform a community service by serving as consultants, members of boards, or volunteers in family planning agencies where adolescent girls are clients.

Many men and women consider contraception and pregnancy *"her problem."* Parents of an adolescent or health workers treating her may not consider her relationship with her partner a serious one and may, therefore, not mention him or consider his influence on the girl's decision. I believe these are outmoded and harmful ideas that we should correct whenever possible.

One way to emphasize that two people are involved in sex and contraception is to include the pregnant patient's partner in the interview or at least to inquire about his feelings about the pregnancy and the possible alternatives to it. Whenever possible the positive aspects of the relationship with the partner should be noted and reinforced. The girl, her boyfriend, and parents may be so caught up in fear, worry, guilt, or shame that they may not be aware of the positive factors that exist between them. Noting these positive factors can strengthen relationships and help each person to be aware of resources he or she has to deal with the problem.

It is essential that an abortion counselor be aware of her state's law concerning medical treatment for adolescents. The law may allow some emergency treatment at a young age and yet require parental consent for the adolescent who receives treatment for venereal disease and pregnancy. I personally believe young adolescents should be able to give their own consent for treatment of VD, pregnancy, and contraceptive counseling. Abortion counselors who work with adolescents may find it necessary to become involved in legislative action that will permit appropriate care for their patients.

REFERENCES

Caplan, G. 1964. *Principles of preventive psychiatry.* New York: Basic Books.
Gedan, S. 1973. Pre-abortion emotional counseling. Paper presented at the American Nurses' Association Convention, Detroit, May 1972. Reprinted in *ANA clinical sessions,* pp. 217–225. New York: Appleton-Century-Crofts, 1973.
Lore, A. 1973. Adolescents: People, not problems. *American Journal of Nursing* 73:1232–1234.

# 32

---

# Divorced Women

---

## EDNA I. RAWLINGS AND
## DIANNE K. CARTER

---

Recent divorce statistics suggest that counselors can expect to see increasingly more clients going through the crisis of divorce. According to Hetherington, Cox, and Cox (1976), if the divorce rate in the U.S. stabilized at the 1974 level, 40 percent of all new marriages would end in divorce. The fact is, however, that divorce has been increasing at an exponential rate during the past decade (1976). Therefore, it is imperative that counselors of women be competent in helping women deal with the unique problems that arise for them following divorce.

## Problem Areas

Three of women's major problem areas precipitated by divorce are autonomy, financial hardship, and loneliness (Carter 1977). An additional stressful problem facing about 80 percent of divorced women is that of being a single parent (cf. Brown et al. 1976; Hetherington, Cox, and Cox 1976). Women going through divorce often need practical information concerning their legal rights, economic resources, and sources of social support. Counselors should have up-to-date information and women-oriented referral sources and contacts to deal with these reality concerns. Douvan (1976) provides much useful information for single parents.

## Emotional Aftermath

The emotional aftermath of divorce is naturally stressful for both females and males (Weiss 1976); the stresses, however, are usually of longer duration for females (Hetherington, Cox, and Cox 1976). The sources of stress also are different for the respective sexes. Males and females both will experience failure following divorce, but women have a heightened sense of personal failure over not succeeding at their most important societal role. The divorced woman's perception of failure is similar to that of a man's following the loss of employment and results in similar psychological consequences: lowered self-esteem, depression, and guilt. In addition, because affiliation plays a central role in women's lives, the disruption of a significant relationship frequently "is perceived not as just a loss of a relationship but as something closer to a total loss of self" (Miller 1976, p. 93).

The intense feelings that result from divorce are often surprising to the women experiencing them. Parkes (1972) referred to the constellation of feelings following the loss of a relationship as the "separation distress syndrome." This syndrome represents ways of adapting to and coping with loss (Otto and Otto 1976). Women going through divorce go through stages similar to the stages of grief experienced by persons in bereavement. Hallett (1974) and Otto and Otto (1976) discuss techniques for saying "good-bye" to the broken relationship.

One of the most disruptive emotions that interferes with "letting go" of the old relationship by divorced women is anger. Anger is a natural and expected reaction to divorce (Weiss 1976; Otto and Otto 1976). Since women have been discouraged or even punished for aggression, divorced women may be in touch with rejection, hurt, guilt, or depression, but not their anger. The counselor must, therefore, be prepared to help women surface their anger and, once surfaced, express it in a constructive fashion. Techniques for dealing with anger in divorced women are discussed in Otto and Otto (1976) and Carter (1977).

## Women Helping Women

For most women, divorce means separation not only from the former spouses but from the community and other meaningful relationships. At a time when the divorced woman's social-emotional needs are greatest, she may have few social contacts. By becoming involved with other women who are sharing her situation she has the opportunity for companionship, affection, and emotional support. Women can also offer each other practical advice and help in coping with loneliness, child care, and other problems common to divorced women. Experience in a group of women also going through divorce reduces a woman's dependency on men as a source of support, self-esteem, and identity. Women in all-women groups may model strength, competency, and problem solving for each other (Johnson 1976; Carter 1977). Orlinsky and Howard (1976), using a small sample, found that young divorced mothers who had female therapists in individual therapy reported greater self-possession and encouragement compared to those with male therapists. Gender of therapist may be a relevant issue in counseling divorced women.

## Crises versus Opportunity

Following divorce, women often find themselves on their own without a significant other such as a husband or parent on which to lean. To be thrust suddenly into adult responsibilities is scary, and the difficulty is often compounded by financial hardship and social isolation (Carter 1977). Sometimes women attempt to resolve this crisis by retreating into new dependency relationships with husbands, lovers, or counselors who encourage traditional role performance. This precludes their opportunity to grow into full adulthood and increased personality integration, and usually results in stagnation or even deterioration. Therapists or counselors should possess knowledge, skill, and values to assist women in achieving personal growth following divorce.

Among the benefits that divorced women discover in the single state are increased personal autonomy and a greater sense of competence (Otto and Otto 1976). Divorced women report that their freedom and control has increased in almost every area of their lives. They experienced increased control in the management of their domestic responsibilities, of their children, their money, and their social and sexual activities (Brown et al. 1976).

If a woman learns to cope with the problems she faces following divorce, she will feel more competent to deal with problems in living and be more in touch with her personal power. She will experience a sense of achievement and greater individuation. The counselor who works with divorced women needs to view this crisis as a potentially positive experience and to help her or his divorced clients to discover the positive elements in the experience.

The following principles are recommended for working with divorced women.

## Recommended Principles

Knowledge:
1. Counselors/therapists are aware of laws for divorce and separation, names of women-oriented lawyers; resources in the community for support groups, career and skill training, job information, and financial support services.
2. Counselor/therapists are aware of stresses that impinge on "single-again" women and the difficulties of single parenthood.

Skills:
1. Counselors/therapists are able to deal with loss and separation.
2. Counselors/therapists are skilled in facilitating support/therapy groups for "single-again" women.

Attitudes:
1. Counselors/therapists view divorce as having the potential of helping women grow and view "single-again" status as a viable option for women and not merely a transitional stage between marriages.

REFERENCES

Brown, C. A., et al. 1976. Divorce: Chance of a new lifetime. *Journal of Social Issues* 32:119–133.

Carter, D. K. 1977. Counseling divorced women. *Personnel and Guidance Journal* 55:537–542.

Douvan, E. 1976. The single parent: Challenges and opportunities. In *New life options—the working woman's resource book,* ed. R. K. Loring and H. A. Otto. New York: McGraw-Hill.

Hallett, K. 1974. *A guide for single parents.* Millbrae, Calif.: Celestial Arts.

Hetherington, E. M., Cox, M., and Cox, R. 1976. The aftermath of divorce. Paper presented at American Psychological Association meeting, Washington, D.C.

Johnson, M. 1976. An approach to feminist therapy. *Psychotherapy: Theory, Research, and Practice* 13:72–76

Miller, J. B. 1976. *Toward a new psychology of women.* Boston: Beacon Press.

Orlinsky, H. E., and Howard, K. I. 1976. The effects of sex of therapist on the therapeutic experiences of women. *Psychotherapy: Theory, Research, and Practice* 13:72–76.

Otto, H. A., and Otto, R. 1976. Maximizing the positive in separation, divorce, and widowhood. In *New life options—the working woman's resource book,* ed. R. K. Loring and H. A. Otto. New York: McGraw-Hill.

Parkes, C. M. 1972. *Bereavement.* New York: International Universities Press.

Weiss, R. S. 1976. The emotional impact of marital separation. *Journal of Social Issues* 32:135–145.

# 33

# Postmastectomy Counseling

## JAMES G. JOINER AND JOAN Z. FISHER

The incidence of breast cancer has increased to the extent that the problem no longer belongs exclusively to medicine, psychology, or any other treatment discipline. It is now considered a rehabilitation concern encompassing all aspects from medical treatment to full personal readjustment. A body of knowledge is becoming available regarding the full range of considerations, that is, psychological, sexual, social, vocational, and counseling. Rehabilitation counseling must consider its role in the full readjustment efforts of mastectomy patients.

The American Cancer Society predicts that one in every thirteen women will develop breast cancer. The greatest proportion of those affected will be between the ages of thirty-nine and fifty-four. Eighty-four percent of those with localized breast cancer are expected to achieve the five-year survival standard by simple or radical mastectomy, chemotherapy, and/or radiation therapy. Physical survival often leads to impaired chances for personal survival. Harrell (1972) states, "to save a woman by surgical intervention and then deny her the emotional support necessary to form a different life-style and accept an altered body-image is a contradiction in terms" (p. 676).

In considering breast cancer as a rehabilitation concern, many life-area adjustments must be evaluated.

## Psychological Adjustment

The patient's psychological adjustment to breast cancer and mastectomy is perhaps the most difficult to achieve and is equally difficult to adequately assess. A woman's psychological adjustment is closely aligned with her individual self-concept. Woods (1975) discussed the cultural emphasis on the female breast as a symbol of femininity and as a reinforcement for the desire for a whole and perfect body. Breast shape and size are presented by the various communications media as a criterion for sexual desirability, and contemporary clothing styles demand an intact body. Bard and Sutherland (1955) related a woman's reaction to her mastectomy to her individual perception of the breast and her personal psychosexual development. They indicated a cultural, physiological, and psychological interaction that determines the individual meaning of the breast to each woman.

As with other physical disabilities and surgical amputation, much of one's self-concept is dependent on one's premorbid personality. Woods (1975) indicated that the value assigned the lost breast will probably be influenced by the extent to which the woman bases her self-worth and acceptability on her appearance. In women who relate to others through physical attractiveness, feelings of self-rejection may develop when they perceive their bodies as having been disfigured by mastectomy. The removal of a woman's breast may eliminate one of her basic ways of relating to others. Preoperative body image plays a significant part in the woman's response to her surgery.

Bard and Sutherland (1955) wrote that after mastectomy many women develop the notion that the entire body has been made weak and vulnerable and can no longer fight off disease or injury. The woman feels that her body has been marred and she is now unacceptable to herself and to others. For many women the simple acts of dressing and undressing each day constitute dreaded emotional crises further affecting body image and self-concept. Some women have reported feeling distorted or crooked, complaining of loss or emptiness in the axilla (Bard and Sutherland 1955).

Recent advances in technology have improved breast prostheses, and the current practice of providing the patient with a prosthesis upon or even before discharge from the hospital is felt to be a positive step in enhancing psychological adjustment. Clients with older, outdated prostheses may benefit from learning of new types of breast prostheses.

## Sexual Adjustment

A number of authors stress the importance of the husband's role in the patient's postoperative adjustment. Bard and Sutherland (1955) recommend the inclusion of the husband in any discussion of radical mastectomy. Renneker and Cutler (1952) stated the importance of involving the husband in the wife's recovery with instructions that the husband express active interest in the state of the surgical wound, to become conditioned to accept the woman's nude body postoperatively and treat it as a normal part of their life together. The husband is counseled that he plays an important part in his wife's adjustment and that his reactions of shock, disappointment, anxiety, and sorrow are normal; that these may be the same feelings his wife is experiencing and that it is important for them to share these experiences.

The male partner's reaction to mastectomy is influenced by his own sexual identity. Woods (1975) points out that a man may feel threatened by the postmastectomy woman if his own sexual identity is dependent upon the sexual image projected by his wife. In addition, if he tends to rely on the assessment of his peers of his partner as "sexy" or attractive, it may be difficult for him to accept her surgery. If the husband's fears of being disfigured are intense, he may have great difficulty accepting the woman's changed body since it may reinforce his own fears of disfigurement. In many cases the woman perceives a feeling of rejection or revulsion on the part of her husband, which in turn may lead to evasion of sexual contact.

As with the postmastectomy self-concept, it has been shown that postoperative marital relations are usually contingent upon the preoperative status of the marriage (Bard and Sutherland 1955). It has been pointed out that among stable marriages in which healthy sexual relationships existed prior to surgery, there tended to be fewer problems in sexual adjustment than among already insecure relationships (Woods 1975). Some women feel they must be partially clothed or protected with a pillow in order to participate in sexual relations. Many feel compelled to keep the room in total darkness to avoid the viewing of their disfigurement. Reach to Recovery, a mastectomy volunteer organization, can provide beneficial lay counseling. In such a setting a woman may discuss some of her fears and anxieties with a fellow mastectomy patient.

Just as the physical appearance of the affected breast can tend to inhibit sexual expression, pain or tenderness in the operative area may initially cause discomfort and preclude the desire for, or ability to participate in, sexual activities (Woods 1975). Fear of disrupting the wound and possibly inducing pain may prevent the resumption of normal sexual relations. The woman who previously enjoyed breast stimulation as an erotic and pleasurable sensation may experience a decrease in arousal after mastectomy.

## Emotional Responses

Bard (1952) outlines a progression of emotional responses following breast surgery: First there is depression followed by self-pity; self-pity is usually accompanied by feelings of misgiving and guilt. Ultimately successful resolution of these feelings results in the resumption of functioning and interest in the environment. A 1973 Gallup survey, "Women's Attitudes Regarding Breast Cancer," indicated that most women think that a normal life pattern can probably be maintained or reestablished after mastectomy; however, there is less confidence among single and young women and among those with low incomes (American Cancer Society 1976).

In a study of the emotional reactions to cancer, Peck (1972) indicated that anxiety was the most common patient response, followed by depression characterized by appearing sad or having lost interest in usual pursuits. Guilt was found to be a frequent emotional reaction in eighteen of fifty patients studied. Six of these expressed feeling much guilt, assuming that their own actions had caused them to develop cancer. Overt anger at having cancer was present in twenty-two out of fifty patients, and anger was directed at doctors, hospitals, and relatives. In addition, defense mechanisms such as denial and displaced anxiety were common. Denial can occur throughout the course of the disease, sometimes beginning with the discovery of a lump or defect and often appearing even in the postoperative phase of recovery.

Bard and Sutherland (1955) see expressions of anxiety and tension as normal emotional reactions during the postoperative period. Patients display eating and sleeping-pattern disturbances as well as increased dependence and expressions of resentment. These postoperative emotional responses are felt to be normal and positive signs. The authors point out that mastectomy patients with such manifestations are informing the environment that they have been through a trying ordeal and are in need of support. Renneker and Cutler (1952) view the development of anxiety in the mastectomy patient as a normal concomitant of the disease that should be anticipated and utilized therapeutically.

In some instances women who have been very independent will

desire nurturant care in a setting devoid of responsibility. Even when adequate care is available in their own homes, some women may seek the homes of friends or relatives (Bard and Sutherland 1955).

# Social Adjustment

The mastectomy patient's role in social and interpersonal situations may be altered in various ways after surgery. Harrell (1972) wrote that a woman must know how to cope not only with herself but with the reactions of others to her surgery. There are indications that the family experiences as much of a crisis as the patient herself (Klein 1971). Bard and Sutherland (1955) found patients reluctant to engage in any activity requiring close contact with groups of people, such as shopping or traveling, because of a belief that the operative site, even when healed, was unable to withstand the slightest trauma and that serious consequences could result from physical contact. Some patients experience fear and anxiety upon discharge from the hospital that was felt to be associated with a fear of not being ready to face people. This feeling signifies an expectation of social unacceptability as a consequence of mastectomy and is evidence of lowered self-esteem. Woods (1975) also relates that many women view dealing with people with apprehension and fear having their children see them undressed. Bard and Sutherland (1955) reflected on the feeling that some women become extremely secretive about their mastectomy, wanting to hide the information from the community. This in turn causes the community to view the individuals with even more suspicion, just as is evidenced in other disabling conditions.

# Occupational Adjustment

The mastectomy and its physical and psychological aftermath can profoundly affect the woman's occupational outlook. The woman whose role is basically that of wife and mother may find that the mastectomy is disruptive to her routine. Physical limitations and residual weakness from the surgery may undermine the ability to perform her usual role of mother and housewife. Women in occupations that depend on bodily attractiveness, such as models, entertainers, hostesses, may find they cannot return to their jobs. Limitations in strength and range of motion may be vocationally handicapping to some women in a variety of occupations that involve lifting, reaching, and pushing, such as factory and assembly work, food service occupations, and other job areas. Bard and Sutherland (1955) referred to the occurrence of hypochondria and somatic symptoms in some women following mastectomy, which may affect a woman's job attendance and performance.

There are a number of medical complications that frequently occur following the mastectomy that can hinder the occupational adjustment in addition to the previously described social adjustment problems. Lymphedema, brachial plexus injury, radiation fibrosis, and shoulder dysfunction can occur as a result of treatment for breast cancer. In addition, Healy (1971) relates psychological sequelae of lymphedema with 95.4 percent of patients surveyed experiencing self-consciousness of their enlarged arm. The occurrence of postoperative physical complications constitutes an additional threat, with most women viewing any complications as evidence of recurrent disease and the need for additional surgery.

Two studies (Craig, Comstock, and Geiser 1974) indicated encouraging statistics with regard to a mastectomy patients' return to preoperative responsibilities. One study revealed that 83 percent of patients surveyed had resumed their preoperative responsibilities within two years of radical mastectomy. A subsequent study revealed that 83 percent of patients surveyed resumed preoperative responsibilities five years later. The former study, however, revealed that with regard to psychosocial disability, only 54 percent of the subjects had a "good" attitude at initial interview with 42 percent "fair," and 4 percent "poor." At an eighteen-month follow-up, the same survey indicated 39 percent "good," 57 percent "fair," and 4 percent "poor." This may have relevance to "in treatment" attitudes supported by treatment staff and later attitudes reflected by reality contacts. As expected there are those whose poor attitudes remain stable.

## Counseling Considerations

Counseling the postmastectomy patient will likely encompass the entire range of rehabilitation counseling concerns, that is, psychological, sexual, social, vocational, and personal adjustment. The usual counseling concerns seem to intensify in postmastectomy counseling because of the perceived devastation to several life areas.

Klein (1971) related postmastectomy counseling to other crisis counseling. Counseling must assist in the patients' performance of certain psychological tasks: (1) expressing feelings; (2) sorting out the real from the unreal; (3) not giving false reassurance; (4) anticipating the future; (5) helping family members express feelings and understand the feelings of the patient; (6) assisting in how and what to tell other significant persons in her life.

The initial sessions are extremely important in postmastectomy counseling. Providing an accepting atmosphere where the counselor presents an "I—Thou" attitude of respect and a mutual search for adjustment potential is essential. The counselor must remember that the client has previously been involved in a kind of *person-to-object* treatment process. The client has probably been told what to do and how to feel to the extent that adjustment by concealment is well ingrained.

The *person-to-object* treatment process creates two problems in the initial counseling sessions. First, the client is reluctant to discuss personally relevant content that has been dealt with in a matter-of-fact, objective manner. This, she may feel, would be an indication of her weakness and inability to adjust to the drastic change in her image. Second, because counselors do not understand the potential dynamics, they may readily accept the client's facade of adjustment. Counselors should gently lead the postmastectomy client to an opportunity to express fears of inadequacy and vulnerability. Conversely, counselors must use discretion in their pursuit of discussion of such emotionally laden content areas.

Bronner-Hurszar (1971) indicates the task for postmastectomy rehabilitation counseling: "remission or recovery after treatment for neoplastic disease can only be considered complete when the patient is able to fully resume work and all significant pre-morbid pursuits, such as social, recreational and sexual activities" (p. 133).

REFERENCES

American Cancer Society. 1976. *Facts and figures.* Washington, D.C.: American Cancer Society.

Bard, M., and Sutherland, A. M. 1955. Psychological impact of cancer and its treatment. *Cancer* 8(4):646–672.

Bronner-Hurszar, J. 1971. The psychological aspects of cancer in man. *Psychosomatics* 12(2):133–138.

Craig, J. J., Comstock, G. W., and Geiser, P. B. 1974. The quality of survival in breast cancer: A care-control comparison. *Cancer* 33(5):1451–1457.

Harrell, H. C. 1972. To lose a breast. *American Journal of Nursing* 72(4): 676–677.

Healy, J. E. 1971. Role of rehabilitation medicine in the care of the patient with breast cancer. *Cancer* 28(6):1666–1671.

Klein, R. 1971. A crisis to grow on. *Cancer* 28 (6):1660–1665.

Peck, A. 1972. Emotional reactions to having cancer. *CA: A Cancer Journal for Clinicians* 22(5):284–291.

Rennecker, R., and Cutler, M. 1952. Psychological problems of adjustment to cancer of the breast. *Journal of the American Medical Association* 148(10):833–888.

Woods, N. F. 1975. Influences on sexual adaptation to mastectomy. *Journal of Obstetric, Gynecological and Neonatal Nursing* 34.

# 34

# Group Work with Widows

ANDRE TOTH AND SUSAN TOTH

Of 12.6 million widowed individuals in the United States in 1976, 10.7 million were women. Furthermore, today the chances that the typical marriage of a bride of twenty and groom of twenty-three will eventually end with the death of the husband are 70 in 100 (Metropolitan Life Insurance Company Statistical Bulletin 1977a, pp. 10–11). In this country, one of every eight women fourteen years or older is widowed (Metropolitan Life Insurance Company Statistical Bulletin 1977b, pp. 8–10).

In response to the grim reality behind these statistics, the authors began planning for a group therapy program for widows. A search of the literature revealed an abundance of books written by widows for widows, but the authors could not find a formally organized group therapy program for this particular population (cf. Caine 1974, 1978; Kavanaugh 1974; Kreis and Pattie 1969; Lewis and Berns 1975; Lindsey 1977; Young 1976).

It was clear from the literature, however, that the death of a husband provided such a strong common denominator among women that the initial question concerning the composition of the group was indirectly answered. The authors believed that women of different socioeconomic backgrounds and ages could be mixed without jeopardizing the quality of the therapeutic experience. This turned out to be correct.

The Sisters of Charity Hospital in Buffalo, New York, agreed to sponsor the group. The authors decided to conduct six sessions, and to limit the size of the group to twelve. A number of issues significant to widows were selected for discussion, and time for clients to express individual concerns was also allotted. Although additional sessions were possible, the authors did not want to keep meeting indefinitely to avoid excessive dependence on the group as well as repetiveness.

To select clients, the authors went through the medical records of the hospital to identify women whose husbands had died there. The authors selected women who had been widowed for no less than six months and no more than fourteen. During the first three or four months after the death of a husband, identified as the shock stage, an individual is less receptive to therapy (Kreis and Pattie 1969). Widows at the other end of this period were excluded because the authors believed the most difficult time was in the eight to ten months following the initial shock. Although these guidelines were somewhat arbitrary in that adjustment is a highly individualized process that hinges on many variables, the authors planned to conduct only one group at first and they wanted to reach those widows who needed the most help.

Women whose present status indicated psychological problems beyond grief and whose presence might have distracted the group process were also excluded. The authors realize that, with more resources, these individuals should also have help, and, as it turned out, some of these individuals were already receiving psychiatric support.

The purpose of the group was to allow individual women to share with each other the meaning of widowhood. The authors, as therapists, would provide a protected environment in which this could occur. It was hoped that a sense of group identity would help these women develop insight and courage to deal effectively with their situation.

## Group Identification

Twelve women attended the first session of the group. They had never seen each other before and their only link was widowhood. After a brief introduction to the program and a statement concerning confidentiality, each widow was asked to narrate the events that led to the death of her husband. Each widow was asked to describe the length and type of illness, where her husband died, memories of their last days, weeks, or months, the funeral and the first few days following it, and anything else they felt was significant about the experience. This was the most dramatic session of the group. As each woman narrated her story, which often was interrupted by tears, the other women in the group nodded every time they heard situations or feelings they recognized. As this process of identification occurred, some of the women's pain lessened. One woman said later:

After listening to each lady tell her sad story, it suddenly became clear that I wasn't alone anymore. I found a place I belonged. I am a widow and so are all the other ladies.

By the end of the first session, twelve strangers had become a cohesive group. So strong was the bond of widowhood that the women appeared to be old friends getting together after a long separation. The occasion was obviously not a happy one, but the feeling of the group lacked the depressing pall it had had at first. The atmosphere was one of nervous excitement—nervous, yes, but excitement nonetheless.

Most women said they began to experience many kinds of somatic problems during the first few weeks after the death of their husband. All group members experienced sleeplessness regularly, as well as headaches, backaches, and a general feeling of malaise, even if they had had no such problems prior to their husband's death. Although attendance at group meetings seemed to produce little change in their various aches and pains, some members did report that they had had their first good sleep in weeks on the night following the first group session. By the end of the sixth session, several group members were sleeping better, if not regularly so. Other women continued to experience troublesome insomnia. One of these women did state to the group, however, "Now when I can't sleep, I know other women are going through the same thing and somehow it helps."

Members of the group felt other symptoms of depression in varying degrees, including a general sense of aimlessness, difficulty in making decisions, and an inability to get going, especially in the mornings. Although group members could talk about their feelings, their insights were largely intellectual. The authors learned that no formula exists to deal with this kind of situational depression, but it is helpful for clients to know that what they are experiencing is part of a normal and healthy process of grieving.

## Discomfort of Others

Realizing the supporting role that friends and relatives can play, the authors asked the group to describe the emotional support they had received before and after their husband's death. No matter how much social workers think that ways of coping with death and dying have become popularized in modern society, it was found that apparently they have reached a very small minority. The women revealed that most people felt uncomfortable with the subject of death and acted clumsily at best in supportive roles.

The group agreed that a conspiracy of silence seemed to exist among many of their friends and relatives. The name of the deceased was carefully avoided in social situations, as was any reference to anything even remotely connected with him. One woman described the feelings as follows:

It was as if he had never existed. I kept on bringing up his name and they kept on changing the subject. I felt a tremendous resentment against them all, even though I realized that it was because they wanted to spare my feelings.

The group agreed that one source of strength for a widow is the realization that her husband has not been forgotten by those who loved him. A woman will feel significant support, although temporary, from hearing people reminisce about positive experiences or humorous episodes they may have shared with her husband.

Many people also expect a widow to exhibit a "stiff upper lip." They would rather not witness any display of emotion and generally seek to handle the whole situation with as many platitudes as possible. This greeting-card mentality is another example of people's discomfort with death. One woman said, "People were asking me, 'How are you?' You know darn well the only answer they wanted to hear was, 'Fine.'" Another widow said:

Everyone was telling me how great I was doing and how fine I looked. All I wanted to tell them was, "What do you want me to do, crawl around and writhe on the floor? Paint my face black?"

## Personal Identity

At a practical level, the cultural notion of thinking of women first as spouses and mothers and only last, if at all, as individuals accentuates the trauma of widowhood. The women commented: "When I walk alone into a room full of people, I feel terribly uncomfortable," "When confronted, even with the simplest situation, I have a very hard time," and "Ever since my husband died, I have had these overwhelming attacks of insecurity. Where do you think they are coming from?" It is not surprising that a woman, having been known for twenty to thirty years as "John's wife," should have tremendous identity problems when John dies. "Now that my husband is gone, who am I?" one woman cried poignantly.

When children grow up and leave the household, a similar identity question emerges, especially for the woman whose primary concept of self derives from motherhood. The difference, of course, is that growing up is a gradual process; the death of one's spouse is not.

The group discussed self-identity theoretically at first. Each woman was encouraged to begin the gradual rediscovery of the self as unique, slowly dissociating herself from labels that had become painful. The search for identity is so complex that it cannot be accomplished simply, however. Intellectual awareness is at least a necessary, if not a sufficient, condition for change.

## Guilt

Many widows seem to feel guilt, although not always at a conscious level; when guilt is not conscious, it may create havoc in the resolution of grief. The obvious advantage of group interaction is that individuals who are able to verbalize vague, uneasy feeling in themselves allow others to recognize their own feelings. Once brought to a level of consciousness, feelings can be confronted directly.

A widow's guilt seems to originate from the sorrow of not doing more to prevent her husband's death. "Had I just taken him to one more doctor, had we tried some different drugs" was a familiar regret. A widow also tends to remember episodes where she perceived her behavior as unacceptable, for example, during arguments, and wishes she could take her words back. Even when a woman is unable to pinpoint the specific origins of her guilt, it is obvious that she feels guilt nonetheless because of a sense of failure: Her husband's death is seen as a direct reflection of her inability to care for him adequately, and that had she been a better person, his death would not have happened. The exchange of supportive feelings was a natural way the group handled these situations. For these women, this exchange was the beginning of insight that, in most instances, led to a healthy resolution of their feelings of guilt.

## Anger

A widow often continues to talk to her deceased husband. This may take many forms. She may simply exclaim at her inability to find a missing document or express annoyance when she has car troubles of the kind her husband used to fix. During a particularly painful moment of loneliness, she may cry, "Oh, why did you leave me?" The women in the group were able to share these conversations. Before the group began they may have experienced doubts about their sanity, but they then recognized that other widows behaved in the same way and that it was perfectly acceptable and normal behavior, as was wearing their husband's favorite robe or sweater or keeping a particularly significant item that was his.

In addition, the group began to explore the feelings connected with some of the widows' comments. One woman acknowledged:

I remember getting stuck in a snowbank at the end of our driveway and saying, "Where are you, John, now that I need you?" And yes, there was anger in me. A few seconds later I felt terrible for feeling this way. How could I possibly feel angry with him. Obviously, he didn't die by choice.

As the group explored similar episodes, it found that a sense of abandonment was a commonly shared feeling. Intellectually, the women knew their husband did not choose to die. Emotionally, however, they felt abandoned. In the abstract, their anger was directed against circumstances; on a more concrete level, however, it was directed toward those who had done the abandoning, their deceased husbands. Although not all the women identified with these feelings, those who did benefited from the realization that what they were feeling was a normal stage in the grieving process and that they were not experiencing it alone.

The authors have now conducted three groups for widows of six sessions each. A follow-up is also scheduled at three, six, and twelve months. Many of the participants have already acknowledged that the experience was worthwhile. As one of the group members stated:

The group did so much for me . . . to be able to talk it all out, all the sorrow, guilt, abandonment, and hurt from friends. There was so much inside of me that I couldn't express to relatives or friends, but with the group, I could say it all.

REFERENCES

Caine, L. 1974. *Widow.* New York: Bantam Books.
———. 1978. *Life Lines.* Garden City, N.Y.: Doubleday.
Kavanaugh, R. E. 1974. *Facing death.* New York: Penguin Books.
Kreis, B., and Pattie, A. 1969. *Up from grief: Patterns of recovery.* New York: Seabury.
Lewis, A. A., and Berns, B. 1975. *Three out of four wives.* New York: Macmillan.
Lindsey, R. 1977. *Alone and surviving.* New York: Walker.
*Metropolitan Life Insurance Company Statistical Bulletin 58.* January 1977a.
*Metropolitan Life Insurance Company Statistical Bulletin 58.* September 1977b.
Young, A. R. 1976. *By death or divorce: It hurts to lose.* Denver, Colo.: Accent Books.

# 35

# Psychosocial Aspects of
# Wife Battering

BARBARA STAR, CAROL G. CLARK,
KAREN M. GOETZ, AND LINDA O'MALIA

Since it has become the object of media attention, few people would question the fact that wife beating represents a serious social problem. However, researchers are only beginning to offer information useful to practitioners working with battered women. For instance, many researchers attribute the phenomenon of wife abuse to early exposure to parental violence (cf. Ball 1977; Gayford 1975; Gelles 1976). Histories of both the abused and the abuser often contain accounts of violence between parents or of violence directed toward themselves as children.

Susan Hanks and C. Peter Rosenbaum (1977) found striking parallels between early and adult life conditions among women married to violent men. Women raised in families characterized by a subtly controlling mother married to a bombastic, but ineffectual, man themselves married men who needed rescuing. Women from families in which the mother was submissive to a dictatorial man emulated their mothers by marrying men whom they knew had violent, alcohol-abusing tendencies like their fathers. Women raised in unstable families headed by an emotionally disturbed mother who had numerous mates tended to enter unstable relationships with a series of inadequate, abusive men.

Although earlier studies have claimed that female masochism is the major dynamic operating in wife-abuse situations, more recent studies focus on descriptive rather than explanatory factors (cf. Deutsch 1944; Reynolds and Siegle 1959; Schultz 1960). Anton Dewsbury (1975) speculates that five of the fifteen battered women he interviewed showed gross personality disorders, another five showed neurotic reactions, and one woman was psychotic. And the literature is replete with reports of low self-esteem, depressive illnesses, suicide attempts, and characterological problems among samples of battered wives (Carlson 1977; Gayford 1975; Snell, Rosenwald, and Robey 1964).

Unfortunately, almost all the research to date relies heavily on information derived from interviews; little hard data exist. The research on which this article is based, however, was designed to present information based on personality tests as well as on questionnaires and interviews. The article describes a study of fifty-seven battered women, delineates three major psychosocial components essential to understanding the predicament of women in abusive situations, and offers treatment considerations.

## The Research Methodology

The study, undertaken from January to June of 1977, used accidental sampling methods to draw a voluntary population of recently battered women.[1] The majority of the sample (80 percent) consisted of battered women living in shelters located in southern California and Arizona. The remainder of the sample came from outpatient programs in Los Angeles and the surrounding area. All participants had spent at least six months in marital or common-law relationships with men from whom they received severe, repeated, and demonstrable injury.

The research design called for all subjects to complete questionnaires and personality tests. In addition, fifteen women, randomly selected from the California shelters and outpatient clinics that participated in this study, engaged in hour-long, semistructured interviews with one of the researchers. To avoid unnecessary disruptions of administrative and treatment routines, personnel from those shelters and agencies involved in the study distributed and collected the research instruments and arranged interview appointments with the women. Because people other than the researchers were involved in the distri-

1. Ninety percent of the women in the sample were battered within the three months prior to initiating the study, and the rest had been battered within the past year.

bution and collection of test instruments, the return rate for the instruments varied. All fifty-seven participants provided demographic information about themselves and their husbands, forty-two completed a psychosocial inventory, and fifty completed the personality tests. Fifteen women were interviewed. This article reports the results of the available data.

*Data Collection Instruments*

Five instruments comprised the test battery. The background information form provided demographic and descriptive data about the age, ethnicity, height, weight, education, religion, and socioeconomic status of the women and their spouses.

The psychosocial inventory for battered women, an original questionnaire developed by the authors, consisted of three sections. The first, personal data, covered such topics as the women's memories of childhood and adolescence, reasons for marrying, perception of marital status, and social and sexual life with their husband or boyfriend. The second section, exposure to violence, dealt with the topics of violence and punishment in the women's childhood home, the nature and severity of the beatings they received from their spouses, suicidal thoughts, and the women's attempts to leave. The final section, self-perceptions, tapped the women's sense of their own competence and strengths in such areas as motherhood, finances, and interpersonal relationships.

A personality profile was drawn from two tests devised by Raymond Cattell, the 16 PF and the Clinical Analysis Questionnaire (Cattell, Eber, and Tatsuoka 1970; Delhees and Cattell 1975). The 16 PF yields information on sixteen normal personality dimensions, with each dimension designated by an alphabetic code and offering two behavioral extremes, for example, reserved versus outgoing. Raw scores are converted to sten scores ranging from 1 to 10. Sten scores of 5 and 6 reflect the standardized balance between the personality extremes and are considered "average." (Because of its lower vocabulary requirements and shorter length, Form C of the 16 PF was selected.)

Part II of the Clinical Analysis Questionnaire, which provides information about twelve factors that are in the pathological domain—for example, low hypochondriasis versus high hypochondriasis—was used. Like the 16 PF, the scores range from 1 to 10 with sten scores of 5 and 6 representing the standardized average. Table 35-1 contains a list of both the personality and psychological factors tested in the 16 PF and the Clinical Analysis Questionnaire.

The final component of the test battery was an interview schedule. The interviews clarified and elaborated information gained from the

TABLE 35-1

*Personality and Psychological Factors of Battered Wives (N = 50)*

| Factor | Mean[a] | Mode |
|--------|---------|------|
| A (reserved vs. outgoing) | 4.34 | 5.00 |
| B (less intelligent vs. bright) | 5.22 | 4.00 |
| C (low vs. high ego strength) | 4.36 | 4.00 |
| E (submissive vs. dominant) | 6.14 | 6.00 |
| F (sober, serious vs. enthusiastic) | 4.84 | 3.00 |
| G (weak superego vs. strong superego) | 5.12 | 4.00 |
| H (shy vs. bold) | 4.66 | 4.00 |
| I (tough minded vs. tender minded) | 6.20 | 8.00 |
| L (trusting vs. suspicious) | 5.96 | 6.00 |
| M (practical vs. imaginative) | 5.94 | 6.00 |
| N (unpretentious vs. polished) | 5.44 | 5.00 |
| O (secure vs. insecure) | 5.80 | 6.00 |
| Q1 (conservative vs. radical) | 5.96 | 7.00 |
| Q2 (group dependent vs. self-sufficient) | 7.04 | 7.00 |
| Q3 (undisciplined self-conflict vs. controlled) | 4.38 | 5.00 |
| Q4 (relaxed vs. tense) | 6.50 | 8.00 |
| D1 (low vs. high hypochondriasis) | 6.02 | 5.00 |
| D2 (low vs. high suicide ideation) | 5.14 | 7.00 |
| D3 (low vs. high brooding discontent) | 5.34 | 4.00 |
| D4 (low vs. high anxious depression) | 6.02 | 6.00 |
| D5 (high energy euphoria vs. low energy depression) | 5.82 | 5.00 |
| D6 (low vs. high guilt) | 5.80 | 6.00 |
| D7 (low vs. high bored withdrawal) | 6.40 | 6.00 |
| Pa (low vs. high paranoia) | 6.78 | 7.00 |
| Pp (low vs. high psychopathic deviation) | 5.68 | 6.00 |
| Sc (low vs. high schizophrenia) | 6.54 | 7.00 |
| As (low vs. high compulsive thoughts) | 5.74 | 6.00 |
| Ps (low vs. high general psychosis) | 6.10 | 7.00 |

[a] Based on scale of 1 to 10 with 5 to 6 as normal range.

*Note:* A test comparing the means of the study sample and the means of a normative sample revealed statistically significant difference (ps .05) if the study sample scored below 4.7 or above 6.3 in any test category.

written instruments. Topics included personality qualities the women perceived in themselves and their husbands, the positive and negative aspects of their relationship, the way problems were resolved, and the decisions involved in continuing or severing the relationship.

# Findings

That most of the women in this sample had left the violent situation and were living in shelters should be kept in mind when reviewing the findings. While, at present, the universe from which such a sample

*429*

might be drawn is unknown, it is known that women electing to seek help from shelters probably represent only a minority of battered women. Therefore the results of this study may not be generalizable to the broader spectrum of battered women. Also, the information in this study was derived solely from the women's perspective, and several sections, especially those regarding spousal characteristics and marital interactions, were subject to rater bias.

### Characteristics of the Sample

The sample consisted primarily of women in their late twenties or early thirties. The mean age for the group was thirty-two, with ages ranging from seventeen to fifty-four. Although the group contained several ethnic and religious minorities, 70 percent were Caucasian and 42 percent were Protestant. Blacks represented the largest ethnic minority (12 percent); and Catholics, the largest religious minority (22 percent). Forty-seven percent, nearly half the sample, were raised by people other than, or in addition to, their natural parents, including stepparents, grandparents, and siblings. When the women selected words to describe their childhood, over half chose only negative words, such as lonely, violent, and troubled. An even greater number (64 percent) described their adolescent years using entirely negative terms. The majority (65 percent) attended at least some high school, but only 28 percent participated in academic or vocational programs beyond high school; the remainder (7 percent) did not progress beyond elementary school.

Although for the purposes of this study all women were considered "married," forty-five women were legally married and twelve were in common-law or living-with relationships. The average age at marriage was twenty-three years. The relationships ranged in duration from six months to thirty-one years, with a mean of nine years. Sixty-four percent of the sample reported that the current relationship represented their first marriage. Over 40 percent of the women had two or more children. The women married men who were, on the average, three years older, Caucasian (61 percent), and a member of the Catholic religion (45 percent). Seventy-five percent of the spouses attended high school, with an additional 20 percent holding college or postsecondary vocational training. However, fewer than 50 percent of the men were employed consistently throughout the relationship.

### Exposure to Violence

The findings indicated that approximately one-third of the sample was exposed to violence in the form of witnessing parental abuse, enduring severe punishment in childhood, being abused by men other than their current spouse, or experiencing sexual assault, even before entering the present abusive relationship. Thirty percent reported witnessing their father beat their mother at least once and 33 percent directly experienced frequent physical punishment from parents or parent surrogates who slapped them with an open hand or hit them on the head or limbs with an object. Thirty-three percent reported being sexually assaulted prior to marriage.

Several women received, but chose to ignore, the warnings of future marital violence. Forty-nine percent of the women witnessed their husband behave violently either toward them or others at least once prior to marriage and 35 percent witnessed such violent behavior several times. Within three months after marriage, 40 percent had received their first taste of physical abuse; by the end of the first year, 67 percent had been battered. However, some (16 percent) did not experience an assault until after their first year of marriage; for others (16 percent), violence played no part in the marriage until they had been together for over three years.

Intimidation and threats reinforced the physical abuse in all cases. All the husbands yelled and screamed at their wives. In addition, many (85 percent) used some combination of banging on furniture or walls, kicking or throwing objects, or lashing out at the children.

Batterings occurred monthly or every few months for most of the women and ranged in severity from receiving a light slap or shove to losing consciousness. In most cases, arguments preceded the assaults and a barrage of cursing accompanied them. The women ranked the severity of the beatings they received on a scale from 1 to 10. The majority of the women (68 percent), having endured repeated blows, placed themselves in the mid-portion of that scale. Five women selected scale scores of 9 as a result of severe injuries, permanent damage, or gunfire. Almost all of the women feared that their husbands might lose control and kill them during the battering incident even though the actual severity of the abuse ranked lower on the severity continuum.

The women received numerous injuries to almost all parts of their bodies. Most injuries were to the head and neck and, in addition to bruises, strangle marks, black eyes, and split lips, resulted in eye damage, fractured jaws, broken noses, and permanent hearing loss. Assaults to the trunk of the body were almost as common and produced a broken collarbone, bruised and broken ribs, a fractured tailbone, internal hemorrhaging, and a lacerated liver. Damage to the extremities occurred least often and mainly took the form of bruises, sprains, and scratches to arms and legs, although one woman reported torn leg muscles and another was burned on the foot several times with a lighted cigarette.

Fifty percent of the women responding to the psychosocial inventory had received medical attention for injuries they sustained during the beatings. The other 50 percent of the sample felt that their injuries required treatment but were unable to seek the medical attention they needed either because their husbands would not allow it or because the women did not want outsiders to know about the beatings.

*Psychological Characteristics*

The scores on the personality test indicated that the battered women in this sample fell solidly within the average range on most of the personality and clinical factors measured. (See table 35–1.) They were of normal intelligence and comparable to the norms on the traits of dominance, enthusiasm, social awareness, self-reproach, and conservatism.

They tended to differ from the norms on six personality traits and three clinical factors. As a group, the women scored below the standardized mean scores on factors A, C, H, and Q3 (see table 35–1). This indicates reserve and caution in emotional expression, low ego strength and a feeling of being unable to cope, shyness and difficulty with self-expression, and low levels of self-sentiment. The only areas in which the women scored above the standardized averages were on factors Q2 and Q4. High scores on these traits signify self-sufficiency, introversion, tension, and frustration. Two other scores warrant attention: A low modal score on factor F and a high modal score on factor I suggest tendencies toward introspection and insecurity.

On the clinical test, three characteristics emerged that differed from the standardized averages. One involved factor D7, the tendency to withdraw and avoid interpersonal contact. Another, factor Pa (paranoia), indicated a belief that they were being mistreated or persecuted. The third involved factor Sc, schizophrenia, a tendency to retreat from reality and give way to sudden impulses. None of the findings is indicative of a clinically deviant population, but rather of a group that holds some distinguishing characteristics from a random sampling of women.

The overall profile depicts women with low self-esteem, a lack of self-confidence, and a tendency to withdraw. The women display an aloof quality, a critical or uncompromising attitude, and a sense of discomfort when interacting with others. The combination of shyness and reserve generally reflects traits developed in childhood as a result of poor early life relationships.

The women are also anxious and have trouble binding their anxiety. Interviews with the women revealed that they faced a great deal of situational stress in their marriages around such issues as finances, household responsibilities, employment, and child rearing. These pressures, combined with their consistent fear about their husbands' violent outbursts, contributed to high levels of tension.

It is important to note, however, that the test measures broad and relatively stable personality traits, and the women's difficulty controlling their anxiety does not necessarily originate in the marital relationship. In many ways these women are immature, lacking clear self-identities because of early deprivations in the form of emotionally restrictive and unstable family situations. The test results reveal an emotionality or sensitivity that leaves them feeling easily hurt, frustrated, perturbed, and overwhelmed. While growing up, they lacked the adult models to show them appropriate and rational ways to express or control their feelings and emotions. Perhaps during situations of marital stress, this sensitivity to threats and criticism contributes to existing disputes. For example, one twenty-six-year-old woman of Mexican origin reported that her Mexican-American husband frequently called her a "stupid wetback" and claimed that she was a terrible lover. The woman would respond to the name calling by crying and physically clinging to her husband, demanding that he hold and embrace her. His response to her clinging and whining was more verbal and physical abuse.

## Marital Relationship

Both the questionnaire and the interviews elicited information that highlighted the social, sexual, and power aspects of the relationship as well as offered insights into the women's motivations for remaining in the relationship. The following information is based solely on the women's perceptions.

Prior to entering the marital relationship, most of the women were dependent on others for their living arrangements. Only a third lived in their own apartments and half were supported by their own earnings. While some denied feeling pressured to marry, others believed that they were not attractive or popular, or worried they were getting too old to find a husband. Seventeen percent were pregnant when they married. Many women reported negative relationships with parents; they married, despite parental objections, so they could leave their parents' homes.

For the most part, the women displayed little social sophistication prior to marriage. They rarely entered into school or community activities. The majority dated fewer than five men, with a third of the sample dating no one else or only one person other than the abusing spouse. Forty percent knew the man three months or less when they married or began living together. They entered marriage with high, and unrealistic, expectations that it would solve all their problems.

Along with their high hopes, the women brought to the marriage very traditional ideas about marital behavior. Although almost all claimed that marriage is a fifty-fifty partnership, a large proportion also believed that the man should be the head of the house and that a woman's greatest joy is to be a wife and mother. In addition, a third of the sample clung to the notion that it is the wife's duty to obey her husband in family matters and to submit to him sexually whenever he wishes.

The balance of power in the relationship reflected the sex-role stereotyping. Decision making was unequally shared. Despite the fact that close to 60 percent of the men did not work continuously, in no case was housework the husband's responsibility. That task was part of the woman's domain even if she held outside employment. The men made the decisions about major expenditures such as appliances and automobiles whereas the women made the mundane decisions about grocery purchases and meal planning. However, bill-paying responsibilities usually fell to the women. The husbands also tended to direct the couples' social life. The men decided when they would go out or when they would invite people to the house. The men also frequently determined their wives' social or education activities. Several of the women said they had virtually no social life because of their husbands' extreme and unfounded jealousy. One woman reported that she was not allowed to see her female friends because her husband would accuse her of having homosexual relationships. Only twenty-three women reported being involved in any type of activity outside of the family. Many commented that they felt like prisoners in their own home.

According to the women, their husbands were not given to frequent demonstrations of affection such as hugging, holding, or kissing. During the early phases of the marriage, however, the women felt sexually satisfied. But, as the relationship deteriorated, so did their sexual pleasure until, toward the end of the marriage, the majority reported their sexual relations were very unsatisfying. In many instances the husbands forced their wives to engage in sexual activities against their will, and a third of the women claimed to have used sexual relations as one way to appease their husbands and prevent physical violence.

As a couple, their shared pleasurable activities were limited, consisting mainly of watching television or going out for a drink. The marital interactions were filled with disagreements, bickering, suicide or divorce threats, and separations. Prolonged arguments usually preceded the physical assaults. The husband's excessive jealousy most often served as the focal point for their disputes. One woman was beaten after talking to the mailman because her husband suspected that she was having an affair with him. Another woman said that she was only able to hold a job for a short period because her husband became jealous when she dressed up for work. He assumed she must be seducing her male bosses. However, several other issues also provoked disputes that led to the beatings. In order of frequency, they included the husband's drinking or use of drugs, finances, housework or child care, inlaws, the husband's work or lack of it, pregnancy, or the woman's jealousy.

Although 88 percent of the women did not believe they deserved the beatings they received, many did think their actions sometimes contributed to triggering the abuse. Sarcasm and shouting were among the most frequently mentioned. Far less prevalent, but occasionally mentioned, was nagging, sulking, silence, threatening divorce, refusing sex, kicking the husband, or throwing an object.

Over 80 percent of the women threatened divorce at least once and close to half considered suicide at some point after the physical abuse began. However, the majority followed neither course of action, preferring instead frequent periods of separation, usually lasting several days or weeks.

The personality makeup of the women and their ambivalence toward the husband clouded decisions to sever the relationship permanently. The women perceive themselves as reserved individuals, not quick to initiate action. They comment: "I was willing to just sit and take everything," or "People think they can run over me. I don't speak up when something's bothering me." They also envision themselves as good and generous, wanting to help and care for others. They view their husbands as men with problems, deserving of sympathy. According to one of the women: "I feel sorry for my husband. My mother says, 'How could you?' I think he's sick. Sometimes I used to hate him when he was doing those things [battering] but I have to feel sorry for him. I don't think he was doing it just for kicks. He had a real lousy childhood."

But fear at two levels also contributed to their indecision. At the interpersonal level, the men reacted with threats to retaliate if the women initiated police action or filed for divorce. However, at the intrapersonal level, the women feared the prospect of their own inability to survive independently from the husband. Taken together, all these factors produced a resistance to leaving a familiar, albeit painful, relationship.

## Treatment Considerations

Even though wife battering clearly indicates the existence of marital problems, it often cannot be treated with the usual forms of marital therapy. The men may deny that anything is wrong with the relationship and either refuse to participate in the treatment process or attend a few sessions as token demonstrations of their reformed behavior. Of even more importance is the potential physical danger faced by the women following conjoint marital sessions in which they air pent-up grievances or disclose information that may arouse their husbands' jealousy. Social workers who discount the violence in the marriage run the risk of exacerbating the situation and placing their female client in jeopardy. Therefore, the treatment procedures outlined below focus on the women and offer what, in the authors' clinical experience, seem to be the most effective interventive strategies, whether working with abused women who are in shelters or who are seen in outpatient settings.

Clearly, the experiences of battered women are not confined to violent marital episodes. Their reactions reflect perceptions and patterns of behavior developed during childhood and adolescence that interact with the conflicts and stresses of their marital situation. Treatment becomes complex when viewed from the needs of battered women and requires a multifaceted process of therapeutic interventions, which include the following components.

*Assess the Immediate Crisis.* The first step is to assess the immediate danger and crisis aspects of the situation. The woman's initial state of high anxiety and fear necessitates a supportive therapeutic response. She needs to feel that someone cares about her tense situation, wants to listen and help, and can offer a much needed sense of security. It is also essential during the first phase of therapeutic contact to assess the suicidal potential of the woman. The woman feels so overburdened and helpless that depression underlies most of her actions and suicidal ideation frequently occurs.

*Take an In-depth History.* An in-depth examination of the woman's marriage, her role in the marital relationship, her feelings about herself and the abusive spouse, and her childhood and adolescent experiences related to violence and separation is necessary for both client and therapist to reach any understanding of the problem confronting battered women. This is the place for specific and open-ended questions, rather than assumptions or guesses that can lead to premature closure. Because of their relative isolation and lack of input from sources outside the marital relationship, battered women may enter a therapeutic situation unaware of the severity of the problems in the marriage and the destructive potential of such problems for themselves and their children. For example, they may fail to connect the husband's excessive drinking, explosive violent displays, and forceful sexual demands to their own feelings of depression and low self-esteem or the various behavior problems that may begin to appear in the children.

*Know Local Resources.* Another aspect of the therapeutic process involves pointing out the alternatives and resources available for battered women. Many of the women in the sample were unfamiliar with agencies and services in their communities that could provide them with various forms of assistance. When working with women with minimal support systems, limited job skills, little or no income, and dependent children, it is incumbent on the social worker both to know the community's provisions for shelters, legal aid, medical assistance, financial aid, vocational training, and educational counseling, and to assist the women in their pursuit of such alternatives when needed.

*Increase Client's Mastery of Environment.* The women's high anxiety level should receive constant attention. They need involvement in a structured therapeutic program containing mutually agreed upon goals and objectives, which diminishes anxiety by increasing their mastery over their environment. Because for so long they occupied the victim's role, which depended on the initiative of others, battered women need to feel they are accomplishing some things on their own. Success attained independently of others will be a relatively new and surprising discovery. Continued self-understanding and progress toward constructive change increases if recognizable and concrete successes occur during the process.

*Encourage Emotional Monitoring.* Learning to overcome their emotional reserve and to express feelings appropriately are essential goals for battered women. Most battered women focus their attention on their spouse's problems and behavior, *his* motivations and feelings. With the exception of guilt and a sense of unworthiness, the women maintain little contact with their own feelings. Emotional monitoring, especially of anger, increases sensitivity to feelings and offers greater potential for emotional expression.

*Anticipate Ambivalence.* Throughout the treatment process therapists will be forced to deal with the women's ever-present ambivalence about whether or not to remain with the abusive spouse. It is not uncommon among any divorcing population for separation to occur more than once before the final termination. The majority of women in our sample had left their spouses more than once, and even after their stay in a shelter, many women returned. Most husbands were apologetic after the beatings and promised their wives they would never beat them again. One man was waiting in front of the doctor's office for his wife. He was openly weeping on bended knees with a crucifix in his hand, begging her to return. For women with fragile self-esteem, who are easily upset, and who already feel guilty about taking the children away from their father, it is not surprising that the return rate is high. Social workers who are aware of the tremendous difficulty that insecure battered women face in leaving their husbands should not be surprised or disappointed if the women decide to stay with, or return to, the abusing spouse. Instead, they should be prepared to help the women take the next step, whether that means marital counseling or leaving again. It is especially critical that battered women not be deprived of their therapist if they choose to remain with the husband.

*Offer Role Model.* The final component in the multistep therapeutic process involves the provision of a constructive role model for the women. Social workers can use their position as consistent and understanding adult figures to establish a much-needed trusting relationship. Because many of the women in the sample grew up in unstable or abusive families, experiencing a corrective relationship benefits the women by (1) allowing the recognition of nonconstructive behavior patterns, (2) offering new ways to perceive reality, and (3) providing the guidance required to act upon their environment effectively.

Because this treatment process is elaborate and difficult to accomplish through traditional therapeutic means, a differential therapeutic approach that applies the qualities and characteristics of each modality to the personality traits and needs of battered women is advocated. Therefore, crisis intervention might form an initial part of the treatment process, but not the entire course of treatment. Much of the needed support, security, and practical assistance may only be found in shelters for battered women. By providing a warm, supportive, familylike environment free from the dangers of physical abuse, shelters are conducive to helping the women bind their anxiety and express feelings without fear of reprisal from their spouses. Perhaps more than any other single form of intervention, they meet most fully the women's immediate needs. But that too, by itself, falls short of the ideal. Other therapeutic avenues stimulate additional forms of personal growth. For example, group therapy is especially effective for developing socialization and interpersonal skills as well as providing participants with feelings of acceptance, while individual counseling offers a more intensive and personalized therapeutic experience and a corrective relationship.

For maximum effectiveness, therapeutic contact with the women must extend beyond crisis treatment or brief respites at shelters and enter the realm of outreach programs, long-term therapy, and ongoing groups. Whenever battered women reach out for help they begin a process of personal and social change. It is extremely important that these women receive continuous support and understanding during this difficult period.

REFERENCES

Ball, M. 1977. Issues of violence in family casework. *Social Casework* 58:3–12.

Carlson, B. 1977. Battered women and their assailants. *Social Work* 22:455–460.

Cattell, R. B., Eber, H., and Tatsuoka, M. 1970. *Handbook for the sixteen personality factor questionnaire.* Champaign, Ill.: Institute for Personality and Ability Testing.

Delhees, K. H., and Cattell, R. B. 1975. *Manual for the clinical analysis questionnaire.* Champaign, Ill.: Institute for Personality and Ability Testing.

Deutsch, H. 1944. *The psychology of women.* New York: Grune & Stratton.

Dewsbury, A. 1975. Family violence seen in general practice. *Royal Society of Health* 95:290–294.

Gaylord, J. J. 1975. Wife battering: A preliminary survey of 100 cases. *British Medical Journal* 1:194–197.

Gelles, R. 1976. Abused wives: Why do they stay. *Journal of Marriage and the Family* 38:659–668.

Hanks, S., and Rosenbaum, C. P. 1977. Battered women: A study of women who live with violent alcohol-abusing men. *American Journal of Orthopsychiatry* 47:291–306.

Reynolds, R., and Siegle, E. 1959. A study of casework with sado-masochistic marriage partners. *Social Casework* 40:545–551.

Schultz, L. 1960. The wife assaulter. *Journal of Social Therapy* 6:103–112.

Snell, J., Rosenwald, R., and Robey, A. 1964. The wifebeater's wife. *Archives of General Psychiatry* 11:107–120.

# 36

# Wife Battering and the Maintenance of Gender Roles: A Sociopsychological Perspective

MARJORIE BAYES

One of the puzzling aspects of the battered-wife/abusive-husband situation is that the woman stays in the relationship, sometimes for many years. She stays even though she is physically damaged, humiliated, devalued, subjugated, placed in the role of helpless victim, and her psychological adult development is retarded or stopped. As research data indicate (e.g., Rounsaville, Lifton, and Bieber 1977), the husband is often controlling, possessive, jealous, restrictive. The women themselves are often puzzled as to why they remain. They may arrive at rationalizations of dubious plausibility, or they may cite their fear of the husbands' retaliation if they leave (Martin 1976).

A woman's remaining in such a relationship has been explained from a social perspective by her lack of resources and options and of economic and social supports. These factors are certainly real and relevant, but perhaps they do not completely explain the phenomenon. From a psychological perspective, the woman is often given the label of "masochist," used in the broad sense of describing a person who fulfills unconscious needs by taking the role of helpless victim in an interpersonal situation. Yet neither the social nor the individual psychological explanation alone seems sufficient to account for what occurs in the relationship and for the responses of others to the situation.

This paper addresses the tenacity of the battering relationship from a combined social and psychological viewpoint, suggesting that, at least in some battering situations, the psychological mechanism of projective identification is used by both partners in the male-female dyad in an attempt to establish and preserve socially dictated and strongly valued gender roles. The use of this mechanism has a binding effect upon the couple. In addition, other members of society, including therapists, interact with the couple in maintaining the battering situation because of the importance of the gender-role stereotypes. Wife battering, then, is behavior that is at the extreme of a dimension on which most men and women participate, the dimension of maintaining gender roles as a significant, perhaps central, aspect of social and personal identity.

## Gender Roles

Bayes and Newton (1978) have discussed the centrality of gender roles in society and in personal identity. Males and females are socialized in a context that both overtly and covertly defines gender roles as total roles. A total role is one that identifies a sense of self and a set of appropriate behaviors, including level and kind of authority, responsibility, and privilege. Gender roles are total roles insofar as they permeate all aspects of life and take precedence over other social roles incompatible with gender.

As is well known, the masculine role is defined by dominance, independence, and strength, while the feminine role is understood as passive, submissive, nurturant (Broverman et al. 1970). These gender roles are learned through early and continuous socialization.

Why are these specific gender roles so strongly held and reinforced in society? Why is it so important that females learn and maintain subservience? Bayes and Newton (1978) state:

The view, pervasive in the culture, that women should be powerless, nurturant, and submissive co-exists with, and is perhaps a response to, the fantasy that women are potentially more powerful and dangerous than men. Neumann (1955) presents substantial anthropological evidence that representations of female goddesses preceded representations of male gods. He discusses various artistic and mythological representations of the archetype of femininity. This archetype, portrayed for thousands of years, has three forms: the Good Mother, who is giving, nurturing, caretaking; the Terrible Mother, who is aggressive, devouring, ensnaring; the Great Mother, who combines all of these attributes.

Currently the essence of desirable femininity, culturally defined, emphasizes the Good Mother image and the avoidance of the Terrible or Great Mother, requiring that women repress or suppress or project anger and aggressiveness. It seems important to society to keep women in a nurturing but otherwise powerless role; this role becomes established as a social fact (Lerner 1974; Neumann 1954), perpetuated in the basic social structure and process of the nuclear family. (p. 8)

Various explanations of the fantasy of women's destructive power have been suggested. Lederer (1968), Harding (1973), and Horney (1967) present reviews of data attesting to men's fears of women throughout history and in many different cultures. Lederer notes that woman has become a symbol for animal nature and for the unconscious. Harding suggests that, early in civilization, the fierceness of the mother's defense of her young and "the voracity of her lust for the male" (p. 59) made women appear threatening and dangerous. Horney believes that the fear is rooted in the "mystery of motherhood," the primitive belief that one who gives life can also take it away.

Freud (1932), Horney (1967), and Lerner (1974) point out that the role of women as primary socializers of children means that women control the child's earliest satisfactions and frustrations, thereby becoming a target for the child's earliest anger and aggression. A child's experience of helpless dependency upon an all-powerful maternal figure arouses persistent affects that are then carried into adult life. Lerner persuasively argues that it is the defensive handling of these affects that leads to the gender-role stereotypes of "masculine" and "feminine" and to the devaluation of women.

As children mature, they must resist maternal authority and become independent. Continued subordination to maternal authority, particularly for males, is regarded with scorn. This has special significance for adult males' reactions to women. Men may feel compelled to challenge a woman's right to any authority, even to her authority over her own life. The fact that women also participate in their own oppression and deny their own authority has often been pointed out (e.g., Lerner 1974; Miller 1976), and suggests their fear of their own power.

We are confronted, then, with strong cultural pressures to maintain women in a powerless role. In response to these pressures, individuals within a male-female dyad are particularly affected, and must act to form and maintain their gender roles in relation to each other. But what is a woman to do with her assertiveness, anger, aggression? What is a man to do with his helplessness, dependency, passivity? Projective identification is one psychological mechanism used in the service of maintaining gender roles, and it may be used in extreme form in the wife-battering situation.

## The Use of Projective Identification

Melanie Klein (1952) describes projective identification as a primitive form of identification that establishes the prototype of an aggressive object relation. Characteristics of the self are split off, projected into another person, and consciously disowned. However, following the projection, the individual becomes locked into a relationship with the other person. An aspect of the self is located in the other person, with which one remains unconsciously identified. The projected parts of the self can now be controlled by controlling the other person. A compulsive bond is created. This process is also seen in a group that chooses a scapegoat to represent an undesirable characteristic of all members; the group then engages in extended attempts at controlling the scapegoat (Eagle and Newton 1977).

We may postulate that this mechanism is often used in the service of maintaining gender roles, which are an important aspect of social structure. In order to maintain these crucial social roles, individuals must engage in actions that rid the self of emotions and behavior contrary to role ideals. In a male-female dyad, the male may project into the female those aspects of the self, such as passivity and dependency, that do not fit his gender-role ideal. The female may project into the male her aggression and strength, which are unconsciously seen as very dangerous. Each then acts for and represents the other in these realms.

In order to easily maintain the gender-role ideal of dominance, men tend to choose women who are younger or who are their intellectual or social inferiors. Reciprocally, to maintain their subservience, women prefer men who are older or superior to them in various ways. There is evidence (Gelles 1974; Rounsaville 1977; Snell, Rosenwald, and Robey 1964; Schultz 1960) that in couples who maintain the wife-battering situation, the women often have superior personal strengths and resources, a circumstance unsuitable according to gender-role ideals. In such a case, a couple must either learn to be comfortable with the deviations from gender stereotypes or use various mechanisms, such as projective identification, to institute the "normal" male-dominance female-submission status. In the latter instance, the couple is vulnerable to an upset of the tenuous balance; when the gender-role balance is threatened, anxiety arises and action is taken to reestablish appropriate roles. Wife battering may be seen as an extreme example of such action.

When a woman has projected her aggression into her mate, she has also given up many elements of strength and power that she could otherwise mobilize on her own behalf. Klein (1952) notes that "the aggressive component of feelings and of the personality is intimately bound up in the mind with power, potency, strength, knowledge, and many other desired qualities" (p. 301). As a woman accepts the projection of the man's dependency, she believes that she cannot survive if she leaves the relationship; nor can she behave independently within it.

When psychotherapists work with a wife-battering couple within this conceptual framework, the task is to assist each member of the couple to recover and integrate those characteristics perceived to be contrary to gender role and to reduce the accompanying anxiety. One problem, however, is that therapists often do not work with the husband. A second problem is that therapists and others all too often act unconsciously as representatives of the social pressure upon men and women to "stay in role." When a wife does try to recover her own authority and assertiveness, the mechanisms of society intervene.

## Case Example

The following is a case example in which a married couple and several mental health professionals appeared to act in ways that maintained a longstanding wife-battering situation.

Mr. and Mrs. X approached a mental health center for help, at the wife's instigation. Throughout their forty-one years of marriage, Mr. X had frequently beaten Mrs. X. Mrs. X presented this as well as other issues of marital discord.

On one occasion several years earlier, when Mrs. X was preparing to take a trip to Europe by herself, Mr. X tried to attack her with a knife. Neighbors intervened. Mr. X then went on a rampage with the knife, causing several thousand dollars' worth of damage to household furnishings. He was adjudicated "temporarily insane," but Mrs. X would not press charges.

The couple was seen for six sessions in couples' therapy and discharged. The male therapist stated that the pattern of "longstanding marital maladjustment" was too tenacious. Mrs. X was described as "an intelligent, resourceful, manipulative woman with a hysterical character structure." Mr. X was described as "easily excited," with "a somewhat passive-aggressive character structure," who "feels himself being emasculated." He was less verbally skilled than his wife.

Four years later, they again presented themselves for therapy, with Mrs. X saying that her husband's intense and delusional jealousy and angry outbursts were "making her crazy." When she spoke of leaving him, she reported, he threatened to kill her. They were seen for ten sessions by a male therapist, who noted that Mrs. X "regularly attempted to get the therapist to sympathize with her and her suffering."

The husband's presenting problems were listed as more numerous and severe than the wife's, yet only Mrs. X received a psychiatric diagnosis—hysterical personality. The therapist stated that Mrs. X "is able to manipulate her husband into having jealous fits." Mr. X "becomes angry," and "because of his inadequate feelings where his wife is concerned, is easily manipulated to a position of looking like the culprit." At the conclusion of the couple's therapy, Mrs. X was referred for individual therapy and "the husband is discharged with the suggestion that he could enter into therapy if and when he desires so."

Mrs. X was seen in individual therapy by a female therapist. Mrs. X was outraged that her husband had been discharged. Her therapist joined her in insisting that Mr. X also be seen in therapy. A male therapist saw him for five sessions and discharged him, stating that change seemed impossible, that Mr. X "comes from a subculture of male dominance and feels himself emasculated and humiliated."

The wife and her therapist again insisted that Mr. X be readmitted. He was seen three times for evaluation by a male therapist, who then discharged him. The process was reinstituted by the wife's therapist. A male therapist met twice with Mr. X and told the wife's therapist that he planned to discharge him. The female therapist discussed the situation with the male therapist's supervisor, who agreed that Mr. X should indeed be seen in treatment.

Throughout this process within the clinical service organization, the male-female battle was picked up by the female therapist and the male therapists, who engaged in angry interchanges about the discharging of Mr. X. The woman insisted that Mr. X be seen, and the men insisted either that there was nothing wrong with him or that he was not an appropriate case for clinical services. At no time did a male clinician discuss the case with the female therapist before discharging Mr. X.

After the supervisor's intervention, Mr. X was referred to a female therapist, who saw him for several sessions and who then discussed the case with Mrs. X's therapist. The two therapists decided to have meetings in which both clients and both therapists were present. During these sessions, Mrs. X continued to insist that the marriage was maintained only because of Mr. X's threats to kill her if she left. It became apparent, however, that when Mr. X would move toward ending the relationship, Mrs. X would effectively prevent him from doing so. For example, when he was going to see an attorney about a separation, Mrs. X told him that the therapists had said they should talk things over first. He allowed himself to be persuaded not to consult the attorney. When this fact was pointed out by the therapists, Mrs. X was unable to see that her actions prevented a separation. The therapy continued for two months, at which time the couple announced that treatment had been very helpful and they wished to terminate it. Both therapists felt that little change had occurred, and that Mr. and Mrs. X were collaborating in a "flight from change." The couple has made no further contact with the therapists for over a year following termination.

In this case example, Mrs. X tenaciously saw herself as victim and was unable to acknowledge her own power in maintaining the relationship. Male therapists perceived her strength, but derogated it as "manipulation," seemed to sympathize strongly with the husband who was "being emasculated," and were unable to intervene in constructive ways. Mr. X, carrying the projections of force and anger, resorted to threats and violence.

In many ways, the society uses the wife-battering situation as an affirmation of appropriate gender roles, both by not providing the wife with social supports and resources and by not wishing to work with the husband at all. According to strongly held cultural dictates, the power of a woman must be restrained, and every effort is made to retain culturally defined gender roles of dominant male and submissive female. However, the blaming of the wife (Mrs. X was said to instigate and ultimately control her husband's behavior) represents a breakthrough of the belief in women's greater power.

## Summary

A woman is seen unconsciously by males and females alike as potentially very powerful and destructive. There is strong cultural pressure to subdue and control woman's power. The feminine gender role is established by society as submissive, passive, and dependent, and every effort is made to train women in such behavior.

In a male-female dyad, each member can deal with those characteristics of the self that are incongruent with gender role by projecting them upon the other. This process is one, not simply of projection, but of projective identification, wherein each remains identified with the projected aspects of the self in the other, forming a strong bond in the relationship.

When one or both partners begin to recover some of their projections—that is, to feel or act upon gender-incongruent aspects of the self—the accompanying anxiety in both leads to measures of restoring the balance. In the preceding case example, when Mrs. X felt strong and independent enough to undertake a long trip alone, Mr. X acted to restore his mastery and her subordinacy in dramatic fashion. In the wife-battering relationship, the technique of physical violence quickly restores the configuration of dominant male and submissive female.

Professional service providers, such as the police, judges, and therapists, function as agents of society, charged with enforcing social norms valued by the majority. They often enforce the norms of gender role. They may collude in a couple's task of maintaining gender roles, and at the same time reveal the general fear of female power that underlies the gender roles.

As in the case example, the wife remains in the situation to the extent that she continues to fear her own power and authority, to project them into her male partner, and to accept his projections of his helplessness and submissiveness. Each is then bound to the other through projective identification. If both partners can acknowledge their own complexity, unrestricted by gender stereotypes, they will no longer need the master-victim dichotomy and can either separate or rebuild their relationship in a different form.

## REFERENCES

Bayes, M., and Newton, P. M. 1978. Women in authority: A sociopsychological analysis. *Journal of Applied Behavioral Science* 14:7–20.

Broverman, I. K., et al. 1970. Sex-role stereotypes and clinical judgments of mental health. *Journal of Consulting and Clinical Psychology* 34:1–7. [Reprinted herein chapter 7.]

Eagle, J., and Newton, P. M. 1977. Scapegoating in small groups: A Sociopsychological, organizational approach. Unpublished manuscript.

Freud, S. 1932. Female sexuality. *International Journal of Psychoanalysis* 13:281–297.

Gelles, R. J. 1974. *The violent home: A study of physical aggression between husbands and wives.* Beverly Hills, Calif.: Sage Publications.

Harding, M. E. 1973. *Woman's mysteries: Ancient and modern.* New York: Bantam Books.

Horney, K. 1967. *Feminine psychology.* New York: Norton.

Klein, M. 1952. Notes on some schizoid mechanisms. In *Developments in psychoanalysis,* ed. M. Klein et al., pp. 292–320. London: Hogarth Press and the Institute of Psychoanalysis.

Lederer, W. 1968. *The fear of women.* New York: Harcourt.

Lerner, H. 1974. Early origins of envy and devaluation of women: Implications for sex role stereotypes. *Bulletin of the Menninger Clinic* 38:538–553. [Reprinted herein chapter 2.]

Martin, D. 1976. *Battered wives.* San Francisco: Glide Publications.

Miller, J. B. 1976. *Toward a new psychology of women.* Boston: Beacon Press.

Neumann, E. 1954. *The origins and history of consciousness.* New York: Pantheon Books.

————. 1955. *The great mother.* Princeton, N. J.: Princeton University Press.

Rounsaville, B. 1977. Perspectives on marital violence: Evidence from study of battered women. Unpublished manuscript, Yale University, Department of Psychiatry.

———, Lifton, N., and Bieber, M. 1977. Battered Wives: Experiences with screening and group psychotherapy. Paper presented at the American Psychiatric Association meetings, Toronto, Canada, May 1977.

Schultz, L. G. 1960. The wife assaulter. *Journal of Social Therapy* 6:103–111.

Snell, J., Rosenwald, R., and Robey A., 1964. The wifebeater's wife: A study of family interaction. *Archives of General Psychiatry* 11:107–112.

# 37

# Rape: Sexual Disruption and Recovery

## ANN WOLBERT BURGESS AND LYNDA LYTLE HOLMSTROM

Rape, long stereotyped as a sexual act, has recently come to be viewed more in terms of its violent aspects. The contemporary understanding of rape takes into consideration physiological functioning; power, anger, and aggression issues; and role socialization. However, rape, by definition, includes some sexual component, as Geis (1977) has noted in cautioning against the adoption of too narrow a focus on the violent nature of the behavior.

The sexual component of rape has received recent attention by researchers in terms of sexual dysfunction of the rapist (Groth and Burgess 1977), victims' subjective sexual response during rape (Holmstrom and Burgess 1978b), husbands' or boyfriends' initial reactions to the rape (Holmstrom and Burgess, in press), and marital adjustment (Miller, Williams, and Berstein, n.d.). Clinical reports of victim counseling, as in the following quote from our sample, also emphasize that, years after the rape, there may still be an association between current situations and the traumatic event:

[Are you able to enjoy sex with anyone now?] It depends how I relate to the man. If I'm in a position to enjoy it—a 50–50 thing—then I'm OK. But if I'm feeling that I'm only doing this for him and not for my own enjoyment, then I feel like the incident again . . . then sex is bad.

The impact of rape on a victim's sex life seems an important area for inquiry, with significant clinical implications. Thus an attempt was made to try to gain a clearer perspective on the subsequent sexual style of adult rape victims, whatever their marital status or living situation. This research was part of a longitudinal follow-up study of rape victims conducted by the same researchers who had provided the crisis counseling to the victims.

## Method

This paper reports part of a three-phase longitudinal study consisting of (1) an interview at the time victims were first admitted to the hospital; (2) short-term follow-up, by telephone or home visit, weekly for the first three months and then at six-month, nine-month, and one-year intervals, including accompanying victims to court; and (3) long-term follow-up by telephone or home visit four to six years after the rape.

The original phase of the research project on rape victims was started in July 1972. Over a one-year period, the authors were notified by the Emergency Department of the Boston City Hospital each time a rape victim was admitted, and went immediately to the hospital to gather data. The sample included ninety-two adult victims (ages seventeen to seventy-three) and twenty-three preadult victims (ages five to sixteen). In 1976 the authors began to contact these rape victims again. The sample for this paper consisted of eighty-one victims, 88 percent of the original adult sample who were reinterviewed (seventy-eight women) or for whom there were good indirect data (three cases). Three women from the original sample have since died; although there are considerable data on them, they are not included in the statistics for this paper. The adult rape-victim group represents a heterogeneous sample in terms of ethnicity, race, religion, social class, employment, education, marital status, and age.

It should be emphasized that the sample consists of victims whose rapes were reported. Other research has suggested that victims are less likely to report if the assailant is known (Smith and Nelson 1976), and that the reactions of women to rape by a known assailant may be different than to rape by a stranger, especially concerning the issue of trust (Bart 1975; Burgess and Holmstrom, n.d.).

In most cases, data for the initial and short-term follow-up project were collected by both authors. Typically one author interviewed while the other author took notes at the time of the victim's admission to the hospital. Data collection methods for the first two phases of the study are described in a prior publication (Burgess and Holmstrom 1979). Victims entering the criminal justice system were accompanied to court, and participant observation methods were used (Holmstrom and Burgess 1978a).

For the longitudinal follow-up study, the authors used a standard schedule of questions that were flexible and open-ended. Some questions asked during the initial interview and during the crisis counseling in 1972–1973 were repeated, and some new questions were asked (Burgess and Holmstrom 1978). For this paper, the four independent variables are (1) sex life prior to rape, (2) changes in frequency of sexual relations, (3) symptoms (flashbacks, discomfort with sex, aversion, and inorgasmic response), and (4) partner's reaction.

The dependent variable in our set of papers on recovery from rape is the time required for the victim to feel recovered. This paper looks at recovery in the specific area of sexuality. The overall classification of length of recovery is based on victims' answers to the following questions:

Do you feel back to normal—that is, the way you felt prior to the rape? If so, when did this occur? If not, in what ways are you not back to normal?

The data consist of subjective reports by victims of their own recovery over the intervening years. The definition of normal was left to the victims, rather than being decided by the authors. This approach provided variations in what victims themselves considered normal. Based on their reports, victims were categorized into three groups: those who felt recovered (1) in months; (2) in years; or (3) not by the time of the long-term follow-up, four to six years after the rape.

The majority of victims (74 percent) judged themselves recovered by the time of the long-term follow-up; half of these ($N=30$) felt themselves recovered within months, the other half within years. The smallest group of victims ($N=21$) did not feel recovered by the time of follow-up (Burgess and Holmstrom 1978).

## Prior Sex Life and Length of Recovery

In order to measure any change in sexual activity, baseline information is needed on victims' sex life at the time the rape occurred. In this study victims were categorized sexually active if they reported having had sexual relations within the six months that preceded the rape. Victims who had not been sexually active, and those who had never had genital sexual contact, were categorized separately. One of the victims who was not sexually active at the time of the rape brought to our attention the need for three separate categories, when she said:

I've had sex . . . I know people think if you aren't a virgin it is not as important . . . But there are lots of categories—not just virgin and nonvirgin.

As shown in table 37-1, most of the adult rape victims interviewed four to six years later (78 percent, or 63/81) were sexually active at the time of the rape. Of the remaining victims, 13 percent were not sexually active and the remaining 9 percent were virgins.

An issue that has been the subject of clinical debate is the impact of rape as a first sexual experience. Thus we hoped that our findings might help to determine whether a woman's sexual history influenced the length of her recovery from rape, and whether it would become a therapeutic issue. The data suggest that prior level of sexual activity does not affect length of recovery from rape. The stereotyped belief that recovery would be especially long for virgins was not supported by our findings. Rather, the data reinforce the contemporary view that trauma of rape involves considerably more than the sexual act; other factors can be identified that influence length of recovery (Burgess and Holmstrom 1978). As one victim, who took years to recover, said:

Having sex again didn't bother me. That was one thing I could separate out. . . . I never equated that rape was sex, so I never had trouble in my sexual life.

Despite the lack of association between prior sexual activity and length of recovery, of clinical importance are descriptive data from victims suggesting that sexual history can become a therapeutic issue in individual cases. One young victim, who reported that her recovery took years, had been raped at age seventeen by her boyfriend while on a date. She had not been sexually active earlier. She did not date

TABLE 37-1
*Sexual Activity at Time of Rape and Length*
*of Recovery, as Reported at Four- to Six-Year*
*Follow-up (N = 81)*

| Recovery Time | Never Active | Inactive | Active |
|---|---|---|---|
| Months | 2 (29%) | 6 (55%) | 22 (35%) |
| Years | 5 (71%) | 3 (27%) | 22 (35%) |
| Not yet recovered | 0 (0%) | 2 (18%) | 19 (30%) |
| Totals | 7 (100%) | 11 (100%) | 63 (100%) |

for well over a year, until after her graduation from high school. The one man she did date she eventually married three years after the rape. Not only did the marriage create psychosocial stress for this young woman, she also experienced vaginismus during intercourse and sought medical advice for her symptoms. She said:

The doctor told me I have tight muscles there. That is why it hurt so bad the first time [the rape] and why it still hurts a lot.

Sometimes objective indicators of victim recovery may mask the subjective indicators. In the case of one twenty-five-year-old woman, the objective indicators six years after rape included strong family network support during and following the rape, no major health issues, graduation from law school, and being in a partner relationship. The only unsettled area in her life she described as follows:

Enjoying sex is the exception rather than the rule. . . . My partner is very loving and understanding . . . couldn't ask for a better partner . . . he has tried everything . . . but I just get to a point and freeze.

## Resuming Sexual Relations

Following rape, victims are confronted with issues regarding sexuality. Sexually active victims are faced with (1) making a decision about resuming sexual relations, (2) having to deal with their own responses—psychological and physiological—to the sexual activity, and (3) the reactions of their partners.

### Frequency of Sexual Relations

A previous paper (Burgess and Holmstrom, in press) analyzed several coping mechanisms that facilitate recovery, such as changing residence as a way to cope with fears relating to the environment in which the rape occurred. It seemed useful to examine whether a change in frequency of sexual relations served as a coping mechanism for victims resuming sexual relations. Our data indicate that the majority of victims who were sexually active did alter the frequency of their sexual relations. Over two-thirds of victims (71 percent, or 45/63) decreased sexual activity, while only 19 percent reported no change. Change in frequency of sexual relations was not associated with length of recovery.

*Abstinence.* The most frequently reported change was abandonment of sexual activity. Following the rape, 38 percent (24/63) of the sexually active victims gave up sex for at least six months. These women made such comments as: "Didn't have sex for over a year," or "It was a long, long time." Several victims went years before deciding to have sex again ("I felt I could go on forever without sex."). And a few victims reported, on follow-up, that they had not had sex since they were raped.

*Decreased Activity.* The second most frequent change was a more modest decrease in sexual activity. One-third of the sexually active victims (21/63) reported a delay in resuming sex and a decrease in usual frequency. Sometimes delaying sex served to pressure the victim into telling her partner about the rape. Some victims would no longer initiate sex ("Only have sex when my husband wants it.").

*No Change.* Of the 19 percent of victims who reported no change in sexual frequency, 92 percent (11/12) reported themselves recovered by the time of follow-up. One might speculate that these women experienced minimal amounts of stress in resuming sexual relations, since they returned to sexual activity so quickly. However, of the twelve, only six also reported experiencing no sexual symptoms. The other six developed subjective and physiological symptoms, including flashbacks, worry about partner reaction, lack of orgasmic response, and aversion to specific sexual acts. Victims often said they were pressured to have sex by their partners or that it was the partners who wished to resume sex. In two cases, the partners wanted sex as soon as they were alone with the victims ("He made me have sex that night . . . said it was good for me to have sex.").

*Increased Activity.* A small number of victims (6/63) reported an increase in frequency of sexual activity. Sometimes the victims desired sex as a means of countering the negative experience ("That spurred me to want sex."). Another victim tried to explain her change in sexual activity as follows:

Right afterwards, I'd do things I wouldn't ordinarily do. It was strange . . . as though I lost all moral values . . . I suppose I was reacting to the rape but not consciously.

Victims spoke of an increase in frequency of sexual activity. ("After I moved, I got promiscuous. . . . It was like I was saying to myself, 'I'll have an upper hand now.' "), as well as indiscriminate selection of partners ("Had very confusing relationships . . . men and women and any type of sex."). Prostitution became a possible sexual style; as one victim said:

Tried prostitution about a year later . . . it is very mechanical. You don't think of men. You just want the money.

## Sexual Response

It was important, in analyzing victims' sexual responses *during* rape, to keep the physical and psychological (subjective) responses analytically distinct (Holmstrom and Burgess 1978*b*). Our follow-up data suggest the appropriateness of a similar approach, since most victims had difficulty on one or both levels in subsequent sexual situations. Thus they will be discussed separately: Overall, data clearly indicated that the more sexual symptoms that developed, the longer the recovery period for the victim.

*Subjective Reaction.* In any sexual situation, a negative psychological reaction to sex has the potential to develop into an aversion. Victims, on follow-up, described sexual aversion *physically* ("I shudder at the thought of sex."); *mentally* ("It is mental anguish having sex. Have to turn myself off."); *subjectively* ("Enjoying sex is the exception rather than the rule."); *in general* ("All sex is unpleasant."); as a *joint issue* ("The sex problem was in my mind and in his attitude."); and *affectively* ("Sex is boring.").

The subjective experience of enjoying sex may become an important issue following rape, even if it was not particularly important prior to the rape.

Before the rape, I didn't care much about my own pleasure as long as I had fun. Now I want things calm and gentle. That is a top priority. I need consideration and time.

Or, in contrast, disinterest in sex may be a subjective reaction ("I can take it or leave it. It is not a big deal.").

Flashbacks were frequently reported by victims. Some women described flashbacks while being alone and thinking of the rape—a non-stimulus-induced reaction—or when having a pelvic examination, as well as during sexual relations. Half of the sexually active victims (32/63) reported having flashbacks to the rape in a variety of situations, and the majority experienced the flashback during sexual activities. Flashbacks ranged from thoughts of the rape and the way that it happened to feelings that the present partner was the rapist ("I close my eyes and freak out with a substitution . . . then have to explain to my partner."). Victims reacted to general behavior ("I always get a chill or freeze up when someone whispers in the dark like the rapist did whispering for me to shut up.") and to the sexual behavior of partners ("My boyfriend was more forceful than I preferred and I started scratching at his chest like he was the guy.").

Victims described changes in the type of sexual activity they engaged in or avoided following rape. Over one-third of the victims (35 percent) were able to identify specific sexual acts that they now found distressing. Oral sex was most frequently identified (*N*=7) as upsetting ("Up until a year ago, oral sex was torturous."). Some victims found all types of sexual activity distressing, and three victims specified anal sex as upsetting. Two victims whose breasts had been handled during the rape could not tolerate anyone touching their breasts subsequently. Other victims listed specific acts that they associated with the sexual details of the rape: the smell of beer on their partner, sudden moves, having sex in the dark, a specific sex position, and certain body parts rubbed.

*Physiological Response.* Physical response to sex is multidetermined and complex. Many victims reported experiencing pain and discomfort on resuming sexual intercourse and difficulty experiencing orgasm. We realize that painful intercourse may fall under either subjective or physiological response. Because much of the data reflect pain, which in turn may affect arousal level and thus inhibit the physiological lubricating function, we have placed painful response to sex here.

Sixteen of the sixty-three sexually active victims reported pain or discomfort when resuming sexual relations. The medical condition of vaginismus involves an involuntary constriction of the outer third of the vagina, caused by spasms of the muscles in that area. Intercourse becomes painful and penetration is difficult or, in severe cases, impossible. Vaginismus may occur when there has been tissue damage to the genital area through lacerations in the supporting structures that separate the vagina from the bladder or rectum. Victims experiencing rape as their first sexual experience may be at high risk of developing vaginismus. There may be additional causes for painful intercourse, such as feeling tense prior to having sex, which could interfere with any lubricating physiological response. Victims associated pain with a psychological cause ("For four months it really hurt. Think it was psychological and I really didn't want sex."). There may be additional physiological trauma. One young married couple had great difficulty eradicating the gonorrhea that the victim contracted from multiple rapists ("Getting VD and passing it back and forth . . . got two shots and for two days in a row. Tested five days later and had to go another day for shots.").

Orgasmic changes are a problem for rape victims. Forty-one percent of the women (*N* = 26) reported having difficulty either experiencing any sexual feelings or being orgasmic during sex. It is important to determine if the lack of orgasmic response is rape-related or a condition that existed prior to the rape. Some victims who previously had difficulty reaching orgasm were particularly aware of the persistence of the condition ("I wasn't able to orgasm prior to the rape and still can't."). Others were quite clear that their loss of orgasmic response was rape-related.

Victims who are nonorgasmic may perceive the problem as physiological (One victim of a gang rape explained, "I was numb afterwards. Even now it isn't like it used to be. Still attribute it to the rape."). Sometimes the problem is seen as more emotional:

Hard to have an orgasm for quite a while. Felt uptight and uncomfortable. It was on my mind how uncomfortable I was and I couldn't concentrate or relax.

Some victims told their partners of their difficulty, while others did not ("I don't really enjoy sex. I fake a response."). Certain victims became resigned to their lack of physiological response to sex ("No orgasm since the rape.... I just go through the motions.").

## Partner Reaction

The theme of partner reactions was common in follow-up interviews. Disruption in a relationship was related to longer recovery, although the direction of cause-and-effect is still an open question. Victims talked of (1) their concerns and worries, which tended to inhibit recovery, and (2) the helpful things that partners did to facilitate their recovery. All except one of the adult victims—all of whom were female—had had male sexual partners prior to the rape. One victim exclusively selected female sexual partners; four victims described themselves as bisexual, and having had both male and female partners prior to the rape.

One interesting observation was the similarity between male and female sexual partners' reactions. Both men and women could react either positively or negatively. The woman who had an exclusive female partner reported that her partner reacted negatively and initiated disruption of the relationship. A bisexual victim described having sexual difficulty with both male and female partners following rape. In contrast, partners can react positively. Another bisexual victim said:

Feel comfortable with women for what I or they want. Don't see any difference in male or female partner since the rape.

*Worries and Concerns.* The victim may be preoccupied with concern about her partner's reaction and feelings. This preoccupation may contribute to her inability to relax and respond positively to sex.

Victims for whom there are data divided fairly evenly on the question of whether they had any worries regarding partners' reactions (30 no, 27 yes). The victims who had worries were concerned about how their partners felt about the rape. Victims themselves held various stereotypes and perceptions about male partners' reactions. Victims worried that partners thought it had been their *fault* ("I wonder if he was

457

thinking of it and if he thought it was my fault."); that they would not be *believed* ("Afraid he wouldn't believe me."); that they were *different* ("Would he think of me in the same way?"); that they would be suspected of having *enjoyed it* ("My boyfriend . . . did ask if I enjoyed it."); that they had had *sex with another man* ("Wondered what he thought about another man bothering me."); that they had *wanted it* ("He might think I was cheating on him or galavanting around and picked up this creep who brought along a lot of guys."); that they were *degraded and soiled* ("My worry was that a lot of times men think women are degraded and soiled after they are raped and the man turns against the woman."); and that they were *undesirable* ("Felt he would feel I was permanently soiled . . . just be undesirable.").

Some victims (11 percent) had such worries about partner reaction that they did not disclose the rape ("I didn't dare chance it and tell."). Other victims did not disclose the incident for additional reasons, feeling they had adequate support and did not believe it would aid the relationship.

In contrast, some victims who did not report any worries said that they always told subsequent sexual partners about the rape. They did this to see if the partner had an *aversion* ("Would always tell a partner first in case he had an aversion because I'd been raped . . . wouldn't want to have sex with the guy if he did."); was *liberal* ("Men I told were liberal. . . . I wouldn't date any man who thought I was unclean."); or was *prejudiced* ("Wouldn't care for a man if I had to worry what his reaction was.").

*Helpful Partner Reaction.* The most beneficial partner attitude was described as sympathetic understanding ("He was worried about me and supportive and wanted to help me."). Over half the victims reported this quality in partners, but in twelve of sixty-three cases it was the new partner ("My new partner was sympathetic . . . not like my boyfriend at the time.").

Victims were divided on the value of talking about the rape with their partners. Some women found it helpful ("He was concerned and wanted to know how it happened and how I felt. That made me calm. I wanted to tell him."). But some victims did not want to talk even if the partner did ("He wanted me to talk about it. I wanted to forget it and I wouldn't talk about it."). Although half of the victims commented on the strategy of talking, twenty-one were in favor and eleven were against the tactic as aiding in recovery.

Victims had comments to make on those aspects of partners' sexual style that they found helpful. Victims described a nonpressuring, gentle approach as the most beneficial. As one victim said:

In the first couple of weeks, it was good enough just to be close . . . didn't have to do anything physical. He was patient. . . . After that initial feeling of aversion died away, it was me who wanted it.

Another theme mentioned involved the victim assuming control of the couple's sex life ("Had sex when I wanted it.").

## Clinical Issues

A number of circumstances deserving of clinical attention were identified by victims during the sexual recovery process:

1. *Rape as a first sexual experience.* It is important to assess the value that the victim has placed on sexual activity in order to try to predict the magnitude of the sexuality issue following rape. One woman who had placed a high value on being a virgin when she married indicated on follow-up that the issue was still very much present ("My memory of the rape was how dumb I was. It hurt so bad and I had such dreams of how the first time would go. I was so idealistic.").

2. *Rape as an unresolved issue.* One victim who was raped at age fifteen by three teenage strangers, and raped a second time at age eighteen by an acquaintance, illustrates the severity of sexual problems that may result when the rape as a first sexual experience remains unresolved:

I don't think anyone recovers from it, especially when the first time they have had sex is a rape. That's what happened to me. Normal people experience love with sex. I never did. I will never recover.

3. *Victims not sexually active at the time of the rape.* Women who have been sexually active at some point in their lives may be inactive at the time they become rape victims. Many times these women decide to continue to abstain from sexual activity with a partner. However, when they do resume sexual relations, problems may arise ("Didn't have sex for two years. When I did, had a flashback and had the feeling of being raped again."). It is important to help victims anticipate some of the issues they may face when they resume sex, whether their resumption is immediate or comes weeks, months, or years later.

4. *Resuming sexual activity.* Victims may be helped to gain control over their sexual recovery by talking about their experiences. One victim who resumed sex immediately said of the experience:

I was afraid to have any sexual contact. I really didn't want any. It was two nights before I could even think of it. Even when we did have sex on the third night, every time I closed my eyes, the scene of the attack went through my mind.

The clinician can help to monitor the victim's reactions to resuming sexual activity, and can note the gradual decrease—or increase—in symptoms and problems. The victim may be overly concerned about resuming sexual relations and need reassurance that the experience went well. One victim who was not sexually active at the time of the rape began dating about a year later. She felt she had to tell her partner, because he said, "What's your story? You act awfully virginal." She told him she had been raped, and she described the first sexual contact with her boyfriend as follows:

I was really shaky. And afterwards I was relieved that I didn't feel the revulsion. But I cried and cried and cried for hours afterwards.

5. *Partner counseling.* Both victim and partner have to readjust to the disruption caused by the rape. The increasing professional trend toward providing counseling services to the couple should be supported. During the counseling, it may be learned that the partner is adding to the victim's sexual stress, as in the following case.

I delayed a couple of weeks, then felt I couldn't say no anymore. Sex repulsed me. He knew it. Kept pressuring me . . . probably thought he was doing it for my own good.

In this situation, the victim and her partner needed to talk about resuming sexual activity, and about the thoughts and feelings each had regarding the subject. Individual counseling with victim and partner might be appropriate, followed by a joint session to help negotiate sexual activity as well as issues in other areas.

6. *Intensification of sexual problems.* Not all victims reported having recovered sexually ("Definitely the sexual area was a hard area to deal with. I'm mentally OK, but not sexually."). For victims who have persistent difficulty in recovering their sexual equilibrium, additional referrals are indicated to clinicians trained in sex therapy and possessing a solid understanding of the physiological and psychosocial trauma of rape.

REFERENCES

Bart, P. 1975. Rape doesn't end with a kiss. Unpublished manuscript, Department of Psychiatry, Abraham Lincoln School of Medicine, University of Illinois, Chicago. (Abridged version in *Viva*, June 1975.)

Burgess, A., and Holmstrom, L. 1979. *Rape: Crisis and recovery.* Bowie, Md.: Robert J. Brady Co.

———. 1978. Recovery from rape and prior life stress. *Research in Nursing and Health* 1(4):165–174.

———. n.d. Rape: The style of attack and victim themes in recovery. Unpublished manuscript.

———. In press. Adaptive strategies and recovery from rape. *American Journal of Psychiatry.*

Geis, G. 1977. Forcible rape: An introduction. In *Forcible rape: The crime, the victim and the offender*, ed. D. Chappel, R. Geis, and G. Geis. New York: Columbia University Press.

Groth, A., and Burgess, A. 1977. Sexual dysfunction during rape. *New England Journal of Medicine* 297(14):764–766.

Holmstrom, K., and Burgess, A. 1978a. *The victim of rape: Institutional reactions.* New York: Wiley.

————. 1978b. Sexual behavior of assailant and victim during rape. Paper presented to American Sociological Association, San Francisco.

————. In press. Rape: The husband's and boyfriend's initial reactions. *Family Coordinator.*

Miller, W., Williams A., and Berstein, M. n.d. The effects of rape in marital and sexual adjustment. Unpublished manuscript.

Smith, L., and Nelson, L. 1976. Predictors of rape victimization reportage. Paper presented to American Sociological Association, New York.

# 38

# Development of a Medical Center Rape Crisis Intervention Program

SHARON L. McCOMBIE, ELLEN BASSUK,
ROBERTA SAVITZ, AND SUSAN PELL

Rape is a physical, social, and psychological attack upon the person. It is the fastest rising violent crime in the United States: The FBI reported a 68 percent increase in rape (from 31,000 to 51,000 cases) between 1968 and 1973, and police figures in Boston show a 43.5 percent increase between 1972 and 1973 (Federal Bureau of Investigation 1973).

Rape has been viewed primarily as a sexual rather than a violent assault. The traditional assumption is that the woman in some way invited the attack. This attitude obscures recognition of the trauma experienced by the victims and interferes with the development of adequate community and institutional resources to treat them. This is reflected in the absence or fragmentation of medical and psychological care for rape victims.

In response to this problem, a comprehensive support system for the rape victim has been developed at the Beth Israel Hospital, a metropolitan teaching facility oriented toward community medicine. Particularly in urban areas, hospital emergency rooms are the typical health care facility utilized by victims at the time of the rape. Prior to the development of our project, emergency room records showed that an average of one victim a week received medical care during 1972–1973. The psychiatric service was consulted only if the victim presented a management problem for the emergency room staff. Follow-up was generally inconsistent. Clinicians were impressed, however, by the number of women who appeared at the Psychiatry Clinic months or years later for whom the rape was a major component in the presenting symptomatology. At the time of the assault, these women had not sought psychiatric assistance. Indeed, many had never told anyone about the rape.

The Rape Crisis Intervention Program is based on the premise that early intervention can prevent the development of psychological and psychosomatic disturbances. The program's aim is to integrate and expand available medical services and provide psychiatric crisis counseling (Bassuk et al. 1975). This paper will describe some of the problems encountered in implementing such programs in a medical setting.

## Rape as a Legitimate Health Issue

There is both community and hospital resistance to recognizing rape as a legitimate health issue requiring medical and psychological services. In the past the psychiatric community has not participated in providing resources for victims. Throughout the country most services come from grass roots women's organizations, which often view psychiatry as a male-dominated, pathology-oriented profession that stigmatizes the victim by labeling her a mental patient.

Because hospitals have only recently acknowledged the needs of rape victims, feminist organizations have tended to regard these institutions as part of the problem. These women's groups have attempted to minimize the victim's contact with health professionals by establishing alternative facilities. However, there is no way to bypass the necessity for professional gynecological services. The medical, surgical, and psychiatric resources of the emergency room, their twenty-four-hour availability, and the legal requirement for medical evidence bring the victim into the health care system. Because of the multidisciplinary makeup of the general hospital, it is a potential center for comprehensive treatment of both the physical and emotional needs of the rape victim.

Hospital resistance to mobilizing supportive services can be traced to two major sources. First, staff prejudices about rape can jeopardize the respectful, thorough treatment of the victim. Second, staff working in a treatment model geared to respond to medical and surgical emergencies may underestimate the significance of emotional crises. If the woman does not exhibit wounds that testify to her victimization and unambiguously signal her need for medical assistance, her status as a legitimate consumer of health services may be questioned. Regardless of the presence or absence of physical injury, the emotional trauma of forced violation—frequently under threat of death—establishes the victim's right to sensitive professional care.

## Program Description

There have been four major objectives in the implementation of our service for rape victims:

1. Providing both immediate and follow-up counseling that is aimed at resolving the psychological crisis.
2. Encouraging emergency room personnel to respond sensitively to the emotional needs of the victim.
3. Developing an understanding of the special needs of this patient population in order to provide expert consultation to community and professional groups.
4. Conducting research on the acute and long-term impact of rape on life adjustment.

There are still many unanswered questions about the psychodynamics of rape trauma and the adult victim's reactions and long-term adaptation (Burgess and Holmstrom 1974; Fox 1972; Sutherland and Scherl 1970). To provide quality crisis counseling and assessment and to gather sound clinical observations, we needed mental health clinicians on the staff of our program. Because of this need and the funding problems we encountered, a volunteer counselor roster was organized. The counseling team is a self-selected group of volunteer personnel from psychiatry, social service, psychology, and nursing. This multidisciplinary approach distinguishes our program from the single-discipline model used in other hospitals (Burgess and Holmstrom 1973; Zuspan et al. 1974).

Training and supervising a multidisciplinary group of volunteers is complicated by the various levels of counseling sophistication that are represented in the team. Individual learning needs are addressed in weekly supervisory sessions based on the model used for teaching psychotherapy. All members of the counseling team are required to attend a series of weekly didactic seminars on crisis intervention techniques and the special problems of rape victims. Nurses, gynecologists, and other interested hospital personnel are encouraged to attend these meetings.

The volunteer model has proved to be cumbersome, unreliable at times, and difficult to coordinate. However, it has had the advantages of sensitizing a large number of hospital personnel to the emotional needs of the rape victim and of encouraging awareness of psychological issues in the treatment of all general hospital patients.

The twenty-four-hour on-call system insures that a counselor will be available to accompany the victim throughout all emergency room medical procedures. The initial role of the counselor is to provide emotional support and information to the victim. The counselor also meets with friends or relatives who have accompanied the victim to discuss their concerns and mobilize their support. Follow-up begins within forty-eight hours after the initial emergency room contact. Subsequent contacts are made at regular intervals for at least one year. The frequency and content of the intervention is based on the needs of the victim, as determined by clinical assessment and timing of anticipated periods of exacerbation of symptoms, such as court appearances.

The counseling goal is to increase the individual's adaptive capacity by delineating and working through the crisis-related issues. If the victim has unusual difficulty resuming her precrisis level of functioning, she is referred for psychotherapy.

## Organizational Interfaces and Policy Issues

Official sanction from the Department of Psychiatry was crucial to the implementation of our program. Staff time was requested for the recruitment, training, and supervision of the counselor team. Initially there was hesitation about supporting the program because of the demands on staff time. There was also a tendency to see rape as a social problem rather than as a crisis warranting psychiatric intervention.

Since crisis intervention techniques could be taught with rape counseling as a model, the program was consistent with the Psychiatry Department's commitment to training and its active hospital liaison program, which integrates psychological understanding with patient care

(Zinberg 1964). At the same time, the growing public awareness of the needs of women helped to offset objections stemming from the controversial nature of our target population.

The chiefs of social service, nursing, and medicine were approached to enlist their cooperation in personnel training and coordination of service delivery. This initiated a continuing dialogue with these departments carried on through periodic visits to their staff meetings.

In order to establish administrative backing, we had to develop a policy regarding payment for counseling services. Currently the woman is charged the routine fee for the emergency room visit and is not billed for the counseling services. The cost is absorbed by the hospital as loss of staff hours from the professional volunteers' regular duties.

There is a continuing debate as to whether the hospital, the community, or the victim should be responsible for the costs incurred. One argument is that, as in all preventive health care programs, the treatment of rape victims is cost effective in the long run. However, because of the economic recession and the rapidly rising overhead of hospitals, each program must demonstrate its cost effectiveness.

A variety of complex factors must be considered before an optimal financial policy can be determined. These include the following:

1. The majority of the victims are young, single women with low incomes, inadequate health insurance, and doubtful ability to pay.
2. Some of the medical procedures are for the collection of evidence for the state's case against the alleged criminal rather than for the victim's health care.
3. There is clinical concern about the meaning transmitted to the victims when they are set apart from other consumers of health care who pay for services.

## Gynecology and Emergency Room Liaison

We have emphasized liaison with the gynecology and emergency room staffs. The mechanics of the gynecological examination are usually handled with skill (Halleck 1962). However, anxiety about how to respond to a woman who has just been raped can lead to staff withdrawal or denial of the event. Female staff members are reminded of their own vulnerability. Male staff members become acutely conscious that they may be the first man the victim sees after the rape. The victim's anger and helplessness are frightening, and there is a tendency to counterattack or to infantilize.

The medical examination of the rape victim occurs in the interface between the health and legal professions, since the physician's findings may become evidence in a court of law (Evrard 1971). Since the doctor can be required to give testimony, he may hesitate to become involved or may respond by trying to judge for himself whether the case is a "real" rape.

The protocol of the American College of Obstetricians and Gynecologists (1970) for the examination of rape victims is a detailed procedure for the gathering and preservation of specimens for evidence. It has the advantage of providing complete and careful documentation. Nevertheless, in the pressures of the emergency room, it may be regarded as a tedious chore. Other factors affecting the physician's response to the rape victim are his concept of his professional role, his personal feelings about rape, and his attitudes toward the legal and penal systems.

Gynecology and nursing meetings have been used as forums to identify and discuss staff concerns. Treating victims of violent sexual assault is openly acknowledged as stressful. Through the use of videotaped interviews with victims, role playing, and discussion, personnel are sensitized to the stresses the victim experiences in the emergency room.

When a woman who has recently been raped takes on the label of patient, she is assuming a role characteristically associated with being damaged and helpless. The victim-as-patient assumes a status that reinforces the helplessness and fears about being damaged that are natural sequelae of the rape experience. Her physical and emotional pain become tangible reminders of her inability to protect and to defend herself. The confusion and lack of privacy in the emergency room can prolong and compound her discomfort. A pelvic examination done abruptly can be experienced as a repetition of internal invasion. The hospital becomes an institutional transference object upon which both negative and positive feelings are focused. The staff must be equipped to deal with the intense affects aroused and to help the victim work through them. The rape crisis counselor is a consultant to medical and nursing staff in the emergency room, and his or her interpretation of the victim's behavior and empathy with the medical staff's feelings reduce anxiety and enhance sensitive treatment of the patient.

The introduction of a new program staffed by nonemergency-room personnel into the routine emergency room system has presented several unsolved problems. For example, while our counselors relieve the nurses of certain pressures and responsibilities, there is also a mixed message about the nurses' role and competency. Although we have explicitly invited them to be trained as rape counselors, few are able to do so because of the demands of their regular duties. We have approached this difficulty by including an emergency room nurse as a member of the program's administrative and planning group; this has resulted in an improved cooperative team effort and, secondarily, has supported nurses' continuing efforts to expand their role.

## Discussion

Although our program is still in the experimental phase, progress has been made in establishing rape as a legitimate health issue and in including the care of rape victims among the repertoire of services provided within a medical center. The liaison work has been essential in successfully setting up a multidisciplinary program of this kind. The most important interfaces have been with the Departments of Psychiatry, Nursing, and Gynecology. Our continuing dialogues with these departments have emphasized the generalizability of our crisis approach to other patients.

As organizational issues are settled, the program will increasingly concentrate its efforts on developing research on the long-range resolution of the rape crisis and will attempt to differentiate the implications for women at various stages in the life cycle. This information is critical for optimally effective service and for evaluation of the preventive impact of early intervention on later adjustment. The didactic series used in teaching our counselors is being refined and compiled into a training manual for use by other hospitals. The Rape Crisis Intervention Program is rapidly becoming a resource center for the community through consultation and education programs for police, educators, health professionals, and the public. Our aim is to encourage and assist other community medical facilities in providing a support system for women dealing with this life crisis.

REFERENCES

American College of Obstetricians and Gynecologists. 1970. *Technical Bulletin Number 14.* Chicago: ACOG.

Bassuk, E., et al. 1975. Organizing a rape crisis program in a general hospital. *Journal of the American Medical Women's Association* 30:486–490.

Burgess, A., and Holmstrom, L. 1973. The rape victim in the emergency ward. *American Journal of Nursing* 73:1741–1745.

————— . 1974. Rape trauma syndrome. *American Journal of Psychiatry* 131:981–986.

Evrard, J. 1971. Rape: The medical, social and legal implications. *American Journal of Obstetrics and Gynecology* 111:197–199.

Federal Bureau of Investigation. 1973. *Uniform crime reports for the United States*. Washington, D.C.: U.S. Government Printing Office.

Fox, S. 1972. Crisis intervention with rape victims. *Social Work* 17:34–42.

Halleck, S. 1962. The physician's role in the management of victims of sex offenders. *Journal of the American Medical Association* 180:273–278.

Sutherland, S., and Scherl, D. 1970. Patterns of response among victims of rape. *American Journal of Orthopsychiatry* 40:503–511.

Zinberg, N., ed. 1964. *Psychiatry and medical practice in a general hospital*. New York: International Universities Press.

Zuspan, F., et al. 1974. Alleged rape: An invitational symposium. *Journal of Reproductive Medicine* 12:133–152.

# 39

# The Rape Victim: Psychodynamic Considerations

## MALKAH T. NOTMAN AND CAROL C. NADELSON

The experiences that we call rape range from surprise attacks with threats of death or mutilation to insistence on sexual intercourse in a social encounter where sexual contact is unexpected or not agreed upon. Consent is crucial to the definition of rape. The importance of mutual consent is often overlooked and misinterpreted; many people assume that certain social communications imply willingness for a sexual relationship. Although men, women, and children are raped, the majority of rape victims are women; this paper will focus on understanding rape as a psychological stress for the woman victim.

Burgess and Holmstrom (1974) divided the rape victims they studied into three groups: (1) victims of forcible completed or attempted rape, (2) victims who were "accessories" because of inability to consent, and (3) victims of sexually stressful situations where the encounter went beyond the woman's expectations and ability to exercise control. Despite the different circumstances, the intrapsychic experiences of rape victims in all categories have much in common.

The rape victim usually has had an overwhelmingly frightening experience in which she fears for her life and pays for her freedom in

470

the sexual act. Generally this experience heightens a woman's sense of helplessness, intensifies conflicts about dependence and independence, and generates self-criticism and guilt that devalue her as a person and interfere with trusting relationships, particularly with men. Other important consequences of the situation are difficulty handling anger and aggression and persistent feelings of vulnerability. Each rape victim responds to and integrates the experience differently depending on her age, life situation, the circumstances of the rape, her specific personality style, and the responses of those from whom she seeks support.

## Rape as a Stress

Rape can be viewed as a crisis situation in which a traumatic external event breaks the balance between internal ego adaptation and the environment. Since it is an interaction between an extreme environmental stimulus and the adaptive capacity of the victim, rape is similar to other situations described in the literature on stress, including community disasters (Tyhurst 1951; Lindemann 1944), war (Glover 1941, 1942; Schmideberg 1942; Rado 1942), surgical procedures (Deutsch 1942; Janis 1958), and so on. The unexpectedness of the catastrophe and the variability of victims' resources for coping with an experience that may be viewed as life-threatening are critical factors in rape, as in other crisis situations.

Although there are cultural and personality style differences, descriptions of stress reactions generally define four stages, which vary in intensity and duration (Weiss and Payson 1967). These responses, listed below, are also found in rape victims.

1. *Anticipatory or threat phase.* In this stage, anxiety facilitates perception of potentially dangerous situations so that they can be avoided. Most people protect themselves with a combination of defenses that maintain an illusion of invulnerability, with enough reality perception to allow them to protect themselves from real danger. When a potential stress is planned (i.e., elective surgery), an individual can protect his or her ego integrity by strengthening those defenses that will ward off feelings of helplessness.

2. *Impact phase.* Varying degrees of disintegration may occur in a previously well-adapted person during this second phase, depending on the degree of trauma and the adaptive capacity of the individual. There may be major physiological reactions, including vasomotor and

sensorial shifts. Tyhurst (1951) reported on the extremes of fire and flood victims' reactions, which ranged from "cool and collected" to "inappropriate" responses, with "states of confusion, paralyzing anxiety, inability to move out of bed, hysterical crying, or screaming." The majority of these victims showed variable but less extreme responses—they were "stunned and bewildered" and demonstrated restricted attention and other fear responses, such as automatic or stereotypical behavior. This picture is also seen in rape victims.

3. *Posttraumatic or "recoil" phase.* Emotional expression, self-awareness, memory, and behavioral control are gradually regained in the recoil phase. However, perspective may continue to be limited and dependency feelings are increased. The individual perceives adaptive and maladaptive responses in him/herself and may question his/her reactions. A positive or negative view of one's ability to cope may affect the course of resolution of the trauma and future capacity to respond to stress, and self-esteem may be enhanced or damaged.

Group support during this phase enables the victim to feel less isolated and helpless. Obviously, the rape victim, who is usually alone during the attack, can only hope for support later. Women are often disappointed by the failure of family, friends, and the community to validate their experience.

Janis (1958), in his study of surgical trauma patients, noted that any threat that cannot be influenced by the individual's own behavior may be unconsciously perceived in the same way as were childhood threats of parental punishment for bad behavior. This results in attempts to control anger and aggression in order to avoid provoking "punishment." The absence of overt anger is also a very prominent finding in rape victims.

4. *Posttraumatic reconstitution phase.* A process occurs during this phase that may alter future life adjustment. The loss of self-reassuring mechanisms that had fostered a sense of invulnerability may result in a decrease in self-esteem. The victim then blames him- or herself for lack of perception or attention to danger. Kardiner and Spiegel (1941) studied war stress and stated, "As soon as fear is directed inward in the form of questioning the individual resources to cope with external danger, or toward the group in the form of questioning its ability to be a protective extension of the individual, then a new and more serious danger situation is created." Maladaptive responses have been reported in the war neuroses of World War II (Kardiner 1941), in which the individual develops mechanisms that are protective against further exposure to trauma but are psychologically costly and may involve loss of pride and self-esteem (Grinker and Spiegel 1945).

The rape trauma syndrome described by Burgess and Holmstrom (1974) can be considered a form of stress reaction that can lead to traumatic neurosis. They reported an acute disorganizational phase with behavioral, somatic, and psychological manifestations and a long-term reorganizational phase with variable components depending on the ego strength, social networks, and specific experiences of the victim. They focused on the violent life-threatening aspects of the crime. Two types of response they noted are: "the expressed style," in which the victim is emotional and visibly upset, and the "controlled style," in which denial and reaction-formation seem to be the most prominent defenses. They also described feelings of shock and disbelief in many victims and the prevalence of guilt and self-blame in the initial phase. The reconstitution phase varies considerably with each individual; however, the patterns of response appear to be similar to those reported in the other types of stress reactions we have discussed.

## The Dynamics of the Response to Rape

The important considerations in understanding the dynamics of women's responses to rape are (1) affects, (2) unconscious fantasies, and (3) adaptive and defensive ego styles.

### Anger

A striking phenomenon in rape victims is the initial display of fear, anxiety, guilt, and shame—but little direct anger. There are several probable reasons for this.

1. Since rape may evoke memories of childhood threats of punishment for misdeeds (Janis 1958), the victim may feel that she is being punished or is in some way responsible. Her anger may be repressed and experienced as guilt and shame, despite her concomitant feelings of helplessness and vulnerability. Most of the angry feelings appear later in recurrent nightmares, explosive outbursts, and displacement of anger as the woman attempts to master the assault.

2. Expression of aggression in women has been highly conflictual because of cultural restrictions and expectations of passivity and greater compliance for women. Women have often tended toward a masochistic orientation, in which anger is transformed into culturally supported patterns of self-blame. Identification with the aggressor, a mechanism that serves as an attempt to gain mastery, may also make it difficult to acknowledge anger toward the rapist.

3. The socially reinforced suppression of aggression in women has a

possible adaptive function, since women are usually smaller and physically weaker than men. Therefore, not responding with a counterattack may prove beneficial. This is an important consideration in understanding the concept of consent. In the past, legal expectations included evidence of force or a struggle in order to establish rape. Current laws accept threat of force as sufficient, recognizing that a woman may submit in fear rather than risk fighting and being overcome.

## Guilt and Shame

Despite the varying circumstances of rape and the different degrees of violence, surprise, and degradation involved, guilt and shame are virtually universal. The tendency to blame the victim, thereby assigning responsibility to her, fosters guilt and prevents her from adequately working through the crisis. It is common for a rape victim to feel that she should have handled the situation differently, regardless of the appropriateness of her actual response. Concerns about the amount of activity or passivity that might have prevented the attack or the rape are frequent. The assumption is that the woman should or could have handled the situation better, that her unconscious wishes perhaps prevented more appropriate assessment and more adaptive behavior.

The guilt of the victim is further increased by focusing on the sexual rather than the violent aspect of the experience. Although aggression is most prominent in the victim's perception, society regards rape as sexual. Since longstanding sexual taboos still persist for many people, even an unwilling participant in a sexual act is accused and depreciated. The popular adage that advises the woman who cannot avoid rape to "relax and enjoy it" misconstrues the attack as a sexual experience. In reality, the rape experience is depersonalizing and dehumanizing. The woman is often a faceless object for the rapist's expression of hostility, and the victim feels degraded and used. Furthermore, since women are expected to exert impulse control in sexual encounters, the rape victim's sense of failure in setting limits, impossible though this may have been, contributes to her guilt.

## Unconscious Fantasies

The question of unconscious wishes translated into provocation of a rape must be seriously considered. While undoubtedly there are unconscious fantasies in which rape plays a part, and some women do have fantasies in which submission to a stronger man may be linked with forbidden oedipal wishes, on the conscious level the woman knows she is submitting because any other behavior would result in real danger to her life. However, this is not so clearly differentiated in the unconscious. The universality of rape fantasies certainly does not make every woman a willing victim—or every man a rapist. The unconscious fantasy does not picture the actual violence of the experience.

An individual's defensive organization usually protects him or her from acting out such fantasies. However, if the defensive barrier breaks down and unconscious destructive, aggressive, or masochistic wishes gain expression, anxiety over the loss of control combines with guilt regarding the impulses. Rape involves an overwhelming confrontation with another individual's sadism and aggression and one's own vulnerability. This challenges the woman's confidence in her ability to maintain her defenses and controls.

Many women feel some ambivalence toward men as a result of past developmental experiences. Women expect men to be their protectors and providers, as well as relating to them sexually. Men may also be seen as potential aggressors and exploiters, and the experience of rape confronts the woman with this violent potential. The betrayal by the supposed protector who turns aggressor has a profound effect. Almost all rape victims say they trust men less after the rape. All men may be suspect, and all are potentially on trial. Uncertainty about one's ability to control the environment reverberates with concerns about the ability to control and care for oneself.

## Men's Responses to Rape

It is important to consider the responses of men who participate in discussions about rape. They often feel indignation and sometimes identify with both the victim and aggressor. They may feel their masculinity is violated by both the attack on a woman who is felt to "belong" to them and by their own helplessness deriving in part from early feminine identification as well as from their actual failure to have prevented the attack. This may be particularly threatening to men who need to reject any latent feminine components of their own personalities and may lead to a defensive identification with the rapist in an attempt to escape the anxiety of their own sense of vulnerability. Some men have difficulty coping with the impulse for revenge, which would reestablish their sense of control and the ability to protect "their" women.

A man whose daughter, girl friend, or wife has been raped may react by becoming overprotective, partly as a result of his sense of guilt for not having been protective enough. However, it may also evolve as a defensive means of handling his anger at the attacker of ·

"his" woman and at the woman for having allowed herself to get in this position. A complex series of feelings about his own sexual impulses may be evoked, and a man may find himself unable to be supportive or helpful to the woman after the rape, despite a previously close relationship. He may have difficulty with his own rape fantasies, his concerns about "used merchandise," and even the breakthrough of homosexual impulses. He may withdraw from the woman as a result of this anxiety. The woman who is deprived of support from a man who is important to her is particularly vulnerable to adverse reactions after a rape. The man may be unaware that he is not supportive, since denial operates to minimize the experience so it can be forgotten.

## Life Stage Considerations

It is difficult for anyone to predict how he or she will actually behave in a crisis. In the state of panic evoked during a rape, most women think about how to behave to avoid being physically injured or killed. Some talk, some resist, and others become passive, depending on their assessment of what is going on and their past styles of managing stress (Burgess and Holmstrom 1976). There are, however, some specific issues related to age and life stage.

### The Young Single Woman

The single woman between the ages of seventeen and twenty-four is the most frequently reported rape victim. She is vulnerable often by virtue of being alone and inexperienced. Her relations with men have frequently been limited to the trusted, caring figures of her childhood or the young men she dated in high school. She enters the adult world with little sophistication in some of the nuances of human interaction, and she may easily become involved in an unwelcome sexual encounter. In this age group, the frequency with which rape victims report prior knowledge of the rapist is striking, and this is often the reason for a victim's refusal to prosecute. A young woman may have been raped by a date, an old friend, or even an ex-husband, and she often reproaches herself because she should have "known better" or been more active in preventing the rape.

As was discussed earlier, feelings of shame and guilt are prevalent regardless of the circumstances of the rape; coupled with the victim's sense of vulnerability, these feelings color the victim's future relationships with men. This is especially true for the very young woman who may have had her first sexual experience in the context of violence and degradation.

The experience of rape may revive concerns about separation and independence. A young woman's sense of adequacy is challenged when she asks, "Can I really take care of myself?" Parents, friends, and relatives often respond with an offer to involve themselves in taking care of her again. Although the offers may be supportive and reassuring, they may also foster regression and prevent mastery of the stress and conflict evoked by the experience.

Problems for the younger rape victim also affect her perception of and tolerance for gynecological examination. She may have suffered physical trauma, she is susceptible to venereal disease, and she may become pregnant. An examination is indicated, but it may be perceived, especially by an inexperienced or severely traumatized woman, as another rape. She is concerned about the intactness and integrity of her body and wants reassurance. However, she may have difficulty dealing with the necessary procedures if they stimulate memories of the original rape experience.

## The Divorced or Separated Woman

The divorced or separated woman is in a particularly difficult position because she is more likely to be blamed and have her credibility questioned. Her life-style, morality, and character are frequently questioned. Her apparent sexual availability makes her seem more approachable sexually. She may experience the rape as a confirmation of her feelings of inadequacy, and she is especially likely to feel enormous guilt that can lead to failure to obtain aid or to report the crime. Her ability to function independently is challenged. If she has children, she may worry about her ability to protect and care for them, and others will probably raise questions about her adequacy as a mother. The woman with children must deal with the problem of what, how, and when to tell them about the rape. If the event is known in the community, its implications for her and her children may be difficult to manage.

## The Middle-aged Woman

For the middle-aged married woman, issues of her ability to have control and her concerns about independence are particularly important. She is often in a period of critical reassessment of her life role, particularly in the face of changed relationships to her grown-up children. Husbands in their own midlife crises are often less responsive and supportive to their wives' sexual and emotional needs.

There is a common misconception that a woman, married or single, who is past her most sexually active period has less to lose than a younger woman. One cannot quantify the self-devaluation, feelings of worthlessness, and shame in any woman—especially a woman who may already be concerned about her sexual adequacy.

## Attitudes of Professionals

Until recently many psychiatrists felt that rape was not a psychiatric issue and that psychiatrists had little to offer the rape victim. They often shared the view that the victim "asked for it," and she was seen as acting out her unconscious fantasies and therefore was not a "true victim." Thus the woman who had been raped did not receive the empathy and understanding usually extended to people in a crisis. There is also the common belief that many accusations of rape are false. We have not found this to be true in the majority of cases seen at the Rape Crisis Intervention Program at Beth Israel Hospital, nor have others in this field with whom we have spoken.

Professionals have shared the image of the rape victim as a young, sexually attractive woman who in some way exposes herself to an avoidable danger or uses the accusation of rape to save herself from criticism. This view of rape implies that it happens only to marginal people, who collude in some way, and this idea fulfills several functions. It protects the individual who accepts the view from anxiety about his or her feelings of vulnerability. It is also another way to deny that rape occurs and that its incidence is increasing. This defensive position is further expressed by the focus on the sexual aspect of rape. If it is sexual, then one can think that the victim and the rapist were both seeking sexual gratification. The professional is thus protected from any sense of guilt or responsibility.

In our own experience in the development of a rape crisis program at Beth Israel, we saw a change of attitudes in participating professionals. An increase in interest results in recognition of the crisis nature of the experience and increased dignity for the individual victim.

# Consequences of Rape

Attention to the long-term effects of rape is important. It is difficult to predict all the long-term needs of the rape victim, since the working out of the trauma proceeds in many different ways. The feelings aroused may lead to behavior that seems out of character and would be puzzling if it were not for the rape. Some of the issues that reemerge in some women at a later time are (1) mistrust of men, with consequent avoidance or hesitation; (2) a variety of sexual disturbances; (3) phobic reactions to situations that are reminiscent of the rape; and (4) anxiety and depression, often precipitated by seemingly unrelated events that in some small details bring back the original trauma.

# Counseling Considerations

Counseling of rape victims should involve an assessment of previous adjustment, including stress tolerance and adaptive resources. In addition, it is also important to learn whom in her environment the victim views as supportive and to attempt to involve these people if possible.

The woman in this situation needs support and reassurance about the way in which she handled the encounter and her efforts to cope afterward, even if she seems volatile, disorganized, or guilty. Negative countertransference feelings may be evoked if she displaces her anger onto those who are attempting to help—for example, friends, doctors, or the police. It is important that she have the opportunity for constructive catharsis with a caring and empathic person. The counselor's patience may be tested by the victim's repetitive retelling of the story. The counselor may need to be available frequently for the more overtly upset rape victim. The more subdued victim may need to be encouraged to communicate and should be offered the opportunity for future counseling.

Each woman presents special considerations and requires the acknowledgment and support of the counselor in verbalizing and working through the complex problems she faces. The young woman needs help in confronting her family, her relationships with men, and her feelings about her sexuality; the woman with children must deal with her communication with them; and the older woman may have to face her sexual anxiety more openly.

REFERENCES

Burgess, A. W., and Holmstrom, L. L. 1974. Rape trauma syndrome. *American Journal of Psychiatry* 131:981–986.
———. 1976. Coping behavior of the rape victim. *American Journal of Psychiatry* 133:413–418.
Deutsch, H. 1942. Some psychoanalytic observations in surgery. *Psychosomatic Medicine* 4:105–115.
Glover, E. 1941. Notes on the psychological effects of war conditions on the civilian population: I. The Munich crisis. *International Journal of Psycho-Analysis* 22:132–146.
———. 1942. Notes on the psychological effects of war conditions on the civilian population: III. The blitz. *International Journal of Psycho-Analysis* 23:17–37.
Grinker, R., and Spiegel, I. 1945. *Men under stress.* Philadelphia: Blakiston.
Janis, I. L. 1958. *Psychological stress.* New York: Wiley.
Kardiner, A. 1941. *The traumatic neuroses of war.* Psychosomatic Medicine Monograph II–III. Washington, D.C.: National Research Council.
———, and Spiegel, H. 1941. *War stress and neurotic illness.* New York: Hocher.
Lindemann, F. 1944. Symptomatology and management of acute grief. *American Journal of Psychiatry* 101:141–156.
Rado, S. 1942. Pathodynamics and treatment of traumatic war neurosis (traumatophobia). *Psychosomatic Medicine* 4:362–369.
Schmideberg, M. 1942. Some observations on individual reactions to air raids. *International Journal of Psycho-Analysis* 23:146–176.
Tyhurst, J. S. 1951. Individual reactions to community disaster: The habitual history of psychiatric phenomena. *American Journal of Psychiatry* 107:764–769.
Weiss, R. J., and Payson, H. E. 1967. Cross stress reaction. In *Comprehensive textbook of psychiatry,* ed. A. M. Freedman and H. I. Kaplan, pp. 1027–1931. Baltimore: Williams & Wilkins.

# 40

# Identification and Treatment
of Incest Victims

## DENISE J. GELINAS

The essential element in working with incest is recognizing that incest does, in fact, exist. There is a common misconception that incest occurs only as a relatively rare form of sexual deviance, in fantasy, or in cultures sufficiently removed from our own that they are best dealt with using anthropology or history. Prior to working with incest victims and their families, we thought the same way.[1]

In the course of our usual clinical work, however, each of us became interested in a certain peculiar pattern. There were several patients, all women, for whom we were having difficulty establishing a diagnosis and, therefore, a treatment approach and information regarding possible medications. Specifically, they all complained of depression, but their depressions were atypical and showed certain "borderline" features. These patients had received a variety of diagnoses, including depressive, hysterical, and dissociative neuroses; incipient psychosis; and latent schizophrenia. As we gathered more information from these patients to establish a more reliable diagnosis, we found that each had been sexually abused by a close family member as a child.

We use a working definition of incest based upon *sexual contact* and

1. "We" refers to the coordinators of the Incest Treatment Program in the Baystate Medical Center's Department of Psychiatry: Barbara Goodman, M.S.W., Donna Nowak-Scibelli, M.S.W., and Denise J. Gelinas, Ph.D. The program provides individual, family, and/or group therapy as well as consultation to clinicians or agencies.

a *preexisting relationship* between the adult and the child. (Legal definitions may vary across states and also because of variations in act, intent, the victim's age, and degree of relationship between offender and victim.) For clinical purposes, we consider incest to be sexual activity between relatives by blood, marriage, or adoption. Sexual companions of parents are not considered unless the relationships are longstanding, the adults consider themselves married by common law, and the child considers the man her father or father-surrogate. The existence of a *parent-child relationship* is the essential criterion. "Sexual activity" refers to genital exposure, fondling, oral-genital contact, and/or vaginal or anal intercourse. Incestuous fantasies, propositions, or attempt at persuasion are not sufficient to meet the criteria. Some form of overt sexual behavior is required for the situation to be regarded as incestuous. Our recommendations about the identification and treatment of incest are based on our work during the past three years.

Our recommendations will address father-daughter or surrogate father-daughter incest. Thus far sexual abuse by surrogate fathers appears indistinguishable in act or effects from that by biological fathers. It is the relationship, not the biology, that is betrayed.

Although we have treated other types of incest (e.g., sibling, father-son, avuncular, and grandparental), the vast majority of cases we have seen have been the father-daughter type (by ratio of 15 to 1).

Whether sibling incest or paternal incest is more frequent remains an open question. As Meiselman (1978) points out, no clinical investigator has observed more sibling than father-daughter cases. Our review of the incest literature reveals that typically authors will assume sibling incest is more frequent, but report that in their own sample, father-daughter incest is more frequent (cf. Boekelheide 1978; Cavallin 1970; National Center on Child Abuse and Neglect 1978). Our inference is that father-daughter incest is probably more frequent than sibling incest.

Several authors have speculated that the low disclosure rate for sibling incest occurs because it is not as destructive. This is likely to be true only if the sexual contact is truly mutual and not coerced, which is more likely if the sister is somewhat older than the brother. Since families express the power dynamics of the society, when brothers and sisters are of approximately equal age the brother is very likely more powerful, both physically and with respect to authority and influence. If the sister is somewhat older than the brother, then she is more likely to be an equal partner and therefore not coerced. When the brother is older, coercion is likely.[2]

2. The only cases of sadistic incest we have seen involved brothers slightly older than sisters. We have seen no cases of sadistic father-daughter incest. In one sibling case,

## Demographics of Incest

*Incidence*

Unfortunately, incest is much more common than most people had thought. Santa Clara (California) County's well-known Child Sexual Abuse Treatment Program estimates that the actual incidence of incest in this country is as high as 800 to 1,000 cases per million population. In 1978 the National Center on Child Abuse and Neglect (NCCAN) estimated that the incidence of child sexual abuse is between 60,000 and 100,000 cases per year.

All forms of child sexual abuse are greatly underreported; a retrospective study of 1,800 college students resulted in approximately one-third reporting that they had been subjected to some form of sexual abuse as a child (not necessarily incest), but that only one-half of the girls and only one-tenth of the boys had reported this, even to their parents (Landis 1956).

One reason children so rarely report sexual abuse is that frequently the people to whom they would most naturally report such abuse, their parents, are themselves the perpetrators. A child is significantly more likely to be abused by a family member or near relative than by the proverbial stranger. The American Humane Association (DeFrancis 1969) reviewed 9,000 cases of child sexual abuse and found that 75 percent were perpetrated by members of the victims' household, neighbors, or acquaintances. Other studies have placed responsibility on a member of the victim's family in 50 percent of cases (Burgess et al. 1978; Sexual Assault Center [SAC] 1979) or in 30 to 80 percent (McGeorge 1964) of cases.

*Other Characteristics of Incest*

As treatment programs become well-known in their communities, the incidence of male children identified as incest victims rises; SAC's increase in male victims rose from 11 to 20 percent in one year (SAC 1979 and Harborview 1980). Despite this surprise, however, female children obviously remain at far greater risk of being the victims of

---

a brother from the ages of twelve to fourteen burned his five- to seven-year-old sister's genitals with cigarettes on several occasions and held her upside down outside windows several stories high. Perhaps these sorts of extreme impulses are inhibited in men who are in a parental role; even though this role is transgressed sexually, it might serve to restrain aggression. Thus sibling incest may have greater potential for noncoerciveness, but also for sadism.

incest. Approximately 98 percent of offenders are male and 2 percent female.

Typically, incest is initiated when the victim is four, five, or six or around nine or ten. Until ages eleven or twelve, sexual activity is usually limited to fondling or oral-genital contact due to the difficulty of vaginal intromission with a prepubertal child.

We have seen several cases, however, where vaginal intercourse was carried out with four- and five-year-old children with resulting injury to the child requiring medical treatment. The SAC (1979) notes that anal intercourse is less difficult at these ages and so appears more often than one would expect. By ages eleven or twelve, vaginal intercourse becomes more common.

Sexual contact is usually terminated at about age fifteen, usually by disclosure, threats of disclosure, and/or running away. The SAC (1979) found that as children get older, actual force is increasingly used by the offender to gain the child's compliance. Thus, within forty-eight hours of last contact, only 15 percent of children younger than twelve had some, usually minor, injury, while 24 percent of the thirteen to sixteen-year-olds showed some injury. In adolescence, fully one-third of the victims reported the use of force or very serious threat of force (guns, knives). As children grow older, they know that intrafamilial sex is prohibited; they are larger, stronger, and have contacts outside the home. Their compliance is more difficult to obtain.

The compliance of a younger child is unfortunately easy to obtain, through the parents' authority and dominance, by the misrepresentation of sex as affection, through threats or bribes. One of our patients remarked that she was ten years old before she learned that what they were doing was called sex. A child's trust, loyalty, affection, needs for affection, and desires to please can easily be exploited. Unfortunately, the victim is often left feeling that she was the one to blame.

Duration of incestuous abuse varies from a single incident (17 percent), less than six months (24 percent), six to twelve months (19 percent), one to five years (31 percent), and finally more than five years (9 percent). These figures from the SAC (1979) indicate that fully 40 percent of these victims were sexually abused by a family member for one to five years. This is more serious than had been thought.

Incest victims sometimes become pregnant because of the repetitive nature of the sexual contact, and because the victim is rather young and cannot easily get birth control counseling or devices. Statistics about the incidence of pregnancy range from 2 pregnancies in 360 victims in the SAC (1979) group (but this sample includes males); 12 percent of 250 incest victims in the 1969 American Humane Association study (NCCAN 1978); and finally 24 percent of 203 incest cases during a 1959 study by Sagarin (1968).

# Negative Effects of Incest

## Trivialization and Blaming the Victim

Many authors have claimed that incest does not have negative effects (Henderson 1975; Lukianowicz 1972; Sloane and Karpinski 1942). In fact, the first modern article on incest, by Bender and Blau (1937), is widely cited as supporting this notion. Others have even claimed that incest has positive effects, including reducing the potential for psychoses (Rascovsky and Rascovsky 1950). While there are interesting historical reasons why these claims were made, the current literature certainly documents negative effects of incest on the victim.

## The "Developmental Trigger"

We have noticed a clinical reason why many negative effects of incest have been overlooked. Simply stated, the effects are not always obvious at the time of sexual contact, or soon thereafter. Often negative effects are not obvious until later, when what we call a "developmental trigger" occurs. A "developmental trigger" is any developmental milestone that causes a negative effect of incest to emerge after some period has elapsed since cessation of sexual contact. The negative effect becomes obvious only when a new area of functioning is required of the victim. For instance, most of the incest victims we have treated have had some type of sexual dysfunction, but this is obviously not a recognized negative effect until the woman is old enough to become sexually active in her own right. Thus marriage or a serious relationship with sexual contact constitutes a developmental trigger when it brings to light anorgasmic functioning related to the prior incest experiences.

Also, we have seen several women hospitalized with serious depressions after they had been given well-deserved promotions at work; their self-esteem was so low they could not tolerate the discrepancy between their self-perceived skills and the demands of the new position. Actually, all were quite competent and, despite chronically damaged self-esteem, were able to function well enough to not only keep their respective jobs, but to get promotions. Only when *recognition* of their competency resulted in a promotion did these incest victims become depressed. The self-esteem problems surfaced for the first time and led to a recognizable depression. Promotions, marriages, the children of victims reaching puberty, death of parents—all of these and other milestones can be developmental triggers. Unfortunately, until this is realized, many of the delayed negative effects of incest will continue to be overlooked. Interviewing children at the termination of sexual contact will not reveal the delayed negative effects that become obvious only after a developmental trigger.

### Degree of Negative Effect

Incest is almost always injurious, and *very* rarely neutral or beneficial. Further, the same negative effects are found *consistently* across patients, and specific treatment recommendations can be made. The degree of negative effect varies according to several factors. The earlier the incest begins, the more destructive it proves to be, particularly for ego development. The longer the duration of sexual contact and the more extensive the contact, the more serious the effect.[3]

The closer the relationship, the more destructive the incest; crossing the generational boundaries as in parental or grandparental incest carries great psychological weight beyond the overstimulating aspects of the sexual contact itself. Finally, the greater the secrecy and the needs for duplicity and silence, the greater the amount of destructiveness, particularly in terms of the victim's isolation, guilt, and self-esteem.

## Recognition and Identification of Incest Victims

Incest is very rarely spontaneously disclosed and is rarely a presenting problem; its occurrence is surrounded by secrecy and shame, and the former victim often blames herself and/or feels a good deal of guilt about it. The subject is a difficult one for victims to broach; if they do so obliquely, testing the therapist's capacity to accept this sort of information, it behooves us all to be able to recognize what is occurring and to encourage the disclosure. Some patients are not able to initiate disclosure and are openly relieved when asked by a therapist if sexual contact with a family member has occurred.

3. We have occasionally found that if some, but not psychologically overwhelming, force is used, then the victim can say to herself that the force precluded her compliance; with force, decision making is taken away and she can more easily perceive that as a young child, she had no choice. Thus the element of guilt can be reduced. (This is most emphatically *not* an argument in favor of the use of force. It merely points out that if force was used, a patient might feel less guilty about the nature of her participation in incest. During psychotherapy, however, as the patient realizes that, as a child, she had had little say in the whole matter of incest anyway, the issue of force emerges, once again, as a gratuitously destructive element.)

We never inquire if "incest" has occurred; the term is too emotionally loaded. Also, some patients have resisted recognizing the experiences they had as "incest"; recognition of this may come only later.

We routinely inquire of each patient, male as well as female, if sexual contact with a family member has ever occurred. At times we can alleviate a patient's lingering fear that certain forms of play have so qualified. Usually, when phrased in this manner ("Have you ever had any sexual contact with a family member?"), patients regard this question as innocuous. Occasionally a patient may balk at the propriety of such a question. Our typical response is "I've needed to ask you a number of personal questions, about your sleep, your appetite, your physical health, and now I'm checking for some things in your sex life." Given this accurate explanation in a matter-of-fact manner changes the context, and patients do not then object. This inquiry is especially important when a patient ranks high on our Suspicious Index, a constellation of presenting problems and personal history we have found closely associated with the prior occurrence of incest.

## Suspicion Index for Incest[4]

Essentially, patients present with complaints of longstanding depression, with a variety of complications, some of which are secondary to a chronic depression and others of which suggest problems with impulsivity and dissociation.

*Presenting problem:* Chronic depression.

*Accompanied by:* Complications of a chronic mood disorder (substance abuse, poor relationships, self-injurious behaviors, impaired judgment, sexual dysfunction).

Dissociative elements (complaints of "confusion" from a nonpsychotic individual, recurrent nightmares or unpleasant memories triggered by a characteristic event or person, depersonalization).

Impulsivity (tantrum, spending or eating sprees, auto accidents, child abuse).

*History of Parentification*

## Depression

*Most incest victims will not request treatment for incest, but for symptoms relating to longstanding depressions.* The criteria for Dysthymic Disorders in the *Diagnostic and Statistical Manual of Mental Disorders,* third edition

4. With children and adolescents, the identifying profile is somewhat different (cf. Bernstein and tenBensel 1977; Brant and Tisza 1977; Burgess et al. 1978; Green 1979; Greenberg 1979; Nakashima and Zakus 1979; Pascoe 1979; Sgroi 1979; Simrel, Berg, and Thomas 1979).

(DSM-III) (1980), provides a good characterization of this type of depression.[5] However, incest victims show atypical depression with strong dissociative and impulsive elements. In treatment, victims appear to be suffering from a disguised delayed posttraumatic syndrome (also in DSM-III) rather than simple depression. Thus patients *present* with depressions but respond best in therapy when treated as posttrauma patients as well, where insight and affect are elicited within a supportive and structured context.

During psychotherapy, certain aspects become more prominent, including chronically low self-esteem, passivity, guilt, needy depressiveness, and isolation. Most obvious is chronically low self-esteem. Victims often state that they feel like "freaks," different, dirty, and of little value. This leads them to tolerate situations not in their best interests, such as bad marriages, poor work situations, and so forth. This is not masochism (as this passivity usually holds no sexual payoffs), but rather passivity engendered by poor self-esteem and experiences of powerlessness, a sort of learned helplessness. Marked lack of assertiveness is usually evident.

All of these depressions show strong currents of *guilt*. Our patients often state they feel responsible for the incest, even if intellectually they know this is not true. Such self-blame reinforces their low self-esteem and lack of assertiveness. *Needy depressiveness* is also evident, and once treatment commences becomes particularly obvious in patients' strong, unmet dependency needs, testing of treatment boundaries, and desires for personal contact with the therapist.

Many incest victims show *isolation* and *distrust*. Some have never previously disclosed the incest; one woman had not told anyone in thirty-seven years until a member of the nursing staff recognized the pattern and asked her about it. Others have disclosed, to find that people could not, or would not, help them or even blamed them. Thus they tend to disclose warily, and typically have few friends and almost no support network—all of which contributes to the longstanding depression. Incest victims often show problems with interpersonal relationships. There can be a strong trend toward transference and projection. Men are often seen as authoritarian, seductive, selfish, and powerful; women are often seen as angry, withholding, cold, or aban-

---

5. The essential feature is a longstanding (at least two years in an adult) mood disturbance involving either depressed mood or loss of interest and/or pleasure in most usual activities. Associated symptoms might be chronic tiredness and decreased effectiveness at school, work, or home, social withdrawal, decreased concentration, sleep problems, loss of self-esteem, tearfulness, and/or suicidal ideation. The mood disorder is not sufficiently severe to be characterized as of psychotic proportions; but it is of sufficient duration that complications and associated features can arise secondary to the continued mood disturbance; these can include suicide attempts, substance abuse, occupational and relational difficulties, and poor judgment.

doning. Obviously these raise treatment considerations, especially in individual psychotherapy, where both transference and projection develop most intensely.

Most incest victims complain of sexual dysfunctions, usually distaste of sexual contact or nonresponsiveness. One young woman raped by her father at age thirteen sought treatment for depression and suicidal impulses because she had been unable to consummate her marriage of three months. She had not disclosed the rape in the intervening seven years, except to her stepmother, who had not believed her. Her husband learned of the assault only during her hospitalization.

## Dissociative Features

The depressive picture is usually complicated by dissociative features. Many victims talk about this process occurring during the incestuous contact. They have talked about feeling as if they were "part of the wall" in rooms where the incest was occurring; some had had experience of watching what was going on from far away or above. Others have felt "removed" from the experience emotionally; at the initial meeting they discuss the incest with markedly little affect, denying it has had any real impact and stating that they would prefer to put it all behind them. Within a couple of sessions, however, a good deal of affect begins to emerge, usually grief, anger, and disbelief. Early selective amnesia for some of the sexual contact is also quite common.

These dissociative features probably account for some of the faulty diagnosis of the past. Many victims have been wrongly diagnosed as psychotic. Once the initial denial and dissociation begin to dissolve, accounts are remarkably vivid, detailed, and affect-laden. This vividness is quite startling, but the victims have been able (during the same session in which they related their experiences) to demonstrate good reality testing.[6] Also, this appears to be the stuff of early psychoanalytic treatment, when insight and affect, carefully rejoined, produce lasting change.

## History of Parentification

Victims typically describe strong parentification. That is, they have had to assume parental roles in the family beyond their developmental capabilities. This can mean assuming excess responsibility at an early age for household chores, child care, and in extreme cases, even

6. None of the above is meant to imply that no incest victims can be psychotic. Some have been or are. It is to differentiate, however, formal thought disorder from those cases where depression is not simple, but complicated by often vivid dissociative elements.

parent the parents, in a complete role reversal. Just helping with the chores is not parentification; having full responsibility is—the child does not help with the laundry; she does it all. Incest victims often care for younger children, even infants as soon as they are brought home from the hospital, when the incest victim is as young as six years old (though nine is more common). What is crucial to this process of parentification is the responsibility the child, in reality, bears and feels, and also the sense of emotional availability to succor the parents' needs.

## Intergenerational Risk

One further negative effect of incest that is not immediately apparent is the increased probability that incest will occur in future generations. The family structure that permitted/induced incest to occur is often perpetuated across generations, as are most other family structures. Although a discussion is beyond the scope of this paper, a strong intergenerational pattern has become increasingly evident and we regard it as a negative effect of incest.

The structure and roles of the family are recapitulated in the next generation, and often the sexual abuse is too. One sixteen-year-old patient had been sexually abused for many years by her stepfather. Her older sister had been sexually abused by one of the mother's previous husbands. During family treatment, it was revealed that mother had also been sexually abused by her stepfather, and she had several compelling reasons to suspect that the same thing had earlier occurred to her own mother (the identified patient's grandmother). While it is unusual to be able to document the intergenerational pattern so clearly, it is a prominent factor in many cases and underscores the importance of recognition and treatment to break the self-perpetuating pattern.

# Treatment Considerations

## Treatment Assumptions

We have found it helpful to make three treatment assumptions.[7] First, whenever there is sexual contact between an adult and a child, it

7. The SAC has reported that 97.5 percent of incest cases reported to them have been

is *always* the adult's responsibility. While we recognize that children sometimes seek affection and attention in ways that can be construed as sexy, it is the adult who has the control *and* the knowledge of the differences between affection and actual sexual expression.

Second, we pay particular attention to the loyalty dynamics in families; whether immediately apparent or initially invisible, family members have tremendous loyalty to each other, especially children for their parents (Boszormenyi-Nagy and Spark 1973; Boszormenyi-Nagy 1980). This is especially true of the incest victim. In her role as parentified child, the daughter is "responsible" for many things, including caring for the father as well as other family members. By acknowledging the daughter's concern for family members, the therapist allows the patient to trust the therapist and to feel that she or he will respect her loyalties; this frees her up to talk. Whether she is initially guilt-ridden and depressed, or angry and rejecting of her parents or the father, attempts by the therapist to have the victim repudiate her father will eventually backfire. Often, in an attempt to elicit some anger toward father from a chronically-depressed patient, therapists will induce or allow a vilification of the father. If this is successful, the patient will be in an untenable position and will be forced to leave treatment rather than betray such fundamental loyalties.[8] Instead, the victim's anger should be elicited within the explicit context of her loyalty; so a therapist might say, "Remembering that in a lot of ways, he was a strong (good, warm, appropriate) father for years, it sounds like he could also be exploiting (harsh, scary, violent, seductive)." Or "So, in many ways he was . . . , but he was also . . ." The aim here is to elicit the underlying affect without forcing the victim to betray her concern and loyalty for her family; this is the case whether the treatment is individual, group, or family therapy.

Third, keeping in mind both the victim's loyalty and the adult's responsibility for the sexual contact, we stress the *accountability* of the parents, and especially the father, for the occurrence of the incest, but we avoid any scapegoating. This can be fully as difficult as it sounds. As therapists, we are hearing obvious exploitation and see some of the negative consequences. It would be easy to become angry and blame

---

"founded," that is, true. For an excellent article on the differentiation of fact from fantasy in reports of incest, see Rosenfeld, Nadelson, and Krieger (1979).

8. One family had sought treatment years earlier, but had terminated contact when, in the first session, the therapist referred to the father as a "creep." The children refused to return, and the family sought help at a second agency, where they again left treatment after the first session, during which that therapist stated to the mother, "Now we'll see how you so failed your husband that he had to turn to your daughter." Both therapists put the adolescent children into the untenable position of getting treatment at the price of loyalty to one or another parent.

the offender or, as some have done, the mother.[9] Instead, again using the contextual approach (cf. Boszormenyi-Nagy 1980), we emphasize accountability for one's behavior but resist character assassination. We use the technique of "multilaterality," that is, we attempt to take everyone's point of view and side in turn, rather than remaining "objective." In this way treatment does not scapegoat one member or leave anyone's accountability out, but rather retains an explicitly relational basis. We also use intergenerational family factors and consider the father's actions in terms of his own childhood. Frequently we find that he was physically or emotionally abandoned as a child; in many cases he was himself physically or sexually abused. With this approach we can refrain from being punitive, yet continue to hold him responsible for his actions as an adult and a father.

## Treatment Alternatives

In treating incest victims, we make three major interventions. These are: (1) prevent further abuse; (2) stabilize the situation; and (3) provide therapy to treat the negative consequences. If the patient is an adult who was victimized as a child, there are usually[10] no interventions necessary to prevent further abuse, and the stabilizers needed are the usual case management techniques that provide structure. Generally patients are referred to our incest groups: groups of six to eight victims with two female co-therapists that meet for one and one-half hours per week for sixteen weeks, using a structured, short-term approach. We screen patients before they enter a group for their ability to tolerate anxiety and a structured group format, and to desensitize them to the idea of talking about incest.

We are explicit in our use of sexual terms and types of contact; we ask about frequency of intercourse (or fondling, fellatio, etc.), degree of coercion, secrecy, mystification, duration of abuse in months or years, previous disclosures; we ask about who in the family knew about the sexual contact, and who else was involved either as offender

9. There is a small, but destructive, thread running through the literature that blames the mother for paternal incest. While some mothers undoubtedly know about the incest and refuse to intervene, most mothers have realized only post hoc what the import of certain patterns or comments might be. Some have confronted husbands and/or daughters and received denials. While it is true that the mothers are active members in the role structure conducive to incest, it is erroneous to claim that most of them knew about it while it occurred; it is far-fetched and an expression of scapegoating to blame them for the actions of the adult husbands.

10. Many incest victims are approached by the offender even after reaching adulthood, marrying, and having children. The victims tend to avoid their fathers as they fear the approaches and experience difficulty asserting themselves, often because they continue to be parentified and do not want to "hurt" father's feelings. They prefer to avoid all contact whatsoever.

or as victim.[11] We ask about problems they have run into (presenting problems) and, toward the end of the evaluation, introduce some questions about symptoms from the constellation reviewed earlier if they seem appropriate (e.g., if a patient talks about always feeling ugly or fat or incompetent, we will follow up on self-esteem issues).

Once in a group, the victims have surprisingly little trouble talking. Some of the benefits of the group are that the incest victim who has always felt isolated and bound in secrecy can share with others who have been there. This is a consensual phenomenon common to groups such as mastectomy patients or men returning from Vietnam: relief at being with people who have "been there" and have experienced roughly the same things. The sense of isolation breaks down. Also, finding commonalities among the incest victims regarding low self-esteem, guilt, passivity, impulsiveness and/or self-destructiveness, poor relationships, and so forth, allows patients to externalize these patterns and see them as consequences of incest rather than as immutable characteristics of the self. This opens the door to change and problem solving.

Early group sessions focus on sharing facts and implications of commonalities; middle-phase sessions have tended to be problem solving. Later group sessions tend to focus on continuing difficulties with parents. At this point we work with group members to go back to their parents and actually talk about some of these issues while they are in treatment. Did mother really not know? Did father really think that she was willing?

All the victims we have worked with become fully capable of going to the relevant persons to talk with them and gain some balance to the relationship. We urge patients to return to their parents and rebalance the set of obligations and entitlements of the family relationships rather than attempt to abandon them altogether.

We prefer treating incest victims in groups (if they are adult) or in family therapy if they are living at home or in their teens. Individual therapy does not confer the benefits of commonality as a group does. Also it is more difficult for the victim to talk about incest in individual therapy than in group, probably because transference issues are more intense in individual therapy and many victims show problems with impulsivity and dissociation. Individual transference can lead to panic and the patient leaving treatment or decompensating. Transference is much easier to deal with in a structured group format.

It is necessary to be firm about the limits and boundaries related to time of starting and ending the group, professional rather than per-

---

11. The SAC points out that in 37 percent of their cases, siblings of the identified patient were also incest victims.

sonal contact with us, where patients will wait for group to begin, allowable number of sessions missed, and so forth. Also, transference issues differ with the gender of the therapist. With women therapists, patients tend to see us as punitively withholding what is perceived to be nearly oceanic amounts of maternal caretaking. Patients can be angry and hurt; some have developed endogenous depressions *during* the course of treatment. Patients often fear their male therapists might seduce them.

Finally, depression or acting-out often occurs during treatment. We require some group patients to be in concurrent individual therapy where the therapist can help set limits and provide support.

If the incest victim is a child and/or living at home, further abuse must be prevented. We prefer to have the offender rather than the victim leave the home temporarily; this assigns responsibility where it belongs. This is a time of crisis for all concerned, especially the victim. She is often initially blamed by mother for the incest, or is the focus of anger from father who feels betrayed that she disclosed. She is also usually regarded ambivalently by her siblings. If legal procedures are pending, the stress is even greater. We attempt to temporarily support *all* concerned, negate scapegoating, and revitalize whatever natural support networks exist in the extended family or social network. This provides continuing support for family members without draining us, the therapists, in the first couple of weeks of treatment.

Also, most mental health professionals are "mandated reporters"; that is, mandated by state laws to file a report with the local children's protective agency on suspected cases of child abuse. Sexual abuse is child abuse. Unfortunately, many mental health professionals are leary of filing these forms. We have treated children and women who were hospitalized with vaginal injuries, where no one filed a complaint. We have also seen several cases where incest was stopped when a minister or mental health worker insisted, but when the contact was stopped, incest was reinstated. For obvious reasons, the victim's hopelessness and sense of betrayal were exacerbated.

The children's protective service report has been very important and helpful in treating the victim of incest. It helps to protect the victim[12] and means prosecution for the offender only if he continues the abuse. Generally, if investigation demonstrates that the incest has stopped and if the offender gets treatment, no legal charges are brought.

When people have questions about filing the report, we suggest that the best thing to do is to phone the relevant agency and sound them

12. The SAC reported that without prosecution approximately 90 percent of the offenders in their treatment sample did not want treatment and that a very significant percentage became repeat offenders.

out. A telephone call for filing information is a benign procedure and usually serves to reduce the therapist's anxiety.

One of the peculiar things about incest is the whole area of therapist anxiety and reactions. In large part, the reason incest is so little recognized, researched, and treated relates to the high degree of anxiety it engenders in therapists. At times the work is demanding. It helps to have a co-therapist, consultant, or colleague who shares in the recognition that incest is destructive, important, and that its victims can and should be treated.

REFERENCES

American Psychiatric Association. 1980. *Diagnostic and statistical manual of mental disorders*, 3rd ed. Washington, D.C.: American Psychiatric Association.

Bender, L., and Blau, A. 1937. The reaction of children to sexual relations with adults. *American Journal of Orthopsychiatry* 8(4):500–518.

Bernstein, G. A., and tenBensel, R. W. 1977. Incest: Detection and treatment by the physician. *Minnesota Medicine* October 1977, pp. 767–770.

Boekelheide, P. 1978. Incest and the family physician. *Sexuality Today* 1(18):3–4.

Boszormenyi-Nagy, I. 1979. Contextual therapy: Therapeutic leverages in mobilizing trust. In *The American family*, ed. Smith, Kline, and French, Report no. 2, pp. 1–12. Philadelphia.

————, and Spark, G. 1973. *Invisible loyalties: Reciprocity in intergenerational family therapy*. New York: Harper & Row.

Brant, R., and Tisza, V. 1977. The sexually misused child. *American Journal of Orthopsychiatry* 47(1):80–90.

Burgess, A., et al. 1978. *Sexual assault of children and adolescents*. Lexington, Mass.: D. C. Heath.

Cavallin, H. 1970. Incestuous fathers: A clinical report. In *Studies in human sexual behavior*, ed. A. Shiloh, pp. 387–397. Springfield, Ill.: Charles C. Thomas.

DeFrancis, V. 1969. Protecting the child victim of sex crimes committed by adults. Denver, Colo.: American Humane Association, Children's Division.

Green, F. 1979. Introduction: Child sexual abuse: The physician's responsibility. *Pediatric Annals* 8(5):11–13.

Greenberg, N. 1979. The epidemiology of childhood sexual abuse. *Pediatric Annals* 8(5):16–28.

Harborview (Seattle, Washington) Sexual Assault Center. 1980. Response to violence and sexual abuse in the family, ed. Center for Women Policy Studies 3(7):7. [Also referenced as Sexual Assault Center.]

Henderson, D. J. 1975. Incest. In *Comprehensive textbook of Psychiatry*, ed. A. M. Freedman, H. I. Kaplan, and B. J. Sadock, vol. 2, 2nd ed., pp. 1530–1539. Baltimore, Md.: Williams & Wilkins.

Landis, J. T. 1956. Experiences of 500 children with adult sexual deviation. *Psychiatric Quarterly Supplement* 30(1) (suppl):91–109.

Lukianowicz, N. 1972. Incest 1: Paternal incest. *British Journal of Psychiatry* 120:301–313.

McGeorge. 1964. Sexual assaults on children. *Medicine, Science, and the Law* (England) 4:425.

Meiselman, K. C. 1978. *Incest: A psychological study of causes and effects with treatment recommendations.* San Francisco: Jossey-Bass.

Nakashima, I., and Zakus, G. 1979. Incestuous families. *Pediatric Annals* 8(5):29–42.

National Center on Child Abuse and Neglect. 1978. Child sexual abuse: Incest, assault, and sexual exploitation. Special report, U.S. Department of Health, Education, and Welfare, Children's Bureau, August 1978.

Pascoe, D. 1979. Management of sexually abused children. *Pediatric Annals* 8(5):44–58.

Rascovsky, M., and Rascovsky, A. 1950. On consummated incest. *International Journal of Psychoanalysis* 51:42–47.

Rosenfeld, A. A., Nadelson, C. C., and Krieger, M. 1979. Fantasy and reality in patients' reports of incest. *Journal of Clinical Psychiatry* (April) 40:159–164.

Sagarin, E. 1968. *Problems of sex behavior.* New York: T. Y. Crowell.

Sexual Assault Center, Harborview Medical Center, Seattle, Wash. 1979. Sexual abuse within the family. Workshop co-sponsored by Franklin/Hampshire Community Mental Health Center and Women's Crisis Center, Brattleboro, Vermont. [Also referenced as Harborview.]

Sgroi, S. 1979. Pediatric gonorrhea beyond infancy. *Pediatric Annals* 8(5):73–99.

Simrel, K., Berg, R., and Thomas, J. 1979. Crisis management of sexually abused children. *Pediatric Annals* 8(5):59–72.

Sloane, P., and Karpinski, E. 1942. Effects of incest on the participants. *American Journal of Orthopsychology* 12:666–673.

# 41

# Incest Between Fathers and Daughters

## JUDITH HERMAN AND LISA HIRSCHMAN

The incest taboo is universal in human culture. Anthropologists generally believe it to be the foundation of all kinship structures. Claude Lévi-Strauss (1969), the French structuralist, suggests that the taboo is our basic social contract, while Margaret Mead (1968) proposes that it is required to preserve human social order. All cultures, including our own, regard violations of the taboo with horror and dread. Nonetheless, in spite of the length of the prohibition, sexual relations between family members occur more frequently than we had earlier imagined. And because of extreme secrecy surrounding the violation of our most basic sexual taboo, we have little clinical literature and no accurate statistics to guide us.

According to the Kinsey et al. (1953) report—probably our most reliable source of data on sexual experiences in America—one woman in seventy-five has had sexual contact with her father during childhood. That is, 1.5 percent of the U.S. female population are incest victims. A number of clinical reports estimate that the figure may be closer to 4 or 5 percent.

Mother-son incest, by contrast, is rare. The most comprehensive American survey ever undertaken, S. K. Weinberg's in 1955, found 164 cases of father-daughter incest, compared with only 2 cases of sexual contact between mother and son. A study of court cases in Germany reported that 90 percent of the cases involved fathers or stepfathers and daughters. Homosexual father-son contact accounted for another 5 percent. Incest between mothers and sons occurred in only 4 percent of these German cases. And according to the American Humane Association (1967), incest appears to follow the prevailing pattern of sexual abuse of children, in which 92 percent of the victims are female and 97 percent of the offenders are male.

The literature fails to account for this striking discrepancy in the behavior of mothers and fathers. It is apparently taken for granted. The failure to question or even speculate on the reasons for the difference reflects the wide acceptance of assumptions about sex roles deeply ingrained in our patriarchal culture.

Because the subject of incest inspires such strong emotional reactions, few experts have even attempted a dispassionate study of its occurrence and effects. Often those who have studied it have been unable to avoid their own defensive reactions.

## Freud's Theory

Clearly the most famous instance of denial occurs in Freud's (1954) work. In an 1897 letter to his colleague Wilhelm Fleiss, Freud reveals why he didn't believe the incest reports he heard from so many of his women patients: "Then there was the astonishing thing that in every case blame was laid on perverse acts by the father, and realization of the unexpected frequency of hysteria, in every case of which the same thing applied, though it was hardly credible that perverted acts against children were so general."

Freud concluded that for the most part the sexual act had never occurred. He could not believe that incest was a common event in respectable families. Since mothers rarely sexually approach their sons, Freud concluded—incorrectly—that the same was true for daughters. Freud's followers also assumed that incestual relations occurred only in fantasy and failed to investigate the facts. They focused on the child's desire rather than on the adult's (and the father's capacity for action). Psychoanalytic study, while it places the incest taboo at the center of the child's psychological development, has done little to uncover the secrecy veiling its occurrence.

Those who have investigated incest often tend to judge the child as the instigator of her own seduction. It reveals an attitude similar to the common belief that the victim of rape is responsible for the crime (particularly if she is attractive).

In the course of just a few years in our practice, we encountered what seemed to us to be a surprisingly large number of patients who were incest victims. Other therapists, we found, had similar experiences. Out of the first ten therapists we questioned, we learned that four had at least one incest victim in treatment. Within a short time, we had collected fifteen case histories.

In our study, we included only those cases where overt sexual contact had actually occurred between parent and child and only those in which there was no doubt in the daughter's mind that explicit and intentionally sexual contact had occurred and where secrecy was required. Not included were the many women who reported seductive behavior on the part of their fathers.

## Remarkably Similar Histories

The incest histories were remarkably similar. Most victims were the eldest or only daughters and had experienced their first sexual approach by their fathers or male guardians between the ages of six and nine. The youngest girl was four years old; the oldest fourteen. Sexual contact usually took place repeatedly, and often the relationship lasted three years or more. Physical force was not used, and intercourse was rarely attempted with girls who had not reached puberty. In all but two of these fifteen cases, the relationship remained a secret.

Previous studies, often based on court referrals, give an erroneous impression that incest occurs predominantly in poor families. But this is not so. The fathers' occupations cut across class lines. Several held jobs that required considerable personal competence and commanded social respect—college administrator, army officer, policeman, engineer, physician. Others were skilled workers, foremen, or managers in offices or factories. All the mothers were houseworkers.

Certain common features emerged in the pattern of these victims' family relationships. Most striking was the almost uniform estrangement of mother and daughter, an estrangement that preceded the occurrence of overt incest.

More than half the mothers were partially incapacitated by physical or mental illness or alcoholism, and either assumed an invalid role in the home or were periodically absent because of hospitalization. Their eldest daughters were often obliged to take over the household duties. At best, the mothers were viewed by their daughters as helpless, frail, downtrodden victims, who were unable to take care of themselves, much less to protect their children.

In particular, the daughters felt unable to go to their mothers for help once their fathers had begun to make sexual advances. In many cases the mothers tolerated a great deal of abuse themselves, and the daughters had learned not to expect any protection. Five of the women said they suspected that their mothers knew about the incest and tacitly condoned it. Two victims who had made attempts to bring up the subject were put off by their mothers' denial or indifference.

At worst, the mother-daughter relations were marked by frank and open hostility. Some of the daughters said they could remember no tenderness or caring from their mothers. In contrast, almost all the victims expressed some warm feelings toward their fathers. Many described them much more favorably than their mothers.

To the outside world, the fathers were often liked and respected members of the community. The daughters responded to their fathers' social status and power and derived satisfaction from being their fathers' favorites. They were "daddy's special girls," but often they were special to no one else.

The victims rarely expressed anger toward their fathers, not even about the incestuous act itself. Most expressed feelings of fear, disgust, and intense shame about the sexual contact, and said that they had endured it because they felt they had no other choice. But though they felt abused by their fathers, they did not feel the same sense of betrayal as they felt toward their mothers. Having abandoned the hope of pleasing their mothers, they seemed relieved to have found some way of pleasing their fathers and gaining their attention.

## Power Within the Family

Although the victims reported that they felt helpless and powerless to resist their fathers, the incestuous relationship did give them some semblance of power within the family. Many of the daughters effectively replaced their mothers and became their fathers' surrogate wives. They were also deputy mothers to the younger children, and were generally given some authority over them. Many girls felt an enormous sense of responsibility for holding the family together. They also knew that, as keepers of the incest secret, they had an extraordinary power that could be used to destroy the family. Their sexual contact with their fathers conferred on them a sense of possessing a dangerous, secret power over the lives of others. Keeping up appearances became a necessary, expiating act, at the same time that it increased the daughters' sense of isolation and shame.

What is most striking to us about this family constellation, in which the daughter replaces the mother in the traditional role, is the underlying assumption about that role shared apparently by all the family members. Customarily, a mother and wife in our society is one who nurtures and takes care of children and husband. If, for whatever reasons, the mother is unable to fulfill her ordinary functions, it is apparently assumed that some other female must be found to do it. The eldest daughter is a frequent choice. The father does not assume the wife's maternal role when she is incapacitated. He feels that his first right is to continue to receive the services that his wife formerly provided, sometimes including sexual services.

This view of the father's prerogative to be served is shared not only by the parents and daughters in these incestuous families, but also by the wider society. Fathers who feel abandoned by their wives are not generally expected or taught to assume primary responsibilities as a parent. We should not find it surprising, then, that fathers occasionally turn to their daughters for services (housework and sexual) that they had formerly expected of their wives.

## Unable to Love

One of the most frequent complaints of the victims entering therapy was a sense of being different, and distant, from ordinary people. They expressed fear that they were unable to love. Their sense of an absence of feeling was most marked in sexual relationships, although most women were sexually responsive in the narrow sense of the word; that is, capable of having orgasms.

In some cases, the suppression of feeling was clearly a defense that had been employed in the incestuous relationship in childhood. Originally, the isolation of affect seemed an appropriate device to protect against the feelings aroused by their molesting father. Passive resistance and dissociation of feeling appeared to be among the few defenses available in an overwhelming situation. Later it carried over into their relations with others.

## Distance and Isolation

These women made repeated and often desperate attempts later in life to overcome their sense of distance and isolation. Frequently it resulted in a pattern of many brief, unsatisfactory sexual contacts. Those relationships that became more intense and lasting were fraught with difficulty. While most expressed suspicion of men, they also overvalued them and kept searching for a relationship with an idealized protector and sexual teacher who would take care of them and tell them what to do. Half the women had had affairs during adolescence with older or married men. In these relationships, the sense of importance and power and the secrecy of the incestuous relationship was regained. The men emerged as heroes and saviors.

In many cases the women became intensely involved with men who were cruel, abusive, or neglectful, and tolerated extremes of mistreatment. One remained married for twenty years to a psychotic husband who beat her, terrorized their children, and never supported the family. Several were rape victims.

Why did these women feel they deserved to be beaten, raped, neglected, and used? Almost all of the fifteen women described themselves as a "witch," "bitch," or "whore" and saw themselves as socially branded even when no social exposure of their sexual relations with their fathers had occurred or was likely to occur. They experienced themselves as powerful and dangerous to men: Their self-image had almost a magical quality. They seemed to believe that they had seduced their fathers and, therefore, could seduce any man.

At one level their sense of malignant power can be understood to have arisen as a defense against the child's feelings of utter helplessness. In addition, however, their self-image was reinforced by the longstanding conspiratorial relationship with their fathers. And, as a matter of fact, as children, they did have the power to destroy the family by exposing the secret.

What's more, most of the victims were aware that they had experienced some pleasure in the incestuous relationship, and together with their fathers they joined in a shared hatred of their mothers. This led to intense feelings of shame, degradation, and worthlessness. Because they had enjoyed their fathers' attention and their mothers' defeat, these women felt responsible for the incestuous relationship. Almost uniformly, they distrusted their own desires and needs, and did not feel entitled to care and respect. Any relationship that afforded some kind of pleasure seemed to increase their sense of guilt and shame. They constantly sought to expiate their guilt and relieve their shame by serving and giving to others, and by observing the strictest and most rigorous codes of religion and traditional morality. Any lapse from a rigid code of behavior confirmed their innate evil. Some of the women embraced their negative identity with a kind of defiance and pride. "There's *nothing* I haven't done!" one woman boasted.

Those women who were mothers themselves appeared preoccupied with the fear that they would themselves be "bad" mothers to their children, as they felt their mothers had neglected them. Several sought treatment when they became aware of feelings of rage and resentment toward their own children, especially their daughters. Any indulgence in pleasure seeking or attention to their own personal needs reinforced their sense that they were unfit mothers. In some, the fear of exposure was felt as dread that the authorities would intervene and take their children away. Other mothers worried that they would be unable to protect their daughters from incest in their own families.

## Therapy

Very little is known about how to help the incest victim. If the secret is discovered while she is still living with her parents, most often the family is destroyed. Since such an outcome is usually terrifying, even to an exploited child, most victims cooperate with their fathers in maintaining secrecy rather than seeing their fathers jailed or risk being sent away from home themselves.

The Santa Clara County Court offers a model treatment center designed for the rehabilitation of the incestuous family. It involves all members of the incestuous family in both individual and family therapy, and benefits from a close alliance with Daughters United, a self-help support group for victims. Several similar treatment centers are now in the process of development. While it offers a promising model for the treatment of the discovered incestuous family, this model does not help families with undetected incest. The vast majority of incest victims reach adulthood still hiding their secrets. Nor are most therapists equipped to treat those patients who come to them for help.

As with many other ancient women's secrets (abortion, rape), public testimony and consciousness raising have often provided better therapy for women than professional services. We believe that increased public awareness of the scope of the problem is the first step toward helping incest victims lose their sense of isolation and shame.

REFERENCES


American Humane Association. 1967. *Sexual Abuse of Children,* ed. V. DeFrancis. Denver, Col.

Freud, S. 1954. *The Origins of Psychoanalysis: Letters to Wilhelm Fliess, Drafts and Notes: 1887–1902.* New York: Basic Books.

Kinsey, A., et al. 1953. *Sexual Behavior in the Human Female.* Philadelphia: Saunders and Co.

Lévi-Strauss, C. 1969. *The Elementary Structures of Kinship.* Boston: Beacon Press.

Mead, M. 1968. Incest. In *International Encyclopedia of the Social Sciences,* ed. D. L. Sills. New York: Crowell, Collier, and Macmillan.

Weinberg, S. K. 1955. *Incest Behavior.* New York: Citadel.

# PART IV / Supplementary Readings

*Developmental Issues*

Abernathy, V. et al. 1976. Family planning during psychiatric hospitalization. *American Journal of Orthopsychiatry* 46:154–162.

Becket, J. O. 1976. Working wives: A racial comparison. *Social Work* 21:463–471.

Flapan, M., and Schoenfeld, H. 1972. Procedures for exploring women's childbearing motivations, alleviating childbearing conflicts and enhancing maternal role development. *American Journal of Orthopsychiatry* 42:389–397.

Jacobs, R. H. 1979. *Life after youth: Female, Forty—what next?* Boston: Beacon Press.

Rubin, L. B. 1979. *Women of a certain age: The midlife search for self.* New York: Harper & Row.

Van Dusen, R. A., and Sheldon, E. B. 1976. The changing status of American women: A life cycle perspective. *American Psychologist* 31:106–116.

*Trauma*

Barrett, C. J. 1977. Women in widowhood. *Signs* 4:856–868.

Burgess, A. W., and Holmstrom, L. L. 1976. Coping behavior of the rape victim. *American Journal of Psychiatry* 133:413–418.

Herman, J., and Hirschman, L. 1977. Father-daughter incest. *Signs* 2:735–756.

Rounsaville, B., Lifton, N. and Bieber, M. 1979. The natural history of a psychotherapy group for battered women. *Psychiatry* 42:63–78.

# PART V

# *Therapies*

# 42

# Psychotherapy with Women Clients: The Impact of Feminism

## ELIZABETH HOWELL

The last decade has witnessed widespread questioning of the appropriateness of the various forms of psychotherapy for women clients. This questioning comes in the wake of the consciousness-raising movement as well as in response to increased awareness of sexism in the practice and theory of psychotherapy. As a result, a new form of therapy, broadly called "feminist therapy," has developed. In addition, so-called "traditional" therapy has broadened its scope to better encompass the needs of women clients and to accommodate feminist concerns. One result is that the impact of the therapist's gender on the psychotherapeutic process has now received greater attention. Such questions as whether a woman should have a male or female therapist, or whether men undertake to treat women at all, are frequently asked. There has been a surge of interest in aspects of the female-female encounter in the psychotherapy relationship, including transference and countertransference and common concerns in the "real" relationship.

The papers collected in part V reflect the impact of feminism on psychotherapy. They present ways in which greater awareness of the issues presented by the woman client and of feminist concerns can be incorporated into the modalities of individual, family, and group psychotherapy. Of particular interest is the suggestion that consciousness raising itself can function as a form of psychotherapy (Lieberman et al. 1979) and as a model for psychotherapy (Brodsky 1973).

Two viewpoints coexist in the concept of the consciousness-raising group as psychotherapy. First, while the aim of the consciousness-raising group is not psychotherapy but social and political change, the group can have a therapeutic effect as a by-product. Second, the proper cure for many women's problems is not "traditional" psychotherapeutic treatment but an awareness of their sociopolitical oppression. Thus it is not the primary task of such groups to examine psychodynamic phenomena or the psychoanalyst's stock-in-trade, transference. While personal change and psychological growth can occur in consciousness-raising groups (and sometimes more dramatically than in traditional therapy), they are not by definition, therapy.

Discoveries of the psychotherapeutic potential of consciousness-raising groups have had a significant impact upon feminist therapy. Yet, the question of what is meant by feminist therapy is important, for by now "feminist therapy" is widespread and "feminist therapists" abound, encompassing women and men of almost all therapeutic orientations. Some maintain that feminist therapy is just "good" therapy, others have specific requirements of it. Various individuals and groups have conceptualized and articulated what they believe are the tenets of feminist therapy. While the differences among these are at times considerable, they share a common focus on sexist aspects of social reality that contribute to women clients' sense of unhappiness and/or to their psychopathology and a common rejection of the adjustment model of mental health (Nutt 1979). As described by Johnson (1980), feminist therapy involves:

(a) interpretation of the client's problems in terms of the social-political context; (b) support for anger, aggression, and initiative taking, when indicated, even when their expression may cause problems with significant others; (c) encouragement of trust and respect for other women; and (d) careful attention to the shared nature of emotional problems—for example, orgastic dysfunction in women is often related to men's premature ejaculation. . . . Many feminist therapists also feel a commitment to support women publicly through participation in women's rights organizations or in the women's caucus of professional societies. (p. 367)

As Johnson goes on to point out, a popular theme in the women's movement has been "The personal is political." Echoing this theme, Thomas (1977) concludes from her research on feminist psychotherapy that:

feminist therapy must be understood more as a part of a social movement than as a type of psychotherapy and less as a theoretical orientation in the traditional sense than as a belief system and a number of ways in which the system is put into practice. (p. 452)

Thus, it appears that feminist therapy retains, at least connotatively, a commitment to political action, and this can be confusing. Feminist therapists understand that as a result of cultural and gender-role bias, social inequities are often unknowingly identified as personal inadequacies of the woman client. This translation occurs within theory as well as in the work of the individual therapist. The feminist therapist may choose to interpret the inequities of the environment, as opposed to the client's psychopathology, as causes of the client's distress. In addition, a woman's pain and symptoms may be viewed as healthy, adaptive responses to a bad situation, rather than as indicators of pathology (Klien 1976.) These are highly important considerations. However, disappointment with the sexist bias of psychological theory can sometimes lead to a flight from a developmental and psychodynamic orientation altogether—in favor of a viewpoint that stresses the usefulness of interpreting the environment. Once we are focused on the environment, though, political action connotations become more cogent, and a different point of view concerning the usefulness of psychotherapy can arise. As expressed by Tennov:

the term "feminist therapist" involves an inherent contradiction. The feminist objective is to change societal institutions so that women may have opportunities equal to those of men in education, employment, participation in government, and so forth. When a woman is depressed or anxious, the feminist looks for a probable cause in the facts of her underemployment—almost every woman in this culture is not only underpaid, but wasted through underemployment in which her work does not utilize her abilities—the burdens of housework and child care, or some other aspect of the role she plays in society. Solutions to these problems are not to be found in individual pathologies, but in changing the behavior of persons in the woman's environment. (Tennov 1976, p. 191)

Discussing the usefulness of psychodynamic theory, Tennov asks:

But if the feminist who wishes to engage in psychotherapy uses the trappings of psychodynamic therapy, is she not misleading her potential clients? If she interprets her client's behavior, is she now engaging in oppressive and abusive actions? (p. 191)

In other words, since the psychological problems of women are really only expressions of social ills, psychotherapy on the basis of individually understood dynamics is a useless proposition. The problem with this view is that it equates Freudian and phallocentric psychology of women with psychology in general (including the whole body of psychodynamic theory); if the first is found lacking or wrong, the second is dismissed also. The fact that psychological theories about the "nature" of woman have been largely unproven empirically and are riddled with sex bias (Weisstein 1971) does not mean that we know nothing about the intrapsychic dynamics of people.

Perhaps the most salient characteristic of feminist therapy as a type of psychotherapy, is its emphasis upon the recognition that social structure has an important impact upon intrapsychic life, as well as upon psychopathology and symptomatology. Of course, this emphasis is typical of the psychotherapeutic activist perspective that has gained increased popularity in recent times. For instance, community organizing, community psychiatry, and community psychology, as part of the greater societal awareness of the ecological model, increasingly have been designated as appropriate forms of remediation of individual ills. In contrast to these, however, feminist therapy has distinguished itself by its address to one primary problem in the social structure: sexism.

Whether one strives to cure social pathology or individual pathology depends to some extent upon one's estimation of the degree to which individual pathology reflects social structure. According to Bart (1974), psychiatry has expanded to include activism within its domain. This legitimization occurs because activism, as well as psychotherapy proper, has as its ultimate goal autonomy rather than victimization of the individual. Feminist therapy, as it is generally practiced, lies somewhere between activism and the view that problems and their solutions arise from intrapsychic processes, described by Bart as "psychotherapeutic quietism" (1974, p. 13). There are complications as well as dangers arising from the overemphasis of either pole. For instance, it is no more desirable for the individual to be relieved of responsibility for personal problems by too much focus on the environment than it is for the victim to be blamed for her or his environmental oppression.

What we need to understand is how the social environment and intrapsychic structure both together and separately contribute to the mental health and mental illness of women. More specifically, we need to pay attention to the ways in which the social context is internalized in psychic structures common to women, and how women, in turn, shape their own environment.

Feminist influence has had a powerful and much-needed impact on the mental health field. We are still struggling with the myriad hard questions it raises. Among these are: How can we best eliminate sexist bias from our theory and our practice? Is psychotherapy the best tool for facilitation of personal change? What is the place of political action? And, if we choose the psychotherapy route, how do we best understand the project before us?—one question, in particular, being the nature of the interaction between the social context and psychodynamics.

REFERENCES


Bart, P. 1974. Ideologies and utopias of psychotherapy. In *The Sociology of Psychothera-py*, ed. P. Roman and H. Trice, pp. 9–57. New York: Jason Aronson.

Brodsky, A. M. 1973. The consciousness-raising group as a model for therapy with women. *Psychotherapy: Theory, Research and Practice* 10:24–29. [Reprinted herein chapter 47.]

Johnson, M. 1980. Mental illness and psychiatric treatment among women: A response. *Psychology of Women Quarterly* 4:363–371.

Klein, M. 1976. Feminist concepts of therapy outcome. *Psychotherapy: Theory, Research, and Practice* 13:89–95.

Lieberman, M. A., et al. 1979. The psychotherapeutic impact of women's consciousness-raising groups. *Archives of General Psychiatry* 36:161–168.

Nutt, R. 1979. Review and preview of attitudes and values of counselors of women. *The Counseling Psychologist* 8:18–20.

Tennov, D. 1976. *Psychotherapy: The hazardous cure.* New York: Anchor Press/Doubleday.

Thomas, S. 1977. Theory and practice in feminist therapy. *Social Work* 22:447–454.

Weisstein, N. 1971. Psychology constructs the female. In *Women in sexist society*, ed. V. Gornick and B. Moran. New York: Basic Books.

# 43

# Women Patients and Women Therapists: Some Issues That Come Up in Psychotherapy

## REBECCA GOZ

Frequently in an initial interview a woman patient will request a woman therapist, but the reasons for this request are unclear, or remain broad and superficial for a long while. Many women couch their requests in the current phraseology of women's liberation, and in that movement's concomitant efforts to have women increase their contacts with other women in a variety of ways instead of primarily relying on men. "Only women can understand women," someone might say. Or "Because you are a professional, and I'm trying to become a professional, we have both probably gone through the same thing, and you can help me." Or "Seeing you gives me the hope that I too can become a professional married woman, with children, and sometimes be pregnant, and be able to do all these things at once." But what does a request for a woman therapist by a woman patient actually signify? What is that patient asking for? Is it true that in general only women can understand women? Is it the hope that the mere combination of two women will somehow supply some sort of underpinnings for a

I would like to acknowledge Roy Schafer, Ph.D., and Rosemary Balsam, M.D., who made useful comments and criticisms on earlier versions of this work.

social and career identification? Or is the language of women, by women, for women, and between women, somehow different from that of, by, for, and between women and men, such that the exclusion of men from the therapy process offers some special magical relief from the perceived sexual demands of men and men's alleged perceptions of the roles of women? Is there something special about "us" versus "them"—men—that allows the patient to talk about her varied feelings toward men, and about herself and her relations with women, more freely? Can the patient become a more aggressive woman, free from the influence of a "male-dominated situation," by seeing a woman therapist? The answers are probably yes, no, and maybe to all of these possibilities. The special request may thus signify many things, all of which must be taken seriously even though the particulars are not clear to begin with.

However, the inherent implication so far is that the woman patient requesting a woman therapist primarily sees her request as an effort to get away from a male therapist for fear of some kind of domination by him, and she sees her direction toward a woman therapist as an effort to establish her separate identity or role as a woman vis-à-vis men, and she usually expresses all of this in some currently socially acceptable terms. Although in my experience it is very rare, once in a while a patient may wish to see a woman therapist expressly in order to work out her relationship to her mother, or to other women. The general thesis of this paper is that the request for a woman therapist by a woman patient is in some major form or other nearly always a disguised request by the patient to duplicate, review, reinstate, reenact, repair, and recreate some powerful unresolved tensions in her relationship to her mother in particular, and the realistic presence of a female therapist before her very eyes in short-term psychotherapy enhances the likelihood that this may occur. Women's lib phraseology provides a convenient frame of reference for her request of a woman therapist, but it may be that the implicit request is less to get away from a male therapist, and more to get with a woman therapist, that is, a surrogate mother for its own sake, regardless of men. Once beyond the initial request with all the socially real and justifiable reasons for which a woman may feel put upon by men, there may be the wish for an *exclusive relationship* with a woman, which is relatively devoid of and divorced from issues of male chauvinism. And even if there is no explicit request for a woman therapist, the assignment to one may bring to the fore significant issues of women in relation to other women and may thereby either enhance or hinder the therapy, or do both. The efforts of this paper are directed toward taking note of some important issues for some women in therapy, which need to be separated out from polemics and particulars of where women stand in society relative to men in any one era, important as those may be. Both the inner and outer realities, and the interaction between them, are crucial for understanding any individual woman patient, but it seems as though all the emphasis on women's lib issues may shortchange a full perspective of inner realities.

What follows is the core of some thoughts about what some women patients may work on to special advantage in their treatment with some women therapists in three areas of female development. These are *pregnancy, symbiosis,* and *homosexuality.* The dynamics of these three are not mutually exclusive, but are separated here for purposes of exposition. Also, they are only a few of the host of topics important to women patients, and the particulars of how they will shape up in therapy may depend largely upon where the therapist and patient are in their respective developmental levels relative to those issues.

This paper is by no means an assertion that these issues are "best" discussed with a woman therapist, for after all women patients come in a variety of shapes, sizes, and forms in their personalities, and women therapists vary in kind as they do in number. And it is possible that for any one woman therapist, her personal biases and fantasies on a particular facet of an issue may lead to unexplored, unverbalized assumptions of mutual understanding or omission between her and the patient, only to create misunderstanding, blind spots, countertransferences, and the wrong focus. Also, many male therapists are especially adept in discussing issues of special importance to women.

In addition, there is no implication here that it is only women who go through these particular experiences in these ways. Nor does the focus here detract from the special relationship of a woman to her father. The emphasis on women patients and women therapists is solely designed to draw attention to, and to highlight, some issues of importance in a woman's relationship to other women. By virtue of having a female body and the opportunity to have played the roles of girl baby, daughter, sister, wife, lover, pregnant woman, mother, divorcee, widow, and grandmother, a woman does have unique experiences, different from men, that she may find especially useful in understanding her women patients, and from which patients may profit. The coalition of woman patient and woman therapist may thus provide special conditions that can evoke fruitful discussion of these topics.

The clinical examples to be presented are excerpts derived from therapy with my own patients, and do not reflect the therapy in its entirety, nor all of the topics discussed with each patient. In order to accentuate a theme, details of what led up to an insight or interpretation or tactic have generally been omitted or condensed. This may give the impression of a more accelerated pace and superficial manner to the therapy than was probably the case.

# Pregnancy

One patient was pregnant when she started treatment, and was due to deliver within the month. I was pregnant then too, but the patient was four months ahead of me.

The pregnancy was causing havoc in the patient's life, because it was an unplanned, unwanted one, occurring fairly early in the marriage. It meant that she could no longer financially support her husband in his studies, as had originally been planned, and it exacerbated the sexual tensions that had already existed. The couple showed their anxiety, as well as other feelings about the pregnancy, in accelerated and seemingly compulsive sexual relations.

At the time various members of the patient's family were having difficulties of their own, and each was preoccupied with his or her own troubles. Her parents had recently been separated. The mother was depressed, and the father was living with another woman. A younger sister had become pregnant and was planning a wedding soon after the patient was to give birth, and the patient was expected to travel to the family home to "stand up" for her sister at the wedding. Thus there was a dearth of familial support for the patient at her time of need, and instead she was expected to be helpful to the others, though this was not without her implicit cooperation.

My approach in the therapy was to focus on the patient's varied, intensifying struggles around the pregnancy, because this is what seemed most important to her considering that her due date was imminent. Full of feelings of shame and guilt, she cried about her deep resentment of the baby and how it could wreck her marriage, as her own birth and her sister's birth had wrecked their parents' marriage. She worried that the baby would resent her in turn, sensing her resentful attitude. Her doubts about her competence as a mother ranged from fears of her inability to change a diaper to fears about handling emotional upsets. The patient wished the baby would be born dead— that would end her troubles. Her terror of the pain and anguish of the birth process was also mounting. How was it, she wondered, that some women looked all aglow when pregnant, and seemed only happy, whereas she felt only resentment? This contrast made her feel envious of other women and even more ashamed of her feelings. It also showed her once again how she could not measure up to her ideals. I pointed out that no one feels just one way about pregnancy, or about anything else. Just as a woman who may seem to be only happy about her pregnancy may also harbor worries, fears, and resentment, as she, the patient, described, she herself seemed to have some feelings of joy about the baby, in addition to her resentment. Interlaced with her complaints, she had already expressed some daydreams, fantasies, and hopes of how she might enjoy motherhood, and what the baby would be like, how she would take care of it, and try to encourage it to feel proud and self-confident, and to talk with her, its mother, about things that troubled him or her. Hopefully she could do some things for her child that she wished her own mother had done for her. Later on the patient volunteered that this notion of two possible sets of feelings—not wanting and wanting the baby simultaneously—helped to carry her through. I offered the interpretation of mixed feelings to the patient when I did, primarily because as the due date approached she was becoming somewhat flooded by her extreme feelings of resentment, which seemed like something of a protest, and there was sufficient evidence to support that part of her that did want the baby.

Other topics we discussed included how she was feeling physically and household preparations for the newborn. She worried that the difference between her own conservative sexual needs and her husband's accelerated ones meant that they were incompatible and should be separated. I advised her to put off thinking about that complex issue until after the birth when she would be more settled and could think more clearly, and also suggested that her husband might be showing his anxieties about the pregnancy through sex. The couple did talk about this, and it emerged that the husband was fearful of losing his wife to the baby, and that the baby would possess his wife and take all her love and affection away from him. We also discussed both her pity for her own mother and her resentment that now, as well as on several previous occasions, when the patient needed her, she seemed unavailable. There was some discussion of how the patient participated in mothering her mother, and the satisfaction the patient seemed to derive from this role.

It was noteworthy that although I was obviously pregnant and wearing maternity clothes, the patient never spontaneously mentioned my pregnancy. I myself mentioned it to her, in the context of explaining what may have been an extensive interest on my part in pregnancy. I brought it up in the way of an assumption that she had noticed it, but it turned out that she had not noticed—at least that's what she said. Her reaction to my telling her I was pregnant was, apparently, pleasure at the similarity of our states. There was some sharing of experiences in the sense of my expressing a knowing acknowledgment of the physical discomforts and mood swings that go with pregnancy.

Around the time of the birth, the couple became more involved with each other and the baby. On two occasions, at the patient's request, therapy took place on the telephone, at appointment times, because the patient was too weak and tired to come in. We talked about the birth, which turned out to be difficult; the baby; the patient's post-partum feelings, including joy, fear, and doubt; and how to balance her own needs against the demands made upon her by her family. The patient told me of some of her feelings and experiences during child-birth and as a new mother, in the manner of a teacher talking to a student. We did discuss her two big reactions to this "reversal," as she called it. On the one hand, she was pleased that she could return to me some of the support and knowledge that she felt she had gained from me; it boosted her self-confidence, which was a contrast to her usual diffidence, to feel an expert at something. On the other hand, it made her feel guilty, too pushy, and as though she had overstepped her bounds to be talking with me in this assertive way.

This patient might also have worked usefully with a male therapist or with a nonpregnant woman therapist. But the fact is that she was treated by a pregnant woman and it does seem as though the treatment with me helped the patient very much during the crisis of her pregnancy. Essentially, and most important, the patient was ultimately able to go through childbirth without too much emotional upheaval. And this result, at least in part, was probably a function of the focus in therapy on the patient's own needs for attention at this time and on her gaining some understanding appreciation of her ambivalance, of her mixed feelings about the baby, her desires for it as well as her resentment of it. My feeling was that the fact of our simultaneous pregnancies lent a special vividness to the verbal and nonverbal lan-guage of our communications, which might have been absent or less so with a different therapist. To some degree, the patient may have identified with me in the sense that she borrowed for herself some of the attitudes I tried to convey to her (some of which were based on my own real-life experiences at the moment) concerning the importance of her need for a special focus on herself and concerning the variety of feelings she was having about her baby. And she also had some chance to express her appreciation to me, by teaching me what she had learned from childbirth and motherhood, as if she were preparing me in a way similar to the way I had prepared her. Thus the transfer-ence in therapy, as well as some of the realistic components of the context, may have provided this patient with a special opportunity during her pregnancy to obtain some wished-for good mothering and at the same time to provide herself some mothering for another, which was part of her usual pattern of living, though not always as constructive.

Yet it is also possible that the therapeutic situation may have com-plicated matters. Since this was an unfamiliar situation to me, with both the patient and myself being pregnant (for the first time) at the same time, and on account of my own blind spots regarding the transference and countertransference, I was much less than diligent in taking up with the patient her reactions to my activity, her resistance to observing the fact of my pregnancy, and some of her probably unconscious reactions to it, including jealousy, and the possibility that some of her guilt feelings over her resentment toward pregnancy may have derived from the feeling that she was attacking me.

## Symbiosis

The wish for exclusiveness in the bond between mother and child shows itself in a variety of ways in psychotherapy. The notion encompasses a nurturant, dependable, consistent, reliable mother, one who is "always there" so to speak, that is yearned for by the girl child throughout her life, and that the mother as well may seek from her child. The wish may be expressed by sticky symbiotic feelings and fantasies in which mother and child are one or nearly so, through a variety of other connections and emotional ties thinner than symbiosis, but just as strong and important, such as availability, mutuality, honesty, and protection, which may derive from symbiosis. The patient may feel as though she has not been able to get enough of her mother exclusively for herself, and in all her other relationships she strives to get more of her mother for her very own, along some dimension of exclusiveness or other, but she may also be in severe conflict about getting this—wanting it and repulsing it at the same time.

One patient, with symptoms of depression and anxiety and emotional ups and downs, portrayed quite vividly her symbiotic struggles with her baby. Although the emphasis in this example is on the patient's role as a mother, the points made are applicable to the discussion because she is also a daughter, and her needs for an exclusive relationship with her baby were derived partly from her relationship to her own mother. This patient was a new mother who had returned to school two weeks after childbirth, for the child was born in the middle of the school year and the mother did not want to miss out on her classes.

In graphic language she described the reactions she endured each time she left her daughter with the baby-sitter. It was as though the patient and the baby were a big mass of molasses, all mixed up and mushed together as one. As the distance between them grew greater, and the patient drove her car closer to the university, but was consequently farther and farther from her baby, it felt as if the ball of molasses were painfully and searingly divided into two, with one portion the baby and the other portion the patient. However, since the stuff was so sticky there was never an actual division, and there were always fantasies of elongated threads of the sticky stuff that kept the two masses of molasses connected. The situation would reverse itself en route home. While away from home, the patient would fantasize all kinds of damage the baby-sitter might be doing to her child in her absence and would magnify the smallest detail into the greatest hazard, each time torn with indecision as to whether it would be best just to get rid of the sitter, quit school, and stay home herself. For example, one day the patient noticed that the baby-sitter had dirty fingernails, and the patient became alarmed and imagined that this probably meant that she was spreading germs all over the food she was feeding the baby. She might be poisoning the baby!

The therapy focused on trying to pin down when the patient felt depressed and when elated, what she felt would happen to her if she stayed home more, and questioning the adamance with which she insisted on continuing her schooling at that time. Our discussions revealed that the patient was unconsciously struggling with her own need to be with her baby girl exclusively, to bask in the joy and terror of being alone with her, feeling extremely close to and united with her, of loving her and letting the baby feed on her and suck nurturance from her. All of this she fought against, for it collided with another need to have something special but unrelated to motherhood for herself, so that she would not feel engulfed by the exclusive demands she felt would be made upon her, and which part of her wanted to give into for her own sake and personal needs. She felt as if she were both mother and child. She knew she was struggling, in part, with the desire to mother herself via the baby, and she also wanted mothering from me. Her own mother's extreme self-centeredness and selfishness, as well as the existence of several siblings, made her feel that as a child she was shortchanged of an exclusive relationship with her mother, and she was constantly engaged in a conflict about this— wanting desperately to possess her mother for her very own, sometimes having snatches of that, but also fighting against it, because a good deal of whatever was exclusive in her relationship to her mother she felt was for her mother's gratification, benefit, and needs for nurturance. The patient fought against her needs for an exclusive relationship to her baby, because somehow she felt that if she didn't go back to school she would end up like her rather unaccomplished mother, who had always remained at home and complained bitterly about it as if the children were responsible. The patient refused to be that way. She would show that she could be a career woman from the very beginning, and she would not depend upon her child. In addition, she somehow identified the baby with her mother such that she felt that by having the baby do something "on her own"—going out for a walk with the baby-sitter—the baby was "getting out of the house," which her own mother complained she was never able to do. The patient thought that the early, partial separation would in itself later on insure a special kind of exclusiveness between mother and child because it would set a pattern and be a reflection of the mother's demonstration that she had other interests and would foster the same in the child. She wanted to show that she did not need to possess the child entirely for herself.

What ultimately emerged quite clearly in the treatment after discussion of these issues is that the patient indeed wanted very much to be at home with her baby, and needed to be as much as she wanted to, and needed to pursue her studies. Prior to childbirth she had not anticipated that she would want to be with the baby as much as she actually did, and the turmoil and turbulence alone that came about were a shock to her. Finally, as a culmination of all of these insights, she was able to arrange a very suitable program for herself, by lightening her course load and staying home more with the baby but remaining a student, and continuing to employ the baby-sitter who by objective standards was, in fact, quite excellent.

My own personal experiences with symbiotic struggles that occurred shortly after the recent births of each of my children helped in major ways to provide a frame of reference for the conflicts that the patient just described was enduring. The lenses through which I viewed the patient partly as a result of my own motherhood made it possible for me to understand in a fuller and more meaningful way than previously the intense emotional pushes and pulls that exist between mother and child, that simultaneously repel and attract the two. At times, when the patient inquired about my family life and how I managed to combine it with a professional life, it became appropriate after some discussion to mention a few facts about myself and to indicate that I too had to contend with very strong feelings and some struggles with my various needs, desires, and responsibilities. These points were very useful and supportive to the patient, and her knowledge of them contributed to her identification with me and enabled her to see various alternatives for herself that might be satisfying. Nevertheless, at times when she was feeling highly vulnerable and especially troubled by her ambivalence, and inwardly pressured to be either a mother or a professional woman, she would project her conflict onto me and accuse me of pushing her to make one choice or another. Frequently these projections were lined up with the conflicts she experienced in relation to her mother, in the sense that a decision for the professional life made her feel guilty and removed from her mother in a variety of ways, and a decision for the maternal role made her feel submerged beneath her mother. Through the patient's relationship to me in which she reenacted some aspects of the mother-daughter tensions, real as well as fantasized, she was able to express some of her conflicts and feelings without recriminations and ultimately to feel much less emotional pain because of the opportunity to do so. Similarly, she was able to clarify and to get some better perspective of her varied feelings toward her mother, and to see her in a more realistic light, which included acknowledgment of her love and sympathy for her.

An important aspect of this vignette is to illustrate what is so often absent in some of women's liberation proselytizing, namely the possibility that a woman herself may have a very strong need and desire to be with her babies, to have an exclusive relationship with each of them. Usually women liberationists attribute demands for women to remain at home to men and to the needs of children, failing to recognize that a mother herself may want this. All the complaints about the unsuitability of baby-sitters and the unavailability of day-care centers, while realistic, may in part be a disguised way of saying that no surrogate mother is as good for a child as she is and she doesn't want anyone invading that relationship. For any individual woman in therapy who discusses her conflicts about motherhood versus career, and who complains about her staunch desire not to identify with her mother who stayed at home rearing her children, it is important for the therapist not to side with the patient's denial of her needs for an exclusive mother-baby relationship. Therapy may be extremely useful to any woman in conflict about motherhood and career, because it may offer her a chance to discuss the various alternatives and choices open to her, without settling in advance on any single choice, and therapy may also offer a woman an awareness of the origins of her conflict. A balance may certainly be struck in satisfying the need to be both a mother and a career woman at the same time. Hopefully, neither role is shortchanged for lack of being a full-time one, but instead each is enhanced by virtue of the simultaneous existence of the other.

During the third month of my second pregnancy, when it was not necessarily obvious that I was pregnant, I was assigned a bizarrely dressed, young schizophrenic woman whose very first words after the introduction were "Are you pregnant? Is this your first baby?" She had a five-year-old out-of-wedlock daughter, so she was very attuned to pregnancy, but more important at that moment I felt she was asking me whether I was hers and hers alone, or was I someone else's mother? Early in her marriage a few years before, she had been in treatment for seven months, then suddenly had to leave psychotherapy in order to join her husband in another state. Because the undiscussed termination of her relationship with that woman therapist was so disruptive to her, and left her feeling so raw and unfulfilled, she was reluctant to enter therapy again but she felt she had no choice as she was feeling so low.

Her presenting problems were severe depression, marked by loss of hope, along with an inability to paint as she used to be able to, especially in front of her husband, who was a talented actor. Somehow she seemed to feel absorbed by him when he was around. She decided that she would like to concentrate her efforts in therapy on handling her daughter, who sometimes overwhelmed her with her questions, noise-making, demands, and efforts at autonomy. With that temporary goal in mind, in the second session we started to talk about the child. When there were fifteen minutes left to the session the patient asked how much more time we had. I replied, "Until eleven twenty." She cringed in disbelief when I said that it was time to stop and marched out the door looking quite pained. The next session she stormed in with a terrific verbal assault. She snarled and screamed incessantly that I was totally incompetent and absolutely unresponsive to her needs, that I obviously had virtually no comprehension of what she was about, that I was extremely abrupt in telling her that we had only five minutes more in the previous session, and then, in ending exactly on time in the middle of what she was talking about, I was even more abrupt. She didn't know whether she would ever come back and came in that day solely to tell me all this. I suggested we talk about it, but she preferred to think about it on her own. She then swept out of the office. Quite shaken by this barrage, and considering that her complaints might be justified, I wondered whether she should see a different therapist, but I was encouraged by a colleague to continue with her and to accept her behavior as a reflection of her sense of her own emptiness, which was being projected onto me. To let her go now, whether or not she requested it, would probably only intensify her feelings of rejection and unworthiness. In fact, she might likely be responding to termination issues at the very beginning of therapy.

In marked contradistinction to what had taken place in the session just described, she returned the next time and seemed quite composed, casually mentioning that she planned to keep seeing me, but noting with a slight grin that she thought I was frightened of her last time. "Yes," I replied, "I was." And after a while, when it was timely, I wondered out loud whether she was trying to see whether I could survive and withstand her outraged assaults on me. She sort of agreed that this was true. We also discussed what she meant by my being "unresponsive." My understanding of her outbursts, which occurred in less violent forms on several other occasions, was that she indeed felt a very special bond with me from the very start, or at least fantasized a bond with me, precisely because she felt that I was tuned into her and that I did understand her, rather than that I didn't. This exclusive relationship with me, which she sensed she could depend upon, gave her a small sense of hope, but such a bond invaded the exclusive hopeless bond she had with her disturbed, frightened, harried, frazzled, violent mother, for whom she had considerable compassion and pity. To allow herself to become hopeful would separate her from her mother, and this made her feel extremely guilty and at a loss, so she felt compelled to remain in a hopeless state in order to remain with her mother. The devastation and threat she experienced in altering this very painful state of affairs forced her to distort my behavior and to make me into her mother, by claiming I wasn't helping her. In therapy she made some strides in understanding all this by my pointing out in each relevant instance how these dynamics showed themselves and how she needed to punish herself.

Part of the reason for the dearth of an exclusively dependable relationship with her mother was that her mother was indeed "abrupt" with her in the sense that the patient had two younger siblings, born when she was one and two years old, respectively. There was very little opportunity to have her mother all to herself. It was no wonder that she was so attuned to my pregnancy, for her mother was nearly always pregnant for the first two years of the patient's life. It was as though at the end of each session with pregnant me the reenactment of the birth of a rival sibling were taking place, and this is what she was referring to when she accused me of being abrupt. To her it would always feel as though she didn't have enough time. I hypothesized to myself that by giving birth to an illegitimate child, the patient reacted in a very self-destructive way to her own infancy. Psychologically, she became her own mother by identification with her mother's pregnancy and motherhood, and thereby probably established an exclusive link with her. She was also her own child, but this time the only child of the fantasized mother.

The extremely primitive rage that was elicited when the patient felt merged or fused with mother, husband, child, or me usually had no place to go but inside her, which made her feel obliterated, like a void, like "nothing." It emptied her out. As a child she had had a skin disease on her legs, and so her mother had prohibited her siblings from hitting her. But the patient had bitten them whenever she felt like it. Their inability to retaliate made her, out of guilt, turn some rage toward herself. Her mother added to this inwardly directed rage by beating her, and because she dared not risk losing any more of her mother than she had already lost, she did not hit back. Perhaps these beatings provided some other form of exclusive relationship with the mother that the patient continued on her own as she continued to fight against herself. Therapy with her pregnant therapist, who did not disintegrate before her very eyes from her outrage, seemed to provide some meaningful opportunity for an outlet of this rage, and also provided much reassurance for her.

Termination, which took place primarily as a function of her moving out of town, was a special opportunity for the patient to verbally and directly express her needs for an exclusive relationship with me. In an extremely poignant session in which she heaved and trembled in her seat as she sobbed, she gasped: "If you really loved me you wouldn't leave me even though it is I who am leaving you." And "If you really loved me you wouldn't be having that baby to take care of instead of taking care of me."

Although she left treatment after five months with many of the same problems that had brought her in, this patient did gain one small ray of hope because she knew something of where the hopelessness and void within her had originated.

## Homosexuality

This discussion of homosexuality is meant to draw attention to a significant aspect of female development that is sometimes overlooked in the short-term therapy of women patients in favor of other less loaded topics.

Though it is not stated, one major reason that patients may request women therapists is that unconsciously they hope to talk about some of their struggles and their sexual feelings toward other women. This may be so even when homosexuality per se is not a stated problem in the initial interview. The patient's presenting symptoms may run the gamut: compulsive eating, difficulty in talking with boyfriend or mate, unresponsiveness in a sexual relationship with the boyfriend or mate, difficulty in social relationships with women, inclinations toward homosexual men as boyfriends, getting into relationships with unsuitable men that never seem to work out, getting into relationships with men that leave the woman wanting in some major ways, flitting from one man to another, giving birth out of wedlock, difficulty in writing papers, difficulty in making decisions, and hypochondriasis. These symptoms may reflect a variety of emotional concerns on several developmental levels, but they may also serve as an effective cover for homosexual concerns as well, concerns that could be left untouched in the treatment because they are so well disguised.

It is likely and reasonable that a conception of female homosexuality encompasses a very broad range of fantasies, behaviors, and feelings including genital sexual aspects, but not necessarily limited to those. These may range from the slightest touch or bumping into between women, through intense feelings of longing for love, affection, and attention, through intense jealousy between friends, through possessiveness, through outright genital contact between women. The original precursor of feelings of eroticism between women lies in the frequent and intense physical contact between mother and child. Watch the intense sensual excitement of breast feeding. Watch a mother changing her girl baby's diapers and cleansing the baby to make her comfortable. There are hundreds of caresses, touches, squeezes, inspections, and strokings involved. And these contacts are all socially acceptable and within the bounds of good mothering. These contacts multiply in number with each clothing change, kiss, hug, and cradling, which build up over a period of years into a whole lot of sexual feelings about one's body and intensify the physical relationship between mother and girl child. It is worthwhile to consider a broad range of fantasies, behaviors, and feelings under the rubric of possible or potential homosexuality, simply because the word inherently neither defines nor describes anything specific. And for any one patient no presumption can be made about what she regards as homosexual unless she talks about what she means. And this is most likely to be very difficult for her to do although she may show her concern more in her actions than in her words.

A married woman with complaints of sexual dissatisfaction expressed great pleasure at sitting face to face with me and felt that our respective chairs were just the right distance apart. She noted that they were "not too close." "Not too close for what?" I inquired. "Well, they were just the right distance for talking about intimate things—not too close and not too far." Therapy seemed to proceed well for we talked about her fears of achievement relative to outdoing her very successful husband who was also a student, her desire for more interest by her mother in her married life, and conflicts about having children. She made great strides in her understanding of all these issues, and many of my interpretations, especially about conflicts over competitiveness, seemed to fit at the time. In a discussion about professional women it came up that she assumed I was unmarried, for she did not notice my wedding ring. After some discussion, when I brought it to her attention that I wore it on my right hand, she seemed vividly upset. From what followed it seemed as though she interpreted my wearing of the ring on my right hand as an indication of marital difficulties on my part, which was disturbing to her since she was using me as a model and placed great faith and store in my being okay in every respect. Yet

527

I had a nagging feeling that something was missing in this interpretation as well as in the others—there seemed to be a shallowness to them, but I didn't know quite what it was. My reevaluation of this case suggests that it was her sexual feelings and concomitant conflicts toward her mother, which were exacerbated by her being an only child and which were transferred to me, that were the missing links in a number of enigmas in the therapy, including the "not too close" reference, the ring reference, and her complaints about her mother and her wish to cut her out of her life by saying that she had no past and no roots. We did discuss the patient's desire for protection and attention from me and her longing to feel close to me as though she were my only patient and child. But her possible feelings of desire toward me were never mentioned, and the focus instead was more on her wish for nurturance. This patient made a number of gains in this brief treatment, but it may have been very helpful to her to understand at least something important that existed within her.

Two years ago I saw a very shy, soft-spoken, socially awkward graduate student who complained of tearfulness; longstanding, unexplained depression; excessive shyness with men; and uncertainty over her career goals. Only with obviously great pain was she able to talk about her family. Her older brother seemed to have had a nervous breakdown while in graduate school. Her mother was described as bright, aggressive, and very intrusive and involved in her daughter's life, which had been the case since she was a little girl, and which was always a great source of distress to the patient. The intrusiveness showed itself chiefly in her mother's persistent questions about everything, which the patient did not answer or otherwise avoided. The father, who was in the wholesale ladies' shoe business, was described as very quiet and reserved, and very much in the background of the family affairs.

Whenever I asked a question or made a comment, the patient appeared to be under great stress and nearly withdrew into a shell, as if to take refuge in hiding within herself. Although we talked about the similarity in her frightened reaction to me and to her mother, this did not alleviate her apprehensions about me, and so I decided to maintain a reserved posture with her for a time. During treatment her father became seriously ill, but she was not very capable of talking about her feelings about this, mostly denying that she felt much, and in fact whatever she was feeling seemed thoroughly ambiguous to me. She terminated treatment unexpectedly after eleven sessions, saying that she felt much better. By this time she was beginning to have a sexual relationship with one of her classmates, the first such relationship, but was reluctant to talk about him with me. Her depression had lifted in good measure. She was still uncertain of her career plans, but she was no longer too troubled about this.

About one year later, looking very buoyant and strong though still tearful, she returned to the clinic and asked me to be her therapist again. With considerably greater verve and emotional reflectiveness than she had ever shown before, she explained her response to her previous therapy experience with me, emphasizing that she knew that she had more or less refused to let me help her then, because she was so highly resistant to my questions and other efforts. Many times she knew what she was feeling, but denied awareness because she was so frightened and because I reminded her of her mother. Therapy had nevertheless helped her quite a bit in her relationship to men, and in her career, in which she was becoming quite successful. Now, however, she came back for something else. Recently a college roommate whom she continued to see regularly told her that she had been having a homosexual affair with another friend, whom the patient admired greatly, and the patient realized consciously for the first time in her life what she had always sensed just under the surface—that she too was sexually attracted to women. She did not know how extensive her interest was, and she was also petrified of it, but she did want at least an opportunity to talk about it, with a woman, because she thought this would be most appropriate. She realized that talking about her sexual interest in women would lead to discussing her relationship to her mother, and this might clarify some of the reasons for her fears of her mother's intrusiveness. All of these possibilities were both attractive and frightening at the same time.

I agreed to treat her. Her ability to relate to me and her fairly ready voluntary willingness to talk about her reaction to me and to my then pregnancy were in marked contradistinction to the stony attitudes she displayed in her earlier therapy experience. When I canceled a session because of a bad cold, she was able to express her bitterness and intense jealousy of the probability of my wanting to take good care of myself, in order to protect my unborn child, and my consequently apparent willingness to let her, the patient, fend for herself that week. This led to associations of how her mother took care of her when she was sick, how she loved the physical comforting and attention, and how these satisfactions may have been some of the reasons she was ill so often as a child. Similarly, her frequent colds now and concomitant need to stay in bed might be reenactments of earlier experiences, but this time she was babying herself. She had some dreams about my pregnancy that reflected her desire to have a child, and to be a child, and to be infantilized. All of what I am describing had definite sexual components that the patient was aware of, even though to a major extent the focus of her discussion was on the nurturance she wished to get from me. Although from time to time she was able to discuss some of the nature of the details of her attraction to women, she did not get far in directly confronting the issue. In part this was because she felt that if she were to do this, then inevitably she would have to discuss her sexual feelings toward me. And this she simply could not do in any direct manner at the time. Merely being able to state aloud to another woman that she was aware of her attractions to women, and letting me know that she had similar feelings toward me and "probably" toward her mother, was enough for her to cope with. And it was. Even discussing her fears of separating from her family, mainly her mother, to study in Europe was a big accomplishment.

In this example the relationship between the patient's needs for, and fears of, nurturance were very much connected to her sexual attractions to women.

I worked for a brief time with a highly flamboyant musician who came in in a severely anxious state, weeping hysterically that she might not be able to complete a composition in time to graduate in June. In addition, she was living with a bisexual man, whom she had known for only ten days before they decided to live together, and who had become a great problem to her. He seemed to be very unkind to the patient, and she seemed very willing to absorb this punishment.

This young woman was previously in therapy in the clinic. According to the richly detailed notes, the emphasis in prior therapy was almost entirely on her feelings toward men, toward her father—her parents had been divorced when she was seven—and consequently on her feelings, sexual and otherwise, toward her male therapist. The patient became quite upset at termination and acted out in a very hostile way toward her female roommate to whom she had been quite close until then. She was seen again by her therapist for three more sessions to help tide her over the termination, during which time she discussed some of her feelings toward her mother and described some things about her that had not come up before. Then she terminated.

The intake interviewer who saw the patient on her recent return to the clinic pointed out that the patient preferred a woman therapist because she did not wish to get into a seductive relationship with a male therapist again, and because she had already noticed in the waiting room that she was attracted to a number of the male therapists. On the basis of this patient's history, as well as the dearth of discussion of her relationship to her mother in psychotherapy, at least according to the notes, plus what seemed like an excessive and overdone emphasis on her sexual attractions to men, I hypothesized to myself that one of her chief struggles was with homosexual feelings.

In the first session, while talking about her boyfriend, she casually slipped in that she had homosexual fantasies about women. In therapy she wanted to focus on her difficulty in writing papers, and suddenly speculated that there might be a connection between that difficulty and sex—a possibility that she had never before considered.

The next time she mentioned that, while masturbating the previous night, she was very turned on by fantasies of the women's role, while she was engaged in sex with a man. She was considering trying out some sex with a woman, asked me some questions about what I thought of the idea, and specifically put the question, "What do I do, put an advertisement in the paper, 'Lesbian Wanted'?" My response to her question of my reactions was to the effect that I couldn't say much about all this because I didn't know her very well and didn't know what all this meant to her. Quite spontaneously she then brought up two important aspects of her relationship to her mother. The first was a vivid and lengthy description in which the patient used her hands to enhance her description of how her mother used to make up and adorn herself in front of the mirror for hours on end, an activity that the patient witnessed and may have found exciting. The making-up led to nothing for the mother did not go out with men. Second, as a teenager, whenever the patient went out on a date she would rush home and provide her mother with explicit details of the kisses— whether they were French kisses or whatever—and the mother would express her opinion about the activity and the boys involved. Much later on at college, when the patient started to sleep with men, she decided against telling her mother about it. She and her friends would make up elaborate stories to tell a parent, in case the parent called the dormitory while the girl was out sleeping with her boyfriend. Once, in the middle of the night, at 3:00 A.M. the mother called the patient, only to learn from the boyfriend that the patient was "in the music studio," which was the standard excuse when the patient was not around. The patient rushed back to her own apartment, in case the mother should doublecheck there, and at 4:00 A.M. called her mother back and subsequently became involved in a four-hour conversation in which they talked about the daughter's sleeping with men. The mother complained that she "could not sleep all night" upon hearing the news that her daughter was "in the music studio," figuring this meant she was sleeping with someone, and she accused the daughter of promiscuity and prostitution, as she had done several times before. Apparently the mother was overinvolved in the daughter's sexual activities, but the daughter may have encouraged this as well. These incidents suggest that there was at least an unwritten homosexual involvement between mother and daughter, which the mother may have originally fostered in her activities around the house. The existence of this mother and child living together for so many years without men may have exacerbated the intensity of the homosexual interaction, even though to my knowledge no overt sexual activity took place.

In addition to the patient's descriptions of her mother, and the implicit sexual connotations that were an inherent part of their relationship, the patient also talked of her attractions to a current female friend. She and her friend had had several discussions about homosexuality and their sexual interest in one another. Generally, the patient appeared to be consciously and unconsciously preoccupied with the homosexual aspect of herself that she had not hitherto explored, and this was both scary and enticing to her.

This patient terminated therapy after a total of five sessions, and about three weeks earlier than she had planned to leave school. By that time her life with her lover had become too emotionally demanding and chaotic, so at her father's and stepmother's invitation she went to live with them in a nearby city, and she came to school for a few days a week. She was pleased at reestablishing a relationship with her father, and was also pleased that her parents now spoke with each other for the first time in twenty years, when the mother called the father's home to speak with her daughter.

The patient considered it a big accomplishment that she came in to tell me of her relatively sudden decision to terminate, rather than doing it by phone. Her decision was based on a few things. There were too many aspects of her life that were fragmented now. Her clothing was in several different places, she was living with various addicts and homosexual friends while at school, traveling to and from her father's home was a hardship, and once-a-week psychotherapy was not enough considering her problems. Her family, including her father, her stepmother, and her mother, was providing plenty of support so she didn't need me for that, and between her stepmother and mother, she had more women than she could handle, she felt. The patient felt that she needed to withdraw from all the stimuli around her, to cease the input and output, and to curtail her relationships in order to write the composition that would enable her to graduate. She had already begun work on it, which pleased her, because it was trouble with that composition that had brought her into treatment in the first place. She was now confident she could get it done. After graduation she would be able to work on her emotional life and to get the therapy she needed.

I tried to encourage the patient to discuss whether there was something in what we had discussed or in her feelings toward me that led to her decision to terminate. When she expressed appreciation for my efforts, I inquired about other feelings as well, and she did express some anger at my suggesting in a previous session that we discuss the meaning to her of her efforts to keep me after the sessions were up. Then she said she was getting a headache, and she was unwilling to pursue the discussion any further. We agreed that in addition to her need to withdraw and to concentrate on her work, a variety of feelings toward me were probably contributing to her decision to terminate now.

It is not possible to come to definite conclusions about the value of the treatment for this patient, but there is a strong suggestion that talking for a brief time with a woman therapist provided relief of some tensions and allowed the patient a special opportunity to discuss her troubling homosexual fantasies and feelings. This view is based on the difference in content in each of the patient's therapy experiences. Of course it may be that the patient may just have been ready to discuss the newer content at this time, regardless of the sex of the therapist. However, the patient herself had anticipated that with a woman she would have some freed energy to deal with some of her major concerns because in contrast to her previous therapy, she would not have to expend so much effort seducing a male therapist. Perhaps consciously or unconsciously what she had in mind was to touch upon her homosexual feelings. Whatever relief that did result from our discussions may have been responsible for her newly found ability to write her composition. At the same time, it is possible that in the transference to me, and in other aspects of her life, namely the relationship to her girl friend, the patient's sexual feelings were aroused to a level that was very difficult for her to tolerate, and that this contributed to her decision to terminate. It would probably be most accurate to say that the therapy, with its built-in limits imposed primarily by the patient herself, afforded the patient an opportunity to relieve some tensions that enabled her to work and renew her relationship to her father, while at the same time those same tensions caused her considerable anxiety.

# 44

# Adaptive and Pathogenic Aspects of Sex-Role Stereotypes: Implications for Parenting and Psychotherapy

## HARRIET E. LERNER

It is fortunate that the current feminist movement has brought issues regarding masculinity and femininity to public and professional attention. A careful reading of the psychiatric literature indicates that there is conceptual confusion about the meaning of the terms "masculine" and "feminine," as well as a confused rationale as to why specific traits, behaviors, or qualities are considered appropriate and healthy for one sex but maladaptive or less appropriate for the other (Lerner 1974). Further, there is considerable controversy related to the impact of our bipolar concepts of masculinity and femininity, that is, whether sex-role stereotypes have an adaptive or pathogenic effect on an individual's development.

The first task of this paper is to evaluate the positive and negative effects of sex-role stereotypes, disregarding any particular definitions

This paper grew out of an inspiring exchange of letters with Dr. Marie R. Badaracco, to whom the author expresses her gratitude. She would also like to thank Drs. Meredith A. Titus-Maxfield and Stephen Lerner for helpful suggestions.

of masculinity and femininity that exist in this culture at present. Second, I will present my viewpoint that the degree to which dichotomous concepts of masculinity and femininity are adaptive and facilitative (as opposed to restrictive and pathogenic) for a particular individual is inversely related to the degree to which that individual has consolidated a stable and clear sense of gender identity. Finally, implications for parenting and psychotherapy will be discussed. I will not attempt to present an exhaustive and definitive account of the issues at hand; rather, my goal is to add balance and conceptual clarity to an important area that has remained clouded by prejudice, cultural mythology, and a counterproductive battle of the sexes.

## Pathogenic and Adaptive Consequences

The pathogenic consequences of sex-role stereotypes have been discussed at length in the feminist and psychiatric literature. There is little question that stereotyped notions of masculinity and femininity have a constricting and inhibiting effect on development. Children are encouraged to conform to idealized generalizations of what males and females "should be" rather than being allowed to develop their own unique potentials, interests, and skills (Lerner 1973; Seidenberg 1970). The inevitable pathogenic consequence of any masculine-feminine dichotomy is that the child will be made to feel that some valued and desired aspect of herself or himself is gender-inappropriate and must be denied or relinquished (Badaracco 1974). The question of biological or constitutional sex differences is not relevant in this regard. Rather the question is whether one respects the temperament and biological predisposition of each unique child, which may or may not conform to statistical group differences between the sexes.

In recent years there has been a growing appreciation of the deep guilt, anxiety, and inhibition that result when a child is told that his or her interests, skills, or behaviors are gender-inappropriate (Badaracco 1974). No little boy can tolerate being called "feminine," and no little girl can tolerate being called "masculine." It is hardly surprising, then, that early in a girl's life she experiences anxiety and guilt about strivings in directions that are not domestic (Seidenberg 1970). Numerous publications in the psychoanalytic literature suggest that many women who seemingly "choose" to relinquish self-seeking ambitious strivings do so because they cannot freely and without guilt fulfill themselves through personal achievement. This guilt is linked to the fact that professional capability and competence are unconsciously experienced as "masculine" (Chasseguet-Smirgel 1970; Moulton 1973). Clinical and life experience demonstrate that few women are resilient enough to tolerate internal and external threats to their femininity. As one psychoanalyst put it, "No woman will treasure any fame or glory she can achieve at the price of being called unfeminine. This below-the-belt blow sends most women into despair" (Seidenberg 1970, p. 143). Pressures on men to relinquish so-called feminine aspects of themselves are equally if not more intense.

In addition to having pathogenic consequences, it may be argued that sex-role stereotypes, irrespective of their content, are conceptually unsound. Dichotomous notions of masculinity and femininity implicitly embrace a dichotomous concept of mental health for the two sexes that is difficult to justify on theoretical grounds. Research findings demonstrating statistically significant differences between the sexes cannot be interpreted to mean that a trait or quality is healthy for one sex and less adaptive or important for the other. Rather it is more likely that a trait, quality, or behavior is either healthy or unhealthy for a particular individual, irrespective of sex. Both sexes, for example, should be able to express a healthy degree of aggression, competition, and self-assertion that allows one to persist and work for what one believes in, even in the face of anger or disapproval from others. However, for both sexes aggression, competition, and self-assertion may have pathological underpinnings; competing, winning, or "measuring up" can become ends in themselves, perhaps to compensate for an individual's underlying feelings of narcissistic inadequacy.

Let us turn now to the positive or adaptive aspects of sex-role stereotypes. First, we should pay due respect to the fact that in all places and times there has existed some masculine-feminine dichotomy that has included a clear division of labor based on sex, as well as a sharp division in the attributes, traits, and qualities valued for each sex. The universality of sex-role stereotypes does not necessarily prove them to be virtuous (scapegoating, prejudice, and war have also achieved such universal status), but it does suggest that a masculine-feminine polarization serves significant adaptive functions.

It is important to note that the defenses of splitting and projective identification that are involved in a masculine-feminine polarization are not just pathogenic defenses—they also facilitate personality organization for the growing organism (Cooper 1976). As Klein noted, the ordering of experiences into bipolarities orders the universe and "allows the ego to emerge out of chaos and to order its experience" (Segal 1967, p. 22). She suggested that splitting might be a precondition for the later, more complicated, although internally more whole, experience of integrating bipolarities within one's self (e.g., good-bad, active-passive, dependent-independent).

One adaptive function of bipolar concepts of masculinity and femininity is to make the consolidation of gender identity a simpler task for the child. The child's cognitive labeling of herself/himself as girl/boy is the basic organizer for subsequent gender experience (Kleeman 1976), and dissimilarities or bipolarities in socialization may facilitate this labeling process. In addition, establishing and reinforcing clear-cut differences between the two sexes may help the child to manage certain anxieties regarding sexual differences, for example, the boy's fear that he will lose his penis and become a girl; the girl's fear that she has lost a penis and is thus a castrated male.

It is likely that dichotomous notions of masculinity and femininity are of greater psychological value to the male child, in part because of the intensity of castration anxiety. In addition, an exaggeration or polarization of the differences between the sexes (whether real or imagined) may help the boy child in the task of achieving autonomy and separation from the mother. This has characteristically been a more difficult developmental task for the girl child, who is anatomically similar to the mother and cannot rely on a sense of masculinity to bolster differences from or defiance of her mother. At the same time, however, the boy is in the uniquely difficult situation of identifying with and learning from a primary caretaker whose qualities he is taught to repudiate within himself.

Although the exaggeration or polarization of sex differences, whether real or contrived, may simplify the establishment of gender identity, it does not follow that a similar sex-role socialization for both sexes would lead to a disturbance in gender identity. Psychiatric writings often suggest or imply that adherence to dichotomous concepts of masculinity and femininity, however culturally defined, is essential for the development of normal gender identity (Kleeman 1976; Stoller 1976). This theoretical viewpoint is put forth without acknowledging or studying those healthy children who are being raised in normal families wherein sex-role stereotypes are neither adhered to by the parents nor especially encouraged in the children. I am speaking of families in which parents have a deep sense of gender identity that transcends and is independent of societally prescribed role behaviors and culturally defined notions of masculinity and femininity.

## Implications for Parenting

The viewpoint that sex-role stereotypes have a consolidating and facilitating effect as well as restrictive and pathogenic consequences raises the question of the optimum degree to which sex-role stereotypes should be adhered to for the growing child. Should parents try to free themselves entirely from thinking in terms of a masculine-feminine dichotomy? Should stereotypes be adhered to rigidly, at least while the child is young? Or is there some middle ground in which we can retain our cultural definitions of masculinity and femininity, while broadening them and making them more flexible, thus providing a wide range of choice for both sexes?

This question, so long as it is posed as a search for general rules and guidelines, cannot be answered. Sex-role stereotypes and bipolar concepts of masculinity and femininity provide a structure for the child. The extent to which this structure is necessary and valuable—or restrictive and inhibiting—depends on the child's unique qualities and the family constellation. My clinical work suggests that the degree to which sex-role stereotypes are adaptive and facilitating (as opposed to restrictive and inhibiting) is inversely related to the extent to which an individual has established a stable and integrated sense of self and has consolidated a solid gender identity.

It may be helpful to define the concept of gender identity as it appears in this paper. Stoller (1976) defines "core gender identity" as "the sense we have of our sex—of maleness in males and of femaleness in females" (p. 61). "Gender identity" is a broader concept involving "a conviction about one's self and one's role," or a sense of masculinity and femininity. The concepts of "masculine" and "feminine" are elusive, since they refer to subjective experiences that can achieve a multiplicity of behavioral expressions. I define gender identity (i.e., masculinity and femininity) as a stable, subjective sense of comfort and liking for one's sex and for those functions that are sex-specific. In women this means comfort and liking for female genitals and reproductive capacities without undue envy or fear of men and the penis. In men this means a comfort and liking for male genitals without undue envy or fear of women and female genitals and reproductive capacities.

Consider first the child who is being reared by two mature parents, each of whom has established a sense of autonomy and self-worth and a stable, nonconflictual gender identity. That is, the mother has a secure and comfortable sense of being female and feminine, and the father of being male and masculine. If such parents are not split along traditional masculine-feminine lines, their child may receive considerable psychological benefits with few costs. If the mother and father are both nurturant and intellectual, if they cook together, clean together, and share authority in a spontaneous collaborative way that defies traditional stereotypes, the child does not become confused or anxious. Rather, such parenting allows the girl (or boy) to incorporate a definition of femininity (or masculinity) that permits or sanctions acknowledgment, appreciation, and enjoyment of a wide range of behaviors, feelings, and experiences.

In contrast, consider the child reared in a family where self-other boundaries between parents are poorly maintained and where the father and/or mother has an unstable or conflict-laden gender identity. For such children, who may be developing unassimilated, confused maternal and paternal imagoes, the parents' adherence to traditionally defined masculine-feminine roles can have a clarifying-consolidating effect. In such families culturally defined bipolar concepts of masculinity and femininity may be reassuring not only to the child but also to the parents. As Kleeman (1976) noted, the parents' cognitive awareness of the child's sex—"my baby is a girl"—organizes and directs a whole set of cues, rewards, and sanctions. Sex-role stereotypes simplify the task of parenting by providing explicit rules and guidelines for child rearing. This is essential for parents who themselves lack stable and clear inner directives.

## Implications for Psychotherapy

The viewpoint that sex-role stereotypes have a consolidating, supportive function for certain individuals and restrictive, inhibiting consequences for others has important implications for treatment. For example, it is not therapeutic to attempt to "liberate" a patient from cultural sex-role stereotypes if that patient relies on them to shore up and maintain a shaky sense of gender identity. The following brief vignette is illustrative.

*Case 1*

*When Ms. A came to her first therapy hour, she had an "ultrafeminine" appearance and manner that had an imitative or "tacked-on" quality. There was a striking absence of so-called masculine strivings in her history. She had never gone through a tomboy stage and had always avoided rough or aggressive play. In many ways she had always been a model if not a caricature of domesticity and femininity.*

*Ms. A had managed to maintain a somewhat stable existence until she began to feel pressure from the feminist subculture in California and from a man with whom she was involved to become more "liberated." As she yielded to such pressure, the potentially disorganizing effects were quickly apparent. For example, on a camping trip she dressed in her first pair of blue jeans and a work shirt and suddenly felt "unfeminine" and unattractive, and the thought crossed her mind that perhaps she was not "totally female." Subsequently she noted that when she was dressed in "men's clothing" (in this category she included women's jeans with a fly front) she "talked differently," took "bigger strides," and began to have mild episodic feelings of depersonalization and unreality. In the face of this anxiety and confusion, Ms. A, at the age of twenty-five, sought psychotherapy.*

*Early in the course of treatment, which by practical necessity was once-a-week therapy, it became evident that Ms. A was a severely disturbed individual who maintained her tenuous sexual identity primarily through strict conformity to behaviors ascribed to her sex that were clearly differentiated from those ascribed to men. Given the practical limitations on the extensiveness of treatment and the very precarious nature of the patient's ego functioning, I chose a supportive approach and helped her to reestablish the sense of femininity that in the past she had been able to consolidate through her strict adherence and even caricature of traditional feminine behaviors. Part of this therapeutic approach was actively helping Ms. A to resist surrounding cultural pressures toward androgyny. A strict feminist therapist might have failed to appreciate the consolidating, supportive effect of sex-role stereotypes for this woman.*

While the severity of Ms. A's disturbance is atypical, the phenomenon illustrated by this vignette is widespread. One neurotic female patient, for example, was unable to assume the top, more active position in intercourse because it made her feel like she "had the penis," a conflicted wish for her. A neurotic male patient was unable to comfortably let his wife drive while he was in the car because this made him feel "feminine." Some conflicts and anxieties about gender identity may be ubiquitous. To the degree that a particular individual experiences such conflicts or anxieties, sex-role stereotypes or the "rules of the game" may be helpful. The therapist's decision to analyze or to support defensive conformity to sex-role stereotypes should be made not on the basis of personal ideology but rather on a careful assessment of the function that sex-role stereotypes may serve for a particular individual.

In treating relatively healthy patients who have established a stable gender identity, the most common therapeutic error is failure to question conformity to sex-role stereotypes. This happens frequently when the patient is seemingly comfortable in complying with her or his culturally defined role. The following vignette is illustrative.

## Case 2

*Ms. B, a twenty-eight-year-old woman in intensive psychotherapy, announced to her therapist that she would be moving to a new city at the end of the year because of her husband's professional advancement. Although she was sad about leaving psychothera-*

*py as well as her friends and her teaching job in a Montessori school, she expressed excitement about the challenges that the move would bring and pride in her husband's success. Initial inquiry by the therapist as to any less enthusiastic feelings she might have met with a restatement of her positive reaction to the anticipated change. Certainly it entailed losses for her, but these were well overshadowed by the gains. Further, Ms. B was thinking about starting a family soon and thought she might stop work entirely for several years. She communicated clearly that she would like the issue dropped, and it was dropped for some time.*

*Months later when Ms. B was discussing some pains and pleasures of her work, the therapist once again commented that he was struck by how easily she made her own job unimportant in regard to the planned move, and how adept she was at convincing him that this was the case. He also speculated as to why she might need to avoid taking her own professional life seriously, and commented that it was difficult for her to be in competition with her husband or to ask him to make professional sacrifices for her, although she had done so earlier for him. His questioning, which occurred in the face of her initial insistence that there were no further issues to discuss, led to her increased understanding of the neurotic anxieties that caused her to devalue her work, to treat it as less important than her husband's, and even to be ready to drop it entirely. The therapist's persistence in this line of questioning also had significant transference implications, since it communicated to the patient that he took her work seriously. The fact that he had dropped the issue, even though she had more than invited him to do so, had for her the unconscious meaning that he, like her mother, did not really want her to be a fulfilled individual. Ms. B and her husband did not move, and she has continued to advance professionally and now has a challenging position with considerable authority.*

This therapist's skillful handling of Ms. B's treatment may be more the exception than the rule. Many therapists fail to analyze defensive and maladaptive aspects of the life choices of patients who conform to predominant cultural stereotypes, especially when the patient is seemingly content (e.g., the "feminine" woman who opts for full-time motherhood because of neurotic anxieties regarding intellectual achievement, competition, and success). This is an especially important issue for women patients who so often begin treatment with intense unconscious guilt and anxiety about acknowledging wishes or longings that are not in keeping with the feminine role. Even therapists who are deeply committed to facilitating women's struggles for self-realization may unwittingly contribute to their inhibitions by an implicit acceptance or approval of a patient's neurotic compliance with culturally defined notions of "femininity."

## Conclusions

It is to be hoped that mental health professionals will continue to re-examine and clarify their thinking regarding sex-role stereotypes and bipolar concepts of masculinity and femininity. While radical feminist writings are sometimes naive in their global damnation of sex-role stereotypes, the traditional psychiatric literature has more frequently erred in the direction of blanket condemnation of the current trend toward depolarization of the sexes. Some of this literature warns of impending pathology for children who are not raised in conformity to traditional masculine-feminine stereotypes and suggests that nonsexist child rearing will lead to identity problems, sexual confusion, and to gray, affectless, "neuter" children (Group for the Advancement of Psychiatry [GAP] 1975). Terms such as "role blurring," "role confusion," and "role reversal" are applied to parents in a pejorative manner, often without discriminating between healthy parents who, for adaptive reasons, do not choose to organize their lives along traditional masculine-feminine lines and those chaotic, unstable parents who may make a similar "choice" for pathogenic reasons.

In addition to being theoretically unsound, such writing has the consequence of discouraging certain people from seeking our services and has led individuals to turn to more progressive nonestablishment therapists who may be less qualified to offer help. There is unquestionably a powerful trend in this country away from dichotomous concepts of masculinity and femininity; many young couples today choose not to live like Jack Spratt and his wife. In fact, a recent GAP report (1975) quoted a study finding that 50 percent of college students expressed a belief in equal and shared parenting. Whether recent trends toward androgyny are healthy or pathogenic is not a question to be answered simply or to be considered out of the context of the unique individual at hand. Perhaps it is because issues related to the topic of masculinity and femininity are anxiety producing and emotionally laden that so much of our writing on this topic fails to do justice to either the precision of scientific thinking or the complexity of human experience.

REFERENCES

Badaracco, M. R. 1974. Recent trends toward unisex: A Panel. *American Journal of Psychoanalysis* 34:17–23.

Chassequet-Smirgel, J. 1970. *Female sexuality.* Ann Arbor, Mich.: University of Michigan Press.

Cooper, L. 1976. Cotherapy relationship in groups. *Small Group Behavior* 7:473–498.

Group for the Advancement of Psychiatry, Committee on the College Student. 1975. *The educated woman: Prospects and problems.* GAP Report 92. New York: GAP.

Kleeman, J. A. 1976. Freud's views on early female sexuality in the light of direct child observation. *Journal of the American Psychoanalytic Association* 24:3–27.

Landman, L. 1974. Recent trends toward unisex: A Panel. *American Journal of Psychoanalysis* 34:27–31.

Lerner, H. E. 1973. Women's liberation. *Menninger Perspective* 4:11–13, 20–21.

———. 1974. Early origins of envy and devaluation of women: Implications for sex role stereotypes. *Bulletin of the Menninger Clinic* 38:538–553. [Reprinted herein chapter 2.]

Moulton, R. 1973. The myth of femininity: A panel. *American Journal of Psychoanalysis* 33:45–49.

Segal, H. 1967. *Introduction to the work of Melanie Klein.* New York: Basic Books.

Seidenberg, R. 1970. *Marriage in life and literature.* New York: Philosophical Library.

Stoller, R. 1976. Primary femininity. *Journal of the American Psychoanalytic Association* 24:59–78.

# 45

# A Feminist Works with Nontraditional Clients

## JOAN ISRAEL

I am very pleased and honored to be here [at the sixtieth anniversary of the Smith College School for Social Work] today—twenty-four years after my graduation. A generation has passed, and for all of us the years have brought their combination of pleasure and sorrow. The years have also brought many other changes—particularly in social relations—which in turn have influenced the functioning of the family. I am happy to speak on the subject, because it indicates Smith's recognition of these contemporary changes in the area of clinical social work.

The traditional nuclear family has been the cornerstone of American society. Historically, the roles of men and women have been rather rigidly defined: for the woman, that of caring for the home and children—being the nurturer; for the man, that of breadwinner and protector. Nadelson and Eisenberg (1977) state, "Traditionally the status of the wife is ascribed rather than achieved . . . derived from the social position of her husband. . . . Census inquiries into the occupation of 'head of household' automatically report that of the husband unless there is no husband present. It is taken as a social given that when the marriage is intact, the male is the head of the household."

During the last ten years, social forces have changed the roles and expectations in the family in ways which the graduates of 1954 would find quite startling. These influences are familiar by now but worth-while reviewing briefly:

1. The increasing number of working women. Forty-six percent are in the paid labor force (including those with children). This has given women a new independent status both in and out of marriage.
2. Women's view of employment not only as a job but also as a career. This affects their view of themselves as well as the nature of marriage, including patterns of child care and household responsibilities.
3. The lower birth rate because of the pill and other contraceptive methods (fewer children and fewer years spent in child rearing).
4. The shift toward later marriage—especially in people with college degrees. This shift allows women to experience a period of self-sufficiency rather than moving directly from the parental home to the marital home.
5. Economic changes resulting in the greater availability of jobs, increased purchasing power, and, now with inflation, the necessity of two incomes.
6. Higher divorce rates resulting in more one-parent families, usually headed by women.
7. The greater acceptance of different life styles (including homosexuality, singleness, and serial marriages).
8. The anti-war and civil rights movements, which challenged conventional attitudes toward youth, minority groups, and life goals in general.
9. The resurgence of the women's movement and the effect this has had upon women's self-image and role expectations, and the secondary impact this has had upon family life because "roles can be considered the mediating link between the social structure and the individual" (Kirsin 1974, p. 326).

Kravetz (1976) states in her article "Sexism in a Woman's Profession" that:

Sex bias and sex role stereotyping pervade clinical theories and literature. Psychoanalytic theories, for example, present women as innately passive, dependent, anatomically inferior, and emotionally immature. Motherhood is required as a universal fulfillment. Unfortunately, standards used to assess the behavior of female clients to evalute their psychological distress and to formulate treatment goals are derived from such concepts. Thus, the prevalence of sex bias in clinical theories is likely to affect practice. A recent nationwide survey identified four areas in which sex bias is evident in psychotherapy: 1) fostering of traditional sex roles, 2) adherence to biased expectations and devaluating concepts of women, 3) sexist application of psychoanalytic concepts, and 4) responding to women as sex objects. In light of such studies and of personal reports of women, many articles in popular literature and professional journals have criticized the mental health profession for helping to perpetuate an adjustment-oriented system that severely limits women's opportunities for personal growth and participation in society. The nature of social work education will determine whether social workers are or can be responsive to women's changing roles and status.

The dictionary defines *traditional* as "following or conforming to tradition, accepted from the past." Nontraditional would mean following or incorporating contemporary or recent trends, being open to change. From a psychological view, *traditional* has meant that because women have always assumed certain roles, they should continue to do so (emphasizing the biological differences between men and women). The focus of my paper today is on some nontraditional solutions as exemplified by six families from my casework practice. My case load may include a greater than usual number of nontraditional clients. Since my feminist activities have resulted in local media exposure, many nontraditional people seek me out in the hopes of working with a feminist therapist.

The Women's Counseling Group in Brookline, Massachusetts has isolated five components that differentiate feminist therapy from more traditional therapy:

1. Feminist therapy assumes in principle that all roles are open to women although the risk taking is greater than in nontraditional roles.
2. Feminist therapists bring a sociological perspective to their work with women. In doing so, they help women sort out which parts of their behavior have been determined by internalized societal norms and which behavior is in response to current societal pressures.
3. Feminist therapists develop with women a new feminist ego ideal. It is important to acknowledge and value the assets of women—nurturing, sensitivity, emphasis on relationships—while at the same time incorporating some of the more aggressive and assertive qualities women have hesitated to develop (a new ego ideal for which there are few role models).
4. Feminist therapists strive to help restore a balance to love and work— usually men have been helped to work and women to love. It is important for both to do both.
5. Feminist therapists reassess the value of women's relationships to other women (which may or may not be sexual in nature) (Ravor et al. 1977).

To illustrate the points outlined above, I have chosen six cases: a woman separated from her husband, a single man, a divorced woman, a lesbian mother, and two married couples.

I chose Sandy because she departs from her family's cultural norms, especially in career choice. Sandy is a twenty-five-year-old woman from a working-class Polish background, the youngest of four daughters and a son. The apple of her father's eye because she was a fast learner, she was encouraged to be independent, skillful with tools, and active in sports. When she came to see me a year and a half ago, she was married, without children, very unhappy, cried a great deal, and felt that her husband tried to dominate her, not letting her make decisions. When she did make decisions, he was very critical. He was very possessive and tried to make her feel guilty if her whole life didn't revolve around him. He was not as bright or self-confident as Sandy, even though he was a high school graduate and the manager of a specialty department in a national department store chain. This was ironic because Sandy had taught him everything he knew about this area. She had gone to a technical school, was very talented, and after three years as an apprentice, opened her own business, now flourishing. Her husband's attitude was: I am a man and I know more than Sandy. Sandy felt that this domination extended to most areas of her marriage. She was uncertain about divorce because she had a hard time thinking of herself as one who hurts others. This was especially relevant because her husband wanted the relationship to continue. In view of this uncertainty, I saw both of them for marriage counseling. After a time it became evident the marriage would not survive. They are now separated with divorce pending. Sandy is feeling stronger but is often perplexed, angered, and disappointed by the reaction of men, and to some degree women, to her. People wonder how she can function without a man in her business. Male customers now feel they can talk or act in a seductive way. Women are amazed, intrigued, and jealous of her success. She would like to develop a mature relationship with a man in which she doesn't have to play "the little woman" and in which men will not be threatened by her self-sufficiency. She is afraid "all men are alike."

My role has been to be supportive of her desire to be independent and firm, to help her understand and clarify the consequences of her behavior, and to point out the contradictions in her and in society where they exist. Some of the pressures exist because Sandy's success is unusual in a person of her youth and because in her Roman Catholic, working-class background, women traditionally stay in the home in a subservient role. Divorce is still not common in her extended family. Sandy's changes have affected all of her family. Her father, who would applaud her success, is dead. Her mother and sisters have had to make allowances in their expectations of the traditional female role, causing some consternation, misunderstanding, and rejection. As for the future, Sandy feels marriage is not a first priority. She is not sure about having children, as the failure of her marriage has made her very cautious. She sees herself as a hard-working, creative individual who is more sure of herself but less sure of the reliability of others. She is hopeful but still feels tentative and uncertain in her developing life.

Jim F. was an unmarried twenty-year-old undergraduate student when he first came to see me three years ago. He had heard me speak at a round-table seminar on feminist therapy at a professional meeting. He worked in a local social welfare agency. His presenting problem was the handling of sporadic outbursts of violent anger. He was also troubled by his relationship to his father, a high-ranking politician whom he admired but from whom he felt distance and disapproval. Jim never felt he was masculine enough to please his father. He alternated between trying to please him (by playing football, building up his body, doing carpentry) and being angry that his father didn't love and accept him as he was. He was much closer to his mother, a warm, affectionate, noncritical woman who acted as a buffer between Jim and his father. Jim had some close friends who were homosexual, but he never felt conflicted about his own sexuality. Jim had difficulty in his long-term relationships with women. He realized that he expected women to be like his mother so that he could continue playing the little boy. This invariably led to his disappointment both in women and in himself, and to the termination of the relationships. Interestingly enough, he worked out his violence rather easily after recognizing that it was both self-destructive and an expression of hostility toward his father. As he recognized the nature of his conflicts, and as he gained approval from me for increased emotional self-reliance, Jim developed more self-confidence and maturity. He was then able to approach his father in confrontational but friendly talks, discussing what was bothering him and what in their relationship he would like to change. In accepting the fact that he could be sensitive and expressive and at the same time mature, Jim developed a conception of what a man is that is very different from that of his father. He will have more room to include a variety of feelings in his conception of the male image.

Alice is a woman in her late thirties, divorced for about five years, with custody of her four children, now eighteen, sixteen, ten, and eight. After the birth of her last child, Alice went back to school to become an occupational therapist, a profession she found very satisfying. She had come from a traditional middle-class family and had married a successful businessman at age eighteen. She said she had never really loved her former husband but had married him because of pressure from her parents ("he was a good catch"). She had a very traditional marriage, having complete responsibility for the children's care. Her former husband had on occasion given lip service to the idea of sharing this responsibility. About a year ago Alice came for help because she felt she wanted to give up permanent custody of the children to her husband. She was tired, irritable, had developed a relationship with another man. She felt that her children had *two* parents and that their father had an equal responsibility toward their care. The children had a good relationship with their father, and he responded positively to Alice's suggestion that he take over custody. He could provide better material and emotional support for them at this time. She was drained. She would like to take the children on weekends—to be the "fun parent." She felt very guilty, however, and wanted to make sure she was doing the right thing. Years ago, acting on this would have been unusual, and Alice would have been thought of as an uncaring person and an unfit mother. As we explored her feelings, it was clear she had indeed been a good mother. I reenforced this after careful examination of how she had related to her children over the years. Her present resentment grew out of the years she had spent renouncing the gratification of her own reasonable needs in favor of the needs of others. The details of the custody charge were handled sensitively, and much time was spent on how this might be done so that the children would experience as little rejection as possible. The three youngest have adjusted quite well. The oldest girl (with whom there was always a strained relationship) reacted with ambivalence and negativism.

Alice has since sold the family home, found an apartment near the university, and changed jobs to a more challenging situation. She has maintained a consistent and positive relationship with her children. Her oldest daughter is preparing to go away to college, and the tension of the change in parental home has subsided for the time being. It was important in this case that all members of the family were open to the changing nature of parental roles and did not interpret this change as a rejection.

Elaine was a lesbian in her late twenties. She was in the process of divorcing her husband and living with a lesbian when she came to see me. She was the mother of two adopted children—a six-year-old girl who was physically handicapped and a fifteen-year-old mentally retarded boy. She realized soon after entering therapy that she had adopted handicapped children because of the challenge to her mothering skills. She needed this extraordinary challenge to feel good about herself. During the ten years she was married, she had worked very hard to be a good homemaker, wife, and so on, because she had wanted to be valued for something. She found that her own dissatisfaction with this role and her husband's nonresponsiveness to what she did led her to start school at a community college. The increased stimulation and fulfillment in these activities hastened the deterioration of the marriage. Soon after separating, she moved in with another lesbian woman, also the mother of two children. The illusion that the relationship would be better because it was with a woman rather than a man quickly ended. Elaine found herself in the same dependent role she had been in with her husband. This woman had a full-time job and Elaine was a student. A power struggle evolved in many areas: the children, sex, household chores, money, and so forth. In the middle of this, Elaine was trying to learn to understand her homosexual feelings and how she should relate to her children (particularly her teenage son) concerning her lesbianism. One of the most difficult things Elaine had to do was to discuss her life style with her son. As she reported to me, this was handled with honesty—but unsureness. Elaine had to stop treatment unexpectedly because of a change in schedules, but we have talked many times by phone. She is now moving to a new home along with her children, feeling that tensions, particularly about the children, were too much to work out with her housemate.

I've chosen to present the last two cases together, as I think they represent an interesting contrast in the conflicting goals and roles that women and their spouses are facing today. These are two situations in which both women are in their middle thirties and are sympathetic to the ideals of the women's movement.

Sally was a full-time homemaker. When the youngest of her three children went to kindergarten, she wanted a job on a regular basis. Up to that time she had been a freelance writer. Her new work schedule and expectations of time for herself created new tension in a marriage that was basically sound but had its ups and downs. Sally had always been the one to give in to her husband's personal and professional needs, since he had a very demanding job in which he could be sent out of town on short notice, had deadlines, and so forth. Sally now felt it reasonable to expect John to share more completely in child care and household responsibilities. I saw John and Sally separately and together as they reexamined the traditional structure of their marriage. A simple task like arranging for a baby-sitter loomed large to John, largely because he had never done it before. Many other facets of their marriage were laid out and struggled with. Here were two intense individuals who needed personal time—the solution: Each had a night to her/himself, either at home or elsewhere. Another area of concern was bringing up their children in a nonsexist way in terms of assignment of chores, the way the parents relate to them, and so on. Sally and John did work out ways of handling old tasks, but they did not find it an easy task.

The other situation is the reverse. Jean had a part-time job in a profession in which she was competent but had not received training. Her husband was a teacher. Both were very compulsive in making sure the other did his or her share in family responsibilities. They were quite critical of each other and showed little sense of humor. A major shift in the relationship occurred when Jean, in a mutual decision with her husband, decided to stop working and return to school. This meant a readjustment in their schedules and how they saw themselves. Jean was no longer bringing in money, a matter about which she felt badly, since she felt she no longer had as much right to decide how the money was spent. After two years in school, Jean decided her two young children were growing up too fast and that she wanted to spend more time with them. There were also problems that she hadn't resolved about the way she related to the homemaker role, problems such as procrastination, lack of organization at home, dislike of certain tasks. She needed to deal with this if she were ever going to be able to cope with a career—the goal for which she had returned to school. Jean was confused by her own mixed messages about the worth of the homemaker role. She needed to find out for herself the parameters of the role. One of the questions she had to work out was what she could reasonably expect from her husband and children (everything used to be split down the middle when she was in school or working outside the home). Jean and her husband are still in the process of working these things out. Both Jean and Sally have had to shift gears in their roles and how they see themselves in terms of the time with their families.

These situations highlight the societal changes we've been talking about. What did I do that was different from what a traditionally oriented therapist would do? Whether I intended to or not, I represented a role model, one who has combined several aspects of life. The therapist-client relationship is usually based on the medical model, with the therapist being all powerful and the client being the dependent one. I try to balance this by being informal in form of address, using first names and having people call me by my first name unless there is some discomfort with this. People are given a choice.

My training at Smith was excellent, but it was heavily, if not exclusively, based upon Freudian theory. As is evident in this paper, I consider current social influences as well as past internal experience to be of considerable importance. This affects my diagnosis and subsequent treatment. In interaction with clients I am quite active verbally, supportive when need be, confronting when it seems appropriate. I am selectively self-disclosing when helpful. There might be discussion of books, plays, politics when it fits in.

In closing, I have presented a view of feminist therapy as an effective tool with which to work with nontraditional clients. I look forward to a stimulating discussion with all of you.

REFERENCES

Kirsh, B. 1974. Consciousness-raising groups as therapy for women. In *Women in therapy*, ed. V. Franks and V. Burtle, pp. 326–354. New York: Brunner/Mazel.

Kravetz, D. 1976. Sexism in a woman's profession. *Social Work* 21:421–426.

Nadelson, T., and Eisenberg, L. 1977. The successful professional woman—on being married to one. *American Journal of Psychiatry* 134:1071–1076.

Ravor, et al. 1977. Issues in feminist therapy: The work of a women's study group. *Social Work* (November).

# 46

---

# A Feminist Approach
# to Family Therapy

---

## RACHEL T. HARE-MUSTIN

---

One might well ask what family therapy has to do with feminist therapy. Have not the family and the institutions that support it been the primary cause of maintaining women in their stereotype sex roles? As feminists can readily point out, "The family has been the principal arena for the exploitation of women, and however deeply rooted in social structure that exploitation may be, it is through family structure that it makes its daily presence felt" (Chase 1977, p. 19). Chase's question, "What does feminism demand of therapy?" (1977, p. 3) is the question I would like to examine in the form "What does feminism demand of family therapy?"

In discussing family therapy from a feminist point of view, I will first briefly consider the principles of feminist therapy and review the structure of the family as we know it today. I will then discuss how family therapy has evolved. Some of the ways in which family therapy differs from the feminist approach will be examined. Finally, I will present in greater detail the ways feminist values can be translated into techniques for working with families.

## Feminist Therapy

Feminist therapy grew out of the theory and philosophy of consciousness raising. Central to feminist therapy is the recognition that (1) the traditional intrapsychic model of human behavior fails to recognize the importance of the social context as a determiner of behavior, and (2) the sex roles and statuses prescribed by society for females and males disadvantage women (Lerman 1974; Marecek 1973; Rawlings and Carter 1977; Sachnoff 1975).

Feminism sees as the ideal for the individual the ability to respond to changing situations with whatever behavior seems appropriate, regardless of the stereotyped expectations for either sex. This idea of the androgynous personality reflects a recent shift away from dualistic notions of masculine-feminine personality types (Kaplan 1976). In helping women develop in line with an androgynous model, feminist therapy has encouraged women not only to become aware of the oppressiveness of traditional roles but also to gain experiences that enhance their self-esteem as they try new behaviors as part of gaining self-definition. The feminist therapeutic relationship itself embodies these principles in its emphasis on greater equality between the therapist and the client. By differentiating what is personal from what is external, feminist therapy may be distinguished from nonsexist therapy or humanistic therapy. These approaches may encourage individual development free of gender-prescribed behaviors, but they do not (1) examine and (2) seek to change the conditions in society that contribute to the maintenance of such behaviors.

## The Family

The American family as we know it from research and clinical practice is one in which the husband bears the main responsibility for the economic maintenance of the family and the wife bears primary responsibility for domestic work and child care. The nature of the family today is a consequence of the dramatic changes that took place during the nineteenth century, chief among which was the separation of work from the home (Peal 1975). Where productivity was rewarded by money, those who did not earn money, such as women, children, and old people who were left at home, had an ambiguous position in the occupational world (Keller 1974). The instrumental role for males and the expressive role for females that evolved were held up as normative by Parsons and Bales (1955) and even necessary for the well-being of individuals, the family, and society.

The employment of women outside the home has not released women from the assigned expressive role that accompanies homemaking responsibility. Employed wives labor longer than either employed men or full-time housewives, and the fact that child care is not available for working women in the United States reinforces the idea that women are not about to be released from their primary responsibility in the home merely because they work outside (Bernard 1974). Recent work patterns for women are actually not innovative but regressive in terms of the decreasing proportion of women in any but low-paying jobs (Rosenthal 1974). Being female is regarded as uniquely qualifying a woman for domestic work, no matter what her interests, aptitudes, or intelligence (Bem and Bem 1970). Equalitarian arrangements by which both parents share equally in domestic areas or by which contributions to the family are based on personal preferences and individual capabilities are rare when these preferences diverge from traditional role expectations.

In marriage, the power of the male in the family is guaranteed by society's expectation that he will be older, bigger, have more education, and come from a higher social class than his wife. This tends to assure that he has the strength, credentials, experience, special knowledge, and training on which power in part is based. Marriages in which this is not the case are regarded as deviant. The power in the female role that derives from the woman's responsibility in organizing the household, the children, and the husband has depended on being married and having children (Keller 1974). With the decline in the importance of the family, such power has been reduced. Women's lack of power is obscured and attributed to women's being more emotional and less able to "handle power" than men. As in other unequal relationships, the dominant group defines the "acceptable" roles for the less powerful, which are those activities like domestic work that the dominant group does not choose to do. There is research demonstrating that loss of power or chronic powerlessness are frequent precursors of psychological disorder (Marecek 1976).

Marriage typically demands that women give up their activities or place of residence to adjust to the needs of men. It has been observed that the partner who sacrifices or gives up the most for the marriage must of necessity be the one most committed to it (Minuchin 1974). The woman, who may have given up her occupation, family closeness, or residence for marriage, must rely more on the marriage to fulfill her needs. The expectation that women will adjust to men's patterns leads to an often unrecognized difference in the number of stressful life events impacting on men and women. Dohrenwend (1973) has found that women are exposed to a relatively higher rate of change or instability in their lives compared with men, which can be seen as contributing to frequent psychosomatic symptoms and mood disorders.

The inequality in the traditional family is rarely recognized by individual or family therapists. It has been observed that power aspects of sex roles are largely disregarded or denied, except when women have power (Millman 1971). The formulation of dominant-mother/ineffectual-father as the cause of practically every serious psychological difficulty is made without regard for the underlying inequality that leads to such a situation. Few therapists recognize that the stress on family members and particularly on women from required sex roles that assign them an inferior position had led to the family becoming the arena of conflicts that arise from the inequity sanctioned by the larger society (Miller and Mothner 1971).

## Family Therapy

In the late 1940s and 1950s, researchers such as Wynne, Lidz, and others, focusing on the schizophrenic patient, identified the overinvolved mother as the source of pathology. In terms of the social events of the time, women who had been more fully involved in activities outside the home during World War II were now being encouraged to return to their natural feminine occupations as wives and mothers and to apply themselves to these responsibilities. The profound impact on the field of Parsons and Bales's (1955) idea of fixed sex roles, with males having the instrumental role and females the expressive, has been pointed out (Klapper and Kaplan 1977). Observations of these stereotyped sex roles in the American family were then used by researchers and therapists as the basis for the argument that these were the necessary conditions for normal family life and successful child rearing. Advances in the 1960s saw the application of principles of general systems theory to the understanding of the family. The most notable change in family therapy in the 1970s, and one that has implications for women, is the growing acceptance of the family developmental point of view that follows from the work of Hill and other sociologists (Hill and Rodgers 1964).

The family developmental orientation is analogous to the individual life cycle perspective in its focus on the stages in family development over the family life span—from the initial courtship phase to the death of the last member of the couple. Stages are defined in terms of the dominant developmental tasks faced by individual members of the family and the family as a system at that point. "Normal" crises in family development are usually identified as those that occur around the addition or loss of a member, whether actually by birth or death, or symbolically by change in activity or residence. The importance of this model is that it can provide an orientation toward prevention rather than pathology by identifying predictable crisis points in advance. Therapeutic interventions are directed at preparing the family for such stress points as well as helping the system move on from crises to resume its characteristic functioning.

If the systems approach to family therapy has adopted a prevention model of mental health and has shifted from a focus on the individual to recognizing social systems as determinants of behavior, one might ask why has it not been discovered and acclaimed by feminists as sex-fair therapy? In point of fact, while espousing a theory that might seem to assure equality for family members, family therapists in practice share the same biases and prejudices as others in the society and often have not freed themselves from their past training in a traditional orientation that views the mental health of males as akin to adulthood and that of females as not (Broverman et al. 1970). For example, Bowen's Differentiation of Self Scale (1966) can readily be identified as a sex-stereotyped masculinity-femininity scale with femininity at the devalued end. Bowen's approach is akin to the Ego Strength Scale based on the Minnesota Multiphasic Personality Inventory (MMPI), which is biased in favor of males by including more masculine than feminine scored items (McAllister and Fernhoff 1976). Bowen ignores the fact that women's socialization encourages them to be emotional and intuitive rather than rational.

To restore the family to healthy functioning, family therapists often intentionally or unwittingly reinforce stereotypic role assignments for man, the doer, and woman, the nurturer, assuming that the traditional roles are the basis for healthy functioning. That some people are more comfortable in these roles for which they were trained cannot be denied, but, as suggested earlier, they may pay a price in psychological functioning. The fact that married women have a higher incidence of mental illness than men but single women do not (Gove 1976) should lead family therapists to question the structure of the traditional family as it affects women. Representative of family therapists who support sex-stereotyped roles as important for healthy development are Boszormenyi-Nagy and Spark (1973). They point out that "A heterosexual [therapy] team permits each individual to function more comfortably in his or her life-long assigned biological-emotional role. . . .

Mutual respect is needed to confirm the differences between masculinity and femininity" (p. 204). They criticize women who live vicariously through their husbands and children, thus avoiding facing their own lack of identity; however, they also criticize women who seek identity elsewhere, as in the following example.

A young married woman who received superior ratings as a school teacher refused to cook or shop for food since she considered this beneath her. . . . She seemed to expect the therapist as well as her family to be completely accepting of her passive, dependent attitude that it was beneath her dignity to fulfill this aspect of a woman's role. (p. 203)

Minuchin (1974) sees himself as modeling the male executive functions, forming alliances, most typically with the father, and through competition, rule setting, and direction, demanding that the father resume control of the family and exert leadership as Minuchin leads and controls the session. In a comparable manner, Forrest (1969) describes the female therapist as using her feminine warmth, wisdom, and interest in men to appeal to their masculine instincts.

These illustrations reveal how the unquestioned acceptance and reinforcement of stereotypic sex roles takes place in much of family therapy, despite the possibilities inherent for change in the systems point of view. As Klapper and Kaplan (1977) point out in their survey of sex-role stereotyping in family therapy literature, current writing has been minimally affected by the emerging consciousness.

Someone being trained as a family therapist would have to maintain stern vigilance in order not to be caught up in the oftentimes subtle reinforcement of behavior patterns which are so debasing and humiliating to women. (p. 28)

## Techniques for Family Therapy

Despite the fact that a feminist approach to family therapy has not developed, I would contend that such an approach is possible. The obstacles can be summed up as (1) the socially reinforced sex roles that exist in the family; (2) the therapist's own family and clinical experience that renders her or him unaware of and insensitive to alternatives to stereotyped sex roles; and (3) the family's concerns, which are rarely identified as related to traditional sex-role assignments. My purpose in what follows is not to analyze family therapy techniques per se but rather to consider certain areas of intervention in which a feminist orientation is important. These areas are the contract, shifting tasks in the family, communication, generational boundaries, relabeling deviance, modeling, ownership and privacy, and the therapeutic alliance with different family members.

## The Contract

Feminists stress the equality in the relationship between the therapist and the client as a departure from the paternalistic medical model in which the doctor is presumed to always know best. Recognizing that the capacity to influence people comes in part from their expectations (the placebo effect), feminists are contending that an equal relationship with mutual respect can still raise expectations that are beneficial in achieving goals (Frank 1973). One method of attaining equality is by use of a contract.

Many family therapists use an informal or unwritten contract with families that come for help that facilitates agreement on arrangements for treatment and goals (Hare-Mustin et al. 1977). As has been pointed out by the Nader group, a contract that is written assures the protection of client rights to an even greater extent (Adams and Orgel 1975). The contract is probably not intended to be legally binding, but it does establish a mutual accountability between the therapist and the family. Furthermore, the negotiation of the contract can be an important part of the therapeutic process itself. The contract can include arrangements for treatment, the amounts and kinds of responsibility to be assumed by the therapist and by the family, issues of confidentiality, the goals of therapy and measurement of their accomplishment, and provisions for renegotiation of the contract.

One of the problems in contracting with families is the need to involve all family members, some of whom are more reluctant to participate than others. Hines and Hare-Mustin (1978) have pointed out the ethical problems in requiring reluctant children and adolescents to participate in family therapy. Most families come because the mother is distressed about something in the family. The father, from his less-involved position, feels that there is nothing to worry about, while the children have little choice. Too strong initial support by the therapist of any one member's point of view is likely to alienate the other members and lead to sabotaging or early termination of treatment. The therapist must reach some shared agreement with all family members.

To the extent that the father is paying for the sessions, he controls the sessions. It is hard to complain about the person paying the bills, as women and children are well aware. Part of the therapeutic process that relates to the contract and the setting of fees is the shifting of the conventional idea that the one who contributes money to the family is the only meaningful contributor. Unpaid services of other family members, primarily the mother, must be viewed as contributing to and subsidizing the person who is bringing in the money. Another aspect of the money economy is the inflexibility of most job schedules that can be pointed out to the family in connection with scheduling appointment times that the father can attend. In like manner, when baby-sitting arrangements are necessary, the value of the mother's unpaid work should be focused on, rather than merely her traditional responsibility for locating baby-sitters.

Beginning with the contract helps the family learn about negotiation and makes explicit the "rules" for the therapy. From the negotiations about the contract, the family can begin to understand how rules regulate the behavior of family members. Many family conflicts center about what the rules are and who makes them, which is basically the issue of power. In family conflicts, Zuk (1972) has pointed out that the weak person traditionally espouses values such as justice, compassion, and relatedness, while the powerful person advocates control, rationality, law, and discipline. In husband-wife conflicts, wives usually espouse values concerned with caring, while husbands espouse rationality. In parent-child conflicts, children espouse the relatedness values, while their parents stress control and discipline. The family therapist can help the family recognize the value differences that accompany the shifts in power among participants in family conflicts.

## Shifting of Tasks in the Family

Family therapists recognize that it is impossible to change the role of one family member without changing the role of another. However, the division of labor and functions in the family is often looked at in very limited perspective. Therapists who ask about the sharing of chores in the family may not recognize that the division of labor in the home is in part a result of the separation of paid work from the home and the consequent devaluing of domestic work. Traditional therapists who see some women having a greater share of responsibility and power within the home than men overlook the fact that men typically have power and status elsewhere. Family therapists should not rush to "restore" the power in the family to the father, thus further reducing the mother's self-esteem and limited authority. As noted earlier, the observation that fathers typically have the instrumental role and mothers the expressive role in families has led family and child-care experts to assume that these role assignments are necessary for normal functioning, an assumption for which the evidence is at best equivocal.

Many couples share responsibilities without regard for traditional stereotypes until the birth of the first child (Rice and Rice 1977). The arrival of a child precipitates a change in power and relationship status between the partners. Resentment can build up at this point in the person who has to shift to the major child-care responsibilities—resentment that can lead to the breakdown of the bonds of affection established in the previous period. At the same time, the woman with authority is too often seen as a monster by her family and by therapists because for a woman to have authority deviates from the stereotype. In point of fact, the limited power that women have to make decisions and guide the lives of family members has declined as the family has declined in importance.

Often women would like others to share more of the decision making in the family (Minturn and Lambert 1964). Mothers are burdened with many small decisions, but the fact that fathers do not participate signals to the mother as well as to the children that the decisions are about matters that are not really important. The family therapist needs to help family members examine how decisions are made and who shares in the process.

The practice of the mother's thanking other family members for household chores also needs to be examined. As long as the mother thanks others and they expect to be thanked, the implication is that they are doing her work, rather than family work, and they are doing it as a favor to her. In addition, children are not going to participate willingly in chores that the father signifies by his nonparticipation are demeaning.

What should take precedence, the job or the family? The feminist therapist needs to be aware of the complexities of this question. The intense pressure on the person working with technology in the money economy often results in a choice having been made in favor of the job. Because men bring in the money, it is expected that women and children will adjust to their needs. Yet when a woman works, the family still demands primary allegiance (Bernard 1974). Women who work are expected to be interrupted by and respond to the demands of the family. I had a case in which an unemployed father and the teenage daughter waited for the working mother to come home and cook supper. Not all therapists would have questioned this practice.

Family therapists need to be aware of the options for women as well as men and not oversell work for women outside the home when the jobs available are frequently repetitious, demeaning, and underpaid. In addition, there are women whose socialization is such that they are genuinely happy with the "professionalization" of housework in their current lives. The encouragement of women to go out to work without a reduction of their workload at home may be but a thinly disguised punitive act. The economic realities are also such that if both individuals work part-time or if the woman works full-time instead of her husband, there will be a loss in family income owing to the differentials in earning power of men and women and the loss of fringe benefits for part-time work. Despite these limitations, outside work can be an enhancing experience. Therapists need to help the family recognize not only the positive aspects but also the enormous societal barriers operating against meaningful change in the family and not advocate facile solutions that may have slight chance of success. On the other hand, counseling women to remain in traditional roles can have repercussions for their families in terms of anger, frustration, and a smothering overinvolvement with their children (Smith 1972).

The mother, as well as other family members, needs to give up the view that she should be totally available to respond to every demand family members make upon her. If she is to give up some of the power associated with being central in the family, she must be connected with areas outside the home where she can have autonomy, respect, earning power, and opportunities to develop her capabilities. Women's ambivalence and resistance to giving up responsibility in the family is often a defense against the guilt they feel about not fulfilling their traditional sex roles and the anxiety they experience when departing from the familiar patterns of wife and mother. Some of the specific directions the therapist can take with the family are drawing up and trying out new schedules of household chores; involving the father in home tasks, child care, and decision making; assigning age-appropriate responsibilities to the children; and helping the family develop network supports that will be encouraging of the anticipated changes. More appropriate assertive behaviors can be developed by the mother at the same time she is learning to set more realistic goals for herself. One of the first things that signals change may be a reduction in the mother's behavior as a critic, which is an often unacknowledged consequence of her inferior position. All family members can benefit from consciousness raising as a part of family therapy. Understanding of different roles develops as parents and children are asked to examine what they like and do not like about being male or female.

### Communication

Many family therapists focus on communication, but few have analyzed the relation of communication styles to male and female roles. Women are typically not listened to as having something important to say because the woman in a family or marital relationship is viewed as an adjunct. ("Hello, Mrs. Smith. What does your husband do?") Like children, women are not taken seriously or, when they talk about serious things, are accused of imitating a man (Beauvoir 1970). Research on nonverbal communication consistently shows that women are treated and behave as inferiors (Mehrabian 1972). There are several consequences of this lack of confirmation experienced by women that therapists should be aware of: Women are regarded as nags because they talk constantly in seeking to be attended to or as devious or vague because they express themselves indirectly and tentatively in order to avoid disapproval.

The transactional nature of family therapy reveals habitual family communication patterns as no other approach has been able to do. For example, the nagging person can be viewed not only in terms of the withdrawn or disinterested partner that provokes the nagging behavior, but also in terms of the third person in the triangle who is being given a lesson, drawn in, distanced, supported, alienated, or the like. Changing communication patterns in the family is regarded by some family theorists as the single most important technique for changing behaviors and attitudes (Haley 1971; Watzlawick, Weakland, and Fisch 1974). The family can practice new ways of communicating, shifting roles through role play, critique, and practice in order to learn new ways of interacting and to understand the confining aspects of one's own or another's traditional role.

Rules for communication have been developed by women's consciousness-raising groups to help women express themselves and be heard. Some of these are similar to those used by family therapists, such as not interrupting, relating the particular experience to the universal (generalizing), becoming specific ("What does that mean to you?"), and attaching significance to feelings, not just to facts. The latter leads to less disqualifying of women's experiences or style of expression than the rational mode to which men have been socialized. The therapist can also reinforce a greater range of genuine emotional expression and sensitivity to emotions in men who have avoided or disparaged emotional expression.

## Generational Boundaries

Clear generational boundaries are often seen as congruent with healthy family functioning (Minuchin 1974). The breakdown in boundaries can occur when one of the parents is more closely allied with a child than with the spouse. The therapist who is not sensitive to the power differences in family roles may not understand the alliance of the powerless mother and child against the powerful father or the father and child against the demanding mother. Sometimes there seem to be no generational boundaries but an amorphous unit consisting of parents and children in which the parents avoid the burden of decisions and responsibility by a spurious equality. Children may find themselves parenting the parent with exaggerated dependency needs.

The low status accorded to older people in our society and particularly to older women needs to be kept in mind by the therapist who sees a mother trying to be an age mate to her daughter. The therapist should work to restore the alliance between the parents without the exaggerated status differences that have evolved between adults and children in modern times.

It has been pointed out that children have a deteriorating effect on the marital relationship in terms of a decline in understanding, love, and general satisfaction (Hill and Rodgers 1964). This could well be a consequence of the mother's dissatisfaction with the burden of her assigned role and the lack of genuine sharing and interest in child care by the father. The availability of the mother to the children leads to close alliances as well as the perpetuation of stereotyped sex roles. Mothers tend to use their daughters (or sons) as confidants because their isolation in the home from other adults confines them to housewife and mothering functions. In this way women pass on their sense of worthlessness and denigration to both daughters and sons. The unavailability of fathers affects sons and daughters as well as mothers, sons because the unavailable father does not provide a model for learning, daughters because the father's unavailability leads them to develop an image of the male as a romantic stranger, an unrealistic ideal that cannot be satisfied when they reach adult life.

During adolescence daughters are particularly torn between identification with the mother and with the father. This is the time when it becomes increasingly apparent to young women that career paths may be closed to them. The daughter who has a close relationship with her mother but is interested in a life different from her mother's may see herself as betraying and competing with her mother. If she aspires to a career path and identifies with her father, this can interfere with her relationship with her mother as well as with the development of feminine aspects of her identity (Nadelson 1974). The therapist who is sensitive to the confusion of young women during this period can provide support to the girl as a facilitative model who values both career and family.

Siblings can sometimes develop a strong subsystem independent of the parents. Freedom from assigned sex roles among siblings can be supported by the therapist and the parents. It is frequently not recognized how much siblings contribute to one another's development through socialization, control, and rescuing operations.

Younger children are often co-opted by one or both of the parents in terms of their own needs. Therapists need to be aware of the extent to which children bring zest and life to a family and misbehave to keep the family system functioning. A range of behaviors should be equally allowed both girls and boys. Children's disturbing behavior may be subtly encouraged by parents who can be united only when dealing with a child's misbehavior. School refusal and other disruptive behaviors may actually be supportive of a depressed parent, usually the mother. To the extent the family therapist can help the mother develop independence and self-esteem, as well as gain the positive regard of the father, the therapist frees the children from the need to rescue the mother by "bad" behavior.

## Relabeling Deviance

Diagnostic labels are not useful in a family systems approach because they carry intrapsychic and causal connotations that do not fit into a systems model. Like the feminist therapist, the family therapist can avoid labels implying that the attribute belongs to the individual rather than the situation. Diagnostic labels, by focusing on the individual, serve to mask the prevalence of particular conditions in society that stress individuals. That behavior has become habitual as a result of socialization patterns of reinforcement does not mean that the therapist should shift to the intrapsychic model. For example, it should be recognized that the unhappiness of women in families is too widespread to be viewed as an individual weakness or defect. As Halleck (1971) has emphasized, treatment that does not encourage the patient to examine and confront her environment merely strengthens the status quo.

The use of language is important because in this way sex differences can be exaggerated, often with disparaging connotations (Gingras-Baker 1976). Some of the pejorative labels used are imposed by the male-dominated culture such as pretty, sexy, ugly, blonde, dumpy, and the like (Kirsh 1974). Others clearly reflect the double standard of terminology for men and women. The use of the generic masculine pronoun denies women's experiences. Consider also, for example, "father absence" and "maternal deprivation." Or the fact that a family is called traditional when the man is breadwinner but matriarchal when the woman is the breadwinner (Millman 1971). "Weak" is a label applied to women and pejoratively to men but, like "strong," its meaning can only be understood in transactional terms. All too often the weak person in the family, by appearing incompetent, is shoring up the strong one in order to prevent the latter's true fraility from becoming apparent. In this way the inadequate housekeeper or the fearful woman is making her partner as well as other family members appear strong, and so in reality she is protecting them.

An example of a pejorative and overused label in contemporary society is "passive-aggressive." What the therapist needs to do is examine the conditions that make individuals use covert and indirect means rather than direct means for gaining their ends. Some behaviors, such as phobic behaviors, can be understood as exaggerations of the dependency and timidity that women are taught or as a consequence of women's inexperience and the taboos against women successfully coping with and overcoming obstacles in a "man's world." Too often therapists, like others, blame women for the dependency in which they have been trained.

There are a number of ways by which therapists who are sensitive to the misuse of labels can bring about change. They can help both women and men free themselves from stereotypic expectations that lead them to try to hide attributes in themselves they have been taught are unacceptable. In addition, therapists can often perceive attributes of family members that are not usually noticed and by drawing attention to them can shift family members' ways of perceiving and interacting. Labels of "good" and "bad" illustrate how labels deny the complexity of persons. In the case of an older "bad" sister who was always in trouble, I was able to shift some of the "good" from the younger "good" child to the "bad" one by drawing the family's attention to the contribution that older children make to younger ones by testing the limits and the rules in the family. This emphasized the similarities between the children rather than their differences.

## Modeling

Feminists recognize that one of the important aspects of consciousness-raising groups is the opportunity for women to model for each other. There are a variety of successful male models available in public life, business, the professions, and the media, but women have lacked female models because of the relatively few women in positions of prominence. Women have also been isolated from others in their daily lives in their homes. The female therapist can model a successful woman for clients. I have found that it is hard for even the most liberal male to acknowledge that a female therapist could provide something that he could not. Some male therapists claim that they are better therapists for female clients because they can provide a different kind of male model than the client is accustomed to (Lazarus 1974). What goes unrecognized is that the male therapist, in providing a different male model, is reinforcing traditional stereotypes by assuming that the female client needs a special male who will treat her differently than other males have done. What a woman needs to learn is not that some men are different but how she can become a different woman.

By modeling different behaviors, the female therapist can help women free themselves from minority-group traits that they have developed because of lack of power and secondary status, traits such as dislike of one's own sex, a negative self-image, "shuffling," insecurity, low aspirations, and appeasing behaviors (Keller 1974). Another quality that female therapists can model for all the family is competency in a woman. However, in family therapy the therapist needs to be careful not to render family members incompetent by being a better parent, a better mother, or a better partner—more wise, just, and all-seeing. Traditional therapy has too often fostered the woman's view of herself as incompetent. The therapist who can acknowledge a lack of knowledge in some areas is a better model for parents and family members than one who is either a superwoman or a superman.

## Ownership and Privacy

Just as Gestalt therapists have sought to develop ownership of an individual's feelings and attitudes by "I" statements, so family therapists can encourage ownership. Women typically have not been sure of their share in family resources that relate to the money world. Therapists may need to help women negotiate with other family members to gain ownership of many aspects of their lives. Women often lack ownership of the means of privacy, such as personal space, their space being that associated with their household job, like kitchen or sewing room (Lennard and Lennard 1977). They also do not own personal time without feelings of guilt or the use of money without accountability. A sensitive therapist can also encourage a woman to own and develop her talents and hobbies, as well as her thoughts and feelings. By encouraging ownership in other areas, the therapist may be able to help women assert ownership of their own bodies. Experiences like menstruation, menopause, hot flashes, tension around menstrual periods, impregnation, lactation, and childbirth can be crisis situations that women never discuss with male therapists.

Is family solidarity incompatible with individual ownership in the family? The therapist needs to point out that personhood for the mother as well as other family members is important, that the family need not be either a fortress or a prison. Since women have been raised to believe that their self-worth and identity is inextricably bound to finding the right husband and caring for a family, they may use therapy to talk about relationships with men rather than about their own identity (Barrett et al. 1974). The family therapist deemphasizes "talking about" in the favor of interaction and can be influential in reinforcing assertive steps toward a sense of self that does not result solely from identification with family goals, family service, and family responsibility.

*Therapeutic Alliances*

An issue raised in modeling and in the interventions and alliances of the family therapist is the therapist's own gender. Does the therapist interact differently with men and women? Can a male be a feminist therapist? Certainly a nonsexist male therapist is better than a sexist female one. The power differential between males and females is still an enormous obstacle. Furthermore, because the stereotyped male role requires men always to appear competent, it may be that men find it harder than women to recognize and acknowledge sex biases in themselves. These therapist blind spots lead to reinforcing traditional patterns, whether the male therapist is allying with a woman to "protect" her, which is really a competitive move against her husband, or allying in a male bond with the husband, against the wife.

An essential aspect of family therapy is that the therapist must be committed to each person in the family (Hines and Hare-Mustin 1978). This means the therapist must frequently shift alliances congruent with therapeutic goals. An alliance does not necessarily mean an "agreement" with. The experienced family therapist can ally with one family member in terms of feelings, attention, or emphasis on syntonic aspects of therapist and client personalities, while supporting the views and attitudes of another family member. For example, an initial alliance of one kind may need to be made with the typically reluctant father in order to assure his attendance and participation in the beginning stages of therapy.

The female therapist will frequently be viewed as allied with the mother because of their common gender, just as the male therapist will be perceived as allied with the male when sometimes this is not the case. The husband and the therapist as the two reasonable (powerful) persons are often assumed to have a natural alliance. Rawlings and Carter (1977) report a family therapy session with two therapists, a psychiatrist and social worker, both males, where the mother felt like a rabbit being attacked by a wolf pack. Women may need the support of a female therapist to oppose traditional alliances and to be able to release pent-up rage, helplessness, and envy of men (Kronsky 1971).

Many married couples who do cotherapy assume that they provide a model of a normal or a liberated couple, as the case may be. I would agree with Sager (1976) that "the therapy couple's use of themselves as role models is a dubious procedure based on the treating couple's idealization of their own self-image" (p. 188). Marriage per se of a cotherapy team is no guarantee of therapeutic effectiveness (Lazarus 1976). If there are differences in experience, training, and status of the cotherapy pair, there is a basis for inequality that is not lost on family members, no matter what roles the cotherapists imagine they are playing in the therapy sessions. Male-female cotherapy teams have been found to reinforce patterns of behavior that are oppressive to women (American Psychological Association 1975). The cotherapy team in which the female rather than the male therapist is the senior member is virtually unheard of. Some therapists prefer a cotherapist because they recognize that family therapy can take on aspects of an adversary proceeding in which each spouse is seeking an ally for a scolding match (Rawlings and Carter 1977).

The family therapist needs to be aware of the alliance-seeking behaviors of some family members who draw the therapist into a triangle at the expense of other family members. Therapists who expect and assume that female behaviors toward males are basically envious or seductive are themselves locked into stereotyped thinking that will interfere with their capacity to be helpful. Nor can one disregard the enormous emotional significance of men qua men in our society. Orlinsky and Howard (1976) have pointed out that the client's emotional reactivity solely to the sex of the therapist may override the experience, talent, and warmth that the therapist brings to bear. A problem for the male therapist may be to deal with the woman's anger as she recognizes the irrelevance and goallessness of the activities that are her daily lot. A problem for the female therapist is the lack of respect and questions of therapeutic competence that are leveled at the female professional. As the husband and children learn to deal with the competent female therapist, they will learn to deal with the wife and mother in the family in a new way.

# Conclusion

Family therapy provides opportunities for social change unavailable in other therapeutic approaches. The therapist is addressing problems in the family that reflect the traditional norms and expectations the parents bring from their own families of origin and attempt to maintain in their current family. The systems approach to family therapy is congruent with feminist therapy in examining behavior in terms of its economic and social determinants rather than using an individual-centered approach. A feminist-oriented family therapist can intervene in many ways to change the oppressive consequences of stereotyped roles and expectations in the family. As consciousness raising takes place in families, family members come to recognize the sociocultural pressures that perpetuate traditional sex roles and seek ways to free themselves from these pressures. A review of family techniques from a feminist perspective indicates that family therapy is indeed possible without encouraging stereotyped sex roles.

REFERENCES

Adams, S., and Orgel, M. 1975. *Through the mental health maze.* Washington D.C.: Public Citizen's Health Research Group.
American Psychological Association. 1975. *Report of the task force on sex bias and sex role stereotyping in therapeutic practice.* Washington, D.C.: American Psychological Association. [Reprinted herein chapter 8.]
Barrett, C. J., et al. 1974. Implications of women's liberation and the future of psychotherapy. *Psychotherapy: Theory, Research and Practice* 11:11–15.
Beauvoir, S. de. 1970. *The second sex.* New York: Bantam Books.
Bem, S. L., and Bem, D. J. 1970. We're all nonconscious sexists. *Psychology Today.* November 1970, p. 22.
Bernard, J. 1974. *The future of motherhood.* New York: Dial.
Boszormenyi-Nagy, I., and Spark, G. M. 1973. *Invisible loyalties: Reciprocity in intergenerational family therapy.* New York: Harper & Row.
Bowen, M. 1966. The use of family theory in clinical practice. *Comprehensive Psychiatry* 7:345–374.
Broverman, I. K., et al. 1970. Sex-role stereotypes and clinical judgments of mental health. *Journal of Consulting and Clinical Psychology* 34:1–7. [Reprinted herein chapter 7.]
Chase, K. 1977. Seeing sexism: A look at feminist therapy. *State and Mind.* March–April 1977, pp. 19–22.
Dohrenwend, B. S. 1973. Social status and stressful life events. *Journal of Personal and Social Psychiatry* 28:225–235.
Forrest, T. 1969. Treatment of the father in family therapy. *Family Process* 8:106–117.
Frank, J. D. 1973. *Persuasion and healing.* Baltimore, Md.: Johns Hopkins University Press.
Gingras-Baker, S. 1976. Sex role stereotyping and marriage counseling. *Journal of Marriage and Family Counseling* 2:355–366.
Gove, W. R. 1976. The relationship between sex roles, marital status, and mental illness. In *Beyond sex-role stereotypes, Reading toward a psychology of androgyny,* ed. A. G. Kaplan and J. P. Bean, pp. 281–292. Boston: Little, Brown.
Haley, J., ed. 1971. *Changing families.* New York: Grune & Stratton.
Halleck, S. L. 1971. *Politics of therapy.* New York: Science House.
Hare-Mustin, R. T., et al. 1977. Rights of clients, responsibilities of therapists: A training module. Unpublished manuscript.
Hill, R., and Rodgers, R. H. 1964. The developmental approach. In *Handbook of marriage and the family,* ed. H. T. Christensen. Chicago: Rand McNally.
Hines, P., and Hare-Mustin, R. T. 1978. Ethical concerns in family therapy. *Professional Psychologist* 9:165–171.
Kaplan, A. G. 1976. Clarifying the concept of androgyny: Implications for therapy. Paper presented in Symposium on Applications of Androgyny to the Theory and Practice of Psychotherapy at the meeting of the American Psychological Association, Washington, September 1976.
Keller, S. 1974. The female role: Constants and change. In *Women in therapy,* ed. V. Franks and V. Burtle, pp. 411–434. New York: Brunner/Mazel.

Kirsh, B. 1974. Consciousness-raising groups as therapy for women. In *Women in therapy*, ed. V. Franks and V. Burtle, pp. 326–354. New York: Brunner/Mazel.

Klapper, L., and Kaplan, A. G. 1977. The emerging consciousness of sex-role stereotyping in the family therapy literature. Unpublished manuscript.

Kronsky, B. J. 1971. Feminism and psychotherapy. *Journal of Contemporary Psychotherapy* 3:89–98.

Lazarus, A. A. 1974. Women in behavior therapy. In *Women in therapy*, ed. V. Franks and V. Burtle, pp. 217–229. New York: Brunner/Mazel.

Lazarus, L. W. 1976. Family therapy by a husband-wife team. *Journal of Marriage and Family Counseling* 2:225–235.

Lennard, S. H. C., and Lennard, H. L. 1977. Architecture: Effect of territory, boundary, and orientation on family functioning. *Family Process* 16:49–66.

Lerman, H. 1974. What happens in feminist therapy. Paper presented in Symposium on Feminist Therapy in Search of a Theory at the meeting of the American Psychological Association, New Orleans, 1974.

McAllister, A., and Fernhoff, D. 1976. Test on the bias: An experiential assessment of sex bias in the psychological battery. *Division 35 Newsletter,* American Psychological Association 3(4):10–12.

Marecek, J. 1973. Dimensions of feminist therapy. Paper presented in Symposium on Liberating Psychotherapy: Changing Perspectives and Roles among Women, at the meeting of the American Psychological Association, Montreal, September 1973.

————. 1976. Powerlessness and women's psychological disorders. *Voices: Journal of the American Academy of Psychotherapists* 12:50–54.

Mehrabian, A. 1972. *Nonverbal communication.* Chicago: Aldine-Atherton.

Miller, J. B., and Mothner, I. 1971. Psychological consequences of sexual inequality. *American Journal of Orthopsychiatry* 41:767–775.

Millman, M. 1971. Observations on sex role research. *Journal of Marriage and the Family* 33:772–775.

Minturn, L., and Lambert, W. W. 1964. *Mothers of six cultures, antecedents of child rearing.* New York: Wiley.

Minuchin, S. 1974. *Families and family therapy.* Cambridge, Mass.: Harvard University Press.

Nadelson, C. M. 1974. Adjustment: New approaches to women's mental health. In *The American woman: Who will she be?*, ed. M. L. McBee and K. A. Blake. Beverly Hills, Calif.: Glencoe Press.

Orlinsky, D. E., and Howard, K. I. 1976. The effects of sex of therapist on the therapeutic experiences of women. *Psychotherapy: Theory, Research and Practice* 13:82–88.

Parsons, T., and Bales, R. F. 1955. *Family, socialization, and interaction process.* Glencoe, Ill.: Free Press.

Peal, E. 1975. Normal sex roles: An historical analysis. *Family Process* 14:389–409.

Rawlings, E. I., and Carter, D. K. 1977. *Psychotherapy for women.* Springfield, Ill.: Charles C. Thomas.

Rice, D. G., and Rice, J. K. 1977. Non-sexist "marital" therapy. *Journal of Marriage and Family Counseling* 3:3–10.

Rosenthal, E. R. 1974. Structural patterns of women's occupational choice. Ph.D. dissertation, Cornell University.

Sachnoff, E. 1975. Toward a definition of feminist therapy. *AWP Newsletter,* Fall 1975, pp. 4–5.

Sager, C. J. 1976. *Marriage contracts and couple therapy.* New York: Brunner/Mazel.

Smith, J. A. 1972. For God's sake, what do those women want? *Personnel and Guidance Journal* 51:133–136.

Watzlawick, P., Weakland, J. H., and Fisch, R. 1974. *Change.* New York: Norton.

Zuk, G. R., 1972. Family therapy: Clinical hodgepodge or clinical science? *Journal of Marriage and Family Counseling* 2:229–304.

# 47

## The Consciousness-Raising Group as a Model for Therapy with Women

By now almost everyone is familiar with a sense of growing unrest among women with many of their traditional sex-role stereotypes. There is no evidence that women are more like each other psychologically than men are like each other. In fact, the bulk of evidence on gender-role differences points out that the differences between individuals of each sex are greater than differences between men and women (Mischel 1966). Yet, for a woman in particular, her sex determines to a large degree her future roles in life, dictating limitations on the options for her development, regardless of intellect, activity level, or physical and emotional capacity (Epstein 1970; Amundsen 1971). This role confinement has been psychologically frustrating to many women and is a major basis for identification as feminists of many of the therapists on the Feminist Therapist Roster of the Association for Women in Psychology (Brodsky 1972). Epidemiological studies (Gurin, Veroff, and Feld 1960; Chesler 1971) reveal that women complain more of nervousness, impending breakdown, and attempts at suicide (and they are beginning to achieve this goal more often). They are more frequently seen in therapy, and more likely to be hospitalized for their mental disorders. As Chesler (1971) points out, women are the most "treated" category in our society. The Task Force on Family Law and Policy (1968) concluded that the married woman, in the traditional feminine role of housewife, has the most difficulty psychologically, and the discrepancy between married women and other groups increases with the years of marriage. Bart (1971) noted that depression in middle-aged women was most likely to occur when there was an overly strong commitment to the mother role so that other forms of individual identity were lacking when the children left home.

Directing women into narrowly confined roles is a long socialization process that starts with the toys and books of young children that encourage specific social models that differentiate instrumental and expressive tools of development (Bardwick and Douvan 1971). The realization that women are not to make a significant impact upon the world, that their role in life is not only different from that of their brothers, but qualitatively inferior in terms of the rewards of the society in which they live, occurs in vivid and demonstrable form by high-school years. Horner (1970) demonstrates dramatic evidence of the suppression of self-esteem and self-actualization in adolescent girls. The motive to avoid success becomes a powerful inhibition on the academic achievement of girls. The fears of loss of femininity associated with being competitive, the social disapproval of intellectual females, and the actual denial in bright women that a woman is capable of high levels of achievement were all themes repeatedly related in projective stories of Horner's subjects. Sixty-five percent of the sample of females, compared to less than 10 percent of the males, showed this phenomenon of avoiding success.

The identity crisis is perhaps most noted in the married, middle-class women who have been overeducated and underutilized. The gulf separating the life style of the upper-middle-class housewife and her mate is perhaps wider than any other strata in our society. By definition these women are happy. They have husbands, families, and household help. Why don't they feel fulfilled? Friedan (1963) refers to the uneasiness and disillusionment of the bored middle-class housewives as the "problem that had no name." These women continued to live out their proscribed roles in spite of vague, undefined needs for more variability and needs for more opportunity to reveal individual talents that were often not consonant with the roles of "kinder, kuche, and kirche" (children, kitchen, and church).

With the reawakening of the feminist movement in the sixties, women began to investigate the problem with no name. Bird (1968) discovered what women in the working world suspected but dared not voice aloud. That is, when a woman leaves the stereotyped roles, she fights a battle of subtle and often blatant discrimination and resentment. The battle is a lonely one for those who can overcome the initial fears of loss of femininity, social disapproval, and disdain of men and women alike for daring to compete in the male domain.

Consciousness-raising (CR) groups grew out of both the sense of restless constraint noted by Freidan and the awareness of being different and alone noted by Bird. These feelings were finally exposed as a common occurrence and CR groups developed a very important aspect of the women's movement, the awareness of women that others shared these same self-doubts.

The small group structure of the women's movement was ideally suited to the exploration of personal identity issues. The technique of heightening self-awareness by comparing personal experiences was as basic to the continuance and solidarity of the movement as any other tactic. Women found themselves eliciting and freely giving support to other group members who often were asserting themselves as individuals for the first time in their lives. They gained strength from members who confronted others, and they learned to ask for their own individual rights to adopt new roles and express new behaviors.

The individual changes that occurred in the context of CR groups were unique from many therapeutic techniques that women had previously experienced. Many CR group members had previously been in therapy (Newton and Walton 1971). Many others had considered the entire mental health profession as implying illness and abnormality and had no contact with individual or group experiences until they joined a CR group.

By education and training, women had been encouraged to be conformists and passive. In their traditional roles, they had been isolated from each other and from events in the larger political and economic world beyond their narrowly confined psychological space. The CR group offered a sense of closeness or intimacy with other women as opposed to a media-produced sense of competition and alienation from each other. The development of the concept of sisterhood arose as a shared understanding of the unique problems of being a woman in a man's world.

Movement women (Allen 1971) and professionals (Newton and Walton 1971) have begun to study consciousness-raising groups for their perspectives on the social movement, and on exploration of new life styles. The present analysis focuses on the psychological impact, with particular reference to the issue of identity crises. In terms of contrast with therapy groups, the CR group starts with the assumption that the environment, rather than intrapsychic dynamics, plays a major role in the difficulties of the individuals. The medical model of abnormal behavior based on biological, innate causes is not acceptable to these groups. They are struggling to redefine these very concepts that have been seen as assigning women to a helpless patient role, destined as victims of their biological nature to behave in certain ways (Weisstein 1969; Chesler 1971).

Women in CR groups do not react in traditional female interaction patterns that are commonly seen in all-female therapy groups. For example, ask a therapist who has dealt with all-female groups of mothers of patients, institutional groups, and so forth. The typical response is that women are catty, aggressive, competitive, and much tougher on each other for digressions than they are toward men.

In CR groups women are confronted with acting as individuals. They are encouraged to examine their uniqueness apart from their roles toward others such as wife, mother, or secretary. It appears easier for a woman to reveal taboo subjects and feelings such as not liking to care for young children, wishing one had never married, feeling more intelligent than one's boss or husband, or being tired of boosting his self-esteem at the expense of her own. Finding that not only are these feelings not abnormal, but common experiences among other women, can have an almost religious conversion reaction in some women (Newton and Walton 1971).

A sense of trust in other women and a closeness based on common problems that arise from external sources as well as internal deficiencies serves to bind the groups into continuing, relatively stable units. The attrition rate for the groups I and my colleagues have encountered as well as those studied by Newton and Walton (1971) appears to be lower than those of typical voluntary therapy groups or sensitivity groups. Members appear to move to an intimacy stage rapidly and maintain a strong loyalty. Dropouts occur early, often due to conflict with male relationships that are threatened by changes in dependency behaviors.

The therapeutic processes that occur in these groups are akin to assertive training, personal growth groups, achievement-oriented training, or simply self-development groups. In assertive training the key technique seems to involve the role models provided by other group members. Women as models are more convincing than male authoritarian leaders for whom the assertive role is a cultural expectation. Likewise, achievement needs are raised more readily in an all-woman group. The identification with other women who achieve is more real than transference to a model outside the situation of direct discrimination experiences. In this sense, like Synanon, Recovery, Inc., or Alcoholics Anonymous, in CR groups some experienced members give strength to the neophyte.

I have seen faculty women return to long-forgotten dissertations and take advanced courses and housewives who have confronted their husbands for more rights or domestic help. Others went through divorces from marriages that had been security traps, and childless women stood up for their right to refuse to have children simply because others thought they should.

One difficulty with the groups comes at a stage when the women try to transfer their newfound behaviors outside the group. In a parallel fashion to the sensitivity group member who expects others outside the group to respond as positively as the group, CR group members often find that the group understands, but the outside world does not change to correspond with the groups' level of awareness. It is at this stage that women tend to become angry with their employers, lovers, and old friends for continuing to act in chauvinistic, stereotyped patterns. A new response from a woman may be either ignored, misunderstood, patronizingly laughed at, or invoke a threatened retaliatory confrontation. Unlike the individual in a more traditional assertive training situation, these women are behaving often in new ways that society usually does not condone. In frustration women may overreact and, as a result, provoke just the response they fear to get. For example, loud demands for better treatment on the job by a previously meek woman may well meet with a backlash response leading to termination of her entire job.

This type of frustration often leads to a period of depression, either of individuals or the group as a whole. They feel that while they can become aware of their situation and make individual changes, they cannot make much of an impact on the outside world. There is little outside reinforcement to carry on their motivation. At this later dropout stage, the faculty woman gets pregnant instead of completing her dissertation, the potential divorcée decides that security is more important after all, the frustrated housewife announces that "Joe thinks this group is making me unhappy and he wants me to quit," or the graduate student cannot find time because she is up nights typing her boyfriend's thesis.

If these regressive tendencies are weathered by the group, the most crucial, and often the most effective, stage of the group experience develops. The women plan to actively alter the environment in a realistic manner to make it more compatible with the developing growth needs of the members. The direction of the group turns from personal, individual solutions (except for occasional booster-shot sessions as the need arises) to some sort of group action. Actions that groups may take vary according to talents, age, and needs. They might consist of organized protests, political lobbying, educational programs, or missionary goals of helping to organize other groups to expand the population of the enlightened. The CR group works to give a sense of social as well as personal worth to the members and, as a by-product, serves to help modify an environment insensitive to the needs of an increasingly growing population of restless women.

The premise of this paper is that the CR groups of the women's movement have implications for the treatment of identity problems of women in therapy. The following ways are suggested possibilities for transferring the CR groups dynamics to use in individual therapy. First, in working with women on identity issues, therapists should be aware of the increasingly wider range of valid goals for healthy functioning of women in terms of roles and personality traits (Maccoby 1971). For example, exuberance should not be interpreted as aggression because the behavior occurs in a female. Second, a good therapist is aware of the reality of the female patient's situation. Many factors are beyond her control. She cannot realistically expect to attain achievement comparable to a man, unless she has greater intellectual and/or motivational abilities. Discrimination does exist (Amundsen 1971; Bernard 1971; Astin 1969; Epstein 1970; Bird 1968; etc.). Because of this discrimination, the importance of encouragement through assertive training and independence from others, including the therapist, is paramount to counteract the many years of discouragement through subtle cultural mores. The therapist can serve as supporter and believer in the patient's competence through the regressive, drop-out stages, and, finally, in the face of individual frustrations he or she can recognize the need for some direct and meaningful activity related to improvement of the social situations.

Working with women's CR groups offers a number of insights to a therapist for the particular problems women face in trying to resolve the difficulties of living in a world that revolves around men's work. For example, those women who report patterns of intrusive male behavior often appear to be oversensitive to slights and minor brushoffs. CR group experiences help women to confirm the reality of such slights rather than deny their existence or pass them off as projections. For a man, such incidents can be overlooked as exceptional and not integrated into the broader experience of being taken seriously and accepted as a thinking individual. For a woman, the experience is more a rule than an exception (unless she is an exceptional woman). Her sensitivity to such slights comes out of an awareness of the situation and a concomitant frustration in being unable to defend herself in the situation without appearing pompous, uppity, or paranoid.

The accumulation of experiences of being interrupted in conversations, of having her opinions ignored or not taken seriously, can severely affect a woman's feelings of competence and self-worth. Her desire to be assertive or to make an impact on the environment is continuously weakened by this lack of affirmation of her self by others.

There are therapists who maintain that women who act insecure or inferior in such situations are doing so in order to get secondary gains from such postures (using feminine wiles) and her verbalizations of a desire for independence or responsibility are not genuine. Such therapists probably do not understand that without role models or encouragement from the environment, these women have no real choice in not accepting the only reality they have been indoctrinated to believe about the capabilities of their sex.

Other major themes that some therapists are apt to misjudge or overlook when dealing with women clients can be briefly mentioned here. Unaware therapists still tend to consider marriage uncritically as a solution for women's problems without realizing that, as with men, divorce or no marriage may often present the best available alternative for the individual. When a woman proposes such a solution, the therapist may become more concerned with her nontraditional life style than with her personal feelings in living out such a style.

Some therapists also automatically assume that a woman's career is secondary to her mate's career. The conflict over "having it both ways," by wanting a career and family, is still seen as the wife's burden, not the husband's also. Unusual patterns of division of household tasks, child care, and so forth, are no longer stigmas that label individuals as deviant. Therapists have been guilty of producing iatrogenic disorders in women who felt comfortable with what they were doing until the therapist suggested that they were selfish, unreasonable, or pointed out how no one expected them to accomplish so much and they would be loved and accepted without this unrealistic drive to compete.

Perhaps related to the foregoing is the frustration women have experienced with therapists who can empathize readily with a man who is stifled by a clinging, nagging wife, but who interprets the same complaint from a woman as her being cold and unfeeling for not responding affectionately to an insecure, demanding husband. The crucial issue surrounding such misunderstandings is an unconscious tendency for many therapists to have a double standard for men and women in mental health and adjustment (Broverman et al. 1970). This attitude restricts their capacity to allow their clients a free expression of the various available roles. Women, after all, have needs for self-esteem, independence, expression of anger and aggression; and men have needs for security, affection and expression of fear and sorrow. While at present men may have more diverse models in our society for the development of an adequate masculine role, women's models have been restricted for the most part to housewives or the more narrow traditional feminine occupations.

Perhaps the strongest message to be seen from the success of these

CR groups is that women are capable of using other women as models. Identification of women with role models of their own sex has been largely limited to the traditional homemaker roles or the feminine occupations such as teaching and nursing. The acceptance of more varied roles and personality traits in women will help to integrate a larger portion of women into the "mentally healthy" categories.

Until this happens to a greater extent, perhaps, as Chesler (1971) suggests, only women should be therapists for other women. On the other hand, if therapists must have the same experiences as their patients in order to help them, we would be a sorry lot indeed. The important lesson for clinicians, male and female alike, is to make a particular effort to study the facts and reasoning behind the women's movement. We help neurotics, psychotics, children, handicapped, any group of which we are not a member by keeping up with the current literature written by those in close touch with large numbers of that particular population. In the same vein, any male therapist who has not kept abreast of current theory and issues relating to women is treating from a position of ignorance. The sample of women in his personal life does not provide sufficient clinical data or theory on which to base therapy. Women have a great need today for allies in their struggles to alter a constricting environment. Legal and political allies are not sufficient. Understanding, enlightened therapists are necessary if we want to avoid psychological casualties of today's transitional cultural changes.

REFERENCES

Allen, P. 1971. *The small group in women's liberation.* New York: Times Change Press.
Amundsen, K. 1971. *The silenced majority: Women and American democracy.* Englewood Cliffs, N.J.: Prentice-Hall.
Astin, H. 1969. *The woman doctorate in America.* Hartford: Russell Sage Foundation.
Bardwick, J., and Douvan, E. 1971. Ambivalence: The socialization of women. In *Woman in sexist society: Studies in power and powerlessness,* ed. V. Gornick and B. Moran, pp. 147–159. New York: Basic Books.
Bart, P. 1971. Depression in middle-aged women. In *Woman in sexist society: Studies in power and powerlessness,* ed. V. Gornick and B. Moran, pp. 99–117. New York: Basic Books.
Bernard, J. 1971. *Women and the public interest.* New York: Aldine-Atherton.
Bird, C. 1968. *Born female: The high cost of keeping women down.* New York: McKay.
Brodsky, A., ed. 1972. *Feminist therapist roster of the Association for Women in Psychology.* Pittsburgh: KNOW, Inc.
Broverman, I. K., et al. 1970. Sex-role stereotypes and clinical judgments of mental health. *Journal of Consulting Psychology* 34:1–7. [Reprinted herein chapter 7.]

Chesler, P. 1971. Patient and patriarch: Women in the psychotherapeutic relationship. In *Woman in sexist society: Studies in power and powerlessness,* ed. V. Gornick and B. Moran, pp. 251–275. New York: Basic Books.

Epstein, C. 1970. *Woman's place: Options and limits in professional careers.* Berkeley, Calif.: University of California Press.

Freidan, B. 1963. *The feminine mystique.* New York: Dell.

Gurin, G., Veroff, J., and Feld, S. 1960. *Americans view their mental health.* New York: Basic Books.

Horner, M. 1970. Femininity and successful achievement: A basic inconsistency. In *Feminine personality and conflict,* ed. J. Bardwick, pp. 45–76. Belmont, Calif.: Brooks/Cole.

Maccoby, E. 1971. Sex differences and their implications for sex roles. Paper presented at American Psychological Association, Washington, D.C., September 1971.

Mischel, W. 1966. A social-learning view of sex differences in behavior. In *The development of sex differences,* ed. E. Maccoby, pp. 56–81. Stanford, Calif.: Stanford University Press.

Newton, E., and Walton, S. 1971. The personal is political: Consciousness-raising and personal change in the women's liberation movement. In Anthropologists look at the study of women, chaired by B. G. Schoepf. Symposium presented at the American Anthropological Association, November 19, 1971.

Reeves, N. 1971. *Womankind: Beyond the stereotypes.* New York: Aldine-Atherton.

Report of the Task Force on Family Law and Policy to the Citizen's Advisory Council on the Status of Women, Washington, D.C., 1968.

Weisstein, N. 1969. Kinder, kuche, kirche as scientific law: Psychology constructs the female. *Motive* 29:6–7.

# 48

## The Psychotherapeutic Impact of Women's Consciousness-Raising Groups

MORTON A. LIEBERMAN, NANCY SOLOW,
GARY R. BOND, AND JANET REIBSTEIN

One consequence of the women's movement has been to direct attention to widespread dissatisfaction with traditional sex-role structures and attitudes toward women. As an early outgrowth of the women's movement, "consciousness-raising" (CR) groups provided women with a setting in which they could draw on the commonalities underlying personal experiences to analyze and understand their discontent (Allen 1970).

The precursors of CR groups were political discussion groups for women involved in the civil rights and antiwar protest movements during the 1960s (Carden 1974). Since then CR groups have generally evolved into support groups serving a psychotherapeutic function

This investigation was supported in part by grant F22 DA 00791–01 to Dr. Bond from the National Institute of Drug Abuse and grant 1 F31 MH 05406 to Ms. Reibstein and Research Scientist Award 5–K05–MH 20342 to Dr. Lieberman from the National Institute of Mental Health.

(Freeman 1975; Warren 1976). This change probably reflected the fact that CR groups lacked the structure and clear-cut objectives of task-oriented political action groups. In a recent national survey of women entering CR groups, it was found that CR attracts a sizable proportion of psychologically distressed women with psychotherapeutic goals (Freeman 1975).

The present study assessed the psychotherapeutic effectiveness of CR by investigating four general areas of impact: (1) mental health status and psychological functioning; (2) life-style decisions and personal values; (3) marital relationships; and (4) feminist attitudes and orientations.

# Method

Two women's centers located in an eastern metropolitan area were contacted. Both held open meetings during which CR "starters" (women who help coordinate and advise CR groups) organized a number of smaller CR groups.

The research was presented to women attending the organizational meeting. Packets containing self-administered questionnaires were distributed to women interested in the study. To insure anonymity, the questionnaires were number-coded and cross-indexed with a post-card identifying the respondent. The postcard was mailed back to the women's center. Approximately 100 questionnaires were distributed in this manner, and an additional 50 were distributed to other newly forming groups known to women at the centers. In all, 73 women returned questionnaires.

## Follow-up Questionnaires

Six months later respondents were mailed a follow-up questionnaire. Eighteen respondents not providing addresses were lost from the sample. In all, forty-three women (76 percent of those contacted at follow-up) completed the second questionnaire. We found no systematic bias on any of the demographic variables in this reduced sample; women completing both questionnaires appeared to be similar to those completing only the first questionnaire. Of the forty-three women returning follow-up questionnaires, thirty-two had continued in the group for four months or more. The evaluation of changes was based on this subsample.

Thirty women indicated that they would participate in a telephone interview; we were able to contact twenty-four of them. In these twenty- to ninety-minute interviews, we asked each woman to discuss her most and least positive meetings, examined specific changes and decisions in her life occurring during the time of her CR participation, and clarified and amplified questionnaire responses.

## Outcome Measures

Outcome measures, listed in table 48-1, reflect the hypothesized areas of change in CR groups. Measures of psychological functioning, personal value systems, and the quality of marital relationships were drawn from the psychotherapy and encounter group literature, while the feminist attitudes scales were used in the aforementioned CR group survey. The questionnaires also examined reasons for joining, expectations, and experiences in the group. In the follow-up questionnaires, we included additional scales of marital stress, strain, and coping.

Reliability coefficients for internal consistency were computed on scales for which such information was not previously available. Using the scores from the initial sample of seventy-three women (fifty-one of whom were married), Cronbach's alpha coefficients were as follows: self-reliance, .56; marital satisfaction, .77; marital communication, .89; marital discord, .81; and discrimination index, .69. The coefficients of reproducibility and scalability, using the Gutmann scaling procedure, were .93 and .51, respectively, for the Gutmann feminist orientation scale.

# Results

*Participants in CR Groups.* Our previous survey of 1,700 CR group participants (Lieberman and Bond 1976) found that CR attracted well-educated, white, upper middle-class women between twenty and fifty years of age. The seventy-three women who completed the initial questionnaire resembled this survey sample. Respondents in the current study ranged in age from twenty-one to sixty-two years, with a mean age of thirty-seven. Sixty-nine percent were married, 23 percent were divorced or separated, and 8 percent were single. Those who were married had been so for a median of fourteen years (range 1 to 31 years); the median number of children was between two and three.

TABLE 48-1
*Outcome Battery*

| Instrument | Chief Source | Format | Content |
|---|---|---|---|
| **Mental health status and psychological functioning** | | | |
| Target problems | Battle et al. 1966 | 3-item open-ended | Ideographic problems and goals in group |
| Self-esteem | Rosenberg 1965 | 10-item scale | Feelings about self |
| Hopkins Symptom Checklist | Derogatis et al. 1974 | 35-item checklist | Symptom distress (e.g., depression, anxiety) |
| Coping strategies | Lieberman, Yalom, and Miles 1973 | 19 Likert scales | Coping styles: defensive, adequate subscales |
| Personal resources | New | 8-item open-ended | Source of social support for stressful events; self-reliance subscale |
| **Personal value systems** | | | |
| Life space | Lieberman et al. 1973 | 12-item open-ended | Personal values; life-style goals and decisions; orientation toward growth |
| **Marital relationship** | | | |
| Marital satisfaction | Landau 1976, adapted from Bradburn and Caplovitz 1965 | 6-item checklist | Extent of satisfaction |
| Marital communication | New, adapted from Jourard 1961 | 15-item checklist | Degree of disclosure to spouse |
| Marital discord | Landau 1976, adapted from Bradburn 1969 | 17-item checklist | Frequency and areas of disagreements |
| Decision making | Landau 1976, adapted from Blood and Wolfe 1960 | 6-item checklist | Actual and ideal ratings |
| **Feminist attitudes and orientation** | | | |
| Feminist identification | New | 7-point Likert scale | Identification with women's movement |
| Discrimination index | Lieberman and Bond 1976 | 6-item checklist | Perception of personal discrimination |
| Feminist orientation scale | Lieberman and Bond 1976 | 7-item scale | Attitudes on feminist issues: ERA, day care, abortion, etc. |
| Feminist affiliations | Lieberman and Bond 1976 | 9-item checklist | Membership in women's groups |

The women were well educated: 44 percent were college graduates, while another 40 percent had attended college. The majority of women were employed outside of the home: 21 percent held professional or managerial positions; 36 percent worked in secretarial or administrative capacities; and 4 percent were skilled or unskilled workers. The remaining 39 percent were either students (6 percent), unemployed (9 percent), or housewives (24 percent). Students were underrepresented in the current sample (16 percent of the women in the national survey were students), while housewives were overrepresented (24 percent as compared to 14 percent in the national survey). On the whole, however, the women in the current study were fairly similar demographically to the survey sample.

The motivations for joining CR groups offered by the women in the present study also were similar to those described by the survey sample. In both samples the predominant reason for entering a CR group was an "interest in women's issues" (e.g., to share thoughts and feelings about being a woman, to learn about other women and their experiences, to examine problems women have with their traditional roles). Often such motivations were accompanied by "help-seeking" concerns, as manifested in the desire "to get relief from things or feelings troubling me," "to solve personal problems," and "to bring about some change in myself." Political motivations, only slightly evident in the national survey, were virtually absent in the current sample. The current sample was less involved in political activity: While 40 percent of those in the survey were members of women's political organizations, only 21 percent in the present study had such affiliations.

The interests of the women in the present study thus seemed to reflect a trend, extending from the late 1960s to the early 1970s, noted in the survey: Women increasingly join CR groups for the enhancement of their personal well-being rather than to induce social and political reform. This preoccupation with self-improvement was also reflected in the women's widespread utilization of professional mental health services. In the present study, 74 percent (55 percent for the national survey) had received psychotherapy within the past five years; of these, 44 percent were undergoing treatment at the time they entered a CR group. The current sample had higher psychiatric distress scores on the Hopkins Symptom Checklist than the women in the national survey; both samples, however, had well above the average distress ratings reported for a normative sample of demographically similar women (Lieberman and Bond 1976).

*The CR Group.* The groups were small (six to fifteen women), leaderless groups structured along a set of guidelines provided by the women's centers. These guidelines merit special attention, for they help to distinguish the CR group process from that of traditional group therapies. Each weekly CR meeting centered around the discussion of a specific topic chosen by the group members; mothers, fathers, sexuality, self-image, and husbands were topics covered by most groups. The guidelines recommended that each woman address the chosen topic from the first-person perspective. Furthermore, while recounting her personal experiences, a woman was not to be interrupted or criticized by other group members, nor was the speaker herself to solicit advice or comments.

From the interviews, we determined that the sample included women from at least fifteen different groups. Three of these disbanded after meeting for less than four months. In one group, a depressed, suicidal woman demanded considerable individual attention; the others decided to disband rather than to continue to deal with the distressed member's suicide threats. A second group experienced two sources of tension: ambivalence about getting involved with the problems of a more distressed member and conflicts between the interests of older, separated or divorced women and younger, married participants. The third group appeared to have multiple difficulties: The members had subgrouped by age and religious affiliations; further, levels of disclosure may have been ill-timed, with women revealing intimate details of their lives (lesbianism, having an abortion) early in the group's existence. Problems of composition and inability to resolve conflict, then, may have contributed to the difficulties of groups that disbanded.

*Dropouts.* The mean number of women initially in a CR group was eleven (range, 7 to 15), and most groups maintained a steady membership of approximately nine active members. In the twelve ongoing groups, on the average approximately three women dropped out (based on questionnaire information of all respondents). Available follow-up information on nine dropouts and thirty-two continuers disclosed that the only demographic characteristic distinguishing dropouts from continuers was marital status: Half of the dropouts were separated or divorced (all within nineteen months prior to joining CR groups) as compared to fifteen of the continuers. Initial mean levels of symptom distress, self-esteem, and coping styles did not distinguish the two groups, nor did attitudes on feminist issues. The dropouts cited reasons for leaving their CR group that were linked to either general group conditions ("dull," "too large," "polarized—older versus younger women"), or to an incompatibility of goals ("the women in the group were about five years behind me in their awareness of women's rights," "others used the group as an adjunct to their psychotherapy"), or to the discomfort with their own quality of participation ("too frightened," "unable to participate," "felt left out").

Dropouts, not surprisingly, had much lower evaluations of their CR experience than continuers, as indicated by percentage of positive responses to the testimony scales: "met goals": 0 percent of dropouts, 59 percent of continuers; "learned a great deal": 13 percent of dropouts, 69 percent of continuers; "enjoyed": 13 percent of dropouts, 86 percent of continuers. Dropouts, while less likely than continuers to encourage others to join CR groups, did not actively discourage others from participation.

## Changes After Six Months in CR Groups

The impact of CR groups was assessed for a sample of thirty-two women who had participated in a CR group for at least four months.

Besides the nine participants just described who voluntarily dropped out, two others were eliminated from the analyses, since one had contracted hepatitis and never actually attended a meeting while the other was asked to leave by the other group members early in the group's history. The results of the analysis of change, therefore, are limited to the outcome for those women who participated meaningfully in their CR group.

*Target Problems.* Prior to their participation, the women indicated three "target" problems or goals (table 48–2). The majority reflected concerns about the self-concept and interpersonal functioning, with 72 percent of the problems sorted into one of these two areas. Only one person described problems concerning neither the self-concept nor interpersonal functioning.

Self-concept problems included concerns about self-esteem, assertiveness, and identity. Some women complained that they lacked the self-confidence to be assertive, while others hoped to become more self-reliant and independent of their husbands. Some women felt inadequate and incapable of making changes in their lives. Others seemed to be experiencing identity confusion. Common goals were "to discover who I am," "to explore my identity as a woman," or "to find a direction in life." Some were reevaluating their social roles; one woman described her target problem as "confusion on happy marriage—I love my home life, yet feel guilty for accepting 'home, wife, mother' as total."

Interpersonal problems centered on a desire to explore marital, family, and female relationship issues. Several women felt isolated and lacking in interpersonal relationships, and believed that CR groups would give them an opportunity "to develop closer relationships with women" as well as "to hear how other women feel," "to learn how others cope with similar problems," and "to like women more." Still

TABLE 48–2
*Target Problems*

| Category | No. (%) of Women Mentioning Problem |
|---|---|
| **Self concept** | |
| Self-esteem | 16 (50) |
| Role dissatisfaction | 7 (22) |
| Autonomy | 6 (19) |
| Identity | 5 (16) |
| **Interpersonal** | |
| With women | 7 (22) |
| With men | 5 (16) |
| Marital | 3 (9) |
| Family | 4 (13) |
| Loneliness | 5 (16) |
| Isolation | 3 (9) |
| Skills | 6 (19) |
| **Symptoms/affective** | |
| Anxiety | 3 (9) |
| Handling of feelings | 2 (6) |
| Depression | 0 (0) |
| **Other** | |
| Career | 5 (16) |
| Women's Movement | 3 (9) |
| Situational | 3 (9) |
| Weight reduction | 2 (6) |
| Sexuality | 1 (3) |
| Physical complaints | 1 (3) |
| Growth | 1 (3) |
| Total | 88[a] |

[a] Based on thirty-two women. Twenty-nine women mentioned three problems, one woman mentioned two problems and two women mentioned one problem. In three instances a woman mentioned two similar problems, which have been counted only once.

others anticipated improving general interpersonal skills by reducing "impatience with others" and by learning to "speak more freely and deal with people in a more relaxed manner."

Problems concerned with affect (depression, anxiety, affect control) were rare, despite the high scores on the Hopkins Symptom Checklist. Here the target goals differed markedly from those reported in psychotherapy studies, which typically find that more than half of the patients mention such problems (Sloane et al. 1975; Yalom et al. 1978). For the most part, they hoped to explore their attitudes and feelings toward the self and significant others and did not expect to deal with symptomatic distress.

*Changes in Mental Health Measures.* The results presented in table 48–3 suggest that CR groups aided the women by improving self-attitudes, but were limited in promoting other changes in psychological functioning. Of the seven measures in this area, significant levels of improvement were found for only two indices. Mean distress on target problems was significantly decreased ($P \leq .001$) and mean level of self-esteem significantly increased ($P \leq .003$). There was also a trend toward an increased reliance on the self rather than on significant others or informal helping networks in dealing with problematic situations ($P \leq .06$). No appreciable changes were evident for symptom distress or the adequacy of coping styles.

The questionnaire data thus portrayed a specific pattern of change: Feelings about and attitudes toward the self improved, while symptoms and coping styles remained unimproved. Since most women had indicated that at least one of their target problems centered on their self-concept, this pattern of change was consistent with their goals. The lack of symptoms reduction in spite of relatively high initial levels was surprising.

Accompanying this increased self-esteem were modest changes in behavior, such as asserting one's right to take the night off from preparing dinner and taking separate vacations from one's family.

Changes were also found in the area of self-reliance, as indicated by responses to a series of dilemmas (e.g., "making an important decision," "facing an embarrassing situation"). Contrary to theoretical expectations, women did not expand their range of utilization of significant others. Rather, they increased in the average number of dilemmas they would deal with on their own, without outside help.

Although such self-reliance is congruent with changes in self-esteem, peer self-help systems would be expected to increase use of such networks. Perhaps their increased self-reliance was part of a general feeling of greater mastery and control over their situation, to assert their needs despite what others thought or felt about them. For one woman, this change involved:

becoming more choosey with the type of person I spend my time with. Before, I wanted everyone to like me—especially my husband's friends. Before, I used to trail along. Now I'm just as happy to be alone. Now if my husband invites some people over who I don't like, I'll go into another room. Other times I just won't go out with my husband. I do what I want to do, which is selfish, but it's good for me.

*Life-Style Decisions and Personal Value Systems.* Were changes in feelings about the self translated into decisions that altered the women's life styles?

In all, 35 percent reported an important change in their career or

TABLE 48-3

*Outcome Results[a] (N = 32)*

| Scale | Pre-CR Group | 6-month Follow-up | p |
|---|---|---|---|
| Mental health status and psychological functioning | | | |
| Target problem distress (1, low; 9, high) | 5.9 | 4.8 | .000 |
| Self-esteem (6, low; 0, high) | 2.3 | 1.5 | .003 |
| Symptom distress (.00, low; 1.00, high) | .29 | .25 | NS |
| Coping strategies | | | |
| Adequate (1, least; 8, most adequate) | 5.6 | 5.7 | NS |
| Defensive (1, least; 8, most defensive) | 5.2 | 4.9 | NS |
| Personal resources | | | |
| Self-reliance (0, low; 8, high) | 1.1 | 1.5 | .06 |
| Personal value systems | | | |
| Growth orientation, % of values growth-oriented (0, none; 100, all) | 65 | 48 | .01 |

| | 6-month Follow-up | | |
|---|---|---|---|
| | More Important | Less Important | No Change |
| Value hierarchy, relative importance of each area | | | |
| Personal growth | 9 | 11 | 12 | NS[b] |
| Family | 19 | 5 | 8 | .01 |
| Instrumental | 10 | 11 | 11 | NS |
| Interpersonal | 3 | 16 | 13 | .07 |
| Hedonistic | 8 | 13 | 11 | NS |

| Scale | Pre-CR Group | 6-month Follow-up | p |
|---|---|---|---|
| Marital relationship (N = 21) | | | |
| Marital satisfaction (1, high; 5, low) | 2.3 | 2.2 | NS |
| Marital discord (0, low; 17, high) | 1.8 | 1.8 | NS |
| Marital communication (0, low; 15, high) | 6.7 | 6.4 | NS |
| Marital decision making (0, low discrepancy from ideal; 4, high discrepancy from ideal) | .39 | .29 | NS |
| Feminist attitudes and orientation | | | |
| Feminist identification (1, positive; 7, negative) | 3.4 | 2.9 | .05 |
| Discrimination Index (0, low; 6, high) | 1.4 | 2.3 | .001 |
| Feminist orientation scale (0, low; 7, high) | 4.97 | 5.0 | NS |
| Feminist affiliations (member of at least one women's group) | 22 | 37 | NS[c] |

[a] All statistical analyses were calculated using *t* tests between pre-CR group and six-month follow-up means, unless otherwise indicated.

[b] Sign test.

[c] McNemar test for the significance of changes.

interpersonal situations. Four returned to college and three previously nonworking women were employed at follow-up. Changes in marital status included one marriage, one separation, and a reconciliation between a separated couple. One woman became engaged, while two single women terminated long-term relationships with men. The woman who separated, whose change scores suggested substantial gains from the CR group, said this about her relationship:

I felt strong enough to question his attitudes and feelings and decided we were getting nowhere together. . . . I got the strength to make the break in my group. I realized I don't have to let someone physically and verbally abuse me. I had a right to leave.

For the most part, however, the women did not consider their CR group experience to play a primary role in initiating such decisions, although groups generally did support the women after they had made their decisions.

Analysis of the women's "life space" values further supported our impression that participation in CR groups itself generally did not initiate life-style changes. The women decreased in their desire for growth, change, and learning ($P \leq .01$), which may indicate that CR group participation lowered rather than raised expectations about how much change was feasible or desirable. Some women appeared to have moved toward greater acceptance of their current situation. One woman, whose initial target problems centered on difficulties in trusting her husband and in feeling close to her family, described her CR group experience as having been significant because:

I felt that I have the happiest life of all the members—a reasonable husband, interesting job, relative freedom, and I had a feeling of being able to cope with whatever may come. . . . It made me feel more content with me.

Nor did CR groups have any dramatic impact on the ordering of priorities in the life space. Using the first five life space values mentioned by each woman, we determined a "hierarchy of values" both for individuals and for the sample as a whole. The sample hierarchy prior to participation in CR groups (1, personal growth; 2, family; 3, instrumental—career, education, etc.; 4, interpersonal; 5, hedonistic) was the same at follow-up, except for an increased emphasis on the family at the expense of interpersonal relationships outside the family. Overall, then, values remained fairly stable, with some suggestion of a slight shift toward a more traditional view of the family.

*Marital Relationships.* Participation in CR groups seemed to have no impact in enabling the women to establish more effective communication, to reconcile differences in various conflict areas, or to adopt decision-making processes closer to their ideals. As indicated by table 48–

3, the women did not manifest significant decreases in marital conflicts or communication; nor did they change their patterns of decision making. Furthermore, no consistent changes were discernible in marital satisfaction or dissatisfaction. Nearly all women who were initially dissatisfied with one or more aspects of their marriage (this included 71 percent of the sample) remained dissatisfied at the six-month follow-up. On the other hand, those women who were initially satisfied were also generally not affected.

Testimonials about the impact of CR groups on marriages gave a different picture. More than half of the married women indicated greater acceptance, if not renewed appreciation, of their marriages. The most prevalent response ($N = 7$) was that the women felt more trusting and closer to their spouses. In several cases the opportunity for comparisons with other women's marriages provided a new framework in which the woman could assess her own marriage. The result of such comparative evaluations was often an increased appreciation of the marriage. Other women ($N = 5$) indicated that their CR groups helped them become aware of their husbands as individuals with their own strengths and weaknesses.

Still others seemed to have reconceptualized the meaning of marriage to them as well as to have reevaluated their roles within the marital relationship. Echoing the general increase in self-assertion, several women ($N = 6$) assumed greater responsibility for their own happiness while decreasing dependence on their husbands. For example, a woman married for twenty-two years recognized that:

[participating in CR] verifies that my relationship with my husband is not what I would want it to be or not on a par with what other women expect and receive. But the point is that I have stopped blaming and come to a new point of actively making more of myself and relying less on him for meaning in life.

Finally, two young women came to the conclusion that they had to give more to the marital relationship. As one self-described feminist explained:

I now realize that I have to give a little too. I was very nervous about going into a marriage as a feminist. I thought I would either have to give up everything or stand so firmly that we would get nothing done as partners. Through CR, I've seen that I have to give a little, I don't have to give up everything, nor do we have to battle constantly.

Many would view this testimonial evidence with some skepticism, especially since it was not collaborated by other evidence. Nonetheless, we conjecture that some women may have adopted different and more functional attitudes about their marriages in ways the scales did not measure.

In order to gain greater perspective on the nature of the women's marriages at follow-up, we took advantage of an alternative frame of reference by comparing the CR group women to a demographically similar group of women (white, married, college-educated, aged twenty-five to forty-five years) drawn from a probability sample of adults living in an urban area (Peralin and Lieberman, forthcoming). The results of these comparisons on standardized scales of marital strain, stress, and adjustment are shown in table 48-4. This approach, while

TABLE 48-4

*Marital Comparisons Between CR Group and Normative Samples[a]*

| | CR Group Sample (*N* = 21) | Normative Sample (*N* = 76) | *p* |
|---|---|---|---|
| Marital stress (1, low; 4, high) | 2.2 | 1.6 | .002 |
| Marital strain (1, low; 4, high) | 2.0 | 1.6 | .01 |
| Marital coping levels (1, maladaptive; 4, adaptive) | 2.9 | 3.0 | NS |
|   Emotionality | 2.4 | 3.1 | .002 |
|   Social comparison | 3.2 | 3.2 | NS |
|   Negotiation | 3.0 | 3.2 | NS |
|   Passivity | 2.8 | 3.1 | .05 |
|   Selective ignoring | 3.0 | 3.1 | NS |
| Comparison with other people's marriages, % | | | NS[b] |
|   Much better | 48 | 29 | |
|   Somewhat better | 33 | 37 | |
|   Same | 10 | 32 | |
|   Not quite as good | 9 | 1 | |
|   Much worse | 0 | 1 | |
| Own marriage over time, % | | | NS[b] |
|   Gets better | 81 | 79 | |
|   Stays same | 10 | 29 | |
|   Gets worse | 9 | 0 | |
| Preoccupation with marital problems, % | | | .02[b] |
|   Very often | 33 | 5 | |
|   Fairly often | 14 | 8 | |
|   Once in a while | 38 | 40 | |
|   Never, almost never | 14 | 47 | |

[a] All statistical analyses were calculated using *t* tests between sample means, unless otherwise indicated.

[b] Kolmogorov-Smirnov test.

not addressing the issue of change, does clarify questions concerning the quality of marital relationships at follow-up.

The findings clearly demonstrate that the CR group sample had significantly greater stress and strain in their marriages ($P \leq .002$ and $P \leq .01$, respectively) than the women in the normative sample, and were also more likely to utilize maladaptive coping strategies such as avoidance and emotionality. Thus the CR group participants' lack of change on the marital scales is probably not explained by the supposition that their marriages were unstressful. Based on the evidence available, it appears that CR groups had little discernible impact on marriages.

*Feminist Orientation and Attitudes.* Concern with changes in ideology are somewhat outside the usual interest of psychotherapy researchers. However, because of the ideological component of CR groups and their historical development within the feminist movement, several indices reflecting changes in feminist orientation and attitudes were included in our battery.

After participating for six months in a CR group, the women reported having experienced significantly higher levels of discrimination than they had prior to their CR experience ($P \leq .02$). There was also a significant increase in perceiving themselves as identified with the women's movement ($P \leq .03$), and eight women who previously had no affiliation with women's organizations joined such associations.

More than half of the women we studied remained uninvolved in any formal political organization after six months' participation in CR groups. Most of the women were reluctant to convert the CR group into a political forum. For example, when a woman tried to get her group involved in a chapter of the National Organization for Women (NOW) that was being formed, she was ignored by other group members. In some respects participants became more sympathetic to the feminist viewpoint, particularly in seeing their own lives as being shaped by discrimination. This identification, however, did not result in activist political involvement in the feminist movement.

## Comment

Our findings should be viewed in light of the strategic and technical problems facing investigators interested in assessing the impact of nonprofessional helping systems. Paramount are the problems of adequate control groups, managing outcome assessment on a turf that is in no way controlled by the investigator, and dealing with ideological differences that emerge when the organization controlling the treatment resources holds values distinct from those of the researcher. We discuss many of these conceptual and methodological problems elsewhere (Lieberman and Bond 1978).

How representative of CR group participants is this small sample of middle-class women from a suburban eastern area? Obviously, they do not represent American women in general, but the sample does appear to mirror the demographic, stress levels, and motivations of our 1974 survey of 1,669 women who were CR group participants (Lieberman and Bond 1976). How representative was the CR group experience for the participants in this sample? The basic format used by NOW (Perl and Abarbanell 1976), which emphasizes guidelines for topics of discussion and procedures, was followed by the groups studied. More direct evidence that this sample of CR groups were similar in method of operation to most other CR groups is provided by a direct comparison between the several hundred groups studied in the survey and the twelve groups used in the present study. Identical instruments, asking respondents to indicate meaningful group experiences that impacted on their learning or change, were administered in both studies. Five factor-analyzed scales represented major therapeutic mechanisms of change. The sample means and standard deviations for the current study and the national survey on these five dimensions were as follows: sharing commonalities, 1.60 (.58), 1.59 (.58); involvement, 1.70 (.71), 1.81 (.75); risk taking, 1.87 (1.00), 1.96 (.74); insight, 1.99 (.72), 2.07 (.72); role analyses, 2.58 (.80), 2.21 (.73). The rank order of importance is identical, with sharing commonalities being the most important and role analyses the least important. These similarities in guidelines and in reported mechanisms of change suggest that the current study did examine women who are in groups "typical" of CR groups in general.

The preliminary and exploratory nature of this study notwithstanding, a number of important and interesting findings have emerged. Consciousness-raising groups appear to have a unique impact that distinguishes them from other helping systems. Unlike psychotherapy, in which symptom reduction nearly always occurs, participation in CR groups did not decrease depression or anxiety. Unlike encounter groups, CR groups did not lead to increasing emphasis on personal growth and change. Rather, the impact involved reassessment of the self, reflected typically in increased self-esteem, renewed self-respect, and acknowledgment of self-importance.

Although not emphasized in this report, the specificity of outcome results, as well as information from the interviews, suggests several important process of change considerations. Consciousness-raising groups are not social microcosms; they do not rely on the examination of the interactive here-and-now that is prototypical of almost all psychotherapy. Rather, they are environments that provide support, attention, and direction for the exploration of personal problems. Frank disclosure of past experiences accompanied by minimal expression of current feelings toward group members—what could be labeled "introspection within a group"—may promote the specific changes found: higher self-esteem and greater reliance on self. A common existential theme, often expressed as "I am responsible for my own happiness," emerged from the interviews. Participants linked this new awareness to the opportunity to examine their personal experiences on chosen topics without the distractions of suggestions, interruptions, and advice giving.

Another element highlighted in CR groups is comparative judgment. Frequently women reported gaining a new perspective or a new view on themselves or their marriages, such as "after having heard others talk about their problems, I realized I was in a much better position than I had previously thought." More often than not, these comparative judgments led to perceptual reorganizations of the life space rather than to decision making. Instead of confirming the feminist imagery of radical life changes, CR group discussions reinforced modest expectations of self, career, and spouse. Private fantasies about major changes in life style were modified by the sharing of experiences.

A major concern among professionals about self-help groups is their psychological safety. Several CR groups did have difficulty when confronted with participants in severe emotional distress. One group asked a severely depressed woman to leave their group (providing her with a transparently false pretext). The woman in question survived the incident and subsequently sought professional treatment, as recommended to her by the group. This anecdote suggests that painful rejection by one's peers may occasionally occur in CR groups.

Another incident involved the sabotage of a group by a suicidal woman. The group disbanded rather than contend with the suicidal threats. The suicidal woman could hardly have benefited from the experience, while the others undoubtedly felt bruised by it. Another group, by disbanding after several sessions, left members who exposed their vulnerabilities with unresolved feelings. The consequences were especially adverse for a fifty-two-year-old divorcee, who described herself as an isolated woman with a "tendency to hide." She summarized her group experience:

I was able to reveal that I had an abortion many years ago. This was significant because I was unmarried and at that time that situation was a disgrace—and I made up my mind at that time I'd never tell anybody about it. I have since regretted telling the group since shortly thereafter the group disintegrated.

Although such unfortunate incidents occur in professional treatment as well, the responsibility for screening applicants and for following up clients, especially after negative experiences, is much clearer for professionals. Back-up for peer-led groups is often ambiguous. As already mentioned, NOW has been giving attention to the quality control of feminist CR groups. Efforts to increase the psychological safety of participants in nonprofessional groups usually involve setting limits on appropriate content and behavior. Within CR groups, time-limited, uninterrupted turn taking is one such step toward greater safety. The approaches of such organizations as Alcoholics Anonymous and Gamblers Anonymous suggest that highly ritualized formats can be fruitful. Yet, ultimately, such constraints result in a concomitant loss in spontaneity and free expression of feeling, so valued in psychotherapy.

Even if psychotherapists experience dissonance created by the competing views of help-giving embodied in psychotherapy and in CR groups and other self-help activities, participants themselves do not. Clients often move back and forth, with no apparent conflict in loyalty, between change induction systems with radically differing ideologies about the causes and solutions for problems (Yalom et al. 1968). Although professional mental health services and peer-led self-help groups are often viewed as antagonistic helping networks, in actuality many women in the present study were receiving professional psychotherapeutic treatment concurrent with their participation in CR groups. Their experiences lend support to a "synergistic" model to describe the relationship between professional and self-help services, since those participating in both changed significantly more than the others, who received no professional help. (However, this finding must be interpreted cautiously: The women receiving professional treatment were initially more distressed, as measured by the symptom checklist, the target problems, and the self-esteem scale.)

The interviews amplified the adjunctive role that CR groups played in psychotherapy. Several women found that the CR group provided important sources of material for later therapy sessions. One woman became aware of a tendency to compete with other women, a problem her therapist had discussed with her but that she did not recognize until she participated in a CR group. For another, a CR group discussion of childhood sexuality stimulated material for "a major breakthrough in therapy."

In addition to opening up new areas and providing new insights into old problem areas, the CR group seemed to play an important role in bolstering changes that had already been initiated in therapy. One woman commented:

My CR group gives very strong reinforcement of the self-confidence that gets built up in therapy. Every week I always get a compliment from someone; someone in the group will comment how I've thought something out well. The group really reaffirms my therapist, who always tells me, "You can do it."

Bearing in mind the need for more research to illuminate the issues raised by this modest study, we venture a number of preliminary conclusions. Participation in CR groups is not a substitute for psychotherapy for those women whose problems are longstanding and involve severe neurotic or character problems. Rather, the groups in the present study provided a forum in which mildly depressed women with low self-esteem could explore their feelings about themselves and their life situations. The major impact of such an experience was a revised self-image. These changes did not lead to modifications in life styles. The lack of change in areas of symptom distress, coping styles, and marital relationships supports our prior speculation that CR group experiences serve a limited, although valuable, psychotherapeutic function.

REFERENCES

Allen, P. 1970. *Free space: A perspective on the small group in women's liberation.* New York: Times Change.

Battle, C. C., et al. 1966. Target complaints as a criteria of improvement. *American Journal of Psychotherapy* 20:184–192.

Blood, R. V., and Wolfe, D. 1960. *Husbands and wives.* New York: Free Press.

Bradburn, N. 1969. *Structure of psychological well-being.* Chicago: Aldine.

————, and Caplovitz, D. 1965. *Reports on happiness: A pilot study of behavior related to mental health.* Chicago: Aldine.

Carden, M. I. 1974. *The new feminist movement.* New York: Russell Sage Foundation.

Derogatis, L. R., et al. 1974. The Hopkins symptom checklist (HSCL): A self-report symptom inventory. *Behavioral Science* 19:1–15.

Freeman, J. 1975. *The politics of women's liberation.* New York: McKay.

Jourard, S. 1961. Self disclosure patterns in British and American college females. *Journal of Social Psychology* 54:315–320.

Landau, I. 1976. Sex-role concepts and marital happiness in middle-aged couples. Master's thesis, University of Chicago.

Lieberman, M. A., and Bond, G. R. 1976. The problem of being a woman: A survey of 1,700 women in consciousness-raising groups. *Journal of Applied Behavioral Science* 12:363–379.

————. 1978. Self-help groups: Problems of measuring outcome. *Small Group Behavior* 9:221–241.

Lieberman, M. A., Yalom, I. D., and Miles, M. B. 1973. *Encounter groups: First facts.* New York: Basic Books.

Peralin, L. I., and Lieberman, M. A. Social sources of emotional distress. In *Research in community and mental health,* ed. R. Simmons. Greenwich, Conn.: JAI Press. Forthcoming.

Perl, H., and Abarbanell, G. 1976. *Guideline to feminist consciousness raising.* Manual prepared for the National Task Force on Consciousness Raising of the National Organization for Women.

Rosenberg, M. 1965. *Society and the adolescent self image.* Princeton, N.J.: Princeton University Press.

Sloane, R. B., et al. 1975. *Psychotherapy versus behavior therapy.* Cambridge, Mass.: Harvard University Press.

Warren, L. W. 1976. The therapeutic status of consciousness-raising groups. *Professional Psychology* 7:132–140.

Yalom, I. D., et al. 1978. Alcoholics in interactional group therapy: An outcome study. *Archives of General Psychiatry* 35:419–425.

# PART V / Supplementary Readings

Laws, J. L. 1975. A feminist view of marital adjustment. In *Couples in conflict: New directions in marital therapy,* ed. A. S. Gurman, and D. G. Rice, pp. 72–123. New York: Jason Aronson.

Klein, M. 1976. Feminist concepts of therapy outcome. *Psychotherapy: Theory, Research, and Practice* 13:89–95.

Kronsky, B. 1975. Feminism and psychotherapy. In *Women, body & culture,* ed. S. Hammer. New York: Harper & Row.

Maracek, J., Kravetz, D., and Finn. S. 1979. Comparison of women who enter feminist therapy and women who enter traditional therapy. *Social Work* 47:734–742.

Tennov, D. 1976. *Psychotherapy: The hazardous cure.* New York: Doubleday, Anchor Books.

Thomas, S. 1977. Theory and practice in feminist therapy. *Social Work* 22:447–454.

Weisstein, N. 1971. Psychology constructs the female. In *Woman in sexist society,* eds. V. Gornick and B. Moran, pp. 133–146. New York: Basic Books.

# PART VI

# *Where Do We Go from Here?*

# 49

# Where Do We Go from Here?

## ELIZABETH HOWELL

In the preceding sections we examined how sexism in society affects women's mental health and how it has pervaded the mental health profession. We considered the particular treatment needs of women and new therapeutic approaches that better address them. The papers included in this section examine how the mental health field both has changed and is changing in order to offer women more extensive and effective therapeutic benefits.

At this point it is important to ask where the field of women and mental health is going and which issues deserve our special concern in contemplating future directions. Three issues that appear to be of particular importance concern: (1) the psychological concepts of normative ideals, (2) the interpretations and applications of biological knowledge, and (3) the meaning and measurability of changes in the social structure.

## Psychological Concepts of Normative Ideals

Over time our concepts of ideal mental health have been and continue to be subject to revision. With its normative division of behaviors and attributes into the domains of "masculine" and "feminine," gender-role stereotyping has been found to be at best mildly deleterious, at worst capable of rendering men and women into "half human beings." The notion of psychological androgyny, or the combination in one person of the traditional male and female social and psychological characteristics, has been proposed as a new normative ideal. While androgyny as an ideal has the advantage of providing for a larger and more flexible repertoire of behaviors, it has the problematic potential of becoming prescriptively stereotypical in itself.

An alternative concept is that of gender-role transcendence (Howell 1975). Part of our difficulty may stem from a reliance on norms. Most developmental paradigms posit a progression through preconformist, conformist, and postconformist stages. Norms and stereotypes correspond to the conformist stage of development. As individuals progress through postconformist stages, they begin to think through, choose, and create their own ideals and values. As they consider what characteristics they most value in themselves and in others, the qualities that are often stereotypically gender-linked (for example, nurturance and competence) cease to be categorized and become simply human qualities. Although these resulting combined qualities may be termed androgynous, androgyny itself has not been the aim. Upon reflection, it is remarkable how normatively evaluative are the terms "masculine," "feminine," and "androgynous." Future scholarship in the field is going to have to grapple with the frequent, denotative unclarity of these terms.

## Biological Knowledge

Though repercussions of the impact of Freud's famous phrase, "anatomy is destiny," have given the concept of biological determinism a bad name, particularly among feminists, today recognition of the importance of biological variables enjoys renewed popularity. Increasingly, biological factors are being found to have an important impact upon psychological phenomena. It should be stressed, however, that the phenomena we see, often attributed to "biology," are virtually always the result of an interaction between the organism and the environment. The conception of a "normal" course of development that is only modified by extrinsic factors is misleading, for the shaping forces of the environment are always present. Nonetheless, the new surge of attention to biological factors is of concern, and understandably so, to many modern feminists. They fear (and upon observation of prece-

dent, with reason) that the recent attention to biologically based explanations of sex differences in behavior (such as hormonal bases for
greater aggression in men or sex differences in cerebral lateralization)
can be used as a means of supporting the social status quo (Lambert
1978; Lowe 1978). Lambert (1978) notes the changing but still commonly held assumption that differences in natural endowments justify
unequal social treatment, whereas inadequacies caused by defects in
the social system are deemed worthy of social restitution. According to
Lambert "arguments about sexual equality often get stuck on whether
sex differences are socially or biologically caused" (p. 116). She notes
that the assumptions concerning the justifiability of unequal treatment
dependent upon whether certain attributes have been biologically or
societally caused that underlie these arguments are often illogical (biological and sociocultural causation are so interwoven that it is extremely difficult to separate discrete influences) as well as morally un-
justifiable. Lambert comments further that feminists would be wise to
stay out of the battleground dealing with biology and social equality
because there an unjustified value status is granted to biological
differences.

Interestingly, one problem in this debate seems to stem from the
unclear meaning and differing usages of the word *equality*. Rapaport
and Rapaport (1975) have proposed the concept of *equity*, by which
they mean "a fair allocation of both opportunities and constraints"
(p. 421). This would eliminate the demand for the sameness implied
by the term *"equality"* yet preserve the emphasis upon fairness.


## Changes in Social Structure


From our current perspective, it is hard to fathom how the mental
health establishment (which treats mostly women) could so underestimate the importance of issues that are relevant to the treatment of
women, such as the characteristically patriarchal structure of the treatment situation. (Chesler 1972). But it is part of our cultural heritage
that such concerns were, at an earlier time, voiced primarily by radical
feminists and thus easily dismissed.

It has by now become highly unfashionable to express sexist views
publicly within the mental health establishment. The eradication of
sexism from the arena of treatment has been widely endorsed as a
positive value. This would seem to indicate its absorption of feminist
concerns. Indeed, recent analogue studies (in which behavior in the

testing situation is assumed to extend by analogy to real behavior outside of the testing situation, for instance, to the therapy hour) generally have not confirmed the earlier findings of Broverman and associates (1970) concerning the prevalence of a double standard of mental health among clinicians (see Chapter 7). Nor have recent analogue studies for the most part yielded other evidence of evaluative prejudice among clinicians against women. Such findings, however, may result as much from the greater sophistication among clinicians as from the diminution of sexist bias in treatment (Davidson and Abramowitz 1980). Davidson and Abramowitz along with others (for example, Striker 1979) are critical of the analogue design. They note that naturalistic investigations have yielded data more indicative of sexist bias in treatment, and they call for more of this type of research.

## Conclusion

It is frequently asked whether the field of women and mental health is simply a passing fad or if it is here to stay. Clearly, the political climate of the future cannot be foreseen. But what can be said is that while this field once was viewed as polemical and radical, it now has been incorporated into the mainstream of substantive thought and research in the mental health arena. It now may be considered, at the very least, legitimate.

REFERENCES

Chesler, P. 1972. *Women and madness.* New York: Avon Books.
Broverman, I., et al. 1970. Sex-role stereotypes and clinical judgments of mental health. *Journal of Consulting and Clinical Psychology* 34:1–7.
Davidson, C. and Abramowitz, S. 1980. Sex bias in clinical judgment: Later empirical returns. *Psychology of Women Quarterly* 4:377–395.
Stricker, G. 1977. Implications of research for psychotherapeutic treatment of women. *American Psychologist* 32:14–22.
Howell, E. 1975. Self presentation in reference to sex-role stereotypes as related to level of moral development. Ph.D. dissertation, New York University.
Lambert, H. 1978. Biology and equality: A perspective on sex differences. *Signs* 4:97–117.
Lowe, M. 1978. Sociobiology and sex differences. *Signs* 4:118–125.
Rapoport, R., and Rapoport, R. 1975. Men, women, and equity. *The Family Coordinator* October: 421–432.

# 50

---

# A Decade of Feminist
# Influence on Psychotherapy

---

ANNETTE M. BRODSKY

---

In 1963, as the first female clinical psychology intern in the U.S. Army, I was assigned a forty-year-old woman client who refused to accept me as her therapist because I was younger than she, and a woman. She was convinced that she was assigned to the lowly female intern because her husband was only a sergeant. Her parting words as we aborted our tenuous relationship were something like "I'm a difficult case, honey. It's not your fault. I hope someday you'll be another Joyce Brothers."

On the other hand, recently a woman client peeked into my office after leaving our initial session and commented, "You know, I'm glad you're a woman. I don't think I could be as honest with a man. I would be worrying too much about whether or not he approved of me."

These two comments reflect more than differences in personality, age, marital status, or some unknown variable. They reflect almost two decades of change in attitudes toward women in positions of authority. They also reflect a change in knowledge of women's roles in society. Individual women may not have made the personal changes that the women's movement has fostered, but they are aware of the potential for such changes and have a sense of where they fit in. Instead of seeing themselves as "difficult cases" that only a strong man can handle, they are more receptive to being independent of men and working with other women.

## Women and Psychotherapy

There has probably been more said and written about the subject of women and psychotherapy in the last decade than in the fifty preceding years. During this period, the women's movement has had a strong influence on many areas of our lives, including new life styles, work situations, and relationships between the sexes. We have been examining and reexamining our stereotypes and their scientific or lack of scientific bases.

Observers of psychotherapy have made very little progress toward a better understanding of what is helpful in insuring that clients achieve mental health and self-actualization. Critics of the institution of psychotherapy, especially women (Fields 1975; Tennov 1975), have been vocal about this. The field of psychotherapy appears to have developed laterally more than it has linearly. There are now hundreds of systems of psychotherapy, each with its own vocabulary, process, and specific goals. Little common ground exists among the psychotherapies other than the assumption that the client, who is experiencing some sort of distress, enters into a verbal relationship with an expert, who through use of specified techniques based on a particular theory of personality facilitates growth toward remediation and well-being.

What we do know from empirical research about the ingredients of good therapy is limited and often elusive. We know that, in general, clients report they feel better after therapy than they did before, no matter what type of therapy they have received (Aronoff and Lesse 1976). Women report more satisfaction with therapy than men (Orlinsky and Howard 1976), but we do not know if their reports of satisfaction correlate with behavioral criteria of improvement. We know that therapy cannot be completely value free, and we suppose that clients are often seen as improved because they become more like their therapists (Welkowitz, Cohen, and Ortmeyer 1967). We have evidence that it is the therapist more than the therapeutic technique that may make the difference in whether or not a client improves (Dent 1978), and we know, therefore, that the therapist's personal traits, values, attitudes, and impressions of the client have a major impact on the client and the course of therapy (Abramowitz and Dokecki 1977).

The influence of therapist variables has only recently been recognized. The empirical basis for evaluating the benefits of psychotherapy remains shaky, even though researchers have for many years been trying painstakingly to isolate the components that make for good psychotherapy outcome. The variables involved in therapy are enormously complex, and researchers have examined effects of therapist, process, and client dimensions, alone and in combination with one another (Strupp and Luborsky 1962). However, the ethics of dealing with human beings in need, controlling pertinent variables, isolating therapy segments from their total context, and so forth have understandably restricted the extent of knowledge that empirical research has been able to provide (Bergin and Strupp 1972).

## Sex Bias in Psychotherapy

From this limited research base, feminists have attempted to examine sex bias in psychotherapy. As a variable superimposed on those applicable to psychotherapy in general, sex bias presents almost formidable problems to the researcher. After all, bias, by definition, implies a lack of awareness of one's actual behavior. Deception therefore becomes necessary in most experimental research designs to avoid any artificial sensitization of subjects to sex-role bias that does not reflect the typical behavior of therapists in the field.

In spite of these difficulties, a need arose to validate empirically the gut feelings of feminists that biases were rampant in therapy. The clinical experiences of feminist therapists and clients convinced them that sex bias and sex-role stereotyping were very real and not at all rare (American Psychological Association [APA] 1975). Thus an era emerged of investigation of therapist, client, and process variables related to sex roles. We started the decade by examining relevant demographic statistics. Several researchers (Chesler 1971; Gove and Tudor 1973) alerted us to the fact that therapists are mostly male, whereas their clients are mostly female, and that the longest treatment relationships are most likely to be between attractive young male therapists and attractive young female clients. Next we learned that diagnostic labels vary by sex; women are deemed depressed, hysterical, anxiety neurotics, and phobic, whereas men are deemed alcoholic, organic, and antisocial (Gove and Tudor 1973; Howard and Howard 1974).

Reeling with this information, we invaded the mechanics of the therapist-patient relationship. Very few main effects indicative of bias were found, however. Sex of the therapist, for example, has not proven to be an important variable in the majority of published studies that investigated sex-role bias toward clients. The impact of the most often cited study that did find a sex-of-therapist effect (Haan and Livson 1973) was softened when Werner and Block (1975) reanalyzed the data using a more appropriate error term and found no differences.

However, the original Haan and Livson study is still being cited today, perhaps because the need to validate personal experience that sex bias in psychotherapy exists is so strong that researchers feel almost compelled to demonstrate it empirically. Even feminist reseachers, however, fail to find the effect they seek (Billingsley 1977; Gomes and Abramowitz 1976; Kaschak 1978). The inability to validate one's personal experiences is frustrating.

In an article in the *American Psychologist,* Stricker (1977) sharply criticized the research on sex bias on a number of methodological grounds. Although he insists that empirical studies be the final determinant of whether bias occurs, his own need to proceed without such empirical evidence surfaces later when he chastizes the Task Force on Sex Bias and Sex Role Stereotyping (APA 1975) for bothering to survey the obvious by asking women psychologists for examples of sexist practices. We certainly would prefer not to have to research what we consider obvious, but many of our colleagues will not believe our experiences unless we are able to present data to validate them. All research is colored by the biases of the investigator, and as long as a certain segment of the profession believes that sex bias does not exist, we will have to demonstrate what we, with feminist biased eyes and ears, know to be true. I am not particularly worried about a Rosenthal (1966) effect in feminist research, as I am fully confident that our detractors are actively counterbalancing it with their own equal and opposite experimenter biases. Feminist research originally emerged to challenge a male bias that has existed for many years.

To return to our failure to find sex of therapist as a significant variable, however, our insights, clinical experiences, and surveys of women therapists (APA 1975; Sherman, Koufacos, and Kenworthy 1978) are being supported empirically, not through main effects, but through higher-order interactions. We are where the more generic psychotherapy research was about twenty years ago. We are finding that only by taking into account the interaction of many relevant variables affecting psychotherapy will we find the effects of sex bias. Thus, for example, Orlinsky and Howard (1976) found the relationship of therapist sex to the therapy experiences of women depended on factors such as age, marital status, and independence of the woman client. Although the dependent variable in this study was not a behavioral indicator from a therapy session but a report by the client after termination, this finding nevertheless is representative of where we are in answering such questions as "Should women clients see male therapists?"

At the beginning of the decade, Phyllis Chesler (1972) concluded that the answer to this question was no. Today, if we believe clients' retrospective reports, there are more likely to be two answers: (1) "no" for young single women uncertain as to their direction in life, or in their relationships with men, or both; and (2) "yes" if the client is older, or married. We do not, however, know what other factors, yet to be studied, may also have a bearing on the answer.

In general, we do not have enough empirical support from well-designed and executed studies to state relationships between psychotherapy and sex bias or sex-role stereotyping with confidence. Because our methodology is restricted, we may never be able to "prove" that certain attributes relevant to sex bias are prominent among therapists. We can point to such attributes in individual cases, however, and we can prepare clinicians for their vulnerability to sexist behavior. Sherman, Koufacos, and Kenworthy (1978) point out from their survey regarding the practices and knowledge about women clients of Wisconsin therapists that there may be less bias than misinformation about women's problems.

There is a bright side to the status of our knowledge about women in therapy, however. For while some feminists have invested their energies in demonstrating empirically that women have suffered, others have approached the issues from more applied perspectives. There is much that we can use now as a result of the theoretical and applied efforts of feminist practitioners in psychotherapy during the last decade.

## Feminist Influences in Assessments

With the rise of the new feminist movement, some women rejected the psychological professions entirely and took advantage of consciousness-raising groups, finding that they could help each other where traditional psychological sources of help had failed. This was in the context of the development of other self-help techniques that enabled women to learn about their bodies, pregnancy, and childbirth. Women also shared their expertise and compassion with each other in crisis situations, such as rape or abortion counseling. Rape centers were established by radical feminists who were not professionals. Feminists in the helping professions were often involved, and it was in this atmosphere of working with women who rejected professional health care that women in psychology and psychiatry began to look at how their own professions were contributing to this widespread dissatisfaction.

With the birth of the Association for Women in Psychology in 1968, presentations on the psychology of women began to surface at APA conventions and in the feminist literature. Naomi Weisstein (1970) attacked the misguided wisdom on which clinical stereotypes were based, and Phyllis Chesler's *Women and Madness* (1972) became an impetus for clinical researchers to examine assessment and treatment issues. Julia Sherman (1971) and others reviewed studies that refuted psychoanalytic concepts used to reify penis envy, moral inferiority of women, and "inner space."

In the area of sexual functioning, Masters and Johnson (1966) reported that women had multiple orgasms. The physiological response to sexual arousal was comparable between men and women, with the clitoris being the major if not the sole source of orgasms in women. These discoveries led to a tremendous amount of debate and discussion of the nature of female sexuality. The psychoanalytic insistence that orgasms experienced during sexual intercourse were superior to those felt through clitoral stimulation was simply physiologically incorrect. Thus the analogous insistence that passivity is a biologically determined trait for sexually mature women was likewise refuted.

Meanwhile, other feminists were challenging the assessment measures used to equate nonconformity with pathology in the female. Thus counseling psychologists became concerned that the Strong Vocational Inventory, with its pink and blue forms for female and male, was prejudiced by having three times as many scorable occupations for males as for females. It was noted that many counselors were giving the male forms to females when they expressed an interest in a more "masculine" occupation. The Campbell-Strong Revision (Campbell 1974) eliminated the male-female dichotomy and provided norms that included women. Intelligence tests also were scrutinized for items slanted toward males. The new revision of the WISC (Wechsler 1974) includes an arithmetic problem involving the counting of hair ribbons.

The Dictionary of Occupational Titles became suspect when feminist researchers discovered that occupations were rated with higher status if they were traditionally male rather than traditionally female. Thus a dog trainer was considered to have more skill dealing with persons, data, and concepts than was a kindergarten teacher (Briggs 1971). In the new revision, titles of occupations have become nonsexist. Thus the former mailman is now a postal worker, and the stewardess is a flight attendant, but the ratings have not yet been changed to reflect more accurately the status of the skills involved (Witt and Nahenny 1975).

When we move into the area of projective testing and evaluation of personality, we approach even more sensitive issues. A study that reanalyzed hundreds of assessment reports of adolescents discovered that descriptors of female clients did not differentiate women from each other, but merely served to stereotype women as a class regardless of their personality characteristics. Thus when a report described a woman as emotional, it did nothing to aid in evaluation other than to indicate that the person described was probably female (Haller 1975). Some Rorschach interpreters were distressed when it was discovered in the early seventies that the symmetrical figures on Card III were producing new norms. Clients were increasingly reporting one figure as female and the other as male. One male psychiatrist even suggested that this reflected sexual identity confusion caused by unisex dressing in our culture. Regardless of the interpretation given, however, there was at least the demonstration that perceptions of women were indeed changing.

## Feminist Treatment Alternatives

It is in the area of providing direct psychotherapeutic services that the most dramatic progress has occurred. In the area of rape, for example, the last several years have seen the protest against the identification of rape victims as seducers and the recognition of the rape trauma syndrome to understand the dynamics of the victim and to work with her on reintegrating her life after the assault. Burgess and Holmstrom (1973) reported on the sequence of shock, disorganization of everyday life, and eventual reintegration of the rape victim. The shock is less that of being sexually violated than the threat of death or the experience of loss of control over one's body. Since then we have seen the development of support systems, family counseling, and follow-up services for rape victims, as well as direct emergency aid for the victims. The updating of archaic corroboration rules of evidence and the differentiation of degrees of rape (so that victims and juries do not feel that a conviction means the death sentence in all cases) were partly a response to the rape crisis center movement.

Another spinoff was concern about family violence, where feminist psychologists had much input on theoretical and practical application. Factors such as poverty, low self-esteem, stigma, and so forth countered the victim-precipitation explanation for the low incidence of reporting. Victims had little free choice to leave their situations due to economic and psychological bondage to their assailants. Needs of battered wives thus emerged as an area of psychological attention, and we are seeing some feminist analyses of the situation that do not blame the victim (Walker 1978).

With regard to abortion, the last decade has seen the legalization of the procedure, changing the counseling process into a more personal decision rather than one based on ability to find the risk the dangers involved. This topic is still fraught with great emotion and controversy on moral grounds. Now, however, at least there is access to a variety of alternatives for the women who have the economic means and good fortune to live in a community that does not try to circumvent the law by enacting local statutes requiring the reading of propaganda including pictures of aborted fetuses.

We are also seeing some changes in the concepts of disorders that are frequently diagnosed for females. For example, many women were laughingly passed off as hysterical personalities because they were flamboyant in dress and manner, constantly demanding attention, seductively and often desperately seeking approval of men, and demeaning of other women. Such a woman was usually termed manipulative and considered to have a style of life that was difficult to change in therapy, because her manipulations usually included her male therapist. Now hysterical personality disorders are being understood as exaggerations of the traditional feminine sex role, an overconditioned reaction in vulnerable women to their dependency on males for their self-esteem. This "disorder" turns out to be something they acquired in the normal process of being rewarded for cute dressing and acting coyly toward their fathers and of being fawned on by adults for performing and catering to their superficial needs (Wolowitz 1972). As adults, these women have continued to manifest these traits past their usefulness and have leaned on approval of others, particularly males, as their sole source of self-esteem. Traditional therapies deal with insight into the inability of the manipulations to work and the substituting of less dramatic means to gain approval. The feminist perspective emphasizes the development of an independent self-identity and self-determination, so that the need for approval diminishes.

The area of depression in women has also seen strong feminist influence as a result of Pauline Bart's (1972) work on "the empty nest syndrome." Women had been socialized to become "supermoms" who depended entirely on this role for a sense of usefulness. Previously we had not paid much attention to the meaninglessness of the role of women who completed their child-rearing tasks by the age of forty and who were not prepared for any other role to occupy their next forty years. Depression has also been associated with a mourning for the lives women have not permitted themselves to pursue and their sense of helplessness in determining the course of their current lives (Beck and Greenberg 1974). The contribution of role conflicts to postpartum and involutional depressions has also been examined (Melges 1972).

Feminists have become involved in a closer look at phobias in women. We are just beginning to discover the extent of inhibiting fears that keep women housebound and dependent. Most agoraphobics are women, and the great majority are married (Fodor 1974). Socialization of dependence in women fosters development of phobic reactions. In fact, assertive training has surfaced as a technique applied so predominantly to women that books and workshops on assertive training for women are requested by men.

## Backlash, Regression, and Apathy

Not all women, however, are reaping the benefits of the procedures that can help them to counteract the years of socialization that convinced them they had no right to put their own needs on a level with that of the rest of the family. Many women do not yet believe they should have this right. In a letter to the editor of the *Tuscaloosa News*, a woman wrote explaining her objection to the equal rights amendment and ended with the statement, "I have no desire to be equal to anyone, especially a man."

For all the progress that has been made in working with women in therapy in the last decade, there are also discouraging aspects to the story. Rapid advances always leave some casualties behind. As Bardwick and Douvan (1972) noted, one way to deal with an expected change with which you are not yet ready to cope is to deny the need for adoption of new behaviors by a reactionary exaggeration of the necessity and desirability of the outmoded roles. Thus in the seventies we have not only contended with the exciting new possibilities and options for women, but we must also deal with a flight to exaggerated, stereotyped feminine roles as prescribed by Marabel Morgan's *The Total Woman* (1975) or Andelin's *Fascinating Womanhood* (1974).

These superfeminine women sincerely believe that the new roles are destructive for them and others, and they hear the women's movement telling them that they have wasted their lives. A therapist cannot tell a fifty-year-old housewife that she has lived her life in vain, that it was not necessary to make all those sacrifices, or that her children should not be expected to repay her for them. Her self-esteem is at stake. Holding on to the last glorious remnants of the past era is one way to survive a confusing transition period. In her *Playboy* (Kelly 1978) interview, Anita Bryant, a friend of Marabel Morgan, told how frightened she was when she realized that she was under great stress and needed psychological help. She finally went to a religious retreat after having rejected the possibility of being helped by a traditional psychiatrist.

So fear of the power and influence of the therapist over the client is not restricted to feminists wanting to be free of stereotypes, but extends also to antifeminists who fear the prospect of change and its responsibilities. In fact, keeping therapists objective and ethical has been a prime goal of feminists in the psychotherapeutic professions.

The Task Force on Sex Bias commissioned by the American Psychological Association (APA 1975) collected data from women psychologists in 1974 and derived a set of guidelines for therapy with women (APA 1978a). Division 17 of the APA (1978b) has just endorsed a set of principles for counseling women. So identification of the problem areas has been accomplished; but getting therapists to abide by these guidelines will be an enormous task. No one identifies him- or herself as sexist. It is very difficult to examine one's own prejudices. It takes openness, sensitivity, and dedication to recognize one's flaws, to learn from them, and thus to modify one's behavior. In a survey Jean Holroyd and I conducted on erotic practices of licensed psychologists (Holroyd and Brodsky 1977), 5.6 percent (1 in 20) of the males and .6 percent (1 in 200) of the females admitted to having sexual intercourse with their opposite-sex clients. The general consensus of those who engaged in such practices was that the incident was destructive to either client, therapist, or both, but most of those who engaged in the activity were repeaters.

This study at least provided some data on the prevalence of a blatantly unethical act after a decade of feminist concern and attention to the practice. The victory, however, was only one battle in the war. The reactions to the study included, "Oh, is that all, I thought the rate would be much higher." *Playboy* magazine treated it with a comment under *Sex News* (1978) in a piece entitled "Kiss my Couch." They noted that "It is as hard to find a good therapist these days as it is to find a good masseuse."

Like violence on TV, there is the danger that the public and profession will become immune to the reports of sex in the therapy hour. When the news no longer is hot, who will continue to monitor the behavior? Interest in rape victims has already passed its prime. Rape centers are struggling for financial support, which is now being diverted to newly exposed abuses of children and battered wives and, most recently, the elderly. We will need steady monitoring to assure reasonable long-term attention to issues that present mental health de-livery problems past their hour in the spotlight.

## An Encouraging Word

In concluding, I think we can feel encouraged by the distance we have traveled in the last decade. Certainly there are still incidents of gross sexism and ignorance of women's unique problems, and large seg-ments of the therapist population are unwilling to admit they may have any biases, much less be educated on how to remediate them. It only seems that we are losing ground every time we see a throwback to the rampant sexism of the fifties and sixties. To appreciate our prog-ress one has to revisit some old issues of our psychotherapy journals. In a 1967 issue on the sexual revolution (*Voices* 1967), under the title of "Women and Other Revolutionaries" (O'Donovan 1967), an author shares with the reader his insights about the woman's movement.

Having obtained many rights, they are dissatisfied with not having more. . . . Indeed there are definite advantages to their present status. There is also some biological evidence supporting their present status. They have not been trained for equal status and responsibility. They seem naturally adapted to their less free, less responsible, more serving role. They are in danger of los-ing what makes them unique and lovable if they gain equal status.

On the preceding page of this issue is a cartoon of a female client lying nude on the office couch, while the therapist at the open door says to a colleague, "I tell you, Fred, it's a shame to cure her." I think our professional journals have improved, even though we may still find much covert sexism. I do not have the fantasy that sexism can be eliminated entirely, but I do feel that by the next decade today's seem-ingly more subtle sexist publications and offhand comments will seem just as blatant to everyone as the 1967 issue of *Voices* seems today.

REFERENCES

Abramowitz, C. V., and Dokecki, P. R. 1977. The politics of clinical judgment: Early empirical returns. *Psychological Bulletin* 84:460–476.

American Psychological Association. 1975. Report of the task force on sex bias and sex-role stereotyping in psychotherapeutic practice. *American Psychologist* 30:1169–1175. [Reprinted herein chapter 8.]

―――――. 1978*a*. Task force on sex bias and sex-role stereotyping in psychotherapeutic practice. Guidelines for therapy with women. *American Psychologist* 33:1122–1123.

―――――. Division 17 Ad Hoc Committee on Women. 1978*b*. Principles concerning the counseling and therapy of women. Paper presented at Annual Meeting of the American Psychological Association, Toronto, Canada, 1978.

Andelin, H. B. 1974. *Fascinating womanhood.* New York: Bantam Books.

Aronoff, M. S., and Lesse, S. 1976. Principles of psychotherapy. In *The therapist handbook: Treatment methods of mental disorders,* ed. B. B. Wolman. New York: Van Nostrand Reinhold.

Bardwick, J. M., and Douvan, E. 1972. Ambivalence: The socialization of women. In *Readings on the psychology of women,* ed. J. M. Bardwick. New York: Harper & Row.

Bart, P. 1972. Depression in middle-aged women. In *Readings on the psychology of women,* ed. J. M. Bardwick. New York: Harper & Row.

Beck, A. T., and Greenberg, R. L. 1974. Cognitive therapy with depressed women. In *Women in therapy,* ed. V. Franks, and V. Burtle, pp. 113–131. New York: Brunner/Mazel.

Bergin, A. E., and Strupp, H. H. 1972. New directions in psychotherapy research: A summary statement. *Changing frontiers in the science of psychotherapy.* Chicago: Aldine/Atherton.

Billingsley, D. 1977. Sex bias in psychotherapy: An examination of the effects of client sex, client pathology, and therapist sex on treatment planning. *Journal of Consulting and Clinical Psychology* 45:250–256.

Briggs, N. 1971. Prejudice: Being down on something you are not up on. The forum (Report no. 2). Madison, Wisc.: Wisconsin Psychiatric Institute, University of Wisconsin.

Burgess, A., and Holmstrom, L. 1973. Rape trauma syndrome. *American Journal of Psychiatry* 131:981–986.

Campbell, D. P. 1974. *Manual for the Strong-Campbell interest inventory.* Palo Alto, Calif.: Stanford University Press.

Chesler, P. 1976. Patient and patriarch: Women in the psychotherapeutic relationship. In *Women in sexist society,* ed. V. Gornick and B. K. Moran, pp. 251–275. New York: Basic Books.

―――――. 1972. *Women and madness.* Garden City, N.Y.: Doubleday.

Dent, J. K. 1978. *Exploring the psycho-social therapies through the personalities of effective therapists.* Rockville, Md.: U.S. Department of Health, Education, and Welfare.

Fields, R. M. 1975. *Psychotherapy: The sexist machine.* Pittsburgh: Know.

Fodor, I. G. 1974. The phobic syndrome in women: Implications for treatment. In *Women in therapy,* ed. V. Franks and V. Burtle, pp. 132–168. New York: Brunner/Mazel.

Gomes, B., and Abramowitz, S. I. 1976. Sex-related patient and therapist effects on clinical judgment. *Sex Roles: A Journal of Research* 2:1–13.

Gove, W. R., and Tudor, J. F. 1973. Adult sex roles and mental illness. *American Journal of Sociology* 78:50–73.

Haan, N., and Livson, N. 1973. Sex differences in the eyes of expert personality assessors: Blind spots? *Journal of Personality Assessment* 37:486–492.

Haller, D. L. 1975. Attribution of sex-stereotypic descriptors to adolescent females in psychotherapy. Master's thesis, University of Alabama.

Holroyd, J. C., and Brodsky, A. M. 1977. Psychologists' attitudes and practices regarding erotic and non-erotic physical contact with patients. *American Psychologist* 32:843–849.

Howard, E. M., and Howard, J. L. 1974. Women in institutions: Treatment in prisons and mental hospitals. In *Women in therapy,* ed. V. Franks and V. Burtle, pp. 357–382. New York: Brunner/Mazel.

Kaschak, E. 1978. Therapist and client: Two views of the process and outcome of psychotherapy. *Professional Psychology* 9:271–277.

Kelly, K. 1978. Playboy interview: Anita Bryant. *Playboy Magazine* 25:240–241.

Masters, W. H., and Johnson, V. E. 1966. *Human sexual response.* Boston: Little, Brown.

Melges, F. 1972. Postpartum psychiatric syndromes. In *Readings on the psychology of women,* ed. J. M. Bardwick. New York: Harper & Row.

Morgan, M. 1975. *The total woman*. New York: Simon & Schuster.

O'Donovan, D. 1967. Women and other revolutionaries. *Voices* 3:38–39.

Orlinsky, D. E., and Howard, K. I. 1976. The effects of sex therapist on the therapeutic experiences of women. *Psychotherapy: Theory, Research and Practice* 13:82–88.

Rosenthal, R. 1966. *Experimenter effects in behavior research*. New York: Appleton-Century-Crofts.

Sex news. 1978. *Playboy Magazine* 25:264.

Sherman, J. A. 1971. *On the psychology of women*. Springfield, Ill.: Charles C. Thomas.

Sherman, J. A., Koufacos, C., and Kenworthy, J. A. 1978. Therapists: Their attitudes and information about women. *Psychology of Women Quarterly* 2:299–313.

Stricker, G. 1977. Implications of research for psychotherapeutic treatment of women. *American Psychologist* 32:14–22.

Strupp, H. H., and Luborsky, L. 1962. *Research in psychotherapy*, vol. 2. Washington, D.C.: American Psychological Association.

Tennov, D. 1975. *Psychotherapy: The hazardous cure*. New York: Abelard-Schuman.

*Voices: The Art and Science of Psychotherapy*. 1967. 3(Special issue, The Sexual Revolution).

Walker, L. E. 1978. Treatment alternatives for battered women. In *The victimization of women*, ed. J. R. Chapman and M. Gates, Beverly Hills, Calif.: Sage.

Wechsler, D. 1974. *Manual for Wechsler Intelligence Scale for Children (Rev)*. New York: Psychological Corporation.

Weisstein, N. 1970. Kinde, kuche, kirche as scientific law: Psychology constructs the female. In *Sisterhood Is Powerful*, ed. R. Morgan, pp. 205–220. New York: Vintage Books.

Welkowitz, J., Cohen, J., and Ortmeyer, B. 1967. Value system similarity: Investigation of patient-therapist dyads. *Journal of Consulting Psychology* 31:48–55.

Werner, P., and Block, J. 1975. Sex differences in the eyes of expert personality assessors: Unwarranted conclusions. *Journal of Personality Assessment* 39:110–113.

Witt, M., and Nahenny, P. K. 1975. *Women's work-up from 878. Report on D.O.T. research project*. Madison, Wisc.: University of Wisconsin Extension Resources.

Wolowitz, H. M. 1972. Hysterical character and feminine identity. In *Readings on the psychology of women*, ed. J. M. Bardwick, pp. 307–314. New York: Harper & Row.

# 51

## New Directions in Counseling Women

JUDITH WORELL

Several of my colleagues raised eyebrows and shrugged shoulders in body-language response to the gist of this article. Is there a revolution in counseling women? There are some who maintain that a good counselor counsels people, and therefore the effective counselor can deal equally with both male and female clients. It follows from this view that there is no need for a separate body of information or unique strategies related to clients who happen to be female. In reviewing the recent literature on counseling women, I came across more than 500 articles dealing with ideologies, goals, needs, rationales, strategies, and research findings related to counseling women. Surely we have the data base now to support a contrary view: There is indeed a revolution in counseling the female client, matched by no other innovation in the field of counseling today.

In the following discussion, I explore four facets of this revolution that seem to represent a significant departure from previous orientations and procedures. The multiple dimensions of the new approach to counseling women is the emergence of a new discipline. The legitimacy of this new discipline is supported by the continuing development and expansion of each of the four factors: (1) a substantial and relative-

I wish to express my appreciation to Beth Doll for her expert assistance in the preparation of this article, and to Pam Remer for her helpful comments on the first draft.

ly new body of knowledge and theory about the biological, psychological, cultural, and political characteristics of the client population; (2) an emergent set of client populations whose nontraditional counseling needs and goals support the development of alternative intervention strategies; (3) sets of procedures specifically tailored to the unique characteristics and goals of these new client populations; and (4) special codes of ethics and standards to monitor the implementation of counseling procedures with women. I will discuss each of these four factors as they relate to current innovations in counseling. I propose that the outcome of this set of innovations will be (1) a new discipline of counseling women, and (2) the development of new training programs to meet the professional needs of counselors who select this discipline as a career specialty.

## The Psychology of Women and Sex Roles

The first requirement for the recognition of a new discipline is a body of knowledge to serve as a data base for theory, explanation, and research. In the past ten years there has been an upsurge in research on differences that may exist between males and females. Several recent review articles consider how the literature on women's concerns relates specifically to counseling practice (Holroyd 1976; Maracek, Kravetz, and Finn 1979; McEwen 1975; Oliver 1975; Rose 1976; Schlossberg and Pietrofesa 1978; Whitley 1979). There are at least three topics for exploration here relevant in the counseling of women: (1) gender differences and special characteristics in development, socialization, and biophysical functioning; (2) the effects of sex-role stereotyping; and (3) the theory and measurement of androgyny. Theory and research within each of these areas provide increasing evidence that gender and sex-role considerations support new imperatives for revisions in content, procedures, and training in counseling psychology.

*Gender differences* are defined here as characteristics that reliably differentiate males from females. Typical research on gender-related attributes selects a set of behaviors or characteristics and compares how boys and girls or men and women perform on measures of these characteristics. Recent gender-related research has investigated, for example, intellectual performance—spatial relations and mathematics; achievement and career patterns; power and dominance relationships; affiliative relations—friendship, attachment, cooperation, and helpfulness; communication styles in verbal and nonverbal spheres; sexuality and biological functioning; mental health variables—self-competency, anxiety, and depression; social role functioning, as in parenting, coupling, and stresses of role conflict; and a variety of life-cycle perspectives (Chafetz 1978; Friedman, Richart, and Vande Wiele 1974; Hoyenga and Hoyenga 1978; Maccoby and Jacklyn 1974; Spence and Helmreich 1978; Tavris and Offir 1977; Williams 1977).

The outcome of these research efforts provides extensive documentation on the differences that do and do not appear between males and females on structural, experiential, and response dimensions. Although it is beyond the scope of this article to discuss specific findings, it is legitimate to conclude that aside from female menstruation, pregnancy, and lactation, few behaviors or experiences are exclusively male or female (O'Leary 1978). Within each of these areas, however, certain behaviors or life experiences are found to be modally more characteristic of one gender than the other. In interpersonal communication, for example, females are more frequently interrupted by males, and they less often initiate new topics in conversation (Key 1975; Michelini, Passalacqua, and Cusimano 1976). In mixed-sex groups, men more frequently disagree with women than with men (Willis and Williams 1976), and they touch women more than they are touched by them (Henley 1973). Consider the possible impact of these findings on either a male-female counseling dyad or a mixed-sex counseling group. How might counselor awareness of these potential differences in communication patterns affect the counseling procedures?

Coupled with an increasing repository of information on sex differences is a reexamination of theories about how males and females develop, what is of importance and value to them, and how each gender can be motivated toward effort, achievement, and participation (Bardwick 1971; Lee and Hertzberg 1978; Sherman 1978; Stein and Bailey 1973; Vetter 1973; Westervelt 1978). Reconsideration of some long-favored theories about human development has led many current theorists to discard at least parts, if not all, of some well-entrenched ideas about how women function (Doherty 1978; Weisstein 1971). The dialogue now suggests that theories constructed from and devised to explain male behavior, such as the formulations of Freud (1965), Erikson (1968), and Kohlberg (1966), are not necessarily relevant to the lives of women. More specific examples of male-oriented views are certain theories of achievement motivation (cf. McClelland et al. 1953) that fail to account for gender differences in task value, expectancies for success and failure, internal and external attributions, role conflicts (e.g., fear of success), and the relative importance of competition and winning. In a similar contradictory position are career-development theories (cf. Super and Hall 1978) that base their ideation and predictions on the experiences, interests, and life choices traditionally faced by males.

What do these newer conceptions of women's development and behavior suggest for counselors? At the very least, we may be constrained to discard some favorite stereotypic ideas about how men and women ought to function. As a self-educational goal, counselors need to keep current and knowledgeable about contemporary theoretical formulations of sex-role development and functioning. Although no supertheory has emerged to dominate the field, several suggestive formulations have recently been proposed that attempt a more realistic account of both male and female development than do traditional theories. Among the new formulations are those that view learning sex roles as analogous to language acquisition (Pleck 1975), as rule-governed behavior (Constantinople 1979), as the outcome of social cognition (Lewis and Weinraub 1979), or as a stage-determined process incorporating cognitive and social tasks (Katz 1979). Clearly we are only at the edge of a comprehensive conception of sex-role development that can apply equally to males and females, to all life situations, and to developmental changes that occur throughout the lifespan. As counselors reconceptualize and restructure their perspectives on women's life cycle, however, they may become better able to provide a counseling milieu that is appropriate to women's continuing growth and development.

*Sex-role stereotyping* is a second critical area of research that demands counselor attention. In contrast to empirical evidence about gender differences, sex-role stereotypes represent categorical judgments about an individual's personal characteristics on the basis of gender and sociocultural role expectancies. Counselor bias occurs when counseling procedures, including assessment, dyadic interactions, evaluations, and recommendations for future behavior, are based on stereotyped opinions about what are appropriate gender-related roles.

The landmark study by Broverman and associates (1970) demonstrated bias in practicing clinicians' tendency to use a double standard when judging the psychological health of males and females on a sex-stereotyping questionnaire. In this study, the healthy male was rated in a manner similar to the ideal healthy adult and was assigned significantly more socially desirable traits than the "healthy" female. Subsequent research provides a considerable array of support for the biasing influences of sex-role stereotyping on counselor judgments and decision making. Counselors have been found to display negative reactions toward women entering nontraditional careers (Pietrofesa and Schlossberg 1970; Thomas and Stewart 1971) and to recommend occupations for female high-school seniors that are lower paying,

623

more highly supervised, and require less education than those recommended for their male counterparts (Donahue 1976). Several studies have found more biased responses from male counselors (Kahn 1977; Sherman, Koufacos, and Kenworthy 1978; Wentworth 1977), but this seems to interact with the problems presented (Hill et al. 1977) and theoretical orientation (Stewart 1978). The report of the American Psychological Association (APA) Task Force on Sex Bias and Sex-role Stereotyping in Psychotherapeutic Practice (1975) found four areas of perceived bias: (1) fostering traditional sex roles, (2) showing bias in expectation and devaluation of women, (3) using sexist theoretical concepts, and (4) responding to women as sex objects.

What are the implications of these findings for counselors who deal with women? Certainly there is a need for increased awareness and sensitivity on the part of counselors concerning their own biased attitudes. Counselors need to be aware, for example, of how they view the nontraditional woman who elects to adopt a unique career, life style, sexual or marital arrangement. Although some trends show increased counselor verbal *acknowledgment* of sex-role stereotyping, *overt behavior* is not always congruent with expressed sex-role attitudes (Reisman 1978; Worell 1979a, 1980a). I believe that universal awareness and behavior change in practicing professionals will not come about without concerted effort and specialized experience. In particular, we need carefully planned training programs that expose counselors to information, experiential activities, and feedback on their behavior in real and simulated counseling situations.

*The theory and measurement of androgyny* is a third major area of current research into the psychological functioning of women and men. New formulations of psychological masculinity and femininity have proposed that they are independent, orthogonal dimensions of personality (Bem 1974; Berzins, Welling, and Wetter 1978; Heilbrun 1976; Spence, Helmreich, and Stapp 1975). In contrast to earlier conceptions of sex-typed behavior, which relied on a single, bipolar dimension of masculinity-femininity, current formulations assume that these personality traits can be measured in varying amounts in the same individual. The most intriguing outcome of this new model of sex typing is androgyny, whereby an individual endorses relatively equal numbers of masculine and feminine traits. Bem's (1974, 1975, 1976) theory proposes that androgynous persons, in comparison to sex-typed individuals, are more adaptive, flexible, and more effective in interpersonal contexts. The androgynous person is able to be both expressive (using traditional feminine characteristics of warmth, support, and nurturance) and instrumental (using traditionally masculine characteristics of assertiveness, competence, and independent action). In contrast, sex-typed persons are assumed to be behaviorally constricted and limited in situations where sex-inappropriate behavior is required because they inhibit and suppress cross-sex behavior.

Although the research literature on validation of androgyny theory is beset with many methodological problems (Kelly and Worell 1977; Worell 1978, 1980b), there is considerable support for the theoretical predictions in interpersonal situations. In several validation studies, highly sex-typed males and females tended to avoid performance of activities that were culturally sex-role inappropriate (e.g., a male baking a cake), and masculine males demonstrated fewer expressive and supportive behaviors when interacting with a baby or a lonely student (Bem and Lenney 1976; Bem, Martyna, and Watson 1976). In an interesting set of studies pairing sex typings of strangers in interactive situations, Ickes and Barnes (1978) found that androgynous males and females interacted most effectively together, and sex-typed males and females produced the most limited and constricted dyadic interaction.

The implications of research and theory on androgyny are multiple. As an ideal, we might desire all counselors to adopt a personal orientation of psychological androgyny, so that they can be optimally effective with their male and female clients. For counselors of both men and women, the theory suggests that androgynous clients, who use both expressive and instrumental (assertive) personality traits, may be more competent, effective, and successful in interpersonal situations. Certainly counselors should be aware of the androgyny research and therefore be prepared to support and encourage progress toward assertiveness and independence in women. Some recent evidence suggests that, at least at a reported attitudinal level, many counselors are integrating the theory of androgyny into their practice (Englehard, Jones, and Stiggins 1976). Training programs for counselors might incorporate modules on assertiveness so that counselors become skilled at direct encouragement of competent interpersonal behavior.

## Emergent Client Populations

The second requirement for a new discipline in counseling is a client population whose emergent needs and goals are not being met by traditional procedures: We have evidence that women have long been the primary consumers of psychotherapeutic services (Chesler 1972; Gove 1976). Where, then, are the new client groups coming from? The dramatic change in economic, political, legal, and family arrangements in the past ten years has produced an upheaval in the expectations, life styles, and goals of at least half the American population. The women's movement, the changing composition of American families, and the 1979 Title IX Amendment to the Civil Rights Act are all sources of cultural change that have motivated individuals to alter their life-style activities and value systems. In particular, women are marrying later, having fewer children, divorcing, and single-parenting more frequently, and they are swelling the ranks of the labor force at an unprecedented rate (Block 1979; Hoffman 1977). These accumulated changes in social organization are creating new sources of personal stress and increased demands for innovative counseling services.

How shall we describe the new client populations? Although not all the demands for services can be construed in completely novel terms, each of the following represents a substantial departure from previously identified client groups.

1. *Career development counseling* includes nonstereotypic educational and vocational options that are freely explored. Family/career/achievement conflicts are examined in depth (Farmer 1978; Fitzgerald and Crites 1979; Hansen and Rapoza, 1978; Harmon 1977; Kincaid 1979; Remer and O'Neill 1980; Vetter 1973; Wolleat 1979).

2. *Life-span development counseling* may incorporate one or more aspects of multiple-role management, including consciousness raising, assertiveness training, decision making, and goal setting (Brodsky 1973; Fitzgerald 1978; Galassi and Lemmon 1978; Jakubowski 1978; Loeffler and Fiedler 1979; Scarato and Sigall 1979).

3. *Reentry and adult counseling* includes women returning to work or school, "displaced homemaker" or "empty nest" women, and aging and retiring women. Reentry counseling incorporates any aspects of counseling mentioned earlier, as well as perspectives on identity crisis management and aging (Resnick 1979; Roach 1976; Scarato and Sigall 1979; Worell 1980*b*).

4. *Family and marital role counseling* focuses on resocializing mothers and partners who are reformulating their stereotyped roles and seek self-identity in family relationships (Hare-Mustin 1979; Wyman and McLaughlin 1979). In contrast to traditional family approaches, the emphasis is on examining the balance of power as it relates to sex-role concerns. Both traditional and dual-career couples fall into this client group.

5. *Divorce, widowhood, and singleness counseling* targets the unique problems of women following loss of spouse through divorce or death. Included here might be financial stress, loneliness, single parenting, developing new relationships, dependency and autonomy, and legal issues (Aslin 1978; Rawlings and Carter 1979).

6. *Sexuality counseling* focuses on the applications of recent findings of female psychosexual functioning. Included here might be aspects of lesbianism, primary and secondary orgasmic dysfunctions, and other physical and psychological aspects of female sexuality (Barbach and Ayres 1976; Liss-Levinson 1979; Sotile and Killman 1977).

7. *Unplanned pregnancy counseling* is of increasing concern as abortion becomes a more available option. Components of crisis counseling are integrated with accelerated decision-making skills, information, and support during the

period of anxiety, grief, and recovery (Frieberg and Bridwell 1978; Kahn-Edrington 1979).

8. *Rape counseling* has moved into public attention as women increasingly report and testify to incidences of sexual assault. Again, crisis counseling deals with the victim's fear, rage, isolation, mistrust, depression, and self-blame. In particular, the counselor needs to help the woman separate her feelings of personal violation from the critical reactions of others. Recovery counseling counters subsequent and frequently long-term reactions to the personal violation and provides for referral to ancillary services and procedures that may be invoked (Burgess et al. 1978; Courtois 1979; Holmstrom and Burgess 1974).

9. *Sex discrimination counseling* is a relatively new resource, emerging fully after the enactment of Title VII of the Equal Employment Act of 1972. The discrimination counselor works with women before, during, and after filing a sex discrimination suit, providing information, support, and direction during the grievance procedures (Jeghelian 1976; Pendergrass et al. 1976).

10. *Other specialized client groups with special needs* can be identified as targets for individualized counseling strategies. Among the groups are such diverse populations as black and minority women, lesbians, handicapped women, female offenders, and managerial or corporate women. Each subpopulation may present a set of relatively homogeneous problems and concerns that call for counseling procedures uniquely tailored to their requirements. Indeed, counseling principles and procedures have been developed and applied separately to each of these groups of female clients, suggesting that there is sufficient justification for viewing them as distinguishable client populations.

The range and diversity of counseling concerns outlined above does not exclude the possibility of client groups overlapping, and a single client may well present several of these diverse problems to a single counselor. The simultaneous appearance of correlated presenting problems does not negate any area as a separate, legitimate professional concern. Each client group has separate and distinct characteristics, however, and efforts should be initiated and maintained to develop appropriate resources, counselor skills, and relevant outcome research.

## Emerging Procedures to Serve New Client Populations

The third requirement for the separate discipline of counseling women is the introduction of innovative procedures and strategies. As in the overlap of client groups, there are unquestionably many standard, validated counselor skills and techniques that are appropriate across all populations and counseling situations. In terms of counseling women, two general approaches have been proposed that are unique to this discipline. First, a broad view of appropriate counseling procedures for women has emerged—*feminist counseling*. This view has a philosophical base and a focused orientation. Second, we see the development of more specific sets of principles and competencies to meet the counseling requirements of specific client populations. I will discuss each approach briefly.

The tenets of feminist counseling cut across diverse theories and specific techniques. Feminist therapists choose to discuss the philosophy and attitudes of feminism rather than to delineate specific procedures. To the extent that the feminist therapist professes certain ideals and belief systems, however, the procedural directions are broadly prescribed. In feminist counseling, the following guidelines are suggested (Brodsky 1973; Lehrman 1974; Maracek, Kravetz, and Finn 1979; Nutt 1979; Rawlings and Carter 1977; Worell 1976).

1. Providing an egalitarian relationship with shared responsibility between counselor and client. The client is encouraged to trust her own judgment and to arrive at her own decisions. In contrast to many traditional counseling relationships, the client is never in a one-down position of having to accept counselor interpretations of her behavior or external prescriptions for appropriate living.

2. Employing a consciousness-raising approach. Women are helped to become aware of the societal restraints on their development and opportunities. Clients are helped to differentiate between the politics of the sexist social structure and those problems over which they have realistic personal control.

3. Helping women explore a sense of their personal power and how they can use it constructively in personal, business, and political relationships.

4. Helping women to get in touch with unexpressed anger in order to combat depression and to make choices about how to use their anger constructively.

5. Helping women to redefine themselves apart from their role relationships to men, children, and home; exploring women's fears about potential role changes that may alienate spouse and children, as well as co-workers and boss.

6. Encouraging women to nurture themselves as well as caring for others, thereby raising self-confidence and self-esteem.

7. Encouraging multiple skill development to increase women's competence and productivity. This may include assertiveness training, economic and career skills, and negotiation skills with important others who resist change.

Although not every counseling situation with women will necessarily incorporate each of these principles equally, the philosophical and procedural base provides a cornerstone for further intervention. To the extent that any counselor openly endorses and actively practices these principles, he or she may be regarded as a feminist counselor. For many current theorists, the professional goal is to incorporate these principles into all counseling situations.

The second innovation in counseling women has been the development of more specific principles to cover particular client needs and goals. Since 1972, three complete issues of the *Counseling Psychologist* have been devoted exclusively to the counseling concerns of women. The major portions of the first two issues now appear in *Counseling Women* (Harmon et al. 1978). The most recent issue (1979, vol. 8, no. 1) contains no less than seventeen sets of differing principles and procedures for dealing with diverse women client groups. The reader is here referred to this publication for a detailed review of these suggestions. For each client group, the principles delineate areas of competence for practitioners. These principles are designed to remediate gaps and distortions in present counseling practice. The three broad areas of competence are (1) knowledge about the developmental, psychological, biological, and mythological aspects of the area, as well as about community resources and alternative options; (2) skills at the individual, group, institutional, and community levels, depending on the client's presenting concerns and unique needs; and (3) attitudes that may effect stereotyped responses to the client group. A careful reading of these principles reveals that they meet the criteria for feminist counseling, and they point the way for further innovative practices that aim to free the woman client for optimal growth and development.

These advances in formulating novel approaches to helping relationships with women represent only a pioneer effort. Many counselors, because of the dearth of knowledge and theory about the lives of women, are operating on a trial-and-error basis. As new procedures and skills are fashioned and tailored to individual needs, research efforts will gradually reveal their efficacy. For example, if we take only the burgeoning research on assertiveness training, it is clear that some procedures are more effective than others. The principles that govern the optimal effectiveness of assertiveness training in various situations are not yet fully determined (Rich and Schroeder 1976). One solution to our knowledge deficit, of course, is to increase the research base on which these procedures are predicated. In the training proposal that completes this article, I suggest that new programs for training counselors of women incorporate a research component that complements the theoretical and practical elements of the program.

## Ethics and Standards in Counseling Women

The fourth and final requirement for a new discipline in counseling women is the development of a set of ethics that specifically addresses itself to women's concerns. At present, at least two such guidelines have been proposed, which incorporate and expand the ethical standards provided by the American Psychological Association (1977).

The first set of ethical guidelines was produced by the APA Task Force on Sex Bias and Sex-role Stereotyping in Therapeutic Practice (1978) and the second by the APA Division 17 (counseling) Committee on Women (1979). The substantive content of these two documents is similar. Both groups call for therapy/counseling practices with women that will (1) meet the APA standards for ethical practice; (2) match in substance the concepts of feminist counseling outlined above; and (3) specifically avoid sexist language and sexual contact between client and counselor. As a start, I recommend that counselors who have not read, discussed with colleagues, and fully internalized the contents of these two guidelines severely limit all further professional contact with women.

What kinds of counselor practices most frequently fail to meet ethical standards for professional practice? Clearly, counselors and therapists as a group desire to uphold the principles of their profession. The APA ethical principles commit the practitioner to (1) promote the welfare of the client by using and recommending procedures that are in the client's best interests; (2) insure and protect the rights and dignity of the client in the therapeutic relationship; (3) practice within the limits of the counselor's own competence; and (4) maintain confidentiality. Most of the violations reported by the APA Task Force fall into one of these four categories. These reported violations include such instances as fostering prolonged dependency relationships; having sexual contact with clients; encouraging women to submit to oppressive and stereotyped sex-role behaviors within marital, sexual, career, and employment situations; blaming the woman who is a victim of assault or of sexist practices by others; interpreting the women's problems in terms of sexist theoretical concepts; failing to establish mutually satisfactory goals and procedures; providing a spouse with unauthorized information about the client/wife; and failing to use appropriate community referral resources. The wide range of these instances suggests that many counselor therapists are practicing beyond the limits of their competence through their lack of knowledge about and application of the psychology of women and sex roles (Hare-Mustin et al. 1979; Worell 1979b). One remedy for this distressing state of the art is contained in the substance of this article: the establishment of training programs to disseminate appropriate information and encourage development of relevant skills and attitudes in counseling women.

## Implications for Training Programs

Revolutions are intended to bring about the establishment of a new order. It has been the thesis of this article that the revolution in counseling women must result in the revision of counseling and psychotherapy training programs. At present, graduate programs for training providers of counseling and psychological services suffer from particular deficits that prevent the establishment of sex-fair counseling practices. These deficits include unequal distribution of male and female faculty and graduate students; absence of courses on the psychology of women and sex roles; text and curricular materials that are insufficient, biased, and sex-stereotyped; lack of experiential and practicum provisions for sex-role awareness and consciousness raising; and inadequate provisions for specific skill development in counseling the special populations of clients presented by contemporary women.

As a start in the appropriate direction, counselor education programs need to increase their female faculty to provide adequate role models for career orientation in women students (Douvan 1976; Harway 1979; Kenworthy, Koufacos, and Sherman 1976). Female counselors have also been shown to be more aware of sex-stereotyped practices than male counselors and are frequently more liberated than males in their attitudes toward expanded roles for women. Harway (1979) reported in a recent survey that 85 percent of counselor educators are male. This imbalance needs to be remediated before we can expect a serious implementation of training program revisions. The remaining provisions for program revisions would necessarily depend on individual resources and faculty commitment to change. I would suggest Harway's (1979) model as one that can be appropriate for all programs to implement. It is quoted here in full:

The model program (a) employs at least 40% women on the faculty; (b) enrolls an equal number of male and female students and provides recruitment programs to equalize the number; (c) provides at least one required course on the psychology of women and sex-role socialization, a practicum experience in counseling women, and workshops to other college women; (d) encourages research on women and women's career development; (e) has a substantial library of significant research and theoretical work in the psychology and counseling of women; (f) requires one or more experiential sessions for all students (and faculty) on sex-role stereotyping, and thus provides an opportunity for each individual to examine his/her biases; and (g) encourages faculty to develop sex-fair materials or books and prohibits the use of male pronouns when referring to both sexes. (p. 9)

The Harway model for sex-fair counseling provides guidelines that should be fundamental for all counseling education programs. I be-

*631*

lieve that we need to progress one step further and evolve a cadre of specialists who possess expertise beyond the basic sex-fair training provisions. The substance of this article supports the concept of establishing a specialty in counseling on women's concerns. Training programs to develop the specialist in counseling women would add to the Harway model by including (1) a balanced core of cognitive and experiential courses related to sex-role concerns (Foxley, 1979, suggests four courses as a minimal standard); (2) active commitment via group cooperative effort to research on the development, psychology, and counseling of women; (3) community outreach by means of workshops, consultation, and program development with community agencies; and (4) intensive practicum and internship experience in several settings concerned directly with counseling women. Of particular significance to the counseling psychologist is the recommendation that practical experiences are gained directly in settings that target women's concerns, and that supervision in these settings be accomplished via group experiences that focus on relevant sex-role issues as well as on general counseling concerns (Kenworthy, Koufacos, and Sherman 1976). The graduate products of such a training program would be prepared not only to counsel in areas of relevance to women, but also to encourage public and institutional policy for change toward equal opportunity for women, and to provide competent and knowledgeable role models for incoming generations of students and faculty.

## Summary and Conclusions

Evidence has been provided here to support the thesis that there is indeed a revolution in the area of counseling women. Recent changes in the economic, social, and legal position of women have brought about an upheaval in traditional values, expectations, and life goals of both men and women. As a result of increased stress and life-style changes, new populations of female clients are emerging. Competent and ethical counseling practices with these client groups demand innovations in counselor knowledge, attitudes, and skills. In response to the needs and goals of these client groups, the trainers of counselors and providers of psychological services will be expected to reorient and revise their programs. The model program would increase the proportion of female faculty and introduce sex-fair curricular materials, courses on sex-role stereotyping and the psychology of women, sex-role awareness experiences, and a practicum in counseling women.

A commitment to research on the development and functioning of women would be infused throughout the education curriculum. A support and outreach component of the programs would provide extramural workshops and consultation to community and professional groups to educate the lay population and reeducate the practicing professional. A long-term goal of these proposals will be the model counselor of the future who provides all clients with appropriate services that are sex-fair, competent, and ethical.

REFERENCES

American Psychological Association. 1975. Report of the task force on sex bias and sex-role stereotyping in psychotherapeutic practice. *American Psychologist* 30:1165–1175. [Reprinted herein chapter 8.]

———. 1977. *Standards for providers of psychological services*, rev. ed. Washington, D.C.: American Psychological Association.

———. 1978. Task force on sex bias and sex role stereotyping in psychotherapeutic practice. Guidelines for therapy with women. *American Psychologist* 33:1122–1133.

———. 1979. Division 17 Ad Hoc Committee on Women. Principles concerning the counseling and therapy of women. *Counseling Psychologist* 8:21.

Aslin, A. L. 1978. Counseling "single-again" (divorced and widowed) women. In *Counseling women*, ed. L. W. Harmon et al., pp. 230–240. Monterey, Calif.: Brooks/Cole.

Barbach, L. G., and Ayres, T. 1976. Group process for women with orgasmic difficulties. *Personnel and Guidance Journal* 54:389–391.

Bardwick, J. M. 1971. *Psychology of women.* New York: Harper & Row.

Bem, S. L. 1974. The measurement of psychological androgyny. *Journal of Consulting and Clinical Psychology* 47:155–162.

———. 1975. Sex-role adaptability: One consequence of psychological androgyny. *Journal of Personality and Social Psychology* 31:634–643.

———. 1976. Probing the promise of androgyny. In *Beyond sex-role stereotypes: Readings toward a psychology of androgyny*, ed. A. G. Kaplan and J. P. Bean, pp. 47–62. Boston: Little, Brown.

———, and Lenney, E. 1976. Sex-typing and the avoidance of cross-sex behavior. *Journal of Personality and Social Psychology* 33:48–54.

Bem, S. L., Martyna, W., and Watson, C. 1976. Sex-typing and androgyny: Further explorations of the expressive domain. *Journal of Personality and Social Psychology* 34:1016–1023.

Berzins, J. I., Welling, M. A., and Wetter, R. E. 1978. A new measure of psychological androgyny based on the Personality Research Form. *Journal of Consulting and Clinical Psychology* 46:126–138.

Block, J. 1979. The changing American parent: Implications for child development. Paper presented at the meeting of the Society for Research in Child Development, San Francisco, March 1979.

Brodsky, A. 1973. The consciousness-raising group as a model of therapy with women. *Psychotherapy: Theory, Research, and Practice* 10:24–29. [Reprinted herein chapter 47.]

Broverman, I. K., et al. 1970. Sex-role stereotypes and clinical judgments of mental health. *Journal of Consulting and Clinical Psychology* 34:1–7. [Reprinted herein chapter 7.]

Burgess, A. W., et al. 1978. *Sexual assault of children and adolescents.* Lexington, Mass.: D. C. Heath.

Chafetz, J. S. 1978. *Masculine/feminine or human? An overview of the sociology of gender roles*, 2nd ed. Itasca, Ill.: F. E. Peacock.

Chesler, P. 1972. *Women and madness*. Garden City, N.Y.: Doubleday.

Constantinople, A. 1979. Sex-role acquisition: In search of the elephant. *Sex Roles* 5:121–134.

*Counseling Psychologist*. 1979. Special issue: Counseling Women III 8(1).

Courtois, C. A. 1979. Victims of rape and incest. *Counseling Psychologist* 8:38–39.

Doherty, M. A. 1978. Sexual bias in personality theory. In *Consulting women*, ed. L. W. Harmon et al., pp. 94–105. Monterey, Calif.: Brooks/Cole.

Donahue, T. J. 1976. Discrimination against young women in career selection by high school counselors. (Ph.D. dissertation, Michigan State University, 1976.) *Dissertation Abstracts International*, 1976, 37A, 802A (University Microfilms No. 76-18, 612).

Douvan, E. 1976. The role of models in women's professional development. *Psychology of Women Quarterly* 1:5–20.

Englehard, P. A., Jones, K. O., and Stiggins, R. J. 1976. Trends in counselor attitude about women's roles. *Journal of Counseling Psychology* 23:365–372.

Erikson, E. 1968. *Identity: Youth and crisis*. New York: Norton.

Farmer, H. S. 1978. Why women choose careers below their potential. In *Career development and counseling of women*, ed. L. S. Hansen and R. S. Rapoza, pp. 118–131. Springfield, Ill.: Charles C Thomas.

Fitzgerald, L. E. 1978. Women's changing expectations . . . New insights, new demands. In *Counseling women*, ed. L. W. Harmon et al., pp. 128–134. Monterey, Calif.: Brooks/Cole.

Fitzgerald, L. F., and Crites, J. O. 1979. Career counseling for women. *Counseling Psychologist* 8:33–34.

Foxley, C. H. 1979. *Nonsexist counseling: Helping women and men redefine their roles*. Dubuque, Iowa: Kendall Hunt.

Freud, S. 1965. *New introductory lectures on psychoanalysis*. New York: Norton.

Frieberg, P., and Bridwell, M. W. 1978. An intervention model for rape and unwanted pregnancy. In *Counseling women*, ed. L. W. Harmon et al., pp. 261–269. Monterey, Calif.: Brooks/Cole.

Friedman, R., Richart, R. M., and Vande Wiele, R. L., eds. 1974. *Sex differences in behavior*. New York: Wiley.

Frieze, I. H., et al. 1978. *Women and sex roles: A social psychological perspective*. New York: Norton.

Galassi, M. D., and Lemmon, M. 1978. Life direction seminars: Facilitating human development at a women's college. *Personnel and Guidance Journal* 57:172–175.

Gove, W. R. 1976. The relationship between sex roles, marital status, and mental illness. In *Beyond sex-role stereotypes: Readings toward a psychology of androgyny*, ed. A. G. Kaplan and J. P. Bean, pp. 281–292. Boston: Little, Brown.

Hansen, S. L., and Rapoza, R. S. 1978. *Career development and counseling of women*. Springfield, Ill.: Charles C Thomas.

Hare-Mustin, R. T. 1979. Family therapy and sex role stereotypes. *Counseling Psychologist* 8:31–32.

———, et al. 1979. Rights of clients, responsibilities of therapists. *American Psychologist* 34:3–16.

Harmon, L. W. 1977. Career counseling for women. In *Psychotherapy for women: Treatment toward equality*, ed. E. Rawlings and D. Carter, pp. 197–206. Springfield, Ill.: Charles C Thomas.

———, et al., eds. 1978. *Counseling women*. Monterey, Calif.: Brooks/Cole.

Harway, M. 1979. Training counselors. *Counseling Psychologist* 8:8–10.

Heilbrun, A. B., Jr. 1976. Measurement of masculine and feminine sex-role identities as independent dimensions. *Journal of Consulting and Clinical Psychology* 44:183–190.

Henley, N. M. 1973. Status and sex: Some touching observations. *Bulletin of the Psychonomic Society* 2:91–93.

Hill, C. E., et al. 1977. Counselor reactions to female clients: Type of problem, age of client, and sex of counselor. *Journal of Counseling Psychology* 24:60–65.

Hoffman, L. W. 1977. Changes in family roles, socialization, and sex differences. *American Psychologist* 32:644–657.

Holroyd, J. 1976. Psychotherapy and women's liberation. *Counseling Psychologist* 6:22–32.

Holstrom, L. L., and Burgess, A. W. 1974. *Rape: Victims of crisis*. Bowie, Md.: Brady.

Hoyenga, K. B., and Hoyenga, K. T. 1978. *The question of sex differences: Psychological, cultural and biological issues*. Boston: Little, Brown.

Ickes, W., and Barnes. R. D. 1978. Boys and girls together. An enacting stereotyped sex roles in mixed-sex dyads. *Journal of Personality and Social Psychology* 36:669–683.

Jakubowski, P. 1978. Facilitating the growth of women through assertive training. In *Counseling women*, ed. L. W. Harmon et al., pp. 106–122. Monterey, Calif.: Brooks/Cole.

Jeghelian, A. 1976. Surviving sexism: Strategies and consequences. *Personnel and Guidance Journal* 54: 307–311.

Kahn, L. G. 1977. Effects of sex and feminist orientation of therapists on clinical judgments (Ph.D. dissertation, Columbia University, 1976). *Dissertation Abstracts International*, 1977, 37B, 3613B (University Microfilms No. 76–29, 598).

Kahn-Edrington, M. 1979. Abortion counseling. *Counseling Psychologist* 8:37–38. [Reprinted herein chapter 30.]

Katz, P. A. 1979. The development of female identity. *Sex Roles* 5:155–178.

Kelly, J. A., and Worell, J. 1977. New formulations of sex roles and androgyny. *Journal of Consulting and Clinical Psychology* 45:1101–1115.

Kenworthy, J. A., Koufacos, C., and Sherman, J. 1976. Women and therapy: A survey of internship programs. *Psychology of Women Quarterly* 2:125–137.

Key, M. R. 1975. *The role of male-female language*. Metuchen, N.J.: Scarecrow.

Kincaid, A. M. B. 1979. Traditional-age college women. *Counseling Psychologist* 8:23–24.

Kohlberg, L. 1966. A cognitive-developmental analysis of children's sex-role concepts and attitudes. In *The development of sex differences*, ed. E. E. Maccoby, pp. 83–173. Stanford, Calif.: Stanford University Press.

Lee, D., and Hertzberg, J. 1978. Theories of feminine personality. In *Women and sex roles: A social psychological perspective*, ed. I. H. Frieze et al., pp. 28–44. New York: Norton.

Lehrman, H. 1974. What happens in feminist therapy. Paper presented at the annual convention of the American Psychological Association, New Orleans, September 1974.

Lewis, M., and Weinraub, M. 1979. Origins of early sex-role development. *Sex Roles* 5:135–154.

Liss-Levinson, N. 1979. Women with sexual concerns. *Consulting Psychologist* 8:36–37.

Loeffler, D., and Fiedler, L. 1979. Woman—a sense of identity to facilitate personal growth in women. *Journal of Counseling Psychology* 26:51–57.

McClelland, D. D., et al. 1953. *The achievement motive*. New York: Appleton-Century-Crofts.

Maccoby, E. E., and Jacklyn, C. N. 1974. *The psychology of sex differences*. Stanford, Calif.: Stanford University Press.

McEwen, M. K. 1975. Counseling women. A review of the research. *Journal of College Student Personnel* 16:382–388.

Maracek, J., Kravetz, D., and Finn, S. 1979. A comparison of women who enter feminist therapy and traditional therapy. *Journal of Consulting and Clinical Psychology*, 47:734–742.

Michelini, R. L., Passalacqua, R., and Cusimano, J. 1976. Effects of seating arrangements on group participation. *Journal of Social Psychology* 99:179–186.

Nutt, R. L. 1979. Review and preview of attitudes and values of counselors of women. *Counseling Psychologist* 8:18–20.

O'Leary, V. E. 1978. *Toward understanding women*. Monterey, Calif.: Brooks/Cole.

Oliver, L. W. 1975. Counseling implications of recent research on women. *Personnel and Guidance Journal* 53:430–437.

Pendergrass, V. E., et al. 1976. Sex discrimination counseling. *American Psychologist* 31:36–46.

Pietrofesa, J. J., and Schlossberg, N. K. 1970. Counselor bias and the female occupational role. Unpublished manuscript, Wayne State University (ERIC CG 006 056).

Pleck, J. H. 1975. Masculinity-femininity: Current and alternative paradigms. *Sex Roles* 1:161–178.

Rawlings, E. I., and Carter, D. K. 1977. *Psychotherapy for women.* Springfield, Ill.: Charles C Thomas.

————. 1979. Divorced women. *Counseling Psychologist* 8:27–28.

Reisman, B. L. 1978. Short-term effects of "Seminar: Counseling Women" on attitudes and behaviors toward women held by its participants (Ph.D. dissertation, Kent State University, 1977). *Dissertation Abstracts International*, 1978, 38A, 5929A–5930A (University Microfilm No. 7727750).

Resnick. J. L. 1979. Women and aging. *Counseling Psychologist* 8:29–30.

Rich, A. R., and Schroeder, H. E. 1976. Research issues in assertiveness training. *Psychological Bulletin* 83:1081–1096.

Roach, R. M. 1976. Honey, won't you please stay home? *Personnel and Guidance Journal* 55:86–89.

Rose, G. 1976. The effects of gender on patient-therapist match. Unpublished manuscript, University of Kentucky.

Scarato, A. M., and Sigall, B. A. 1979. Multiple-role women. *Counseling Psychologist* 8:26–27.

Schlossberg, N. K., and Pietrofesa, J. J. 1978. Perspectives on counseling bias: Implications for counselor education. In *Counseling women*, ed. L. W. Harmon et al., pp. 59–74. Monterey, Calif.: Brooks/Cole.

Sherman, J. C. 1978. Views of women in counseling and psychotherapy (Ph.D. dissertation, Idaho State University, 1977). *Dissertation Abstracts International*, 1978, 38, 4589A–4590A (University Microfilms No. 7730626).

Sherman, J., Koufacos, C., and Kenworthy, J. A. 1978. Therapists: Their attitudes and information about women. *Psychology of Women Quarterly* 2:299–313.

Sohle, W. M., and Killman. P. R. 1977. Treatments of psychogenic female sexual dysfunctions. *Psychological Bulletin* 84:619–633.

Spence, J. T., and Helmreich, R. L. 1978. *Masculinity and femininity: Their psychological dimensions, correlates, and antecedents.* Austin, Texas: University of Texas Press.

————, and Stapp, J. 1975. Ratings of self and peers on sex-role attributes and their relation to self-esteem and conceptions of masculinity and femininity. *Journal of Personality and Social Psychology* 32:29–39.

Stein, A. H., and Bailey, M. M. 1973. The socialization of achievement orientation in females. *Psychological Bulletin* 80:345–366.

Stewart, E. V. 1978. A study of sex-role stereotyping in psychotherapy with women as a function of therapeutic orientation and sex of therapist (Ph.D. dissertation, California School of Professional Psychology, 1976). *Dissertation Abstracts International*, 1978, 38B, 3418B (University Microfilms No. 77-17, 173).

Super, D. E., and Hall, D. T. 1978. Career development: Exploration and planning. *Annual Review of Psychology* 29:333–372.

Tavris, C., and Offir, C. 1970. *The longest war: Sex differences in perspective.* New York: Harcourt.

Thomas, H., and Stewart, N. R. 1971. Counselor response to female clients with deviate and conforming career goals. *Journal of Counseling Psychology* 18:352–357.

Vetter, L. 1973. Career counseling for women. *Counseling Psychologist* 4:54–67.

Weisstein, N. 1971. *Psychology constructs the female, or, the fantasy life of the male psychologist.* Andover, Mass.: Warner Modular Publications.

Wentworth, V. R. 1977. An investigation of sex-role stereotypes in student counselor descriptions of the healthy adult man and the healthy adult woman and their responses to hypothetical male and female clients (Ph.D. dissertation, Indiana University, 1977). *Dissertation Abstracts International*, 1977, 38A, 2570-A (University Microfilms No. 7-24, 043).

Westerveldt, E. M. 1978. A tide in the affairs of women: The psychological impact of feminism on educated women. In *Counseling women*, ed. L. W. Harmon et al., pp. 1–33. Monterey, Calif.: Brooks/Cole.

Whitley, B. E., Jr. 1979. Sex roles and psychotherapy: A current appraisal. *Psychological Bulletin* 86:1309–1321.

Williams, J. H. 1977. *Psychology of women: Behavior in a biosocial context.* New York: Norton.

Willis, F. N., Jr., and Williams, S. J. 1976. Simultaneous talking in conversation and sex of speakers. *Perceptual and Motor Skills* 43:1067–1070.

Wolleat, P. L. 1979. School-age girls. *Counseling Psychologist* 8:22–23.

Worell, J. 1976. Issues in counseling women. Paper presented at the meeting of the Southeastern Psychological Association, New Orleans, April 1976.

——— . 1978. Sex roles and psychological well-being: Perspectives on methodology. *Journal of Consulting and Clinical Psychology* 46:777–791.

——— . 1979a. Changing sex roles. Paper presented at a meeting of the Southeastern Psychological Association, New Orleans, March 1979. (ERIC Document No. ED 170 066).

——— . 1979b. Ethical issues in counseling women. Paper presented at a meeting of the Kentucky Psychological Association, Lexington, April 1979.

——— . 1980a. Psychological sex roles: Significance and change. In *Psychological development in the elementary years,* ed. J. Worell. New York: Academic Press.

——— . 1980b. Gender and sex role contributions to life-span development. In *Individuals as contributors to their development: A lifespan perspective,* ed. R. Lerner. New York: Academic Press.

Wyman, E., and McLaughlin, M. E. 1979. Traditional wives and mother. *Counseling Psychologist* 8:24–25.

# PART VI / Supplementary Readings

Kaplan, A., and Bean, J., eds. 1976. *Beyond sex-role stereotypes: Readings toward a psychology of androgeny*. Boston: Little, Brown.

Maracek, J., and Kravetz, D., 1977. Women and mental health: A review of feminist change efforts. *Psychiatry* 40:323–329.

Millman, M., and Kanter, R. M., eds. 1975. *Another voice: Feminist perspectives on social life and social science*. Garden City, N.Y.: Anchor Books/Doubleday.

Rapoport, R., and Rapoport, R. N. 1975. Men, women and equity. *The Family Coordinator* October: 421–432.

# SOURCES

Early Origins of Envy and Devaluation of Women: Implications for Sex-Role Stereotypes, by Harriet E. Lerner, originally was published in the *Bulletin of the Menninger Clinic* 38, 1974, pp. 538–553. Copyright © 1974, The Menninger Foundation. Reprinted by permission.

Psychological Consequences of Sexual Inequality, by Jean Baker Miller, originally was published in *The American Journal of Orthopsychiatry* 41, October 1971, pp. 767–775. Copyright © 1971, the American Orthopsychiatric Association, Inc. Reprinted by permission.

The Conflict Between Nurturance and Autonomy in Mother-Daughter Relationships and Within Feminism, by Jane Flax, is reprinted from *Feminist Studies* 4(2), June 1978, pp. 171–189, by permission of the publisher, Feminist Studies, Inc., c/o Women's Studies Program, University of Maryland, College Park, Md. 20742.

Sex-Role Stereotypes and Clinical Judgments of Mental Health, by Inge K. Broverman et al., appeared originally in the *Journal of Consulting and Clinical Psychology* 34, 1970, pp. 1–7. Copyright © 1970, the American Psychological Association. Reprinted by permission.

Report of the Task Force on Sex Bias and Sex-Role Stereotyping in Psychotherapeutic Practice, by Annette M. Brodsky and Jean Holroyd, was written under the auspices of the American Psychological Association and was published in *American Psychologist*, December 1975, pp. 1169–1175. Copyright © 1975, the American Psychological Association. Reprinted by permission.

The Psychiatrist-Woman Patient Relationship, by P. Susan Stephenson and Gillian A. Walker, is reprinted from the *Canadian Journal of Psychiatry* 24, 1979, pp. 5–16, with permission.

A Review of Women's Psychotropic Drug Use, published originally in the *Canadian Journal of Psychiatry* 24(1), 1979, 29–34, appears with permission of the author, Ruth Cooperstock, and the journal.

Psychiatry's Problem with No Name: Therapist-Patient Sex, by Virginia Davidson, is reprinted by permission of the Editor, *The American Journal of Psychoanalysis* 37(1), 1977, pp. 43–50.

Sex Differences and the Epidemiology of Depression, by Myrna M. Weissman and Gerald L. Klerman, originally was published in the *Archives of General Psychiatry* 34, 1977, pp. 98–111. Copyright © 1977, American Medical Association.

The Hysterical Personality: A "Woman's Disease" first appeared in *Comprehensive Psychiatry* 15, 1974, pp. 157–164. Reprinted by permission of Grune & Stratton, Inc., and the author, Harriet E. Lerner.

Madness in Women is reprinted from *Psychic War in Men and Women* (1976), by Helen Block Lewis. Copyright © 1976 by Helen Block Lewis. Published by permission of New York University Press.

Phobias after Marriage: Women's Declaration of Dependence, by Alexandra Symonds, is reprinted by permission of the Editor, *The American Journal of Psychoanalysis* 31 (2), 1979, pp. 144–152.

A Starving Family: An Interactional View of Anorexia Nervosa, by Dorothy Conrad Mazur, originally was published in the *Bulletin of the Menninger Clinic* 41, 1974, pp. 487–495. Copyright © 1974, by The Menninger Foundation. Reprinted by permission.

Cinderella's Stepsisters: A Feminist Perspective on Anorexia Nervosa and Bulimia, by Marlene Boskind-Lodahl, is reprinted from *Signs* 2(2), 1976, pp. 342–356, by permission of the University of Chicago Press and the author. Copyright © 1976 by the University of Chicago. All rights reserved.

Group Process for Women with Orgasmic Difficulties, by Lonnie Garfield Barbach and Toni Ayres, appeared originally in *Personnel and Guidance Journal* 54, 1976, pp. 389–391. Copyright © 1976, American Personnel and Guidance Association. Reprinted by permission.

The portions of Issues in the Treatment of Female Addiction: A Review and Critique of the Literature, by Walter R. Cuskey et al., appeared originally in *Contemporary Drug Problems* 6(3), 1900, pp. 307–353. Copyright © Federal Legal Publications, Inc., 157 Chambers St., New York, N.Y. 10007. Reprinted by permission.

The Female Alcoholic, by Judy Fraser, appeared originally in *Addiction*, Fall 1973, and is reprinted with permission of the Addiction Research Foundation of Ontario. Copyright © 1974, the Alcoholism and Drug Addiction Research Foundation, Toronto, Ontario.

A Study of Attitudes Toward Menarche in White Middle-Class American Adolescent Girls, by Lynn Whisnant and Leonard Zegans, appeared first in the *American Journal of Psychiatry* 132, 1975, pp. 809–814. Copyright © 1975, the American Psychiatric Association. Reprinted by permission.

Teenage Pregnancy: A Research View, by Catherine Chilman, copyright © 1979, National Association of Social Workers, Inc. Reprinted by permission from *Social Work* 24 (6), November 1979, pp. 492–498.

Attitudes Toward Parenting in Dual-Career Families, by Colleen Leahy Johnson and Frank Arvid Johnson, appeared originally in *American Journal of Psychiatry* 34, 1977, pp. 391–395. Copyright © 1977, the American Psychiatric Association. Reprinted by permission.

Female-Headed Families: Trends and Implications, by Esther Wattenberg and Hazel Reinhardt, copyright © 1979, National Association of Social Workers, Inc. Reprinted, with permission, from *Social Work* 24(6), November 1979, pp. 460–467.

Lesbian Families: Cultural and Clinical Issues, by Marny Hall, copyright © 1978, National Association of Social Workers, Inc. Reprinted, with permission, from *Social Work* 23 (5), September 1978, pp. 380–385.

Midlife Concerns of Women: Implications of the Menopause, by Malkah T. Notman, originally was published in the *American Journal of Psychiatry* 136, 1979, pp. 1270–1274. Copyright © 1979, the American Psychiatric Association. Reprinted by permission.

Abortion Counseling, by Marla Kahn-Edrington, is from *The Counseling Psychologist* 8 (1), 1979, pp. 37–38. Reprinted by permission.

Abortion Counseling with Adolescents appeared originally in the *American Journal of Nursing* 74(10), October 1974, pp. 1856–1858. Copyright © 1974 by the American Journal of Nursing Company. Reprinted with permission.

Divorced Women, by Edna I. Rawlings and Dianne K. Carter, is from *The Counseling Psychologist* 8(1), 1979, pp. 37–38. Reprinted by permission.

Postmastectomy Counseling, by James G. Joiner and Joan Z. Fisher, was published originally in the *Journal of Applied Rehabilitation Counseling* 8, 1977, pp. 99–106. Reprinted by permission.

Group Work with Widows, by Andre Toth and Susan Toth, copyright © 1980, National Association of Social Workers, Inc. Reprinted, with permission, from *Social Work* 25(1), January 1980, pp. 63–65.

Psychological Aspects of Wife Battering, by Barbara Star et al., is reprinted from *Social Casework* 60, 1979, pp. 479–487. Reprinted with permission of the publisher, Family Service Association of America.

Rape: Sexual Disruption and Recovery, by Ann W. Burgess and Lynda L. Holmstrom, was first published in the *American Journal of Orthopsychiatry* 49, October 1979, pp. 648–657. Copyright © 1979, The American Orthopsychiatric Association, Inc. Reproduced by permission.

Development of a Medical Center Rape Crisis Intervention Program, by Sharon L. McCombie et al., originally was published in the *American Journal of Psychiatry*, 133, April 1976, pp. 418–421. Copyright © 1976, the American Psychiatric Association. Reprinted by permission.

The Rape Victim: Psychodynamic Considerations, by Malkah T. Notman and Carol C. Nadelson, originally was published in the *American Journal of Psychiatry* 133, April 1976,

# Sources

pp. 408–413. Copyright © 1976, the American Psychiatric Association. Reprinted by permission.

Incest Between Fathers and Daughters, by Judith Herman and Lisa Hirschman, is reprinted from *The Sciences* 17, 1977, pp. 4–7, with permission. Copyright © 1977 by the New York Academy of Sciences.

Women Patients and Women Therapists: Some Issues That Come Up in Psychotherapy, by Rebecca Goz, appeared first in the *International Journal of Psychoanalytic Psychotherapy* 2, 1977, pp. 298–319. Reprinted by permission.

Adaptive and Pathogenic Aspects of Sex-Role Stereotypes: Implications for Parenting and Psychotherapy, by Harriet E. Lerner, originally was published in the *American Journal of Psychiatry* 135, 1978, pp. 48–52. Copyright © 1978, the American Psychiatric Association. Reprinted by permission.

A Feminist Works with Nontraditional Clients, by Joan Israel, appeared first in the Smith College School for Social Work *Journal* 6(2):20–22, and is reprinted with permission.

A Feminist Approach to Family Therapy, originally published in *Family Process* 17, June 1978, pp. 181–194, is reprinted with permission of the author, Rachel T. Hare-Mustin, and *Family Process*.

The Consciousness-Raising Group as a Model for Therapy with Women, by Annette M. Brodsky, was published originally in *Psychotherapy: Theory, Research and Practice* 10, Spring 1973, pp. 24–29. Reprinted by permission.

The Psychotherapeutic Impact of Women's Consciousness-Raising Groups, by Morton A. Lieberman et al., was published first in the *Archives of General Psychiatry* 36, February 1979, pp. 161–168. Copyright © 1979, American Medical Association. Reprinted by permission.

A Decade of Feminist Influence on Psychotherapy was published originally in *Psychology of Women Quarterly* 4, Spring 1980, pp. 331–343. Copyright © 1980 by Human Sciences Press. Reprinted by permission.

New Directions in Counseling Women, by Judith Worell, appeared originally in *Personnel and Guidance Journal* 58(7), March 1980, pp. 477–484. Copyright © 1980, American Personnel and Guidance Association. Reprinted with permission.

Psychology of Women: Perspectives on Theory and Research for the Eighties, by Emilie F. Sobel, and Identification and Treatment of Incest Victims, by Denise J. Gelinas, appear by permission of the authors.

# NAME INDEX

Abramowitz, S., 84, 100, 606
Adams, P. W., 178
Addiction Research Foundation, 296
*Addictions,* 296n
Addiction Services Agency (ASA), 270
Adolescent Health Services and Pregnancy Care Act, 336
Adorno, Theodor W., 64n11
Aid to Families with Dependent Children (AFDC), 332-33, 361-64, 366-67
Albee, Edward, 47
Alcoholics Anonymous, 297, 575, 597
Allen, R., 115
*Always Ask a Man,* 200
American Cancer Society, 411, 414
American College of Obstetricians and Gynecologists, 467
American Humane Association, 484, 498
American Psychiatric Association, 144, 179, 220-21, 379
American Psychological Association (APA), 83-84, 98, 98n, 99, 110-11, 378, 616, 624, 630
*American Psychologist,* 610
Andelin, H. B., 615
ARF Detoxification and Rehabilitation Programs, 300, 302-303
Aries, Elizabeth, 280
Arnon, W. E., 274, 286
Association for Women in Psychology, 572, 611
Ayres, Toni, 265


Badaracco, Marie R., 534n
Bailey, Holly, 252n2
Bales, R. F., 555-56
Balsam, Rosemary, 514n
Bandura, A., 73
Bane, M. J., 370n11
Barbach, Lonnie, 263, 365
Bard, M., 412-16
Bardwick, J. M., 72, 615
Barker, R. G., 313
Barnes, R. D., 625
Barnett, R., 15, 385
Bart, Pauline, 100, 180, 221-22, 391, 512, 573, 614
Baruch, G., 385

Bayes, M., 441
Baystate Medical Center, 481n
Beck, Aaron, 213
Becker, E., 259
Beckman, Linda J., 120, 304
Bell Canada, 303
Bell, R. Gordon, 297, 302
Belote, B., 144-45
Bem, S. L., 76, 624
Benedek, T., 342, 390-91
Berger, D. M., 202-203
Bergman, Ingmar, 144
Bernstein, B., 362
Beschner, G., 282n2
Beth Israel Hospital, 462, 478
Bettleheim, Bruno, 12, 27
Bhrolchain, M., 183
Binger, Carl, 236
Birchmore, Doreen, 301
Bird, C., 573-74
Blanck, Gertrude and Rubin, 53n5
Blitzer, J. R., 241
Block, J., 609
Blos, P., 322
Bonaparte, Marie, 7
Bond, Gary, 581n
Boston City Hospital, 450
Boston Strangler, 121
Boston Women's Health Book Collective, 341-42, 397
Boszormenyi-Nagy, I., 557
Bourne, R., 116
Bowen, M., 557
Boys Clubs, 335
Boy Scouts, 335
Brett, Elizabeth, 311n
Breuer, Josef, 142
Brocher, Tobias, 26n
Brodsky, Annette, 98n
Bronfenbrenner, Urie, 368n9
Bronner-Hurszar, J., 417
Brothers, Joyce, 607
Broverman, D. M., 70, 74-75, 83
Broverman, I. K., 83, 119, 122, 157, 185, 623
Brown, C., 84
Brown, G., 183
Brownmiller, Susan, 121
Bruch, H., 241, 249, 251, 253-55, 258
Brunswick, Ruth Mack, 7, 30, 32

*643*

# SUBJECT INDEX